TRANCEWORK

"Of the many excellent books Dr. Yapko has authored, both for health professionals and the general public, *Trancework* is the most detailed and comprehensive. This book is a must for every health professional who uses or wants to learn to use the powerful tool of hypnosis to help patients and clients. I highly recommend *Trancework* and will personally refer to it often in my own work."

Jordan I. Zarren, M.S.W., DAHB, DCSW
Past President: American Society of Clinical Hypnosis
Diplomate: American Hypnosis Board for Clinical Social Work & National Association of
    Social Workers
Co-Author: *Brief Cognitive Hypnosis: Facilitating the Change of Dysfunctional Behavior*

"Michael Yapko delivers a state of the art sourcebook that spans the depth and breadth of the hypnotic tradition. Up to date chapters on neuroscience and social psychology, as well as on the practical application of hypnosis, provide beginning and seasoned practitioners alike with creative ways to design and implement effective interventions. If you want to add a book to your library that is destined to be a classic, *Trancework* is a safe bet!"

Maggie Phillips, Ph.D.
Co-Author: *Healing the Divided Self: Clinical and Ericksonian Hypnotherapy for
    Posttraumatic and Dissociative Conditions*
Author: *Finding the Energy to Heal: How EMDR, Hypnosis, TFT, Imagery and Body Focused
    Therapy Help to Restore Mindbody Health* (2000)
Current Book Editor: *The American Journal of Clinical Hypnosis*

"Yapko has made the best text on hypnosis even better. His commitment to sound science, clarity of reason and pragmatic applications is communicated with a passion in this new edition of *Trancework*. The freshness of information and skills, built on the wisdom of former editions, make this a state-of-the-art book for every therapist who wants to be (and shouldn't we all be?) a state-of-the-art practitioner."

George W. Burns, B.A. (Hons.), clinical psychologist.
Author: *101 Healing Stories and Standing Without Shoes*
Director: The Milton H. Erickson Institute of Western Australia

"This is a definitively broad and seminal coverage that accurately and articulately covers leading approaches, events, people, and topics in the field of hypnosis. Clinicians, students, and researchers in hypnosis will undoubtedly find this the best single book they can read on the topic."

Stephen R. Lankton, MSW, DAHB, Founding Editor, *Ericksonian Monographs*, and
    co-author, *The Answer Within* and *Tales of Enchantment*

"Yapko finds the balance in *Trancework*. The mix of theory and practice is right: section one helps readers understand contemporary concepts and findings, with enough links to practical matters to keep readers grounded; section two helps readers apply specific hypnotic techniques in the context of therapy, with appropriate references to theoretical issues in hypnosis and beyond. The mix of simplicity and sophistication is right: readers new to hypnosis will be engaged by the clarity of exposition; those experienced in hypnosis will be impressed by the depth of knowledge that is conveyed. *Trancework* will be a major resource for those with therapeutic knowledge and skills who wish to integrate evidence-based proficiency in hypnosis into their interactions with clients."

Kevin M. McConkey, Ph.D., Professor of Psychology, The University of New South Wales

TRANCEWORK

An Introduction to the Practice of Clinical Hypnosis (3rd Edition)

by

MICHAEL D. YAPKO, Ph.D.

BRUNNER-ROUTLEDGE

New York and Hove

Published in 2003 by
Routledge
Taylor & Francis Group
270 Madison Avenue
New York, NY 10016

Published in Great Britain by
Routledge
Taylor & Francis Group
2 Park Square
Milton Park, Abingdon
Oxon OX14 4RN

© 2003 by Michael D. Yapko
Routledge is an imprint of Taylor & Francis Group

Printed in the United States of America on acid-free paper
15 14 13 12 11 10 9 8 7 6

International Standard Book Number-10: 0-415-93589-X (Hardcover)
International Standard Book Number-13: 978-0-415-93589-0 (Hardcover)
Library of Congress Card Number 2003009290
Author photo by Bradford Photography, LaCosta, California
Cover design by Pearl Chang

Library of Congress Cataloging-in-Publication Data

Yapko, Michael D.
    Trancework : an introduction to the practice of clinical hypnosis /by Michael D. Yapko.—3rd ed.
      p. cm.
    ISBN 0-415-93589-X (hc)
    1. Hypnotism—Therapeutic use. I. Title.
    RC495.Y373 2003
    615.8'512—dc21   2003009290

Visit the Taylor & Francis Web site at
http://www.taylorandfrancis.com

and the Routledge Web site at
http://www.routledge.com

This book is dedicated with love to my wife, Diane,
who has kept me deeply absorbed
in the happiest of hypnotic states

Contents

CONTENTS   ix

Frames of Reference

Interesting and insightful comments from leading figures in the fields of hypnosis and psychotherapy

List of Tables

Acknowledgments

Preparing this book has been a challenge and a delight. It has given me an opportunity to develop new friendships and deepen existing ones. It has given me a chance to re-examine some of what I think I know and discover yet again that "knowing" is a dynamic and changing process. It has given me a sense of drive to keep expanding my "comfort zone" by exploring issues and learning things that have taken me beyond the easy and familiar.

No one does a sizeable project such as this one truly alone, even though it sometimes seems that way when it's 2:00 a.m. and it's just me, my computer, and some strong coffee. In truth, there are many people who have helped support, encourage and needle me in the best of ways. My wife, Diane, has been and continues to be my greatest find in roaming the planet and searching for what matters. Her unwavering love, honesty, and the sheer strength of her being is a continuous reminder of how lucky I am to have a life partner who is so very special.

I have many professional colleagues who have helped teach and inspire me. I want to acknowledge with great appreciation the wonderful people who helped shape my views over the years of what it means to be a clinician and teacher. I'm expressive of my appreciation for these people, so I have good reason to believe they know who they are. I also want to thank all those friends and colleagues around the world who have invited me to come and teach some of what I know. The clinical trainings keep me well informed about what clinicians want to know and what issues are on their minds, and help provide the encouragement to continually evolve ever-clearer ways of describing and demonstrating hypnotic interventions.

My friends and family have also taught and inspired me in more profound ways than I could possibly describe. Every day I am gifted with their love and support for all I do. No matter where I am in the world or what I'm doing, they are always in the forefront of my mind.

Finally, I want to acknowledge the many people at Brunner-Routledge who brought this intensive project to completion. Brunner-Routledge has been my professional publishing home for a very, very long time, and I am grateful for their support of my work.

Foreword to the 3rd Edition

I attended my first hypnosis workshop more than 30 years ago, and it shines vividly in my memory. While learning the rudiments of clinical hypnosis, I was privileged to witness Dr. Erika Fromm conduct fascinating demonstrations of hypnotic phenomena including analgesia, time distortion, and age regression. At the time, there was only a modest empirical foundation for the use of hypnosis in psychotherapy and, in the public eye, and even in some professional circles, hypnosis was as much linked with hocus pocus, flummery, charlatanism, and the like, as it was associated with bona fide clinical practice. Nevertheless, I had an immediate sense that hypnosis would play an important role in my professional life, and not long after, I decided to be a serious student of hypnosis. I now believe that virtually every clinical practitioner can benefit from being a student of hypnosis, and I am delighted to introduce Michael Yapko's superb sourcebook on clinical hypnosis: *Trancework: An Introduction to the Practice of Clinical Hypnosis.*

Why use hypnosis as an adjunctive procedure in the first place? Over the years I have learned that hypnosis can instigate profound transformations in the way people think, feel, and act. Fundamental to the practice of hypnosis is the idea that deep and enduring change is possible when people are fortified by the belief that they can change and are able to integrate new ideas, perspectives, and growth-oriented experiences into their lives. When clinicians introduce hypnosis into the therapeutic relationship, it is a dramatic indication of their intention to be helpful, as well as of their professional expertise and readiness to employ efficient techniques to assist clients create themselves anew. I have often observed how the mere expectancy of pain relief for the hurting, the balm of relaxation for the anxious, and a rosier worldview for the depressed can engender hope and forge a positive therapeutic alliance and mental set toward treatment in general. Practitioners of hypnosis are likely to be attuned to the helpful as well as the harmful effects of words and nonverbal communications, and are trained to devise therapeutic suggestions that can target the cognitive and behavioral under-pinnings of diverse psychological disorders and medical conditions with exquisite precision. A suggestive approach, at its best, involves an intimate collaboration with the client geared toward determining some combination of effective strategies and techniques. It is to Michael Yapko's credit that he has captured and made explicit in this volume many of the details and fine points of how effective therapy can occur when hypnosis is used as a core component of the intervention. In this way, the author achieves one of his central goals: to convey the "artistry" of hypnosis to the reader.

An emerging body of research supports the idea that hypnosis can be an effective catalyst to therapies ranging from cognitive-behavioral to psychodynamic (Barber, 1985; Lynn, Kirsch, Barabasz, Cardeña, & Patterson, 2000). Nevertheless, newcomers to hypnosis are often chary about learning hypnosis given the cultural myths that have surrounded it from the time of Mesmer, and are intimidated by the prospect of crafting inductions and suggestions and of not "doing hypnosis right." If you are such a newcomer, *Trancework* is an authoritative primer that will start you on your way. In a step-wise, logical sequence, you will learn the nuts and bolts of how to: (a) establish rapport and demystify hypnosis, (b) create an hypnotic induction and devise a plethora of useful therapeutic suggestions, (c) assess responsiveness to suggestions, and (d) minimize untoward reactions to hypnotic procedures.

Readers already familiar with hypnotic procedures will appreciate the nuanced and engaging discussions of influential hypnosis theories, the role of informed consent in treatment, recent developments in cognitive neuroscience in understanding hypnosis, the pros and cons of formal versus informal hypnotic suggestibility assessment, and the advantages and disadvantages of different types of hypnotic suggestions (e.g., direct, indirect, permissive, authoritative) and manualized versus individualized treatment approaches. Novice and seasoned readers alike will appreciate the humor and wit, good advice, anecdotes, and rich case material that is the author's stock-in-trade. I found myself flipping through the pages like I was reading compelling nonfiction, and like some of the novels I treasure, I was disappointed when the book ended.

The title, which features the controversial term "trance," might dissuade some readers from perusing the book. That would be a mistake. As the author explains, the title is a vestige of previous editions of the book, and was retained in this thoroughly updated revised edition in order to identify it with its two immensely successful predecessors. Although Yapko acknowledges that the term "trance" is obsolete, there is nothing obsolete about the contents of the book. In fact, *Trancework* brims with virtually up-to-the-minute references to research, contemporary hypnosis theories, clinical issues and techniques, and intellectually stimulating controversies and theoretical debates. The author's presentation of controversies regarding the nature of hypnosis and the role of hypnosis in creating false memories is fair to different theoretical perspectives, faithful to the empirical literature, and accessible to a wide audience.

It is evident that writing this book was a labor of love for Michael Yapko. He speaks with the authority of many years of clinical experience, shared in this and his many other excellent books. But he is also a knowledgeable, clear, and compassionate teacher who takes seriously the challenge of making the skills of hypnosis accessible to a broad audience. I heartily recommend Michael Yapko's *Trancework* to what I hope will be a growing legion of students of hypnosis around the world.

–Steven Jay Lynn, Ph.D., ABPP
Professor of Psychology
Binghamton University
Binghamton, NY

REFERENCES

Barber, T. X. (1985). Hypnosuggestive procedures as catalysts for effective psychotherapies. In S. J. Lynn & J. P. Garske (Eds.), *Models and methods of psychotherapy* (pp. 333–76). Columbus, OH: Charles E. Merrill.

Lynn, S. J., Kirsch, I., Batabasz, A., Cardeña, E., & Patterson, D. (2000). Hypnosis as an empirically supported adjunctive technique: The state of the evidence. *International Journal of Clinical and Experimental Hypnosis, 48,* 343–61.

Introduction to the 3rd Edition

Welcome to this new edition, the third, of *Trancework: An Introduction to the Practice of Clinical Hypnosis*. It has been a labor of love to prepare this new edition. Being in this field for as long as I have, it is a wonderful thing to feel even more enthusiastic about it than when I began. I hope my enthusiasm will come shining through, and that you will find *Trancework* a valuable introduction to a dynamic and fascinating field.

WHAT'S NEW IN THIS EDITION

First, let me say a few words about why a new edition was necessary, and what you can expect to find in this volume. The second edition of *Trancework* came out in 1990, more than a dozen years ago, and so much has happened in the field in the interim that this revision is actually quite long overdue. In fact, so much has evolved that I considered changing the title of the book simply to eliminate the use of the obsolete word "trance" just to keep in step with the times. But, the title *Trancework* is so well known within the field that it made practical sense to keep it, thereby requiring people to look beyond the title to see what's new.

So, what's new in this third edition? Two brand new chapters have been added, as have many entirely new chapter sections spread throughout the book. Other chapters have been substantially modified, a response to the explosion of good recent studies revealing and clarifying many aspects of hypnosis. An invaluable addition to this edition are the many hundreds of reference citations provided throughout the text. For careful readers who want to be pointed in the direction of supportive research for points made, or who simply want further information on a particular topic, the extensive reference sections at the end of each chapter will be welcome.

Every field has its share of distinguished contributors, and clinical hypnosis is no exception. You will be introduced to many of them in this book through special sections throughout called "Frames of Reference." In these sections, you will hear pioneers and innovators in the field of hypnosis present some of their ideas on principles and applications of hypnosis. I am pleased to have the chance to introduce you to some of the field's most influential figures.

Trancework is a textbook meant to guide your training in hypnosis. It is meant to inspire you, of course, but also to teach the skills to be effective in applying hypnosis. The chapters are filled with practical information, and at the end of almost every chapter, you will be presented with "Things to Discuss" and "Things to Do." I hope and expect you will find these an invaluable part of the learning process.

WHAT'S NEW IN THE FIELD

Clinical hypnosis has been the subject of serious scientific inquiry for only about 70 years, but has been the source of fascination for students of human experience for more than two centuries. Only in the last two decades, however, has hypnosis research reached a level of sophistication that offers some objective evidence for its clinical value.

Three powerful forces converged in the 1990s and continue to the present that re-shaped many of our understandings of clinical hypnosis. The first of these forces has been the growing emphasis in the field of psychotherapy on proving its worth with empirical data affirming its effectiveness. The drive for developing so-called empirically supported psychotherapies has pushed and pulled the field in different, and sometimes even contradictory, directions, taking hypnosis along with it since hypnosis is most commonly applied in the psychotherapeutic domain. A direct result is the division within the field of those who see hypnosis as a vehicle for delivering "standard" psychotherapies (e.g., cognitive-behavioral, psychodynamic, etc.) and not a therapy in its own right, and those who see hypnosis as a special form of therapy reflected in the self-defining term "hypnotherapy." Regardless of one's position, the salient research questions have been, "Does hypnosis enhance treatment results?" and, "Can hypnosis correctly be considered an 'empirically supported' style of intervention?"

The second force re-shaping clinical hypnosis in recent years directly and explosively collided with the first. I'm referring to the so-called repressed memory controversy. In the mid 1990s, the controversy reached its zenith, bitterly dividing the mental health profession over the presumed role of repressed memories of childhood sexual abuse as the underlying cause of a client's current symptoms. Extreme positions by "experts" dominated the field, encouraging clinicians to either believe all memories excavated in treatment through hypnosis and other suggestive memory retrieval techniques or to disbelieve all such memories as fabrications in response to untoward influence by therapists or others. (The controversy has since quieted as evidence for both/all points of view helped define an informed clinical practice.) Suddenly, hypnosis and the phenomenon of human suggestibility was in the center spotlight as experts in persuasion, interrogation, memory, trauma, and hypnosis squared off against each other, both in the journals and the tabloids, further confusing an already confused public about what it all meant. Meanwhile, each day's headlines blared a new story of some trusted figure being accused of abuse on the basis of memories recovered in hypnosis. The field of clinical hypnosis was forced to redefine itself more scientifically while directly addressing and correcting many of the common myths held about the nature of human memory and how it is affected by hypnotic procedures.

The third major force reshaping the field has been the advances in cognitive neuroscience. There is something about the experience of hypnosis that invites careful neurophysiological inquiry. After all, unusual things happen: A person has normal bodily perceptions one minute, then focuses on suggestions for experiencing a dramatic change in bodily sensations, and the next minute the person actually experiences those suggested changes. How does the mind influence the brain in hypnosis, and vice versa? Newer scanning technologies, such as functional Magnetic Resonance Imaging (fMRI), have made it possible to begin investigating the brain during hypnotic procedures in ways that simply were not possible years ago. The possibilities in this new domain of research are very exciting and may eventually help us focus our clinical efforts.

RESEARCH AND CLINICAL PRACTICE

Has a state of hypnosis, what used to popularly be called a "trance state," been identified? No, nor do people in hypnosis generally think of themselves in some unique altered state of consciousness. The use of the term "trance" to characterize the experience of hypnosis is not particularly descriptive of anything either scientifically precise or clinically relevant, and so I have dropped it from the body of this volume. Instead, I will talk about the subjective experiences of hypnosis from the standpoint of the person in hypnosis, and the processes of hypnosis from the standpoint of the person conducting the hypnosis session. I will generally use the term "client" to refer to the former, and either "clinician" or "therapist" to refer to the latter.

With data being the new currency in the field, researchers have taken a newly ascendant position, and clinicians a largely defensive one, struggling to continue to do what they feel works, even if the evidence is not yet there to validate them. Clinicians understand that no matter how much scientific data are generated, clinical practice will always require a high level of artistry. Consequently, I think it is imperative to provide you with some exposure to the scientific side of hypnosis, citing many (but only a small percentage of) the good research studies available. And, I think it even more imperative to highlight the actual skills that go into developing and delivering effective hypnotic processes. After all, no matter how much data and scientifically supported rationales you might have for a specific intervention, it means next to nothing if the client doesn't benefit from it. (Frankly, it's why I'd prefer we "validate" *therapists* rather than therapies.) As you can tell, I'm a pragmatist. My emphasis throughout this book will reflect that orientation, highlighting what is practical and effective.

Helping you evolve the artistry in both conceptualizing and applying clinical hypnosis is a primary goal of this volume, especially in light of recent clinical controversies and the demands of modern clinical practice in an age of accountability. I hope you will enjoy learning both the art and science of clinical hypnosis. And, I especially hope you will discover both the personal and professional enrichments as well as the many benefits to your clients when you integrate clinical hypnosis into your practice.

–Michael D. Yapko, Ph.D.
June 2003
www.yapko.com

Foreword to the 2nd Edition

Although I am not a practitioner of the Ericksonian approach, nor a strategic therapist, and hold different opinions on aspects of hypnotism from Michael Yapko, I believe I can correctly state that *Trancework* is an excellent exposition of current teachings on Ericksonian therapy or, as the author prefers to say, of the naturalistic approach originated by Milton H. Erickson.

The naturalistic approach to therapy and to hypnotism can be summed up in a few words: It is the "utilization," that is, the use by the therapist of whatever capacities and kinds of responses the patient has and is capable of giving at any particular moment; even his or her symptoms can be used.

Trancework is also an excellent introduction to strategic therapy, which is an outgrowth of this naturalistic approach. Strategic therapy was originally defined quite broadly by Jay Haley (as a result of his study of Erickson's therapeutic work) as any therapy in which the therapist takes the responsibility of directly influencing the patient according to a plan of treatment determined by the presenting problem. But to be a true reflection of Erickson's approach, as it was intended to be, this definition should have added that the plan is also determined by what can be utilized out of what is offered by the patient at any given moment, a plan that is both fluid and unique for each patient. It is in this sense that I see *Trancework* as an exposition of strategic therapy.

However, *Trancework* is not just an exposition of Ericksonian methods or of strategic therapy. It is more; it is a reflection of Michael Yapko's personal understandings, skills, and experience as a psychotherapist and psychologist. One way of summing up Erickson's approach to psychotherapy is to say that it is an integration of hypnotic and nonhypnotic phenomena brought about naturalistically for therapeutic purposes. It is to Yapko's credit that he not only has been able to capture the essence of this approach, but he has also been able to make it available in a practical way.

While the author's subject matter is primarily clinical hypnotism as viewed from within a naturalistic framework, he does not ignore matters pertaining to traditional hypnotism and introduces the reader to its principal concepts and methods. With fairness, he points out the strengths and weaknesses of the two approaches as he sees them, although clearly giving his overall preference to the naturalistic approach.

There is considerable didactic material in *Trancework*, but the book remains above all a practical work aiming not only to teach the reader the art of doing hypnotherapy but, more importantly, the art of doing effective psychotherapy. For, as already intimated, it is in the nature of the Ericksonian approach not to separate the use of hypnotic patterns of communication from therapeutic communications in general. For both Erickson and Yapko, effective communication is the key to both the skilled use of hypnotic phenomena and to effective psychotherapy. One may not necessarily agree with the author that all influencing communications constitute hypnosis—which seems to be his position—but there is no question that readers who practice the communication techniques he details will be well on their way to becoming skilled clinical hypnotists and therapists.

A valuable pedagogical feature of the work that should not be overlooked are the lists of topics for discussion and the assignments with which each chapter terminates. Readers would be well advised to give them their attention.

Trancework will be a good starting point for beginners, and a good review for more advanced workers. It brings together a great deal of material, and should be particularly instructive for practitioners who have thus far limited themselves strictly to the traditional approach.

—André M. Weitzenhoffer, Ph.D.
Nathrop, Colorado

Introduction to the 2nd Edition

When *Trancework* first came out in 1984, it was riding on a wave of enthusiasm for the creative approaches to hypnosis and hypnotically based psychotherapy of the late Milton H. Erickson, M.D. The focus on Erickson and his innovative methods has spawned a whole new generation of clinicians interested in hypnosis and the applications it may have in various clinical contexts. *Trancework* is not a book about Erickson, though. It is a book about practical methods for developing the kinds of relationship and communication skills that will increase the effectiveness of your clinical methods, regardless of the context in which they are applied. I am a practical-minded fellow who is interested in therapeutic patterns that work. Erickson's emphasis was also a practical one, which I can appreciate. His influence on the material contained here is significant.

This second edition represents an effort to make the acquisition of skills to apply hypnosis more easily accomplished by the reader. The exercises and discussions can be the most powerful teachers of hypnotic skill, but this revised edition presents new features that will enhance the learning process. First, two new chapters have been added. Chapter 19 contains transcripts of portions of actual hypnosis sessions conducted with bona fide clients. Chapter 20 presents a verbatim clinical session in its entirety, including commentary intended to amplify points of interest in the learning of hypnotic communication. Both new chapters are intended to provide greater insight into the clinical applications of hypnosis and are considered a valuable addition to the text.

Another new feature is the Frames of Reference sections, which include worthwhile quotes on a variety of stimulating topics from leading figures in the field. These Frames of Reference provide an enjoyable glimpse into the thinking and the history of notable authorities. The reader will note that the Frames of Reference are listed separately, immediately following the table of contents.

Also new to this edition are 20 tables that clearly and succinctly provide key information. These tables can be easily memorized, allowing more rapid integration of the material. What makes hypnosis so potentially useful a tool? Is it the emphasis on acknowledging and respecting the subjective reality of each individual client? Is it the emphasis on the cooperative nature of the therapeutic relationship? Is it the enhanced appreciation and use of the recognition that words can heal? Certainly, all these are factors contributing to the effectiveness of hypnotic patterns, but the strength of doing trancework comes from undefinable sources within each human being. Whether these are termed the "unconscious," "inner wisdom," "the God within," or some other equally ambiguous name, there is a remarkable potential in each person that surfaces during those states of absorption called "trance" that one can readily appreciate. If there is a more dynamic and potent means of empowering individuals than by working hypnotically, I am not yet aware of it.

It is unfortunate, but nonetheless true, that the field of hypnosis remains an internally conflicted one. The focus on the clinical approaches of Erickson has been substantial in the last decade, and it is a basic truth that every movement creates a countermovement. While many were (noncritically) touting the wonders of "Ericksonian hypnosis," others were openly criticizing the apparent lack of objectivity in such strong claims. Just as there are divisions in the field of psychotherapy, there are those who align themselves with one model of hypnosis and openly express disapproval for any other model. It is my hope that *Trancework* will permit you to sidestep issues of alignment and instead focus on issues associated with discovering how you as an individual practitioner can best apply these approaches in a manner congruent with your training and personality. While I generally favor the flexibility of less direct and imposing techniques, I am quite aware that what works well for me may not work as well for someone else.

Knowing what I know about trance states and ways to induce and utilize them, I am inclined to integrate the seemingly irreconcilable views about hypnosis. I generally promote the perspective that while the experimental production of specific trance phenomena is not an apparent capability of all people, the "real life" utilization of specific trance phenomena to create reality (including wellness and illness) is evident in all. The question of what is and what is not "trance" is interesting fodder for debates which cannot be won, but is irrelevant when a client is in distress and needs a skilled, flexible, creative therapist to interrupt self-limiting patterns while building self-enhancing ones.

Technique is inevitably bound to context. What succeeds in one context can be faithfully duplicated but still yield unfortunate results in another context. What *Trancework* is ultimately about is synthesizing what is known about social influence, communication, psychotherapy, and clinical hypnosis in order to sensitize you to the healing power of words, the healing power of beliefs, and the healing power of relationships.

In that regard, I have chosen not to focus on facts and issues unrelated to the development of actual skills in using hypnosis. Detailing the ancient history of hypnosis or reporting unusual experiments with hypnosis that lead to nonclinical questions such as whether or not hypnosis can be used to get someone to rob a bank is simply not consistent with my aim in writing *Trancework*. I am all too aware that most professionals do not get their hypnosis training in academic institutions—they get it in privately sponsored workshops. If you are taking a university-sponsored course in hypnosis, consider yourself fortunate to have some progressive aspects in your curriculum. Most hypnosis training takes place in small groups of interested and experienced clinicians. As one who routinely offers such training, I am aware of the participants' desire to focus on skill-building above all else. For this reason, I have included things to discuss and things to do in every chapter. The conceptual framework of the first part of the book is simply a foundation for more easily assimilating the techniques of the second part of the book. The true skills, however, come only with practice, as you would naturally expect.

I would like to make one final point about usage in this edition. Rather than refer to people exclusively as male, as tradition suggests, or exclusively as female, as I did in the first edition, I have consistently made use of both male and female pronouns in an inconsistent way, throughout the book. Male and female therapists; male and female clients. Just like in the real world.

I hope you find *Trancework* a valued ally in your efforts to learn clinical hypnosis. More importantly, I hope you find resources in yourself you can appreciate as you learn.

—Michael D. Yapko, Ph.D.
San Diego, California

Foreword to the 1st Edition

Milton Erickson was known for his flexible and effective therapeutic communication which was predicated to a great extent on his ability to read nonverbal behavior. Early in my training with Erickson, I asked for instruction to be able to better understand nonverbal behavior. In an amused fashion, he asked if I knew the definition of "zyzzyx." I replied that I did not and asked what it meant. He instructed me to look it up in the dictionary, stating that you first learn the alphabet, then the words, then the grammar. There is no substitute for direct experience and, before one goes on to complex tasks, it is important to really know the basics.

In this volume, Michael Yapko presents the alphabet of hypnotic influence communication based in part on Erickson's strategic and symptom-based therapy, a methodology that uses hypnosis both formally and naturalistically to promote change. Whereas traditional therapy made understanding and insight primary, Ericksonian methods center on promoting effective living independent of the therapeutic situation. To accomplish goals and to maximize patient-based change, Erickson pioneered indirect techniques, noting that communication occurs on multiple levels, including the verbal content, the implications, and such extraverbal factors as tone, duration, intensity, and body language. In fact, some experts maintain that only a small fraction of our response to communication is due to the verbal content.

Traditional therapists interpret the patient's multiple level communication, that is, describe back to the patient what he "really means." Modern Ericksonian methods, however, are predicated on the idea that if the patient is intelligent enough to communicate on more than one level, the therapist should be equally intelligent. Therapeutic communication does not need to be interpretive, concrete, direct, or linear to be effective. In fact, therapeutic communication is best when the therapist is flexible, uses indirect techniques, and focuses as many output channels of communication as possible (Zeig, 1980).

Yapko gently eases us into the world of hypnotic communication. He provides a balance between direct and indirect techniques, integrating clear examples of each approach into the text. Examples also are given of content and process techniques (roughly, those that are specific and those that are more general). Direct and indirect techniques along with process and content suggestions have their place in therapy. Yapko does not tell us which to use or when to use them; rather, he examines possibilities, presenting the advantages and disadvantages of each, reminding us that the amount of indirection to be used is directly proportional to the perceived resistance.

Yapko's approach to hypnosis is a radical departure from other authorities. He defines hypnosis as influence communication—a position sure to be considered controversial because some might think that definition too general, thereby unnecessarily diluting the territory. However, Yapko presents his arguments cogently and has a position that deserves recognition in the literature and can be supported by citations and references.

Trancework was written to promote clinical hypnosis and make it more available to psychotherapists. It will motivate many to enter the field and broaden their interests so that there will be active use of and research into hypnotic communication.

I find this book particularly interesting when it describes the induction process, the utilization of trance phenomena, and the wording of different types of suggestions. Professionals will appreciate the attention given to the ethical use of hypnosis. In good Ericksonian fashion, we are admonished to attend to individual differences and meet the patient at his frame of reference; the emphasis is on communication skills, not on rigid formulas.

Trancework provides the building blocks necessary to learn the vocabulary and grammar of hypnotherapy and effective forms of influence communication. We look forward to other expositions from this talented writer.

     —Jeffrey K. Zeig, Ph.D.
      Director, The Milton H. Erickson Foundation
      Phoenix, Arizona

REFERENCE

Zeig, J. (1980). Symptom prescription techniques: Clinical applications using elements of communication. *American Journal of Clinical Hypnosis, 23*, 23–32.

Introduction to the 1st Edition

If the word "hypnosis" conjures up images of a powerful, magician-like figure dangling a gold watch in the face of a stuporous subject while giving the command to "sleep deeply," then you are in a for a pleasant surprise. Not only is that not what clinical hypnosis is all about, but that old stereotype of hypnosis has little relevance to the current perspective of hypnosis as a rich system of communication.

Hypnotic patterns are evident wherever influential communication occurs. The artistry of meaningful applications of hypnosis can be appreciated when one considers the dynamics of how one person can use communication to alter the experience of another.

It is my hope and anticipation that hypnosis will become a significant part of your range of interactional skills, even if after reading this book you never formally induce a trance in anyone for the remainder of your life. Although that may seem a grandiose goal for a hypnosis book, many years of teaching hypnosis to practicing professionals and graduate students have convinced me that the skills in communication described in this book can make a positive difference in the work you do and in the relationships you form with virtually everyone.

So much has happened in recent years in the fields of clinical hypnosis, clinical psychology, communications, linguistics, neurology, and other fields relevant to understanding human behavior that the impact has yet to be fully appreciated. Certainly a revolution has taken place in perspectives on hypnosis, described throughout this book. In the past there have been numerous theories explaining the various phenomena associated with the trance state, yet the practice of hypnosis was generally limited to one of two forms: (1) the "traditional" application of hypnosis emphasizing the power of the hypnotist in relationship to an obedient subject (this approach is best represented by the stage hypnotist), and (2) a "standardized" approach emphasizing the responsibility of the client to adapt herself to a scripted, and therefore nonindividualized, program of the hypnotist (best represented by prepackaged tapes and "cookbook" treatments). Both approaches have been quite limited in their ability to obtain positive results reliably (see Appendix A).

Fortunately, the field of hypnosis has evolved past these two limited approaches in recent years. This development is due in large part to the innovative and untiring work of the late psychiatrist and hypnosis pioneer Milton H. Erickson, M.D. Erickson evolved his own unique techniques which could recognize and use the creativity and individuality of each person. Recently, numerous texts and articles have flooded the hypnosis literature promoting Erickson's methods, collectively called the "utilization" approach, though also referred to as "Ericksonian hypnosis." In this model, emphasis is placed upon the utilization of as many dimensions of the client's inner world as possible, particularly the unconscious mind's unique resources.

The progression of hypnosis as a field beyond demanding blind obedience and offering scripted routines has radically changed its conceptual and practical frameworks. Hypnosis is no longer the "occultish" mystery it once was, although undeniably there are still things about hypnosis remaining to be explained. With the progression in understandings about hypnosis has also come acceptance. Although most people encountering hypnosis for the first time still do so in a stage show context, increasing numbers of people are also being made aware of its clinical and other appropriate professional uses. Typically, they have been made aware through the media, which frequently runs programs and articles on hypnosis, or through friends who have obtained help through hypnosis.

The sole purpose of this book is to introduce professionals to the rich and complex world of clinical hypnosis. I hope it will allow you to acquire a comprehensive understanding of the concepts and issues related to its practice, and to acquire the basic skills that only years of regular practice and continued pursuit of excellence can build upon. Re-read, if you don't mind, the last sentence. It is one written with great sincerity. To become truly skilled in the use of hypnosis (or any other worthwhile endeavor for that matter) takes a great deal of time and commitment. This book can provide a broad and solid framework of understanding and experience that more advanced, specialized studies of hypnosis can build upon.

There are plenty of books, cassette and videotape packages, and training programs that promise to make you a hypnotist "overnight." They are not lying, either, for you can be a hypnotist overnight. Guiding a person into trance is not particularly difficult, nor is reading a prepared script to the hypnotized subject. Such approaches may even get some positive results occasionally. However, obtaining consistent results across a wider range of client concerns requires a sensitivity and deeper knowledge that is not available in such approaches. Developing sensitivity to the individual needs of the client and learning how to best develop her unique inner resources is not taught in the "overnight hypnotist" programs. Only rigid formulas are. The oversimplifications of the traditional and standardized approaches make them, in many instances, undesirable for use.

Unfortunately, a powerful tool like hypnosis can be placed in the hands of people who are not in a position to appreciate the full implications of its use. This is another reason why anyone can be a hypnotist: It is legal for anyone who wants to to hang out the "hypnotist" shingle on her door with no formal credentials, not even a high school diploma. Hypnotists who are untrained in the health professions are routinely providing physical and psychological health care, under ambiguous names of course, but health care nonetheless. Some are really quite good at what they do, but the potential dangers should be apparent.

After you have read this book you will be faced with decisions about how much more, if any, training and proficiency you want to obtain. Beyond what you will be aware of learning, you can learn a great deal more without even realizing you are learning, and perhaps you can decide to learn just enough to take pride in your knowledge and skills. This is a book for training in hypnosis. There are exercises to do, concepts and terms to master, and points to discuss. I encourage you to experience and practice all the techniques you can. Ultimately, you can read about hypnosis, then read more about it, and talk about it, and then read still more about it, but there is no substitute for hours and hours of working with it. A lot of commitment, but the payoff is most rewarding.

—Michael D. Yapko, Ph.D.
San Diego, California

SECTION I
Conceptual Framework

1
What Is Hypnosis and Can it Help?

Vicki knew something was physically wrong with her, but she didn't know how wrong. The numerous doctors she presented her symptoms to seemed unconcerned, and she reported that several were even abrupt and dismissive of her. She assumed the unwelcome reactions she received from her doctors were probably because her patient file was so thick and included an extensive history of mental health issues. The doctors reasoned, and apparently more than one even said it to her directly, that anyone with such an accumulation of hospitalizations and doctor visits, most of them psychiatric, must be a deeply troubled woman. Presumably, she must be prone to exaggeration at least, and she may be a frustrating and time-consuming hypochondriac, or perhaps she is even delusional. She rationally countered, "But, even hypochondriacs get sick!" and asked for appropriate medical tests. By the time she was finally diagnosed with terminal cancer, it was too late for her to be heard. The cancer had already spread throughout her body, and was in her brain, bones, lungs, and adrenals. She was told she had a very short time left to live, probably just weeks. There were no apologies or expressions of regret from her dismissive doctors.

Vicki had tumors growing in her body that caused her considerable pain at times. She was told by her newly sympathetic doctors that she could have whatever pain medications she might need or want to make her last days comfortable. But Vicki didn't want to take any pain medications at all, if possible, out of concern that she would be negatively affected mentally by them. She wanted to be fully alert mentally and as physically active as possible in whatever time she might have left. She found her way to me in order to explore whether it might be possible for her to learn how to use her mind to manage pain without drugs. She had heard that clinical hypnosis was a valuable therapeutic tool that could even be used by patients to undergo major surgeries without the use of any chemical anesthesia. (She was informed correctly.) Vicki wanted to develop as much control over her pain as she could so she could function as well as possible right up to the very end.

What a remarkable woman! In the face of her impending death, she sought personal growth. Instead of focusing on despair, she chose to focus on increasing her sense of fulfillment. Vicki was inspiring, and I wanted to help her in any way I could. But, what could I say to ease her pain? What could I teach her about her inner experiences and hidden resources that would help her manage dying with the kind of dignity and clarity she wanted?

By the time we began the hypnosis session, Vicki had revealed many facets of her Self that were extraordinary: courage, determination, resilience, focus, and so many more. All that she had experienced in her life, right up to age 42 when I saw her, had come to serve as powerful personal resources. What hypnosis does best is amplify people's abilities, including their hidden abilities such as the capacity to reduce the subjective experience of pain or the capacity to better adapt to a change in one's circumstances. Hypnosis empowers people to discover and develop strengths in themselves they didn't know they had, and the consequences in people's lives are often nothing short of extraordinary.

Hypnosis helped Vicki find the comfort she wanted. A full transcript of my entire session with Vicki, including commentary and analysis, can be found in chapter 20. When you have learned what's in the chapters between here and there, you'll likely find the session a moving example of how hypnosis can be used to make a meaningful difference for someone struggling with issues as deep and powerful as life and death.

The power of hypnosis. The "magic" of hypnosis. The mystery of hypnosis. The very word has an aura of intrigue associated with it.

What is hypnosis? How is hypnosis relevant to clinical intervention in treating client problems? And, how can you begin to acquire the skills for incorporating hypnosis into your clinical practice? These three questions provide the foundation for this text, and aspects of the complicated answers will evolve as each chapter unfolds. This book will provide clinicians wanting to learn hypnosis with both perspectives and methods that are based on current scientific understandings of hypnosis as well as the realities of modern clinical practice.

Hypnosis has no single agreed upon definition (Lynn & Rhue, 1991). A widely cited definition is the one offered by the American Psychological Association's hypnosis division, called the Society of Psychological Hypnosis (1993): "Hypnosis is a procedure during which a health professional or researcher suggests that a client, patient, or subject experience changes in sensations, perceptions, thoughts, or behavior." This broad definition acknowledges the role of the person doing hypnosis, the context in which it is done, and the role of the person experiencing hypnosis. What happens in the mix of these three factors that makes it possible for someone to essentially direct someone else to have an experience that, under normal conditions, would seem, at the very least, unlikely? For example, telling someone to have a sense of numbness in a particular physical location is not typical conversation! Something very special is going on in the world of hypnosis, as I hope and expect you will discover here.

Hypnosis has been up and down on the roller coaster of acceptability to both layperson and professional alike. To help gain acceptance for hypnosis (or themselves), some practitioners have made some pretty wild claims, sensationalized treatment results, and, in general, built hypnosis up into a magical, mystical process that seems to have everything going for it but a formal endorsement from the Almighty. Unfortunately, the more grandiose a claim for *any* product or service, the more skeptical the careful consumer must become, and the more extreme a position its advocates are subsequently pushed into. The result is almost inevitably more turn-offs than turn-ons.

In recent years, however, hypnosis has increasingly become the subject of serious scientific inquiry, effectively scaling down the grandiose claims while steadily increasing what can be said in its favor with substantive evidence. Thousands of articles have been published in the best of scientific journals (Nash, Minton, & Baldridge, 1988; Weitzenhoffer, 2000), and membership in the professional societies has encouraged more and more clinicians and researchers to join together to investigate the merits of hypnosis (Baker, 1987; Lynn, Kirsch, Neufeld, & Rhue, 1996).

Hypnosis is an innately fascinating topic to most people. It's a phenomenon that invites lively discussion, curious speculation, and even profound philosophizing about the nature of human consciousness and the complex, confusing relationship between mind and brain. Hypnosis has been at the heart of major controversies in recent years, and it continues to confound the general public who, understandably, can't readily grasp how hypnosis can be in the spotlight in cheesy stage acts (that don't seem to, but probably should, embarrass everyone involved), and yet it can be taken seriously by prominent researchers and clinicians who unequivocally declare it an effective vehicle of treatment.

More and more frequently, I encounter people who have had positive exposure to the applications of clinical hypnosis. There have been some wonderful segments showing hypnosis which have aired on popular television programs in recent years, some excellent articles describing clinical hypnosis have appeared in popular magazines, and hypnosis has been featured favorably in a variety of other media avenues available to both the general public and the professional community alike. As a direct result of these and other influences (such as highly respected individuals and institutions aggressively promoting its use), hypnosis has steadily grown in depth and breadth to become an important and more widely utilized component of the health treatment team. There is still a long way to go in making hypnotic principles and methods a part of most helping professionals' repertoire of fundamental skills. But, my experience in teaching clinical hypnosis to health professionals of diverse backgrounds and interests suggests that when hypnosis is made a more practical and understandable tool, its positive use grows and the appreciation for its potentials spreads.

HOW HYPNOSIS INFORMS CLINICAL PRACTICE

This book doesn't seek to sensationalize hypnosis, nor is it intended to make a statement about how hypnosis is "the answer to all of life's challenges." Rather, hypnosis is conceptualized and treated as a means of helping clients develop powerful personal resources that can be purposefully directed toward achieving their therapeutic goals. The evidence for the effectiveness of hypnosis is substantial and ever growing (Kirsch, Montgomery, & Sapirstein, 1995; Lynn, Kirsch, Barabasz, Cardeña, & Patterson, 2000).

Therapeutic intervention of *any* type inevitably involves skilled communication between client and clinician. Therapy's *interpersonal* (i.e., social) aspects are a primary focus in studying hypnosis, since a primary question we routinely ask ourselves as clinicians is the one posed above in the Vicki vignette: What can I say to ease this person's pain? Studying hypnosis teaches us a great deal about *how to present ideas* and *how to structure interactions* for maximum therapeutic benefit (J. Barber, 1991; T. Barber, 2000).

Just saying something with an intention to be helpful isn't enough, however. How a client hears what we say is an obviously crucial piece of the interaction. The study of hypnosis offers substantial insights into *how human beings construct their individual realities*, and how the various *intrapersonal* components of human experience can be assembled to help generate wellness at one end of the continuum and pathology at the other (Lynn & Sivec, 1992; Brown, 1992).

Studying hypnosis will no doubt change your understandings of people and their problems by encouraging you to look for client strengths in ways you may not have considered before. Acquiring skills in the use of clinical hypnosis will be an invaluable means for enhancing your clinical abilities. Integrating hypnosis into your treatment plans can allow you to obtain lasting results in the therapy work you do. Perhaps best of all, use of hypnosis can be a way to promote self-sufficiency and independence in the clients you work with, helping them to feel more in control, resourceful, and self-assured (Lynn, Kirsch, Barabasz, Cardeña, & Patterson, 2000; Schoenberger, 2000).

THE CLINICIAN-CLIENT RELATIONSHIP
IS THE FOUNDATION

Clinical hypnosis has many different facets, each reflecting a different dimension of the phenomenon. In this book, I will primarily pay attention to the clinical context in which hypnosis is applied. By focusing on the clinical use of hypnotic principles and approaches, I will be paying greater attention to the essential skills of using words and gestures in particular ways to achieve specific therapeutic outcomes. Thus, the emphasis throughout this text will be on the use of hypnotic processes as agents of therapeutic influence involving patterns of effective relationship and communication skills. This is not to say that hypnosis is only about the skills of the clinician, particularly when it is well established that hypnosis only happens when the client permits it and has the salient resources for it (Woody, Bowers, & Oakman, 1992; Hilgard, 1992). But, the skills of the clinician are a large part of the hypnosis equation, and these skills are the focus of this book. The orientation toward hypnosis emphasizing skillful relating to the client minimizes the use of ritualistic or impersonal approaches to hypnosis, instead encouraging an assessment of and flexible responsiveness to individual client needs. Identifying and responding to the unique attributes of each client is more demanding than adopting a "one-size-fits-all" approach, and accounts in large part for the considerable effort involved in becoming skilled with hypnosis. I would say the same thing, of course, about developing *any* clinical skill.

My emphasis throughout will generally lean heavily in the direction of being "practical" and "understandable." I intend to present the concepts and techniques of hypnosis in a way that will allow you to evolve clinically useful understandings. In doing so, I would like to avoid, whenever possible, the unanswerable philosophical questions that knowledgeable people have debated about endlessly, such as whether there is such a thing as "reality" or whether Adam was in hypnosis when God took his rib to make Eve. Instead, I will focus on specific clinically relevant skills that can be obtained through the study of hypnotic phenomena and patterns of hypnotic communication.

THE CHALLENGE OF NEGATIVE BIAS

Almost everyone has an established attitude about hypnosis. Most people have seen or heard of it, and whatever they saw, heard, or felt at the time left an impression as the basis for their attitude. Hypnosis has been demonstrated in movies, kiddie cartoons, television programs, stage shows, state fairs, and night clubs everywhere. You may have seen someone dabble in the art at parties (usually just before his lampshade-on-the-head routine). It may have caused someone you know to try to quit smoking in one of those "instant success" programs and feel even worse when they may have failed to do so. It was rumored to be the reason that the kid in your neighborhood joined a cult. With these kind of negative exposures, it is little wonder that many people feel certain that *whatever* hypnosis is, it is beyond understanding . . . and probably dangerous.

For stage performers, keeping the mystery in hypnosis means more bread and butter. Unfortunately, these are the people least able to use hypnosis effectively to its greatest potential as a legitimate clinical tool for helping people improve their lives. Instead, they misrepresent hypnosis to the public, both layperson and professional, as an apparent mind-controlling instrument with frightening implications. As sophisticated and enlightened as many people are becoming in many areas, change of mind seems to come a bit harder in the field of hypnosis. It is difficult to bridge a gap as wide as the one between the crudeness of stage hypnosis and the refined applications of clinical hypnosis.

Few fields have had the ups and downs hypnosis has had. Hypnosis as a recognizable phenomenon has been around, in various forms and with various names, for thousands of years. Acceptability has ranged from moderate to none. People who practiced hypnosis had their rituals ("techniques") and superstitions ("this induction worked pretty well on the last client I had with freckles . . ."), but they had very little scientific understanding of what they were actually doing. The assumption was that there was something inherently powerful about the technique itself, thus too little attention was paid to the inner processes of the client or the nature of the situation in which the hypnosis was applied. With ever-increasing evidence of the effectiveness of hypnosis in catalyzing positive clinical outcomes, and with acceptability and applicability of hypnotic processes growing in scope as a result, the need for a sensible, understandable approach is more necessary than ever for maximizing positive exposure to the merits of hypnosis. That is a primary goal of this book.

IS THERE EMPIRICAL EVIDENCE
THAT HYPNOSIS REALLY WORKS?

The current climate for clinical practice, and the climate that will likely prevail for the foreseeable future, is one that heavily emphasizes empiricism. Clinicians in all fields are now routinely being asked to explain and justify their methods in terms of objective data attesting to the merits of their interventions. In the practice of psychotherapy, clinicians are expected (by insurance companies, employers, and even clients) to use only those methods that have a strong base of support in clinical research. Some in the field have even gone so far as to promote the idea of manualizing treatment such that therapy is performed according to a specified format developed on the basis of controlled research indicating its value.

The field of hypnosis has been directly influenced by the push for what are generally termed "empirically supported treatments." In recent years, substantial high-quality research has been done in order to assess what, if anything, hypnosis can contribute to the positive effects of treatment. Thus, a growing body of good hypnosis research is becoming available to clinicians of all types, especially since this valuable research is no longer being published only in hypnosis specialty journals.

What does the hypnosis research say about hypnosis as an empirically supported treatment? How should we view such research? These are important questions to consider at the outset of your study of hypnosis. As you evolve your own individual conceptual framework and style for applying hypnotic approaches, you will be better equipped to determine for yourself the significance and relevance of particular research findings for your work.

Let's briefly consider the issue of how to view hypnosis research before discussing general or specific findings. Much more will be said about these issues later, of course, but in this first chapter it seems necessary to address the research issue, even if only superficially. Let's pose the question directly: Does hypnosis work, that is, is it an effective therapy? The question seems deceptively simple, as if there should be a clear response. Unfortunately, though, the issue isn't clear because of one confounding factor: The debate still goes on to this day as to whether hypnosis should be considered a therapy, or simply a therapeutic tool and not a therapy in its own right (American Psychological Association, 1999; Kirsch, Lynn, & Rhue, 1993). There are prestigious and persuasive advocates for both positions. For those who view hypnosis as a therapy in its own right, a therapy which employs hypnosis is termed "hypnotherapy" and it implies that hypnosis is the principal mechanism of intervention. Hypnosis is viewed by hypnotherapists as a style of treatment that is as well-defined and as distinct in character as, say, behavior therapy. On the other side of the issue are those who view hypnosis as a tool of treatment, integrated into a larger conceptual and practical framework that transcends the hypnotic procedures themselves. Rather than hypnosis or suggestive procedures being "stand alone" methods, hypnosis is used to further the aims of other, more well defined interventions, such as cognitive therapy. (It may seem like an annoying semantic issue to some, especially in the United States, but in many European countries the issue is substantial because how you define your work determines whether or not you are eligible for payment from government insurance resources.)

Whether hypnosis enhances treatment results is not dependent on resolving the issue of whether to define hypnosis as a therapy or a therapy tool. The dividing line between a therapy and a therapy tool in this case is sufficiently ambiguous to arouse debate by the experts. What matters more is the growing body of objective evidence that when hypnosis is part of the treatment process, it generally increases the benefits of treatment (Kirsch, Montgomery, & Sapirstein, 1995; Lynn et al., 2000; Schoenberger, 2000).

Hypnosis has been effectively applied in the treatment of far too many conditions and disorders to name them all, but some of the best known applications are in the domains of pain (Chaves, 1999; Eimer, 2000; Montgomery, DuHamel, & Redd, 2000), anxiety (Kirsch et al., 1995; Schoenberger, 2000), post-traumatic stress disorder (Brom, Kleber, & Defare, 1989; Spiegel, 1996), depression (Yapko, 1992, 2001a, 2001b, 2001c), phobias (Crawford & Barabasz, 1993; Weitzenhoffer, 2000), children's disorders (Milling & Costantino, 2000; Olness & Kohen, 1996), irritable bowel syndrome (Galovski & Blanchard,1998; Gonsalkorale, Houghton, & Whorwell, 2002) and dissociative disorders (Phillips & Frederick, 1995; Spiegel, 1993).

Hypnosis can differ dramatically from the way one clinician applies it to the way another clinician applies it. Thus, when one researcher concludes hypnosis did not significantly increase positive effects, or, conversely, when another researcher concludes it did, it bears more careful scrutiny by the reader to determine what kinds of procedures were used, and whether they reflected a particular style or orientation to hypnosis that enhanced or diminished the value of the findings.

Thus, the question, "Does hypnosis work?" is a complicated question. Is it the hypnosis itself that "works," or is it the larger treatment plan of which hypnosis is only a part that is effective? *In the most general sense, though, it can be said with confidence that hypnosis helps improve treatment outcomes.* That in itself justifies the time and effort it takes to learn hypnosis.

BUYER BEWARE

When people discover I apply hypnosis in clinical practice, they are usually both fascinated and skeptical. Almost everyone has had some direct or indirect experience with hypnosis, and it is often incorrectly assumed that whatever I do with hypnosis is similar to whatever anyone and everyone else who uses hypnosis does with it. Few people have had enough exposure to hypnosis to be able to differentiate the types and applications of hypnosis from one another. This is a drawback to being an overt practitioner of therapeutic hypnosis; the general public assumes that "hypnosis is hypnosis is hypnosis," and all they have to do as consumers is shop around in order to find the most inexpensive deal with the most promises attached.

Used skillfully, however, this problem can become an asset. By exploring the various treatment approaches and possibilities with the person seeking information about my work, I can help that person become knowledgeable enough to make meaningful decisions. Helping consumers have the information necessary to make an informed decision about treatment should, in my opinion, be basic to any professional practice. Just because someone doesn't ask questions doesn't mean he or she has none. It usually means the person just doesn't know what to ask.

By involving people in a brief discussion about their needs and the nature of clinical hypnosis as part of the treatment process, one can provide information that helps consumers more realistically assess their needs and the best means for meeting them. Often, formal hypnosis (i.e., a procedure clearly defined as hypnosis) aimed at symptom removal alone is neither a desirable or realistic treatment alternative, but was turned to by the person for some "magic" and a chance to avoid the maze of pursuing other, more personally challenging, approaches to treatment.

The fact that hypnosis is used as a stage act in the media (live shows especially, but also in cinema and television) contributes to popular stereotypes of hypnosis as a magical means for instant problem resolution through powerful suggestions. I wish I had a nickel for every person who has asked for a "quick suggestion" to stop some unwanted behavior. Rational explanations of why the work to be done might be a little more involved than they think are often met with puzzled looks and some variation of the question, "Then how does a stage hypnotist just snap his fingers to get his subject to do whatever he wants him to?" Unrealistic concepts can lead to disappointment and disillusionment in the client.

Clarifying the purposes and capacities of hypnosis is almost always beneficial for the client. If the unusual situation arises where it may be of benefit to the client to *not* be directly active in treatment, one might choose not to hold an informative discussion—occasionally an appropriate alternative. Clarification, however, leads the person to face the fact that there will likely be no miracle cures other than the ones he or she provides for him- or herself. It means both accepting personal responsibility for the problem and being active in its resolution.

Almost as dangerous as the stage hypnotist in promoting misconception, perhaps even more so, is the hypnotist who, through ignorance or greed, uses hypnosis in a practice that caters to public misconception. Such people usually have little or no formal education in hypnosis and the clinical sciences, but know just enough to mislead people with claims of sensational power.

These are just a few of the challenges faced by hypnosis as a field in its quest for greater visibility and appreciation. Others are discussed in later sections of the book. The point is made throughout that if hypnosis is to be considered a serious treatment alternative, it must be promoted with a sensitivity to the issues of concern both to consumers and other health care providers. It starts with you, the reader.

BROADENING PERSPECTIVES

LABELING EXPERIENCES

Sometimes when one tries to describe or define an experience, attaching a specific label to the experience limits the way the experience will be perceived. For example, if a new co-worker is introduced to you as a patient recently released from a psychiatric unit, how will your perception of the person be influenced by the label "psychiatric patient"? Would you react to the person in the same way if no such introduction was given?

When you consider a simple, concrete object, such as a chair, the tendency for labels to bias you and get in the way of open-minded experience is not so troublesome. The word "chair" represents something tangible that most people can experience similarly. In considering something as abstract, complex, and subjective as "hypnosis," however, the difficulties arise almost immediately. The word represents different experiences to different people, literally preventing the attainment of a precise shared meaning.

Traditionally, hypnosis has been considered a subjective *state* of experience ("in hypnosis") in which the individual has capabilities or experiences generally regarded as atypical of the "normal waking" state (Dixon & Laurence, 1992). Hypnosis has also been considered to be a *process* ("doing hypnosis") in which a hypnotist offers suggestions to a subject or client (Weitzenhoffer, 2000). Both of these concepts are correct, yet both are limited in using the word "hypnosis" to describe an individual, subjective state and also a process of offering suggestions to another person.

Hypnosis as a word has been overused to the point of robbing it of any real meaning. When one word comes to describe as many different experiences as "hypnosis" has, there is ample opportunity for misunderstanding, mislabeling, misconception, and ultimately, confusion. As a direct result, the field of hypnosis is internally divided, much as the field of psychotherapy is internally divided (Kihlstrom, 1997; Lynn & Rhue, 1991). Different practitioners and researchers each tend to emphasize a different facet of hypnosis in striving to explain it. While each viewpoint adds to our understandings of the phenomenon, they also frustrate efforts to achieve a unity within the field.

Because hypnosis is one word for many different kinds of experiences, most people's exposure to hypnosis remains quite general. The average person is led to believe that "hypnosis is hypnosis," regardless of context. Furthermore, because the word "hypnosis" is used for many different experiences, even helping professionals untrained in hypnosis are skeptical about its use in clinical contexts, uncertain whether it differs appreciably from the silliness demonstrated in stage shows. As you will learn, though, the context in which hypnosis is applied is ultimately what defines it and gives it substance.

Proponents of hypnosis have long recognized the difficulties in getting people to be open to its clinical use when their previous exposure to hypnosis has only been to the stage variety. Some have even tried to rename hypnosis with more scientific sounding names, yet the term "hypnosis" remains virtually unchanged in common usage. It seems imperative to be clear in describing the clinical context in which hypnosis is used so others may be continually reminded of the variety of applications. Thus, "clinical hypnosis" is preferable to "hypnosis," and "medical hypnosis" is even more descriptive than "clinical hypnosis."

DESCRIPTIONS OF HYPNOSIS

Arranging the broad concepts and techniques of hypnosis into a meaningful description is an exceedingly difficult task. There are simply too many unknowns about both mind and brain, too many contradictory and paradoxical findings, and too many unique and idiosyncratic aspects of human experience highlighted in hypnosis to develop a single, well-elaborated description of it. Moving in that idealistic direction, though, some of the leading perspectives may help illuminate some of the facets of hypnosis. These definitions include:

1. *Hypnosis is guided daydreaming.* The hypnotist, either another person (heterohypnosis) or one's self (autohypnosis, self-hypnosis) acts as a guide for an experience regarded as fantasy (Barrett, 1979).
2. *Hypnosis is a natural, altered state of consciousness.* The person enters a state called "hypnosis," a state distinctly different from the person's "normal" state, through a natural process which does not involve either the ingestion of any substances or other physical treatments (Tart, 1972).
3. *Hypnosis is a relaxed, hypersuggestible state.* The person enters a very relaxed state of mind and body, and subsequently is less vigilant and more responsive to suggestion (Edmonston, 1991).
4. *Hypnosis is a dissociated state.* The hypnotic state is considered to involve a disconnection between conscious and unconscious mental processes presumably allowing the unconscious mind to be more readily accessible and receptive to suggestion (Hilgard, 1977).

Each of the above descriptions of hypnosis contains an element of truth, but is limited in its usefulness. All describe hypnosis from the standpoint of the person in the hypnotic state, with no mention of either the role of the hypnotist or the quality of the relationship between the two. All imply a passive responsiveness to suggestion on the part of the hypnotic subject, a tendency to accept offered suggestions due to the presence of a state ambiguously called "hypnosis." Other descriptions will be offered along with the theories of hypnosis in chapter 3, Conceptualizing Hypnosis.

COMMUNICATION AND YOUR CONCEPTUAL
FRAMEWORK

When people think of hypnosis, they typically think of the hypnotized person behaving in unusual and even paradoxical ways in response to a hypnotist's suggestions. Some theoretical models of hypnosis incorporate hypothetical constructs of the mind and human personality to explain hypnotic phenomena. Such explanations have generally been quite narrow in their focus and are usually bound to one theoretical view. Perhaps the most obvious example is a psychoanalytic view of hypnosis as a transference response involving psychological regression in which the hypnotist is responded to as a symbolic parent figure (Fromm, 1992; Nash, 1991).

Is there any compelling reason to want to adopt a single theoretical framework for understanding and applying clinical hypnosis? How do we distinguish between our own conceptual framework and the actual experience of the client? The hazard, as in any clinical practice, is in not seeing phenomena that lie outside the boundaries of what you tend to look for. The fact that most clinicians describe themselves as eclectic in orientation is an indirect statement by professionals that they want to have the freedom to do what is effective, independent of an allegiance to one specific model of intervention.

It becomes possible to transcend hypothetical considerations of the structure of the mind or personality when you consider how you detect such structures. In other words, *if* there are detectable structures of the mind and personality that can be recognized and developed into explicit theories or models, perhaps the level of consideration that is most worthwhile to study is the means by which such structures are evidenced in the person. What exactly does a client *say* and/or *do* that reveals the presence of these hypothetical structures to a clinician? The person somehow *communicates* them. By focusing on the client's communications, the clinician can come to better understand something of the subjective experience of the client, and can therefore strive to better understand what aspect(s) of experience needs attention and intervention.

Every person who works with people in a clinical capacity makes continuous assessments of clients' needs, motivations, skills, and limitations (Geary, 2001; Lynn et al., 1996). Each further assesses the likelihood of success in reaching the goals of their relationship. These assessments are made in a variety of ways, not the least of which is in accordance with how the clinician chooses to conceptualize the problem from the way it is communicated, that is, the framework he or she uses to organize perceptions while working with the client.

Your framework is your way of viewing people and their problems. It varies from clinician to clinician according to formal training, personal experience, and the resulting belief system from the interaction of the two. Someone who believes in one particular theory will conceptualize a problem's dynamics very differently from someone else who believes in and practices from a different theory. For example, someone with a weight problem will be given different alternatives and instructed in different concepts while undergoing cognitive-behavioral treatment than will someone undergoing treatment for the same problem while undergoing psychoanalysis. Likewise, a 12-step approach to the problem will be different in structure from a medical approach.

Arguments about theoretical perspective are hard to avoid since competing views can each be credible, but they can be sidestepped to some degree when one appreciates that such arguments can not be won. No one theory to date adequately explains why people do what they do or how to intervene therapeutically in a uniformly successful way. There are hundreds of psychotherapies currently in use (Hubble, Duncan, & Miller, 1999). Each has its advocates, and each has at least anecdotal support in the literature. Despite the wide array of approaches for providing treatment, no therapist succeeds with all clients, perhaps not even with most. Psychotherapy is able to help people, but it is not 100% effective, nor is it ever likely to be, given the varied and unpredictable nature of human beings. The idealistic goal is to learn its limitations and strive to transcend them.

This, then, is my point: It seems to me that taking a client's communications about his or her problems and altering them from their original form in order to fit with some preferred theoretical belief is a step that is both arbitrary and unnecessary. Responding to a client's communications in their original form as a reflection of what the person is experiencing can lead you to communicate in a more meaningful way that can enhance the quality of the interaction.

The approach to hypnosis promoted in this book is essentially a way of organizing your therapeutic communications to best fit an individual's needs, using words and gestures selectively in order to arrive at some worthwhile outcome. Which therapeutic framework you choose to work from is not an issue here. *All* the therapeutic approaches work some time with somebody, which is why each has devotees. The clinical skill lies in knowing *which* approach to use at any given moment.

The client who senses being understood by the clinician is the client more likely to benefit from the relationship. Of course, this is not an original idea, for every clinician is trained to appreciate the importance of the quality of the relationship with the client. Literature in hypnosis and psychotherapy generally employs the word "rapport" to describe the ideal positive interrelationship between hypnotist/clinician and client. How one attained rapport was left up to the individual clinician, as it must be, but such noticeable lack of consideration has resulted in a de-emphasis of the interpersonal components of effective clinical hypnosis. Consequently, rigid approaches that pay little heed to specific individual differences between people have flourished. A global "low" or "high" hypnotizable label doesn't count as an assessment of an individual's capabilities, in my opinion.

The process of clinical intervention can correctly be described as a series of communications between a clinician and client. No matter what your orientation, you are using the communications of the client to make assessments, and you are using communications as the vehicle for delivering your therapy. A therapeutic communication is defined as one that influences the person in distress to think, feel, or behave differently in a way that is considered more adaptive or beneficial. In producing a beneficial result, the client's experience matters, the clinician's skills matter, and the relationship between them and the context in which they interact matter.

The essence of what I am discussing here is communication and interpersonal influence, and that is precisely where hypnosis comes in. If one rejects the passive, exclusively intrapersonal view of hypnosis as only an individual's subjective state, and instead considers the dynamics of interpersonal communication a skilled clinician employs in order to influence a client to have a suggested therapeutic experience, then a rich and complex new world opens up. Somewhere in the interpersonal communications of the client and clinician are some components that enable a client's subjective experience to be altered and therapeutic influence to take place. Hypnosis, like psychotherapy, involves multiple components on multiple dimensions in order to be effective (T. Barber, 2000; Evans, 2000).

To use your words and gestures skillfully in the deliberate creation of therapeutic experiences for an individual in distress (or any other person one would want a specific outcome with) is the "nuts and bolts" of what hypnosis is all about. Approaching hypnosis from this standpoint places emphasis on being an effective communicator, one who is able to recognize and competently relate and respond meaningfully to the communications of others.

When you shift the focus away from mere techniques to consider dimensions of communication that increase the potential for influencing another person's experience, the emphasis is much less on ritual or attaining particular levels (i.e., depths) of hypnosis, and much more on the use of words and gestures in specific ways. *Thus, elements of any piece of communication can have hypnotic qualities associated with them without formally being called "hypnosis"* (Watzlawick, 1985; Zeig & Rennick, 1991). Simply put, you don't have to incorporate the rituals of hypnosis in order to be hypnotic in your wording or demeanor. Even if you were to choose not to pursue expertise in doing formal hypnosis in your clinical practice, you can still benefit greatly from learning about the power of effective communication through the study of hypnotic approaches.

INFLUENCE IS INEVITABLE

More often than should be the case, in my opinion, clinicians see themselves as separate from their interactions with their clients. They may think they can ask questions without influencing the quality of the answers they get, or they may think they can be neutral in avoiding offering direct advice when asked for some. There are even those who genuinely believe that when they do hypnosis with someone, they are simply eliciting—not directing—the client's hypnotic talents. They do not see themselves as playing a significant role in what surfaces at all. I find that incredible, and it greatly concerns me. How can you be conscious of using your skills deliberately and with integrity if you deny you have any influence?

It is an important starting point in studying hypnosis to recognize the ever-present nature of interpersonal influence. In studying the fascinating realm of social psychology in particular, you learn almost right away that influence is inevitable *simply by your being there*. Think about this statement: "You will do things when you are by yourself that you will not do if even one other person is around." The mere presence of another person alters your behavior. It is not a question of *whether* you will influence your client—you undoubtedly will—but rather a question of *how* you will influence him or her. Learning to use patterns of influence responsibly while respecting the integrity of those we work with is a demanding challenge. After all, an insensitively used word can hinder or prevent a positive treatment result. Likewise, a sensitively used phrase can engender a positive belief that dramatically improves the chances for a successful treatment outcome (McNeilly & Brown, 1994).

Patterns of influence do not just exist in the contexts of therapy or hypnosis, though. If you are observant, you will see them literally everywhere you see social interaction. When you learn to recognize hypnotic elements in everyday situations, it will help you to use hypnosis more naturally, flexibly, and with greater success.

HYPNOSIS AND POSITIVE PSYCHOLOGY

In describing hypnosis early in this chapter as a means for amplifying people's abilities, empowering them to find and use their resources for their benefit, there was an implicit point I now want to make more explicit in this last section of my opening chapter. Before I do, let me pose a question to you: Do you believe that people in general and clients in particular are "sick" and need to be healed, or do you believe, despite their problems, they are basically all right and can be helped to be even better?

There is a growing movement in the field of psychology, largely catalyzed by Martin E. P. Seligman, Ph.D., a noted researcher and former President of the American Psychological Association. Seligman challenged the field to focus less on the pathologies of humankind and to focus more on increasing its strengths—for example, loyalty, compassion, generosity, perseverance, and so on. Seligman called for the development of what has come to be called a "positive psychology," whose mission would be to research, characterize, and teach those principles that lead to better adjusted individuals, communities, and institutions (Seligman, 2002; Seligman & Csikszentmihalyi, 2000).

Seligman did not originate the concept of studying what's right with people. Significant luminaries like Milton H. Erickson, Abraham Maslow, Virginia Satir, and Carl Rogers all called for developing a deeper understanding of the best parts of human experience. But Seligman has been particularly effective in turning an abstract goal into a domain of well-defined research that has the potential to offer much more than inspiration alone.

THE FIRST LESSON: WHAT YOU FOCUS ON YOU AMPLIFY IN YOUR AWARENESS

The field of hypnosis has largely been a field of positive psychology almost from the start. The very first thing to understand about hypnosis, whether experiencing hypnosis yourself or guiding someone else through it, is that when you focus on something, you amplify it in your awareness (Gendlin, 1981, 1997; Polster & Polster, 1973). If you do cognitive therapy, you focus more on peoples' thoughts than on other aspects of their experience. If you do behavior therapy, you focus more on behavior. If you prescribe medication, you focus more on physiology. Key considerations in doing therapy are determining what dimension of a person's experience you want to amplify in his or her awareness, and why you want to amplify it. If I'm going to ask you, "So, how do you feel about that?" and thereby encourage you to focus on and amplify your feelings, is there a sound therapeutic rationale for doing so, or am I just doing a technique out of habit?

Hypnosis generally focuses on and amplifies people's strengths. Hypnosis begins with the premise that the client has valuable abilities that are present but hidden, abilities that can be uncovered and used in a deliberate way to overcome symptoms and problems (Lankton, 2001;Yapko, 2001c). Hypnosis starts with a belief that people are more resourceful than they realize. When a clinician helps a client discover the ability to manage pain without drugs; helps a client discover the ability to move comfortably through situations that used to cause panic, or helps a client develop the ability to shift his or her focus onto more of what's right instead of only what's wrong, and reduces his or her despair in the process; such a clinician is connecting with and enhancing the strongest and healthiest parts of those clients (Lankton & Lankton, 1983; J. Barber, 1991). Can you focus on symptoms and address the negative factors in people's lives? Of course, and to be therapeutic you *have to*, at least some of the time. But, the greater issue is one of how your beliefs and methods serve to increase or decrease your chances of noticing and amplifying what's *right* with people.

Is the goal of treatment to reduce pathology, or to expand wellness? How you answer this question will help determine much of your reaction to the material in this book, and will shape how you ultimately use hypnosis in your own practice. Whatever your answer may be right now, though, I hope your study of hypnosis will gradually highlight for you the wisdom of evolving a positive psychology that can help inform your understandings of yourself and the people you treat.

For Discussion

1. Why do you want to learn hypnosis? What do you find appealing about hypnosis?
2. What things have you heard are possible to do with hypnosis? What is your reaction to these claims?
3. What previous exposure have you had to hypnosis? What were the circumstances, and what were the outcomes?
4. Do you think the use of hypnosis should be restricted in some way, such as by qualified doctors only? Why or why not? If you think it should, how would you recommend it be done?
5. What things, if any, are you apprehensive about in learning hypnosis? What is the basis for your apprehensions?
6. What do you think makes one an effective communicator?
7. What is your belief system about why people do the things they do? How might your beliefs both help and hurt your ability to interact with others?
8. How do you predetermine what a person is capable of doing? For example, how do you decide that someone is trustworthy?
9. What is your definition of "rapport"? How do you know when you have rapport with someone?
10. Why do definitions of abstract terms, such as "love," differ so much from person to person? What are the implications for effective communications?

Things to Do

1. Watch the media for stories on hypnosis. How is it represented? Keep a scrapbook of articles that appear over the next few months as you study hypnosis.
2. Interview a variety of health professionals (such as physicians, dentists, psychologists, etc.) about their attitudes toward hypnosis. What do you discover?
3. Go through the Yellow Page listings under "Hypnotism." Are there unrealistic or exaggerated claims made for what hypnosis can do? How do you react to these claims?
4. Give your discussion partner instructions not to communicate for three minutes while you observe him or her. Does he or she communicate anything to you in spite of your instructions? What? Why is it not possible to prevent communication?
5. List and define the basic constructs of personality from your perspective. How *specifically* do you become aware of these constructs in the people you interact with?
6. List those people closest to you whom you influence. How do you do so? Do you influence them in ways you would like to?

REFERENCES

American Psychological Association, Division of Psychological Hypnosis (1993). Hypnosis. *Psychological Hypnosis*, 2–3.

American Psychological Association, Division of Psychological Hypnosis (1999). *Policy and procedures manual, 4–5*. Washington D.C.: American Psychological Association.

Baker, E. (1987). The state of the art of clinical hypnosis. *International Journal of Clinical and Experimental Hypnosis, 35*, 203–14.

Barber, J. (1991). The locksmith model: Accessing hypnotic responsiveness. In S. Lynn & J. Rhue (Eds.), *Theories of hypnosis: Current models and perspectives* (pp. 241–4). New York: Guilford.

Barber, T. (2000). A deeper understanding of hypnosis: Its secrets, its nature, its essence. *American Journal of Clinical Hypnosis, 42*, 208–72.

Barrett, D. (1979). The hypnotic dream: Its relation to nocturnal dreams and waking fantasies. *Journal of Abnormal Psychology, 88*, 584–591.

Brom, D., Kleber, R., & Defare, P. (1988). Brief psychotherapy for post-traumatic stress disorder. *Journal of Consulting and Clinical Psychology, 57*, 607–12.

Brown, D. (1992). Clinical hypnosis research since 1986. In E. Fromm & M. Nash (Eds.), *Contemporary hypnosis research* (pp. 427–58). New York: Guilford.

Chaves, J. (1999). Applying hypnosis in pain management: Implications of alternative theoretical perspectives. In I. Kirsch, A. Capafons, E. Cardeña, & S. Amigo (Eds.), *Clinical hypnosis and self-regulation: Cognitive-behavioral perspectives* (pp. 227–47). Washington, D.C.: American Psychological Association.

Crawford, H., & Barabasz, A. (1993). Phobias and intense fears: Facilitating their treatment with hypnosis. In J. Rhue, S. Lynn, & I. Kirsch (Eds.), *Handbook of clinical hypnosis* (pp. 311–38). Washington, D.C.: American Psychological Association.

Dixon, M., & Laurence, J-R. (1992). Two hundred years of hypnosis research: Questions resolved? Questions unanswered! In E. Fromm & M. Nash (Eds.), *Contemporary hypnosis research* (pp. 34–66). New York: Guilford.

Edmonston, W. (1991). Anesis. In S. Lynn & J. Rhue (Eds.), *Theories of hypnosis: Current models and perspectives* (pp. 197–237). New York: Guilford.

Eimer, B. (2000). Clinical applications of hypnosis for brief and efficient pain management psychotherapy. *American Journal of Clinical Hypnosis, 43:1*, 17–40.

Evans, F. (2000). The domain of hypnosis: A multifactorial model. *American Journal of Clinical Hypnosis, 43*, 1–16.

Fromm, E. (1992). An ego-psychological theory of hypnosis. In E. Fromm & M. Nash (Eds.), *Contemporary hypnosis research* (pp. 131–48). New York: Guilford.

Galovski, T., & Blanchard, E. (1998). The treatment of irritable bowel syndrome with hypnotherapy. *Applied Psychophysiology and Biofeedback, 23*, 4, 219–32.

Geary, B. (2001). Assessment in Ericksonian hypnosis and psychotherapy. In B. Geary & J. Zeig (Eds.), *The handbook of Ericksonian psychotherapy* (pp. 1–17). Phoenix, AZ: The Milton H. Erickson Foundation Press.

Gendlin, E. (1981). *Focusing* (2nd edition). New York: Bantam.

Gendlin, E. (1997). The use of focusing in therapy. In J. Zeig, *The evolution of psychotherapy: The third conference* (pp. 197–210). New York: Brunner/Mazel.

Gonsalkorale, W., Houghton, L., & Whorwell, P. (2002). Hypnotherapy in irritable bowel syndrome: A large scale audit of a clinical service with examination of factors influencing responsiveness. *American Journal of Gastroenterology, 97*, 4, 954–61.

Hilgard, E. (1977). *Divided consciousness*. New York: Wiley.

Hilgard, E. (1992). Dissociation and theories of hypnosis. In E. Fromm & M. Nash (Eds.), *Contemporary hypnosis research* (pp. 69–101). New York: Guilford.

Hubble, M., Duncan, B., & Miller, S. (1999). *The heart & soul of change: What works in therapy*. Washington, D.C.: American Psychological Association.

Kihlstrom, J. (1997). Convergence in understanding hypnosis? Perhaps, but not so fast. *International Journal of Clinical and Experimental Hypnosis, 45*, 324–32.

Kirsch, I., Lynn, S., & Rhue, J. (1993). Introduction to clinical hypnosis. In J. Rhue, S. Lynn, & I. Kirsch (Eds.), *Handbook of clinical hypnosis* (pp. 3–22). Washington, D.C.: American Psychological Association.

Kirsch, I., Montgomery, G., & Sapirstein, G. (1995). Hypnosis as an adjunct to cognitive-behavioral psychotherapy: A meta-analysis. *Journal of Consulting and Clinical Psychology, 63*, 214–20.

Lankton, S. (2001). A goal-directed intervention for decisive resolution of coping limitations resulting from moderate and severe trauma. In B. Geary & J. Zeig (Eds.), *The handbook of Ericksonian psychotherapy* (pp. 195–214). Phoenix, AZ: The Milton H. Erickson Foundation Press.

Lankton, S., & Lankton, C. (1983). *The answer within: A clinical framework of Ericksonian hypnotherapy*. New York: Brunner/Mazel.

Lynn, S., Kirsch, I., Neufeld, J., & Rhue, J. (1996). Clinical hypnosis: Assessment, applications, and treatment considerations. In S. Lynn, I. Kirsch, & J. Rhue (Eds.), *Casebook of clinical hypnosis* (pp. 3–30). Washington, D.C.: American Psychological Association.

Lynn, S., Kirsch, I., Barabasz, A., Cardeña, E., & Patterson, D. (2000). Hypnosis as an

empirically supported clinical intervention: The state of the evidence and a look
to the future. *International Journal of Clinical and Experimental Hypnosis, 48*, 239–59.

Lynn, S., & Rhue, J. (Eds.) (1991). *Theories of hypnosis: Current models and perspectives.* New
York: Guilford.

Lynn. S., & Sivec, H. (1992). The hypnotizable subject as creative problem-solving agent.
In E. Fromm & M. Nash (Eds.), *Contemporary hypnosis research* (pp. 292–333). New
York: Guilford.

McNeilly, R., & Brown, J. (1994). *Healing with words.* Melbourne, Australia: Hill of Content.

Milling, L., & Costantino, C. (2000). Clinical hypnosis with children: First steps toward
empirical support. *International Journal of Clinical and Experimental Hypnosis, 48*, 109–
33.

Montgomery, G., DuHamel, K., & Redd, W. (2000). A meta-analysis of hypnotically
induced analgesia: How effective is hypnosis? *International Journal of Clinical and
Experimental Hypnosis, 48*, 134–49.

Nash, M. (1991). Hypnosis as a special case of psychological regression. In S. Lynn & J.
Rhue (Eds.), *Theories of hypnosis: Current models and perspectives* (pp. 171–94). New York:
Guilford.

Nash, M., Minton, A., & Baldridge, J. (1988). Twenty years of scientific hypnosis in
dentistry, medicine, and psychology: A brief communication. *International Journal
of Clinical and Experimental Hypnosis, 36*, 198–205.

Olness, K. & Kohen, D. (1996). Hypnosis and hypnotherapy with children (3rd edition).
New York: Guilford.

Phillips, M., & Frederick, C. (1995). *Healing the divided self: Clinical and Ericksonian hypnotherapy for post-traumatic and dissociative conditions.* New York: Norton.

Polster, E., & Polster, M. (1973). *Gestalt therapy integrated.* New York: Brunner/Mazel.

Schoenberger, N. (2000). Research on hypnosis as an adjunct to cognitive-behavioral
psychotherapy. *International Journal of Clinical and Experimental Hypnosis, 48*, 154–69.

Seligman, M. (2002). *Authentic happiness: Using the new positive psychology to realize your potential for lasting fulfillment.* New York: Free Press.

Seligman, M., & Csikszentmihalyi, M. (2000). Positive psychology: An introduction.
American Psychologist, 55, 1, 5–14.

Spiegel, D. (1993). Hypnosis in the treatment of post-traumatic stress disorders. In J.
Rhue, S. Lynn, & I. Kirsch (Eds.), *Handbook of clinical hypnosis* (pp. 493–508). Washington, D.C.: American Psychological Association.

Spiegel, D. (1996). Hypnosis in the treatment of post-traumatic stress disorder. In S.
Lynn, I. Kirsch, & J. Rhue (Eds.), *Casebook of clinical hypnosis* (pp. 99–112). Washington, D.C.: American Psychological Association.

Tart, C. (1972). Measuring the depth of an altered state of consciousness, with particu-
lar reference to to self-report scales of hypnotic depth. In E. Fromm & R. Shor
(Eds.), *Hypnosis: Research development and perspective* (pp. 445–77). Chicago: Aldine-
Atherton.

Watzlawick, P. (1985). Hypnotherapy without trance. In J. Zeig (Ed.), *Ericksonian psychotherapy Vol.1: Structures* (pp. 5–14). New York: Brunner/Mazel.

Weitzenhoffer, A. (2000). *The practice of hypnotism* (2nd edition). New York: Wiley.

Woody, E., Bowers, K., & Oakman, J. (1992). A conceptual analysis of hypnotic responsiveness: Experience, individual differences, and context. In E. Fromm & M. Nash (Eds.), *Contemporary hypnosis research* (pp. 3–33). New York: Guilford.

Yapko, M. (1992). *Hypnosis and the treatment of depressions: Strategies for change.* New York: Brunner/Mazel.

Yapko, M. (2001a). Hypnosis in treating symptoms and risk factors of major depression. *American Journal of Clinical Hypnosis, 44:2,* 97–108.

Yapko, M. (2001b). Hypnotic intervention for ambiguity as a depressive risk factor. *American Journal of Clinical Hypnosis, 44:2,* 109–17.

Yapko, M. (2001c). *Treating depression with hypnosis: Integrating cognitive-behavioral and strategic approaches.* Philadelphia, PA: Brunner/Routledge.

Zeig, J., & Rennick, P. (1991). Ericksonian hypnotherapy: A communications approach to hypnosis. In S. Lynn & J. Rhue (Eds.), *Theories of hypnosis: Current models and perspectives* (pp. 275–302). New York: Guilford.

2

The Myths about Hypnosis and a Dose of Reality

The interpersonal process of clinical hypnosis can be viewed as a complex interaction in which the qualities of your relationship and communications with your client help determine their eventual worth in treatment. As a clinician, you use hypnosis to focus clients on important aspects of their experience that can serve as resources, and you introduce to them what you hope and expect will be helpful possibilities (e.g., new ideas, helpful skills, etc.). Even those clinicians who think of hypnosis as something that only happens within the person find themselves in the position of saying and doing things to guide their clients to develop their internal resources (Spiegel & Spiegel, 1987).

By describing the hypnotic interaction in broader social terms of communication and influence, much of the mystery of "hypnotic power" can be eliminated. The more we learn about what makes for good clinical hypnosis, the more we come to recognize that the important skills to have as a good hypnotist are the same ones needed to be an effective clinician. These include an ability to establish a strong therapeutic alliance and positive expectations for treatment; flexibility and a willingness to experiment with new ideas, perceptions, and behaviors; and many other equally important abilities (Haley, 1973; Hubble, Duncan, & Miller, 1999; Kirsch, 1990).

Clinical hypnosis with both intra- and interpersonal emphases on creating a context for therapeutic influence is a meaningful perspective with a great deal to offer professional communicators. It brings into harmony the extensive research and clinical literature which make good cases for seemingly contradictory viewpoints by emphasizing their common denominators of a shared relationship, a specific context, and individual abilities each person brings to the interaction (Bowers & Davidson, 1991; Spanos, 1991).

SETTING THE STAGE FOR HYPNOSIS

Since hypnosis from the multidimensional perspective offered here is burdened with the same name as any other hypnosis, the tendency of people who have previous knowledge or experience with hypnosis is to assume that what they already know is accurate. People do not know they may be misinformed until their existing information and beliefs come into direct conflict with some new information. The clinical implication of this point is that it is especially important to spend time with clients discussing directly or indirectly their views and expectations about the therapeutic relationship. Only through such discussion can a clinician discover the client's expectations, needs, and wishes in order to assess whether they are realistic and to evolve a means for incorporating them into the therapy (Duncan, Miller, & Coleman, 2001; McNeilly, 2001).

DEALING WITH MISINFORMATION

In the practice of clinical hypnosis, the opportunity for dealing with misinformation is constant. Most misconceptions people hold are predictable, which can make their identification and rebuttal easier. The single most common misperception that people seem to hold is that hypnosis is a powerful form of mind control in which the hypnotized person has no free will. Most of the other common misconceptions are based on that erroneous notion of surrendering one's will (Frauman, Lynn, & Brentar, 1993).

It is difficult to change people's thinking when they are convinced they are knowledgeable in their opinions. In fact, the more knowledgeable a person views him- or herself, the more difficult it is to introduce conflicting information (Zimbardo & Leippe, 1992). In general, people ignore contradictions or twist them around until everything they believe fits together comfortably, even if incorrectly. I had what seemed to me to be my ten thousandth experience of this recently when I was unable to convince an obstetrician that hypnosis would not be harmful to his pregnant patient who requested hypnosis for reducing stress and increasing her physical comfort during pregnancy. I pointed out ways that hypnosis would, in fact, be helpful to her, and though he could agree at an intellectual level, he could not bring himself to give her permission to experience hypnosis, so strong were his fears and doubts. Instead of empowering his patient to strive to enhance her own experience, he unintentionally reinforced the idea that she should have doubts about her own resources. With many people, unfortunately, the predominant attitude is, "Don't bother me with facts, my mind is made up!" Too often, the client is the one who suffers and loses an opportunity for improvement.

Involving the client in a direct discussion about his or her beliefs and expectations for the hypnotic and psychotherapeutic experience is necessary to make certain he or she is knowledgeable enough to make sensible treatment decisions (Scheflin, 2001). Since the client's understanding of the therapy process may be inaccurate, incomplete, or both, the ethical and competent professional can provide the person with as much information as he or she may require in order to be fully involved in the process in a cooperative and positive way. You may note that I say that as much information should be provided as the person "requires," implying that on some occasions the amount of information dispensed may be marginal, while in other instances it is substantial. Individual client needs differ, and only by communicating clearly with your client will you discover his or her needs. Generally, though, a well-informed client is in a better position to make therapy a more meaningful collaboration (Lynn, Kirsch, & Rhue, 1996).

Many clinicians are helpful in reaction to questions and concerns the client raises, but this may be only a portion of what is required in order for the client to be positively involved in the treatment. The client is sometimes too self-conscious to ask questions of the clinician, and the risk of seeming ignorant in addition to already having presented one's self as experiencing problems that are out of control and in need of professional help is a risk too great for some to take. The result is a silent hope that the clinician is skilled enough to read minds and take the necessary steps to effect a cure with as little self-disclosure and involvement as possible on the part of the client. Another facet of the concern for providing information to the client whether or not you are asked for it is the observation that many people simply don't know what to ask. If a client already feels comfortably knowledgeable about hypnosis, perhaps from past experience, he or she is unlikely to seek new information. But, if hypnosis is something totally new to the client, he or she may not know what questions to ask the clinician. Only a gentle inquiry will help you decide what this person might need to know.

The hazard of not giving the client enough information is matched by the hazard of giving *too much* information to a client who is not ready for it or wanting it. A favorite story of mine illustrates the point: A boy about six years old came home from one of his first days at school and with an aura of great intensity asked his mother, "Mommy, where did I come from?" The mother got a pained look on her face, took a deep sigh and said "Well, I had desperately hoped we wouldn't have to have this talk for a few more years yet, but since you've asked I may as well tell you. The psychologist on the talk show said that if you're old enough to ask, you're old enough to know." The mother proceeded to explain the "facts of life" in vivid detail, describing anatomical differences between males and females, the process of intercourse, the fertilization process, pregnancy, and finally the birth process.

The little boy sat unmoving and wide-eyed while listening to his mother throughout the entire explanation. Finally, the mother completed her explanation and asked her son, "Does that answer your question?" The boy replied, "No, mommy, it doesn't. My friend Mitchell says he comes from Detroit. Where did I come from?"

FINDING OUT WHAT THE CLIENT REQUESTING HYPNOSIS BELIEVES

Only by engaging the person who directly asks for hypnosis in discussion can you discover how much he or she knows and simultaneously use the opportunity to support or challenge the person's beliefs. Some basic questions that have been useful for me to ask are: Have you ever had experience with hypnosis before? Was it personal experience or was it something you saw, read, or heard about? What impression did you form? What leads you to believe it might be helpful to you?

If the client *has* had personal experience with hypnosis, good questions to ask might include: What was the situation in which you experienced hypnosis? Who was the hypnotist and what were his or her qualifications? What was the explanation given to you about hypnosis at the time? What was the specific technique used with you? Was it successful? Why or why not? How did you feel about the experience? What is the basis for your seeking further experience with hypnosis? Such information will be vital in helping determine your approach. Asking a lot of questions can be threatening and tiresome to the client, and so must be done gently; aggressive interrogations under a bright light are not recommended.

If the person *has not* had personal experience with hypnosis, good questions to ask might include: What is the basis for your requesting hypnosis? Have you heard about clinical applications of hypnosis before? How have you heard hypnosis may be used? Do you know anyone personally who has experienced hypnosis? What did he or she tell you about it? What is your understanding of how hypnosis works? How specifically do you believe it might be helpful to you? Have you seen hypnosis demonstrated? If so, in what context? In asking some or all of these questions, you can elicit the client's experiences and attitudes concerning hypnosis. Misconceptions can be dealt with, unrealistic fears and magical wishes can be alleviated, and a positive belief system can be established (Argast, Landis, & Carrell, 2001).

Asking about specific hypnotic techniques the client may have previously experienced is very important. If he or she experienced a process that was ineffective or even unpleasant, then your using a similar technique almost guarantees a similar failure. Unless you specifically ask about prior experience, you run the risk of duplicating past negative experiences. Why?

The client's associations to that approach are negative. If you want to create a positive experience with hypnosis, it makes good sense to do something different.

If the client has not had personal experience with hypnosis before, but is only indirectly familiar with it through entertainment media or the experiences of an acquaintance, it becomes even more important to discover his or her beliefs and attitudes. Second- and third-hand stories about hypnosis from "knowledgeable" friends have a tendency to get distorted and can sometimes be as misleading as the entertainer's version of hypnosis. Many clients who seek hypnosis are fearful of the "mind-control" potential, but seek the associated "magic wand" for the "instant results" they've been told are possible. "Instant results" (i.e., single session interventions) *are* sometimes possible, in fact, but the larger issue here is to help unrealistic people avoid the "magical thinking" that complex problems can be solved instantaneously through hypnosis.

THE ISSUE OF CONTROL

The major issue that arises for most people, experienced with hypnosis or not, is that of "control." In fact, the client's fear of losing control of him- or herself is the single greatest obstacle you are likely to encounter in your practice. In one form or another, almost every common misconception is grounded in this fear. Unless you acknowledge and deal with it in a sensitive and positive way, it will undoubtedly hinder or even prevent the attainment of therapeutic results. The belief that hypnosis has the power to take self-control away has been fostered in ways mentioned previously, and until one has had the experience of therapeutic hypnosis in a positive atmosphere of caring and professionalism, the fear is a real one.

Stage hypnosis and variations of it found in the entertainment media seem to be the biggest culprits for making control an issue of such huge proportions. The typical viewer of a hypnosis stage act has no idea how the hypnotist can "make" seemingly normal volunteers do all those strange and silly things on stage before an audience. The erroneous conclusion is that the hypnotist has some mysterious power that can make people do things they would not ordinarily do.

THE SECRETS OF STAGE HYPNOSIS

How stage hypnotists get their subjects to perform is not difficult to understand if you have an appreciation both of hypnotic principles and of certain aspects of human behavior perhaps best described in the literature of social psychology. Let's consider how it's done.

Stage shows formally begin with a call for volunteers. The volunteers are asked to come up on the stage only if they "truly *want* to be hypnotized." Some stage hypnotists are so well known that volunteers eagerly make themselves available as soon as the opportunity arises, literally rushing to the stage to offer themselves. When a stage hypnotist gets volunteers, he or she knows several things about these people with a high level of certainty:

1. They are aware of what they are volunteering for, and thus are probably willing to perform as directed. There is an exception to this discussed shortly.

2. A general trait common to volunteer performers is some degree of exhibitionism; the greater the degree, the more useful the subject. Someone shy and introverted is unlikely to go on stage to perform before a crowd. If someone shy were to go on stage, one of two things would probably occur: Either the person would "let loose" and consider hypnosis responsible for his or her behavior, or the person would fail the hypnotist's tests for determining subject acceptability and be returned to the audience. For the most part, however, the people who go on stage to become a part of the show are fully aware of what their role will be. In volunteering they are actively seeking the role and are agreeable to carry out its demands. You may notice my use of the word "role." There is a well-defined script the hypnotist creates for the volunteer subject to follow, even though to the members of the audience it all seems so spontaneous. It's why the faces and names of hypnotic subjects change from show to show, but not the routines themselves. Undeniably and invariably, the volunteer subject knows what is expected and agrees to provide it.

3. The experienced stage hypnotist also knows that some individuals are volunteering to participate with the "hidden agenda" of proving to the hypnotist that he or she is *not* omnipotent. Others are intent on proving to themselves that their personal will is strong, evidenced by the inability of the hypnotist to "control" them. Insecure people may have their fragile self-esteem temporarily boosted by an *inability* to be hypnotized if they interpret it as "having too strong a will."

In order to discover which subjects are entertaining performers and which are the ones intent on "proving themselves" through noncooperative behavior, the hypnotist next administers a series of structured hypnotic suggestibility tests to the group of volunteers. This may be done off stage while the audience waits, or may be done on stage with the lights dimmed so the audience isn't privy to the conditioning process of the volunteers. Suggestibility tests are discussed in greater detail in a later chapter, but are defined here simply as brief hypnotic interactions that can reveal the degree to which the subject will likely respond to the hypnotist's suggestions. The stage hypnotist does a focusing technique or induction, then offers suggestions of specific feelings and behaviors, such as "You can't open your eyes." The most responsive subjects are kept on stage to be used in the show, and the others are told to return to their seats in the audience. Typically, the hypnotist offers an indirect suggestion to those remaining on stage about how good and responsive they are as subjects by stating directly to those dismissed from the stage how unfortunate it is that they were not (open, secure, smart . . .) enough to succeed as hypnotic subjects. What does that kind of insult do to the rejected person's self-esteem? One can't be certain, but nothing positive seems possible from such an interaction.

At this point, where the subjects have now been chosen, the pressure to perform becomes very intense. The subjects have been chosen for whatever qualities (primarily obedience) they possess that will help put on a good show. There is a great deal of pressure to meet the expectations of the hypnotist, the expectations of the crowd, and, not least, of themselves. The pressure is to be successful, and *success in this context is directly proportional to the level of obedience* displayed. Now that the subjects have been chosen and motivated to obey, the show can go on. From the perspective of the audience, the show is ready to begin, but from the hypnotist's perspective, the work for the night is essentially over! Subjects have been properly conditioned to comply, and now the show becomes a matter of simply running them through "tricks."

The hypnotist has cultivated almost unquestioned cooperation in the subject by running the person through tests and then "passing" him or her, in essence telling the subject, "You are the person I want here because I know you will do as I suggest." The literature of social psychology calls attention to how much more valuable a position of membership or a relationship is viewed by someone if it is difficult for him or her to attain it. Being accepted as a demonstration subject is a position you have to earn. It is not one given charitably.

The audience expects the hypnotic subject to behave in particular ways, just as the subjects themselves know they will be "made" to act in certain entertaining ways. When a group of people have an expectation of how one is supposed to act, a temporary social norm is established. Deviation from a norm in almost any situation is generally undesirable, and the strong sense of independence it takes not to conform to the norm (the expected behavior) in the stage show context is virtually absent in the chosen subjects. Research on the need for peer approval and its relationship to the phenomenon of conformity describes this concept clearly (Bordens & Horowitz, 2002). Thus, conforming behavior in order to get hypnotist and audience approval is a major ingredient in the stage show formula.

To appreciate the lengths to which the perceived desirability of conforming will drive someone, you may find it helpful to review some of the literature on conformity. (Some of this is described in chapter 6.) You will discover that the need to conform to others' expectations has led research subjects to express obviously incorrect judgments, adopt others' perceptions of ambiguous events, and even to comply with mistrusted authorities. Compromising one's self even in potentially damaging situations is possible if the rewards for doing so are viewed as worthwhile enough. Witness the number of people seriously injured doing hazardous stunts or the number of people subjected to embarrassing and even disgusting circumstances while looking for just a brief moment's exposure on national television.

In a situation like a hypnosis stage show, where the subject is confident he or she will not be injured, being the center of attention and the source of a large group's amusement may be reward enough to justify complying with the hypnotist's suggestions. Any negative side-effects (e.g., embarrassment, self-recriminations) from the performance can be readily attributed to the hypnosis, and not to the subject him- or herself.

Research consistently shows that people are far more willing to take risks, exercise questionable judgment, and even hurt others when they are not held accountable for their actions. If someone else assumes responsibility, or the person can act anonymously, or some other factor (such as alcohol or hypnosis) is a viable alibi, then inhibitions may diminish or even disappear (Spivey & Prentice-Dunn, 1990). Hypnosis is made the culprit for silly behavior, and the subject is free to act "as if" out of personal control. It is to the hypnotist's advantage to maintain this illusion, for if the subject appears to not be maintaining personal control, then it must be the hypnotist who is in control of the subject. This conclusion on the part of the audience is the very perception of special power the hypnotist strives to foster. It's all a part of the act, and it is very convincing for most people.

Last, but not least, the expectations the subject has toward him- or herself are involved in this process. The smart hypnotist uses the person's desire for a positive self-image by making the subject's positive self-image contingent on carrying out the suggestions. Essentially, the hypnotist is saying, "Smart (secure, strong, successful . . .) people respond in this way to this suggestion. Now, how are *you* going to respond?" Unless you want to be viewed by yourself and others negatively, you will likely respond in the suggested manner. People generally want to succeed, not fail; in this context, success is defined as following the given suggestions to the letter.

All the forces described here are working on the subject in the hypnotist's favor. The competent stage hypnotist, before giving any suggestions at all, knows all these things and knows that if all the pressures to perform are developed carefully and used properly, the subject will be most cooperative. If the pressures to perform have not been developed and used well, or if a suggestion is perceived by the subject as too threatening to carry out, the subject is unlikely to respond as well to the hypnotist.

The structure of the suggestions given to stage show subjects is another factor in the apparent ease with which the hypnotist seems to control his or her subjects. The typical layperson in the audience does not understand how saying, "You wouldn't forget your name, would you?" can induce someone to forget her name. This is an example of "indirect negative suggestion," which carries the hypnotist's requests in a more subtle form but is recognizable all the same. Suggestions for an inability to remember being hypnotized (i.e., amnesia) are typically given in the same covert way, furthering the illusion that the hypnotist has control of the subject's mind. These and other types of suggestions are described in later chapters.

At *all* times, *the subject is fully able to refuse to accept suggestions* should he or she choose to. Given the great amount of personal and situational pressure to accept them, however, this capacity is rarely used. It is actually easier just to go ahead and comply than it is to refuse; it takes more energy and inner drive to actively reject a suggestion than it does to passively comply and then blame hypnosis as responsible. The subject is able to reject the hypnotist's suggestions, but for the reasons given typically chooses not to.

Stage hypnotists are, as a group, skilled in their use of hypnosis. In fact, many of the principles and techniques of stage hypnosis are nearly identical to those of clinical hypnosis. Only the application is different. I can respect their skills and knowledge in hypnosis, but I must admit I have strong negative feelings about their chosen application. Using something potentially beneficial to people in a misleading and even degrading way seems unethical and I believe should be discouraged. Many people who could benefit from hypnosis and many clinicians who could use hypnosis to help their clients will not seek out hypnosis as a therapeutic alternative. They cannot even begin to comprehend how what they have seen in a night club show can be used clinically to help someone in distress, and they just don't want the "baggage."

Colleagues of mine have presented an opposing viewpoint, namely that many people seek out hypnosis in therapy *because of* the stage hypnotist. That may well be true, but such people are more likely to believe that hypnotists have mysterious powers. So, they approach treatment unrealistically, an undesirable consequence. Stage hypnosis and its negative connotations rob good people in need of help of what could be a valuable choice as a treatment alternative by promoting misconception and mystery. The entertainment value gets lost for me as a result.

There are those who have suggested that in the same way stage hypnosis is primarily an artifact of compliance, so might hypnosis in the clinical context be an artifact of compliance. In chapter 6 I will discuss this along with other social psychological issues pertaining to hypnosis, but suffice it to say here that the research evidence is unambiguous in its conclusion that hypnosis involves much, much more than mere compliance. When some-

one generates physiological changes or shifts in perceptions, there is something else going on of a greater magnitude that represents the essence of
hypnosis (Dixon & Laurence, 1992; Orne, 1959).

Having a good understanding of how stage hypnosis works will be invaluable to you in terms of understanding dynamics of influence and assisting you in dealing with the general public's fears and doubts about hypnosis.
Addressing misconceptions directly is the subject of the next major section
of this chapter.

RESPONDING TO MISCONCEPTIONS

If someone were to come to you, take you by the hand and say, "Come with
me," would you go? Or, would you first demand to know where you are
being taken? Try this simple exercise on a number of people you know in
varying degrees of closeness. It should highlight to you the recognition that
different people respond differently to direction and uncertainty, an important observation relevant to doing clinical hypnosis. The issue of "control"
surfaces immediately.

Taking the time to identify and correct misconceptions can help you
sidestep the issue of control, particularly if you emphasize the natural qualities of hypnosis through the use of common examples taken directly from
the client's everyday experience (e.g., driving while absorbed in thought,
getting deeply immersed in imagination). Furthermore, you can reinforce
for the client the virtually total self-control the hypnotized person maintains during the experience of hypnosis (Lynn, Rhue, & Weekes, 1990).

Clinicians need to be sensitive to the issue of control and respond to it
in some meaningful way, either directly or indirectly. Avoiding the issue of
control can increase the anxiety of an already uncertain client, and may
generate a force ("resistance") that works against the aims of treatment. If a
client fears an imminent loss of control, the typical result is a "power struggle"
with the clinician. Would *you* want to be hypnotized if you thought you would
lose control of yourself? The sensible goal in therapy is to do all you can to
avoid a power struggle and define the relationship as a cooperative one.
After all, there is really no way to win a power struggle with the client. To
defeat your very best efforts, all he or she has to do is . . . *nothing*!

THE POWER TO CHOOSE

Using the power struggle, and any other interpersonal factors that arise for
that matter, as a hypnotic device to enhance the therapy is possible when
you recognize the paradox present in hypnosis and psychotherapy. Jay Haley

(1963) described this paradox in terms of the hypnotist's seemingly contradictory messages: "I can only hypnotize you by you hypnotizing yourself; I can only help you by you helping yourself." Essentially, the message emphasizes the responsibility and control on the part of the client, but which is shared with the clinician. If I say to you, "Here. I'm giving you control of me," then who is really in control? If I have the control to give you control, then all I am really doing is suspending my decision to exercise my choices and instead use yours. I remain free, though, to begin exercising my choices again at any time I either have to or want to.

If you have ever been involved in a group decision-making process, you may think of the dynamics in that situation as analogous to what takes place in the hypnotic interaction. If it seems unnecessary to express your opinion because others are already acting in a way that is consistent with your beliefs, then you are less likely to make any further contributions to a system that is already working in a desirable way. If the group acts in ways contrary to your belief system, however, you can either: (1) go along with them peacefully but not really internalize their beliefs; (2) resist and contradict them overtly; or, (3) you can resist covertly in a passive-aggressive manner. If you choose to just go along, you have control of yourself, but that control is not overtly expressed by choice in order to avoid contradictory encounters.

The client in hypnosis, likewise, is free to overtly or covertly reject suggestions that don't fit for *whatever* reason. So, even though the client seems to be saying, "Control me," the clinician can appreciate that control of the client is not his or hers to assume. Rather, *the responsibility of the clinician is to structure suggestions responsibly and competently to maximize the likelihood that they will be accepted and translated into a therapeutic change.* There is never a guarantee that even the most well-formed suggestion will be accepted and acted upon. Sensitivity to the client's unique needs only increases the probability.

The role of choice in the hypnotic encounter cannot be overemphasized. Hypnosis has occasionally been accused of making good people do bad things, but such accusations do not consider realistically the choices the individual made (or *didn't* make, which is also a choice). *At any given time, a person in hypnosis is in a position to choose to lighten, deepen, maintain, or end the experience.* You cannot be forced to focus your attention, dissociate and respond, the core components of hypnosis. You may choose to suspend judgment or decision-making, but that is a choice and *not* a surrendering of your will.

WHAT ABOUT THE OTHER SIDE OF THE CONTROL ISSUE?

Control has been identified thus far as an issue for persons seeking clinical hypnosis, but what about control from the clinician's side of the interaction?

Teaching hypnosis to many people over many years has led me to realize that students of hypnosis inevitably confront the issue of control from an opposite perspective. If the typical client is fearful of being controlled, it is easy to appreciate how the misinformed clinician can be fearful of being the "controller" and having an awesome responsibility (J. Barber, 1995).

Typically, persons entering their first course in clinical hypnosis are intrigued and excited by the potential applications of hypnotic phenomena. There is usually also an appropriate sense of concern, even fear, that they will be developing powers they might "lose control" of to someone else's detriment. Developing skills in hypnosis presupposes a directive style (i.e., taking responsibility for initiating and guiding the course of therapy), and there arises for some students the issue of how they will deal with the "power" they think they will obtain from studying hypnosis. For some, the ability to direct another person's experience is used in self-serving ways, evidenced in arbitrary demonstrations of power by requiring the "subject" to respond to such degrading things as finger-snaps. Usually, I become aware of the concerns in a more positive way, however, when students express their thoughts and feelings about developing hypnotic skills in the course of training.

As you become more experienced with hypnosis, the issues of power from the clinician's standpoint become less prominent. Actual experience with hypnosis will demonstrate to you quickly and repeatedly that your suggestions can be, and often will be, rejected. Any sense of omnipotence you might naively begin with is rapidly lost, a fortunate outcome of failure. The fear of losing control of the hypnosis and of the hypnotized client comes to be recognized as an unnecessary concern, since control is ultimately maintained by the client. Adopting this view affords you the comfort of knowing that even if and when a client reacts in unexpected ways, the person is choosing (at some level) to do so and your role is to be as supportive and helpful as possible.

FICTIONS AND NON-FICTIONS

Listed in the remainder of this chapter are many of the most frequently encountered misconceptions about clinical hypnosis. Following each is a discussion containing ideas that can help you clarify the issues related to the misconception. As you become more familiar with hypnosis, and you find yourself talking more about hypnosis to others, responding to these and other misconceptions will gradually become quite automatic for you. You may be surprised how many people, including your colleagues and even self-described "hypnotists," believe some of these erroneous ideas.

MISCONCEPTION: HYPNOSIS IS A GOOD THING

In a very broad perspective, we can think of hypnotic experiences as a basis for the subjective realities we come to accept as our personal truths. This "reality" includes our world views, values, views on right and wrong behavior, and emotional makeup. In this hypnotic view of a self-suggested experience of life, you can appreciate how your quality of life is largely dictated by what you tell yourself about yourself and the world around you. How does it affect your mood, behavior and physiology when you tell yourself, "Life is so unfair!" Likewise, how does it affect you when you tell yourself, "I can do this!" Each person has countless thoughts each day, ranging from profound to (mostly) mundane. Which ones you focus on, which ones you absorb as true, can generate symptoms ("I'm afraid to fly because what if the plane crashes?") or, conversely, can generate healthy choices ("I love the freedom to be able to go anywhere in the world I want to go!"). Suggestion can be used to help or harm, and in that respect hypnosis isn't innately a good thing. It has the *potential* to be *very* good as a tool to help people when it is applied skillfully (Gilligan, 1987; Stanley, 1994).

MISCONCEPTION: HYPNOSIS IS CAUSED BY THE POWER OF THE HYPNOTIST

Most stage hypnotists are skilled at creating the illusion that they possess a magical and mysterious power over other people. The communication and contextual variables of stage hypnosis were detailed earlier in this chapter, and through the systematic and deliberate manipulation of these variables the hypnotist attains and maintains the illusion of power. In the clinical context, the clinician is able to use his or her skills in communication to make acceptance of suggestions more likely, but there is no control over the client other than the control the client gives to the clinician. The hypnotist directs the client's experience, but only to the degree that the client permits it. It is a relationship of mutual responsiveness.

Hypnosis involves concentration on some stimulus (such as the clinician's words or the client's own internal associations). When used formally, hypnosis usually involves a relaxation process as well. You cannot force someone to concentrate or relax; thus, technically, entering hypnosis is a personal choice. Even in the use of covert or indirect techniques, people are capable of resisting having their attention directed. Without the client's cooperation on some level, the likelihood of therapeutic gain is greatly reduced or eliminated. Allowing the client to feel accepted, understood, and likely to be helped is important for that reason.

Realistically, the clinician is given power by the average client because of his or her title, education, reputation, etc. That power can be given suspiciously or openly as an indicator of the level of trust involved. If the clinician were truly in absolute control, then treatment results would be uniformly successful. It is because the client is in control that treatment results vary so much from individual to individual. The clinician is a guide for the experience, but the client permits that role and thus is the ultimate check in the process (T. Barber, 1969; Lynn, Rhue, & Weekes, 1990; Zeig, 2001).

MISCONCEPTION: ONLY CERTAIN KINDS OF PEOPLE CAN BE HYPNOTIZED

This is a tricky issue, and pertains primarily to the induction of formal hypnosis. In theory, almost anyone can be hypnotized, whether directly or indirectly. Even the people whom many clinicians claim are unhypnotizable or "low" hypnotizables (such as depressed individuals) can, in fact, experience hypnosis to some degree, however slightly, but will require the use of specialized techniques (Bányai, 1991; Spanos, 1991).

In practice, there is a spectrum of responsiveness in people ranging from what are generally termed "low" hypnotizables to "high" hypnotizables to "very high" hypnotizables, sometimes referred to as the "hypnotic virtuosos" (Hilgard, 1977). These are designations based on responses to formal tests of hypnotizability (described in chapter 11). Clearly there are some people in whom it is more difficult to induce hypnosis than in others. What that means exactly is the subject of considerable debate within the field. Does it mean the person has some inherent limitation (e.g., a genetically or perhaps neurologically defined capacity for hypnosis), or might it mean that the test protocol used to assess hypnotizability somehow "misses the mark" for the person? There are experienced and bright people arguing for each side (Cohen, 1989; Lynn & Shindler, 2002).

The issue is a critically important one, because if you conclude a person isn't hypnotizable due to some innate limitation, then there is no need for you to continue trying. If you believe those persons deemed "lows" are not significantly less capable than others, but may be less responsive for any of a wide range of reasons (e.g., fear of losing control, inability to distinguish ambiguous internal states such as tension or relaxation, fear of impending change, negative situational factors, etc.), then you may strive to find and resolve the point(s) diminishing the person's responsiveness. Can the "difficult" person be transformed from a poor hypnotic subject into a reasonably responsive one? Many experienced clinicians and researchers would say yes (Gfeller, 1993; Wagstaff, 1996).

WHAT DO THE HYPNOTIZABILITY STATISTICS MEAN?

In some of the literature addressing this issue, there are often statistical averages provided describing what percentage of the population can reach a given level of hypnosis, and even what percentage of the population cannot be hypnotized at all. For example, one such source states that of "normal adults," 5% cannot go into hypnosis at all, 95% can attain a light level of hypnosis, 55% can attain a medium level, and only 20% are capable of attaining a deep level of hypnosis (these figures appeared in the *American Society of Clinical Hypnosis' Syllabus on Hypnosis and Handbook of Therapeutic Suggestions*, 1973. There are many other, differing estimates).

When a clinician states that any percentage of the population cannot be hypnotized, the responsibility to obtain the greatest results possible is taken from the clinician. When someone has difficulty experiencing hypnosis using some standardized (i.e., impersonal) procedure, he or she may be dismissed as "one of those impossible types." That takes the clinician off the hook for having to be more responsible for making greater effort to reach that person—and other "difficult" clients as well.

Statistical averages for hypnotizability are not particularly helpful to a clinician, in my opinion, despite their necessity in research contexts. They say too little about a given individual's capacity for experiencing hypnosis, and they predict too little about clinical outcomes. Furthermore, they are derived under circumstances that have little bearing on the therapeutic interaction. The figures are based on getting a sample of research subjects, running each of them through a standardized procedure as required by research, and then determining how many of them were able to demonstrate behavior thought to be associated with specific levels of hypnosis. The flaws in such studies are numerous:

(1) The most serious fault of such hypnotizability studies is that standardized induction procedures do not recognize individual differences in subjects. Assessing individual differences and then specifically forming suggestions on the basis of those differences is the most fundamental prerequisite for successful clinical hypnosis in my view. Using the same technique with each person without variation is one way of assuring failure with a significant number of people.

Realistically, standardization of procedure is essential for objective studies of hypnosis, but to use standardization to measure hypnotizability as a general trait is unnecessarily misleading. Experimental subjects who can respond to impersonal procedures are demonstrating considerable flexibility. Subjects who don't respond well to such standardized procedures may well be hypnotizable, but may require greater individual consideration. In one-on-one psychotherapy with a competent clinician, such individuals would likely get that kind of individual consideration and thus be more likely to respond favorably. Furthermore, the motivations for research subjects are quite different from the motivations of therapy clients. Personal distress has a different effect on responsiveness than does intellectual curiosity.

(2) In studies of hypnotizability, the person's depth of hypnosis is measured by the demonstration of particular behaviors associated with presumed levels of hypnosis. For example, in order for a subject to demonstrate a hypnotic phenomenon such as age regression, the subject is assumed to be in at least a medium level of hypnosis. Traditional concepts of hypnosis assume that if you can demonstrate phenomenon "X," then you must be at hypnosis level "Y."

This is an invalid assumption, for people demonstrate hypnotic phenomena continually in their everyday "waking" state. For example, almost everyone has had the experience of being engrossed in a task, and only upon its completion noticing they have injured (e.g., cut, bruised) themselves slightly: "I'm bleeding! Now how did that happen?" According to some, such a demonstration of hypnotic anesthesia is possible only in medium to deep levels of hypnosis! In the skilled use of indirect techniques of hypnosis, and in spontaneous hypnotic experiences arising routinely in people, hypnosis has not even been formally induced with a procedure of any sort, yet subjects can still demonstrate various hypnotic phenomena.

(3) Formal studies of hypnotizability also make the assumption that you must employ formal hypnotic inductions in order for hypnosis to occur, which is not necessarily the case. People often enter spontaneous, informal experiences of hypnosis, and these transient episodes of absorption can be every bit as useful to a clinician who knows how to recognize and utilize them as are the formally induced hypnotic experiences.

This last point, especially, is a source of contradiction for the misconception under consideration. Since people enter hypnotic (focused, absorbed, responsive) experiences spontaneously on a regular basis (while engaging in absorbing conversations, while watching television, while reading, while making love ...), it is not unreasonable to conclude that conscious, information-processing people with a capacity for attentional absorption can be induced either formally or informally.

What factors determine hypnotizability? The theorizing and debating in the field continues even now, just as it has for well over a century. The vital issue of hypnotizability will be addressed in greater detail later. (Continued on page 44)

FRAME OF REFERENCE: ANDRÉ M. WEITZENHOFFER, PH.D., M.A., SC.M., SC.B.

One of the most knowledgeable researchers and clinicians to ever study and practice hypnosis is André M. Weitzenhoffer, Ph.D. (1921–). With a strong "hard science" background in physics, engineering, and physiology, and an insatiable appetite for understanding the nature of hypnosis, Dr. Weitzenhoffer gathered and integrated a broad array of hypnosis literature that eventually became his first book, a 1953 classic called *Hypnotism: An Objective Study in Suggestibility.* After its completion, Dr. Weitzenhoffer was contacted by Dr. Ernest ("Jack") Hilgard, Ph.D., who initiated a collaborative attempt to establish a hypnosis research laboratory at Stanford University, which the two successfully did. (Dr. Hilgard is the subject of another Frame of Reference in chapter 11.) Major effort was put forth by the two to develop a scale to measure hypnotic responsiveness, and the result was the *Stanford Scales of Hypnotic Susceptibility, Forms A, B, and C.* These scales are widely considered to provide the best "objective" measure of the elusive trait called "hypnotizability," and so continue to be a backbone of the research wing of the field of hypnosis. Dr. Weitzenhoffer has published dozens of scientific articles and lectured internationally. He has been and continues to be a strong advocate of the need for scientific rigor in the study of hypnosis, and is persuasive in his arguing for continuing the search for what many researchers consider the "Holy Grail" of hypnosis, namely the definitive proof that a state of hypnosis even exists.

The Stanford lab closed over two decades ago, and Dr. Hilgard has since passed away. Dr. Weitzenhoffer enjoys his "retirement" by working almost as hard as ever. He has recently published the second edition of his classic work, *The Practice of Hypnotism* (2000, Wiley), a critical and detailed consideration of many of the most important issues in the field as seen through Dr. Weitzenhoffer's wise eyes.

On the Beginning of His Interest in Hypnosis: "I think, initially, it was a demonstration at a summer camp, done by a camp counselor, that kind of intrigued me. He did postural sway tests. He was a mesmerist, so he used passes. He would put people into a sort of hypnotic sleep, which was kind of weird. Later on, I went to a stage show and saw a magician that I don't think hypnotized anyone, but everyone was convinced he was hypnotizing people. So, I began to look it up in the encyclopedia to find out more about it. I had an inquisitive mind for most of my childhood, and it sometimes got me into trouble, too. But, that's how my interest arose."**

On the Start of the Stanford Hypnosis Research Laboratory:
"Jack Hilgard came down just as I was doing the last six months of my dissertation. He told me at the time that he had read my book and that he was very impressed by the fact that there seemed to be a good scientific basis for hypnotism. He asked me if I would like to join him at Stanford and jointly start a laboratory. Before doing so, we both spent a year at the Center for Advanced Study in Behavioral Sciences, located in Palo Alto. Jack and I spent most of that time working on the details for the laboratory, what he and I had thought of doing, to see if we could work together.

"I think, at that time, about 10 years of research was mapped out. . . . But the first thing we both agreed was necessary was some kind of good instrument to measure suggestibility, to measure depth."**

On Defining Suggestibility and Suggestions: "For me, suggestibility is the capacity to produce responses to suggestion. Okay, that's very broad, so, I also specify that the response must at least be nonvoluntary . . . If the non-voluntary aspect is not there, you do not have a suggestion. By definition, suggestibility is the capacity to respond to a suggestion, that is, to produce a non-voluntary response . . . My definition of suggestion is that there must be something non-voluntary I can establish as taking place or be satisfied it is non-voluntary. The basic idea in the suggestion also must be fairly directly and clearly reflected by the behavior, either at the level of experience or at the level of actual behavior."**

On the Idea of Everyday Hypnotic States: "For me, it is important to distinguish what is hypnosis—to define what it is and to define what it is not . . . I don't like the idea of the everyday trance state because I don't think it has been clearly demonstrated that there *are* everyday trance states. If there are, I think the question obviously is: Are they a hypnotic state or not? . . . I'm willing to say that people go into altered states of awareness. There are all kinds of altered states of awareness, and I think that of all the altered states of awareness that exist, there is a certain class of these states that probably we can call trance states. I don't think all altered states of consciousness should be called 'trance,' however. Certain trances are hypnosis. Others are probably not. Likewise, I believe that hypnosis can probably be identified with a class (really a subclass) of trance states and that while one can probably say that hypnosis is a trance, one cannot say that all trances are hypnosis." **

On the Quality of Hypnosis in Laboratory versus Clinical Contexts: "I reserve the word 'hypnosis' for the state or condition that has thus been named. I have no reasons for believing that it is fundamentally different when produced in the laboratory and produced in a clinical situation. However, it certainly can be experienced and outwardly manifests itself in different ways, and I cannot be certain at this stage in my knowledge that these differences might not be associated with some fundamental (but not just qualitative) differences in the state itself. I know that some have said that laboratory and clinical 'hypnosis' were different, but I have always understood this to be a reference to the production and use of the state rather than the state itself." *

On Lab Findings Directly Relevant to Clinical Practice: "My main interest has been in checking out the reality and properties of hypnosis, of suggestions (and suggestibility), and of a few induced hypnotic effects. My work has provided a scientific foundation to the subject matter of hypnotic phenomena including the clinical uses of hypnosis. The three findings with the most relevance are: 1) the fact that, all other things being equal, all individuals do not respond equally well to direct suggestions; 2) the fact that under certain conditions, communications not intended to be suggestions will act as suggestions; and, 3) the fact that direct suggestions give rise to automatisms (non-voluntary, and even non-conscious responses)."*

On Assessing Hypnotizability in Clinical Practice: "Unless a patient is taking part in a study that calls for such an assessment, doing one probably has no clinical value.* In clinical practice, I do not see that the scales are particularly useful unless you want to be rigorous. Because, for one thing, a good clinician, a good hypnotist, is going to very quickly get a good feeling for what the patient can do by just watching how the patient responds, whether he does it like Milton Erickson or he does it in a more traditional fashion. He gets some feedback which will tell him if the subject/patient is capable of developing specific responses under hypnosis . . . The other thing is that they are an intrusion in the clinical situation. They are an element that seems to have nothing to do with therapy. Of course, you can tell the patient that, 'In order to help you, I've got to spend an hour testing you with this instrument.' . . . Anything else I'm going to find out would be in the course of working with the patient. If the patient can develop amnesia, I'll find that out presently. I start giving suggestions for it under the hypnotic state. Later, by asking questions I'll get some idea of how much amnesia is present. So that's why I say I don't see the use of the scales in the clinical setting as desirable." **

On the Skills of Good Hypnotists: "The really skilled hypnotists have skills other than just giving a suggestion. They have skills in interpersonal relations, including the ability to empathize, establish rapport, and observe what the client is doing, keeping that in mind, integrating their responses into what is going on. " **

On Pleasant Findings and Disappointments: "My biggest pleasant finding (I would not say 'surprise') was finding evidence that suggested effects had a certain reality as elicited automatisms, that is, as
non-voluntary responses to communications. My biggest disappointment
has been not being able to date to show beyond doubt that the state of
hypnosis exists or does not exist." *

*Sources: * Personal communication, August, 2002*
**Personal Communication, December, 1988.

MISCONCEPTION: ANYONE WHO CAN BE
HYPNOTIZED MUST BE WEAK-MINDED

This particular misconception refers to the all-powerful Svengali image of
the hypnotist, and is based on the belief that in order for a hypnotist to
control someone, the individual must have little or no will of his or her own.
Modern "scare stories" about evil hypnotists who control people and force
them into doing terrible things play on this misconception. As discussed
earlier, the average person does not understand how the hypnotized person
can be in control of him or herself while demonstrating unusual behaviors
at the direction of the hypnotist.

Each person has a capacity for will, but some people choose not to
exercise their capacity to make choices, essentially giving the responsibility
for themselves to others to manage. Such individuals assume a "victim" role
relative to others. The label of "weak-minded" is quite inappropriate for
such persons (Kirsch, Lynn, & Rhue, 1993; Lynn, Kirsch, & Rhue, 1996).

To counteract any negative effect this particular misconception may
have had on the hypnosis-seeking public, many clinicians have made claims
to the effect that people with higher intelligence and stronger personalities
will be better hypnotic subjects. The ability to be hypnotized is not reliably
correlated with specific personality traits, or other such factors as age or
gender (Kirsch & Council, 1992). Despite it not being fully true, some clinicians see a potential value in making the claim that intelligent people do
better as hypnotic subjects than their less intelligent counterparts. The potential value lies in the hope that the client will view him- or herself as intelligent, and so will be motivated to respond more readily. The other side of
the coin, however, is that the person is seeking help at a time when his or
her self-image may not be particularly good from having attempted to cope

with problems independently and been unsuccessful in resolving them. If a clinician sets a client up to respond positively on the basis of intelligence or any other seemingly desirable personal characteristic, and then the client has a less than satisfactory experience with hypnosis, the client may use the negative experience to validate his or her negative self-appraisal. This is only one example of how a well-meaning clinician can inadvertently do damage to a client. Rather than trying to get the person to identify with and become a model client, the clinician may better employ his or her skills in accepting what the client offers and using it as the basis for further hypnotic interaction.

MISCONCEPTION: ONCE ONE HAS BEEN HYPNOTIZED, ONE CAN NO LONGER RESIST IT

This misconception refers to the idea that a hypnotist controls the will of his or her subject, and that once one "succumbs to the power" of the hypnotist, one is forever at his or her mercy. As you now know, nothing is farther from the truth, since the hypnotic process is an interaction based on mutual power, shared in order to attain some desirable therapeutic outcome. If a client chooses not to go into hypnosis for whatever reason, then he or she will not.

The nature of the hypnotic process is *always* context-determined, at least in part, since hypnosis always occurs in some context (T. Barber, 2000). Even the most responsive clients can refuse to follow the suggestions of a clinician if they so choose. Prior experience with hypnosis, whether good or bad, is not the sole or even a primary determining factor of whether hypnosis is accomplished or not. The personal characteristics of the individual, communication and relationship factors as well as situational factors are all key variables beyond the client's history that will help determine the outcome.

One of the sources for this misconception is the stage hypnotist's use of "cues," specific words or gestures that have become associated within the subject to the experience of entering hypnosis, allowing him to re-enter hypnosis quickly. From the perspective of the audience, the hypnotist's use of a simple word or gesture to rapidly induce hypnosis is yet another dramatic demonstration of the hypnotist's power.

In clinical practice, it is often convenient to establish a cue in order to make subsequent inductions swifter and easier, but the power to induce hypnosis does not reside in the cue itself. Rather, it is the individual's willingness to respond to the cue that makes the cue a viable trigger for hypnosis. Should the client be given the cue but choose not to enter hypnosis, he or she will not. The cue, also called a "rapid induction signal," is only effective when the client chooses to respond to it. Beginning or ending the experience of hypnosis is fully in the client's control.

MISCONCEPTION: ONE CAN BE HYPNOTIZED TO SAY OR DO SOMETHING AGAINST ONE'S WILL

This is among the most argued issues in the entire field of hypnosis. It raises many complex issues about notions of free will, personal responsibility for one's actions, boundaries in the therapeutic relationship, the potential for abuse of one's position, and other such issues related to professional and personal conduct. In the clinical context, the relationship between clinician and client is necessarily one of mutual responsibility and accountability. In theory, the clinician offers entirely benevolent suggestions which the client can freely choose to either accept or reject. In practice, however, this is far too simplistic to be entirely true given what we have come to know about the phenomenon of iatrogenesis (i.e., client symptoms either caused or aggravated by treatment), the exploitation of naïve or vulnerable clients, and the hazards of working with people who are sometimes psychologically quite disturbed. But, these circumstances represent the exceptions and are atypical of therapeutic environments.

The capacity to influence people to do things against their will exists. There is little room for doubt that people can be manipulated negatively to do things seemingly inconsistent with their beliefs and attitudes (Bordens & Horowitz, 2002). To put it quite bluntly, brainwashing exists. However, the conditions necessary to effect such powerful influence do not correspond very closely to the typical therapeutic encounter. In other words, controlling a person *is* possible under certain conditions, but those conditions are not in and of themselves hypnosis (Laurence & Perry, 1988). And, they are quite far removed from the respectful and empowering approaches to clinical hypnosis promoted in this book. Further discussion of these issues is contained in Chapters 6 and 7.

MISCONCEPTION: BEING HYPNOTIZED CAN BE HAZARDOUS TO YOUR HEALTH

This misconception is a strong one in raising people's fears about hypnosis. In fact, there is some legitimate basis for concern about the use of hypnosis, but the concern should not be about the experience of hypnosis harming anyone. Instead, the concern should be about who practices hypnosis. *Hypnosis itself is not harmful, but an incompetent clinician can do some damage* through sheer ignorance about the complexity of each person's mind, ignorance about the condition to be treated, or through a lack of respect for the integrity of each human being.

The process of formal (i.e., structured and overt) hypnotic induction is an absorbing process in which one's concentration is directed—perhaps to an idea, or to a voice, or to an internal experience, but always to something. There is a slowdown of physiological functions (e.g., breathing, heart rate) and typically the person's body is lethargic. Such physical responses are healthy, effectively reducing stress and discomfort. Many people do not recognize the amount of stress they carry within themselves until they experience the comfort of hypnosis. Then they are able to distinguish more clearly their internal states and gradually develop greater control over their degree of tension. People suffering from hypertension, symptoms of stress, anxiety and pain can get substantial relief from hypnosis. Hypnosis is physically beneficial to any client, though. Experience with hypnosis highlights the extraordinary amount of self-control one can attain, even of physical processes that are generally regarded as involuntary (Brown & Fromm, 1987; Rossi, 2000).

MISCONCEPTION: HYPNOSIS CAN'T HARM ANYONE

In terms of potential emotional harm, it is not hypnosis itself that may cause someone problems, but difficulties may arise due to misdiagnosis, the inappropriate content of a session, or the inability of a clinician to effectively guide the client (J. Barber, 1995; Kleinhaus & Eli, 1987). The same conditions exist in *any* helping relationship where one person is in distress, vulnerable, and seeking relief. An inexperienced or uneducated helper may inadvertently (rarely is it intentional) misdiagnose a problem or its dynamics, offer poor advice, make grandiose promises, impose an antitherapeutic point of view, or simply waste the person's time and money.

Hypnosis often gives the client access to memories and feelings long outside of conscious awareness (McConkey, 1992; Sheehan, 1995). The content of such memories may be distressing, as they often are in therapy, and an inexperienced clinician may feel unable or unqualified to handle the client's issues effectively. In such instances, the clinician may have gotten more than he or she bargained for, although someone else may have been able to use the exact same information or responses to great therapeutic advantage.

The less skilled clinician may have helped to "open up" another person, but it's a wasted and even potentially damaging opportunity if the person has no capacity to do any real therapy. An unfortunate example is one self-proclaimed "hypnotist, healer, psychic counselor" I once encountered who attempted to impress me by describing his use of hypnosis with a woman who presented to him the problem of intense guilt feelings over an abortion she'd had. He used hypnosis to have her vividly imagine the fetus was still alive within her. He then directed her to have a dialogue with it, even giving it a name, in order to explain to it why she needed to abort it. He thought this would be a good technique for settling the matter, and wondered why such a "reasonable" approach didn't fare too well. She left him feeling much worse than when she came in. His thoughtlessness confirmed her worst fears— that she had killed a person with a name and personality. Regardless of your views on abortion, you can probably recognize the inappropriateness of the intervention when the goal was to reduce the client's distress.

This type of encounter is a basis for the misconception that hypnosis does harm. Clearly, hypnosis does not cause harm, but ineffective or inappropriate use of hypnosis can. Ineffective use of *any* skill, whether it be surgery, psychological testing, or giving haircuts can hurt someone. Just as dentistry is not dangerous, but a poor dentist is, hypnosis is not dangerous, but a poor hypnotist is. Theoretically, we have governmental agencies for regulating clinical licensure and practice, but, unfortunately, at the practical level, it is literally impossible to separate those who are competent from those who are not. To compound this problem, in most places people can and do practice hypnosis without any academic requirement or clinical training, much less licensure. (A smart consumer will have to do some "shopping" for a competent, well-trained clinician.)

The flip side of this delicate issue, and the best of all reasons for developing skills in hypnotic approaches, is the emotional good that hypnosis can help generate. In its ability to give people greater feelings of self-control and a subsequent increase of self-confidence, hypnosis is a powerful means for resolving emotional problems and enhancing emotional well-being. It is essential that the clinician have enough knowledge and skill to use it toward that end.

MISCONCEPTION: ONE INEVITABLY BECOMES DEPENDENT ON THE HYPNOTIST

Hypnosis as a therapeutic tool does not in and of itself foster dependencies of any kind, any more than other tools such as a behavioral contract, analytical free association, or an intelligence test can. Dependency is a need, a reliance, that everyone has to some degree. To a greater or lesser extent, we all depend on others for things we feel are important to our well-being. In the helping professions especially, people are seeking help at a time they are hurting and vulnerable. They depend on the clinician to help, to comfort, and to care.

Clinicians know that the ultimate goal of responsible treatment must be to help each client establish self-reliance and independence whenever possible. Rather than foster dependence by indirectly encouraging the client to view the clinician as the source of answers to all of life's woes, hypnosis used properly helps the person in distress turn inwards in order to make use of the many experiences and resources the person has acquired over his or her lifetime that can be used therapeutically. Consistent with the goal of self-reliance and the use of personal power to help one's self is the teaching of self-hypnosis to those you work with (Alman, 2001).

There is an old saying: "If you give a man a fish, you have given him a meal. If you teach him how to fish, you have given him a livelihood." Teaching self-hypnosis to those you work with is a means for helping to ensure that your clients can continue to work independently and grow in your absence. Furthermore, teaching them strategies for problem-solving along with self-hypnosis can allow for the emergence of a self-correcting mechanism that can assure those you work with that they do have control over their lives. It gives you an assurance that you have done your work well.

MISCONCEPTION: ONE CAN BECOME "STUCK" IN HYPNOSIS

Hypnosis necessarily involves focused attention, which may be either inwardly or outwardly directed. It is controlled by the client, who can initiate or terminate the hypnosis session as he or she chooses. It is literally impossible to become "stuck" in a state of concentration. Can you imagine getting "stuck" reading a book?

A source for this misconception is the infrequent occasion where a clinician has given suggestions to the client to "wake up" yet the client remains in hypnosis. The inexperienced clinician may get anxious or even panic when the client does not respond to direct suggestions to open his or her eyes and return to the usual "waking" state. In such situations, the client is not "stuck," but instead simply chooses not to terminate the hypnosis session for at least one of a couple of reasons: Either the client is quite comfortable where he or she is, or the client is still working on completing the experience, that is, getting closure. The best thing to do in such a circumstance is offer an open-ended suggestion that the client can bring him- or herself out of hypnosis when he or she wants to—and then leave him or her alone to do so! In time, usually a short time, the person will return to his or her typical "waking" state. Never can someone not return, so this is one issue you need not lose any sleep over. Respect the choices of the person in hypnosis. If he or she does not follow a particular suggestion, there is a reason for it, so don't press your wants; just let yourself go with the flow.

MISCONCEPTION: ONE IS ASLEEP OR UNCONSCIOUS WHEN IN HYPNOSIS

Hypnosis is not sleep! Observed from outside the experience, someone in hypnosis may physically resemble someone who is asleep, showing minimal activity, muscular relaxation, slowed breathing, and so on. However, from a mental standpoint, objectively measurable in a variety of ways, the client is relaxed, conscious, and alert. Ever-present is *some* level of awareness of current goings-on, even when in deep hypnosis. In the case of spontaneous hypnosis, as well as in the condition of so-called "alert hypnosis" where the person has his or her eyes open and is engaged in some focused task, conscious awareness is even more marked. Physical relaxation need not be present in order for hypnosis to occur (Cardeña, Alarcón, Capafons, & Bayot, 1998).

Misinformation circulated for years about hypnosis being comparable to learning while asleep. "Sleep learning" was soundly disproven years ago, however. Although you may not learn while you're asleep, you can learn while in the transition phases, that is, while falling asleep and awakening at those midpoints between being asleep and awake commonly called "twilight states."

A source of this misconception is the word "hypnosis" itself, a word derived from the Greek word "Hypnos," the word for sleep and the name of the Greek God of Sleep (Gravitz, 1991). The word "hypnosis" was coined early in the nineteenth century and has been used to describe hypnosis ever since. Many early theorists, most notably Hippolyte Bernheim in France in the late 19th century, thought of hypnosis as a special form of sleep, and this viewpoint was widely taught to students of hypnosis (Hull, 1933/2002). Thus, early practitioners reinforced this erroneous viewpoint each time they offered the ritualistic suggestions to "sleep deeply" and "wake up" to their clients. Hypnosis is not sleep, and even the client in deep hypnosis is oriented to external reality to some degree. Therefore, the use of obsolete phrases like "sleep deeply" are neither relevant to or indicative of the client's experience, and so should not be used in doing hypnosis.

MISCONCEPTION: HYPNOSIS ALWAYS INVOLVES A RITUAL OF INDUCTION

When you consider the interpersonal and contextual aspects of hypnosis, you can more easily appreciate how hypnosis can occur to some degree whenever someone focuses his or her attention on experiences (e.g., ideas and feelings) and internal associations elicited by the communications of the guide. The more removed (i.e., dissociated) the person becomes from immediate realities while getting absorbed in the suggested experience, the more absorbing and potentially hypnotic the experience. For as long as your attention is directed in an absorbing way either inwardly on some subjective experience, or outwardly on some external stimulus (which, in turn, creates an internal experience), and you are responsive to suggestions to alter your experience in some way, you can reasonably be said to be in hypnosis (Matthews, Lankton, & Lankton, 1993; Zeig, 2001).

It should be apparent that hypnosis does not have to be formally induced through some ritual in order to occur. Likewise, the various hypnotic phenomena can and do arise spontaneously even when no induction has taken place. You may recall my earlier description of times when you were deeply absorbed in doing something, and only afterward did you notice you were injured or bleeding. That is an example of a spontaneous anesthesia, one of the classic hypnotic phenomena to be discussed at length later. When this happens to you quite spontaneously, you probably didn't think of it as a hypnotic experience, one you could learn to produce deliberately should you want to control pain. Yet, that is what the art and science of clinical hypnosis is ultimately about—creating helpful experiences through suggestive strategies involving focused attention, amplifying and making use of abilities people have they generally don't realize they have, as in the example of anesthesia. It helps to be able to recognize hypnosis as a more common phenomenon than most people realize, and thereby take it out of the realm of "strange" or a place too far removed from everyday experience.

MISCONCEPTION: HYPNOSIS IS SIMPLY RELAXATION

Relaxation feels good, but it is, at best, simply a stepping-stone in the direction of facilitating more complex experiences, like an age regression (experiential memory) or an anesthesia. No one would simply do a relaxation process and then expect the client to undergo a painless surgery. Hypnosis involves the deliberate structuring of experiences like anesthesia that go well beyond simple relaxation.

Hypnosis has been described as an experience of focused attention and absorption in experience that can be quite removed from immediate goings-on. The involvement in the experience of hypnosis can vary in intensity according to a number of factors, such as the client's level of motivation to participate in the process, the person's ability to focus, the relevance of the clinician's suggestions, and so forth. Must someone be relaxed, sitting with eyes closed in order for hypnosis to occur? No. Briefly mentioned earlier was the phenomenon called "alert hypnosis," or what some call "waking hypnosis" (Bányai, Zseni, & Tury, 1993). In these conditions, clients or research subjects are given suggestions to focus intensely on some activity (e.g., riding a stationery bike or running on a treadmill), and with their eyes open while physically active, they are exposed to a hypnotic induction and then given suggestions to generate various hypnotic phenomena, which they may readily do (Bányai & Hilgard, 1978).

As you're learning, hypnosis can occur spontaneously while conversing, reading, and in countless other instances where one's attention is fixed. You can be anxious, even in suspense, and still be wonderfully focused, as in "glued to a mystery." Thus, *physical relaxation is not a necessary prerequisite for hypnosis to occur.*

In clinical practice, however, relaxation is usually a part of the intervention, since it is comforting and soothing, and reduces the stress and anxiety often associated with people's problems. Relaxation generally makes it easier to enlist cooperation on the part of the client, as most clients want or expect it as part of the process. Relaxation also makes access to the client's unconscious (i.e., hidden) resources easier. Furthermore, relaxation can highlight the subjective differences between the experience of hypnosis and the usual "waking" state, convincing the client that he or she has, in fact, experienced an altered state of consciousness that fits with expectations of what hypnosis "should" be like (Sarbin, 1997).

MISCONCEPTION: CLINICAL HYPNOSIS IS A SPECIFIC SCHOOL OF THERAPY

Is hypnosis a therapy in its own right? Hypnosis is quite unique as an approach. After all, how many other therapy approaches emphasize generating and utilizing a client's dissociated and suggestible state for increasing therapeutic responses the way practitioners of hypnosis do? On the other hand, whatever resources you try to mobilize and whatever skills you try to teach the client may be better described in other specific models of psychotherapy. Thus, there is a legitimate basis for saying clinical hypnosis is not a specific school of therapy in its own right, like behavior therapy or analytic therapy, despite the popular use of the term "hypnotherapy." Clinical hypnosis is a therapeutic tool that is not aligned with any one theoretical or practical orientation (Kirsch et al., 1993).

So, what of the term "hypnotherapy?" Does it mean anything? It implies therapy delivered hypnotically, that is, the creation and utilization of the subjective experience of hypnosis in order to enhance treatment effects. And, as you have already learned, hypnosis can enhance treatment effects. There *is* something special about hypnosis that warrants giving it a unique position in the realm of treatment. But should it be considered a distinct form of therapy?

There are nearly as many approaches to the use of hypnosis as there are clinicians who use hypnosis, and inevitably they use it in a way that is consistent with their beliefs about therapy and the way they believe therapy should be done. So, for some clinicians, hypnosis is integrated with cognitive-behavioral approaches, and for others it is integrated with psychodynamic approaches. For some, it is integrated with mind-body healing approaches, and for others it is integrated with preventive approaches. Whatever belief system and style of therapy you currently practice will likely continue to be meaningful to you as you discover ways to enhance what you already do by applying hypnotic approaches.

I have always been amused that whenever I state that I use patterns of hypnosis in my work, my professional peers smile and think they know what I do. Few of them actually do. What one clinician who uses hypnosis does with it and what another does with it may be as different as night and day. Almost any procedure that involves the induction of hypnosis and the use of suggestions has been called "hypnosis," unfortunately, and the countless variations of such general methods that are possible get lost under the generic label. Learning methods and principles of hypnosis is much like learning a language. You learn a common set of rules, words, and structures, yet you will still inevitably express yourself in your own unique way.

WHAT ABOUT HYPNOSIS SCRIPTS?

A primary basis for this misconception is the incredible over-standardization of hypnotic procedures some hypnosis experts promote. Many books and clinical trainings on hypnosis advocate the verbatim use of prepared scripts that have been written for all types of general problems, such as overweight, smoking, phobias, and so on. In such approaches, if you encounter a smoker wanting to stop smoking, for example, you are encouraged to turn to a particular section of the hypnosis book and then read the anti-smoking set of suggestions to the client (after you have read the hypnosis induction script on a previous page!).

The use of scripts robs hypnosis of its real potency, the strength derived from the recognition and use of each individual's unique experiences and needs. Spontaneity and flexibility are essential for best results in doing hypnosis. Even when a therapeutic strategy is worked out beforehand, as good treatment planning may require, a skilled clinician will still incorporate the spontaneous responses of the client into the procedure.

The use of scripts promotes the misconception that hypnosis in clinical practice can be standardized and that each client is identical as long as they have the same presenting complaint. Reading the same script to all smokers as if they are the same simply because they all share a bad habit is an obvious gross oversimplification, and when such an approach fails, typically the client gets blamed, rather than the approach.

The dynamic and spontaneous nature of skilled applications of clinical hypnosis is what makes it so complex and demanding an ability to acquire. Hypnosis as a therapeutic tool is ever-changing with the context in which it arises, and must therefore be adapted to the individual needs of the client and situation. People will likely continue to use the term "hypnotherapy" to offer a label for what they do, but it only implies the use of hypnosis and suggestion in the most general sense, and reveals very little else about what they actually say and do with their clients.

MISCONCEPTION: HYPNOSIS MAY BE USED TO ACCURATELY RECALL EVERYTHING THAT HAS HAPPENED TO YOU

Clinicians need to understand how memory works in order to best utilize this most important aspect of the individual. Some have compared the mind to a computer in which every memory is presumed to be accurately stored and available for eventual retrieval under the right conditions. The computer metaphor is highly inaccurate, however, and has the potential to be hazardous if an unwary clinician operates on that premise (Loftus & Yapko, 1995; Yapko, 1994a, 1994b). The research on memory makes it abundantly clear that the mind does not take in experience and store it in exact form for accurate recall later. In fact, memories are stored on the basis of perceptions, and so are subject to the same potential distortions. People can "remember" things in vivid detail that did not actually happen. Likewise, people can remember only selected fragments of an experience, or they can take bits and pieces of multiple memories and combine them into one false memory. Memory, simply put, is not reliable; if you are looking for "truth," you are unlikely to find it in memory (Sheehan, 1995).

Can a memory be considered more reliable because it was obtained through hypnosis? Can hypnosis be used to uncover the truth of what actually happened in someone's past? The answer to these two critically important questions is no. The effects of hypnosis on memory will be explored in greater detail later. Suffice it to say here that hypnosis does not increase the probability of accurate recall (Lynn & Nash, 1994).

CLOSURE ON MISCONCEPTIONS

As you may have come to appreciate from this chapter, hypnosis carries with it a considerable amount of old baggage. However, it is a dynamic field undergoing a major renovation as serious-minded clinicians and researchers strive to better understand the components of effective intervention and the range of human capabilities. How you as an individual conceptualize the natures of therapy, hypnosis, and the mind, and how creative you are in applying the methods, will determine almost entirely how you will use hypnosis clinically.

At this point, I hope, you have a clearer understanding of some of the most important characteristics and issues associated with hypnosis, and are ready to begin exploring some of the dynamics of communication and influence relevant to your use of hypnotic patterns in your interactions with others.

For Discussion

1. What is peer group pressure? How does it cause one to conform?
2. What personal qualities might allow one to resist peer group pressure? In general, are these positive or negative qualities?
3. How do one's expectations influence one's experiences? How is a "self-fulfilling prophecy" likely to be part of a stage hypnosis show?
4. How does a fear of losing control of one's self surface in everyday behavior? Offer some examples.
5. What fears did you or do you have about experiencing hypnosis? What apprehensions do you have about hypnotizing others?
6. When might a client's misconceptions about hypnosis be an asset to the clinician? A liability?
7. Why do treatment approaches become standardized? What are the advantages and disadvantages of standardization?
8. What is a "power struggle"? Why do they arise? Can they be prevented? If so, how?
9. What types of people do you think would be harder to hypnotize than others? Why do you think so?
10. How might a clinician inadvertently encourage dependency in his or her clients? What may be the underlying motivations?
11. What is the basis for the statement that a person's emotional problems may be as much a consequence of hypnosis as the solutions? How is "reality" determined?

Things to Do

1. When appropriate, tell people you work with or socialize with that you are studying hypnosis. What positive or negative reactions do you get? Are you surprised?
2. See a stage hypnosis show, if you have one in your area. How is hypnosis represented to the public? How might misconceptions be created? How does the hypnotist engender obedience? How are subjects recruited?
3. Ask acquaintances to describe their understandings about what hypnosis is and how it works. What common misconceptions are present in their descriptions?
4. Take peers on a "trust-walk" in which you lead them around while they have their eyes closed. What feelings do they become aware of? What increases or decreases their willingness to be led?
5. Interview hypnotists in your area and ask them what percentage of people cannot be hypnotized. What reasons do they give for their answer?
6. Find books that contain entire scripts for interventions and choose a script of particular interest to you to read closely. What sort of person would this script seem to be ideal for? Why? What sort of person would the script likely be terrible for? Why?

REFERENCES

Alman, B. (2001). Self-care: Approaches from self-hypnosis for utilizing your unconscious (inner) potentials. In B. Geary & J. Zeig (Eds.), *The handbook of Ericksonian psychotherapy* (pp. 522–40). Phoenix, AZ: The Milton H. Erickson Foundation Press.

Argast, T., Landis, R., & Carrell, P. (2001). When to use or not to use hypnosis according to the Ericksonian tradition. In B. Geary & J. Zeig (Eds.), *The handbook of Ericksonian psychotherapy* (pp. 66–92). Phoenix, AZ: The Milton H. Erickson Foundation Press.

Bányai, É. (1991). Toward a social-psychobiological model of hypnosis. In S. Lynn & J. Rhue (Eds.), *Theories of hypnosis: Current models and perspectives* (pp. 564–98). New York: Guilford.

Bányai, É. & Hilgard, E. (1978). A comparison of active-alert hypnotic induction with traditional relaxation induction. *Journal of Abnormal Psychology, 85,* 218–24.

Bányai, É., Zseni, A., & Tury, F. (1993). Active-alert hypnosis in psychotherapy. In J. Rhue, S. Lynn, & I. Kirsch (Eds.), *Handbook of clinical hypnosis* (pp. 271–90). Washington, D.C.: American Psychological Association.

Barber, J. (1995). Dangers of hypnosis: Sex, pseudo-memories and other complications. In G. Burrows & R. Stanley (Eds.), *Contemporary international hypnosis* (pp. 13–26). Chichester, UK: Wiley.

Barber, T. (1969). *Hypnosis: A scientific approach.* New York: VanNostrand Reinhold.

Barber, T. (2000). A deeper understanding of hypnosis: Its secrets, its nature, its essence. *American Journal of Clinical Hypnosis, 42*: 3–4, 208–73.

Bordens, K. & Horowitz, I. (2002). *Social psychology* (2nd ed.). Mahwah, NJ: Erlbaum.

Bowers, K. & Davidson, T. (1991). A neodissociative critique of Spanos's social-psychological model of hypnosis. In S. Lynn & J. Rhue (Eds.), *Theories of hypnosis: Current models and perspectives* (pp. 105–43). New York: Guilford.

Brown, D. & Fromm, E. (1987). *Hypnosis and behavioral medicine.* Hillsdale, NJ: Erlbaum.

Cardeña, Alarcón, A., Capafons, A., & Bayot, A. (1998). Effects of suggestibility of a new method of active-alert hypnosis. *International Journal of Clinical and Experimental Hypnosis, 3,* 280–94.

Cohen, S. (1989). Clinical uses of measures of hypnotizability. *American Journal of Clinical Hypnosis, 32,* 4–9.

Dixon, M. & Laurence, J-R. (1992). Two hundred years of hypnosis research: Questions resolved? Questions unanswered! In E. Fromm & M. Nash (Eds.), *Contemporary hypnosis research* (pp. 34–66). New York: Guilford.

Duncan, B., Miller, S., & Coleman, S. (2001). Utilization: A seminal contribution, a family of ideas, and a new generation of applications. In B. Geary & J. Zeig (Eds.), *The handbook of Ericksonian psychotherapy* (pp. 43–56). Phoenix, AZ: The Milton H. Erickson Foundation Press.

Frauman, D., Lynn, S., & Brentar, J. (1993). Prevention and therapeutic management of "negative effects" in hypnotherapy. In J. Rhue, S. Lynn, & I. Kirsch (Eds.), *Handbook of clinical hypnosis* (pp. 95–120). Washington, D.C.: American Psychological Association.

Gfeller, J. (1993). Enhancing hypnotizability and treatment responsiveness. In J. Rhue, S. Lynn, & I. Kirsch (Eds.), *Handbook of clinical hypnosis* (pp. 235–50). Washington, D.C.: American Psycholgical Association.

Gilligan, S. (1987). *Therapeutic trances: The cooperation principle in Ericksonian hypnotherapy.* New York: Brunner/Mazel.

Gravitz, M. (1991). Early theories of hypnosis: A clinical perspective. In S. Lynn & J. Rhue (Eds.), *Theories of hypnosis: Current models and perspectives* (pp. 19–42). New York: Guilford.

Haley, J. (1963). *Strategies of psychotherapy.* New York: Grune & Stratton.

Haley, J. (1973). *Uncommon therapy: The psychiatric techniques of Milton H. Erickson, M.D.* New York: Norton.

Hilgard, E. (1977). *Divided consciousness: Multiple controls in human thought and action.* New York: Wiley.

Hubble, M., Duncan, B., & Miller, S. (1999). *The heart & soul of change: What works in therapy.* Washington, D.C.: American Psychological Association.

Hull, C. (1933/2002). *Hypnosis and suggestibility.* Williston, VT: Crown House Publishing.

Kirsch, I. (1990). *Changing expectations: A key to effective psychotherapy.* Pacific Grove, CA: Brooks/Cole.

Kirsch, I. & Council, J. (1992). Situational and personality correlates of hypnotic responsiveness. In E. Fromm & M. Nash (Eds.), *Contemporary hypnosis research* (pp. 267–91). New York: Guilford.

Kirsch, I., Lynn, S., & Rhue, J. (1993). Introduction to clinical hypnosis. In J. Rhue, S. Lynn & I. Kirsch (Eds.), *Handbook of clinical hypnosis* (pp. 3–22). Washington, D.C.: American Psychological Association.

Kleinhauz, M. & Eli, I. (1987). Potential deleterious effects of hypnosis in the clinical setting. *American Journal of Clinical Hypnosis, 29,* 155–59.

Laurence, J-R, & Perry, C. (1988). *Hypnosis, will and memory: A psycho-legal history.* New York: Guilford.

Loftus, E. & Yapko, M. (1995). Psychotherapy and the recovery of repressed memories. In T. Ney (Ed.), *True and false allegations of child sexual abuse: Assessment and case management* (pp. 176–91). New York: Brunner/Mazel.

Lynn, S., Kirsch, I., & Rhue, J. (1996). Maximizing treatment gains: Recommendations for the practice of clinical hypnosis. In S. Lynn, I. Kirsch, & J. Rhue (Eds.), *Casebook of clinical hypnosis* (pp. 395–406). Washington, D.C.: American Psychological Association.

Lynn, S. & Nash, M. (1994). Truth in memory.: Ramifications for psychotherapy and hypnotherapy. *American Journal of Clinical Hypnosis, 36*, 194–208.

Lynn, S., Rhue, J. & Weekes, J. (1990). Hypnotic involuntariness: A social-cognitive analysis. *Psychological Review, 97*, 169–84.

Lynn, S. & Shindler, K. (2002). The role of hypnotizability assessment in treatment. *American Journal of Clinical Hypnosis, 44*:3–4, 185–98.

Matthews, W., Lankton, S., & Lankton, C. (1993). An Ericksonian model of hypnotherapy. In J. Rhue, S. Lynn, & I. Kirsch (Eds.), *Handbook of clinical hypnosis* (pp. 187–214). Washington, D.C.: American Psychological Association.

McConkey, K. (1992). The effects of hypnotic procedures on remembering: The experimental findings and their implications for forensic hypnosis. In E. Fromm & M. Nash (Eds.), *Contemporary hypnosis research* (pp. 405–26). New York: Guilford.

McNeilly, R. (2001). Creating a context for hypnosis: Listening for a resource theme and integrating it into an Ericksonian hypnosis session. In B. Geary & J. Zeig (Eds.), *The handbook of Ericksonian psychotherapy* (pp. 57–65). Phoenix, AZ: The Milton H. Erickson Foundation Press.

Orne, M. (1959). The nature of hypnosis: Artifact and essence. *Journal of Abnormal and Social Psychology, 58*, 277–99.

Rossi, E. (2000). In search of a deep psychobiology of hypnosis: Visionary hypotheses for a new millennium. *American Journal of Clinical Hypnosis, 42*: 3–4, 178–207.

Sarbin, T. (1997). Hypnosis as a conversation: "Believed-in imaginings" revisited. *Contemporary Hypnosis, 14*, 4, 203–15.

Scheflin, A. (2001). Caveat therapist: Ethical and legal dangers in the use of Ericksonian techniques. In B. Geary & J. Zeig (Eds.), *The handbook of Ericksonian psychotherapy* (pp. 154–67). Phoenix, AZ: The Milton H. Erickson Foundation Press.

Sheehan, P. (1995). The effects of asking leading questions in hypnosis. In G. Burrows & R. Stanley (Eds.), *Contemporary international hypnosis* (pp. 55–62). Chichester, UK: Wiley.

Spanos, N. (1991). A sociocognitive approach to hypnosis. In S. Lynn & J. Rhue (Eds.), *Theories of hypnosis: Current models and perspectives* (pp. 324–61). New York: Guilford.

Spiegel, H., & Spiegel, D. (1987). *Trance and treatment: Clinical uses of hypnosis.* Washington, D.C.: American Psychiatric Press.

Spivey, C. & Prentice-Dunn, S. (1990). Assessing the directionality of deindividuated behavior: Effects of deindividuation, modeling, and private self-consciousness on aggressive and prosocial responses. *Basic and Applied Social Psychology, 11*, 387–403.

Stanley, R. (1994). The protection of the professional use of hypnosis: The need for legal controls. *Australian Journal of Clinical and Experimental Hypnosis, 22*, 39–52.

Wagstaff, G. (1996). Compliance and imagination in hypnosis. In R. Kunzendorf, N. Spanos, & B. Wallace (Eds.), *Hypnosis and imagination* (pp. 19–40). Amityville, NY: Baywood.

Yapko, M. (1994a). Suggestibility and repressed memories of abuse: A survey of psychotherapists' beliefs. *American Journal of Clinical Hypnosis, 36*, 163–71.

Yapko, M. (1994b). *Suggestions of abuse: True and false memories of childhood sexual trauma.* New York: Simon & Schuster.

Zeig, J. (2001). Hypnotic induction. In B. Geary & J. Zeig (Eds.), *The handbook of Ericksonian psychotherapy* (pp. 18–30). Phoenix, AZ: The Milton H. Erickson Foundation Press.

Zimbardo, P. & Leippe, M. (1992). *The psychology of attitude change and social influence.* New York: McGraw-Hill.

3

Conceptualizing Hypnosis

How you think about clinical hypnosis has profound implications for what you perceive to be its potential applications. Over the years there have been many different perspectives offered by clinicians and researchers to characterize the phenomenon of hypnosis (see Lynn & Rhue's 1991 volume, *Theories of Hypnosis*, for an excellent elaboration of many of these models). As you would predict, these viewpoints often differ sharply. Each of these perspectives considered individually has played a role in both illuminating and confounding our understandings of hypnosis. In general, theories have a paradoxical effect: They catalyze understanding by helping one discover meanings and relationships in an otherwise apparently random universe, and yet theories can often confound matters by limiting one's observations to only what the theory allows for.

With a subject as complex as hypnosis, the inadequacy of a single theory to explain the broad range of responses on so many different dimensions of experience becomes glaringly apparent. The complexities of the subject of hypnosis, and the even greater complexities of the human being capable of hypnosis, are so great that it seems highly improbable that a single theory can evolve to explain its origin and character.

My direct comment about the inadequacy of a single theory's ability to account for all hypnotic phenomena is actually an indirect comment in favor of believing a little of everything, and all of nothing. The theories of hypnosis that have been developed over the years are each useful in their own way for describing one or more aspects of hypnosis, but none can be considered the final word in describing the process or experience of hypnosis.

This chapter provides an overview and discussion of some of the more influential theoretical perspectives of hypnosis informing today's clinicians and researchers. I'd like to encourage you to think critically about each viewpoint, perhaps by first considering what it assumes and evaluating for yourself whether its assumptions seem reasonable and helpful to you. It would be especially helpful for you to consider each model of hypnosis from the perspective of the clinician operating within it, then the individual perspective of the client experiencing it, and finally as a result of the interaction of the two. This may help you distinguish between what may be intellectually interesting versus what is clinically meaningful and effective.

The various models of hypnosis can be differentiated from one another in a variety of ways. I have found it helpful to think in terms of two general categories of hypnosis which may exist singly or in combination that encompass the diverse models:

1. *Intrapersonal* models which emphasize the subjective traits and states of the hypnotized person as the basis for hypnosis;
2. *Interpersonal* models which emphasize the social or relational aspects of the hypnotic interaction.

Models of hypnosis can also be differentiated, as Lynn & Rhue (1991) suggested, according to single or multifactor conceptualizations. Single factor models suggest a single variable influencing hypnotic experience, such as relaxation as described in the last chapter (Edmonston, 1977, 1981, 1991). Multifactor conceptualizations consider a variety of interactional forces combining to produce hypnotic phenomena, such as client expectations and clinician demands (Kirsch, 2000).

Let's briefly consider some of these models.

THE NEODISSOCIATION MODEL: HYPNOSIS AS A DISSOCIATED STATE

The neodissociation model of Ernest Hilgard (1974, 1986, 1991, 1992) has exerted profound influence on the field. Most clinicians learn about dissociation in terms of pathological conditions, such as Dissociative Identity Disorder. However, dissociation represents a human capacity for compartmentalizing different elements of subjective experience. This capacity can be helpful in a variety of ways if utilized skillfully.

Hilgard's neodissociation model is based on the view that humans have multiple cognitive systems capable of functioning simultaneously. These are arranged in a hierarchy under the control of an executive system, called an "executive ego" or a "central control structure." Cognitive subsystems may include habits, attitudes, prejudices, interests, and other latent abilities. The executive system is tasked with monitoring and formulating responses to ongoing subjective experience. In the condition of hypnosis, the various cognitive systems can function autonomously, effectively dissociated from one another to a significant degree. Hilgard described it this way:

The central executive functions in hypnosis are typically thought to be divided between the hypnotist and the hypnotized person. The latter retains a considerable portion of the executive functions from his or her normal state—the ability to answer questions about his or her past and plans, as well as to accept or refuse invitations to move about or to participate in specific kinds of activities. At the same time the subject turns over some of his or her executive functions to the hypnotist, so that within the hypnotic contract, the subject will do what the hypnotist suggests, experience what the hypnotist suggests, and lose control of his or her movements if this is indicated. (Hilgard, 1992, p. 94)

The research sparked by the neodissociation model has been extraordinary in both volume and quality of findings and has led to some of the most important understandings within the field of hypnosis (Kihlstrom, 1985, 1997). Primarily an intrapersonal model, Hilgard's research, and that of other neodissociationists, has focused on the dissociative and other hypnotic capacities of individuals as the eventual determinants of successful hypnosis. Hilgard has made a strong case for viewing hypnotizability as a measurable difference between and a stable trait across individuals (Hilgard, 1965, 1967).

HYPNOSIS AS A PASSIVE OR PERMISSIVE STATE

In this theoretical perspective rooted in the origins of modern hypnosis in the mid-19th century (Bernheim, 1886/1957) and still being researched today with a greater emphasis on the changes in physiology associated with hypnosis (Rossi, 2000), special emphasis is given to what is presumed to be the passive role of the client, whose position is defined as one of responding to the directives of the clinician. Is hypnosis a state of passivity or arousal? It's both. This primarily intrapersonal model explores the active-passive paradox of hypnosis that has confused and divided clinicians about what is happening in the subjective experience of the client. It has led to an emphasis on striving to understand the phenomenological experience of the client, and good research has been done to make it easier to define and to measure such experience (McConkey, 1986; Pekala & Kumar, 2000; Pekala, 2002).

One of the ways to describe a clinician's style of hypnotic intervention is in terms of the degree of authoritarian or permissive suggestions employed (discussed in chapter 12). An authoritarian practitioner is characterized as one who is direct and commanding. The stage hypnotist is a classic example of the authoritarian approach, evidenced by such common direct suggestions as, "You are going to go deeper asleep when I snap my fingers.... When you open your eyes you will laugh uncontrollably as if you're viewing the funniest movie you've ever seen. . . . When I clap my hands, you will stutter and be unable to say your name . . . " (clever stuff, isn't it?). A permissive style is one that emphasizes possibilities without making specific demands on the client, as in a suggestion such as, "*Perhaps* you'll be more comfortable if you let your eyes close."

The authoritarian approach of some clinicians is the basis for this theory's description of the demeanor of the client in hypnosis as a passive, permissive one. Specifically, a permissive client is characterized as one who permits the clinician to direct his or her experience, seemingly expressing no will of his or her own. The client is expected to fully respond to the suggestions of the clinician, and no initiative on the part of the client is either expected or deemed necessary. Due to the secondary, reactive role taken in the therapeutic relationship, the client is essentially viewed as a passive receptacle for the authoritarian clinician's suggestions. The client's only task is to simply comply. If the client fails to respond to the clinician's direct suggestions to the clinician's satisfaction for some reason, the client is deemed "resistant." The resistance is presumed to be evidence of some defense mechanism or pathology of some sort that needs to be identified and "worked through." The possibility that the client simply finds the suggestions unsuitable is not well considered in this model.

If a clinician adopts a permissive style in guiding the client, a style that may be less direct and is certainly less demanding, the client is defined as an active participant in the process of making suggested possibilities come to life. In such a client-activated approach, the "permissive state" theory of hypnosis is no longer as plausible.

The "permissive state" theory contains some truth that is even verifiable physiologically (Sturgis & Coe, 1990) but is most relevant only to a style of practice rather than representative of the phenomenon of hypnosis. One can view the quiet, cataleptic (fixed, unmoving) client as a passive receptacle for suggestions. One can view the formation and verbalization of suggestions on the part of the clinician as an active process. Superficially, the hypnotic interaction may thus seem to be one of the clinician being the active one and the client the passive one. Discussed earlier, however, was the notion that if you allow another person to guide your experience, the person in control is the one who has the power to "allow" the actions of another. The role of the client, therefore, is *not* a passive one. Rather, it is an active one in the sense that it is the client's ability and responsibility to respond, in whole or in part, to the suggestions of the clinician that makes hypnosis happen. And, a response is inevitable, since even no response is a response!

Furthermore, more recent concepts of hypnosis emphasize the need for the clinician to flexibly follow the leads of the client, rather than expecting the client to obediently follow the arbitrary leads of the clinician. This is quite different in concept and practice from the client, facing an authoritarian hypnotist who requires compliance, and who has the responsibility of adapting him- or herself to the suggestions of the clinician. Adapting yourself to authoritarian suggestions that may not even be particularly well suited and yet finding a way to make them meaningful is not a passive state at all. In reality, may of the clinicians who practice in such an authoritarian style succeed *in spite of* themselves, with the client's help, rather than because of themselves. How does a clinician employing an induction method such as counting down from 10 to 1, for example, cause someone to enter hypnosis, unless the client is working hard at making such arbitrary suggestions meaningful?

The metaphor some people use of "programming" the client is based on this model. However, as you will discover as soon as you start doing hypnosis with people, people aren't easily "programmed." Therapy, especially therapy with hypnosis, would be a much more successful endeavor if doing inductions and telling people what to do was all that was required. But, if the clinician offers suggestions that are unacceptable to the client for some reason, the "permissive client" can passively reject them, in essence "doing nothing," a condition the authoritarian clinician is likely to call "resistance." The client's role in many ways is an active one of making use of the clinician's suggestions if and when those suggestions are appropriate and can be meaningfully utilized. The paradox inherent in this theory is the active role of passivity.

HYPNOSIS AND SOCIAL ROLE-PLAYING

There is a considerable amount of confusion and speculation over whether there really is a condition of human experience that can be called "hypnosis." A large and growing body of evidence indicates that the phenomena of hypnosis are not best explained by the notion of a specific state of experience called "hypnosis" (T. Barber, 2000; Wagstaff, 1986). In light of advanced neuro-imaging technology, discussed in the next chapter, is there a discrete and consistently measurable change that takes place we can point to and say, "There! That's hypnosis!"? Unfortunately, as André Weitzenhoffer lamented in last chapter's Frame of Reference, no evidence for a specific state called hypnosis has yet been found. Graphs of brain waves, measurements of biochemical changes in the body, and objective readings on the activity of the nervous system are revealing ever more about the internal workings of hypnotic experience, yet they are still ambiguous enough to prevent us from defining hypnosis in purely, or even primarily, in physiological terms.

Consequently, there are some theorists (T. Barber, 1969; Sarbin, 1950; Sarbin & Coe, 1972) who long ago adopted the perspective that hypnosis is nothing separate from normal experience and that the unusual behaviors associated with hypnosis can be accomplished by anyone sufficiently motivated to so behave in the absence of any mention of hypnosis (Kihlstrom, 1991). Hypnotic phenomena thus occur as a consequence of an interpersonal context labeled by the participants as "hypnosis." In their view, hypnosis exists only when someone is willing to play the socially prescribed role of a hypnotized individual. Theodore Sarbin, Ph.D., at the University of California, Santa Cruz, is a principal architect of the model characterizing hypnosis as a social role. Sarbin's concept of role enactment as central to hypnosis led him to coin the phrase describing hypnosis as "believed-in imaginings" (1997). He described his view this way:

> Role conceptions have been fruitfully employed to describe social behavior of all kinds, not only hypnosis. Of central importance, both for social actions generally and for hypnosis particularly, is that the person is regarded as a doer, a performer, an agent, not an inert object that passively processes information. Instead of happenings in the mind, the focus of role theory is on what the person does and how he or she does it, taking into account immediate and remote contexts in which the performance occurs. (Sarbin, 1997; p. 204)

Thinking of hypnotic behavior as role-governed social behavior obviously defines this hypnosis model as an interpersonal one, taking into account socially prescribed roles, expectations, power, and influence. Support for this perspective comes from a variety of research, addressing issues of whether hypnosis is mere compliance (Spanos & Coe, 1992; Wagstaff, 1991) or whether responses are, in fact, nonvolitional (Lynn, Rhue, & Weekes, 1990). Classic studies conducted by Martin Orne, M.D., Ph.D., who was Emeritus Professor of Psychiatry and Psychology at the University of Pennsylvania (see his Frame of Reference in chapter 9), were among the very first to address the issues of the confounds of distinguishing simulating versus "genuinely" hypnotized subjects and the demand characteristics of hypnosis encounters that could yield responses that were merely compliant rather than hypnotic (Orne, 1959, 1962a, 1962b, 1966, 1971). An experimental scenario might involve a group of subjects who are instructed to behave "as if" they were hypnotized and mixed with a group of subjects who were overtly and willingly formally hypnotized. A number of "experts" in hypnosis are then challenged to discover which individuals were and were not "truly" hypnotized. Subjects who role-played hypnotic behavior were extremely convincing in their manifestations of hypnotic phenomena and were able to successfully confound the experts.

It is not particularly difficult to appreciate the elements of truth in this perspective for its emphasis on the motivation to adhere to a social role. Consider an extreme example to make the point: Imagine someone holding a gun to your head who says, "I am going to poke you in the stomach with a safety pin, and if you so much as flinch I'll pull the trigger." Most probably, you would be highly motivated to immediately develop a means for withstanding pain that defies objective measurement, but is clearly present nonetheless. Likewise, if someone offered you a huge sum of money, or something else that you find rewarding, to motivate you to demonstrate some feat normally considered beyond your means, it probably wouldn't surprise you much to discover capabilities you did not know you had. Creating unusual circumstances to yield unique and beneficial responses in people that involve hidden resources is at the heart of strategic psychotherapies, as well as many hypnotic interventions.

Role-playing hypnotic behavior is a significant component of the stage show process. Subjects may not "feel hypnotized" in the way they may have expected to experience some altered state, but because of the flow of the stage process they are likely to go along and conform to the demands of the role. One of the classic techniques of hypnosis plays on this, called the "As if" technique in which a person is asked to act "as if" he or she can do the thing he or she feels unable to do (e.g., relax, go into hypnosis) long enough to actually do it and experience what it's like to do it. The issue then becomes one of whether it really matters if the action is real or a pretense if the outcome is the same regardless of the intention. In other words, if a client is not really hypnotized, but acts as if he or she is hypnotized well enough for the clinician to get whatever hypnotic responses are desired, then does it really matter that the person doesn't feel genuinely hypnotized? (As a clinical example, if a phobic person acts as if he or she isn't phobic in some context that normally generates anxiety, and he or she doesn't become anxious, is it a pretense—or a cure?) Frequently, stage show hypnotists will ask their subjects at the end of the show whether they were hypnotized, and a common response is a hesitant, "I don't think so." Yet just a few minutes ago that same person was responding enthusiastically to the suggestion to hallucinate the nudity of the entire audience, the suggestion to be unable to remember his or her own name, and other such "entertaining" suggestions.

Role-playing has long been recognized by social scientists as a way of absorbing a person's attention by encouraging him or her to "get lost in the role." Many therapeutic strategies (e.g., psychodrama, behavioral rehearsals, family therapy role-reversals) regularly involve role-playing as a way of rehearsing positive responses in troublesome situations or developing empathy for another person. Initially, the client typically feels self-conscious and uncomfortable in the role, but gradually adapts to the role demands and is soon immersed in it. If you have never seen this kind of phenomenon, perhaps you can use your own experience as an illustration. Can you recall a time when you were in a bad mood, perhaps even depressed, sitting around your house when the doorbell rang unexpectedly? After you wondered to yourself, "Who could that be?" you answered the door and there was a friend of yours just coming by for a casual visit. Charitably, you decided you didn't want to depress this person by being in a bad mood, so you began to act "as if" you were in a semi-decent, or perhaps even good, mood. Did you notice that after a brief while you genuinely were in a good mood? Almost everyone has had this kind of experience, and it is a useful example to illustrate the power associated with playing a role.

Playing a role can even change someone's behavior quite dramatically beyond the time he or she stops playing the role. This is a point long recognized, for even at the turn of the last century, the philosopher and psychologist William James asked the question, "Does a person smile because he is happy, or is he happy because he smiles?" In some powerful research done by psychologist Philip Zimbardo at Stanford University, a mock prison was set up in the psychology building, and a group of student experimental subjects were divided into "guard" and "prisoner" roles. The results of the experiment were both startling and dramatic. A mentality associated with the role evolved, with guards becoming abusive and even brutal, and prisoners becoming passive, obsessed with escape, and ultimately depressed and agitated. Role playing behavior became so intense, the experiment had to be called off for everyone's well-being.

Role-playing as a theoretical perspective on the phenomenon of hypnosis is useful up to the point, wherever that may be, where the artificial experience becomes genuine, a "believed-in imagining" as Sarbin termed it. A client or research subject may begin by playing at hypnotic behavior, but at a certain, idiosyncratic point along the way, a true hypnotic experience begins. Role-playing involves a conscious effort to adhere to the behaviors scripted by a role. Until one's involvement in the role is deep enough to allow unconscious identification with that role, role-playing hypnosis is an experience occurring largely on the conscious level. Consciousness is limited (how many things can you pay attention to at one time?); the unconscious mind is less so. When responses become unconscious (i.e., nonvolitional), the role-play is over and a true hypnotic absorption begins.

HYPNOSIS AS A SOCIOCOGNITIVE PHENOMENON

A dominant model in the field of hypnosis today, and growing ever more influential over time, the sociocognitive model emphasizes social roles but also focuses intently on the cognitive makeup of the individual, including his or her expectations, beliefs, attitudes, attributional style, and other such factors influencing social responsiveness (Lynn & Sherman, 2000). Psychologist Theodore X. Barber, Ph.D., has been especially prolific in his writings and research into the multiple factors comprising hypnotic responsiveness.

(He is featured in a Frame of Reference section in chapter 6.) Barber has considered both intrapersonal characteristics of the client, such as fantasy proneness and imaginative ability, and interpersonal characteristics of the social context of hypnosis. His view is that there are four especially important behavior-determining factors regulating the hypnotic experience:

> (a) *social factors* that obligate the socialized subject to cooperate and try to actualize or realize the hypnotists's expectations and explicit suggestions; (b) *the hypnotists's* unique skills and personal characteristics (including creative ideas, communicative ability, and interpersonal efficacy) and the nature of the hypnotist-subject interpersonal relationship; (c) the effectiveness of the *induction procedure* in guiding the subject to think-with the suggestions; and (d) the depth of meaning, creativity, and "force" or "power" of the *suggested ideas.* (T. Barber, 2000)

Other prominent sociocognitive theorists, including Nicholas Spanos, Ph.D. (1991; Spanos & Chaves, 1989), Irving Kirsch, Ph.D. (1991; Kirsch & Lynn, 1995), Graham Wagstaff, Ph.D. (1991), and Steven Lynn, Ph.D. (Lynn & Rhue, 1991; Lynn & Sherman, 2000) have all conducted significant research on the social and contextual forces affecting hypnosis as they interface with personal variables. As a result, sociocognitve models have exceptionally strong empirical support.

HYPNOSIS AS AN ALTERED STATE OF CONSCIOUSNESS

As described briefly in the previous chapter, the experience of hypnosis has been conceptualized by some as an altered state or states of consciousness featuring absorption and shifts in perception (Tart, 1969; Tellegen & Atkinson, 1974). In this primarily intrapersonal perspective, hypnosis is considered to be a unique and separate state of consciousness, relative to one's "normal" state of consciousness. The hypnotic state, in this view, is created by the hypnotic induction process, which alters the person's consciousness through the narrowing of attention to the offered suggestions. The altered state is thought to feature reduced defenses, greater emotional access and responsiveness, and greater access to unconscious processes (J. Barber, 1991; Nash, 1991).

This view of hypnosis as a distinctly altered state, or perhaps altered states, has historically been popular because of its recognition that people in hypnosis can experience things seemingly beyond their usual capacity. The idea of altered states of consciousness conveniently allows for that possibility, and also allows for the variable proportion of people who can experience such states as described in susceptibility statistics.

Despite its early popularity and seeming obviousness, the view of hypnosis as an altered state of consciousness has less utility than other conceptual frameworks. Unique physiological correlates of hypnosis have not been found, and hypnotic phenomena can be produced without the benefit of hypnotic induction (Lynn & Rhue, 1991).

The term "altered states of consciousness" is, like "hypnosis," very imprecise. Consciousness is a subjective experience. What is "normal consciousness" relative to an "altered state of consciousness"? Aren't I altering your consciousness with each word, each page you read? WAIT! Think of a purple elephant with green ears! Did I just alter your consciousness? How much? Any time your awareness is shifted from one stimulus to another, your consciousness has been altered. The question, then, is this: If hypnosis is an altered state of consciousness, what is it altered *from*? Yet, when a hypnotized person experiences his or her body as numb, that is not a routine experience. Clearly, *something* has changed, but what and how it changed remain a mystery.

Recently, Cardeña (manuscript submitted for publication, 2003) has convincingly made the case for viewing hypnosis as reflective of altered states (plural) rather than a single altered state.

THE REALITY-TESTING VIEW OF HYPNOSIS

Can you estimate how far it is from where you are sitting to the nearest door? About how far apart are your hands from each other right now? What direction is that sound you hear now coming from?

These questions are answerable by you because you are able to use your visual, auditory, and tactile senses to gather information from the world around you. Consciously, but more so unconsciously, you are continually engaged in the processing of huge amounts of sensory input flooding your nervous system that tells you where you are relative to your immediate environment. Information is continuously coming to you through virtually all of your available senses, and all of these tiny bits of information give you a sense of where your body is, what position it is in, and how it is distanced from objects and outside experiences near and far. This is referred to as a "generalized reality orientation" (Shor, 1959, 1970). You are probably not consciously aware of the sensations in your left shoulder until I draw your attention to it. Yet your shoulder (its nerves) is processing information, such as the gentle rub of your clothing against it, and that information is available to you consciously if you strive to notice it, or nonconsciously if you don't.

Obtaining feedback from our senses about the world around us and striving to validate its accuracy is a process called "reality-testing." Proponents of this primarily intrapersonal view claim that people are continually reality-testing in order to preserve personal integrity and alleviate the anxiety of uncertainty in not knowing our position in the world. This process is generally so unconscious we take it for granted. Ronald Shor, Ph.D., a pioneering contributor to hypnosis, described it this way:

> In all our waking life we carry around in the background of our awareness a kind of frame of reference or orientation to generalized reality which serves as a context or arena within which we interpret all of our ongoing conscious experiences. Under certain conditions—of which hypnosis is just one—this wide frame of reference or orientation to generalized reality can fade into the very distant background of our minds so that ongoing experiences are isolated from their usual context. When that happens, the distinction between imagination and reality no longer exists for us. (1970, p. 91)

However, if you have the experience of working with people deemed psychotic, you will often find them consciously and desperately engaged in reality-testing. In such individuals, reality-testing is evident in such activities as feeling the walls for guidance as they walk, touching you repeatedly as they speak to you to make sure you are "real," touching themselves to assure themselves that they exist, and repeating simple cause-effect behaviors such as opening and closing a door apparently to show themselves they can affect their environment.

The process of sensation is simply the neurological response to a stimulus and is purely a biological phenomenon. Perception, however, is the interpretation of the neurological experience, the meaning attached to a sensation. A person's perception is a person's reality. The role of perception on experience is so profound that it literally cannot be overstated. Your perception of events is the determining factor in the course of action that you take. A false perception about a person or situation leads to a very different response than a more accurate perception might.

The reality-testing view of hypnosis theorizes that when someone is first entering and is then in hypnosis, his or her ongoing process of reality-testing is affected, perhaps by an increased comfort with seemingly contradictory bits of information as Orne (1959) suggested when he described what he termed "trance logic" and as prominent Australian psychologists and hypnosis researchers Peter Sheehan and Kevin McConkey elaborated in some of their excellent research (Sheehan, 1992; McConkey, 1991; Sheehan & McConkey, 1982). When someone suspends the process of obtaining feedback from the world around him or her by focusing inwardly as is characteristic of most (but not all) hypnotic experiences, the person is minimally oriented to much other than internal experience (Hilgard, 1986). The suspension of objective reality-testing frees the person to accept whatever reality is suggested. The suggested reality, like any perceived reality, whether true or false, will determine the quantity and quality of behavioral and emotional responses. As Sheehan and McConkey (1982) showed, however, affirmed in later research by Lynn, Weekes, and Milano (1989), suspending or reducing reality-testing in order to accept suggestions for perceptual shifts does not preclude reality awareness. People in hypnosis retain the ability to monitor and, if necessary, respond to situational realities and cues.

Living in San Diego as I do, and as the majority of my clients do, I can do hypnotic processes such as one involving relaxing at the beach if I care to, since most people here are familiar with and enjoy that experience. The hypnotic suggestions might involve incorporating all the sights, smells, sounds, tastes, and tactile experiences associated with being at the beach into the process in such great detail that the client can genuinely feel as if he or she is really at the beach. If I ask the person, "Where are you right now?" he or she might well answer, "The beach." If I then ask, "No, really, where are you right now?" the person will almost surely say, "Your office." But, in doing hypnosis, the reality of being in my office several miles away from the beach is suspended long enough to accept suggestions related to the "realities" of being at the ocean.

The degree to which the client is successful in letting go of the need to have an objective reality immediately at hand (a need whose strength is directly proportional to the person's degree of insecurity) is the degree to which the person can accept the suggested experience.

THE CONDITIONING PROPERTY
OF WORDS AND EXPERIENCES

Three of the most advantageous properties of having evolved consciousness for us as a species are our ability to reason, ability to learn on multiple dimensions of experience, and ability to communicate about experience (Brown, 1991).

Many animal species communicate; complex behaviors such as competition for social position and such dynamic needs as territoriality are examples of routine communications in the animal world. In recent years, interspecies communication has been attempted between human and dolphin, human and ape, and humans and other species. These attempts at communication have had marginal success, due in large part to the limited capacity (according to the human perspective) of animals, evidenced in their inability to invent symbols, using only the symbols provided for them.

Evolution has allowed us to attach words to experience and thus represent experience abstractly. Instead of our communication concretely being tied to a current need or experience, we can communicate about things that occurred millions of years ago or about things yet to come centuries from now.

Language and communication will be discussed repeatedly throughout this book. When we seek to evolve a theoretical perspective for the various phenomena of hypnosis, the recognition of the role of your words as triggers for complex, multidimensional, nonvolitional, focused, socially responsive, contextually valid (did you get all that?) experience is absolutely crucial to the attainment of sophistication with hypnotic techniques. Hypnosis encompasses so many variables, but my ultimate aim with this book is to help you evolve a framework for being able to say something to your clients that will help. Regardless of theoretical orientation, I know of no one who would suggest that what you say to the client is unimportant. How do mere words, those sequences of sound you produce, attain such power?

You are reading this book, specifically this page with lots of black ink marks all over it in various configurations. The patterns of configuration form what you have come to recognize (from years of learning and experience) as words. As you read each word in a fixed left-to-right sequence, line by line, you are taking the words and attaching them to your experience of what they represent to you. The words on this page don't mean anything at all to you until you attach a meaning to them, and the meaning can come from nowhere other than your own experience of having learned what experiences the words represent. Without your attaching meaning to the words, the words on this page are meaningless. When you see the lines and squiggles of written words or hear the sounds of words from a language that is unfamiliar to you, those markings and sounds are meaningless because you have no internal frame of reference for understanding them. Meaning is in you, not in the words themselves. And, since you use your own individual experience to attach meaning to a word, you can appreciate how the same word will *inevitably* mean different things to different people. The more abstract a word, meaning the more room for individual projection, the more this is true.

Exercises suggested throughout this book will help make this point clearer to you, but you have probably already had experiences in which your interpretation of a word or phrase differed from another person's interpretation sufficiently to make you wonder whether that person was from this planet. The differences in interpretation between people account for most communication problems in whatever context problems exist. My idea of what the "right" thing for you to do may be very different from your idea is of what the "right" thing to do is.

In the practice of clinical hypnosis, you need to be sensitive to the words and phrases you use because of the idiosyncratic nature of your client's interpretation. The phrase that works well in helping you develop relaxation, for example, may sound like fingernails on a chalkboard to your client. The word that fits well for your understanding of a particular kind of experience may represent something entirely different to your client.

Words are conditioned stimuli representing internal experience (Watzlawick, 1978). Gestures are also conditioned stimuli arising from socialized experiences (e.g., head nods, hand gestures). Ultimately, though, people are unique individuals, each communicating in his or her own way. Thus, flexible communication both expects and allows clients to interpret and respond in their own unique ways.

The model of hypnosis regarding the conditioning property of words and the experiences words represent is a valuable one in explaining hypnotic experiences. The process of attaching words to experience in linguistics is called "transderivational search," and has been a subject of considerable study in that field. How experiences create habitual response patterns has been described in numerous places, and generally operates on various principles of learning and reward structures. Basically, people do what they are reinforced (rewarded) for doing; the reward may be the comfort of familiarity from having done something the same way before (even if it appears to be a useless or harmful behavior), the favorable reaction of people nearby, the attainment of a goal, or literally countless other possible reinforcements.

Responses may be conditioned, "wired-in" so to speak, on the basis of a single experience. Behaviors have emotional counterparts and emotions have behavioral counterparts and physical responses occur with each, thus creating the holistic nature of the mind-body relationship. In hypnosis, the conditioning property of words and experience is apparent both in the process of the transderivational search the client undergoes (in attaching the clinician's words to experience), and the resulting physical, emotional, and sensory changes that occur while the client is mentally absorbed. These changes, subtle but present, occur quite naturally all of the time, but are accentuated in hypnosis (Zeig & Rennick, 1991). When listening to someone describe the pleasure they had in eating at a good restaurant, why do you get hungry, salivate, and want to go to that restaurant at the first available opportunity? The experience of transderivational search involves you in attaching their words to experiences of pleasurable eating, and while your mind is absorbed to whatever degree, you react to the mental experience on motoric, sensory, and affective levels automatically and, to a large degree, unconsciously.

The motoric, or physical, response is called an "ideomotor response," and is a basic feature of hypnotic processes you will be exposed to later. The ideomotor response is one of several automatic responses collectively called the "ideodynamic" responses. Automatic thoughts are called ideocognitions, automatic sensory associations are called "ideosensory" responses, and automatic emotional associations are called "ideoaffective" responses (Gilligan, 1987).

The relationship between mind and body is a close and powerful one. How the medical establishment was able to successfully separate mental involvement from physical treatment for so long has continued to be a mystery to me, but I am greatly encouraged by the movement toward a reintegration of all the human resources available to people in the process of healing. The more research is done exploring the merits of hypnosis with treating medical illness, the more we learn the power of words and ideas in healing.

Transderivational search and ideodynamic processes are deceptively simple but highly sophisticated characteristics of communication in general and hypnosis in particular. The inevitable role of personal experience in attaching meaning to words accounts for a great deal of the individuality and uniqueness of each person's response to hypnosis. This primarily intrapersonal model does not, however, consider the relationship and situational dynamics that are inevitably a part of all hypnotic work.

HYPNOSIS AS A SPECIAL INTERACTIONAL OUTCOME

In older views of hypnosis, the induction of hypnosis was something a hypnotist "did to" a subject with specific incantations or prepared scripts. The late psychiatrist, Milton H. Erickson, M.D., is widely credited with transforming the clinical practice of hypnosis from such ritualistic approaches to a more refined hypnosis defined in broader interactional terms (Haley, 1973; Zeig, 1980). His methods have collectively come to be called Ericksonian approaches, or, synonymously, utilization approaches (Erickson & Rossi, 1979; Rossi, 1980) Hypnosis, in this view, is a result of a focused and meaningful interaction between clinician and client. The clinician, to be successful, must be responsive to the needs of the client and tailor his or her approach to those needs if the client is going to be at all responsive to the possibilities for change the clinician makes available. The relationship is one of mutual interdependence, each following the other's leads while, paradoxically, at the same time leading.

The idea that the participants in the relationship are both leader and follower is a key point in this theoretical perspective. A client's behaviors and/or feelings are fed back to him or her verbally and/or nonverbally, thereby creating a sense in the client of being understood—the essence of rapport. Tied to verbalizations of what he or she is experiencing as true are respectful suggestions of what *can* become true. Instead of imposing on clients the clinician's belief system of what they should do, the possibility is made available to them of something progressive they can do in their own way and at their own rate.

More will be said later on this idea of accepting and utilizing client behavior, but the important point here in describing this theoretical perspective is that hypnosis is considered a natural outcome of a relationship where each participant is responsive to the sensitive following and leading of the other. Thus, the generally undesirable approach of imposing your beliefs and values on your client is avoided to whatever degree is humanly possible. (I think it is impossible to entirely avoid the sharing of your values, and I also believe that, in some cases, it is quite desirable to openly make your values available to the client as a model to consider.)

The interactional view emphasizes responsiveness and respect for the client, which is ideal in therapeutic contexts. However, clearly these factors need not be present for hypnosis to occur. After all, the stage show hypnotist has no special personal relationship to his or her subjects, and is certainly not sensitive or responsive to their unique personal characteristics and personalities, yet can still obtain hypnotic responses from them.

HYPNOSIS AS A PSYCHOBIOLOGICAL PHENOMENON

The 1990s were dubbed "The Decade of the Brain" by the American Psychiatric Association (to which the American Psychological Association responded with a successful lobby to get this decade named "The Decade of Behavior"). Major funding went to brain and drug research, and the landscape of mental health treatment in particular has been forever transformed as a result. Drug treatment in particular has, in many cases, seemingly relegated psychotherapy to a secondary position.

The new technologies for studying the brain and nervous system did not escape the notice of the hypnosis community. In the next chapter, I will detail some of the findings about the cognitive neuroscience of hypnosis. These findings have been a consequence of the influence of those theorists who have suggested hypnosis is best understood as a neurological or psychobiological phenomenon (Bányai, 1991; Rossi, 2000; Spiegel & Spiegel, 1987).

Psychologist Ernest Rossi, Ph.D., has been an especially prolific researcher and writer in the area of the mind-body relationship in hypnosis and the physiological correlates to hypnotic experience. Rossi (1982) proposed that hypnosis was a natural part of the body's regularly alternating cycles of attentiveness and relaxation called "ultradian rhythms" that occur every 90–150 minutes. More recently, continuing his research on hypnosis and physiology, Rossi has been focused on the potential for neurogenesis as well as hypnotic influence at the genetic level (2001).

Psychiatrists Herbert Spiegel and David Spiegel (1987) hypothesized that hypnotic abilities are the product of the interrelationship of the brain hemispheres. Together they evolved a "biological marker" assessment in the form of an eye-roll test (described in chapter 11) to indicate an individual's hypnotic susceptibility.

From his study of what he calls "broken brains," famed neuroscientist Michael Gazzaniga, Ph.D., evolved what he called a "modular unit" model of the brain (1985). While not specific to hypnosis, it provides a neuroscientific basis for many of the key phenomena of hypnosis, particularly dissociation. Gazzaniga described how different portions of the brain can function together but can also function autonomously. These separate but related sets of neurons, which he termed modular units, can each have their "triggers," creating experiences, or, more accurately, perceptions of experiences that are modifiable with input from other sources. For example, a person goes to a party, has a good time and goes to bed feeling perfectly fine. He or she wakes up feeling depressed the next morning, and naturally strives to understand why. The modular units for mood may have been activated by a dream, but since the person doesn't know that, he or she starts to hypothesize (e.g., "Maybe I was upset about that joke the others made about me that I thought I had just laughed off. But, maybe I was really hurt by it and just didn't know it.") Gazzaniga terms ours "The Social Brain" for its reliance on social cues for making meaning of our experience. It could reasonably be said that hypnosis is a condensed form of such interaction: Accessing modular units of the brain with suggestions and organizing them in therapeutic configurations.

CLOSURE ON PERSPECTIVES

Having presented a few of what I consider to be among the most useful explanations for the phenomenon of hypnosis in this chapter, you may now have an appreciation for my earlier comments about the applicability of aspects of each, and the inadequacy of any single one as a means for understanding hypnosis. As you continue to get more involved in the actual use of hypnosis, you will discover that the complexity of people and the diversity of peoples' responses necessitate your keeping an open mind about the specific elements of each model that seem to be operating in an interaction at any given time. The greater the flexibility you have in making use of the many models there are to work from, the better the response you will get to the work you do.

For Discussion

1. How do one's expectations affect one's ability to observe objectively?
2. What is your reaction to the often-used analogy between the human mind and a computer? Do you believe the mind is "programmed" and that a person needs to have "old tapes erased" when undergoing change? Why, or why not?
3. What is "normal" consciousness? Do you experience altered states of consciousness? When? What defines it as an altered state?
4. How do the transderivational search and ideodynamic processes necessitate careful word choice in doing hypnosis?
5. What is your concept of holistic health treatment? In what ways do you acknowledge the mind-body relationship in your work?
6. What is "personal integrity"? As each class member gives their definition, what do you discover about the variety of experiences attached to an abstract term?

Things to Do

1. Do a role-play in which you and your partner both (in turn) pretend to be deeply hypnotized. What do you experience?
2. Contact health care providers in your area who identify themselves as "holistic" in approach. What do you discover about the variety of approaches called "holistic"?
3. Choose a role to play for a day. For example, if you are basically shy, play the role of someone very outgoing. If you are basically assertive, play the role of someone passive. Whatever role you choose to play for a day, really stay in the role, but make sure it is a safe one to do! What do you discover about the role? How does it affect your perception of yourself?

REFERENCES

Bányai, É. (1991). Toward a social-psychobiological model of hypnosis. In S. Lynn & J. Rhue (Eds.), *Theories of hypnosis: Current models and perspective* (pp. 564–98). New York: Guilford.

Barber, J. (1991). The locksmith model: Accessing hypnotic responsiveness. In S. Lynn & J. Rhue (Eds.), *Theories of hypnosis: Current models and perspectives* (pp. 241–74). New York: Guilford.

Barber, T. (1969). *Hypnosis: A scientific approach.* New York: VanNostrand Reinhold.

Barber, T. (2000). A deeper understanding of hypnosis: Its secrets, its nature, its essence. *American Journal of Clinical Hypnosis, 42*: 3–4, 208–273.

Bernheim, H. (1886/1957). *Suggestive therapeutics: A treatise on the nature and uses of hypnotism.* Westport: Associated Booksellers.

Brown, P. (1991). *The hypnotic brain.* New Haven: Yale University Press.

Cardeña, E. (2003). *The phenomenology of deep hypnosis: A quantitative and qualitative inquiry.* Manuscript submitted for publication.

Edmonston, W. (1977). Neutral hypnosis as relaxation. *American Journal of Clinical Hypnosis, 20*, 69–75.

Edmonston, W. (1981). *Hypnosis and relaxation: Modern verification of an old equation.* New York: Wiley.

Edmonston, W. (1991). Anesis. In S. Lynn & J. Rhue (Eds.), *Theories of hypnosis: Current models and perspectives* (pp. 197–237). New York: Guilford.

Erickson, M. & Rossi, E. (1979). *Hypnotherapy: An exploratory casebook.* New York: Irvington.

Gazzaniga, M. (1985). *The social brain: Discovering the networks of the mind.* New York: Basic Books.

Gilligan, S. (1987). *Therapeutic trances: The cooperation principle in Ericksonian hypnotherapy.* New York: Brunner/Mazel.

Haley, J. (1973). *Uncommon therapy: The psychiatric techniques of Milton H. Erickson, M.D.* New York: Norton.

Hilgard, E. (1965). *Hypnotic susceptibility.* New York: Harcourt, Brace & World.

Hilgard, E. (1967). Individual differences in hypnotizability. In J. Gordon (Ed.), *Handbook of clinical and experimental hypnosis* (pp. 391–443). New York: Macmillan.

Hilgard, E. (1974). Toward a neo-dissociation theory: Multiple cognitive controls in human functioning. *Perspectives in biology and medicine, 17*, 301–16.

Hilgard, E. (1986). *Divided consciousness: Multiple controls in human thought action* (rev. ed.) New York: Wiley.

Hilgard, E. (1991). A neodissociation interpretation of hypnosis. In S. Lynn & J. Rhue (Eds.), *Theories of hypnosis: Current models and perspectives* (pp. 83–104). New York: Guilford.

Hilgard, E. (1992). Dissociation and theories of hypnosis. In E. Fromm & M. Nash (Eds.), *Contemporary hypnosis research* (pp. 69–101). New York: Guilford.

Kihlstrom, J. (1985). Hypnosis. *Annual Review of Psychology, 36*, 385–418.

Kihlstrom, J. (1991). Review of hypnosis: The cognitive-behavioral perspective. *Contemporary Psychology, 36*, 11–2.

Kihlstrom, J. (1997). Convergence in understanding hypnosis? Perhaps, but not quite so fast. *International Journal of Clinical and Experimental Hypnosis, XLV*, 3, 324–32.

Kirsch, I. (1991). The social learning theory of hypnosis. In S. Lynn & J. Rhue (Eds.), *Theories of hypnosis: Current models and perspectives* (pp. 439–66). New York: Guilford.

Kirsch, I. (2000). The response set theory of hypnosis. *American Journal of Clinical Hypnosis, 42*:3–4, 274–93.

Kirsch, I. & Lynn, S. (1995). The altered state of hypnosis: Changes in the theoretical landscape. *American Psychologist, 50*, 846–58.

Lynn, S. & Rhue, J. (Eds.) (1991). *Theories of hypnosis: Current models and perspectives.* New York: Guilford.

Lynn, S., Rhue, J., & Weekes, J. (1990). Hypnotic involuntariness: A social cognitive analysis. *Psychological Review, 97*, 169–84.

Lynn, S. & Sherman, S. (2000). The clinical importance of sociocognitive models of hypnosis: Response set theory and Milton Erickson's strategic interventions. *American Journal of Clinical Hypnosis, 42*: 3–4, 294–315.

Lynn, S., Weekes, J., & Milano, M. (1989). Reality versus suggestion: Pseudomemory in hypnotizable and simulating subjects. *Journal of Abnormal Psychology, 98*, 137–44.

McConkey, K. (1986). Opinions about hypnosis and self-hypnosis before and after hypnotic testing. *International Journal of Clinical and Experimental Hypnosis, 34*, 311–19.

McConkey, K. (1991). The construction and resolution of experience and behavior in hypnosis. In S. Lynn & J. Rhue (Eds.), *Theories of hypnosis: Current models and perspectives* (pp. 542–63). New York: Guilford.

Nash, M. (1991). Hypnosis as a special case of psychological regression. In S. Lynn & J. Rhue (Eds.), *Theories of hypnosis: Current models and perspectives* (pp. 171–94). New York: Guilford.

Orne, M. (1959). The nature of hypnosis: Artifact and essence. *Journal of Abnormal and Social Psychology, 58*, 277–99.

Orne, M. (1962a). On the social psychology of the psychological experiment: With particular reference to demand characteristics and their implications. *American Psychologist, 17*, 776–83.

Orne, M. (1962b). Antisocial behavior and hypnosis: Problems of control and validation in empirical studies. In G. Estabrooks (Ed.), *Hypnosis: Current problems* (pp. 137–92). New York: Harper & Row.

Orne, M. (1966). Hypnosis, motivation and compliance. *American Journal of Psychiatry, 122*, 721–26.

Orne, M. (1971). The simulation of hypnosis: Why, how, and what it means. *International Journal of Clinical and Experimental Hypnosis, 19*, 183–210.

Pekala, R. (2002). Operationalizing trance II: Clinical applications using a psychophenomenological approach. *American Journal of Clinical Hypnosis, 44*:3–4, 241–56.

Pekala, R. & Kumar, V. (2000). Operationalizing "trance" I: Rationale and research using a psychophenomenological approach. *American Journal of Clinical Hypnosis, 43*, 2, 107–36.

Rossi, E. (Ed.) (1980). *The collected papers of Milton H. Erickson on hypnosis* (Vols. 1–4). New York: Irvington.

Rossi, E. (1982). Hypnosis and ultradian cycles: A new state(s) theory of hypnosis? *American Journal of Clinical Hypnosis, 1*, 21–32.

Rossi, E. (2000). In search of a deep psychobiology of hypnosis: Visionary hypotheses for a new millennium. *American Journal of Clinical Hypnosis, 42*: 3–4, 178–207.

Rossi, E. (2001). Psychobiological principles of creative Ericksonian psychotherapy. In B. Geary & J. Zeig (Eds.), *The handbook of Ericksonian psychotherapy* (pp. 122–53). Phoenix, AZ: The Milton H. Erickson Foundation Press.

Sarbin, T. (1950). Contributions to role-taking theory: I. Hypnotic behavior. *Psychological Review, 57*, 255–70.

Sarbin, T. (1997). Hypnosis as a conversation: "Believed-in imaginings" revisited. *Contemporary Hypnosis, 14*, 4, 203–15.

Sarbin, T. & Coe, W. (1972). *Hypnosis: A social psychological analysis of influence communication*. New York: Holt, Rinehart, & Winston.

Sheehan, P. (1992). The phenomenology of hypnosis and the experiential analysis technique. In E. Fromm & M. Nash (Eds.), *Contemporary hypnosis research* (pp. 364–89). New York: Guilford.

Sheehan, P. & McConkey, K. (1982). *Hypnosis and experience: The exploration of phenomena and process*. Hillsdale, NJ: Erlbaum.

Shor, R. (1959). Hypnosis and the concept of the generalized reality-orientation. *American Journal of Psychotherapy, 13*, 582–602.

Shor, R. (1970). The three-factor theory of hypnosis as applied to the book-reading fantasy and to the concept of suggestion. *International Journal of Clinical and Experimental Hypnosis, 18*, 89–98.

Spanos, N. (1991). A sociocognitive approach to hypnosis. In S. Lynn & J. Rhue (Eds.), *Theories of hypnosis: Current models and perspectives* (pp. 324–61). New York: Guilford.

Spanos, N. & Chaves, J. (1989). The cognitive-behavioral alternative in hypnosis research. In N. Spanos & J. Chaves (Eds.), *Hypnosis: The cognitive-behavioral perspective* (pp. 9–16). Buffalo, N.Y.: Prometheus Books.

Spanos, N. & Coe, W. (1992). A social-psychological approach to hypnosis. In E. Fromm & M. Nash (Eds.), *Contemporary hypnosis research* (pp. 102–30). New York: Guilford.

Spiegel, H. & Spiegel, D. (1987). *Trance and treatment: Clinical uses of hypnosis*. Washington, D.C.: American Psychiatric Association.

Sturgis, L. & Coe, W. (1990). Physiological responsiveness during hypnosis. *International Journal of Clinical and Experimental Hypnosis, 38*, 3, 196–207.

Tart, C. (Ed.) (1969). *Altered states of consciousness: A book of readings*. New York: Wiley.

Tellegen, A. & Atkinson, G. (1974). Openness to absorbing and self-altering experiences ("absorption"), a trait related to hypnotic susceptibility. *Journal of Abnormal Psychology, 83*, 268–77.

Wagstaff, G. (1986). Hypnosis as compliance and belief: A socio-cognitive view. In P. Naish (Ed.), *What is hypnosis? Current theories and research* (pp. 59–84). Philadelphia, PA: Open University Press.

Wagstaff, G. (1991). Compliance, belief and semantics in hypnosis: A nonstate, sociocognitive perspective. In S. Lynn & J. Rhue (Eds.), *Theories of hypnosis: Current models and perspectives* (pp. 362–96). New York: Guilford.

Watzlawick, P. (1978). *The language of change*. New York: Basic Books.

Zeig, J. (Ed.) (1980). *A teaching seminar with Milton H. Erickson, M.D.* New York: Brunner/ Mazel.

Zeig, J. & Rennick, P. (1991). Ericksonian hypnotherapy: A communications approach to hypnosis. In S. Lynn & J. Rhue (Eds.), *Theories of hypnosis: Current models and perspectives* (pp. 275–300). New York: Guilford.

4

The Brain
in Hypnosis

The inner workings of the human brain have been a source of both fascination and mystery for as long as human brains have strived to understand themselves. In just considering "simple" or routine tasks, like remembering your address or deciding what you'd like to have for lunch, the brain is a marvel. When you go beyond the simple tasks to consider the ability of a gifted musician to play from memory thousands of notes on a piano or a guitar in a specific sequence and rhythm while coordinating the necessary finger movements at lightning speeds, or consider the mastery of complex and abstract principles and formulas of physics and chemistry in order to place a human being in space and bring him or her back again safely, the talents of the brain are truly spectacular.

The brain, until recently, has been thought of as a "black box," an unknown and seemingly unknowable entity that runs all of our mental and even many of our physical processes. As a "black box," the brain's functions could only be inferred from studying people with gross abnormalities, ones that were pervasive enough to show up on relatively crude scanning and measuring devices. Or, they could be inferred from evaluating the consequences of invasive brain procedures, such as the dramatic surgeries separating the brain hemispheres (called cerebral commissurotomies) of severely epileptic patients, and then assessing functional differences arising from the procedure. Thus, learning about the inner workings of the human brain was (and still is) limited to what was and is technologically possible.

What is technologically possible, however, has changed dramatically in recent years, and the advances in technologies for observing the brain in action have changed the face of neuropsychophysiological research. The brain is a "black box" no longer. Brain research has proliferated during the last decade and continues to do so even now as newer brain research technologies continue to evolve. These allow us an unprecedented opportunity to study detailed aspects of brain functioning never before possible. To study the changes in a person's brain from microsecond to microsecond as he or she engages in some specific activity, such as listening to music or reading a book, measuring these changes in "real time," and determining where such changes may take place, is remarkable. These new technologies, and newer ones still being developed, hold the potential to answer many of the most basic questions about ourselves, such as what physically drives our thoughts, feelings, behavior, and what constitutes the physical basis for conscious experience and unconscious processes under various conditions.

Hypnosis poses a special challenge to our understandings of the brain. In hypnosis, there are cognitive, physical, and behavioral changes that occur that generally manifest as a greater responsiveness to suggested experiences. And, these occur in an interpersonal context in which one person performs an induction on another. Not everyone is equally responsive to hypnotic procedures, though. Researchers separate subjects into groups of so-called "high hypnotizables" and "low hypnotizables" by formally testing for responsiveness to suggested experiences (see chapter 11 on this subject). By focusing brain research on those who appear to have greater presumed hypnotic capacity, researchers attempt to address such questions as these: Is hypnosis a specific state in the realm of human experience? Is there a physiological correlate to the experience of hypnosis? If there is, can it be identified and measured? And, if there is one, what might it mean to the clinician applying hypnosis in treatment? In this chapter, I will describe some of the current research on the neuropsychophysiology of hypnosis, highlighting some of the important findings and what they may imply for clinical practice.

WHY STUDY THE BRAIN IN HYPNOSIS?

The obvious answer to this question must nonetheless be stated directly: The brain is instrumental in generating the experience of hypnosis as well as the various hypnotic phenomena derived through hypnosis. As the principal organ of information processing, sensation, perception, volition, memory, imagination, and all the countless other mental processes it controls, understanding the brain holds the promise for providing us with information that is vital to better understanding ourselves, and better understanding ways to improve the human condition.

Helen J. Crawford, Ph.D., of Virginia Polytechnic Institute and State University, is one of the leading researchers in the field of neuropsychophysiology today. (See her Frame of Reference section later in this chapter.) She has been intensively studying the phenomenon of hypnosis for well over a decade, publishing some of the key research in the field (Crawford, 1990, 2001; Crawford & Gruzelier, 1992; Crawford, Kapelis, & Harrison, 1995; Crawford, Clarke, & Kitner-Triolo, 1996a; Crawford, Corby, & Kopell, 1996b). For Dr. Crawford, the goals in studying the physiology of hypnosis are clear: "I want to take hypnosis out of the realm of mysticism and bring it into the realm of science, and I want to reduce the myths and misunderstandings about hypnosis" (personal communication, June 17, 2002). These are obviously very important goals, whether you are a brain researcher or a clinician introducing hypnosis as a treatment alternative to a new client. Choosing to use hypnosis or any other tool of treatment is a choice that can be made with relevant data.

What makes it possible for someone to focus intently on a quiet induction process in a noisy room? What makes it possible for someone to focus on a suggested sensation of numbness that allows him or her to undergo a surgery without the use of any chemical anesthesia? As researchers strive to understand the cascade of neurophysiological events that take place when one person tells another to "just relax and listen to my words," the quality of research questions grows more complicated, and the quality of research methods designed to answer such questions grows more sophisticated.

It is often the case in life that the quality of your questions significantly affects the quality of the answers you get. What are some of the questions researchers studying the brains of hypnotized individuals want to know the answers to? Pause for a moment before you read on and think about what questions *you* would want to know the answers to about the brain in hypnosis. Here are some of the most basic questions brain researchers try to answer:

Are there morphological differences between the brains of high and low hypnotizables?

Are there cognitive differences between high and low hypnotizables that have a neuropsychophysiological basis?

Are there physiological correlates of the hypnotic state that can be identified and measured?

Are neurophysiologically measurable state changes a cause or reflection of the hypnotic experience?

To what extent do the neurophysiological data reflect the hypnotic induction process(es) used rather than the hypnotic state itself?

How does a suggestion get converted into a (cognitive, behavioral, or physical) response?

Something changes during the experience of hypnosis: Before the induction procedure, the research subject could focus on nothing but the pain in his or her arm. Following the induction procedure and some direct suggestions for numbness (e.g., "your arm will feel completely and comfortably numb as all the sensation seems to drain out of it"), the pain is all but gone from the person's awareness. *Something* has changed—but *what*? Has research fully answered this basic yet very complex question for us? Currently, the answer is no. But, quite a bit has already been learned about what changes in the brain, and more is being learned about brain functioning all the time that can help lead us one step at a time in the direction of (we hope) being able to fully answer the question of what changes as well as the other questions posed above.

As you can infer, the underlying premise in much of the brain research involving hypnosis has been that there is a specific measurable state called "hypnosis" even though it has not yet been identified and defined biologically. In fact, André Weitzenhoffer, Ph.D., a leading proponent of the belief that there is a distinct hypnotic state yet to be discovered and measured, wrote, "The *only* argument with some weight that has been offered against accepting the reality of hypnosis is the impossibility thus far to find consistent and meaningful physiological correlates of the state." He goes on to ask, "But have we found physiological correlates of other mental activities whose reality is not questioned?" (2000, p. 224). For Weitzenhoffer and many researchers, there is a condition called "hypnosis" that *must* exist in an objectively provable way. (See the Frame of Reference with Dr. Weitzenhoffer in chapter 2.) The assumption is that our current technologies, sophisticated as they might be, are simply not yet sufficiently advanced to fully achieve the task. What technologies have been used to study the neuropsychophysiology of hypnosis?

HOW IS THE BRAIN STUDIED?

There are numerous technologies available to neuropsychophysiological researchers to employ in their investigations of the brain in hypnosis. These include computerized electroencephalographic (EEG) frequency analysis, positron emission tomography (PET), regional cerebral blood flow (rCBF), single photon emission computed tomography (SPECT), and functional magnetic resonance imaging (fMRI) (Crawford & Gruzelier, 1992; Crawford, 2001). Each of these has a different means of assessing brain functions, thus yielding distinct though related findings. A comprehensive review of the large body of neuropsychophysiological data is beyond the scope of this chapter. (For an excellent review of such literature, see Crawford, 2001.) However, it would be valuable to look at a few of the approaches to assessing brain function and consider some of the recent findings.

EEG FREQUENCY ANALYSIS:
ALPHA, THETA, HEMISPHERIC ASYMMETRY
AND NEUROFEEDBACK

Electrical activity of the brain is recorded from electrodes placed on the scalp. The brain's relatively weak electrical signal is amplified and then decomposed into its frequency components. The traditional frequency bands studied are *theta* (4–8 Hz.), *alpha* (8–13 Hz.), *beta* (17–30 Hz.), and *gamma* (30–60 Hz.). Electrode locations are designated according to the corresponding brain areas (e.g., F = frontal, T = temporal, C = central, P = parietal, and O = occipital). Odd numbers refer to the left side of the brain, even numbers refer to the right side of the brain, and "z" is the designation for the midline (Ray, 1997).

Some of the earliest brain research regarding hypnosis involved use of the EEG. For example, in the early days of hypnosis some eminent theorists and practitioners held the view that hypnosis was a special form of sleep. In fact, there are still hypnotists today who will instruct their clients to "Sleep deeply!" as a part of their induction process, despite its obvious incorrectness as an instruction to experience hypnosis since hypnosis is *not* sleep. Such outmoded terminology is simply a carryover from the early days when the misconception of hypnosis as sleep was commonly held. (Related to the "hypnosis as sleep" perspective is the misconception that someone in hypnosis is unconscious and unaware of whatever is going on.) EEG research in the late 1940s (Gordon, 1949) and subsequent replications with ever-improving EEG equipment made it clear that the EEG pattern of sleep was distinctly different from the wakeful and aware EEG patterns of hypnosis.

EEG Frequency Analysis today tends to focus on the issue of band frequencies associated with hypnosis, specifically the question of whether one band frequency, such as alpha or theta, is most representative of the hypnotized brain. Early studies in this area suggested that hypnosis is an "alpha state" (London, Hart, & Leibovitz, 1968; Nowlis & Rhead, 1968). This notion was widely popularized, even leading to "higher consciousness" workshops on learning to generate alpha rhythms and the creation of special "alpha wave synchronizing" machines made commercially available to help you do so. However, hypnosis is *not* simply an "alpha state." The research on alpha waves as an indicator of hypnosis is quite ambiguous, but some research regarding alpha waves suggests they may indeed have some relationship to hypnotic susceptibility either before or during hypnosis (Williams & Gruzelier, 2001). Future research will be necessary to clarify this point.

Earlier EEG research has been criticized on a number of counts: Inadequate establishment of hypnotic susceptibility profiles of research subjects, limited number of electrode placements on the scalp, and poor amplification and signal-processing capabilities of the equipment (Perlini & Spanos, 1991; Ray, 1997). Newer EEG research, however, is considerably more sophisticated (there are now multi-channel recording technologies and more refined signal-processing capabilities available) which has obviated many of the previous problems.

Studies of EEG brain-wave activity tend to show that the theta band is associated with higher levels of hypnotic susceptibility both in eyes-open and eyes-closed pre-hypnosis baselines and also during the induction of hypnosis (Crawford, 1990, 2001; Graffin, Ray, & Lundy, 1995; Ray, 1997; Ray, Blai, Aikins, Coyle, & Bjick, 1998). Theta is also associated with focused attention (Schachter, 1977), clearly a necessary component of the hypnotic experience. Thus, as individuals enter hypnosis, EEG theta power tends to increase. This increase may be observed in low hypnotizables as well as highs, but is more pronounced in highs (Crawford, 1990, 2001; Sabourin, Cutcomb, Crawford, & Pribram, 1990). However, research by Williams and Gruzelier (2001) suggests that increased theta is not a trait index of hypnotic susceptibility, though it may be one for simple relaxation. Thus, although theta seems likely to be positively associated with hypnosis, current research findings remain equivocal.

There is another EEG "marker" that is currently receiving a great deal of interest from researchers. It is the so-called "40 Herz band." The 40 Herz band is a high frequency, low amplitude EEG rhythm that centers around 40 Herz that is associated with a condition of focused attentional arousal (Crawford, 2001). DePascalis and Penna (1990) reported that high hypnotizables showed greater 40 Herz production in their right hemispheres during hypnosis, while low hypnotizables showed reduced activity in both brain hemispheres during hypnosis. DePascalis and colleagues (1987, 1989, 1998) also showed that high hypnotizables, compared to lows, both in waking and hypnosis conditions, have a greater capacity to access both positive and negative life-emotional experiences, a capacity associated to task-related hemispheric shifts of fast EEG activity in the 40 Herz band. It has been suggested that the 40 Herz band is the physiological marker of focused arousal (Sheer, 1989), which, presumably, further research will either affirm or deny.

Riding the wave of popular interest in the so-called "split brain" patients who had the corpus callosum connecting their two brain hemispheres surgically severed (Gazzaniga, 1970; Sperry, 1968), the theory of a hemispheric asymmetry was proposed to explain hypnosis and hypnotic phenomena (Watzlawick, 1978). The theory suggested, despite no hypnosis-specific objective evidence to support it at the time, that hypnosis was a process involving "blocking the left hemisphere" while utilizing "right-hemispheric language patterns." Some went a step further and even declared the right hemisphere the "location" of the unconscious, an incorrect position in light of current data which shows a distribution of brain functions—conscious and unconscious—in both hemispheres (Crawford & Gruzelier, 1992).

Is there a hemispheric asymmetry in hypnosis? There is evidence to suggest the answer is yes. Is it the right or left hemisphere that is dominant in hypnosis? The answer appears to be neither and both. Neither one dominates as a reliable force in hypnosis, and either one can dominate depending on the specific task assigned to it. The same can be said to be true in nonhypnotic conditions. Highly hypnotizable individuals seem to show greater emotional arousal, faster emotional arousal, and greater EEG activity in the right parietal region (Crawford et al., 1995, 1996a; Gruzelier, 1998; Heller, 1993).

Gruzelier (1998) proposed a three-stage model of the neuropsychophysiology of hypnosis that features cerebral asymmetric changes in the process. In the first stage there is increased frontal lobe activity in the left hemisphere associated with focusing on the hypnotist's voice. In the second stage, there is a frontolimbic inhibitory process as the hypnotized individual "lets go." The third stage is marked by the person showing a "redistribution of functional activity and an augmentation of posterior cortical activity, particularly of the right hemisphere in high susceptibles" (p. 2). Gruzelier claimed low hypnotizables fail to show engagement in either or both of the first two stages. DePascalis (1998) came to a similar conclusion, showing that early in the hypnotic induction the left hemisphere was more active, but as the induction progressed the left hemisphere's activity was inhibited.

The issue of frequency bands associated with hypnosis is a charged one as researchers hope and strive to identify the physiological markers of hypnosis. It has become charged in another way as well, as an applied newer technology involving brain waves draws the interest of both researchers and clinicians. Popularly known as "neurofeedback," but also known as EEG biofeedback, the premise of neurofeedback is that much of psychopathology can be attributed to problems in brain timing, specifically the person's brain waves being "off" (disruptions in brain self-regulation called dysrhythmias). Self-regulatory deficits have been associated by proponents of neurofeedback to various symptom patterns, such as various arousal disorders (e.g., anxiety), attention disorders, mood disorders, seizure disorder, and specific learning deficits (Sterman, 1996). Neurofeedback involves brain exercises that are directed at teaching the individual to self-correct their brain wave patterns. The presumption is that if you correct the brain, the person's problems may correct as well. Research has shown that brain waves may be retrained on an operant conditioning basis, and there are now some studies suggesting that neurofeedback may be a viable treatment for disorders such as those mentioned earlier (Lubar, 1995; Sterman, 2000). Barabasz and Barabasz (1996) described the use of neurofeedback with alert hypnosis in the treatment of attention deficit hyperactivity disorder (ADHD). Research on EEG conditioning and possible associated neurobehavioral changes is ongoing, and given the relative newness of the technology, future research will help determine its ultimate worth as a means of intervention.

Recently another strategy to manipulate brain wave patterns for the purpose of improving both hypnotizability and clinical symptom presentations has been investigated, called EEG entrainment. Unlike neurofeedback which encourages self-regulation, EEG entrainment involves the use of a stimulus, binaural-beat sound stimulation, to drive the brain. Binaural-beat sound stimulation is part of a brainwave changing process that may also include breathing exercises, guided relaxation, imagery processes and binaural beats (Atwater, 1995). A binaural beat takes place when two different sound waveforms are presented stereophonically through headphones to a subject who will have the subjective perception of a third "beat" frequency occurring due to the difference between the two soundwaves. The effects of listening to the binaural beats may be subjectively experienced as relaxing or stimulating, depending on the frequencies used. In a study by Brady & Stevens (2000), binaural-beat sound stimulation was utilized to attempt to increase theta activity in a small sample of six subjects, which it did in five of them. They also showed significant increases in hypnotic susceptibility in the low and medium-susceptible groups, and no change in the high. Can hypnotic responsiveness really be increased by manipulating brain waves? It is tempting to think so, but it is far too early in such research to answer in the affirmative.

EEG AND EVENT-RELATED POTENTIALS (ERPS)

One of the relatively recent developments in EEG technology is the study of the EEG patterns of the individual either while he or she is listening to or watching some stimulus (called an exogenous or evoked potential), or psychologically responding to some stimulus (called an endogenous potential). These stimuli are called events, and the brain's electrical changes (a series of peaks and troughs) in response to these events are called event-related potentials, or ERPs. To get an accurate read of an ERP, a stimulus must be presented many times, then the researcher averages the EEG time-locked to the stimulus presentation in order to reduce any random background brain activity to zero. By measuring the time it takes for an ERP to occur after the presentation of some stimulus, and by taking multiple recordings from various areas of the brain (the more electrodes that are placed, the better to determine where activity is taking place), it becomes possible to determine the sequence and the timing of the areas in the brain activated by the stimulus.

An endogenous ERP that has been studied extensively is known as the P300, or, in EEG shorthand, a P3 wave. It is typically seen in response to either rare or meaningful stimuli, and appears at about 300 milliseconds after the presentation of the stimulus. (It may take longer, perhaps as long as 1,000 milliseconds, depending on the complexity of the stimulus.)

ERPs have been studied extensively in relation to hypnosis for their potential as either markers distinguishing brain activity in low and high hypnotizables in waking and hypnosis conditions or at least as reflectors of underlying processes. ERPs are affected by information-processing strate-gies that arise in response to the type of task demanded of the person, as well as the emotional aspect of a stimulus, such as surprise (Duncan-Johnson & Donchin, 1980). Thus, studying ERPs in studies of hypnotic alterations of perception and emotional states has been a fruitful avenue of research (Barabasz & Lonsdale, 1983; Crawford et al., 1996b; De Pascalis, 1994). Two recent studies in particular (Barabasz et al., 1999; Jensen, Barabasz, Barabasz, & Warner, 2001) were quite persuasive in showing that when subjects were carefully chosen and grouped for hypnotizability, and suggestions were care-fully worded, the ERPs showed significant differences between groups, sup-porting the notion of identifiable alterations in consciousness in hypnosis.

More specific are the somatosensory event-related potentials (SEPs) which have been studied in relation to human pain responses. As Crawford (2001) reported, hypnotically suggested analgesia results in significant de-creases in the later SEP components (100 msec or later after stimulus) in hypnotically responsive patients. This suggests an inhibitory process that affects the anterior cingulated cortex, a portion of the brain known to show increased activation during pain. (Continued on page 93)

FRAME OF REFERENCE: HELEN J. CRAWFORD, Ph.D.

Helen J. Crawford, Ph.D. (1943–), is professor of psychology and director of the Psychological Sciences Graduate Program at Virginia Polytechnic Institute and State University in Blacksburg, Virginia. Dr. Crawford is one of the most highly visible and influential researchers in the field, having published dozens of scientific articles and book chapters on com-plex aspects of the neuropsychophysiology of hypnosis. Dr. Crawford re-ceived her doctoral degree in experimental psychology in 1974 from the University of California, Davis. From 1975 to 1978, Dr. Crawford was a research assistant in the Laboratory of Hypnosis Research in the Depart-ment of Psychology at Stanford University, under the leadership of Dr. Ernest Hilgard, a leading figure in hypnosis and the subject of a Frame of Reference section in chapter 11. Dr. Crawford's work is known interna-tionally, and she has been an invited Visiting Professor and Scholar at some very prestigious institutions, including the Imperial College of Medi-cine in England, Aalborg University in Denmark, the University of Rome in Italy, and the Hungarian Academy of Sciences. Her scholarly work has earned her a number of awards, including the Bernard B. Raginsky Award for Leadership and Achievement from the Society for Clinical and Ex-perimental Hypnosis for being a "Distinguished Teacher, Scientist, and Pioneer in the Field of Hypnosis." Dr. Crawford's enthusiasm for and commitment to her research is a contagious force when she describes what she does, despite her scientific modesty that sometimes lends itself to pleasant understatement.

On the Biology of Hypnosis: "There are physiological changes that accompany hypnosis. When a person is controlling pain, for example, there are shifts in frontal lobe involvement that interact with other systems in the brain. It's not just the frontal lobe. With our fMRI, we see changes in the anterior cingulated. It's all reflective of something that's differing—the person is cognitively processing, but in a different manner."

On Whether Hypnosis Is a State or a Trait: "There's a shift in cognitive processing in hypnosis. I think the use of the term "state" is dangerously inaccurate. There's a shift in conscious awareness and that's as much as I can say about it. I'm not in either a 'state' or 'trait' camp."

On Using Physical Evidence of Hypnosis to Build Client Responsiveness: "Most people know very little other than what is in the media, and they have many misunderstandings about hypnosis. So, I tell them, "It looks as if hypnosis is focused attention," and then I make an analogy to what they do when they're focused. In the process, I'm giving them facts about where I want to go with them. I explain that when a person is hypnotized, even though they're very relaxed, it appears as if the brain is quite active. Therefore, they have control over themselves, and they can make decisions as to whether they want to participate or not. It really goes over very well. . . . They like the idea that they're getting more control."

On Distinguishing Ability from Attitude: "I make a distinction between ability and attitude. I'm not one of the advocates who says everybody is hypnotizable. There's a range of responsiveness in people, as measured by standardized scales. It's neurologically and genetically influenced. If someone is interested in knowing what a person's responsiveness is, tests can help. And, they help the subjects themselves when they discover they have hypnotic ability."

On Going beyond Biology into the Social Context of Hypnosis: "The relationship with the subject or client is highly important. If a subject doesn't trust me, they won't be hypnotized. You have to develop rapport ahead of time. When I walk into a classroom or a setting where hypnosis is involved, I'll talk to them for 10 or 15 minutes before I ever start the experimental hypnosis session. I'll tell them about hypnosis, address their beliefs and any misunderstandings, and I usually tell them about working in the area of pain control, which I publish on. It gives them a feeling that, 'Oh, this is possible.' It's good for developing rapport and building expectancy."

On Why Psychotherapists Should Know about Brain Physiology: "I think the more you know about brain physiology the better you are in recognizing whether your patient's problems are psychological or whether there might be some underlying neurological problem. I respect therapists a lot, but too often they just don't understand clinical neurophysiology, and they miss physical reasons for their patient's problems. They need to be able to address the physical as well as the psychological."

Source: Personal communication, June 17, 2002.

POSITRON EMISSION TOMOGRAPHY (PET) STUDIES AND HYPNOSIS

First developed in the 1970s, PET measures the emission of positrons from the brain after the subject has received an injection into the bloodstream of a small amount of radioactive isotopes, or tracers. The tracers allow the activity of different parts of the brain to be measured by gauging the volume of blood flow to the region. As a region is activated, the amount of blood flowing to that region increases. By gauging the blood flow with the radioactive tracers, the result is a three-dimensional map with different colors representing different levels of brain activity.

A number of studies of hypnotic phenomena have been done using PET scan technology. In one study, Szechtman and his colleagues (1998) at McMaster University in Ontario, Canada, used PET to image the brain activity of high hypnotizables prescreened for their ability to hallucinate in hypnosis who were given suggestions for an auditory hallucination. While in the PET scanner with their eyes covered, the subjects brain activity was monitored under four conditions: (1) at rest; (2) while presented an audiotaped stimulus of a voice saying, "The man did not speak often, but when he did, it was worth hearing what he had to say"; (3) while simply imagining the voice on the tape; and, (4) while hallucinating the voice after being told the tape was playing when, in fact, it was not.

The PET scans showed that a region of the brain called the right anterior cingulated cortex was equally active when the subjects were hallucinating as when hearing the actual taped voice. But, that same part of the brain was not active when the subjects were simply imagining the voice on the

tape. Remarkably, the brains of these subjects had registered the hallucinated voice as if it were real.

In another PET study of hypnosis, this one conducted by Pierre
Rainville and his colleagues at the University of Montreal (1997), the goal
was to learn something about the brain structures associated with relief from
pain during hypnosis. PET scans were done on hypnotized volunteers whose
hands were immersed in painfully hot water. The somatosensory cortex,
which processes painful stimuli, showed no significant differences when
suggestions were given that either the water would be painfully hot or would
be minimally unpleasant. But, the anterior cingulated cortex, a part of the
brain known to be more active in individuals in pain, showed much less
activity when suggestions were given that the water would be minimally
unpleasant.

A third study using PET scan technology, one that received considerable media attention, was conducted at Harvard University by Stephen
Kosslyn and his associates (including David Spiegel, M.D., who is featured
in a Frame of Reference in chapter 17) (Kosslyn, Thompson, Constantini-
Ferrando, Alpert, & Spiegel, 2000). The study was designed to find out
whether hypnosis could be used to modulate color perception. Research
subjects chosen for their high hypnotizability were shown a series of patterns some involving colors and some only shades of gray while in waking
and hypnotized conditions. Color stimuli were shown to be processed in a
separate region than the gray stimuli are. Researchers suggested that the
subjects visualize each image shown them as either color or black and white
while the PET scan measured brain activity. When subjects were hypnotized, the color areas of the brain were less active when told to see color as
only gray, and likewise, the color areas were more active when told to see
(i.e., hallucinate) the gray stimulus as colorful. The brain areas used to perceive color were activated in both brain hemispheres, despite exposure only
to shades of gray, just as they would activate when genuinely exposed to
color stimulus. When subjects were not in hypnosis, and were told to simply
visualize the colors, only the right hemisphere became active. Thus, the
brains of hypnotized individuals responded to the suggested experiences
rather than the actual stimuli in measurable ways. The researchers concluded that hypnosis is a psychological state with distinct neural correlates.

OTHER NEUROPSYCHOPHYSIOLOGICAL
RESEARCH FINDINGS

Hypnosis clearly involves attentional processes, specifically selective focusing. Neuropsychological studies have suggested that the frontal lobe is associated with attentional functions (Stuss, Eskes, & Foster, 1994). During
hypnotic analgesia, Crawford, Gur, Skolnick, Gur, & Benson (1993) showed

an increased cerebral blood flow in the orbitofrontal cortex, which may be interpreted as a sign of greater attentional effort on the part of subjects. In fact, Gruzelier (1988, 1990) and Crawford and Gruzelier (1992) have theorized that differences in hypnotizability are, at least in part, due to varying capacities for attention across individuals, measurable with frontal lobe activation. Some behavioral research suggests that high hypnotizables have greater ability to focus and to sustain their focus (Roche & McConkey, 1990). However, Kallio, Revonsuo, A., Hamalainen, Markela, & Gruzelier (2001) did not find any evidence of frontal differences between high and low hypnotizables.

The ability of the hypnotized person to focus and respond nonvolitionally has often been deemed an effortless process (Bowers, 1992; Ruehle & Zamansky, 1997; Weitzenhoffer, 2000). Indeed, in the majority of hypnotic interactions, the client appears to be sitting passively and merely absorbing noncritically the suggestions of the clinician (or researcher). However, despite the appearance of effortless passivity, the client is active, participating in the process, and searching for the relevance or salience of suggestions, particularly when they hold the potential to help with solving personally distressing problems. These observations about the active experience of the client in hypnosis have been lent substantial support in recent EEG and cerebral blood flow studies (Crawford, 1994; Crawford & Gruzelier, 1992) as well as psychological research (Kirsch, Burgess, & Braffman, 1999) which show that hypnosis involves substantial cognitive effort.

Problem solving, whether in the course of daily life or specifically in the context of attempting to resolve troublesome physical and/or psychological symptoms, requires some degree of cognitive flexibility. Cognitive flexibility implies an ability to view a situation from a variety of perspectives rather than only one (Beck et al., 1979), an ability to refocus attention and shift cognitive strategies, and other abilities such as vivid imagination and holistic thinking (Crawford & Gruzelier, 1992). Cognitive differences between high and low hypnotizables have been documented in a variety of studies (Spiegel & Spiegel, 1987; Wallace, 1990; Weitzenhoffer, 2000). High hypnotizables tend to have greater cognitive flexibility, more focused attention involving the frontal attentional system, and greater capacity for emotional arousal (Crawford, 1989).

NEUROPSYCHOPHYSIOLOGY IS A YOUNG FIELD

The technologies for being able to peer into the brain as it functions are relatively new ones, and each new technological innovation holds the promise to reveal ever more about how our brains function in various conditions. The fact that brain research involving hypnosis has sometimes shown contradictory findings should not come as a surprise to anyone. Similar contradictory findings are to be found in even less objective psychological research. Why is this so? There are many reasons:

The experience of hypnosis represents a subjective state that, at best, researchers try to define and quantify in some way. But, subjective states cannot easily be defined or quantified. If I say, "I love chocolate," and then I say, "I love my wife," will we find neurological correlates to these seemingly differing subjective experiences of love?

Subjective states cannot usually be measured directly. They must be inferred from some agreed-upon markers. How valid are the inferences in representing the actual phenomenological experience?

When there is a negative finding, that is, nothing measurable happens in a hypnotic experience or in response to a hypnotic suggestion, does that mean the hypnosis procedure was actually ineffective? Or that the experience of hypnosis wasn't attained by the research subject (or client)?

The research currently focuses on those deemed "high hypnotizables" as a sensible place to look for the markers of the hypnotic experience. The research on low and medium hypnotizables is less well developed, and it is still a subject of considerable debate as to the actual differences between lows and highs in terms of brain functions.

The studies vary substantially not only in the way they define hypnotizability (or is it susceptibility?), but also as to which specific test instruments they employ to differentiate highs from lows.

The technology used to assess changes in brain functions in response to hypnosis can only measure what they can measure. As Dr. Graham Jamieson of the Department of Cognitive Neuroscience and Behavior of the Imperial College Faculty of Medicine commented to the members of a scientific hypnosis computer listserv (June 12, 2002), ". . . perhaps it is time to move beyond course (*sic*) grained concepts such as 'focused attention' to consider the internally fine grained models now emerging in the cognitive-neurosciences. These models emphasize the rapid reciprocal flow of information between functionally and anatomically distinct subsystems. Traditional measures such as averaging (ERPs) and (frequency) bandpower are poorly suited to tap these relationships."

The studies vary substantially in the way the researchers word the suggestions they offer their research subjects.

The brain research on hypnosis is an invaluable source of information about hypnosis and hypnotic phenomena. Such sophisticated research represents the crossroad where subjective perceptions intersect with their neuropsychophysiological correlates. Future research involving ever more advanced neuroimaging strategies and devices are already on the horizon. Researchers are beginning to employ combinations of existing devices (such as fMRI, or PET, or SPECT neuroimaging in combination with EEG or magnetoencephalography, known as MEG), and newer technologies such as diffuse optical tomography (DOT). (DOT is a noninvasive optical-imaging process involving near-infrared light applied to tissue surface providing an absorption spectrum for the tissue. See Diamond, Howe, Boas, Stanley, & Denner, 2002.)

WHAT DOES BRAIN RESEARCH MEAN TO CLINICIANS USING HYPNOSIS?

First and foremost, EEG, MEG, PET, SPECT, fMRI, and other scanning technologies offer an unprecedented opportunity to probe the workings of the brain. Involving hypnosis in the process as a research variable can be a valuable means of studying cognitive phenomena that can yield insights affecting the course of treatment (Raz & Shapiro, 2002).

Despite the gains to be made from brain research, however, there are a number of issues complicating the treatment process that clinicians should consider. These include: Can we—should we—attempt to define peoples' experiences, especially their problems, in solely biological terms? As advocates of neurofeedback suggest, should we define depression, anxiety, and numerous other disorders merely as brainwave dysrhythmias? Similarly, the drug industry has strived to define such disorders as evidence of a neurochemical imbalance requiring medications. However, the evidence is overwhelming that almost every disorder has psychological and social correlates, as well as physical ones. Depression, for example, is about much more than just "bad chemistry" (Yapko, 2001). Likewise, the experience of hypnosis takes place in a physical context, a social (interpersonal) context, and it involves personal characteristics such as motivation to attend and expectations. Hypnosis is much more than brainwaves, cerebral blood flow, and hemispheric activation. Despite this point, clinicians should be aware that brain physiology matters, and that what could be interpreted as psychologically based symptoms may well have biological underpinnings. Medical and even neuropsychological evaluations are a sensible first step in treatment.

Does experience alter brain chemistry and even brains themselves? Recent studies suggest the answer is yes. In studies by Dr. Lewis Baxter at the University of California, Los Angeles (UCLA), School of Medicine, depressed patients were exposed to either an SSRI or cognitive behavioral therapy. Ten weeks later, both groups showed nearly identical changes in their brains in PET scans. In another study (Brody et al., 2001), also at UCLA, the results were the same in a 12-week trial of antidepressants compared to interpersonal psychotherapy. In a third study (Martin, Martin, Rai, Richardson, & Royall, 2001) conducted in England, interpersonal therapy compared to the antidepressant Effexor yielded similar results. These studies showed that in response to psychotherapy alone, patients demonstrated decreases in prefrontal cortex activity, increased activity of the cingulated gyrus, and increased activity of the caudate nucleus. Such studies raise more questions than they answer. But, every clinician must consider that in the multiple entry points into the subjective world of the client, each interaction has an effect, as well as potential effects, on multiple levels.

When is hypnosis a treatment tool of choice for someone? Dr. Crawford weighed in on this issue when she recommended using hypnosis early on in the treatment of pain, a domain where the biological evidence for a hypnotic effect is substantial (Crawford et al., 1998) before the patient develops strong pain memories and before surgery and long courses of drug treatment are initiated. One might offer similar criteria for someone suffering distress of *any* sort: Helping the person by using hypnosis before acute distress becomes chronic, and (when appropriate, of course) before techniques other than self-regulation approaches are employed.

Does hypnotizability testing in order to distinguish between high and low hypnotizables bias the clinician's treatment or inform it? There are good arguments for either viewpoint, and these will be explored later. Suffice it to say here that wanting to assess and enhance someone's cognitive and behavioral flexibility is of primary importance in doing treatment, given the implicit (and often explicit) messages to the client, "Look at your circumstances differently" and "Do something different."

Hopefully, you have now begun to develop an appreciation for the complexities associated with striving to understand hypnosis and hypnotic phenomena on a neuropsychophysiological basis. There are profound issues to consider in evaluating the relevance of such work for your specific applications of hypnosis. Some of them have already been raised in this and previous chapters, but others will receive attention in future chapters for you to consider as you evolve your own style of thinking about the clinical practice of hypnosis. At the very least, though, you are now aware that suggestions given in hypnosis can have a powerful effect not only psychologically, but physically as well.

For Discussion

1. What are some of the questions you have about brain functions in hypnosis that you think research may eventually be able to answer? Which ones, if any, do you think no amount of research will ever be able to answer? Why do you think so?

2. Why do you think people are attracted to scientific sounding descriptions of hypnosis (e.g., "Alpha state" or "Theta state") that more often cloud issues than clarify them?

3. In your opinion, is it a reasonable assumption that if you correct "faulty" brain wave patterns the associated problems will also be corrected? Why or why not?

Things to Do

1. Have a session or two with a biofeedback or neurofeedback expert. How might this approach be helpful to some people?

2. Pass an everyday object around the room and have each member of the class generate a novel or unintended use for it. What do you discover about cognitive flexibility?

REFERENCES

Atwater, F. (1995). The Monroe Institute's Hemi-Sync Process (on-line). Available at URL http://www.monroeinstitute.org/research/hemi-sync-atwater.html.

Barabasz, A., & Barabasz, M. (1996). Neurotherapy and alert hypnosis in the treatment of attention deficit hyperactivity disorder. In S. Lynn, I. Kirsch, & J. Rhue (Eds.), *Casebook of Clinical Hypnosis* (pp. 271–291). Washington, DC: American Psychological Association.

Barabasz, A., Barabasz, M., Jensen, S., Calvin, S., Trevisan, M., & Warner, D. (1999). Cortical event-related potentials show the structure of hypnotic suggestions is crucial. *International Journal of Clinical and Experimental Hypnosis, 47,* 5–22.

Barabasz, A., & Lonsdale, C. (1983). Effects of hypnosis on P300 olfactory–evoked potential amplitudes. *Journal of Abnormal Psychology, 92,* 520–3.

Beck, A., Rush, A., Shaw, B., & Emery, G. (1979). *Cognitive therapy of depression.* New York: Guilford.

Bowers, K. (1992). Imagination and dissociation in hypnotic responding. *International Journal of Clinical and Experimental Hypnosis, 40,* 4, 253–75.

Brady, B., & Stevens, L. (2000). Binaural-beat induced theta EEG activity and hypnotic susceptibility. *American Journal of Clinical Hypnosis, 43,* 1, 53–69.

Brody, A., Saxena, S., Stoessel, P., Gillies, L., Fairbanks, L., Alborzian, S., Phelps, M., Huang, S-C., Wu, H-M., Ho, M., Au, S., Maidment, K., & Baxter, L. (2001). Regional brain metabolic changes in patients with major depression treated with either paroxetine or interpersonal therapy: Preliminary findings. *Archives of General Psychiatry, 58(7),* 631–40.

Crawford, H. (1989). Cognitive and physiological flexibility: Multiple pathways to hypnotic responsiveness. In V. Ghorgui, P. Netter, H. Eysenck, & R. Rosenthal (Eds.),

Suggestion and suggestibility: Theory and research (pp. 155–68). Berlin: Springer–Verlag.

Crawford, H. (1990). Cognitive and psychophysiological correlates of hypnotic responsiveness and hypnosis. In M. Fass & D. Brown (Eds.), *Creative mastery in hypnosis and hypnoanalysis: A festschrift for Erika Fromm* (pp. 155–68). Hillsdale, NJ: Erlbaum.

Crawford, H. (1994). Brain dynamics and hypnosis: Attentional and disattentional processes. *International Journal of Clinical and Experimental Hypnosis, 42,* 4204–32.

Crawford, H. (2001). Neuropsychophysiology of hypnosis: Towards an understanding of how hypnotic interventions work. In G. Burrows, R. Stanley, & P. Bloom (Eds.), *International Handbook of Clinical Hypnosis* (pp. 61–84). New York: Wiley.

Crawford, H. Personal communication. June 17, 2002.

Crawford, H., Clarke, S., & Kitner–Triolo, M. (1996a). Self–generated happy and sad emotions in low and highly hypnotizable persons during waking and hypnosis: Laterality and regional EEG activity differences. *International Journal of Psychophysiology, 24,* 239–266.

Crawford, H., Corby, J., & Kopell, B. (1996b). Auditory event–related potentials while ignoring tone stimuli: Attentional differences reflected in stimulus intensity and latency responses in low and highly hypnotizable persons. *International Journal of Neuroscience, 85,* 57–69.

Crawford, H., & Gruzelier, J. (1992). A midstream view of the neuropsychophysiology of hypnosis: Recent research and future directions. In E. Fromm & M. Nash (Eds.), *Contemporary hypnosis research* (pp. 227–66). New York: Guilford.

Crawford, H., Gur, R. C., Skolnick, B., Gur, R. E., & Benson, D. (1993). Effects of hypnosis on regional cerebral blood flow during ischemic pain with and without suggested hypnotic analgesia. *International Journal of Psychophysiology, 15,* 181–95.

Crawford, H., Kapelis, L., & Harrison, D. (1995). Visual field asymmetry in facial affect perception: Moderating effects of hypnosis, hypnotic susceptibility level, absorption, and sustained attentional abilities. *International Journal of Neuroscience, 82,* 11–23.

Crawford, H., Knebel, T., Kaplan, L., Vendemia, J., Xie, M., Jameson, S., & Pribram, K. (1998). Hypnotic analgesia: I. Somatosensory event-related potential changes to noxious stimuli, and II. Transfer learning to reduce chronic low back pain. *International Journal of Clinical and Experimental Hypnosis, 46,* 92–132.

De Pascalis, V. (1994). Event–related potentials during hypnotic hallucination. *International Journal of Clinical and Experimental Hypnosis, 42,* 39–55.

De Pascalis, V. (1998). Brain mechanisms and attentional processes in hypnosis. Presented at INABIS '98–5th Internet World Congress on Biomedical Sciences at McMaster University, Canada, Dec. 7–16th. Invited symposium. Available at URL http://www.mcmaster.ca/inabis98/woody/de_pascalis0311/index.html.

De Pascalis, V., Marucci, F., & Penna, M. (1989). 40–Hz EEG asymmetry during recall of emotional events in waking and hypnosis; Differences between low and high hypnotizables. *International Journal of Psychophysiology, 7,* 85–96.

De Pascalis, V., Marucci, F., Penna, M., & Pessa, E. (1987). Hemispheric activity of 40-Hz EEG during recall of emotional events: Differences between low and high hypnotizables. *International Journal of Psychophysiology, 5,* 167–180.

De Pascalis, V., & Penna, P. (1990). 40-Hz EEG activity during hypnotic induction and hypnotic testing. *International Journal of Clinical and Experimental Hypnosis, 38,* 125–138.

Diamond, S., Howe, R., Boas, D., Stanley, G., & Denner, J. (2002). Functional brain imaging of mind–body inter-stroke recovery. Available from Harvard Biorobotics Laboratory at URL http://hrl.harvard.edu/hrsl/research/sol.html.

Duncan-Johnson, C., & Donchin, E. (1980). The relation of P300 latency to reaction time as a function of expectancy. *Progress in Brain Research, 54,* 1717–22.

Gazzaniga, M. (1970). *The bisected brain.* New York: Appleton.

Gordon, B. (1949). The physiology of hypnosis. *Psychiatric Quarterly, 23,* 317–43.

Graffin, N., Ray, W., & Lundy, R. (1995). EEG concomitants of hypnosis and hypnotic susceptibility. *Journal of Abnormal Psychology, 104,* 123–31.

Gruzelier, J. (1988). The neuropsychology of hypnosis. In M. Heap (Ed.), *Hypnosis: Current clinical, experimental, and forensic practices* (pp. 68–76). London: Croom Helm.

Gruzelier, J. (1990). Neurophysiological investigations of hypnosis: Cerebral laterality and beyond. In R. van Dyck, P. Spinhoven, & A. van der Toes (Eds.), *Hypnosis: Theory, research and clinical practice* (pp. 37–51). Amsterdam: Free University Press.

Gruzelier, J. (1998). A working model of the neurophysiology of hypnotic relaxation. Presented at INABIS '98—5th Internet World Congress on Biomedical Sciences at McMaster University, Canada, Dec. 7–16th. Invited symposium. Available at URL http://www.mcmaster.ca/inabis98/woody/gruzelier0814/index.html.

Heller, W. (1993). Neuropsychological mechanisms of individual differences in emotion, personality, and arousal. *Neuropsychology, 7,* 476–89.

Jamieson, G. (June 12, 2002). Re: EEG correlates, theta, and hypnosis. Listserv message to members. (#2002-83).

Jensen, S., Barabasz, A., Barabasz, M., & Warner, D. (2001). EEG P300 event–related markers of hypnosis. *American Journal of Clinical Hypnosis, 44,* 2, 127–40.

Kallio, S., Revonsuo, A., Hamalainen, H., Markela, J., & Gruzelier, J. (2001). Anterior brain functions and hypnosis: A test of the frontal hypothesis. *International Journal of Clinical and Experimental Hypnosis, 49,* 2, 95–108.

Kirsch, I., Burgess, C., & Braffman, W. (1999). Attentional resources in hypnotic responding. *International Journal of Clinical and Experimental Hypnosis, 47,* 3, 175–91.

Kosslyn, S., Thompson, B., Costantini–Ferrando, M., Alpert, N., & Spiegel, D. (2000). Hypnotic visual illusion alters color processing in the brain. *American Journal of Psychiatry, 157,* 1279–84.

London, P., Hart, J., & Leibovitz, M. (1968). EEG alpha rhythms and susceptibility to hypnosis. *Nature, 219,* 71–2.

Lubar, J. (1995). Neurofeedback for the management of attention deficit hyperactivity disorders. In M. Schwartz (Ed.), *Biofeedback: A practitioner's guide.* (pp. 493–522). New York: Guilford.

Martin, S., Martin, E., Rai, S., Richardson, M., & Royall, R. (2001). Brain blood flow changes in depressed patients treated with interpersonal psychotherapy or venlafaxine hydrochloride: Preliminary findings. *Archives of General Psychiatry, 58,* 641–9.

Nowlis, D., & Rhead, J. (1968). Relation of eyes-closed resting EEG alpha activity to hypnotic susceptibility. *Perceptual and Motor Skills, 27,* 1047–50.

Perlini, A., & Spanos, N. (1991). EEG alpha methodologies and hypnotizability: A critical review. *Psychophysiology, 28,* 511–30.

Rainville, P., Duncan, G., Price, D., Carrier, B., & Bushnell, M. (1997). Pain affect encoded in human anterior cingulated but not somatosensory cortex. *Science, 277,* 968–71.

Ray, W. (1997). EEG concomitants of hypnotic susceptibility. *International Journal of Clinical and Experimental Hypnosis, 45*, 3, 301–313.

Ray, W., Blai, A., Aikins, D., Coyle, J., & Bjick, E. (1998). Understanding hypnosis and hypnotic susceptibility from a psychophysiological perspective. Presented at INABIS '98–5th Internet World Congress on Biomedical Sciences at McMaster University, Canada, Dec. 7–16th. Invited symposium. Available at URL http://www.mcmaster.ca/inabis98/woody/ray0556/index.html.

Raz, A., & Shapiro, T. (2002). Hypnosis and neuroscience. *Archives of General Psychiatry, 59*, 85–90.

Roche, S., & McConkey, K. (1990). Absorption: Nature, assessment, and correlates. *Journal of Personality and Social Psychology, 59*, 91–101.

Ruehle, B., & Zamansky, H. (1997). The experience of effortlessness in hypnosis: Perceived or real? *International Journal of Clinical and Experimental Hypnosis, 45*, 2, 144–57.

Sabourin, M., Cutcomb, S., Crawford, H., & Pribram, K. (1990). EEG correlates of hypnotic susceptibility and hypnotic trance: Spectral analysis and coherence. *International Journal of Psychophysiology, 10*, 125–42.

Schachter, D. (1977). EEG theta waves and psychological phenomena: A review and analysis. *Biological Psychology, 5*, 47–82.

Sheer, D. (1989). Sensory and cognitive 40-Hz EEG event-related potentials: Behavioral correlates, brain function, and clinical application. In E. Basar & T. Bullock (Eds.), *Brain dynamics* (pp. 339–74). Berlin: Springer-Verlag.

Sperry, R. (1968). Hemispheric deconnection and unity in conscious awareness. *American Psychologist, 23*, 723–33.

Spiegel, H. & Spiegel, D. (1987). *Trance and treatment: Clinical uses of hypnosis.* Washington, DC: American Psychiatric Press.

Sterman, M. (1996). Physiological origins and functional correlates of EEG rhythmic activities: Implications for self–regulation. *Biofeedback & Self-Regulation, 21*,1, 3–33.

Sterman, M. (2000). Basic concepts and clinical findings in the treatment of seizure disorders with EEG operant conditioning. *Clinical Electroencephalography, 31*, 1, 45–55.

Stuss, D., Eskes, G., & Foster, J. (1994). Experimental neuropsychological studies of frontal lobe functions. In F. Boller & J. Grafman (Eds.), *Handbook of neuropsychology* (Vol. 9, pp. 149–84). Amsterdam: Elsevier.

Szechtman, H., Woody, E., Bowers, K., & Nahmias, C. (1998). Where the imaginal appears real: A positron emission tomography study of auditory hallucinations. *Proceedings of the National Academy of Sciences of the United States of America, 95*, 1956–60.

Wallace, B. (1990). Imagery vividness, hypnotic susceptibility, and the perception of fragmented stimuli. *Journal of Personality and Social Psychology, 58*, 354–59.

Watzlawick, P. (1978). *The language of change.* New York: Basic Books.

Weitzenhoffer, A. (2000). *The practice of hypnotism* (2nd ed.). New York: Wiley.

Williams, J. & Gruzelier, J. (2001). Differentiation of hypnosis and relaxation by analysis of narrow band theta and alpha frequencies. *International Journal of Clinical and Experimental Hypnosis, 49*, 3, 185–206.

Yapko, M. (2001). *Treating depression with hypnosis: Integrating cognitive-behavioral and strategic approaches.* Philadelphia, PA: Brunner/Routledge.

5

Contexts of Hypnosis

One of the questions I am most frequently asked by others when they discover my involvement with clinical hypnosis is, "Can hypnosis be used in the treatment of such and such?" I used to think that I should instantly be able to cite a variety of scientific studies to support my typically affirmative response, but I have changed tactics in recent years. Citing studies doesn't make the larger point I think needs making when someone wonders aloud about the applications of hypnosis. Now I am much more likely to respond to their question with such counter questions as: Do you think there is any mental or emotional involvement with that disorder you are asking about? Do you think someone's attitude, expectations, or belief system plays a role, however major or minor, in his or her experience of the problem? Are someone's feelings, personal needs, or self-image a factor in the way his or her particular physical and/or mental health problem is experienced?

In asking people such questions, I can't recall anyone ever responding, "No, the person's frame of mind is not a factor at all." I suppose one day I may run into someone who believes their psychological makeup has no effect on their experience of life, including physical symptoms. After I get over the initial shock, I'll try to give that person some insight into ways to use the mind for a level of self-control that might previously have seemed impossible.

I think the most important philosophical place to begin a study of hypnosis or to start developing a realistic appreciation for its merits is with the simple yet profound recognition that people have more abilities than they tend to realize. Furthermore, it helps in the study of hypnosis to appreciate the many ways that the mind and body are interconnected. I think most people seem to have an intuitive understanding that the mind affects the body, and, likewise, one's physiology affects one's mental experience.

Unfortunately, while most people can accept this point with relative ease, they often tend to think of this relationship simply as one in which the person's mental makeup can cause him or her to be physically sick, especially as evidenced in the psychophysiological disorders (Gauld, 1992; Hollander, 2001). The relationship between lifestyle and disease is commonly acknowledged, with stress-related symptoms rampant in our society (D. Brown, 1992; Wickramasekera, 1998). But, if the mind can cause sickness, can't it also foster wellness? It is encouraging that many forms of hypnotic approaches (e.g., visualization, guided imagery, focusing techniques) are being used with considerable success as adjunct treatments in the intervention of physical disease, usually in behavioral medicine programs (Brown & Fromm, 1987). Clinicians working in such contexts are usually wonderfully aware that wellness is not merely the absence of illness, and that hypnosis can play a significant role in absorbing people in healthier lifestyles.

Essentially, my response to the question of whether hypnosis can be used in the treatment of some particular disorder promotes the *general* idea that hypnosis can be used as a tool in the treatment of (not *cure* of) almost any human condition in which a person's attitude is a factor. (Pragmatically speaking, the research evidence, though growing exponentially and affirming this point, is much less abundant than the anecdotal evidence from generations of clinicians applying hypnosis with almost every condition you can name.)

Thus, even if the disease is an entirely organic one, such as a physical injury, the person's mental resources can still be focused to help manage discomfort more easily, and perhaps even to enhance the healing process (Kroger, 1977; Rossi, 2000). In physical disorders where there is no known path to recovery, hypnosis can ease the discomfort, allow some rest, encourage a positive attitude, and lessen any associated emotional trauma. Hypnosis may not facilitate a cure for an illness, but it can still help the person on a variety of levels and in meaningful ways (Barretta & Barretta, 2001; Sylvester, 2001).

A person's mental involvement in the various psychological disorders is far more obvious, and seems to be the basis for a more widespread acceptance of hypnotic principles and techniques among psychotherapists compared to medical practitioners. Psychotherapists are generally quite good at incorporating methods for empowering their clients into their therapies. They seem to more easily recognize hypnosis can be very useful in altering people's self-limiting perceptions (T. Barber, 1985).

Wherever there is involvement of the person's mind in a particular problem, which is *everywhere* to one degree or another as far as I can tell, there is some potential gain to be made through the application of hypnotic patterns. With that point in mind, this chapter will consider specific clinical contexts where hypnosis may be used to facilitate therapeutic outcomes. But before we consider clinical contexts, let's first consider the most public and therefore visible context in which hypnosis is applied, the stage hypnosis show. I can safely predict, if you develop your skills in hypnosis and start using it in your clinical practice, you will end up having to address clients' questions about the stage show phenomenon quite frequently, so it will help you to know how these shows operate and how they relate to hypnosis in clinical contexts.

STAGE HYPNOSIS

Stage hypnosis is the application of hypnotic principles and techniques for the purpose of entertaining an audience. Such shows are commonly found in nightclubs, at state fairs, parties, and in other similar contexts where entertainment is desired. I have already shared my distaste for stage shows involving hypnosis, and I have described the dynamics of how they work (see chapter 2).

In the stage context, hypnosis appears to be a relatively benign method of mind control yet suggests something bordering dangerously close to brainwashing. People in hypnosis are made to look silly (entirely with their permission, of course), and audiences typically have a difficult time understanding how the entertaining routines in the show could possibly be used in a professional context for therapeutic purposes. Consequently, hypnosis is not considered as a serious treatment alternative, and people are inadvertently robbed of what should be widely considered a valuable treatment option. It is also true that some people know better, and may actually become attracted to therapeutic hypnosis as a result of their exposure to stage hypnosis. But such people seem to be in the minority, in my experience.

MEDICAL HYPNOSIS

Traditional medicine has long recognized the "placebo effect." In some instances, a patient's positive belief that he or she is getting an active drug when she is really getting no drug at all, only a sugar pill resembling a drug, will generate the same level of therapeutic effect as if the patient had been given an active drug. Conversely, negative expectations can foster a "nocebo" effect, a negative therapeutic effect. A person's expectations and attitudes can obviously have profound effects on mental and physical experience. With this growing recognition of the influence of client expectancy on both physical and psychological treatments, there is a growing use of hypnosis and hypnosis-related techniques. Psychologist Irving Kirsch, Ph.D., has evolved a specific sociocognitive model of hypnosis, known as the response set theory, which heavily emphasizes the role of expectations in treatment (1985, 2000). In fact, Kirsch detailed considerable evidence that much of the positive effect of hypnosis is due to positive expectations on the part of the client, and Kirsch has even come to refer to hypnosis as a "non-deceptive placebo," unlike the sugar pills clients are fooled into believing are active drugs (1994). There is a considerable body of empirical evidence attesting to the power of expectations in both psychological and medical conditions (Harrington, 1997).

Given a foundation for appreciating how expectancy can influence physiology and behavioral responses, is hypnosis only a placebo? Certainly there is some truth in that perspective, and if that's all hypnosis was, it would still be worthy of intensive study. After all, the need to engage clients in their treatment is vital to enhancing treatment effects and minimizing a sense of victimization and even depression when such reactions delay or even prevent recovery (Lynch, 1999; Yapko, 2001).

The quantity of literature describing the applications of hypnosis to medical problems is growing quickly, and empirical evidence for its value is readily available (Montgomery, DuHamel, & Redd, 2000; Pinnell & Covino, 2000). For specific applications you are encouraged to refer to the various scientific hypnosis journals in which such research is published. Some of these are mentioned in Appendix A.

In general, hypnosis can be a useful adjunct to more traditional medical treatments for several reasons, the first of which relates to the discussion at the beginning of this chapter regarding the mind-body relationship and the role of the mind (attitudes and related emotions) in medical disorders. "Miracle cures" that defy current medical understanding, which have evolved out of a patient's refusal to give up, are not uncommon in the literature. Pragmatically speaking, why not encourage—or at least *permit* "miracles"? Why place limitations on the patient that he or she would not place on him- or herself?

A second reason for making use of hypnosis in the medical context is because of its emphasis, by its very nature, on the responsibility of each person for his own health and well-being. Use of hypnosis gives people a direct experience of having some control over their internal experiences, whether of pain or distress. I have worked with many people who actually cried tears of joy or relief in a session for having had an opportunity to experience themselves as relaxed, comfortable, and positive when their usual experience of themselves was one of pain and despair. Finding resources of comfort or the ability to shift perceptions of their body within themselves was a dramatic experience, and allowed them to take on a new and higher level of responsibility for themselves and their own well-being.

Specific applications of hypnosis in medical contexts are greatly varied, but can generally be described as a way of attaining a significant degree of control over physical processes. One possibility is the reduction or elimination of pain without the use of medication (Chaves, 1993; Montgomery, DuHamel, & Redd, 2000). Pain management is one of the more sophisticated uses of medical hypnosis, and is applicable to the patient in both chronic and acute pain. Pain management techniques can be used before, during, and after surgery, to facilitate easier childbirth, and to help manage physical trauma of any sort. Methods of hypnotic pain management are generally very sophisticated, and you are advised to have a very strong background of education and experience in hypnosis before working with individuals in pain. Working with people in physical pain presupposes appropriate medical licensure or appropriate medical supervision in all cases.

Hypnosis is commonly used in the treatment of anxiety and stress disorders, and is considered to be a most effective treatment (Schoenberger, 2000). Teaching the medical patient techniques for preventing negative stress wherever possible, techniques for identifying stress well before it reaches a level where it is likely to cause debilitating symptoms, and techniques for relaxing and managing stress positively are all elements in teaching a hypertensive patient to manage his or her condition positively and responsibly.

Hypnosis in the treatment of serious diseases, as an adjunct, not a replacement, for more traditional approaches, has demonstrated the necessity of addressing the emotional needs while using the mental resources of the patient as a part of treatment. This is true even for diseases that seem, and probably are, entirely organic in nature. The exact mechanism whereby a doctor can mumble a few hypnotic phrases and effect changes in the patient is unknown. In general, hypnosis is thought to strengthen the body's immunological functions and assist in fighting disease. How it does this exactly has been the focus of a relatively new field called psychoneuroimmunology (Kalt, 2000; Kropiunigg, 1993). Much research still needs to be done, of course, but the lack of precise explanations for mechanisms of action should not inhibit the use of techniques that can assist in the healing of a human body. Hypnosis doesn't replace other treatments—it adds to them.

There are a couple of special issues associated with hypnosis and mind-body healing approaches that I'd like to draw to your attention. The first concerns the responsibility of a patient for his or her health. The goal is to positively encourage a person to use all of his or her resources to help him- or herself. *Pointing out responsibility for one's self is not meant to translate into blaming the person for his or her condition.* One of the most distressing (to me, at least) things to arise from the recognition of patient responsibility is when the doctor, or other well-meaning health professional, further burdens the suffering patient with blame for having caused his or her illness. It's not bad enough the person is sick, he or she is also told he or she caused it ("You're ill because you have unresolved feelings of anger toward your mother"), and is even asked why he or she did this to him- or herself! ("Do you have an unconscious need to suffer?") No, this is not the intent; personal responsibility in health care is positive, blame is not. Helping the person to feel guilty about having made him- or herself sick is a poor outcome of a careless interaction.

The second issue, mentioned in passing earlier, relates to the use of hypnosis in the treatment of medical problems. Specifically, unless you are a physician, or have the proper training and credentials to treat a person's physical disorders, you are working out of your field and are inviting trouble for both you and your patient. If you want to assist someone in the treatment of a physical disorder, it is imperative from an ethical, legal, and humane standpoint that you have the support and involvement of the appropriate medical practitioners. You cannot simply assume, for example, that a patient with migraines is "just stressed." With that symptom, and all others, the patient should have a thorough physical examination, and you should have medical backup as you treat individuals with what may well turn out to be organically induced symptoms. Call the patient's doctor directly, and ask if your treatment plan will interfere with his or hers, at the very least. Rarely, if ever, will it interfere and treatment can be coordinated between you. Knowledge of medications the patient may be taking and the physical impact of his or her symptoms is also essential to effective suggestion formulation.

The growing use of hypnosis in a broad range of medical conditions is evidence of the influence of all those who have called for a more person-centered practice of medicine. Physicians, to their credit, have generally evolved a style of practice that invites the patient to be an informed and active participant in treatment. Hypnosis amplifies this partnership and thereby empowers patients to mobilize their own resources to supplement whatever other treatments they might also be receiving.

DENTAL HYPNOSIS

The powerful mind-body relationship evidenced in medical applications of hypnosis is also evident in dental applications. Many of the desired outcomes sought in medical contexts are also desirable in the dental setting because of the physical nature of dental work. Physical parts of the body (i.e., teeth, gums, and associated structures) are under treatment. Furthermore, attached to every mouth under treatment is a human being whose attitudes about the work being done, the dentist, and his or her self (self-image) will affect the outcome of the intervention.

Dentists are aware, perhaps acutely, that most dental patients do not mark their calendar months in advance of their appointment and wait with eager anticipation for the big day to arrive. Far more common is the patient coming for treatment who can be described as somewhere in between mildly reluctant and terrified.

Hypnosis as a means of effectively communicating with and enhancing the treatments of the dental patient has been well documented. Helping a patient reduce his or her anxiety about receiving dental treatment with a few well-chosen statements can make a huge difference in the outcome. In one case, a dental phobia was successfully treated by suggesting to the patient that a previous negative experience with dentistry could be altered and remembered as having been a positive experience (Baker & Boas, 1983). Finkelstein (1991) also described ways hypnosis could be used to reduce anxiety in fearful patients. Clearly, one good dental experience—real or imagined—can skillfully be used as a prototype for future dental experiences. The person may not eagerly await the next appointment, but he or she won't have to live in dread, either.

A second good use of hypnosis in dentistry involves the use of pain management techniques. Many people either cannot or choose not to use chemical anesthesias (or analgesias) such as novocaine or nitrous oxide, and prefer to rely on their own resources when undergoing dental treatment. Hypnosis techniques for creating the experience of analgesia or anesthesia allow the patient to reduce to a more easily managed level the degree of discomfort experienced, and many are able to eliminate the discomfort altogether (J. Barber, 1977; Chaves, 1993).

A third use of hypnosis in dentistry is for its ability to assist in directing the flow of blood. With proper techniques, ones that really fit well with the patient's experience of himself, hypnosis can reduce blood flow to the area under treatment (Holroyd, 1992; Newman, 1971). The result is a less traumatic experience for the patient and greater clarity for the dentist in seeing what he or she is doing. A related use of hypnosis is for the enhancement of the healing process following treatment. Use of hypnosis techniques involving the imagining of healing (e.g., images, feelings, and sounds associated with rebuilding, repairing, and strengthening) can both shorten the recovery period and allow greater comfort during that time.

Another use of hypnosis in dentistry has been to counter bruxism, or teeth grinding. In one study by Clarke and Reynolds (1991), bruxism patients were given suggestions to develop a greater awareness of and control over the muscles in their jaws. The results were quite impressive, as both bruxism and reports of pain were significantly reduced.

Finally, hypnosis to encourage better dental health practices has been successfully employed (Kelly, McKinty, & Carr, 1988). Suggestions to increase time brushing and flossing can be given to encourage prevention of dental problems.

Many dental practices could easily incorporate hypnosis into treatment through the use of generalized relaxation tapes the patient can listen to (through headphones) during the dental procedures. Of course, better responses occur with more individualized approaches, but unusual is the dentist who has the time, interest, and means for the greater involvement in hypnosis such a practice would require.

FORENSIC HYPNOSIS

In decades past, hypnosis had frequently been used in the course of criminal investigations to refresh or enhance eyewitness testimony, whether that of a witness, victim, or suspect (Sheehan & McConkey, 1993). In light of the considerable research evidence that hypnosis was given more credibility in the domain of memory enhancement than it deserved, a subject I'll explore in depth later, hypnosis has lost much of its value as an investigative tool.

As a part of the investigative process, particularly when information simply can't be obtained in any other way, hypnosis may be used to facilitate a person's recall in an attempt to recover details of the crime the person could not consciously remember. Often, a person's conscious mind is so absorbed in feelings (e.g., fear, fascination, confusion) during the experience of witnessing or being victimized by a crime that conscious memory is poor (Udolf, 1983). Because of the dual nature of the human mind (i.e., conscious and unconscious), memories and details that may have been repressed or else simply escaped conscious detection may not have escaped the person's unconscious (Scheflin & Shapiro, 1989; Kroger, 1977).

A number of famous, or perhaps infamous, criminal cases have been solved through hypnotically obtained information, one such case being the "Chowchilla Kidnapping" case in which a school bus driver and his bus full of students were kidnapped in the small town of Chowchilla in northern California. Three men commandeered the bus to a nearby rock quarry where it and the people inside were buried, and then they issued a ransom demand. The bus driver managed to escape, and the children were soon rescued. Dr. William Kroger, a pioneer and long-time contributor to the field of hypnosis, was called in to use hypnosis with the driver, who was then able to recall the license plate number (though numbers were reversed) of one of the kidnappers' vans. This hypnotically obtained information helped lead to their arrest and subsequent conviction for the crime. (Continued on page 113.)

FRAME OF REFERENCE: WILLIAM KROGER, M.D.

William S. Kroger, M.D. (1906–1995), was one of the primary early catalysts driving the development of the field of clinical hypnosis. Dr. Kroger became fascinated with hypnosis at an early age, and his interest endured throughout his long, distinguished career. He was inspired to be a physician out of compassion for people's suffering, and early professional influences on him nudged him in the direction of psychosomatic medicine. Dr. Kroger co-founded the Society for Clinical and Experimental Hypnosis, and together with Dr. Milton Erickson, co-founded the American Society of Clinical Hypnosis. He also organized the Academy of Psychosomatic Medicine. Not only did Dr. Kroger write the book that was long considered *the* book on hypnosis, *Clinical and Experimental Hypnosis in Medicine, Dentistry and Psychology* (2nd ed., 1977), but he authored and co-authored many other important works, including his 1976 book with William Fezler called *Hypnosis and Behavior Modification: Imagery Conditioning*. Dr. Kroger's deep interest in ways the mind can influence physical responses in particular led him to apply hypnosis in a wide variety of ways, but especially in pain relief.

Dr. Kroger's precedent setting demonstrations more than half a century ago of surgical procedures done under hypnosis remain landmark events in propelling the young and questionable field of hypnosis onto its current level of acceptability and interest. His commitment as a clinician and teacher inspired many of the most prominent people in the field to help bring hypnosis into mainstream research and practice. Anyone who professionally practices hypnosis owes a great deal to Dr. Kroger, whose pioneering efforts paved the way for the field to grow to its current proportions.

On the Origin of His Interest in Hypnosis: "My interest in hypnosis started in 1919. My father had a fur store in Evanston, Illinois. In order to stimulate business, he hired a professional hypnotist to hypnotize a woman as a publicity stunt in order to create interest in the Main Street Businessmen's Association. This, I can see as if it was yesterday. The girl's name was Florina, and she was dressed in purple flowing gowns and veils. And he, with the piercing eyes, approached her and said, 'Florina, sleep!' He stared in her eyes and she fell backwards and they put her in a coffin and buried her in the ground. I was a curious little cuss, and so I went by and paid a nickel to see this sleeping beauty in the ground. She lay there in a vault for two days, and I thought, 'Gee, that's fantastic!' On the third day, they dug her up. 'Florina, wake up!' She opened her eyes, she blinked, she stood up—it was the same thing you'd see on the stage today. So I went around to the kids in the neighborhood and I looked into their eyes and said, 'Sleep!' And to my amazement, half of them fell over. I did the usual things; like I could put pins in their arms, and I'd say, 'Jeez, I could be a doctor some day. This would be great for anesthesia.' So, I didn't realize that hypnosis was anything more than a stage tool until I got to Northwestern University. At Northwestern University, I met the late Dr. J. D. Morgan, whose book you may be familiar with on abnormal psychology. We had several lectures on hypnosis, and I said, 'My God, this is a scientific tool!'"

On Early Prejudices Against Hypnosis: "I was the only doctor who was using hypnosis in the Chicago area. I was laughed at, ridiculed, vilified, and abused, and made to walk seven steps behind everybody else like I was a leper. I was persecuted by the Illinois State Medical Society for an exhibit. They were just against hypnosis, [even just] the word . . .

"The difficulties I went through. . . . You don't know how difficult it really was! [For the first movie ever showing thyroid surgery done with only hypnotic anesthesia] . . . it was an historic moment. First one in the world, and we pulled it off! [The medical director] was sitting downstairs in his office, getting a 'blow-by-blow' description of how the surgery was going, hoping it was going to fail [because hypnosis was involved].

"Individuals who have never gone through things like that can't understand it. See, today hypnosis has some respectability, but in those days, they said, 'Walk seven steps behind me, you're a leper!' They didn't want to associate with me; they said, 'You're a hypnotist.'"

On "Trance" and Hypnosis: "Most people refer to it as a 'trance.' It's not a 'trance.' To me, that term is like fingernails scratching on a chalkboard. That's the most ridiculous term for it. [Hypnosis] is a state of increased awareness. If you're more aware, whatever you hear is going to sink in better. If it sinks in better, you get a better response, whether it's hitting a golf ball or having an erection. As Bernheim said, 'There is no hypnosis, only suggestion.' That's how I conceptualize it. I conceptualize it in terms of neural science concepts as a method of transmitting a message in a minimal noise environment. If the signal to noise ratio is reduced, the message is clearly received. "No other living system can do [what humans can]. Ideas have representations and names. You can't say to a dog, 'Go to the toilet.' He doesn't understand 'toilet.' But a human can—and that makes humans unique, because they can manipulate symbolic communication. The cortex is uniquely different in a human than in any other living system. And it's that cortex that you get out of the way (in terms of its criticalness) that allows you to induce a feeling of belief.

So, what is hypnosis? It's the induction of conviction. All these guys talk about 'hypnosis is this and that'—it's a very simple thing that's [been made] complex, enormously complex."

On Inductions and Beliefs: "Now, an induction technique is an interesting study on feedback control. I'd say, 'You are looking into my eyes, your eyes are getting heavy.' They're not getting heavy because of what I'm saying. They're getting heavy because of the fact that he is gazing up at the ceiling. But the subject imputes to you a magical omnipotence, and he says, 'My God, my eyes did get heavy! This guy's got power!' If he accepts A, B, C, and D suggestions, then he'll accept X, Y, and Z ones. All the time you say, 'You are a good hypnotic subject and yes, that's why that happened.' And all the time, it had nothing to do with what the operator was saying, it had more to do with restructuring his beliefs."

On Cybernetics and Hypnosis: "I'm going to continue to emphasize the cybernetic principles of feedback systems relative to theories of hypnosis, as well as some of the very important neuropsychophysiological aspects by making the computer analogies. The brain functions like a computer. I'm not saying the brain is a computer—I'm only saying I think we can better understand the brain's chemical qualities and neurophysiological mechanisms in terms of cybernetic principles and feedback mechanisms."

Source: Personal communication, 1987

The use of hypnotically obtained testimony in the courtroom is embroiled in controversy even now. Experts are at odds over the issue of whether hypnotically obtained testimony is valid because of the potentially detrimental effects of hypnosis on memory (e.g., intentionally or unintentionally suggested misrememberings). On one side of the issue are those who claim that the information obtained from a hypnotized person is as usable and reliable as any other information obtained from memory, and that hypnosis does not *necessarily* distort memory. On the other side of the issue are those who claim that hypnosis invariably alters memory, that the hypnotized witness can lie while in hypnosis, and is likely to fill in missing details either with fantasy material or with information contained in the subtle leading questions of the investigator. San Francisco attorney and hypnosis expert Alan Scheflin, J.D., has been integral to the field in sorting out the legal implications of the use of hypnosis in clinical as well as forensic contexts (Scheflin, 1995, 2001).

The issue is really one concerning the nature of memory. In a sense, both views on hypnosis and memory are correct. The conflict is a pseudo-conflict, a conflict arising because of its "either-or" nature, which is not a useful dichotomy in this case. All human memory is a distortion of experience—a memory is an internal representation of an event and not the event itself. The process of experiencing and then remembering is regulated by many factors, including values regarding what is important to notice; mood; internal or external focus; expectations; previous experiences in similar situations; and a variety of other factors that must be considered.

Memory, whether in a formally induced hypnotic condition or in the less specific condition called "life," can be reliable to a large extent, such as in "objective" experience when many people reach agreement on the object of observation. Likewise, memory in or out of hypnosis can distort experience because of all the factors described earlier that comprise one's conscious and unconscious information-processing capacities. Why else can ten people (presumably not all in hypnosis) standing on a street corner all see the same accident yet their police reports offer ten different versions?

Hypnotically obtained information should be considered in the same way as information obtained by any other means, in my view. It should be considered, evaluated, and substantiated by other means. If one has a motivation to lie, though, hypnosis has no preventative powers. If one must distort or misrepresent an experience, it won't be because of hypnosis. One doesn't require formal hypnosis to fill in gaps or rely on others' leads; these processes are ongoing in all human beings. I fully agree with Australian memory and hypnosis researchers Peter Sheehan (1995) and Kevin McConkey (1992) that blaming hypnosis for the memory distortions is not reasonable when the evidence is clear that memory distortion is not unique to hypnosis.

The other potential use of hypnosis in the forensic context is to help alleviate the stress and distress in having witnessed or been victimized by a crime. A skillful practitioner can help lessen the trauma by easing the person into a different frame of mind, either by helping the person shift his or her focus away from what has happened to another experience, or by helping the person shift from one uncomfortable dimension of the experience to another that is relatively neutral (neutral at least, but positive if possible). The things one concludes and the things one says to one's self after a traumatic experience play a huge role in the rate and degree of recovery.

Special consideration for the emotional state of the person who recalls details of the trauma must be an integral part of the use of hypnosis in the forensic sciences. Mechanisms to assure the emotional security and well-being of the person must be part of the process, for being left alone to carry the hurt of memories brought out hypnotically is otherwise one more trauma for an already vulnerable human being (Spiegel, 1993).

HYPNOSIS IN EDUCATION

Teaching and learning are highly refined skills which require a great amount of information processing on multiple levels. Teaching is a learning experience—learning how to capture students' interest and attention (a skill necessary for induction of hypnosis, not coincidentally), learning how to present information in such a way that the student can use it (a skill necessary for utilization of hypnosis, not coincidentally), and learning how to allow students to become self-sufficient learners (a skill necessary for consolidating treatment results with hypnosis, not coincidentally) so they may be competent and motivated to learn in the absence of the teacher. Whether a teacher is teaching preschoolers or doctoral candidates, effective teaching involves these steps paralleling hypnotic patterns.

Learning is a multiple step process. For the sake of simplicity (learning theory is a complex world in its own right), effective learning must include the following basic steps: First, there must be some degree of attentiveness to the material to be learned. Second, there must be some method for bringing the material from the outside world into the internal world. One's senses (e.g., sight, hearing, etc.) are the means for gathering information from the world around us. There is nothing we experience of the external world that does not enter our conscious or unconscious mind through one or more of our senses. Which sense is the dominant one at a given time determines, to a large degree, how much and what kind of information can be acquired (Lankton, 1979). For example, a high level of awareness for your (internal) feelings while trying to memorize a set of graphs or charts (external visual information) is likely to result in ineffective learning. Third, there must be some method for organizing the information internally as it mingles with previously acquired information while simultaneously building a framework in which to incorporate future learnings. Fourth, and last, there must be some method for being able to retrieve the information from within as necessity dictates.

Does hypnosis enhance learning by enhancing memory? As you learned in the previous section, hypnosis does not seem to do much for enhancing accurate memory. Studies on using hypnosis to increase recall of meaningful as well as nonsense material generally reinforce this point (Dywan, 1988; Holroyd, 1992).

Hypnosis as a tool has been used successfully, however, to assist in the learning process both by enhancing concentration and diminishing anxiety. Anxiety can interrupt any of the above steps (e.g., "going blank at exam time") and poor concentration can distract one from adequate exposure to the information as well as disrupt its internal organization (Stanton, 1993).

Many creative teachers at all levels are using hypnosis in their teaching, encouraging students' creativity and guiding students with relaxation procedures, for example (Wark, 1996; Wolf, 1986). Many students are developing themselves with self-hypnosis exercises, learning to manage anxiety and increase their ability to notice and organize their subject of study. Hypnosis in the educational context, whether formally or informally used, can enhance teaching skills, creativity, and student performance (Shames & Bowers, 1992).

HYPNOSIS IN BUSINESS

In the business context, formal hypnosis in the sense of overt hypnosis induction procedures is less applicable than is the use of the hypnotic communication principles. Communication that influences is a vital component of any comprehensive view of hypnosis; in the business context the principles of effective communication can either make or break a company. Discussing specific skills in suggestion formation is the subject of later chapters; suffice it to say here that for the businessperson who is able to communicate his or her ideas in flexible ways to those he or she interacts with, there is a greater likelihood of success at all levels. Communication skills in such interactions as the presentation of a marketing plan, the handling of a troublesome employee or supervisor, the job interview, performance evaluations, job standard clarification, the creation of a desirable work atmosphere, and the many other dimensions of the business world are all ultimately interpersonal interactions where skilled communication and influence can occur.

In the business consultations I occasionally do, identifying rigid and dysfunctional communication patterns and replacing them with more flexible approaches helps enhance the business on multiple levels. I don't call my interventions "hypnosis" while there, but hypnotic patterns are evident to the trained eye in my recommendations.

SPORTS HYPNOSIS

Engaging in athletics with any degree of intensity involves a large measure of physical control and mental concentration. Hypnosis as a tool can provide both with extraordinary efficiency. For the athlete, having precise control over one's body is essential to outstanding performance. Athletes often describe what they call "muscle memory," the body's keen awareness of how each limb, each muscle must be positioned in order to perform successfully. The physical control through the amplification of the mind-body relationship can help an athlete push his or her body to the upper limit of his or her talents. The requirement for intense concentration is obvious, and hypnosis as a technique for narrowing one's attentional focus to the task at hand is a powerful tool to have available (Liggett, 2000; Morgan, 1993).

In addition to building concentration and physical control, hypnosis can help in better managing the tension inherent in competing. Furthermore, building positive expectations and positive communication with one's self through self-hypnosis can enhance performance dramatically. Often, the troubled, slumping athlete has mental images of failure, which all too easily get translated into real failure. Building positive images through hypnosis and self-hypnosis can turn an athlete's performance around completely. Certainly, hypnosis does not provide extra talent to the athlete; it simply amplifies the talent the athlete has, giving greater access to as much of his or her talent as possible. A lot of athletes appreciate that, as you can well imagine.

HYPNOSIS IN PSYCHOTHERAPY

Being a psychotherapist by training and in practice, I have developed a profound appreciation for the possibilities hypnosis has to offer in the treatment of behavioral and emotional problems. Hypnosis as a part of therapist training programs seems an essential need, yet only a handful of formal programs offer the opportunity to develop expertise in hypnotic skills. Most people who become knowledgeable in hypnosis do so through involvement with workshops and seminars organized by private practitioners and professional hypnosis societies.

The interesting thing about the omission of direct hypnosis training courses in many schools is that they are teaching aspects of hypnosis indirectly anyway. Every psychotherapy involves influencing a troubled person in some way so the person may feel better. There are countless approaches for helping others to grow, adapt more successfully to the demands of life, or carry out whatever you think therapy should assist people to do. Each of them can show positive results, too (Hubble, Duncan, & Miller, 1999). What are the elements of each approach that influence the person seeking help to change? Whatever model for conceptualizing the human condition you might work from, clearly you are attempting to influence another human being's experience in a way that is beneficial. The way you do this, regardless of what you say or do (which is the difference in content from approach to approach), is through communication.

How do you know where to step in and offer help in a client's world? Only from the way the client communicates about his or her world can you come to know enough of it to discover where and how much to intervene. Only through the way you speak (including what you say and what you don't say) and move can you effect a change in another human being. The client seeking psychotherapy cannot *not* respond to your communications; the sophistication of a good therapist is getting the desired, therapeutic response.

Whatever therapies a clinical training program offers will indirectly include hypnosis because every therapy includes hypnosis (T. Barber, 1985). Even the classic hypnotic phenomena (such as age regression and dissociation) described in later chapters are evident in every therapy, but the concepts and uses for those phenomena are typically not taught. Why? Simply because these phenomena have other names and characterizations in other models of psychotherapy. For example, the father of modern cognitive therapy, psychiatrist Aaron Beck, M.D., claimed he does not do hypnosis (personal communication, December, 1990). But, he has no hesitations about encouraging his clients to close their eyes, relax, and focus on imagining themselves successfully carrying out some new behavior they're learning. He calls this a "success imagery." Structurally, however, he is doing an induction of focusing suggestions, he is orienting the person to the future, he is associating the person to new behaviors or thought patterns in some familiar context, and he is fostering a dissociation from old ineffective patterns. *That is hypnosis!* (For a detailed discussion of how hypnosis is evident in other therapies, especially cognitive therapy, see Yapko, 1992).

A willingness to develop many therapy skills based on a variety of perspectives assures a greater likelihood of success. All of the various therapeutic approaches work in a general sense (Miller, Duncan, & Hubble, 1997). The skill is in knowing what will work with *this* specific person.

Why use hypnosis to effect a dissociation and then look to unconscious resources for trying to help the client? It *is* a different way of doing therapy. But, the person seeking help has quite likely already tried to consciously change (perhaps through sheer willpower or by seeking greater self-understanding from reading self-help books) and failed to do so. The resources the person can get to consciously aren't the ones that have solved matters. In simpler terms, the perceptual frame the person has used to solve the problem hasn't been helpful; the solutions are more likely to be outside the person's usual experience of him- or herself. Hypnosis helps people "step outside" their usual experience of themselves, allowing new associations to be formed in their inner lives (whether on cognitive, emotional, behavioral, and/or physical levels). *Hypnosis by itself cures nothing. It's what happens during the hypnosis that has the potential to be helpful to people.*

Hypnosis in psychotherapy can be used in at least two general ways: (1) to suggest symptom relief; and, (2) to teach specific skills (e.g., cognitive, behavioral, relational) that can help someone better cope with and resolve ongoing issues and problems as well as deal with their presenting symptoms. How someone uses hypnosis clinically is a direct reflection of his or her own beliefs about what constitutes appropriate clinical practice.

Hypnosis that involves simply performing an induction procedure and then giving suggestions for symptom relief is the most superficial and least sophisticated use of hypnosis. (And, amazingly, it still helps a lot of people!) Telling someone in hypnosis that his or her anxiety will diminish a little each day so that by next week "you'll be fine," or telling someone who wants to feel better about him- or herself the old hypnotic suggestion, "Everyday in every way you are getting better and better," is an insult to the intelligence of a client, not to mention a bore to the clinician. This kind of hypnosis is used on a purely symptomatic basis, and is the kind of hypnosis almost all lay hypnotists practice and even many trained psychotherapists use. It can and will be effective with a certain percentage of people; of course, there are some people who will change when you look at them harshly and say in a stern voice, "Stop doing that!" simply because they are ready to change. Since a symptomatic approach can and does work with many people, it is a viable choice to use in some therapies. Be aware, though, that this is only a small fraction of the usefulness of hypnosis.

More complex and skilled applications of hypnosis involve the use of techniques aimed at resolution of deeper conflicts (resolving the symptoms as well) and teaching key skills that can be helpful in resolving current concerns and preventing future ones, if possible. This kind of clinical hypnosis involves more of an interactional approach and works more comprehensively on multiple dimensions of the individual. What that means exactly will become clear to you in later chapters when you learn about structuring therapies using hypnosis.

How you ultimately incorporate hypnosis into your practice is determined by the assumptions you make about people (Ritterman, 2001). A view of people that appreciates each person's uniqueness would preclude you from approaching each client in the same way. To diagnose and categorize, and then treat the category rather than the person in a "cookbook" manner is undesirable, in my view. Likewise, a view of people that assumes all people seeking help are "sick" and need to be made "well" would preclude you from making use of the wealth of their personal resources that would be available to another clinician who views people as uniquely special and potentially powerful in their ability to make use of their resources for growth.

Use of hypnosis in the context of psychotherapy is a potent means for facilitating the client's movement toward a more empowered and satisfying existence. Practice with hypnotic techniques will demonstrate to you repeatedly the diversity, creativity, and power of people. That is one last great reason for its use; you will grow a lot, too!

In whatever context you choose to apply hypnosis, you cannot help but notice that the increased flexibility and sensitivity you demonstrate toward others will receive an appreciative response.

For Discussion

1. Why do you think the mind-body relationship has been a divided one in Western society? What impact has this division had on people's attitude about health care?
2. What does "responsibility for one's health" mean? Do you agree or disagree with those who claim that all sickness is psychogenic? Why or why not? If you get a cold and people ask you, "Why do you let yourself get sick," how do you answer? Is it a reasonable question?
3. What ways can you think of to apply hypnosis in addition to those mentioned in this chapter? How might you encourage people working in that specific area to employ hypnotic methods?
4. Are there any contexts in which hypnosis should not be used? What is the basis for your response?
5. What are the implications of calling hypnosis a "tool" and not a "therapy"?

Things to Do

1. Review recent issues of the *American Journal of Clinical Hypnosis* and the *International Journal of Clinical and Experimental Hypnosis* in order to discover the many ways hypnotic patterns are clinically used. These journals are likely to be available at the nearest university library.
2. In your chosen field, what are the assumptions you find the most limiting? Make a list of what things are and are not possible in your field as a direct consequence of these assumptions. For example, psychoanalysis does not generally allow for a rapid cure. How do you overcome such limiting assumptions?
3. Visit a book or tape store that sells motivational tapes employing standardized hypnosis. How many different applications of hypnosis do you find? Ask the salespeople about these tapes and people's reactions to them. What impression do you form?

REFERENCES

Baker, S., & Boas, F. (1983). The partial reformulation of a traumatic memory of a dental phobia during trance: A case study. *International Journal of Clinical and Experimental Hypnosis, 31,* 14–18.

Barber, J. (1977). Rapid induction analgesia: A clinical report. *American Journal of Clinical Hypnosis, 19,* 138–49.

Barber, T. (1985). Hypnosuggestive procedures as catalysts for psychotherapies. In S. Lynn & J. Garske (Eds.), *Contemporary psychotherapies: Models and methods* (pp. 334–76). Columbus, OH: Merrill.

Barretta, N., & Barretta, P. (2001). Hypnosis: Adjunct to medical maneuvers. In B. Geary & J. Zeig (Eds.), *The handbook of Ericksonian psychotherapy* (pp. 281–90). Phoenix, AZ: The Milton H. Erickson Foundation Press.

Brown, D. (1992). Clinical hypnosis research since 1986. In E. Fromm & M. Nash (Eds.), *Contemporary hypnosis research* (pp. 427–58). New York: Guilford.

Brown, D., & Fromm, E. (1987). *Hypnosis and behavioral medicine.* Hillsdale, NJ: Erlbaum.

Chaves, J. (1993). Hypnosis in pain management. In J. Rhue, S. Lynn, & I. Kirsch (Eds.), *Handbook of clinical hypnosis* (pp. 511–32). Washington, D.C.: American Psychological Association.

Clarke, J., & Reynolds, P. (1991). Suggestive hypnotherapy for nocturnal bruxism: A pilot study. *American Journal of Clinical Hypnosis, 33*, 4, 248–53.

Dywan, J. (1988). The imagery factor in hypnotic hypermnesia. *International Journal of Clinical and Experimental Hypnosis, 36*, 312–26.

Erickson, M., & Rossi, E. (1979). *Hypnotherapy: An exploratory casebook.* New York: Irvington.

Finkelstein, S. (1991). Hypnotically assisted preparation of the anxious patient for medical and dental treatment. *American Journal of Clinical Hypnosis, 33*, 3, 187–91.

Gauld, A. (1992). *A history of hypnotism.* Cambridge, UK: Cambridge University Press.

Haley, J. (Ed.) (1967). *Advanced techniques of hypnosis and psychotherapy: Techniques of Milton H. Erickson, M.D.* New York: Grune & Stratton.

Harrington, A. (Ed.) (1997). *The placebo effect.* Cambridge, MA: Harvard University Press.

Hollander, H. (2001). Ericksonian approaches to psychosomatic conditions. In B. Geary & J. Zeig (Eds.), *The handbook of Ericksonian psychotherapy* (pp. 272–80). Phoenix, AZ: The Milton H. Erickson Foundation Press.

Holroyd, J. (1992). Hypnosis as a methodology in psychological research. In E. Fromm & M. Nash (Eds.), *Contemporary hypnosis research* (pp. 201–26). New York: Guilford.

Hubble, M., Duncan, B., & Miller, S. (1999). *The heart & soul of change: What works in therapy.* Washington, D.C.: American Psychological Association.

Kalt, H. (2000). Psychoneuroimmunology: An interpretation of experimental case study evidence towards a paradigm for predictable results. *American Journal of Clinical Hypnosis, 43*, 1, 41–52.

Kelly, M., McKinty, H., & Carr, R. (1988). Utilization of hypnosis to promote compliance with routine dental flossing. *American Journal of Clinical Hypnosis, 31*, 57–60.

Kirsch, I. (1985). Response expectancy as a determinant of experience and behavior. *American Psychologist, 40*, 1189–1202.

Kirsch, I. (1994). Clinical hypnosis as a nondeceptive placebo: Empirically derived techniques. *American Journal of Clinical Hypnosis, 37*, 95–106.

Kirsch, I. (2000). The response set theory of hypnosis. *American Journal of Clinical Hypnosis, 42*, 3–4, 274–93.

Kroger, W. (1977). *Clinical and experimental hypnosis in medicine, dentistry and psychology* (2nd edition). Philadelphia, PA: Lippincott.

Kropiunigg, U. (1993). Basics in psychoneuroimmunology. *Annals of Medicine, 25*, 5, 473–79.

Lankton, S. (1979). *Practical magic.* Cupertino, CA: Meta Publications.

Liggett, D. (2000). Enhancing imagery through hypnosis: A performance aid for athletes. *American Journal of Clinical Hypnosis, 43*, 2, 149–58.

Lynch, D. (1999). Empowering the patient: Hypnosis in the management of cancer, surgical disease, and chronic pain. *American Journal of Clinical Hypnosis, 42*, 122–31.

McConkey, K. (1992). The effects of hypnotic procedures on remembering: The experimental findings and their implications for forensic hypnosis. In E. Fromm & M. Nash (Eds.), *Contemporary hypnosis research* (pp. 405–26). New York: Guilford.

Miller, S., Duncan, B., & Hubble, M. (1997). *Escape from Babel: Toward a unifying language for psychotherapy practice.* New York: Norton.

Montgomery, G., DuHamel, K., & Redd, W. (2000). A meta-analysis of hypnotically induced analgesia: How effective is hypnosis? *International /Journal of Clinical and Experimental Hypnosis, 48*, 134–49.

Morgan, W. (1993). Hypnosis and sport psychology. In J. Rhue, S. Lynn, & I. Kirsch (Eds.), *Handbook of clinical hypnosis* (pp. 649–70). Washington, D.C.: American Psychological Association.

Newman, M. (1971). Hypnotic handling of the chronic bleeder in extraction: A case report. *American Journal of Clinical Hypnosis, 14*, 126–27.

Pinnell, C., & Covino, N. (2000). Empirical findings on the use of hypnosis in medicine: A critical review. *International Journal of Clinical and Experimental Hypnosis, 48*, 166–90.

Ritterman, M. (2001). The philosophical position of the Ericksonian psychotherapist. In B. Geary & J. Zeig (Eds.), *The handbook of Ericksonian psychotherapy* (pp. 187–92). Phoenix, AZ: The Milton H. Erickson Foundation Press.

Rossi, E. (2000). In search of a deep psychobiology of hypnosis: Visionary hypotheses for a new millennium. *American Journal of Clinical Hypnosis, 42*, 3–4, 178–207.

Scheflin, A. (1995). The current assaults on hypnosis and therapy. Canadian Society of Clinical Hypnosis, Alberta Division, *News & Views* (Fall/Winter).

Scheflin, A. (2001). Caveat therapist: Ethical and legal dangers in the use of Ericksonian techniques. In B. Geary & J. Zeig (Eds.), *The handbook of Ericksonian psychotherapy* (pp. 154–67). Phoenix, AZ: The Milton H. Erickson Foundation Press.

Scheflin, A., & Shapiro, J. (1989). *Trance on trial.* New York: Guilford.

Schoenberger, N. (2000). Research on hypnosis as an adjunct to cognitive-behavioral psychotherapy. *International Journal of Clinical and Experimental Hypnosis, 48*, 150–65.

Shames, V., & Bowers, P. (1992). Hypnosis and creativity. In E. Fromm & M. Nash (Eds.), *Contemporary hypnosis research* (pp. 334–63). New York: Guilford.

Sheehan, P. (1995). The effects of asking leading questions in hypnosis. In G. Burrows & R. Stanley (Eds.), *Contemporary international hypnosis* (pp. 55–62). Chichester, UK: Wiley.

Sheehan, P., & McConkey, K. (1993). Forensic hypnosis: The application of ethical guidelines. In J. Rhue, S. Lynn, & I. Kirsch (Eds.), *Handbook of clinical hypnosis* (pp. 719–38). Washington, D.C.: American Psychological Association.

Spiegel, D. (1993). Hypnosis in the treatment of posttraumatic stress disorders. In J. Rhue, S. Lynn, & I. Kirsch (Eds.), *Handbook of clinical hypnosis* (pp. 493–508). Washington, D.C.: American Psychological Association.

Stanton, H. (1993). Using hypnotherapy to overcome examination anxiety. *American Journal of Clinical Hypnosis, 35*, 3, 198–204.

Sylvester, S. (2001). A warrior's approach in dealing with chronic illness. In B. Geary &

J. Zeig (Eds.), *The handbook of Ericksonian psychotherapy* (pp. 263–71). Phoenix, AZ: The Milton H. Erickson Foundation Press.

Udolf, R. (1983). *Forensic hypnosis: Psychological and legal aspects.* Lexington, MA: Lexington.

Wark, D. (1996). Teaching college students better learning skills using self-hypnosis. *American Journal of Clinical Hypnosis, 38*, 4, 277–87.

Wickramasekera, I. (1998). Secrets kept from the mind but not the body or behaviors: The unsolved problems of identifying and treating somatization and psychophysiological disease. *Advances in Mind-Body Medicine, 14*, 281–98.

Wolf, T. (1986). Hypnosis and Ericksonian interventions with children in the elementary school. In M. Yapko (Ed.), *Hypnotic and strategic interventions: Principles and practice* (pp. 209–14). New York: Irvington.

Yapko, M. (1992). *Hypnosis and the treatment of depressions: Strategies for change.* New York: Brunner/Mazel.

Yapko, M. (2001). *Treating depression with hypnosis: Integrating cognitive-behavioral and strategic approaches.* Philadelphia, PA: Brunner/Routledge.

6

The Social Psychology
of Human Suggestibility

We live in a social world, a world populated with other people who have the potential to exert influence on us merely through the things they say and do, even if those things are not directed at us specifically. Haven't you been influenced by a movie you saw or a lecture you attended, nonspecific as it might have been to you as an anonymous member of the audience? Realistically, how can we *not* be influenced by others (Aronson, 1999)?

The responsiveness to suggestions, that is, direct and indirect messages imparting information and perspective, and the associated vulnerability to the influence of others (and to our self-suggestions as well) is the essence of human suggestibility. John Kihlstrom, Ph.D., is a prominent psychologist and hypnosis researcher at the University of California, Berkeley. An influential advocate for a cognitive-dissociative view of hypnosis, Kihlstrom defined hypnosis this way: "Hypnosis may be defined as a social interaction in which one person, designated the subject, responds to suggestions offered by another person, designated the hypnotist, for experiences involving alterations in perceptions, memory and voluntary action" (1985, p. 385). His definition of hypnosis is a general one that involves clear role definitions existing within a social framework from which the various alterations (i.e., hypnotic phenomena) and cognitive shifts are derived.

Kihlstrom's definition does not suggest a separate and discrete state of hypnosis, but rather a hypnosis that can be viewed within the larger context of social influence. Social-psychological theorists of hypnosis do not typically think of hypnosis as a state of experience that is distinct in its own right. Rather, they think of hypnosis as something better explained in terms of social principles of behavior that are found in many contexts, not just the hypnotic one (T. Barber, 1969, 2000; Spanos, 1991; Spanos & Coe, 1992; Wagstaff, 1991).

Is hypnosis the same as suggestibility? Can we accurately say that hypnosis increases suggestibility, and the evidence for hypnosis is an increase in suggestibility? The circular relationship between the phenomena of hypnosis and suggestibility is both apparent and confusing: Hypnosis occurs because people are suggestible, and people are suggestible because they're in hypnosis.

The relationship between suggestibility and the clinical benefits to be derived from hypnosis is an important domain of inquiry. Is suggestibility simply an individual personality trait that exists in stable form across different contexts? Or is it determined by additional factors beyond the person's capacity to respond to suggestion, such as the salience of a suggestion or the demeanor of the person who offers it?

My response to these important questions is *both*: Suggestibility *in a general sense* is a relatively stable quality of response over time (Piccione, Hilgard, & Zimbardo, 1989). And, in a particular context, such as a clinical interaction, suggestibility is mediated by a variety of personal, social, and situational factors that can serve to increase or decrease it in someone (T. Barber, 2000). The phenomenon of suggestibility will be explored in this chapter.

THE ILLUSION OF THE INVISIBLE CLINICIAN

Some clinicians are of the belief they can do therapy or do hypnosis without influencing the dynamics of the process. For example, they think they can hypnotically "dig" for memories without influencing the types of memories that emerge (Calof, 1993; Fredrickson, 1992), or they think they can be therapeutically neutral by refusing either to take sides with a family member or to offer a client direct advice (Rogers, 1986; Sanford, 1987). It is an illusion to believe you can be in a therapy relationship with someone yet not play a direct role in what happens in that relationship.

Hypnosis in the clinical context is invariably a directive approach, meaning it is purposefully applied with a therapeutic goal in mind. Influence is an overt goal, not a hidden agenda, which some clinicians may have difficulty with if they are of the belief that influencing clients is somehow either wrong or undesirable. To believe you can do therapy or hypnosis with a client—by definition an interpersonal process—yet only elicit the client's intrapersonal dynamics ignores the roles of the clinician and the social context in the process.

Similarly, as the trend continues in the field of psychotherapy to empirically validate treatments and even manualize them, the illusion persists that therapeutic effectiveness is entirely in the technique and not the relationship that provides the context for making the technique viable (Hubble, Duncan, & Miller, 1999). *When more than one person is in the room, social influence is inevitable.*

The field of social psychology in particular offers many valuable insights into the dynamics of interpersonal influence that are immediately relevant to the clinical context in general and to the use of hypnosis in particular. Social psychology as a field evolved out of the recognition that people will do things when they are alone that they will not do if even just one other person is around (Aronson, 1999). An individual's behavior changes in the presence of another individual, often in systematic and predictable ways. Social psychology's task as a field is to identify what kinds of interactions between people are likely to cause specific types of behavior, and has as its ultimate (and idealistic) goal the establishment of organizations and environments that will maximize positive behaviors in individuals (Bordens & Horowitz, 2002). Interpersonal influence has been studied in a variety of ways and contexts by social psychologists, yielding a substantial amount of information that is extremely valuable in describing many of the dimensions of the hypnotic relationship. Some of these are conscious, while many others are unconscious factors in the relationship. Knowledge of these factors may allow you a greater recognition of them when they arise in treatment, and a greater flexibility in deliberately applying them. Let's take a look at social influence in specific contexts.

THE INFLUENCE OF ADVERTISING

In America, many billions of dollars are spent yearly on advertising products and services. Does all that advertising really work? To the corporations who budget hundreds of millions or even billions of dollars annually for television commercials, radio and magazine ads, internet "pop-ups," and direct mail ads, the answer is clearly Yes! Advertisements come at us from all sides and we tend to absorb them whether we consciously realize it or not. Once absorbed, they can influence our buying habits. Why do you buy the products you buy when you shop? How do you choose one brand over another? Why are you likely to feel you are making a sacrifice if you buy the cheaper house brands or plain wrapped brands instead of the familiar name brand you really want (because of its perceived greater attractiveness) (Philipchalk & McConnell, 1994)?

Advertising as an industry makes great use of suggestive techniques to attempt to influence you to buy a product. How do advertisers do this? They typically begin by creating a need for a product (for many centuries, bad breath or body odor was not on the forefront of people's consciousness). Then they use techniques such as promoting an identification with the person in the ad so you'll realize you can solve your problem by using the product in the same way it was modeled for you. Finally, they strengthen your buying habit by rewarding you for having made such a fine choice, essentially telling you how enlightened you are and how much better your life will be for having the wisdom (or guts, or sex appeal, or some other trait) to choose their product. Ads try to generate feelings (e.g., pleasure) or other associations (e.g., scientific data confirming its superiority) that will be tied to the product that may induce you to purchase it instead of another brand (Pratkanis & Aronson, 1991). The field of advertising is obviously much more complex than this brief description may suggest, but the salient point here is that advertising uses words and images in a way that is intended to influence your buying behaviors and perhaps even your lifestyle. And it works! Can the field of hypnosis learn something from studying the dynamics of influence evident in advertising? Specifically, how does an image or idea translate into a change of behavior?

An ad may last only a matter of seconds, or perhaps as much as a minute on television (not counting the lengthier "infomercials" that can last up to half an hour!). Ad time typically costs a great deal of money, yet advertisers know most people don't pay much conscious attention to the commercial, their attention often drifting off to other places. Can the commercial still be influential even if it is not focused upon? Social psychological and cognitive research suggest messages may be absorbed at an unconscious level, where a feeling of recognition can be triggered when you see the product in the store, a phenomenon known as "priming" (Lynn & Sherman, 2000; Sherman, 1988). Social psychology has shown in many different studies that the more familiar an item is to us, the more positive regard we tend to have for it (familiarity is generally positive; for example, when you are in an unfamiliar location while traveling, and you become hungry, you may be relieved to see a familiar hamburger restaurant). Repetition and familiarity are positive means for getting messages across. In our conscious experience, repetition is often boring, but the unconscious mind seems to respond to it when the message isn't perceived as threatening (Aronson, 1999).

THERAPY, INFLUENCE, AND ADVERTISING

Every day, human beings are bombarded by hundreds, and by some researchers' estimates, thousands, of messages (Philipchalk & McConnell, 1994). Each message is, in a sense, an advertisement—some quite overt (such as television commercials), some less so (such as when your friends comment favorably on a particular restaurant). Each interaction you are involved in will influence your experience in some way, whether the interaction lasts only a moment or many hours. Can you think of any interaction in *any* context in which one person is not influencing another? Even in your own internal dialogue, is there anything significant you can say to yourself that *doesn't* affect you in some way?

Therapeutic intervention involves influencing other people sufficiently to alter their experience of themselves in a beneficial way. Therapy in any modality requires guiding the client from a state of distress and dissatisfaction with some portion of his or her experience to a new, more satisfying and effective way of living. Therapy encourages the development of a more adaptive means for coping with life circumstances, especially stressful ones. *Whatever* form therapy takes, from taking pills to recording and correcting dysfunctional thoughts, the client is learning to experience him- or herself in a new way, one that allows for greater flexibility, new possibilities, and inner satisfaction. How does a clinician do this? What is it a therapist says or does that influences the client in a beneficial way? Is this ability to influence someone positively a property of the clinician? Certainly the therapist's skill, demeanor, and knowledge are factors. Is the ability to be influenced a property of the client? Certainly a motivation to change and a willingness to experiment with new behaviors are factors. Is being a catalyst for change in the therapeutic context (or any other context, for that matter) an interaction of the two? The relationship between hypnotist and client (or you and your friend, or a barber and his customer, or a talk show guest and the audience) is one that involves the unique characteristics of each party relating to the other such that the whole is greater than the sum of the parts. The characteristics of each affect the other, and an outcome of some sort—a quality of relationship—is inevitable.

What is suggestibility in hypnosis? It is an openness to accepting new ideas, a willingness to absorb new information or perspectives. Furthermore, it is a focused capacity to translate ideas into suggested responses. As new information is acquired, depending on its subjective value, it can alter the person's experience anywhere from a little to a lot. In the therapeutic interaction, the person to be influenced (i.e., the client) is, to some unknown degree, suggestible and wants to acquire new information or experience that will reduce his or her distress. The person is unhappy with some aspect of him- or herself, and seeks help from an experienced clinician who might be able to say or do something to make a difference.

Few people are completely noncritical in accepting information, and so there is an important difference between suggestibility and gullibility (T. Barber, 1969). Suggestibility as a trait exists because each person recognizes that he or she is limited; after all, no one person knows all there is to know about everything. *No matter how knowledgeable you are in an area, your information remains incomplete.* When we brush up against those areas we recognize we know little about, we tend to become more suggestible to the influence of others we believe may know more.

THE NEED FOR CLARITY AND CERTAINTY

When people experience uncertainty, both social psychology and common sense have taught us that other people become very important as sources of information. The old saying, "When in Rome, do as the Romans do," reflects our reliance on other people's judgments and behaviors as models of what to do when faced with our uncertainty about what is proper. You can probably recall a situation you were in recently that was new to you, and how uncomfortable you felt because you really weren't sure whether you were doing things in the proper way. Pause for a moment and think about such a situation. How much did you rely on others to guide your behavior? Everyone has had an experience like that simply because it's an inevitable part of the socialization process. You may not have acted properly, but at least you're not alone!

The old *Candid Camera* television show played on the themes of uncertainty and conformity by deliberately confusing people and enjoying their confusion as they would try to figure things out, desperately trying to make sense out of an absurd situation. (For example, in one episode a "special" car rolls into a gas station, and the driver asks for service. Upon lifting the hood of the car, the attendant is astonished to discover the vehicle has no engine! The look of utter bewilderment on the attendant's face made for great television.) Typically, people's first response in the scenarios they found themselves in was to look for outside guidance, asking someone else to help them figure out what to do. Often the person they'd turn to was an accomplice to the hoax, further complicating things for the poor "victim."

The principle of increased conformity in the face of uncertainty is immediately relevant to the clinical context (Erickson, 1964). A clinician will have some potential influence arising from the client's perception that he or she is mismanaging some portion of his or her life. The problems are seemingly beyond control, and are a source of confusion and uncertainty as to what to do to solve them. Attempts at self-correction have failed, and so the person then seeks help from someone presumed to be more knowledgeable about solving the problem by virtue of having advanced clinical training. (Some people would rather talk to a hairdresser than a doctor, some would rather confide in a co-worker than a psychologist, and still others would rather write a letter to "Dear Abby" than talk directly to anyone at all. People may invest power in someone simply because they think, rightly or wrongly, the person is more knowledgeable than they are.)

If someone has attempted change and failed (who hasn't?), the suggestion may be accepted that one who is professionally trained in such matters will be able to help. The helping professional is perceived as an authority on a personal problem because he or she has been trained to recognize causes and administer treatments. The person seeking help has already accepted his own ignorance and powerlessness about the situation, and with a strong sense of hopefulness, looks to the therapist as the person who can make the hurt go away.

The quality of the relationship between the clinician and the client has been well established as a primary basis for the therapeutic experience in general and the hypnotic experience in particular. Every therapy I am aware of emphasizes the importance of the therapeutic alliance (Hubble, Duncan, & Miller, 1999). In the application of clinical hypnosis, the therapeutic alliance has the potential to be well defined when one develops a recognition of the factors that contribute to it. These are discussed throughout the remainder of this chapter.

CLINICIAN POWER

When someone comes in for help to deal with a distressing problem, that person is making an investment in the clinician as a person of authority and, hopefully, a source of relief. Power is not typically something the clinician simply has; rather, it is acquired from the client's reaction to him or her (Spinelli, 1994). Thus, power is a capacity and a potential, and not a personality trait. A clinician has the *potential* to be influential, but every clinician learns the hard way through unsuccessful cases that influence is hardly a given in doing therapy. How do some clients come to see the clinician as allpowerful and readily comply with his or her directives, while others successfully resist the influence of the clinician, even to their own detriment?

STANLEY MILGRAM AND OBEDIENCE TO AUTHORITY

A famous and highly controversial set of experiments on the dynamics of power were done by social psychologist Stanley Milgram (1974). These illustrated most dramatically how much power can be given to a person in a position of authority, and worked so well that seemingly normal people could be led to apparently inflict harm on others in the name of compliance.

Milgram devised a basic experiment which was eventually performed in a variety of ways (i.e., varying the proximity, location, etc.). It involved deceiving naïve experimental subjects, misleading them to believe they were involved in an experiment on learning. Directions were simultaneously given to the naïve subjects and to confederates (accomplices) of the experimenter (whom naïve subjects naturally assumed were also naïve subjects like themselves) indicating that the purpose of the study was to discover whether the use of punishment, in the form of electrical shocks, would increase a subject's ability to learn word pairs. Naïve subjects would be assigned the role of teachers, and confederates the role of learners. Teachers watched as the learners were strapped into a chair and hooked up to the shock-delivering electrodes. Teachers listened as the learner disclosed having a heart condition. Then they were placed in a nearby room and positioned in front of the shock generator. The shock generator was marked with specific escalating voltage levels (e.g., 15, 30, 45 volts, etc.), as well as qualitative descriptors (e.g., mild, moderate, severe, extreme shock). Teachers were then instructed to deliver to learners a shock of increasing intensity with each incorrect response.

Teachers were convinced that the learners were getting shocked by their action of pressing the button. As the shock levels escalated ever higher as the experiment progressed, the shrieks (e.g., "Owww!!") and pounding on the wall (e.g., "Let me out of here . . . my heart is starting to bother me!") coming from the learner's room seemed ample evidence that learners were truly being shocked at their initiation. In reality, however, the learners were not being shocked at all. Not knowing that, though, meant teachers had to determine for themselves how far they were willing to carry the experiment. Most subjects in the teacher position were very anxious and became reluctant to let the experiment progress, often turning to the experimenter for guidance and permission to end the experiment. The experimenter's job was simply to say, "You must go on. You have no choice but to continue. The experiment must go on."

More than 50% of the teachers delivered the highest possible shock level, past the point on the machine labeled, "Danger: Severe Shock" and past the point where the shrieking learner became eerily silent and may literally have been dead, for all the teacher knew. This dramatic experiment, one that could not be done by today's standards of research ethics, was based on the "obedience to authority" phenomenon evident in the Nuremberg War Crimes Trials following World War II. Many Nazis charged with exceptionally atrocious crimes claimed as a defense that, "I was just following orders." Milgram wanted to know whether this was a phenomenon unique to Nazis, or whether anyone might be induced to harm another person in the name of obeying an authority. The inescapable conclusion is troubling: People will go to great lengths to obey an authority they perceive as credible and/or if they see no choice other than to obey. If the person perceives that there are no viable alternatives, he or she will likely follow orders even if they are destructive ones. Some subjects in Milgram's experiment, when told "You have no choice . . . you must continue with the experiment," planted their arms firmly on their chests and said, "On the contrary, I have a lot of choice, and I refuse to continue." Such subjects were in the minority, however. Most people simply obeyed. The phenomenon of obedience to authority is observable in many routine contexts, including business ("Do this or you're fired"), education ("Do this or you'll be dropped from the program"), and even some intimate relationships ("Do this or I'll leave you"). Relationships are inevitably built on a markedly disproportionate balance of power, yet not everyone is willing to use power abusively to deliberately hurt others for personal gain. Those that are, though, can make our lives considerably more difficult.

The social psychological issue of obedience to authority has generated research into the question of whether hypnosis as a phenomenon exists or whether it is merely compliance with the hypnotist's suggestions. Lynn & Sherman addressed this issue directly and clearly when they said, "Of course if hypnosis were nothing more than compliance or faking it would be of little interest to anyone. However, hypnosis is interesting to sociocognitive theorists precisely because of the 'believed in' subjective alterations it evokes (2000, p. 296)." As Nicholas Spanos, Ph.D., a leading hypnosis researcher on the issue concluded from the research, ". . . the available data also suggest that compliance, in and of itself, cannot account adequately for hypnotic behavior (1991, p. 336)." The wary clinician should appreciate that compliance is a factor in treatment, with or without hypnosis, and the demands made on the client must therefore be chosen with care. Beyond compliance, though, hypnosis engenders a responsiveness that is special and worthy of additional consideration in its use.

POWER AND THE CLINICIAN

Where does the power of a clinician (or a researcher like Milgram) come from? The status of the therapist is one key factor, and his or her perceived expertness is another. Probably the greatest capacity for power, however, comes from the social role the therapist is in; the clinician-client relationship is generally not, and usually never is, one of equals (Spinelli, 1994; Szasz, 1978). The person coming in for help must divulge personal and sensitive information to a person about whom he or she knows very little—only his or her professional status, and, for the more inquisitive, academic background and clinical training.

The client is in a position of revealing his or her problems, inadequacies, and fears to a person who seems to be going through life successfully and relatively carefree for the most part. This is more or less true depending on the amount of self-disclosure an individual clinician feels comfortable in making. Sometimes too much self-disclosure can hurt the relationship, other times not enough can be detrimental. Regardless, the relationship is characterized by the clinician being the expert, the authority, and a client's uncertainty about how to solve a problem or an inability to detect personal choices can easily induce obedience to the authority of the clinician. Consider how extreme some forms of treatment are, and even many that are just silly, yet how willingly people comply with what they are told by the "expert" to do.

There are at least five different types of power: (1) coercive (derived from the ability to punish); (2) reward (derived from the ability to give benefits ranging from monetary to psychological); (3) legitimate (derived from position, including elected and selected positions); (4) expert (derived from greater knowledge in an area); and, (5) referent power (derived from personal characteristics, such as likeability or charisma). All five of these powers may be operational in almost any context to one degree or another, but they are especially prevalent in the therapeutic context.

The role of a clinician can be a powerful one in the therapeutic relationship. The capacity for influence in using principles and techniques of clinical hypnosis must lead each one of us to consider the phenomenon of power in relationships if we are to use power sensitively for the benefit of the client. Those who deny their power to influence and see themselves as separate from the client's treatment process are at the highest risk for being oblivious to their impact. As you will discover, this point became especially critical in the acrimonious debate over the repressed memory controversy which peaked in the middle of the last decade. Many therapists simply didn't grasp that they played a role in the type and quality of memories that emerged from their digging.

THE NEED FOR ACCEPTANCE

A person seeking professional help, or even just some information, is typically feeling deficient or incomplete in some way. A basic need people seem to have, which is the foundation of any society, is other people. When you combine a feeling of deficiency with a need for others, the drive for acceptance begins to emerge. Acceptance is something we all want in varying degrees. Is there anyone who is truly indifferent to the reactions of others? Or anyone who genuinely *likes* rejection? How far are *you* willing to go to get the approval of others who are important to you?

One of the fears often in the mind of clients coming in for help is, "If I open myself up to you, and let you see all my fears, doubts, quirks, and imperfections, will you like me and accept me? Or will you find me weak, repulsive, and reject me?" The potential for acceptance or rejection by the clinician is a risk the client takes in seeking help, and in light of all the evidence for the potential power of the therapeutic alliance, it is a legitimate concern (Rogers, 1963). Recognizing and respecting the client's need for acceptance is an important factor to consider in addressing the issues of whether and how the client conforms to the demands of clinical intervention. How far is *your client* willing to go to get *your* approval?

SOLOMON ASCH AND CONFORMITY

Among the most well-known studies in the literature of social psychology is the classic work of Solomon Asch on conformity (1951, 1955, 1956). Asch designed numerous studies to determine how others might influence us in terms of our perceptions, decisions, and attitudes. In a famous one, Asch brought in three confederates to interact with a lone naïve subject for an experiment on perception, or so the naïve subject was told. In reality, the experiment was one studying the dynamics of conformity, defined as a person changing behaviors, beliefs, or attitudes in the direction of others around him or her.

Asch presented to the group a series of different sized lines, labeled lines A, B, and C, and a fourth line, X. The task of the group members seemed a simple one: They were to identify which one of lines A, B, and C was closest in size to line X. The discrimination task was an easy one since the lines were generally of distinctly different sizes. The first few rounds, by design, found all four subjects in total agreement with each other. In later rounds, though, the confederates had been given instructions to give an obviously incorrect answer. To the naïve subject, the three other people in the group were generating a seemingly incorrect answer, but they were unanimous and their previous judgments had been just fine. This unexpected wrinkle generated a great deal of uncertainty and anxiety in the naïve subjects. The typical naïve subject was so confused that when the other three subjects all agreed on an answer that seemed wrong, the subject conformed and also gave that incorrect answer! Follow-up revealed that privately the person's perceptions hadn't actually changed. He or she simply conformed to the group.

Why would experimental subjects express obviously incorrect opinions as their own in the group context? Through earlier trials of total agreement, a group identity had formed, a group belongingness and even an interdependence. "Belonging" meets a basic need of people. To openly disagree and act as a nonconformist, effectively cutting oneself off from the others, was too uncomfortable a prospect for many of Asch's subjects to bear. People want the emotional and other intangible benefits of being enough like others to have a sense of belonging. A basic principle guiding relationships according to the literature of social psychology, and verifiable in your own experience, is that similarity is rewarding, dissimilarity is punishing.

The need for acceptance and the need to belong are also factors present in the hypnotic relationship. Avoiding confrontations with the authority, doing things to please him or her (ranging from generating therapeutic results to knitting a sweater for him or her), and conforming to his or her language style, values, and theoretical ideas are all ways this need can be discovered within the therapy relationship. Relative to the above discussion on power, this is where a clinician's reward power can become a considerable force in the treatment process.

Spanos, Flynn, & Gabora (1989) conducted an experiment involving hypnosis which closely paralleled Asch's conformity experiments. They gave 45 highly hypnotizable hypnotic subjects a suggestion that when they opened their eyes during hypnosis they would see a blank piece of paper. In fact, the paper shown them had a number 8 drawn on it that was large and clearly visible. Fifteen of the 45, a full third of them, stated repeatedly the paper was blank. After the hypnosis was ended and another experimenter professing neutrality about their experience questioned them about what they "really" saw, and asked them to draw what they had seen. Fourteen of the 15 who originally claimed the paper was blank drew a number 8. There is clearly a difference between what people may claim to experience versus what they *actually* experience. No clinical context can fully avoid what are known as the "demand characteristics" of treatment, but an aware clinician can strive to foster less compliance and more internalization on the part of the client.

EXPECTATIONS

The effects of our expectations on our experience can be profound. The power of expectation has been demonstrated in numerous places and called by many names, and virtually all models of psychotherapy emphasize the value of positive expectations in enhancing treatment results (Kirsch, 1990; Lynn & Garske, 1985). Probably the most widely used term is "self-fulfilling prophecy," describing how our behavior is unconsciously aligned with our expectations, whether good or bad, increasing the likelihood of their eventual fulfillment.

When someone comes in for help, or for information, typically that person has an expectation of how things are going to turn out. The more emotional investment the person has in that expectation, the less likely he or she is to experience anything that contradicts it. For example, if someone has the idea that a problem he or she is trying to solve is hopeless or unsolvable, then potential solutions people might offer him or her go untried. This causes the problem to remain unsolved, and reaffirms the "correctness" of his or her view that it is unsolvable. In another example, if someone has the self-flattering idea that he or she is a wonderful person whom everyone sees as kind and sensitive, and someone comes along and tells him or her that he or she did something really mean, he or she might dismiss it as evidence of envy, reaffirming to him- or herself that he or she really is kind and sensitive. This circular kind of process is called a "calibrated cycle" in the world of systems theory, and essentially it describes a mechanism whereby people can work very hard at staying the same, whether the effect is to maintain a good or poor self-image.

Expectations can either work for or against the attainment of desired outcomes, depending on their positive or negative quality. In the course of clinical practice, people may specifically seek you out because they have been referred to you by someone else you impressed, increasing the odds of your being able to impress that person, too. Or, the person has a positive expectation because of your affiliation with an institution he or she holds in high esteem, or because of your title and status, or for any of dozens of possible reasons. Unfortunately, people can have negative expectations for equally arbitrary reasons: They don't like your gender, your age, your walk, the institution you work for, the length of time they had to wait to see you, and on and on. Addressing the issue of expectations—both yours and the client's—makes good clinical sense.

Some of the older hypnosis rituals aim to build positive expectations in the client that he or she can have, or already is having, the experience of hypnosis. Some of the tests associated with various susceptibility measures discussed earlier are included solely to convince the test subject that he or she has experienced some altered state. For example, when a subject is given suggestions for being unable to open his or her eyes (called "eye catalepsy") and then is challenged to do so, if he or she passes that test by being unable to open his or her eyes, then he or she is better convinced of being in hypnosis. This may create an expectation of benefit from hypnosis and foster greater receptivity to further suggestions of the hypnotist.

Many of the things that are considered basic to a professional practice are intended to build positive expectations on the part of the client. Why hang your diplomas on a wall? Why print business cards with a fancy title? Why adopt a professional demeanor, other than to instill confidence your client? My work with depressed clients in particular, people who suffer hopelessness and despair and thus have only negative expectations, has taught me how vitally important positive expectations are for eventual recovery. The clinical challenge is to build hopefulness out of hopelessness, and I have described some ways of doing that hypnotically elsewhere (Yapko, 1992, 2001). Suffice it to say here that helping clients co-create a compelling vision of what's possible in their lives is one of the most important things that can happen in therapy.

Psychologist Irving Kirsch, Ph.D., of the University of Connecticut has been an especially vocal proponent of a view of hypnosis that claims hypnosis is *mostly* about expectancy (1990, 1991, 1994, 1997). He said, "expectancy is an essential aspect of hypnosis, perhaps its most essential aspect" (1990, p. 143). His research has been quite compelling in demonstrating how hypnotic responses are influenced by the clients' beliefs and expectations. Thus, for the client, a good hypnotic induction is one that the client believes is a good one, and a good hypnotic experience is one that fits with what the client believes one to be (Kirsch, 1990). Kirsch's recommendation that clinicians need to present convincing reasons for introducing hypnosis into the therapy and in ways that fit with the client's needs and beliefs is sound advice (1994).

What it takes to build positive expectations for treatment in a person varies from individual to individual. Skillfully finding out what a person needs in order to build positive expectations can be a major catalyst to getting hypnosis and the therapeutic process going in a helpful direction. (Continued on page 142)

FRAME OF REFERENCE: THEODORE X. BARBER, PH.D.

Theodore Xenophon Barber, Ph.D. (1927–) has had a remarkable professional career, having been continuously involved with practicing and researching hypnosis since his early training in the 1950s as a stage hypnotist. He had first been drawn to hypnosis as a graduate student, crediting the work of Dr. A. A. Mason from a case study published in the *British Medical Journal* involving the use of hypnosis to help improve an intractable skin condition in a 16-year-old boy. It catalyzed his lifelong fascination with hypnosis, the mind-body relationship, and how suggestions translate into multi-dimensional responses.

By the early 1960s, research publications bearing the name of T. X. Barber became both frequent and highly influential. Dr. Barber posed an immediate intellectual challenge to the field of hypnosis that simply could not be ignored. His experience as a stage hypnotist and his early experiments had made it clear to him that the notion of some vaguely defined and esoteric phenomenon called "trance" was an unnecessary creation in order to explain hypnotic behavior. Instead, Dr. Barber proposed that the phenomenon of hypnosis was best understood in social terms, a concept well ahead of its time. While others at the time were heavily invested in the notion of a special state of consciousness, Dr. Barber was conducting research which illustrated his key point: When the setting was appropriate, and subjects were motivated to carry out the suggested task, their responses were not significantly different from those who had gone through the rituals of hypnosis. His view of hypnosis as grounded in social phenomena has only grown stronger over time. In an exceptionally detailed and clear exposition of his research findings and their implications which he published in the *American Journal of Clinical Hypnosis* in January 2000,

Dr. Barber said: "We can view hypnosis in its broader context, as a social phenomenon par excellence, when we see how much of it is explained by basic principles of the social sciences which have been thoroughly documented by several generations of cultural anthropologists, sociologists, and social psychologists" (p. 232).

Dr. Barber's clinical experience has been almost as varied as his research interests. He has worked with hypnosis in the psychiatric setting with patients considered seriously disturbed; he has worked with elderly patients in a geriatric facility; and he has employed hypnosis in the course of private practice. Dr. Barber's research interests have included the relationships between personality and hypnotizability (especially emphasizing the responsiveness of fantasy prone and amnesia-prone individuals), hypnosis and altered states of consciousness, hypnosis and learning, hypnosis and human potential, hypnosis and healing, and hypnosis and almost *everything*! His interests are exceptionally varied, and have led to writings on unexpected topics, including his observations about animal intelligence which he addressed in a provocatively titled book called *The Human Nature of Birds*. He has authored dozens of significant articles and book chapters on hypnosis, and several classic books in the field, including *Advances in Altered States of Consciousness and Human Potentialities* (1980); *Hypnosis, Imagination and Human Potentialities* (with Nicholas Spanos and John Chaves, 1974); and his landmark work, *Hypnosis: A Scientific Approach* (originally published in 1969 and reprinted in 1995).

Dr. Barber is a past president of the American Psychological Association's Division 30, now called the Society of Psychological Hypnosis, having served from 1971 to 1972. During his career in Massachusetts, he has been associated with Harvard and Boston Universities, Medfield (State) Hospital, and Cushing (Geriatric) Hospital, and is now at the Research Institute for Interdisciplinary Science in Ashland, Massachusetts. Dr. Barber's work has been and continues to be a major influence on my thinking about and practice of hypnosis despite our never (yet) having met in person.

On His Early Academic Training: "My first undergraduate major, focusing on the great philosophers, stimulated my interest in such questions as, What is the nature and essence of reality—Life and Death, Mind and Matter, God and the Universe? I then went on to a second undergraduate career concentrating on the "hard" sciences, especially the vast realms of biology. These studies led me to conclude that serious work on basic questions, especially those pertaining to mentality, consciousness, and the mind-body problem, required a deeper understanding of psychology."**

On His Hypnosis Training: "While working on the Ph.D. in psychology, I read widely in the fascinating history of hypnotism, and I realized that hypnosis was a "royal road" for attacking fundamental questions by scientific methods. Since academic and professional training in hypnosis was not available in those years, I studied with a stage hypnotist and I used this training to help earn a living while in graduate school. After carrying out a series of experiments on hypnosis as part of my doctoral dissertation at American University and post-doctoral research work at Harvard, I was fortunate to receive continuous research grants from the National Institutes of Health which enabled me to investigate hypnosis and its ramifications intensively over several decades."**

On Effective Hypnosis *without* a Formal Induction: "With or without a preceding hypnotic procedure, experimental subjects obtain relatively high scores on hypnotic susceptibility or suggestibility scales (which include tests for arm levitation, arm rigidity, analgesia, age regression, sensory hallucination, post-experimental behavior and amnesia) when they have positive attitudes toward the hypnotic or suggestive situation, positive motivations to experience hypnosis (or the suggested effects), and positive expectancies that they can experience what is suggested. These positively set subjects experience a variety of suggested effects (of the type associated with hypnosis) because they think and imagine along with the suggestions while letting go of interfering thoughts."*

On Situational Factors and Hypnosis: "The extent to which subjects experience suggested effects varies with a series of situational factors. These include a variety of social factors such as social demands, roles, and expectations that obligate socialized individuals to cooperate and comply. They also include: the experimenter's or hypnotist's characteristics and skills (such as communicative abilities, creative ideas, and ability to bond with the subject); the effectiveness of the preliminary procedures or hypnotic induction procedures in guiding the subject to think and imagine with the suggestions; and the suggested ideas themselves—their depth of meaning, their creativity, and their potency for the particular subject."*

On Exceptional "Fantasy Prone" Hypnotic Subjects: "A small proportion of the experimental subjects have unusual life histories and personality characteristics that predispose them to respond easily and dramatically to hypnotic procedures and suggestions. We called one group, comprising less than 4% of our subjects, "fantasy prone" individuals because of their unique life histories. During childhood, each spent an incredibly large proportion of time in fantasy-based activities such as pretend-play, make-believe, imagining companions, vivid daydreaming, and imaginative reliving of pleasurable sexual experiences. As adults, they secretly continue to spend much of their time fantasizing, and they typically insist they see, hear, feel, and experience what they fantasize. In hypnosis experiments they use their well-developed talent for vivid, realistic fantasy to perceive and interact in a profoundly realistic way with the suggested (hallucinatory) object, to experience vivid age regression (as they supplement their early memories with their fantasies of the suggested earlier time), to experience analgesia by deliberately fantasizing they are in a different situation (without the pain stimulus), and so on."*

On Exceptional "Amnesia Prone" Hypnotic Subjects: "The second group of exceptionally responsive subjects, who we labeled as "amnesia prone," comprise about 1% of a student sample. They are characterized by the many kinds of amnesias they have experienced in their lives, typically including amnesia for virtually all of their childhood, amnesia for other scattered periods in their lives, "lapses" or micro-amnesias in their daily lives, and amnesia for their dreams. In hypnotic situations they typically respond like deep trance subjects or somnambules, manifesting a sleep-like appearance, passivity, automatic-like responsiveness to suggestions, and convincing post-hypnotic amnesia. Both their trance-like hypnotic behavior and their various amnesias are related to childhood physical, psychological, and, often, sexual abuse during which they learned to "blank out" or enter an "away" state, and to mentally compartmentalize (or repress, dissociate, or forget) particular stimuli or events."*

On His Varied Experiences Informing His Views: "Our experimental research played the biggest role (in shaping my views). However, my clinical work using hypnotic procedures in therapy, in which I became well-acquainted with the life experiences of a substantial number of subjects, was important in delineating the "fantasy prone" and "amnesia prone" subjects. Experience in stage hypnosis contributed to the conclusion that social situational variables, such as high expectancy, together with careful selection of highly responsive subjects and forceful suggestions is all that is needed to present a dramatic stage demonstration. My experience in self-hypnosis buttressed the conclusion that subjects with positive attitudes, motivations, and expectancies toward the suggested situation can experience a wide variety of suggested effects."*

On His Most Pleasant Surprise in His Work with Hypnosis: "I was pleasantly surprised to realize that our research on producing physiological or bodily changes by suggestions (for example, successfully suggesting that localized warts would disappear) indicated a new and exciting solution to the mind-body problem. In brief, the ability to produce precise, localized changes in the body by words or suggestions indicate that nerve cells literally communicate precise messages to other cells in the body which understand and implement the suggestions carried by the meaningful messages. The indication that cells literally communicate precisely and *understand* the meaning of the communications, in turn, indicated that cells (and the organisms they constitute) are *physicalmental* entities or *bodyminds*. The mind-body problem disappears (or is solved) when cells and organisms are seen to be mentalized matter or embodied minds."*

On His Personal Interests: "Like most people, I enjoy my family and friends. I also enjoy the rain and the sun and the beautiful, boundless Earth. My unique "hobby" goes back to that part of my childhood that took place on a Greek island, when I learned to relate "person-to-person" with the ubiquitous animals (donkeys, pigs, sheep, goats, squirrels, birds, and even ants) and to appreciate the trees and wild plants and the magic of crops rising from the Earth. Thus, my unique present-day pleasure, which began in childhood and was greatly amplified and conceptualized by immersion in the literature on animal behavior, consists of literally interacting and communicating (in a "shockingly" intimate way) with the animals in my surroundings. A related pleasure is documenting with numerous studies that have been buried in the literature, the (scientifically-tabooed) human-like intelligence of animals, which I began in a book published in the 90's and which I expand in a book I am writing now."**

Sources: *Personal communication, October 10, 2002*
Personal communication, November 13, 2002

THE NEED FOR INTERNAL HARMONY

Often when I flip through magazines, I am astonished by the claims made by many advertised products. There are weight loss products that guarantee this product is so good that you can lose weight just by looking at it (only a slight exaggeration); there are books for sale that assure you of being able to acquire the dynamic personality that will get you into the most elite social circles; there are products that promise to clear up your skin, grow hair in your bald spots, cure your arthritis, make you a multimillionaire, turn your house into a showcase, give you "washboard abs" in just a few weeks, and so on. . . .

Who buys these things? Who are the people in those pesky infomercials and magazine ads who enthusiastically describe how this product essentially gave them a reason to go on living? This is a modern version of an old theme. Now the "medicine show" testimonials are filmed in front of an enthusiastic studio audience, or put in print as a part of the advertisement, to show you, the skeptical buyer, that real people, not unlike yourself, have purchased this product and experienced a desperately wanted magical transformation as a direct result. One hundred fifty years ago, the medicine show was a con man traveling in a covered wagon from town to town, with a confederate (or two) sent in advance, who would publicly purchase a bottle of the "Doc Marvel Health Tonic" and instantly experience relief from every known ailment. Others wanting similar relief would purchase the tonic, earning the con man a nice profit. Mysteriously, though, some of them would feel better, too.

Certainly, the person's positive expectation, a placebo effect, is at work in such instances. But there is also another factor to consider operating here: the need for internal consistency, or harmony, based on Leon Festinger's classic "cognitive dissonance" concept (1957). People need to maintain their sense of themselves and part of how we do that is by striving to alleviate confusion and contradictions within ourselves. So we may omit contradictory bits of information, or we may twist (i.e., distort) such information around until it all fits within us comfortably.

Consider the issue of control from a different angle than that described earlier as an example. If I want to feel in control of myself, how can I comply with your demands without feeling like I'm losing control of myself? Social psychological research has shown repeatedly that, like clients in psychotherapy, research subjects in experiments perform far less well when they are aware of the induction of change, the goals of the situation, and the techniques of influence that are being used (Sherman & Lynn, 1990; Lynn & Sherman, 2000). Imagine Stanley Milgram or Solomon Asch informing research subjects "We're testing how obedient to authority you are" or "We're testing how likely to conform to others' incorrect judgments you are." Indirection and even deception were used to elicit spontaneous behavior, and research subjects had to find ways within themselves to feel okay about themselves even while doing things that probably didn't feel very good. People are generally quite adept at finding ways to make disparate pieces of experience fit together. But, the larger point here concerns appreciating many clients' resistance to what they may perceive as overt manipulation. Without a sense of control, people can feel helpless, and so they may wishfully even perceive control where they have none, developing an "illusion of control." Effective use of hypnosis has to consider ways to reinforce peoples' sense of control yet paradoxically encourage them to step outside their "comfort zone" in order to do something differently.

People have a strong desire to feel certain, and when in an uncertain frame of mind, perhaps because of the novelty of the situation they're in, they will often turn to others to find out what to think. The more the explanation provided them fits their personal needs, the more easily the explanation is taken in at a deeper level. Thus, much of what we come to believe is less about "truth" and is more about what's personally desirable or believable.

In an illustrative piece of research by Schachter and Singer (1962), the point about uncertainty and turning to others to explain one's feelings is made clear. If you are chased by a bear and you experience a rapid pulse and heart rate, you can easily attribute the changes to fear. What if you were to experience those same physiological changes, but have no apparent explanation for why? Schachter and Singer's experiment involved injecting subjects either with epinephrine, a synthetic form of adrenaline causing physiological excitation, or with a placebo. Subjects were told they were receiving a vitamin supplement. Some of the subjects were told they would experience an increased heart rate as a side effect of the drug, but other subjects were not similarly informed. For those subjects who were not told of the side effects of the epinephrine, what were they to conclude when their hearts started to pound in their chests and their hands began to shake? Because they did not know what to make of it, they typically incorporated within themselves the reactions of those around them.

Confederates of the experimenters were introduced into the experiment, and research subjects were told that this subject, like them, was also given an injection of the vitamin supplement. The confederate had been given instructions on how to behave. In some instances, he or she was to act as if euphoric, in others he or she was to act angry. Experimental subjects, uncertain as to the cause of their physical reactions, generally behaved in the same manner as the confederate. Maslach (1979) failed to replicate Schachter and Singer's study, yet their study continues to be cited as illustrative of the principle of conformity in the face of ambiguity (Bordens & Horowitz, 2002).

When subjects were certain as to the cause of their reactions, the behavior of those nearby had little or no effect on them. When they were uncertain, though, others' reactions had considerable impact on them. This research further illustrates how the ambiguity of subjects' feelings led them to conform to others' perspectives. The need to make sense of our own reactions is an important part of developing self-awareness and being mentally healthy. But the influence of others clearly affects even the meanings we attach to our own internal experiences. What does this suggest to you about the potential vulnerabilities of our clients to the interpretations we make about the meaning of their experiences?

The experience of hypnosis is a highly subjective, often ambiguous, one that frequently leads clients to open their eyes after your hypnosis session and ask, "Was that hypnosis? Was I hypnotized?" If you choose to answer directly by saying "Yes, that was hypnosis" and then offering what sounds to the client like specific indicators such as, "Did you notice the changes in your breathing? And the changes in your musculature? And how relaxed you felt? . . . ," then quite probably the client will adopt your apparently expert perspective of the ambiguous interaction as if it were his or her own. The need for certainty and the need to have a perceptual frame into which the experience can be integrated may motivate the person to simply accept your explanation of the hypnotic experience.

The need for cognitive consistency sometimes shows up in funny ways that highlight peoples' often quirky natures. In one now classic study, researchers investigated an experimental confederate's ability to cut in front of a long line of people waiting their turns to use a copy machine (Langer, Blank, & Chanowitz, 1978). When the confederate simply asked people in line for permission to cut in front, compliance was only about 60%. (Aren't people nice?) When the confederate wanted to cut in front of the others but offered a meaningful reason, e.g., "I have an important meeting and I'm running late," the rate of compliance rose to 94%. But, when the confederate asked to cut in line and also offered a reason, but a totally uninformative one stating, "Because I have to make some copies," the rate of compliance was 93%! As Lynn and Sherman concluded (2000, p. 306), "The presence of a request plus a reason seems to automatically trigger a compliance response . . ." Do you have a reason to suggest hypnosis to your client, and how good a reason do you have for wanting to do hypnosis?

The need for cognitive consistency surfaces in yet another way as a need, more or less depending on the individual, to derive at least *some* benefit from having received professional help. When people invest money, hope, and time in something, they usually genuinely want it to work, even if "only a little." There is the need to justify the investment to themselves. This need increases with the amount of effort they have put into the treatment process. It's why many clinicians are quite forceful in their requirement that the client be a proactive and collaborative partner in the treatment process from the earliest stages of the therapy. "Behavioral activation," as it may be called (Martell, Addis, & Jacobson, 2001), is a vital force in not only empowering clients, but getting them positively invested in the treatment. And it's based on people's need to believe hard effort and personal (including financial) investment is only justified by success. This same need is evident in the testimonials of people who have bought products that are virtually valueless, whose benefit was derived solely from their own wishful expectations.

There can be a negative side to the role of expectation and the need for cognitive consistency. Consider the person who views him- or herself as a hopeless case, and then goes to great lengths to prove it. Some people, like the ones described earlier who go on stage to prove they cannot be "hypnotically controlled," have a need to prove their commitment to failure. It's a strange psychology, but unfortunately not a rare one, when success is determined by how much you fail. The patient who has been to every doctor in town and is inexplicably proud of his or her inability to be helped is a perfect example; the client who spends fruitless years in psychotherapy going from therapist to therapist is another.

Testimonials in ads for junk products are sometimes a deceptive ploy, made up by the advertiser. Often, however, they are the true feelings of consumers who attributed great power to a useless product. After all, they watched the whole infomercial twice, called within the time frame to get their "bonus gift," and they paid their $29.95, plus tax. And shipping and handling.

COMMUNICATION STYLE

Your style of communication is another significant factor shaping the quality of your client's suggestibility. By communication style, I refer to the manner with which you convey information and communicate possibilities to your client. There are many different styles, each having a different range and quality of impact on how receptive the client will be to the information and perspectives you present (T. Barber, 2000; J. Barber, 1991; Zeig, 2001).

If a clinician wants to get a message across to a client, he or she must consider what style of communication this person is most likely to respond to in the desired way. Should the interaction be one of rationality and reason, or would an emotional appeal perhaps work better? Should the techniques used be direct or indirect? Should the position adopted be a supportive one, or a confrontive one? Would it be better to be demanding of this person, or nondemanding? Will an incongruent message ("mixed message") have greater impact, or a congruent one? The structures and styles of hypnotic suggestions will be dealt with in great detail later; suffice it to say here that there are many ways to package ideas, and no single style is going to be effective with everyone. Suggestibility is a general human trait, but what a specific individual requires in order to respond well can vary dramatically.

CONCLUSION

Special attention has been paid throughout this chapter to developing an appreciation for the social psychology of hypnosis, examining how people's social nature has the potential to empower and disempower them. Directly and indirectly, I have addressed such fundamental topics as beliefs, expectations, attitudes, conformity, obedience, self-justification, and compliance. If you read this chapter carefully, you may have discovered that hypnosis in the clinical context might best be understood and perhaps most sensitively applied with an appreciation for your power to influence your clients. The challenge is how to do that in the most effective and respectful ways possible.

Each of the factors of human suggestibility discussed in this chapter is important to consider in striving to understand what makes for good therapy as well as good hypnosis. There are no established rules about what makes for the most influential communication or the best hypnosis. What appeals to one person will not appeal to another. Some people appreciate and seek out professional help when distressed, while others would rather keep their problems to themselves or seek out the advice of a friendly neighbor. Some people want to be told exactly what to do in a rigid step-by-step fashion and follow such directions happily, while others fight against such explicit directions, perhaps seeing them as attempts to dominate them, and so prefer to be left alone to figure things out for themselves. Some people respond better if they have to go through rigorous demands to reach a goal (e.g., a therapist with a long waiting list is a frustration to such a new client who may perceive that therapist as better than he otherwise would have when he finally does get to see him or her), while others won't even consider putting up with such demands (if faced with a long waiting list they'll just go see another therapist). Some require scientific evidence for backing up almost everything you say, while others are suspicious of science and of those who promote it. Some people open up to the ideas of others when they're confused, while others close off and try to resolve the confusion within themselves, even if they do so with misinformation.

In order to be truly effective in doing hypnosis, the task of the clinician is to discover under what conditions, both internal and external, a person is most receptive to new information and suggested perspectives. The innate suggestibility of each individual, to one degree or another in one context or another, makes change possible and allows growth to take place. The process of discovering what your client wants and how to best reach him or her is the process of building the therapeutic alliance, the relationship between you that serves as the foundation for the techniques you eventually introduce him or her to in your interventions (T. Barber, 2000; Geary, 2001).

For Discussion

1. What commercials seem to have the most impact on your buying behavior? What can you identify about them that makes them so influential?
2. What products or services do you feel almost entirely ignorant about (for example, car repairs, dental work, etc.)? How does ignorance about these things affect your role as a consumer?
3. Do you think Milgram's experiment on "Obedience to Authority" would have the same results today? Why or why not?
4. Describe an example or two of times when you gave in to peer group pressure. How did you feel? What penalties did you think you'd face by not conforming? Did you have control of yourself?
5. Describe an example or two in which you obeyed an authority when you thought he or she was wrong in demanding what was asked of you. Why did you obey? How did you feel about the experience at the time? How do you feel about it now?
6. When you meet someone new, what impresses you? How does someone create positive expectations in you?
7. How does a therapist have each of the five powers described in this chapter?

Things to Do

1. Interview a number of physicians in regard to their ideas about the "placebo effect." What is their description of the phenomenon, and how do they account for it? In what kinds of cases, if any, do they employ it?
2. List some of your most valued characteristics. How do you react when you are given feedback that contradicts your beliefs about yourself? Does your belief about you change? Why or why not?
3. List the feelings or situations in which you find yourself most suggestible to others in a positive sense (i.e., open, receptive). How might you say things or do things that would create these same feelings in someone else?

REFERENCES

Aronson, E. (1999). *The social animal* (8th edition). San Francisco: Freeman.
Asch, S. (1951). Effects of group pressure on the modification and distortion of judgments. In H. Guetzkow (Ed.), *Groups, leadership and men*. Pittsburgh, PA: Carnegie.
Asch, S. (1955). Opinions and social pressures. *Scientific American, 193*, 31–5.

Asch, S. (1956). Studies of independence and conformity: A minority of one against a unanimous majority. *Psychological Monographs, 70,* 9.

Barber, J. (1991). The locksmith model: Accessing hypnotic responsiveness. In S. Lynn & J. Rhue (Eds.), *Theories of hypnosis: Current models and perspectives* (pp. 241–74). New York: Guilford.

Barber, T. (1969). *Hypnosis: A scientific approach.* New York: VanNostrand Reinhold (Reprinted 1995: Northvale, NJ: Aronson).

Barber, T. (January/April, 2000). A deeper understanding of hypnosis: Its secrets, its nature, its essence. *American Journal of Clinical Hypnosis, 42:3/42:4,* 208–72.

Bordens, K., & Horowitz, I. (2002). *Social psychology* (2nd edition). Mahwah, NJ: Erlbaum.

Calof, D. (September/October, 1993). Facing the truth about false memory. *Family Therapy Networker, 17,* 5, 39–45.

Erickson, M. (1964). The confusion technique in hypnosis. *American Journal of Clinical Hypnosis, 6,* 185–207.

Festinger, L. (1957). *A theory of cognitive dissonance.* Stanford, CA: Stanford University Press.

Fredrickson, R. (1992). *Repressed memories: A journey of recovery from sexual abuse.* New York: Fireside.

Geary, B. (2001). Assessment in Ericksonian hypnosis and psychotherapy. In B. Geary & J. Zeig (Eds.), *The handbook of Ericksonian psychotherapy* (pp. 1–17). Phoeniz, AZ: The Milton H. Erickson Foundation Press.

Hubble, M., Duncan, B., & Miller, S. (Eds.) (1999). *The heart & soul of change: What works in therapy.* Washington, D.C.: American Psychological Association.

Kihlstrom, J. (1985). Hypnosis. *Annual Review of Psychology,* 36, 385–418.

Kirsch, I. (1990). *Changing expectations: A key to effective psychotherapy.* Pacific Grove, CA: Brooks/Cole.

Kirsch, I. (1991). The social learning theory of hypnosis. In S. Lynn & J. Rhue (Eds.), *Theories of hypnosis: Current models and perspectives* (pp. 439–466). New York: Guilford.

Kirsch, I. (1994). Clinical hypnosis as a nondeceptive placebo: Empirically derived techniques. *American Journal of Clinical Hypnosis, 37,* 95–106.

Kirsch, I. (1997). Response expectancy theory and application: A decennial review. *Applied and Preventive Psychology, 6,* 69–79.

Langer, E., Blank, A., & Chanowitz, B. (1978). The mindlessness of ostensibly thoughtful action: The role of "placebic" information in interpersonal interaction. *Journal of Personality and Social Psychology, 36,* 635–42.

Lynn, S., & Garske, J. (1985). *Contemporary psychotherapies: Models and methods.* Columbus, OH: Merrill.

Lynn, S., & Sherman, S. (January/April, 2000). The clinical importance of sociocognitive models of hypnosis: Response set theory and Milton Erickson's strategic interventions. *American Journal of Clinical Hypnosis, 42:3/42:4,* 294–315.

Martell, C., Addis, M., & Jacobson, N. (2001). *Depression in context: Strategies for guided action.* New York: Norton.

Maslach, C. (1979). Negative emotional biasing of unexplained arousal. *Journal of Personality and Social Psychology, 37,* 6, 953–969.

Matthews, W. (2001). Social influence, expectancy theory, and Ericksonian hypnosis. In B. Geary & J. Zeig (Eds.), *The handbook of Ericksonian psychotherapy* (pp. 31–42). Phoenix, AZ: The Milton H. Erickson Foundation Press.

Milgram, S. (1974). *Obedience to authority*. New York: Harper & Row.

Philipchalk, R. & McConnell, J. (1994). *Understanding human behavior* (8th edition). New York: Holt, Rinehart, & Winston.

Piccione, C., Hilgard, E., & Zimbardo, P. (1989). On the degree of stability of measured hypnotizability over a 25-year period. *Journal of Personality and Social Psychology, 56,* 289–95.

Pratkanis, A., & Aronson, E. (1991). *Age of propaganda: The everyday use and abuse of persuasion*. San Francisco: Freeman.

Rogers, C. (1963). A concept of the fully functioning person. *Psychotherapy: Theory, research, and practice, 1,* 1 17–26.

Rogers, C. (1986). Client-centered therapy. In I. Kutash & A. Wolf (Eds.), *Psychotherapist's casebook: Theory and technique in practice* (pp. 197–208). San Francisco: Jossey-Bass.

Sanford, R. (1987). An inquiry into the evolution of the client-centered approach to psychotherapy. In J. Zeig (Ed.), *The evolution of psychotherapy* (pp. 188–97). New York: Brunner/Mazel.

Schachter, S., & Singer, J. (1962). Cognitive, social and physiological determinants of emotional state. *Physiological Review, 69,* 379–89.

Sherman, S. (1988). Ericksonian psychotherapy and social psychology. In J. Zeig & S. Lankton (Eds.), *Developing Ericksonian therapy: State of the art* (pp. 59–90). New York: Brunner/Mazel.

Sherman, S. & Lynn, S. (1990). Social psychological principles in Milton Erickson's psychotherapy. *British Journal of Experimental and Clinical Hypnosis, 7,* 37–46.

Spanos, N. (1991). A sociocognitive approach to hypnosis. In S. Lynn & J. Rhue (Eds.), *Theories of hypnosis: Current models and perspectives* (pp. 324–61). New York: Guilford.

Spanos, N. & Coe, W. (1992). A social-psychological approach to hypnosis. In E. Fromm & M. Nash (Eds.), *Contemporary hypnosis research* (pp. 102–30). New York: Guilford.

Spanos, N., Flynn, D., & Gabora, M. (1989). Suggested negative visual hallucinations in hypnotic subjects: When no means yes. *British Journal of Experimental Hypnosis, 6,* 63–7.

Spinelli, E. (1994). *Demystifying therapy*. London: Constable.

Szasz, T. (1978). *The myth of psychotherapy: Mental healing as religion, rhetoric and repression*. New York: Doubleday.

Wagstaff, G. (1991). Compliance, belief and semantics in hypnosis: A nonstate, sociocognitive perspective. In S. Lynn & J. Rhue (Eds.), *Theories of hypnosis: Current models and perspectives* (pp. 362–96). New York: Guilford.

Yapko, M. (1992). *Hypnosis and the treatment of depressions: Strategies for change*. New York: Brunner/Mazel.

Yapko, M. (2001). *Treating depression with hypnosis: Integrating cognitive-behavioral and strategic approaches*. Philadelphia, PA: Brunner/Routledge.

Zeig, J. (2001). Hypnotic induction. In B. Geary & J. Zeig (Eds.), *The handbook of Ericksonian psychotherapy* (pp. 18–30). Phoenix, AZ: The Milton H. Erickson Foundation Press.

7

Matters of the Mind

The neurophysiology of the brain in hypnosis is clearly a fascinating realm of inquiry. How the brain functions in response to suggestion, which parts of the brain "light up" with increased neural activity under suggested conditions, and how brain waves can be deliberately conditioned through structured training experiences all represent intriguing frontiers of exploration into human consciousness. To the clinician wanting to apply hypnosis in treatment, however, the more immediate consideration is how a person's *brain* gives rise to a person's *mind*. What characteristics of mental functioning influence people's ability to respond meaningfully to hypnosis?

Exposing individuals to standardized tests of hypnotizability yields overwhelming evidence that not everyone is equally hypnotizable, even with the most flexible of approaches to induction and the broadest definitions of what constitutes the condition of hypnosis. Assessing hypnotizability with standardized tests and even striving to enhance someone's level of responsiveness will be discussed in chapters 8 and 11. But the appropriate question to address at this point is this one: What do we know about the relationship between conscious and unconscious mental processes and hypnosis? For the sake of simplicity, I will sometimes refer to the "conscious mind" and the "unconscious mind" at points in this chapter, as if they are distinct entities. However, you should be informed this is only convenient shorthand and not an accurate portrayal of the mind. It is more accurate to speak of conscious processes and unconscious processes, reflecting the dynamic nature of mental functioning.

In the most general sense, the rationale for employing hypnosis is to access, organize, and direct a client's mental resources for therapeutic purposes. "Mental resources" covers a lot of ground. Are these resources consciously available to the individual, that is, generally in his or her awareness? Some of them are. Are these resources unconscious, that is, generally outside of the person's awareness? Some of them are. Thus, characteristics of both conscious and unconscious processing become immediately relevant in forming and delivering suggestions to the client. In the remainder of this section, we will explore some of these characteristics.

As you have learned, while there are different theories or philosophical frameworks for describing the phenomenon of hypnosis, there is a broad base of agreement as to what Ernest Hilgard (1973) called the "domain of hypnosis," referring to the various hypnotic phenomena such as posthypnotic amnesia and perceptual distortions. People absorbed in the experience of hypnosis are able to organize their mental processes differently. Conscious awareness becomes more acute, and unconscious processes become more accessible (Kihlstrom, 1985; McConkey, 1991).

Suggestions are responded to simultaneously yet differently on multiple levels by the person in hypnosis, the principal observation leading to Hilgard's development of his influential neodissociation model featuring multiple cognitive controls working on multiple levels. Some of what one experiences in hypnosis may not get processed or retained on conscious levels at all; the person has responses he or she isn't aware of at all, such as smiles or frowns in response to specific suggestions or internal experiences, such as memories, that arise. And, the person may remember little about the experience consciously after ending the hypnosis session, called posthypnotic amnesia. The fact that meaningful responses to suggestions can occur with little or no conscious involvement is some of what gives hypnosis the aura of "magic." It is a curious thing, indeed, when someone follows a suggestion given during hypnosis that he or she has no recollection for having received, or has no conscious understanding for how a response, like numbness in a part of the body, was achieved. For purists like Weitzenhoffer (2000), such nonvolitional responses to suggestion define hypnotic responding.

In using hypnotic patterns, suggestions may deliberately be formed in an effort to convey meaning to the client's unconscious while his or her conscious awareness is occupied elsewhere. Thus, acknowledging the differences between conscious and unconscious characteristics is immediately relevant to the formulation of effective suggestions.

CONSCIOUS AND UNCONSCIOUS CHARACTERISTICS

The conscious and unconscious each have a different set of functions, but also share a considerable number of functions between them (Kihlstrom, 1990). The overlap allows them to work together, while the differences can and sometimes do surface in internal conflict. The conscious has the ability to analyze things, to reason, and to make judgments as to what is right or wrong. The conscious ultimately decides what is possible to do and what is not possible to do, although such decisions may well be—and usually are—based on influences (perhaps from past experiences, cognitive styles, or personality dynamics) that are largely unconscious (Fromm, 1992; Nash, 1992).

Thus, it can reasonably be said that the limitations in one's life are based on a conscious appraisal of experience. Everyone has the ability to seek out or create experiences that challenge their beliefs or expectations, if they so choose. In fact, isn't that how personal growth takes place? You tell yourself you can't, circumstances require you to, and then you happily discover you could. It doesn't always happen that way, of course, but it happens often enough to highlight that if you believe in your expectations noncritically, they become your reality (Kirsch, 1990). If you challenge them, your vision of what's possible grows. Hypnosis can work on both levels: boosting a conscious willingness to challenge oneself, and minimizing unconscious interferences that are the basis for being unnecessarily self-limiting. Directing and absorbing the client's conscious mind elsewhere in order to elicit responses at an unconscious level is often fundamental to the successful utilization of the more complex hypnotic phenomena.

How many things can you pay attention to at one time? Awareness is limited to just a few things at a time, and if too much comes in at once, the mind selectively attends to whatever is given high priority based on personal values, motivation, experience, and other such factors. Selective attention is a characteristic of hypnosis in the client's focusing on the clinician's communications. Beyond the hypnotic interaction, selective attention is a general characteristic of human information processing. Since we cannot pay attention to everything at once, the world is reduced to a manageable level through our conscious or unconscious selection of focal points. Communication to absorb and occupy the client's conscious mind is the starting point in the hypnotic interaction; such communication is called an "induction."

The unconscious mind is, metaphorically, a reservoir of all the multidimensional experiences acquired throughout your lifetime, including your historical experience, personal and social learnings, manner (drives, motivations, needs) for interacting with one's world, and your automatic functioning in countless behaviors each day. The unconscious mind, in contrast to the conscious mind, is not as rigid or analytical. It can respond to inferences between the lines, is capable of symbolic interpretation, and tends to be global in view (Fromm, 1992; Zeig, 1980).

While a hypnotized client has his or her conscious mind occupied, absorbed and focused through the process of selective attention, he or she continues to process information on multiple levels. The conscious mind may be minimally involved, as in deeply dissociated states historically called "somnambulism," with a limited degree of awareness in which he or she is not outwardly responsive by choice. For example, assuming your attention is selectively focused on what you are reading here because you are interested in learning about hypnosis, your consciousness is involved in the reading process. If you are deeply engaged in what you are reading here, then you are either entirely unaware of the routine things occurring around you, or you have some awareness for them but you choose not to respond to them because you do not want to be distracted from reading. If someone else is nearby and calls you by name, for example, perhaps you do not hear him or her at all. Or, perhaps, you hear him or her in the "back of your mind," but are too involved in reading to respond; you'd rather not divert your attention. And when he or she finally calls you for the fourth time and yells, "Hey! I'm talking to you!" you may have an awareness that you heard him or her all along!

UNCONSCIOUS PROCESSING

Just because a person isn't aware of taking in information doesn't mean the person hasn't done so. As a simple example, haven't you found yourself singing some song, only to realize seconds later it's what's on the radio? Information absorbed at an unconscious level can be as powerful as information processed at a conscious level, and often even more so. Simply put, people can take in and respond to information at levels outside of awareness, and hypnosis crystallizes this process. While a client is in hypnosis, his or her conscious mind will naturally wander from thought to thought. He or she may well report having "lost track" of you and whatever you were saying. During those periods of time that can be long or short, the client's unconscious can still take in the clinician's suggestions, and is still quite capable of responding to them. The client might not remember some or all of the suggestions given (amnesia), yet the suggestions may still exert an influence on him or her. Interestingly, many times my clients will come back, or call, quite some time after our hypnosis session and describe to me "new" insights and learnings that have caused a beneficial change in their experience of themselves. When they tell me what they've realized, almost word for word it will be things I said to them during our hypnosis session! But for the client, the important learning is experienced as arising "spontaneously" from within. The sense of personal empowerment as a result is one of the many benefits of hypnosis. (The phenomenon of guided learning at an unconscious level is an interesting one that represents the larger paradox of psychotherapy: The client is empowered by the therapist empowering him or her.)

One's unconscious can process information at a more symbolic, metaphorical level than one's conscious (Lynn & Sivec, 1992; Watzlawick, 1978). While the conscious mind is occupied with rationally analyzing the words, the unconscious is more concerned with meanings. This is the basis for the multiple level nature of hypnotic communication—using wording and phrasing of suggestions to appeal on one level to the client's conscious mind by matching its understanding of things, while simultaneously providing possibilities of new understandings to the unconscious mind (Erickson & Rossi, 1979, 1981). The suggestive mechanisms for doing so will be described in detail in later chapters.

THE UNCONSCIOUS AND SYMPTOM FORMATION

The metaphorical nature of the unconscious mind may be more easily understood when we consider the nature of symptoms. How does a person develop a particular symptom? Why do two different people under similar stresses react with different symptoms? There are many different viewpoints, of course, as to why people develop symptoms. For some, it's about genetic predispositions, for some it's about conditioning, and for others it's about maladaptive or ineffective coping strategies.

Some clinicians think of symptoms as metaphors for the client's experience (Frederick & Phillips, 1995; Ginandes, 2002). For example, a symbolically oriented therapist might interpret a person's obesity as a protective layer of fat used for deterring unwanted sexual advances, or as a pattern of "swallowing anger." Symptoms are thus viewed as purposeful and unconscious. Therapy generally takes the form of trying to provide the client with insights about his or her unconscious needs or motivations to maintain the symptom. In short, they try to force unconscious information into the client's consciousness to be critically dismantled.

This raises an interesting clinical issue: Should the therapist make interpretations about the presumed unconscious meaning of a client's symptoms? How many different ways can a symptom like obesity be plausibly interpreted? The clinician's role is not necessarily to impose his or her solutions on the client, but rather can be to help the client find his or her own solutions. Realistically, imposing one's values and beliefs on the client is an inevitable byproduct of the therapeutic relationship, but it is to be minimized, in my opinion, while maximizing respect for that person's integrity.

Understanding the unconscious, metaphorical nature of client symptoms leads to a different level of appreciation for the makeup of the person, clearly indicating there can be factors outside of consciousness that influence our experience. The unconscious mind's contribution to a person's experience highlights the need to be able to communicate with the unconscious; hypnosis is the most effective tool I know of for this purpose. If the symptom is unconscious and metaphorical, why should the treatment only be conscious, rational, and intellectual? It seems apparent, to me at least, that a conscious approach is valuable to some degree and in some contexts, but a style of therapy that also appeals to the unconscious can be of even greater value. The empirical evidence indicating enhanced treatment effects with hypnosis offers support to this view (Lynn, Kirsch, Barabasz, Cardeña, & Patterson, 2000).

TREATMENT AT AN UNCONSCIOUS LEVEL

The late psychiatrist Milton H. Erickson was an instrumental force in shaping modern psychotherapy. He evolved a style of treatment that operated on the premise, in part, that if a symptom may be metaphorical, so can its treatment be, innovating both direct and indirect approaches to the use of hypnosis and psychotherapy that were aimed at nonconscious aspects of experience (Erickson & Rossi, 1979; Haley, 1973; Zeig, 1980). His work continues to be enormously popular with clinicians for its practicality and ingenuity.

Erickson argued convincingly that the opportunity to communicate with the client's unconscious mind in hypnosis through a variety of suggestive mechanisms (detailed later) is a more respectful approach to addressing his or her needs without *necessarily* having to confront directly his or her conscious fears and limitations. Furthermore, he asserted that such communication is more respectful of the client's personal integrity because it does not force the clinician's values into the person's conscious mind by demanding conformity to the clinician's beliefs or theories. Rather, such communication allows the client the opportunity to keep unconscious whatever he or she wishes to, and likewise to make conscious what he or she cares to, and the clinician's responsibility is to utilize (hence the name "utilization approach" for Erickson's style of intervention) the client's choices in the process of treatment (Duncan, Miller, & Coleman, 2001; Yapko, 2001; Zeig, 1980, 2001; Zeig & Rennick, 1991). In that sense, Erickson's approach is highly individualized and client-centered.

Often, a client will open up with information from the unconscious at opportune moments in the therapy simply because the clinician has not been demanding (i.e., threatening the person's defenses), and the client's unconscious has made the choice that he or she is ready to deal with this information. For some, this is where the misconception about hypnosis having the ability to make people say or do things against their will comes from; information comes out that the client did not consciously expect to discover or release, yet the client has made a nonconscious choice that "now is the time and this is the place" to finally unload useless emotional baggage.

Perhaps this story will illustrate the point I am making. Early in my clinical training in hypnosis, I worked with a woman who had come to therapy to quit smoking. Helping someone to stop smoking is not usually a particularly difficult procedure, and is generally the kind of intervention that is brief and superficial in nature. After interviewing her, I began the induction of hypnosis, which went smoothly. As I began to offer her suggestions to help her achieve her goal, an ambulance happened to go by, its siren blaring. For a few moments that seemed an eternity to me, she stopped breathing, her face went white and then red, and her body tensed up everywhere as she began shaking. A moment later, she began crying and screaming hysterically. She'd had the hallucination that her son, who had been killed in the Vietnam War just a few years earlier, was in the ambulance that had gone by. Her emotions were very intense, and bubbling right on the surface. While I was not expecting a session to stop smoking to turn into an intense one of this type, I was well trained to anticipate and deal with this sort of phenomenon, called an "abreaction," as part of my training. (Abreactions will be discussed at length in chapter 22). I was acutely aware that this woman had made a choice at some level. She obviously needed to resolve her hidden grief and anger (in her view she'd had to be strong for everyone else), and in this case her smoking apparently became of secondary importance to her.

Unexpected as her emotional release was given the originally stated purpose of the session, is that *losing* control or *using* control? Richard Whiteside, Ph.D., in his book, *The Art of Using and Losing Control* (1998) made the point skillfully that what superficially seems like a loss of control can be a therapeutic opportunity in disguise. That was certainly the case in working with this particular woman. Certainly, she had heard other ambulances in recent years without reacting that way. Why did she react that way at that moment and in that context if not to use the opportunity to feel better, to grow?

In supporting her, guiding her, encouraging her, and helping her gain a perspective on her loss and her responsibilities to herself, what started out as a session for stopping smoking became an emotional turning point in her life. She was not out of control, nor was hypnosis forcing her to reveal something against her will. Rather, it was a choice to acknowledge and come to terms with feelings that had been buried along with her young son. How and why she made that choice (was it my age, my name, my height, a phrase I used or some other unconscious association?) is not known, nor was it necessary to know in order to be helpful to her.

The larger point is, the client's unconscious mind is capable of making choices, and those choices should be accepted and respected in the course of treatment. Milton Erickson was way ahead of his time in recognizing this point. (Continued on page 161.)

FRAME OF REFERENCE: MILTON H. ERICKSON, M.D.

Milton H. Erickson, M.D. (1901–1980), is considered by many to be the most innovative and influential figure in the modern practice of clinical hypnosis and psychotherapy. His unique background, perspectives, and approaches to treatment are of nearly mythic proportion, having become the focal point for recent generations of hypnosis practitioners through the scores of publications and countless workshops teaching variations of his methods.

Dr. Erickson's personal history was remarkable. He was stricken with polio at age 17 and nearly died. Paralyzed and unable to move anything more than his eyelids, he had a lengthy and difficult recovery. He often commented later what a good teacher the polio had been, forcing him to relearn the most basic patterns of movement and perception. In later life, he suffered post-polio syndrome, and eventually lost the use of both his legs and an arm, thus confining him to a wheelchair. Yet, his spirit was unbroken, and the many distinguished scholars who came to study with him right up to the very end of his life were awed by his stamina and grace in the face of intractable pain from the residuals of the polio (which, incidentally, he managed with self-hypnosis).

Dr. Erickson attended the University of Wisconsin, and as an undergraduate was exposed to the work of Clark L. Hull, Ph.D., an extremely influential experimental psychologist and expert on hypnosis. Dr. Erickson reacted strongly to the ritualized (i.e., impersonal and inflexible) approaches to hypnosis he saw Hull and others doing, independently evolving an ever-growing awareness of individual differences between people and ways to acknowledge and use those individual differences in the course of therapy. Consequently, Dr. Erickson's work has had a widespread appeal to clinicians in particular, who have found his emphasis on the unique attributes of each person a respectful and necessary way of organizing therapeutic interventions with hypnosis. Dr. Erickson further popularized the use of more natural, conversational approaches to hypnosis which employed indirect methods such as storytelling and paradox. Dr. Erickson's optimistic belief that people had unconscious resources that could be organized and directed for therapeutic purposes has led to a diversity of approaches to and applications of hypnosis that strive to actualize his optimism.

Dr. Erickson published extensively and lectured widely. Not all of Dr. Erickson's ideas have held up to the rigors of modern scientific inquiry, but a great many of his teachings have proven to be not only clinically effective, but also fundamentally correct. His emphases on achieving specific treatment results, involving family members in treatment, and the necessity of the clinician to be an active agent in creating contexts of change, all revolutionary concepts a half century ago, are now standard parts of treatment. His use of strategic task assignments, often seemingly strange in nature, have also become mainstream as current research evidence affirms the therapeutic benefits of behavioral activation. One literally cannot be a serious student of hypnosis without studying Dr. Erickson's work in detail.

So popular is Dr. Erickson's work amongst clinicians that The Milton H. Erickson Foundation, organized in 1980 by Jeffrey K. Zeig, Ph.D. (see Dr. Zeig's Frame of Reference in chapter 13), holds annual national and international meetings devoted to Erickson's methods that are consistently the largest meetings held anywhere in the world on the subject of hypnosis. Furthermore, the Foundation serves as the "hub of the wheel" for the more than 100 Milton Erickson Institutes located all over the world, each dedicated to spreading Dr. Erickson's ideas and methods ever farther.

Unlike nearly all the other distinguished individuals featured in the Frame of Reference sections in this book, Dr. Erickson passed away before I had the chance to meet him personally. The following quotes are taken from a variety of sources noted at the end of each quote.

On Empowering Clients: "Properly oriented, hypnotic therapy can give the patient that necessary understanding of his own role in effecting his recovery and thus enlist his own effort and participation in his own cure without giving him a sense of dependence upon drugs and medical care. Indeed, hypnosis offers the patient a sense of comfort and an attitude of interest in his own active participation in his therapy." (Erickson, in Rossi, 1980, Vol. IV, p. 34)

On the Role of the Clinician: "In hypnosis what you want your patient to do is respond to an idea. It is your task, your responsibility, to learn how to address the patient, how to speak to the patient, how to secure his attention, and how to leave him wide open to the acceptance of an idea that fits into the situation." (Erickson & Rossi, 1981, p .42)

On Confident Expectations: "Every effort should be made to make the subjects feel comfortable, satisfied, and confident about their ability to go into a trance, and the hypnotist should maintain an attitude of unshaken and contagious confidence in the subject's ability. A simple, earnest, unpretentious, confident manner is of paramount importance." (Erickson, in Rossi, 1980, Vol. IV, p. 18)

On Words and Meanings: "Now, every word in any language has usually a lot of different meanings. Now, the word "run" has about 142 meanings . . . the government can run. A run of luck in cards. The girl can run. A run of fish. A run in a lady's stocking. A road runs uphill and downhill, and still stands still . . . And so, you ought to be acquainted with the linguistic patterns of your patients." (Zeig, 1980, p. 78)

On Recognizing Individual Differences: "And I do wish that Rogerian therapists, Gestalt therapists, transactional analysts, group analysts, and all the other offspring of various theories would recognize that not one of them really recognizes that psychotherapy for person #1 is not psychotherapy for person #2. I've treated many conditions, and I always invent a new treatment in accord with the individual personality." (Zeig, 1980, p. 104)

On Hypnosis and Changing People: "It is hardly reasonable to expect a hypnotized subject, upon the snap of the fingers or the utterance of a simple command, to develop at once significant, complex, and persistent changes in behavioral functioning. Rather, it is to be expected that time and effort are required to permit a development of any profound alterations in behavior. Such alteration must presumably arise from neuro- and psychophysiological changes and processes within the subject, which are basic to behavioral manifestations, and not from the simple experience of hearing a command spoken by a hypnotist." (Erickson, in Rossi, 1980, Vol. II, p. 50)

On Putting the Patient First: "You see, I think the important thing in working with a patient is to do the thing that is going to help the patient. As for my dignity . . . the hell with my dignity. (Laughs) I will get along all right in this world. I don't have to be dignified, professional. I do the thing that stirs the patient into doing the right thing." (Zeig, 1980, p. 143)

On Getting Clients to Do Strange Task Assignments: "That is what my family says: "Why do your patients do the crazy things you tell them to do?" I say, "I tell it to them very seriously. They know I mean it. I am totally sincere. I am absolutely confident that they will do it. I never think, 'Will my patients do that ridiculous thing?' No, I know that they will." (Zeig, 1980, p. 196)

On Orienting the Patient to the Future: "Insight into the past may be somewhat educational. But insight into the past isn't going to change the past. If you were jealous of your mother, it is always going to be a fact that you *were* jealous of her. If you were unduly fixated on your mother, it is always going to be the fact. You may have insight, but it doesn't change the fact. Your patient has to live in accord with things of today. So you orient your therapy to the patient living today and tomorrow, and hopefully next week and next year." (Zeig, 1980, pp. 268–9)

On How to Live a Long Life: "Do you know a good recipe for longevity? . . . Always be sure to get up in the morning. And you can insure that by drinking a lot of water before you go to bed." (Zeig, 1980, p. 269)

Erickson's influence amongst clinicians has been profound, and many of his ideas have been echoed by clinicians who are prominent in their own right. Paul Watzlawick, Ph.D., is a psychologist long associated with the Mental Research Institute (MRI) of Palo Alto, California, one of the earliest and most influential "think-tanks" in the world of therapy. The members of MRI have been instrumental in bringing family therapy and strategic therapy to life, and included such luminary early members as Watzlawick, Jay Haley, Virginia Satir, Gregory Bateson, Richard Fisch, John Weakland, and Donald Jackson. Each of them advocated for the value of hypnosis in their work. In Watzlawick's classic book, *The Language of Change* (1978), he described eloquently the need to communicate with the unconscious mind of the client in order to be as influential as possible in therapeutically altering his or her experience. Rather than the intellectual, computer-like jargon that appeals to the limited conscious mind of the client, Watzlawick asserted that language that is descriptive, emotional, and appealing to the senses will likely make greater contact with the client's powerful unconscious resources. What about the other side of the coin, though? Can hypnosis be used to bypass conscious awareness and leave the client defenseless against the hypnotist's suggestions?

IN DEFENSE OF THE MIND

The fact that information can be and often is processed without much conscious awareness is a major factor in the fear many have that destructive or harmful information from the hypnotist is going to get in at an unconscious level and damage the client. Can people be negatively influenced? Unquestionably. Yet, in general, the mind has an uncanny ability to protect itself. Every student of psychology, and anyone who has spent some time in the company of other people, learns about the classic defense mechanisms people employ to ward off threats from entering consciousness. The classic defenses such as repression, projection, rationalization, sublimation, and all the others are unconscious coping mechanisms; no one consciously says, "I can't accept responsibility for my feelings so I think I'll attribute these feelings to that person over there" (e.g., projection). The defenses are unconscious, and are rooted in the person's need for self-esteem and the desire to avoid internal conflict if at all possible. These defenses are certainly relevant to hypnosis (Fromm, 1992; Nash, 1992).

There is a substantial difference between suggestibility and gullibility (T. Barber, 1969). For an individual who is motivated to gather and weigh information, and to consider the relative merits of what he or she is being told, hypnosis does not preclude the ability to do so. For someone who conforms to others' judgments, even obviously incorrect ones as we saw were possible in the last chapter, hypnosis will not amplify the willingness or need to do so. Each person is as psychologically safe as he or she wants and needs to be. If someone wants to reject suggestions, no matter how deeply in hypnosis he or she might be, the ability to do so is retained (Lynn, Rhue, & Weekes, 1990). The defenses someone can employ are both conscious and unconscious, and so even suggestions that escape conscious scrutiny will still encounter unconscious defenses. When, if ever, is hypnosis potentially hazardous? When someone credible intentionally or unintentionally feeds misinformation to an individual who has no ready means for evaluating the merits of what they're being told. This is a primary reason why I advocate hypnosis be done permissively, encouraging expanding the range of empowering choices in client experience rather than demanding mere compliance. Hypnotic hazards and ethical guidelines for using hypnosis are discussed throughout this book, but are the special focus of chapter 22.

As a final point about this issue of the mind's ability to protect itself, it seems to me that if there were a group of powerful humans called "hypnotists" who could control others through manipulation of the unconscious mind, hypnosis would be a uniformly successful tool in practice. It isn't.

THE MYTH OF A BENEVOLENT, ALL-POWERFUL UNCONSCIOUS

Conflicting views about the nature of the unconscious mind, including its abilities to manage conflicting information (McConkey, 1991; Sheehan & Grigg, 1985), generate entirely nonvolitional responses (Lynn et al., 1990), retrieve accurate details of forgotten historical events (Sheehan, 1995), alter physiology and cure some diseases (Phillips, 2000; Rossi, 2002), tap latent creativity (Lynn & Sivec, 1992; Shames & Bowers, 1992), and resolve and manage various psychological problems (Crasilneck & Hall, 1985; Kroger,

1977; Rossi, 1980) have been a part of the field from the very beginning. As the field grows in depth and sophistication, some questions about hypnosis and the unconscious get answered, and as they do, many more new ones evolve as a result.

With such a large and ever growing body of good evidence that hypnosis is helpful in so many types of problems, there has been a growing but noncritical acceptance of the admittedly attractive belief that any problem can be solved, any condition or disease cured, if the "healing powers of the unconscious" are appropriately tapped. Many advocates of hypnosis have made some rather extreme statements out of their enthusiasm for hypnosis. Most of these tout the "wonders" and "unlimited capabilities" of the unconscious mind, suggesting that being in hypnosis and receiving the appropriate suggestions will almost magically resolve nearly every problem. They tell stories to their clients during hypnosis and tell them to "trust your unconscious" to derive the therapeutic meaning; they offer suggestions and tell clients to "trust your unconscious" to integrate them; and they tell clients to be patient in allowing therapeutic progress because they can "trust your unconscious" to know when the best time will be to change, and on and on. *If only* it were the case that all you have to do is offer a sensible suggestion to someone's unconscious and then sit back to wait while his or her unconscious mind magically takes it in and puts it to work. Life as a clinician would be so much easier, if that were the case.

The philosophy of a powerful and benevolent unconscious is appealing for many reasons. It's nice to think that each person has a core of health and power. It's nice to think our fundamental nature is positive and goal-directed. It's encouraging to think we know at some deep nonverbal level what is right and that we should just trust our intuition. It's reassuring to believe that when we get sick with even life-threatening diseases that we can find the cure inside that's just waiting to be let loose.

The belief in an all-powerful unconscious inspires an optimism in people they find spiritually satisfying in the same way they love the motivational speakers who tell us we can "have it all." Well, we can have a lot, but . . . no, you can't have it all. Why? Simply because every choice precludes other choices. If you choose to sit and read this hypnosis text, it means you're not at the movies right now.

The "unconscious" is a global construct psychologists use to talk about parts of human functioning that take place beyond conscious awareness. It's an abstraction, a shorthand. There isn't really a well defined entity called "the" unconscious that we can say predictably and reliably does this or that. Instead, we infer principles of its functioning from experimentation and observation. We learn that the unconscious has some very impressive resources and potentials. And, we learn that unconscious minds make some pretty serious mistakes, enough to warrant skepticism about those approaches that encourage people to simply "trust your unconscious." One can still be enthusiastic about hypnosis, as I obviously am, without overstating what hypnosis can do or, more accurately, what the unconscious can do through hypnosis. The impressive results speak for themselves, but the belief that anyone can achieve similar results is potentially misleading.

CONCLUSION

However you conceptualize the mind, there is a multidimensionality present. Conscious and unconscious dimensions of the mind each have some unique characteristics as well as some overlapping ones and each offers its own contributions to subjective experience. Due to the enormous complexity of the human mind, and because of the extraordinary uniqueness of each human being, respect for the personal power and integrity of each person is not just desirable, but mandatory.

For Discussion

1. Why do people transmit messages incongruously? Is it safe to assume they are being deceptive in doing so?
2. How do you characterize the key differences between the conscious and unconscious minds?
3. Do you trust your unconscious mind? Why or why not? Do you trust your conscious mind? Why or why not?
4. Do you believe in an "inner healer?" Why or why not?

Things to Do

1. Research the functions of the left and right brain hemispheres. Which functions overlap? Which do not?
2. Have one person talk to you for a minute, then two people simultaneously, then three simultaneously, and so on. At what point do you feel overwhelmed in trying to attend to each? What can you conclude from this exercise about the attentional capacities of the mind?

3. Make a list of 10 common disorders, and then make a list of underlying feelings or motivations the problem may be metaphorical for. For example, a weight problem may be viewed as a person surrounding him- or herself with fat for protection against some threat. How do you know your interpretation of a symptom is really what that symptom is about?

4. Collect newspaper and magazine ads that perpetuate the myth of a benevolent, all-powerful unconscious accessible through hypnosis. Discuss the merits and liabilities of each.

REFERENCES

Barber, T. (1969). *Hypnosis: A scientific approach.* New York: Van Nostrand Reinhold.

Crasilneck, H., & Hall, J. (1985). *Clinical hypnosis: Principles and applications* (2nd edition). New York: Grune & Stratton.

Duncan, B., Miller, S., & Coleman, S. (2001). Utilization: A seminal contribution, a family of ideas, and a new generation of applications. In B. Geary & J. Zeig (Eds.), *The handbook of Ericksonian psychotherapy* (pp. 43–56). Phoenix, AZ: The Milton H. Erickson Foundation Press.

Erickson, M. & Rossi, E. (1979). *Hypnosis: An exploratory casebook.* New York: Irvington.

Erickson, M. & Rossi, E. (1981). *Experiencing hypnosis: Therapeutic approaches to altered states.* New York: Irvington.

Frederick, C. & Phillips, M. (1995). De-coding mystifying signals: Translating symbolic communications of elusive ego-states. *American Journal of Clinical Hypnosis, 38,* 187–96.

Fromm, E. (1992). An ego-psychological theory of hypnosis. In E. Fromm & M. Nash (Eds.), *Contemporary hypnosis research* (pp. 131–48). New York: Guilford.

Ginandes, C. (2002). Extended, strategic therapy for recalcitrant mind-body healing. *American Journal of Clinical Hypnosis, 45,* 2, 91–102.

Haley, J. (1973). *Uncommon therapy: The psychiatric techniques of Milton II. Erickson, M.D.* New York: Norton.

Hilgard, E. (1973). The domain of hypnosis: With some comments on alternate paradigms. *American Psychologist, 28,* 972–82.

Kihlstrom, J. (1985). Hypnosis. *Annual Review of Psychology, 36,* 385–418.

Kihlstrom, J. (1990). The psychological unconscious. In L. Pervin (Ed.), *Handbook of personality: Theory and research* (pp. 445–64). New York: Guilford.

Kirsch, I. (1990). *Changing expectations: A key to effective psychotherapy.* Pacific Grove, CA: Brooks/Cole.

Kroger, W. (1977). *Clinical and experimental hypnosis in medicine, dentistry and psychology* (2nd edition). Philadelphia, PA: Lippincott.

Lynn, S., Kirsch, I., Barabasz, A., Cardeña, E., & Patterson, D. (2000). Hypnosis as an empirically supported clinical intervention: The state of the evidence and a look to the future. *International Journal of Clinical and Experimental Hypnosis, 48,* 2, 239–59.

Lynn, S., Rhue, J., & Weekes, J. (1990). Hypnotic involuntariness: A social cognitive analysis. *Psychological Review, 97,* 169–84.

Lynn, S. & Sivec, H. (1992). The hypnotizable subject as creative problem-solving agent.

In E. Fromm & M. Nash (Eds.), *Contemporary hypnosis research* (pp. 292–333). New York: Guilford.

McConkey, K. (1991). The construction and resolution of experience and behavior in hypnosis. In S. Lynn & J. Rhue (Eds.), *Theories of hypnosis: Current models and perspectives* (pp. 542–63). New York: Guilford.

Nash, M. (1992). Hypnosis, psychopathology, and psychological regression. In E. Fromm & M. Nash (Eds.), *Contemporary hypnosis research* (pp. 149–69). New York: Guilford.

Phillips, M. (2000). *Finding the energy to heal: How EMDR, hypnosis, TFT, and body-focused therapy can help restore mind-body health.* New York: Norton.

Rossi, E. (Ed.) (1980). *The collected papers of Milton H. Erickson on hypnosis* (Vols. I–IV). New York: Irvington.

Rossi, E. (2002). A conceptual review of the psychosocial genomics of expectancy and surprise: Neuroscience perspectives about the deep psychobiology of therapeutic hypnosis. *American Journal of Clinical Hypnosis, 45*, 2, 103–18.

Shames, V., & Bowers, P. (1992). Hypnosis and creativity. In E. Fromm & M. Nash (Eds.), *Contemporary hypnosis research* (pp. 334–63). New York: Guilford.

Sheehan, P. (1995). The effects of asking leading questions in hypnosis. In G. Burrows & R. Stanley (Eds.), *Contemporary international hypnosis* (pp. 55–62). Chichester, UK: Wiley.

Sheehan, P., & Grigg, L. (1985). Hypnosis, memory and the acceptance of an implausible cognitive set. *British Journal of Experimental and Clinical Hypnosis, 3*, 5–12.

Watzlawick, P. (1978). *The language of change.* New York: Basic Books.

Whiteside, R. (1998). *The art of using and losing control.* New York: Brunner/Mazel.

Yapko, M. (2001). Revisiting the question: What is Ericksonian hypnosis? In B. Geary & J. Zeig (Eds.), *The handbook of Ericksonian psychotherapy* (pp. 168–86). Phoenix, AZ: The Milton H. Erickson Foundation Press.

Zeig, J. (Ed.) (1980). *A teaching seminar with Milton H. Erickson, M.D.* New York: Brunner/Mazel.

Zeig, J. (2001). Hypnotic induction. In B. Geary & J. Zeig (Eds.), *The handbook of Ericksonian psychotherapy* (pp. 18–30). Phoenix, AZ: The Milton H. Erickson Foundation Press.

Zeig, J., & Rennick, P. (1991). Ericksonian hypnotherapy: A communications approach to hypnosis. In S. Lynn & J. Rhue (Eds.), *Theories of hypnosis: Current models and perspectives* (pp. 275–300). New York: Guilford.

8

Responsiveness
to Hypnosis

Can anyone be hypnotized? The complex issue of who can be hypnotized (and, likewise, who cannot) has been researched and written about at great length by some of the most respected people in the field. The net result is the conclusion that although the great majority of people can experience hypnosis to some degree, not everyone is equally responsive to hypnosis (E. Hilgard, 1965; Weitzenhoffer, 2000). Research subjects exposed to standardized and different forms of hypnotic induction and offered standardized and differing suggestions show variable levels of responsiveness across conditions (Spiegel & Spiegel, 1987; Lynn, Neufeld, & Matyi, 1987). Thus, many experts conclude that hypnotizability, generally defined in the research as an ability to respond positively to suggested experiences, is substantially more about personal factors than interpersonal or contextual ones. In this chapter, we will explore some of the characteristics of the individual (the intrapersonal factors) that may influence hypnotic responsiveness.

Research into the capacity to experience hypnosis has examined many different personal variables including personality types (T. Barber, 1964; Malinoski & Lynn, 1999), imaginative ability and fantasy proneness (J. Hilgard, 1979; Wilson & Barber, 1981, 1983), capacity for absorption (Roche & McConkey, 1990; Council & Huff, 1990), expectancy (Kirsch, 2000), gender (Weitzenhoffer, 2000), age (Morgan & E. Hilgard, 1973), and many other factors.

The hypnotic responsiveness issue was first touched on in chapter 2, specifically in the discussion of the misconception that "only certain kinds of people can be hypnotized." Despite the growing body of research evidence that level of hypnotizability is a variable trait across individuals, but a stable trait within individuals over time (E. Hilgard, 1965; Piccione, E. Hilgard, & Zimbardo, 1989), many hypnosis experts in actual clinical practice prefer to focus on maximizing client responsiveness rather than assessing hypnotizability. Instead, they operate on the premise that hypnotizability, when assessed through a standardized instrument of some sort, misses the synergistic qualities of therapeutic interaction that can enhance responsiveness (Geary, 2001). Later in this chapter I will consider the notion of enhancing hypnotic responsiveness in individuals. Before doing so, let's explore the literature on intrapersonal factors affecting hypnotizability.

PERSONALITY FACTORS AND HYPNOTIZABILITY

Many researchers have explored the relationship between dimensions of personality and responsiveness to hypnosis. Test scores from personality inventories such as the Minnesota Multiphasic Personality Inventory (MMPI), Thurstone Personality Schedule, the Rorschach, the Thematic Apperception Test (TAT), the California Psychological Inventory (CPI), and many other standardized personality measures have all been studied relative to hypnotizability as measured by standardized tests and all have yielded similar results: No specific positive correlations exist between hypnotic responsiveness and scores on these assessment instruments (Kirsch & Council, 1992). In one recent study (Nordenstrom, Council, & Meier, 2002), the "Five Factor" model for describing individual differences in personality (Costa & McCrae, 1997) was studied in regards to hypnotizability. The five factors include openness, conscientiousness, neuroticism, agreeableness, and extraversion. And, once again, no meaningful relationships were found to exist between hypnotic responsiveness and these personality characteristics.

IMAGINATIVE ABILITY, FANTASY PRONENESS, AND HYPNOTIZABILITY

Josephine Hilgard, Ph.D., in her 1970 book, *Personality and Hypnosis: A Study of Imaginative Involvement*, asserted that hypnotizability was best predicted by the capacity for imaginative involvement, which she defined as the capacity for nearly total immersion in some activity to the exclusion of irrelevant competing stimuli. She clearly advocated for the perceptual process of selective attention, but added in the extra element in her formulation of being selectively focused on or immersed in imaginary experience. Perhaps surprisingly, the research for this view has been equivocal, however, that may be because of the broad range of imaginative abilities in human populations.

People vary in their abilities and styles for processing information; some people are quite concrete (i.e., tied to the immediacy of their experience), not very imaginative, and require highly detailed descriptions of experience they have already had in order to experience hypnosis. Others are capable of high level abstraction (i.e., having experiences that are not part of past or present experience) in which imagination and fantasy can run loose in their minds and generate meaningful experiences for them. How concrete or abstract someone is in their thinking is a factor in responsiveness to hypnosis because of the subjective nature of the hypnotic experience. There are no rockets that go off, no sirens that sound, no marching bands that come by waving banners that confirm "this is hypnosis!" The experience of hypnosis can range from being a subtle one, barely distinguishable from one's normal waking state, or it can be a very profound, distinct experience characterized by certain intense sensations and perceptions collectively identified as "hypnosis." To the concrete and unimaginative individual experiencing the subtleties of a lightly hypnotic experience, the reaction is often "I wasn't hypnotized . . . I heard everything you said." The concrete subject should generally be spoken to in parallel concrete terms of verifiable experience. Using abstract terms such as a person's "energy flow," or people's "essence," or their "groundedness," or "letting your energy flow unrestricted in order to achieve a harmony with the universe," and other such nondescript abstractions is likely to result in a cosmic failure. Some people's imaginative powers are very concrete, others' are more abstract. This is one more variable to consider in formulating one's approach.

Building on the research regarding imaginative involvement, the "fantasy-prone" individual was "discovered" by Theodore X. Barber and Sheryl Wilson (Barber, 2000) when studying highly responsive individuals. These are commonly known in the hypnosis research as the "highs," while others still use the older Ernest Hilgard label, "virtuosos" (E. Hilgard, 1977), to describe such highly responsive individuals.

Recently, Barber reviewed the development of and evidence for the fantasy-prone "high" (2000) as a strong factor in his multifactor model of hypnotizability, reviewed in chapter 3. Fantasy-prone individuals are described as those who become immersed in a private and highly subjective world of daydreams and fantasy, and even paranormal experiences.

ABSORPTION AND HYPNOTIZABILITY

The capacity to become absorbed in experience is yet another way for viewing the perceptual process of selective attention so clearly evident in hypnotic responsiveness. Tellegen and Atkinson (1974) described absorption as "an openness to self altering experiences," and devised an instrument called the Tellegen Absorption Scale (TAS) to measure one's quality of absorption. The 34-item TAS questionnaire is a widely used measure of absorption, and it has, in fact, predicted hypnotic responsiveness in research subjects to a significant degree (Council & Huff, 1990; Radtke & Stam, 1991). An interesting finding, though, is that the TAS has only a modest correlation with established hypnotizability scales (described in chapter 11). Whatever ways that might be interpreted, fostering absorption in doing hypnosis benefits the process.

EXPECTANCY AND HYPNOTIZABILITY

The role of expectancy in shaping responsiveness to hypnosis, psychotherapy, medicine, and life experience has been discussed previously. Psychologist Irving Kirsch, Ph.D., has studied expectancy in depth, particularly as it relates to hypnotic responsiveness, evolving his "response set theory" in the process (Kirsch, 2000). In it, he assimilates a wide variety of research supporting the notion that a person's expectations about his or her ability to respond to suggestions mediates his or her eventual experience. He said,

> Suggestions are statements that (are) explicitly aimed at eliciting the expectation of a change in experience and behavior. This is particularly clear with respect to direct suggestions, such as "your arm is getting lighter," "your arm is becoming numb," and "you will forget everything that has happened during this session." To accept a suggestion is to believe or expect that these events will, in fact, happen. (Kirsch, 2000, p. 279)

Kirsch goes even further, suggesting these expectations can lead individuals to develop responses that others call a manifestation of hypnosis without the necessity of any hypnotic induction. Kirsch wrote: "There are good experimental data indicating that for the most part, hypnotic responses reflect genuine changes in experience . . . However, the experiential and physiological changes produced by hypnosis do not require that the person be in a trance" (Kirsch, 2000, p. 278). Expectancy is an especially strong factor mediating hypnotic responsiveness. I would suggest, and have suggested in previous writings (Yapko, 1988, 1989, 1993, 2001), that imparting positive expectations to the client represents the single best focal point for doing hypnosis and the most important initial target of therapeutic intervention.

GENDER AND HYPNOTIZABILITY

Early studies done addressing the issue of whether there are gender differences in hypnotizability yielded some data to support the belief that, in general, women may be slightly more hypnotizable than men (E. Hilgard, 1965). Subsequently, any gender differences in hypnosis have not held up over time. Weitzenhoffer summarized his findings on the subject this way:

> (The difference) between men and women has been equivocal. That is, in general there has been a consistent small difference found favoring women

over men, but never at even the 5% level of significance. This has led past researchers to reject the existence of a difference . . . The difference is much too small to be of practical importance or to indicate something that would be theoretically important. (2000, p. 281)

Despite the lack of difference in hypnotizability based on gender in a general sense, there is certainly good reason to take gender into account given the substantial data showing different rates of vulnerability, differential courses, and differential responses to treatments in a variety of conditions (Waalen, 1997). In recent years, there has been a growing emphasis on acknowledging and incorporating gender differences into hypnotic procedures. Women's issues in particular have received a growing attention within the field (Hornyak, 1999; Linden, 1995, 1997, 1999). These have been catalyzed, in part, by the exceptional contributions of one of the most skilled, forceful, and important figures in the evolution of the field, Kay Thompson, D.D.S. (Continued on page 173.)

FRAME OF REFERENCE: KAY THOMPSON, D.D.S.

Kay Thompson, D.D.S. (1930–1998) was an extraordinary woman and an inspiring contributor to the field of hypnosis. Dr. Thompson graduated in 1953 as the only woman in her class from her dental school, the University of Pittsburgh. Years later she was the first woman to be elected president of the Pennsylvania Dental Association in its 120-year history.

Shortly after graduating from dental school, Dr. Thompson received a brochure in the mail advertising a course in hypnosis. She attended the training out of curiosity, and so began her lifelong fascination with and appreciation of clinical hypnosis. Just a few years later, in 1957, the American Society of Clinical Hypnosis (ASCH) was formed by Dr. William Kroger and Dr. Milton Erickson, and Dr. Thompson joined and continued her training and professional development through ASCH. She was especially close to Dr. Erickson, and once said that, "He had more influence on me than anyone but the woman who gave birth to me." Theirs was a creative and fruitful professional collaboration over the years. She soon became an instrumental teacher in ASCH, and was recognized nationally and internationally for her skill, clinical acumen, sensitivity, and creativity. Eventually, she served ASCH as its president, its first female president, and was a recipient of the highest awards offered by ASCH as well as the other major professional hypnosis society in the United States, The Society for Clinical and Experimental Hypnosis. Generous in sharing her advanced knowledge and skills, Dr. Thompson mentored young dental students and also donated time to provide dental services at a residential facility for physically and mentally handicapped adults. She was a role model for everyone, but being the first woman in positions of power and authority allowed her to be an especially important role model for women everywhere, a fact Dr. Thompson was well aware of and took very seriously.

Dr. Thompson lectured all over the world on the intricacies of the language patterns of hypnosis, continually emphasizing the importance of using language deliberately and with an awareness that meanings are in people and not the words themselves. She also spoke regularly about pain control and the use of hypnosis in dentistry and other physical procedures where managing pain was desirable and necessary. She was creative in her work and her use of hypnosis, and was a co-inventor of one of the most interesting approaches to hypnosis, an overloading technique known as the "dual induction." The dual induction is a process involving two people performing hypnosis *simultaneously* on a single client.

Dr. Thompson loved elephants and collected elephant statues, elephant pictures, elephant *anything*. When I had the unique and life-transforming experience of working on an elephant-breeding program at the San Diego Wild Animal Park, applying some of my skill-building strategies with trainers and keepers, I got to know many elephants firsthand through daily contact. Dr. Thompson was mesmerized by some of the stories of elephant behavior I shared with her. It seemed a too small gift to give back to her, though, for all the times she had mesmerized me with her skills, knowledge, and humanism.

On Becoming a Dentist: "I grew up an only child in the only professional family in the community—my father was a dentist. My father was always there to help others, and I saw it as a very caring profession. And no one told me I couldn't be a dentist! I have always had a strong work ethic and a huge sense of responsibility."*

On Learning Hypnosis: "Somehow I attracted all the frightened and phobic patients. I got a brochure on hypnosis, and went to the course looking for some "magic" for dealing with difficult patients, and I've been involved with hypnosis ever since . . . I think there are two kinds of people who work with hypnosis: the people who are truly interested in using it as a modality to help their patients or their clients, and the other people who get into it because of the need for self-aggrandizement."*

On Meeting Erickson: "I met Erickson in October, 1953. Erickson terrified me! I was fascinated but terrified by anybody who could see into your soul like that. He demonstrated that ability with every demonstration he did. I used to try to hide when it was deep trance demonstration time, but there were many times I had to "volunteer." I worked very closely with him until his death." *

On Hypnotic Interventions in Medicine and Dentistry: "Dental and medical procedures are more physiologically invasive than psychotherapy, and we have less time to help patients resolve their issues about what we are going to do with them and to them. So we have to do brief therapy if we do any therapy . . . Hypnosis is too important a tool to be limited to the pure therapeutic aspect. There are so many physiological benefits that can be obtained with it." **

On Tailoring Interventions to the Individual: "I always emphasize that inductions cannot be a recipe. Each induction must be individualized. Certainly a dual induction cannot be either another's words or a script. I have seen experienced people read an induction and I don't understand why. Subjects always sense if an induction is not for them. That is something that Erickson certainly stressed, and so do I." **

Advice on Developing Skills in Hypnosis: "Practice, practice, practice basic, formal induction techniques. Practice, practice, practice. Observe, observe, observe. Learn to go from formal structured techniques where you learn to observe, and slide into the utilization of metaphor. . . . It takes a long time—years and years of putting things into your unconscious in order to be able to rely upon it to be spontaneous . . . Learn to improve, improve by learning . . . You can't always know what to expect, but you can learn to handle the unexpected." **

*Sources: * Personal communication; December 8, 1988*
*** Interview with Betty Alice Erickson published in The Milton H. Erickson Foundation Newsletter,*
Spring 1994

Acknowledging gender differences between men and women may well influence the quality of your communications with different clients. Language choices, the quality of your demeanor, and the emphasis you place on particular concepts or awarenesses you hope to impart can be well tailored to your client. Certainly people are more than their gender, but gender is undeniably a factor shaping perceptions and so should be considered in treatment planning.

AGE AND HYPNOTIZABILITY

Does an individual's age influence his or her responsiveness to hypnosis? The answer is, in a general sense of course, yes. In particular, the issue of age and hypnosis has revolved around the differences in responsiveness between children and adults. Research in this domain has typically examined hypnotic responsiveness in children using standardized test items of hypnotic responsiveness adapted to children's developmental stage (Cooper & London, 1966, 1976, 1979). Since the test items are much the same as for adults, it becomes possible to characterize hypnotic responsiveness over the course of a lifetime (Cooper & London, 1971).

The available evidence suggests that responsiveness to hypnosis emerges at a low level around age 5, rises sharply to a peak responsiveness around ages 7 to 9, begins a gradual decline in early adolescence, and stays fairly level throughout adulthood (J. Hilgard, 1979; Morgan & E. Hilgard, 1973).

Children are, in general, responsive to hypnosis, but naturally require different approaches than adults do (Vandenberg, 2002). After all, the range of personal experiences is considerably more limited, and both cognitive and social abilities are less well developed. As a counterbalance, though, children also tend to have less rigid notions of reality, a greater capacity for play, including role play, and a higher level of responsiveness to authorities.

One of the most common reasons why some practitioners come to question the responsiveness of children to hypnosis is because of the active nature of most children. As will be discussed in the next chapter, adults generally inhibit voluntary activity when in hypnosis, a phenomenon associated with hypnosis called "catalepsy." In contrast, children often fidget and outwardly appear restless even though they may be very involved with the clinician and what he or she is doing (Olness & Kohen, 1996). If one has an inflexible expectation of how a client in hypnosis must look and behave, a fidgety child will seem unaffected by hypnotic procedures. Sometimes, perhaps much of the time, a procedure with children can encourage and make use of the child's energy by engaging him in some activity (e.g., a game) that distracts him or her from what the clinician intends to communicate. (As you have previously learned, suggestions can engender meaningful responses even when they are not one's principal focal point.)

Observation of the child's interactions with his parents and siblings can provide a great deal of useful information about the kind of relationship (i.e., friend, ally, teacher, doctor) one may build with him or her in order to best influence him or her (Olness & Kohen, 1996). Knowledge of his interests and emotional needs will also help one discover the best avenue of intervention. An exceptionally creative example of an engaging approach to a child's problem is one of Milton Erickson's cases, described by Jay Haley in *Uncommon Therapy* (1973). A young boy with the problem of enuresis was literally dragged in by his parents to see Dr. Erickson. Alone with the child in his office, Erickson angrily complained aloud about the audacity of the boy's parents. How *dare* they order him to cure the boy's enuresis! Erickson went on complaining about the parents for quite some time, and meanwhile the boy was entranced by this strange doctor's unexpected rants against his parents, whom, *not* coincidentally, he was pretty angry with, too. When Erickson finally said he'd prefer not to deal with the boy's bedwetting at all, he shifted their "conversation" to talking about the muscle coordination necessary for the sport of archery, an interest of the boy's. By talking at length about growing up and the development of muscle control, Erickson was able to indirectly offer suggestions for the boy establishing control of his bladder muscles. Erickson's unusual intervention was a successful one, and it began by utilizing the boy's anger, first forming an alliance with him against his parents, or so it seemed, and then using the alliance to teach something the boy wanted to learn that was a perfect parallel to solving his problem. Such a case example illustrates points made earlier about using states of absorption to build new associations within the client, even associations not immediately in the person's awareness.

In general, age is a relatively minor consideration in assessing the capacity to respond hypnotically. Age is a factor to consider, though, in determining an effective approach for the induction and utilization that is appropriate to the age and background of the client.

SELF-ESTEEM AND HYPNOTIZABILITY

Every person has a self-esteem, a value they place on themselves in terms of their perceived self-worth. The self-esteem of a person can range from very low to very high. Self-esteem is not necessarily a stable trait that remains fixed throughout one's lifetime; rather it can go up or down with experience. Yet, self-esteem is self-regulating in that it can unintentionally motivate one to work very hard at staying the same in many important ways. If a person has a poor self-esteem, he or she is unlikely to take even small risks in his or her own behalf. New opportunities to grow, perhaps by leaving behind people and situations long outgrown, may be ignored. For example, a person may be unhappy with a certain life situation, but at the same time feel fearful and uncertain about changing it, and thus be immobilized. The person with a higher self-esteem, by contrast, is better able to take sensible risks, trusting him- or herself enough to manage new situations and opportunities appropriately.

The self-esteem of the client is a significant variable in his or her ability to respond meaningfully to the clinician's suggestions. Self-esteem, in part, determines what one views as possible for oneself. The little boy who says, "Mommy, I can't do math," is not likely to be reassured by a simple,

"Oh, sure you can." It creates dissonance between Mom's feedback and the boy's self-image.

If you consider the typical cigarette smoker as another example of cognitive dissonance (Festinger, 1957), you find that the smoker may view him- or herself as intelligent, sensitive, rational, and as having other positive intellectual qualities as well. If you ask this intelligent, sensitive, rational person why he or she inhales toxic gases voluntarily at great risk to his or her health, the reaction is likely to be defensive, perhaps even angry. You have posed a question that brings his or her irrational actions into awareness, suggesting that his or her way of managing him- or herself is not an entirely sensible one. A typical response to the contradictory feedback you provide is rationalization: "I only smoke a few each day. . . . I'd rather smoke than be overweight (as if they are a tradeoff). . . . I plan on quitting as soon as the stress I'm under eases up. . . ." The rationalizations are virtually endless in an attempt to maintain the belief that "I'm smart even though I smoke."

The point of cognitive dissonance and its importance for hypnotic communication is that information contradictory to what the person believes to be true is defended against through a variety of means in order to maintain the original belief. A person with a terrible self-image who is told, "You have so much to offer," is not likely to take that message in. The real skill of hypnotic communication is in knowing how to package a communication for someone in such a way as to maximize its likelihood of becoming internalized.

Self-image is directly related to how much control a person feels the need to have at all times. Control as an issue for some people was discussed previously as a factor affecting your work with hypnosis. If a client is terrified of losing control, then a formal, ritualized approach to hypnosis that emphasizes the need to respond obediently will be marginally successful at best. Conversely, if a client's self-image is a strong one and there is self-trust, the client can be comfortable that no one can do anything to him or her. For such people, control is not a significant issue. Such people are confident they can respond as they wish.

Self-esteem is an entirely learned phenomenon, not a trait present at birth. Your experiences and, more important, the conclusions you draw from those experiences, determine how you will view yourself. Confronting a client's self-image directly in the form of contradicting it is rarely a successful maneuver for changing it. Typically, the client just gets the feeling the clinician really doesn't understand him or her.

MENTAL STATUS AND HYPNOTIZABILITY

There have been numerous studies attempting to determine whether there is a relationship between hypnotizability and the development of specific clinical disorders. Using standardized measures of hypnotic responsiveness, higher levels of hypnotizability have been associated with phobias (Frankel, 1974, 1976), post-traumatic stress disorder (Spiegel, Hunt, & Dondershine, 1988), dissociative identity disorders (Bliss, 1986), sleep disturbances featuring nightmares (Belicki & Belicki, 1986), and eating disorders (Nash & Baker, 1993; Pettinati, Horne, & Staats, 1985) to name just a few. An increased responsiveness to suggestion, a greater capacity for dissociation, a deeper quality of experiential absorption—any or all of these and other factors, too, may combine to serve as a foundation for various disorders. The parallel notions of a "negative self-hypnosis" (Araoz, 1985) or a "symptomatic hypnosis" (Gilligan, 1987) have been valuable in underscoring the point made earlier that hypnosis is a neutral phenomenon, capable of generating a broad range of experiences, deemed either helpful or harmful depending on their outcome.

When hypnotizability can be associated (correlationally, not causally) with various disorders, does that mean you shouldn't do hypnosis with people suffering those disorders? The answer is unambiguous: You can do hypnosis with any category of disorder, but each category requires its own specialized approaches. For example, the approach you would use with someone who is highly dependent and other-oriented would differ from the approach you'd use with someone socially avoidant and inner-directed. More to the point, though, *we treat people, not diagnostic categories.* Some of the most limiting myths about hypnosis involve the "dangers" of doing hypnosis with particular clinical populations. In fact, much of my professional focus has been on the disorder of depression, a disorder for which hypnosis was taught for decades to be contraindicated. In my 1992 book, *Hypnosis and the Treatment of Depressions,* to my knowledge the very first book on the subject of applying hypnosis in the treatment of depressed individuals, I described at length the myths (such as that hypnosis would "strip" peoples' defenses and leave them suicidal), where they came from, and why they were myths in light of recent data.

I had also been taught that psychotic persons cannot be hypnotized. It is claimed they are unable to attend to the hypnotist's guidance due to their hallucinations, delusions, and confusion. Some psychiatrists have even said they are likely to rediagnose someone labeled psychotic if the person is found to be hypnotizable. There are others, though, who have described good clinical work involving hypnosis with psychotic patients (Baker, 1983; Brown, 1985; Murray-Jobsis, 1993; Rossi, 1980). When one teaches such disturbed patients formal, concrete relaxation procedures, makes contact with their idiosyncratic views, addresses any manipulative aspect there might be to the psychotic's behavior and removes the payoffs when possible, and metaphorically intervenes, psychotic patients may well improve.

Of course, the degree of psychosis is a variable to consider. I doubt a bipolar patient in peak manic phase, for example, can be affected by a good hypnotic suggestion or anything else verbal. The cause of the person's psychosis is an important factor as well. Drug-induced psychosis is difficult to overcome, as is psychosis associated with aging. Senility, though, depending on its degree, may not preclude hypnotic approaches. Many older patients suffering senile dementia can't remember what they were doing five minutes ago, but can remember with remarkable clarity things that occurred 50 years ago. Regressive techniques to early experiences can have a calming, soothing effect for them. Likewise, providing basic care of these and other psychotic patients, such as routine bathing and dressing, can have very positive effects when calming and supportive suggestions are simultaneously employed.

The mental status of the individual is obviously a pervasive factor influencing whether and how he or she will relate to you and your suggestions. As long as the focus stays on any given person's strengths and limitations rather than his or her diagnosis, the potential to help someone exists. This all-important point will be brought to life in a powerful way when when you experience Vicki, the terminal cancer patient in chapter 20, who got lost behind her labels. It cost her her life.

SINGLE FACTORS, MULTIFACTORS, AND HYPNOTIZABILITY

After all the research unsuccessfully attempting to relate single factors of personality, age, or whatever, with hypnotizability, it becomes clear that hypnotic responsiveness is a function of multiple factors operating together in some way. Woody, Bowers, and Oakman (1992) described three possible models of performance that involve a multifactor explanation. They are additive, synergistic, and disjunctive models of performance, and each has different implications for explaining performance in hypnosis. They wrote:

> It is the additive model that is generally presumed. This model suggests that social-psychological and special-trait effects are in principle separable, but in practice, on hypnosis scales, simultaneously coexisting. By contrast, the synergistic model would suggest that the essence of hypnotic performance may inhere in the holistic combination of the two kinds of mechanisms. Finally, the disjunctive model would suggest that a substantial proportion of subjects . . . can enact a given suggestion in either a social-psychological fashion or a dissociative one, depending, presumably, on situational factors. . . . Unfortunately, just as scores on a hypnosis scale do not specify the underlying mechanisms that produced them, neither do they allow us to track down how these mechanisms work together. (p. 19)

Despite the inability to tease out which hypothetical factors within someone create hypnotic responsiveness, the theories abound. Fred Evans (2000) proposed a multifactorial model of hypnotic behavior that emphasized a "complex mix" of four factors: expectations, suggestion, a cognitive component (including relaxation, imagery, and "trance logic"—the ability to withstand inconsistencies in information), and dissociation (described by Evans as a function of selective attention). Theodore X. Barber (2000) proposed the four-factor model described in detail in chapter 3.

Test-retest studies of hypnotizability show a high correlation, suggesting it is a relatively stable phenomenon over time. This has led many experts to consider responsiveness to hypnosis as a personality trait comparable to other personality traits. In their view, it is unclear whether one is born with a high, low, or absent "hypnotic susceptibility" gene structure, or whether this trait is acquired as a learned phenomenon through the socialization process. Regardless, in this view the presence or absence of the hypnotizability trait is a condition that remains relatively stable over time. In other words, if a person lacks responsiveness to a formal hypnosis induction procedure, he or she is deemed a poor subject, a "low." Further research studies on the reliability of this conclusion support it: Poor subjects seem to remain poor over time (in repeated attempts to induce hypnosis in the same person with the same or similar procedures), and good subjects seem to remain good over time. Is hypnotic responsiveness a fixed capacity, or can someone's responsiveness to hypnosis be enhanced?

ENHANCING HYPNOTIZABILITY

A practical concern of the clinician is how to maximize the client's responsiveness to the treatment. If responsiveness is viewed as innate to the client, then there is no need to experiment with different suggestion structures and styles. Either the client has "it," or he or she doesn't. Similarly, in manualizing treatments, either the technique "works," or it doesn't. Clinicians are generally highly skeptical, though, not easily persuaded that what they do is either reduceable to a ritualized treatment or irrelevant to how the client responds. Consequently, the motivation has existed on the part of many clinicians and researchers to go beyond the data declaring hypnotizability a fixed trait in an effort to explore ways of enhancing responsiveness.

Research demands standardization. Every research subject, regardless of whether it is in research on hypnosis or research in some other area, must experience the exact same procedure in order for a study to be considered scientific (i.e., controlled, replicable). In standardizing hypnotic inductions, the process must be the same: The timing, the hypnotist's voice dynamics, the degree of formality of the relationship between researcher and subject, the recording of responses to the procedure, the place, the lighting, and virtually every other variable must be carefully controlled. Consequently, a large number of research subjects are exposed to the same hypnosis procedure, then are given a test to determine their degree of responsiveness. The resulting statistics are published as evidence of the degree of hypnotizability of the general population of which the research population is a sample.

The standardization of techniques in order to promote a scientific hypnosis is a double-edged sword. On the one hand, a deeper, more scientific understanding of hypnosis is desirable if we are to better understand its mechanisms and range of applications. On the other hand, summarizing clients as a "low," "medium," or "high" (or some diagnostic label) reduces the ability of the clinician to notice and respond to the uniqueness of each person. Hypnosis, like therapy, will *never* be only science. It will always involve art (i.e., clinical judgment, creativity, and flexibility). I have gone to great lengths to make sure this book emphasizes *both*.

The important point for this section that follows the above is that hypnotizability may not be as fixed a trait as some believe. Looking back over the sections of this chapter, you can appreciate that there's not much you can do about someone's age, but what about all the other factors? For example, can skills in imagination, and fantasy-proneness be taught? What about improving self-esteem or changing someone's expectations and mental status?

Nicholas Spanos proposed a cognitive skills model which viewed hypnotic responding as a consequence of a variety of skills such as many of those already discussed (e.g., absorption, expectations). He argued quite convincingly that each of these factors is modifiable when people are given helpful information and training (1982). Michael Diamond (1977, 1989) took a similar position to Spanos and stated flatly that "hypnotizability is modifiable" (1977, p. 147). Jeffrey Gfeller (1993) named four specific ways from within the cognitive skills model that hypnotizability might be enhanced, making hypnotic treatment more readily accessible to a wider range of individuals. Gfeller's four strategies are:

Portraying hypnosis as a cognitive experience not far removed from many everyday life phenomena

Discussing the concept of goal-directed fantasy or imaginative involvement and its role in hypnotic experience

Elaborating on the importance of absorption and suspension of reality orientation for facilitating optimal hypnotic responsiveness

Explaining hypnosis as an active process to be learned by the patient as a coping skill (p. 240)

Irving Kirsch added his voice to the possibility of enhancing hypnotic responsiveness by offering specific suggestions for enhancing positive expectancy, including:

> Be permissive. Present and respect choices as therapeutic double binds, so that either choice promotes improvement. Prevent failure by beginning with easy tasks that the patient is almost certain to accomplish. Proceed gradually to more and more difficult tasks. Define tasks so that failure is impossible. Structure expectations so that even small improvements are seen as significant beginnings. Be alert to random fluctuations and capitalize on those that occur in a desired direction. Prepare patients for setbacks by labeling them in advance as inevitable, temporary, and useful learning opportunities. (1994, p. 104)

Steven Lynn and Steven Sherman (2000) offered an integrative model of hypnosis that also emphasizes the malleability of the hypnotic responsiveness of the individual. They wrote:

> To optimize responsiveness in clinical situations and to tailor the procedures to the unique characteristics of the individual, the integrative model implies that it is essential for the therapist to: (a) develop a positive rapport and therapeutic alliance with the patient that promotes the free-flowing quality of hypnotic experience; (b) understand the patient's motives and agenda (i.e., constellation of plans, intentions, wishes, and expectancies) in relation to experiencing hypnosis; (c) identify the personal connotations that hypnosis has for each patient, including their conflict and ambivalence about experiencing hypnosis; (d) assess the individual's stream of awareness and internal dialogue during hypnosis; (e) modify suggestions and hypnotic communications so as to minimize resistance and increase a sense of perceived control when it is lacking; (f) encourage patients to adopt lenient or liberal criteria for passing suggestions (e.g., "You don't have to imagine what I suggest as being real, even a faint image is fine"); and (g) encourage involvement in suggestions, the use of imagination, and attention to subtle alterations in experiences and responses. (pp. 303–4)

CONCLUSION

The advice offered by each of the experts quoted above is good, sound advice. Enhancing responsiveness to therapy, delivered hypnotically or otherwise, requires a flexibility and respectfulness of the client's experience that encourages the best in the person. The "positive psychology" in doing hypnosis is to go beyond labels, discover the unique resources of each person that can be mobilized in the service of the therapeutic goal, and build genuinely therapeutic relationships that foster responsiveness.

For Discussion

1. What do you think of the statement that "anyone who can be socialized can be hypnotized"?
2. Why do some researchers and clinicians seem to conclude that if they can't hypnotize someone, no one can?
3. What age-related factors should one take into consideration when formulating a hypnosis session? In what ways might an approach to a 60-year-old differ from an approach to a 20-year-old?
4. Is intelligence related to the ability to concentrate? Why or why not?
5. When should you strive to meet a client's expectations? When shouldn't you? Why do you say so? What personal and interpersonal dynamics should be taken into account in deciding whether or not to meet the client's expectations?

Things to Do

1. If possible, arrange to tour a psychiatric hospital or nursing home. In observing the residents of the facility, can you determine their degree, if any, of responsiveness to hypnosis? Can you specify any approaches that might be effective with them?
2. Make a list of every rationalization you have ever used to maintain a behavior of yours that you would consciously like to change. Can you see "cognitive dissonance" at work? In what ways?
3. Spend a week or two closely watching someone you know well in a variety of situations. In which situations does he or she seem open-minded and receptive? In which ones does he or she seem closed-minded? What factors can you list that seem to shape this person's responsiveness?

REFERENCES

Araoz, D. (1985). *The new hypnosis*. New York: Brunner/Mazel.

Baker, E. (1983). The use of hypnotic techniques with psychotics. *American Journal of Clinical Hypnosis, 25*, 283–8.

Barber, T. (1964). Hypnotizability, suggestibility, and personality: V. A critical review of research findings. *Psychological Reports, 14* (Monograph Suppl. 13), 299–320.

Barber, T. (2000). A deeper understanding of hypnosis: Its secrets, its nature, its essence. *American Journal of Clinical Hypnosis, 42*, 3–4, 208–73.

Belicki, K., & Belicki, D. (1986). Predisposition for nightmares: A study of hypnotic ability, vividness of imagery, and absorption. *Journal of Clinical Psychology, 42*, 714–18.

Bliss, E. (1986). *Multiple personality, allied disorders, and hypnosis.* New York: Oxford University Press.

Brown, D. (1985). Hypnosis as an adjunct to the psychotherapy of the severely disturbed patient: An affective development approach. *International Journal of Clinical and Experimental Hypnosis, 33*, 281–301.

Cooper, L., & London, P. (1966). Sex and hypnotic susceptibility in children. *International Journal of Clinical and Experimental Hypnosis, 14*, 55–60.

Cooper, L., & London, P. (1971). The development of hypnotic susceptibility: A longitudinal (convergence) study. *Child Development, 42*, 487–503.

Cooper, L., & London, P. (1976). Children's hypnotic susceptibility, personality, and EEG patterns. *International Journal of Clinical and Experimental Hypnosis, 24*, 140–48.

Cooper, L., & London, P. (1979). The children's hypnotic susceptibility scale. *American Journal of Clinical Hypnosis, 21*, 170–85.

Council, J., & Huff, K. (1990). Hypnosis, fantasy activity, and reports of paranormal experiences in high, medium, and low fantasizers. *British Journal of Experimental and Clinical Hypnosis, 7*, 9–15.

Costa, P., & McCrae, R. (1997). Four ways 5 factors are basic. In D. Funder & D. Ozer (Eds.), *Pieces of the personality puzzle* (pp. 163–72). New York: Norton.

Diamond, M. (1977). Hypnotizability is modifiable: An alternative approach. *International Journal of Clinical and Experimental Hypnosis, 25*, 147–65.

Diamond, M. (1989). The cognitive skills model: An emerging paradigm for investigating hypnotic phenomena. In N. Spanos & J. Chaves (Eds.), *Hypnosis: The cognitive-behavioral perspective* (pp. 380–99). Buffalo, NY: Prometheus Books.

Evans, F. (2000). The domain of hypnosis: A multifactorial model. *American Journal of Clinical Hypnosis, 43*, 1, 1–16.

Festinger, L. (1957). *A theory of cognitive dissonance.* Stanford, CA: Stanford University Press.

Frankel, F. (1974). Trance capacity and the genesis of phobic behavior. *Archives of General Psychiatry, 31*, 261–3.

Frankel, F. (1976). *Hypnosis: Trance as a coping mechanism.* New York: Plenum.

Geary, B. (2001). Assessment in Ericksonian hypnosis and psychotherapy. In B. Geary & J. Zeig (Eds.), *The handbook of Ericksonian psychotherapy* (pp. 1–17). Phoenix, AZ: The Milton H. Erickson Foundation Press.

Gfeller, J. (1993). Enhancing hypnotizability and treatment responsiveness. In J. Rhue, S. Lynn, & I. Kirsch (Eds.) (2002). *Handbook of clinical hypnosis* (pp. 235–49). Washington, D.C.: American Psychological Association.

Gilligan, S. (1987). *Therapeutic trances: The cooperation principle in Ericksonian hypnotherapy.* New York: Brunner/Mazel.

Haley, J. (1973). *Uncommon therapy: The uncommon psychiatric techniques of Milton H. Erickson, M.D.* New York: Norton.

Hilgard, E. (1965). *Hypnotic susceptibility.* New York: Harcourt Brace.

Hilgard, E. (1977). *Divided consciousness: Multiple controls in human thought and action.* New York: Wiley.

Hilgard, J. (1970). *Personality and hypnosis: A study of imaginative involvement* (2nd ed.). Chicago: University of Chicago Press.

Hornyak, L. (1999). Empowerment through giving symptoms voice. *American Journal of Clinical Hypnosis, 42*, 2, 132–39.

Kirsch, I. (1994). Clinical hypnosis as a nondeceptive placebo: Empirically derived techniques. *American Journal of Clinical Hypnosis, 37*, 95–106.

Kirsch, I. (2000). The response set theory of hypnosis. *American Journal of Clinical Hypnosis, 42*, 3–4, 274–93.

Kirsch, I., & Council, J. (1992). Situational and personality correlates of hypnotic responsiveness. In E. Fromm & M. Nash (Eds.), *Contemporary hypnosis research* (pp. 267–91). New York: Guilford.

Linden, J. (1995). When mind-body integrity is traumatized by problems with physical health: The women's response. In G. Burrows & R. Stanley (Eds.), *Contemporary international hypnosis* (pp. 169–75). Chichester, UK: Wiley.

Linden, J. (1997). On the art of hypnotherapy with women: Journeys to the birthplace of belief and other recipes for life. *Hypnos, 24*, 3, 138–47.

Linden, J. (1999). Discussion of symposium: Enhancing healing: The contributions of hypnosis to women's health care. *American Journal of Clinical Hypnosis, 42*, 2, 14–145.

Lynn, S., Neufeld, V., & Matyi, C. (1987). Inductions versus suggestions: Effects of direct and indirect wording on hypnotic responding and experience. *Journal of Abnormal Psychology, 96*, 76–9.

Lynn, S., & Sherman, S. (2000). The clinical importance of sociocognitive models of hypnosis: Response set theory and Milton Erickson's strategic interventions. *American Journal of Clinical Hypnosis, 42*, 3–4, 294–315.

Malinoski, P., & Lynn, S. (1999). The plasticity of early memory reports: Social pressure, hypnotizability, compliance, and interrogative suggestibility. *International Journal of Clinical and Experimental Hypnosis, 47*, 320–45.

Morgan, A., & Hilgard, E. (1973). Age differences in susceptibility to hypnosis. *International Journal of Clinical and Experimental* Hypnosis, 21, 78–85.

Murray-Jobsis, J. (1993). The borderline patient and the psychotic patient. In J. Rhue, S. Lynn, & I. Kirsch (Eds.), *Handbook of clinical hypnosis* (pp. 425–51). Washington, D.C.: American Psychological Association.

Nash, M., & Baker, E. (1993). Hypnosis in the treatment of anorexia nervosa. In J. Rhue, S. Lynn, & I. Kirsch (Eds.), *Handbook of clinical hypnosis* (pp. 383–94). Washington, D.C.: American Psychological Association.

Nordenstrom, B., Council, J., & Meier, B. (2002). The "Big Five" and hypnotic suggestibility. *International Journal of Clinical and Experimental Hypnosis, 50*, 3, 276–81.

Olness, K., & Kohen, D. (1996). *Hypnosis and hypnotherapy with children* (3rd ed.). New York: Guilford.

Pettinati, H., Horne, R., & Staats, J. (1985). Hypnotizability in patients with anorexia nervosa and bulimia. *Archives of General Psychiatry, 42*, 1014–16.

Piccione, C., Hilgard, E., & Zimbardo, P. (1989). On the degree of stability of measured hypnotizability over a 25 year period. *Journal of Personality and Social Psychology, 56*, 289–95.

Radtke, H. & Stam, H. (1991). The relation between absorption, openness to experience, anhedonia, and hypnotic susceptibility. *International Journal of Clinical and Experimental Hypnosis, 34*, 39–56.

Roche, S., & McConkey, K. (1990). Absorption: Nature, assessment, and correlates. *Journal of Personality and Social Psychology, 59*, 91–101.

Rossi, E. (Ed.) (1980). *The collected papers of Milton H. Erickson, M.D., on hypnosis* (Vols. I–IV). New York: Irvington.

Spanos, N. (1982). Hypnotic behavior: A cognitive social psychological perspective. *Research communications in Psychology, Psychiatry and Behavior, 1*, 199–213.

Spiegel, D., Hunt, T., & Dondershine, H. (1988). Dissociation and hypnotizability in posttraumatic stress disorder. *American Journal of Psychiatry, 145*, 3, 301–05.

Spiegel, H., & Spiegel, D. (1987). *Trance and treatment: Clinical uses of hypnosis.* Washington, D.C.: American Psychiatric Association.

Tellegen, A., & Atkinson, G. (1974). Openness to absorbing and self-altering experiences ("absorption"), a trait related to hypnotic susceptibility. *Journal of Abnormal Psychology, 83*, 268–77.

Vandenberg, B. (2002). Hypnotic responsivity from a developmental perspective: Insights from young children. *International Journal of Clinical and Experimental Hypnosis, 50*, 3, 229–47.

Waalen, J. (1997). Women in medicine: Bringing gender issues to the fore. *Journal of the American Medical Association, 277*, 1404.

Weitzenhoffer, A. (2000). *The practice of hypnotism* (2nd ed.). New York: Wiley.

Wilson, S., & Barber, T. (1981). Vivid fantasy and hallucinatory abilities in the life histories of excellent subjects ("somnambules"): Preliminary report with female subjects. In E. Klinger (Ed.), *Imagery: Concepts, results, and applications* (pp. 133–49). New York: Plenum.

Wilson, S., & Barber, T. (1983). The fantasy-prone personality: Implications for understanding imagery, hypnosis, and parapsycholgical phenomena. In A. Sheikh (Ed.), *Imagery: Current theory, research, and application* (pp. 340–87).New York: Wiley.

Woody, E., Bowers, K., & Oakman, J. (1992). In E. Fromm & M. Nash (Eds.), *Contemporary hypnosis research* (pp. 3–33). New York: Guilford.

Yapko, M. (1988). *When living hurts: Directives for treating depression.* New York: Brunner/Mazel.

Yapko, M. (1989). Disturbances of temporal orientation as a feature of depression. In M. Yapko (Ed.), *Brief therapy approaches to treating anxiety and depression* (pp. 106–18). New York: Brunner/Mazel.

Yapko, M. (1992). *Hypnosis and the treatment of depressions: Strategies for change.* New York: Brunner/Mazel.

Yapko, M. (1993). Hypnosis and depression. In J. Rhue, S. Lynn, & I. Kirsch (Eds.), *Handbook of clinical hypnosis* (pp. 339–55). Washington, D.C.: American Psychological Association.

Yapko, M. (2001). *Treating depression with hypnosis: Integrating cognitive-behavioral and strategic approaches.* Philadelphia, PA: Brunner/Routledge.

9

The Phenomenology
of Hypnosis

Imagine yourself at work in your usual clinical context. You have a person in front of you who is in some form of distress, and you genuinely want to help make a positive difference in this person's life. You gather salient information you believe will help you form a sensible intervention, and simultaneously you establish a nice rapport with the person. You suggest hypnosis may be helpful in the treatment process and invite the person to begin to focus on your words. You suggest beginning by shifting his or her focus inwardly and then you proceed with your induction. What happens to the person as he or she participates in this process? What's qualitatively different, more or less, about the person experiencing hypnosis that makes performing hypnosis a worthwhile endeavor?

Hypnosis is a highly subjective experience, for no two people experience it in exactly the same way. Appreciating the uniqueness of each person you interact with is a worthy goal in general, but if you want to learn to apply hypnotic patterns effectively, it is a strict requirement. There are certain assumptions that are beyond question and are unfailing when doing clinical hypnosis. One concerns the uniqueness of each person and all that uniqueness implies about each person's individual personal history and responses being unlike anyone else's. A second assumption is that each person is going to have his or her own way of experiencing hypnosis; what specific subjective associations your communications will trigger in the client will be unknown to you until they are somehow communicated to you (unless you are a board-certified mind-reader). A third assumption concerns the multidimensionality of hypnotic experience: Whatever the client is experiencing will have cognitive, behavioral, emotional, spiritual, relational, and physical features. Which dimension(s) you choose to focus on and amplify will be a product of your own style of intervention.

As you are now aware, the efforts to quantify and measure hypnotic phenomena in various research populations have been the backbone of the scientific study of hypnosis. However, as Australian psychologist Peter

Sheehan (1992) pointed out, "Adopting a phenomenological framework is a very useful means of exploring hypnotic phenomena. It enables us to look at processes, for example, in more detail than many other approaches afford, and it reveals the diversity and richness of hypnotic experience and behavior" (p. 364). In this chapter, we will briefly consider many of the most common phenomenological or subjective experiences of the person in hypnosis on a variety of dimensions, divided for simplicity's sake into two broader categories: "psychological" and "physical" characteristics of hypnosis.

PSYCHOLOGICAL CHARACTERISTICS OF HYPNOSIS

EXPECTANCY

As many of the sociocognitive theorists have pointed out, the client is encouraged to expect a change in his or her experience and to accept those suggestions that will fulfill that expectation (Barber, 2000; Kirsch, 2000; Wagstaff, 1998). Many clients actively seek out hypnosis as an intervention because they have the expectation that the experience of hypnosis will be powerful, dramatic, and effective (Lynn & Rhue, 1991; Spanos & Coe, 1992). The mind-set of the client is ideally one consistent with the aims of treatment, and building positive expectancy in order to enhance responsiveness is given deliberate attention by the clinician (Yapko, 1992, 2001).

SELECTIVE ATTENTION

If you have ever heard or used the phrase, "He only sees what he wants to see," then you have an awareness that people can notice what they choose to notice. By implication, we can also *not* notice what we choose not to. This perceptual phenomenon is referred to as "selective attention," that is, the ability to focus on one portion of an experience while "tuning out" the rest. Focusing on a specific stimulus (usually your words or your gestures) to the near-exclusion of other ongoing stimuli is a foundation of hypnotic experience upon which the other phenomena rest. Without the focus to attend to the suggestions of the clinician, not much else that's useful is likely to happen (Spiegel & Spiegel, 1987).

The conscious mind is limited in its ability to pay attention to numerous things occurring simultaneously. We consciously notice only a relatively small part of a total experience. How do you decide which part of an experience to pay attention to? For example, at a concert are you more likely to notice how the musicians look, the words to their songs, or how you feel while you're there? Which part of the concert sticks in your memory? Why *that* particular part?

There are a number of complex factors that determine what works its way into one's field of attention. These include: The degree of sensory stimulation (how weak or strong the stimulus is); the novelty of the stimulus; the person's response tendencies (arising from a complex interplay of socialization and genetics); the person's motivation in the context under consideration; the person's mood; and the kinds and amounts of other sensory stimulation co-existing in the environment.

The client must gradually selectively attend to the provided suggestions and narrow her attention to the associations the suggestions stimulate. The client's focus is generally inward, and so although external events may be noticed and responded to, they typically account for only a small portion of the client's attention. And, while the person's conscious awareness is focused on specific aspects of their experience, the unconscious mind becomes more prominent in its ability to respond to things outside of the person's attentional field. This is a basis for the next characteristic I will discuss: Dissociation.

DISSOCIATION

Ernest Hilgard's neodissociation model of hypnosis (1991) conceptualizes hypnosis as a relaxation of or decreased reliance on the executive cognitive functions. The "executive ego," or "central control structure," is tasked with planning and monitoring various functions of the personality, including the various cognitive subsystems subservient to the executive ego. Hilgard believes that in hypnosis, the various subsystems can become independent of or *dissociated* from one another and can thus respond independently to the clinician's suggestions.

Dissociation, in effect, means that normally integrated and synergistically functioning parts of a person are increasingly able to function autonomously. Stated more simply, while the person in hypnosis has his or her attention selectively focused on the suggestions of the clinician and whatever unconscious associations may be triggered as a result, there is a type of separation occurring between the conscious and unconscious minds. The conscious mind tends to be occupied with the details of the hypnotic process, while the unconscious tends to actively search for symbolic meanings, past associations, and appropriate responses relevant to the suggestions received. This separation of conscious and unconscious during hypnosis is accomplished in varying degrees with different people, and is called "dissociation." Dissociation is so critical a component of the experience that it can reasonably be said that hypnosis cannot take place without *some* degree of dissociation being present. In general, the greater the degree of dissociation, the deeper the person's experience of hypnosis. The fact that the conscious and unconscious minds can be divided and utilized as interdependent yet independent entities is thus the backbone of the clinical applications of hypnosis.

A second aspect of dissociation refers to the sense of detachment people may experience in some situations, especially traumatic ones (Spiegel, 1993). A third aspect of the dissociative nature of the hypnotic experience is evident in the "parallel awarenesses" people typically report they have during hypnosis. The person may well report about his or her experience something like, "*Part of me* was aware of you and what you were saying, and *part of me* was totally into my own experience and tuned you out."

ERNEST HILGARD'S "HIDDEN OBSERVER"

The client in hypnosis can have multiple awarenesses, each operating on a separate level. One of these levels is a mostly objective one that has a relatively realistic understanding of the nature of the experience, a part of the person Hilgard (1977) called the "hidden observer." The "hidden observer" is separated (dissociated) from the immediacy of the suggested experiences, and can maintain a degree of objectivity about the experience. Hilgard described it this way: "The 'hidden observer' was intended merely as a convenient label for the information source capable of a high level of cognitive functioning, not consciously experienced by the hypnotized person" (1992, p. 77). This dissociative characteristic of hypnosis allows the client to attend to and respond to suggestions with a "believed-in imagination" (Sarbin, 1997), while at the same time observing him- or herself go through the experience more objectively. The implication of the hidden observer is that even in deeper hypnotic experiences the client knows what he or she is doing and what is going on. As the field has learned the hard way, due primarily to the acrimonious repressed memory controversy, there are extreme conditions in which the person loses clarity for the line separating fantasy from reality and can adopt as "true" experiences that are not. In the great majority of cases, however, and when sessions are structured appropriately by the clinician, the individual does maintain a strong enough reality orientation to discard offensive or even merely irrelevant suggestions (Lynn & Rhue, 1991; Sheehan & McConkey, 1982).

MARTIN ORNE'S "TRANCE LOGIC"

In a seminal contribution to the literature of hypnosis, Martin T. Orne, M.D., Ph.D., claimed that one of the most important attributes of hypnotic experience is the ability to comfortably tolerate incongruities or inconsistencies in suggestions that in the usual so-called "waking" state would be disturbing (Orne, 1959). Orne offered this example of a subject's stated perceptions of transparency of another person: "This is very peculiar: I can see

Joe sitting in the chair and I can see the chair through him"(p. 295). Orne termed this phenomenon "trance logic."

In clinical practice, trance logic refers to the client's lack of need for objectifying his or her experience. In other words, the client can accept a suggested reality, however illogical and even impossible it may be, as if it were the only reality. For example, if I want to do an intervention hypnotically involving the client's currently inaccessible parents (who may live in a distant place or perhaps are deceased), I can suggest to the client that he or she see his or her parents and interact with them on the issue(s) needing resolution. There may be an element of role playing present, but trance logic allows the client to respond to his or her parents in the "here-and-now" as if they are really there, rather than responding with an intellectual assessment such as, "How can my parents be here when they live in Europe?"

Things that don't make much logical sense can make perfect sense to the hypnotized person engaging in trance logic. This affords the clinician the opportunity to conduct clinical sessions that can be highly creative and imaginative, unfettered by a conventional sense of reality. Trance logic is a voluntary acceptance of suggestions on the part of the client, without the critical evaluation taking place that would, of course, destroy the validity or meaningfulness of provided suggestions. The opportunity to act "as if" something were real can be a gateway to deeper feelings and issues appropriate for therapeutic intervention.

FRAME OF REFERENCE: MARTIN T. ORNE, M.D., PH.D.

Martin T. Orne, M.D., Ph.D. (1927– 2000) was one of the most influential hypnosis researchers of all time. Unfortunately, I never had the occasion to meet Dr. Orne in person, one of my few professional regrets. (Consequently, the quotes in this section are taken from his writings and not from personal communications as in most of the other Frame of Reference sections.)

As a teacher, scientist, and practicing physician, Dr. Orne's expertise was primarily in the domains of hypnosis and memory distortion. Throughout his illustrious career, Dr. Orne collaborated with his wife, psychologist Emily Orne. Their research on hypnosis and its effects on the accuracy of recall was cited in more than 30 legal cases by state supreme courts and the U.S. Supreme Court. His work was so highly regarded and influential that he was given awards for his lifetime contributions from the American Psychological Association, the American Psychological Society, and the American Academy of Psychiatry and the Law.

Born in Vienna, Austria, to a surgeon father and a psychiatrist mother, Dr. Orne moved with his parents to the United States in 1938. The Orne family settled in New York, then eventually moved to Boston. Dr. Orne received his bachelor's degree from Harvard University, his medical degree from Tufts University in 1955, did his residency in psychiatry at Massachusetts Mental Health Center, and returned to Harvard to receive his Ph.D. in Psychology in 1958. He was a professor of psychiatry and psychology at the University of Pennsylvania for 32 years before retiring as emeritus professor in 1996. Besides his seminal contributions to our understanding of the effects of suggestion on memory, Dr. Orne was also widely recognized for his work in biofeedback, pain management, sleep disturbances, and his exceptional analysis of the role of demand characteristics in hypnotic research in particular and psychological research in general. His contributions to our understanding of the social context in which hypnosis takes place are profound. He was a prolific writer, publishing hundreds of scientific papers, many of which are referred to throughout this book and should be considered essential reading. Dr. Orne was also editor of the *International Journal of Clinical and Experimental Hypnosis* for 30 years. His interest in encouraging scientific research on the relationship between the mind and physical health and emotional well-being led him to establish the nonprofit Institute for Experimental Psychiatry Research Foundation. He served as its Executive Director until, shortly before he died, his declining health precluded him from continuing.

Dr. Orne's expertise in memory distortion arising from suggestive influences and even from coercion led to his involvement as an expert witness in a number of famous and infamous cases. Among them was the 1981 trial of Kenneth Bianchi, the former security guard who confessed to being the so-called Hillside Strangler, the killer of five women in the late 1970s. Bianchi contended he suffered from multiple personality disorder, but Dr. Orne was able to cleverly prove to the court's satisfaction that this explanation was a fabrication. Dr. Orne was also an expert witness in the sensational Patty Hearst case. Hearst was the heiress who took part in a 1974 bank robbery after being kidnapped and held captive by a radical group known as the Symbionese Liberation Army. Dr. Orne testified to the role of coercion in her participation, and drew upon his extensive knowledge of the phenomenon of mind-control tactics he had researched as part of his interest in demand characteristics and suggestibility.

Dr. Orne's research again took center stage when the false memory controversy developed in the mid-1990s. He helped expose the unfortunate methods of some psychotherapists who were unwittingly encouraging the creation of false memories of childhood sexual trauma. Dr. Orne used his considerable authority to drive home the point in his last years of work that he had first made as an undergraduate at Harvard in his very first published paper: Age regressed adults are not literally reliving their early childhoods, but are recalling them through the filters of adult understandings and perspectives.

Dr. Orne's lifetime achievements helped shape the modem practice of hypnosis in many ways. The following quotes from his writings can give you a glimpse of this very special man.

On Suggested Realities in Hypnosis: ". . . an important attribute of hypnosis is a potentiality for the (subject) to experience as subjectively real suggested alterations in his environment that do not conform with reality" (Orne, 1959, p. 297).

On Demand Characteristics in Human Research: "A particularly striking aspect of the typical experimenter-subject relationship is the extent to which the subject will play his role and place himself under the control of the experimenter. Once a subject has agreed to participate in a psychological experiment, he implicitly agrees to perform a very wide range of actions on request without inquiring as to their purpose, and frequently without inquiring as to their duration. Furthermore, the subject agrees to tolerate a considerable degree of discomfort, boredom, or actual pain, if required to do so by the experimenter. Just about any request which could conceivably be asked of the subject by a reputable investigator is legitimized by the quasi-magical phrase, "This is an experiment," and the shared assumption that a legitimate purpose will be served by the subject's behavior" (Orne, 1962, p. 777).

On the Potential Harm to Clients When the Therapist is Misguided: "The therapist using hypnosis, like any other therapist, will strive to ally himself with the healthy wishes and aspirations of the patient, but it is of course possible for a disturbed therapist to ally himself with destructive aspects of a patient's personality and facilitate destructive behavior" (Orne, 1972, pp. 113–4).

On Being Blinded By Our Desire to Help: "We should keep in mind that psychologists and psychiatrists are not particularly adept at recognizing deception. We generally arrange the social context of treatment so that it is not in the patient's interest to lie to us, and we appropriately do not concern ourselves with this issue since in most therapeutic contexts it is helpful for the therapist to see the world through the patient's eyes in order to ultimately help him view it more realistically" (Orne, 1979, p. 334).

On More Detailed Memories Not Necessarily Being More Accurate Memories: "Typically, age regressed individuals will spontaneously elaborate a myriad of details which apparently could only be brought forth by someone actually observing the events as they transpired. It is these details which sophisticated clinicians find most compelling and occasionally cause them to testify that they know with certainty that the individual was truly regressed. It is rare indeed, however, for the clinician to have the time, energy, or need to be certain that would cause him to verify the accuracy of an individual's description of events that transpired many years ago in childhood. Unfortunately, without objective detailed verification, the clinician's belief in the historical accuracy of the memories brought forth under hypnosis is likely to be erroneous" (Orne, 1979, p. 316).

On Hypnosis and the Courts: "Since it is widely believed by laymen that there is a virtual certainty of obtaining truthful information when a subject's critical judgment is diminished by either hypnosis or a drug, it is hardly surprising that efforts have been made to introduce hypnotic testimony in court as a way for the defendant to demonstrate his innocence to a jury. The courts, however, have recognized that hypnotic testimony is not reliable as a means of ascertaining truth and appropriately rejected both of these techniques as means of determining factual information" (Orne, 1979, p. 313).

On the Efficacy of Hypnosis in Relation to Individual Hypnotizability: ". . . there is ample clinical evidence that the efficacy of hypnotic procedures is often unrelated to an individual's hypnotic talent . . . This is not to say that the changes achieved necessarily rely on the same processes for persons with differing levels of hypnotizability. In some circumstances, the therapeutic benefit of a hypnotic intervention can be traced to nonspecific aspects of the therapy, yet the treatment response may be no less profound. . . . Hypnotic procedures can have an important effect on the response of even low hypnotizable individuals, particularly in circumstances where the response does not require extraordinary hypnotic talent" (Orne, Whitehouse, Dinges, & Orne, 1996, p. 355).

On Friendship: "Friendship is a complex process. It is sometimes hard, and often difficult to maintain. But it is joyous, too, and full of unexpected rewards. All that is really needed is the patience and commitment to make it work" (quoted by Bloom, 2000, p. 104).

THE TENDENCY TOWARD LITERAL INTERPRETATION

One of the potential complications, especially in the beginning phases of working with hypnosis, is the phenomenon known as "literalism" or a tendency toward the "literal interpretation" of communication by the person in hypnosis. André Weitzenhoffer, Ph.D., described it this way: The term *literal* and its derivatives has at least a half dozen different but related dictionary meanings that focus on the fact that all words have a primary, basic, habitual, literal meaning, as contrasted to a figurative metaphoric one acquired over time. Some people are more prone to act in terms of this literal meaning even when a figurative one is clearly intended. Applied to the hypnosis situation, a subject who would respond to the statement about someone present as being "bright," meaning "intelligent," by seeing the person as surrounded by light, would correctly be considered to have responded literally to the term *bright* (2000, p. 185).

Milton Erickson (1980) reported on his subjective assessment of 1,800 hypnotized and 3,000 nonhypnotized individuals regarding the phenomenon of literalism. He claimed that the great majority of hypnotized subjects responded literally while the overwhelming majority (95%) of nonhypnotized individuals did not. (He asked them, "Do you mind telling me your name?", and a literal response was either a simple yes or no without offering the name).

Green et al. (1990) and Lynn et al. (1990) conducted more well-controlled experiments to test the presence of literalism in hypnotic subjects. Their findings indicate that while literalism may be found in some subjects, the number is relatively small. They conclude that compliance with perceived task demands better accounts for Erickson's seemingly inflated results.

Thus, rather than a predictable characteristic of the hypnotic experience, a tendency toward literal interpretation may best be thought of as a possible response style which might lead the client to react to your words at their face value, in spite of what you may actually have meant. This is the basis for developing a careful approach to clients in terms of your word choices. My earliest mentor, clinician Neil Simon, used to tell this story reflecting one of his earliest experiences with literal interpretation in hypnosis. He was working with a woman who wanted hypnotic anesthesia to manage a minor surgery she was going to have on her wrist to remove a growth. Neil provided an induction of hypnosis and directly suggested that she *"develop an anesthesia in your arm."* She did this quite readily. In order to test her degree of anesthesia, Neil took a pin and gently poked her arm in a series of spots progressively downward from her shoulder. Each poke was met with a comfortable "No, I can't feel that." When Neil poked the back of her hand, she yelled "Ow!" Neil asked, "What's wrong?" and the woman responded "You said my *arm* was numb, not my *hand*!" Well, Neil knew what he meant—an arm is everything from the shoulder down. To his client, though, an arm is an arm and a hand is a hand, and they're not the same! Needless to say, Neil learned quickly to be more specific about what he suggests.

A gentle reminder: How a given person will respond to a word or phrase is unpredictable. Remember, the person is using his or her own frame of reference (i.e., experience, understanding) to make meaning out of your words. The best you can do is use words carefully enough to leave as little room (or as much room, as the case may be) for misinterpretation. Training in clinical hypnosis with peers allows for the kind of feedback on the impact of your words and phrases that your clients are highly unlikely to provide. Finding out which things you said that enhanced the hypnotic experience and which hindered it are valuable aspects of small-group training in clinical hypnosis.

INCREASED RESPONSIVENESS TO SUGGESTION

The attentional and dissociational factors described above can lead to an increased responsiveness to suggestion. Increased responsiveness is evidenced as a greater willingness in the client to be guided by the suggestions of the clinician, that is, to experience the perceptual shifts being suggested. Furthermore, by definition, the person in hypnosis would be more responsive to experiences that, outside of hypnosis, he or she would not be.

From a clinical point of view, when you are concerned about maximizing a client's responsiveness to your treatment, the increased responsiveness hypnosis affords makes it an especially valuable clinical tool. Why are clients more likely to respond? It may be the lowered defenses, the greater focus, the calmer attention to problem-solving, the support of the clinician, and any or all of dozens of such contributing factors.

Responsiveness is not to be confused with gullibility, or noncritical acceptance of suggestions (Barber, 1969). Contrary to the mythology, the hypnotic experience in a respectful clinical or research context actually *amplifies* a person's range of choices, including the choice to reject a suggestion that isn't desirable or relevant. The increased responsiveness to suggestion is a choice on the part of the client to be guided by someone he or she trusts and feels is benevolent in wanting to help. If the personal, interpersonal, and contextual dynamics are not favorable, responsiveness is nonexistent and the result is what is classically termed a "poor response" or even "resistance."

COGNITIVE AND PERCEPTUAL FLEXIBILITY

There are different cognitive styles, that is, ways of thinking about experience. This is true not only across individuals, but also within individuals.

You have different styles of thinking about different types of experiences. For example, some things you may approach more globally or "holistically," while other things you approach more specifically or in "detail" (Crawford & Allen, 1983), and how you think naturally influences your perceptions.

Cognitive styles of the hypnotized person have been studied by a number of researchers (Evans, 1991; Labelle, Laurence, Nadon, & Perry, 1990). Peter Sheehan (1992) described different cognitive styles of response to hypnotic suggestions, but concluded ". . . no one style typifies the response of hypnotic subjects to suggestion, and it is interesting to note that vastly different styles of response may be adopted by equally susceptible subjects" (p. 367). He further noted that, "A subject may use one or more of these styles during the same hypnotic session, and to a considerable extent the choice of style varies with the task complexity . . ." (p. 367). The ability to move in and out of different cognitive styles, and the different perceptual experiences associated with them, as demand dictates, and as hypnosis enhances, is the essence of cognitive flexibility.

As you have learned already, many of the cognitive changes associated with hypnosis surface in the arenas of memory, awareness, absorption, rationality, imaginative ability, imagery, and attention (Barber, 2000; Holroyd, 1992). These have been and continue to be heavily researched since they represent the more compelling aspects of hypnosis. *Every clinician who uses hypnosis is doing so for the express purpose of creating perceptual shifts that enhance the client's quality of life.* Thus, encouraging a cognitive style that permits excruciating pain to be transformed in perception to a mere annoyance, for example, is an invaluable application of such cognitive research. Encouraging a perception of accelerated time that permits a long unpleasant medical procedure to subjectively seem to go by quickly (i.e., "time distortion") is another example of helpful hypnosis. Frederick Evans (1991) has been particularly interested in the greater ease the hypnotized person has in making the transition from one cognitive style to another, or from one form of consciousness to another. He concluded that dissociation is clearly a relevant factor as the person moves from one seemingly discrete portion of experience to another.

Cognitive flexibility in a clinical context has a different connotation than in the research environment, however. Given how often so-called "cognitive distortions" (i.e., errors in information processing) are associated with various disorders (Beck, Rush, Shaw, & Emery, 1979), it becomes an even more vital application of hypnosis to be able to catalyze cognitive shifts and promote cognitive restructuring. The value of hypnosis for enhancing flexibility, whether cognitive, behavioral, perceptual, or on many other dimensions, is a primary reason for integrating hypnosis into psychotherapy in general, and cognitive-behavioral therapies in particular (Yapko, 2001). The empirical evidence supports such applications (Schoenberger, 2000).

PHYSICAL CHARACTERISTICS OF HYPNOSIS

When you perform an induction of hypnosis on a client, how do you know your client is in hypnosis? The answer is a definite . . . you don't. As you know, there is no clearly defined, unambiguous state called "hypnosis." From a clinical point of view, rather than theoretical or experimental points of view, we are interested in the client getting focused on suggested ideas, absorbed in generating positive possibilities, and building meaningful internal associations to the resources needed to live life better. At just what moment a person has gone from his or her usual awareness to a more focused and "hypnotized" experience is not definable with scientific precision. Instead, there are more general indicators of hypnotic absorption that clinicians can use to evolve a practiced sense of when the person is hypnotically engaged (Erickson, Rossi, & Rossi, 1976; Erickson & Rossi, 1979; Weitzenhoffer, 2000).

Physical characteristics of hypnosis are usually the only indicators you will have available for assessing your client's experience unless you specifically ask for verbal or nonverbal feedback about the client's internal experience. Asking for feedback *during* the hypnosis session is a good idea if you want to avoid the trap of "reading body language" (i.e., projecting your interpretations onto what someone's behavior "means").

You can be an excellent observer of your client's physical responses to hypnosis without having to interpret them. Noticing your client shifting his or her position in the chair, for example, allows you to comment on it in a helpful way: "As you adjust your position, you can make yourself even more comfortable allowing you to become even more deeply absorbed in the experience." Noticing the physical changes that take place in the client simply provide information that can be used to further the goals of treatment. You can't use the information, though, if you don't notice it. Thus, it is valuable to practice skills in close observation of others. Physical indicators that may be useful for you to observe include:

Muscular Relaxation

One can be in hypnosis without being relaxed, but the relaxation of mind and body is a general characteristic most people associate with hypnosis. Most hypnotic processes involve relaxation as a way of facilitating dissociation of the conscious from the unconscious mind. Relaxation feels good to clients, alters their experience of themselves in a marked way, and may even convince them that they have, in fact, been hypnotized. Notice the person's level of tension carried in the body and especially the facial muscles both before and during your work for comparison. When you can see muscles relaxing, clearly an internal shift is taking place.

Muscular Twitching

As the body and mind relax, often there are spasms that are wholly involuntary and are related to the neurological changes that take place with relaxation.

Lacrimation

As the person relaxes, occasionally his or her eyes may water. Some clinicians automatically assume the person is upset and shedding a tear, but that is an unjustifiable leap to a possibly (and probably) erroneous conclusion. Whenever you are in doubt about what the client is experiencing, ask him or her for direct feedback using neutral (i.e., non-leading) questions (e.g., "Can you describe what you are aware of right now?").

Eye Closure with Fluttering Eyelids

As the person begins to shift his or her focus and experience hypnosis, his or her eyelids may flutter at a very fast rate and usually outside of awareness. Also, rapid eye movements under the eyelid are observable throughout much of the hypnosis session, even more so if the process involves a lot of suggestions for visualization.

Change in Breathing Rate

A change, either speeding up or slowing down, of breathing is typical. Observe the client's breathing patterns before and during the process for comparison. When you see changes in the rate and quality of the person's breathing, some internal shift is clearly taking place. Some people's breathing becomes shallower as they get absorbed in the process, some people's becomes deeper. Some breathe from the chest, others breathe from the diaphragm. What's significant is the change in breathing, not necessarily the specifics of the change.

Change in Pulse Rate

A change in the pulse rate of the person, either speeding up but usually slowing down, is also typical of hypnosis. When the client is sitting back, you can usually observe pretty easily the pulsing of the carotid artery in his or her neck. Some clinicians prefer (after asking for the client's permission) to hold the client's wrist "to be supportive" during the session, and use the opportunity to take a reading of his or her radial pulse.

Jaw Relaxes

Often the person's lower jaw drops and seems subjectively to weigh so much that it takes conscious effort to close his or her mouth.

Catalepsy

The term "catalepsy" refers to an inhibition of voluntary movement that is reflective of the absorption of the hypnotic experience. Unlike routine states of consciousness or even a sleep state in which one is in almost constant motion, the client in hypnosis makes very few, if any, movements. It just takes too much effort for the relaxed and focused client. Furthermore, the client in hypnosis typically feels dissociated (i.e., detached) from his or her body anyway, and so tends to simply forget about it.

Every once in a while, and this is especially true of children, you may experience someone who moves around a lot rather than being immobile as you might expect. In one training course, I had a student in the class nick-named "The Thrasher." When he experienced hypnosis he liked to roll on the floor and wriggle around quite a bit. On ending the hypnosis, he described how good it felt to relax his body through movement. Interestingly, though, further questioning revealed that a lot of the movements he was making he wasn't even aware of! Even though a client's movement may seem excessive or disruptive, or interpreted as evidence that he or she isn't "getting into it," in fact the client may still be in hypnosis. You can use the other physical indicators to support your assessment of the client's degree of involvement.

Sensory Shifts

The person's body awareness may change in any of a variety of ways: Some people develop feelings of heaviness, as if each limb weighs a ton, while others develop feelings of lightness, as if they're floating weightlessly. Some start to feel physically large, and some start to feel very small. Some people feel more closely associated to their body and become ultrasensitive to physical sensations, and others become quite detached and unaware of their body, even to the point of developing a spontaneous (i.e., one not suggested) analgesia or anesthesia.

Each of the physical characteristics described above may be used as general indicators of hypnosis, but no one sign alone can tell you what your client is actually experiencing internally. In a sense, the clinician is a visitor to someone else's inner world, and so should be observant, cautious, and above all, respectful.

Your assessment as to when to shift from one phase of your hypnosis session to another, for example, going from induction into therapeutic utilization of the hypnosis, will be based on how well you observe changes in the client's body and demeanor. Taking an initial baseline of level of muscular tension, breathing, and pulse rates, and anything else you can notice before beginning to do hypnosis gives you the opportunity to notice changes which suggest the development of an experience that is different from the baseline. You can't always know what the content of the person's experience is, but you can observe changes that suggest an impact from the your guidance. The more skilled you become in observing such changes, the more comfortable you can be in adapting to the ongoing changes in the experience of the client. Many of these changes are listed in Table 1 below.

ASSESSING THE PHENOMENOLOGY OF HYPNOTIC EXPERIENCE

Assessing hypnotic *behavior* is understandably popular as a research method, since behavior can be observed. However, in doing clinical work, as valuable as objective instruments scoring hypnotic behavior might be, what ultimately matters the most is the individual client's actual *experience*. Thus, some researchers have taken on the task of developing ways to better understanding the phenomenology of the client's hypnotic experience. Peter Sheehan and Kevin McConkey developed an instrument called the *Experiential Analysis Technique* (EAT) for evaluating the heterohypnosis experience

---

Table 1. The Experience of Hypnosis

Experiential and selective absorption of attention
Effortless expression
Experiential, nonconceptual involvement
Willingness to experiment
Flexibility in time/space relations
Alterations of perceptions
Fluctuations in degrees of involvement
Motoric/verbal inhibition
"Trance logic"; reduction in reality testing
Symbolic processing
Time distortion
Spontaneous amnesia

(Sheehan & McConkey, 1982; Sheehan, 1992). Erika Fromm and Stephen Kahn (1990) developed one for evaluating the self-hypnosis experience called the Self-Hypnosis Proper Questionnaire (SHPQ). More recently, Ron Pekala and V. K. Kumar (Pekala & Kumar, 2000; Pekala, 2002) have developed an instrument called the *Phenomenology of Consciousness Inventory* (PCI), also for heterohypnosis experiences. These instruments, and others developed by other researchers, represent important steps in the direction of learning more about the range and quality of peoples' hypnotic experiences.

CONCLUSION

This chapter has attempted to give you some insight into the internal experience of the hypnotized person. An experience as subjective as hypnosis will inevitably differ in quality from person to person. Therefore, all the general characteristics of hypnotic experience described in this chapter are likely to be present in most clients, but in varying degrees. In some cases, they may even be absent. The single most valuable source of knowledge about your client's experience is your client. If you want to know something about his or her experience, you'll just have to ask. You may not always get as truthful or as insightful a response as you'd hoped for, but the person in hypnosis is still the best source of information.

For Discussion

1. Why are some people so intense while others are so easily distracted? What are the advantages and disadvantages of each style?
2. Based on your own experiences of hypnosis, do you think hypnosis can be used to generate antisocial behavior in someone? Why or why not?
3. Have each person in the class describe their experience of hypnosis in as much detail as possible. What experiences seem to be common? Which ones do you recognize as being unique to that person?
4. When in the course of daily living is having a parallel awareness an asset? A liability?
5. How is suggestibility different than gullibility?

Things to Do

1. Share an experience with the class of a vacation or some similarly complex experience. Which kinds of details do you tend to focus on? Why? What sort of details do class members identify as being missing or minimally present in your story? Does this indicate anything about you? What, if anything, might it indicate?
2. Do something, such as walk around the room and pick up objects of interest to you. While doing this, verbally describe your every movement. How does it feel to both participate and observe yourself doing something? Is it easy or hard to do? Why?
3. What commonly used phrases can you and your classmates think of that might generate unwanted responses in someone who responded to the phrase with literal interpretation?

REFERENCES

Barber, T. (1969). *Hypnosis: A scientific approach*. New York: Van Nostrand Reinhold. (Reprinted 1995: Northvale, N.J.: Aronson).

Barber, T. (2000). A deeper understanding of hypnosis: Its secrets, its nature, its essence. *American Journal of Clinical Hypnosis, 42*, 3–4, 208–73.

Beck, A., Rush, A., Shaw, B., & Emery, G. (1979). *Cognitive therapy of depression*. New York: Guilford.

Bloom, P. (2000). Martin T. Orne, MD, PhD: A celebration of life and friendship. *American Journal of Clinical and Experimental Hypnosis, 44*, 4, 354–69.

Crawford, H., & Allen, S. (1983). Enhanced visual memory during hypnosis as mediated by hypnotic responsiveness and cognitive strategies. *Journal of Experimental Psychology: General, 112*, 662–85.

Erickson, M. (1980). Literalness: An experimental study. In E. Rossi (Ed.), *The collected papers of Milton H. Erickson, M.D., on hypnosis* (Vol. 3, pp. 92–9). New York: Irvington.

Erickson, M., Rossi, E., & Rossi, S. (1976). *Hypnotic realities: The induction of clinical hypnosis and forms of indirect suggestion*. New York: Irvington.

Erickson, M., & Rossi, E. (1979). *Hypnotherapy: An exploratory casebook*. New York: Irvington.

Evans, F. (1991). Hypnotizability: Individual differences in dissociation and the flexible control of psychological processes. In S. Lynn & J. Rhue (Eds.), *Theories of hypnosis: Current models and perspectives* (pp. 144–68). New York: Guilford.

Fromm, E., & Kahn, S. (1990). *Self-hypnosis: The Chicago paradigm*. New York: Guilford.

Green, J., Lynn, S., Weekes, J., Carlson, B., Brentar, J., Latham, L., & Kurtzhals, R. (1990). Literalism as a marker of hypnotic "trance": Disconfirming evidence. *Journal of Abnormal Psychology, 99*, 16–21.

Hilgard, E. (1977). *Divided consciousness: Multiple controls in human thought and action*. New York: Wiley.

Hilgard, E. (1991). A neodissociation interpretation of hypnosis. In S. Lynn & J. Rhue (Eds.), *Theories of hypnosis: Current models and perspectives* (pp. 83–104). New York: Guilford.

Hilgard, E. (1992). Dissociation and theories of hypnosis. In E. Fromm & M. Nash (Eds.), *Contemporary hypnosis research* (pp. 69–101). New York: Guilford.

Holroyd, J. (1992). Hypnosis as a methodology in psychological research. In E. Fromm & M. Nash (Eds.), *Contemporary hypnosis research* (pp. 201–26). New York: Guilford.

Kirsch, I. (2000). The response set theory of hypnosis. *American Journal of Clinical Hypnosis, 42*, 3–4, 274–93.

Labelle, L., Laurence, J-R, Nadon, R., & Perry, C. (1990). Hypnotizability, preference for an imagic cognitive style, and memory creation in hypnosis. *Journal of Abnormal Psychology, 99*, 222–8.

Lynn, S., Green, J., Weekes, J., Carlson, B., Brentar, J., Latham, L., & Kurzhals, R. (1990). Literalism and hypnosis: Hypnotic versus task-motivated subjects. *American Journal of Clinical Hypnosis, 23*, 113–9.

Lynn, S., & Rhue, J. (1991). An integrative model of hypnosis. In S. Lynn & J. Rhue (Eds.), *Theories of hypnosis: Current models and perspectives* (pp. 397–438). New York: Guilford.

Orne, E., Whitehouse, W., Dinges, D., & Orne, M. (1996). Memory liabilities associated with hypnosis: Does low hypnotizability confer immunity? *International Journal of Clinical and Experimental Hypnosis, 44*, 4, 354–69.

Orne, M. (1959). The nature of hypnosis: Artifact and essence. *Journal of Abnormal and Social Psychology, 58*, 277–99.

Pekala, R. (2002). Operationalizing trance II: Clinical application using a psycho-phenomenological approach. *American Journal of Clinical Hypnosis, 44*, 3–4, 241–56.

Pekala, R., & Kumar, V. (2000). Operationalizing "trance": I: Rationale and research using a psychophenomenological approach. *American Journal of Clinical Hypnosis, 43*, 107–35.

Sarbin, T. (1997). Hypnosis as a conversation: "Believed-in imaginings" revisited. *Contemporary Hypnosis, 14*, 4, 203–15.

Schoenberger, N. (2000). Research on hypnosis as an adjunct to cognitive-behavioral psychotherapy. *International Journal of Clinical and Experimental Hypnosis, 48*, 150–65.

Sheehan, P. (1992). The phenomenology of hypnosis and the Experiential Analysis Technique. In E. Fromm & M. Nash (Eds.), *Contemporary Hypnosis Research* (pp. 364–89). New York: Guilford.

Sheehan, P., & McConkey, K. (1982). *Hypnosis and experience: The exploration of phenomena and process.* Hillsdale, N.J.: Erlbaum.

Spanos, N., & Coe, W. (1992). A social-psychological approach to hypnosis. In E. Fromm & M. Nash (Eds.), *Contemporary hypnosis research* (pp. 102–30). New York: Guilford.

Spiegel, D. (1993). Hypnosis in the treatment of posttraumatic stress disorders. In J. Rhue, S. Lynn, & I. Kirsch (Eds.), *Handbook of clinical hypnosis* (pp. 719–38). Washington, D.C.: American Psychological Association.

Spiegel, H., & Spiegel, D. (1987). *Trance and treatment: Clinical uses of hypnosis.* Washington, D.C.: American Psychiatric Association.

Wagstaff, G. (1998). The semantics and physiology of hypnosis as an altered state: Towards a definition of hypnosis. *Contemporary Hypnosis, 15*, 149–65.

Weitzenhoffer, A. (2000). *The practice of hypnotism* (2nd ed.). New York: Wiley.

Yapko, M. (1992). *Hypnosis and the treatment of depressions: Strategies for change.* New York: Brunner/Mazel.

Yapko, M. (2001). *Treating depression with hypnosis: Integrating cognitive-behavioral and strategic approaches.* Philadelphia, PA: Brunner/Routledge.

10

Conditions for Conducting Hypnosis Sessions

In previous chapters I have explored in some detail the personal and interpersonal factors influencing hypnotic responsiveness. In this chapter, I would like to explore some of the other variables that can affect your work. These are discussed in three separate sections: Environmental, Physical, and Legal variables.

ENVIRONMENTAL VARIABLES

There was a treatment center here in San Diego years ago that invested a considerable amount of money on creating the "ideal" conditions for conducting hypnosis sessions. They had large egg-shaped chairs you had to crawl into, and once enveloped by the chair, the room with thickly carpeted walls became soundless. Clients would sit in the chairs and listen to hypnosis tapes. These special chairs were equipped with numerous sound speakers, lights that flashed in sequence, electronic gadgetry to move the arm rests slowly downward while the client heard suggestions for arm levitation, a fragrance-releasing device that might, for example, release the smell of baby powder fragrance while the client heard suggestions for age regression, and a variety of other such clever tricks.

If you were to ask the clinicians at this center about the "best" environmental conditions for performing hypnosis, I suppose they'd say the environment they created is the ideal. I would disagree. (Apparently, their clients disagreed as well, for they are no longer in business!) From my perspective, and that of virtually every clinician and researcher who emphasizes the importance of the therapeutic alliance, forming an intense, warm, goal-directed relationship with the client is a necessary precursor to making worthwhile therapeutic interventions. Everything else, including the environment in which you do hypnosis, is secondary. Secondary, yes, but *not* unimportant. There have not been any studies that I am aware of to suggest that one environmental condition (e.g., furniture arrangement, lighting) is more likely to produce hypnotic phenomena than another. In fact, very few writers in the field have even addressed this topic. In the real world, clinicians who use hypnosis do so in all kinds of environments, from sterile laboratories with fluorescent lighting and chairs (apparently chosen by someone who was having a bad day); to hospitals or clinics where monitors are beeping and someone in the next room or even the next bed is moaning in pain; to classrooms or lecture halls where it seems every chair creaks at 90 decibels; to offices that look more like living rooms, with fireplaces, couches, soft lighting and soft music playing in the background. Not surprisingly, successful hypnosis has been achievable in all of these environments. There are certain environmental conditions that are desirable for doing hypnosis, but they are clearly not essential.

A Quiet Atmosphere

Working in a relatively quiet atmosphere is especially helpful. An atmosphere free of intrusive or, even worse, obnoxious noise, is less bothersome to the client, allowing him or her to focus more on internal experiences rather than external distractions. Realistically, however, phones ring, doors get knocked on, people converse outside your door (if you even *have* a door), traffic zooms by, planes pass overhead, people upstairs drop heavy objects, people sneeze, pets knock over vases, kids argue, and the list of possible distractions goes on and on. No environment is perfectly quiet and free from external noise, nor does it have to be. A key to helping the client focus internally without being unduly distracted by (though not unaware of) external events lies in your ability to tie those events into your process. By commenting on them and framing them as "normal," the client can let the distractions recede into the background.

Near the beginning of the hypnotic process, it may help the client diminish external awareness by offering a general suggestion to the effect that: "Whatever sounds you may hear in the environment around you . . . as you get more deeply absorbed internally . . . are routine, everyday sounds . . . and you can let them pass through your awareness just as quickly as they enter . . . the sounds of the environment are so routine that you can just let them drift out of your awareness . . ."

By not specifying which sounds you are referring to, you're offering a blanket suggestion to cover all the possibilities. Also, you are avoiding the inappropriate use of negative suggestions such as, "Don't notice the phone ringing," which will, of course, cause the person to notice it.

Perhaps the best thing to do if an intrusion occurs is to use a "chaining" suggestion structure in which you can comment on the current reality of the intrusion, and then chain (i.e., associate) the desired response to the comment. For example, if the phone rings during the hypnosis session, you might comment directly by saying something such as, "Isn't it nice to know the phone can ring and since you don't have to answer it you can just relax even more deeply." Or you can comment on it indirectly by saying something such as, "As you relax, your unconscious mind can *call a message* up to your conscious mind about relaxing even more deeply."

Ignoring the intrusion can inadvertently lead the client to pay even more attention to it. But using the "accept and utilize" structure in which you acknowledge and make use of ongoing events, *whatever* they are, allows the person to more readily "let it go." Intrusions are integrated as part of the experience, transforming their impact from a negative to a positive one.

Gentle Lighting

The use of soft, soothing lighting may be helpful in doing hypnosis. Lighting helps create atmosphere, and soft lighting can help facilitate comfort. I would not recommend lighting that is too dim, nor would I recommend darkness. Candlelight may be all right for some, but too esoteric for others (including me).

Comfortable Furniture

As the client relaxes, his or her body tends to become heavy and immobile. Neck and backaches can easily result if the client doesn't get adequate physical support. Furniture should be comfortable and, most important, support the client's head and body. Recliner chairs or chairs with footstools are quite good for this reason. Beds or couches to lie prone on may be too suggestive and, furthermore, are likely to put the client to sleep, which you definitely *don't* want to happen during typical hypnosis sessions.

As a final environmental consideration, Australian psychologist George Burns in his book, *Nature-Guided Therapy* (1998), made a compelling case for wanting to move at least some of the therapy outdoors, if possible, making use of the natural environment as a stimulus for greater comfort. The sounds and sensations of being in a natural setting can be quite conducive to the hypnotic experience.

PHYSICAL VARIABLES

Physical conditions are also worthy of consideration in doing hypnosis. I refer here not to the client's physical health, but to transient physical experiences that may influence a client's hypnotic responsiveness.

Physical Comfort

It helps if the client is physically comfortable; the body is adequately supported, clothing is not restrictive or binding, the room temperature is comfortable, and the client isn't feeling rushed either by you or life circumstances demanding immediate attention.

It is important that the client have nothing in her his or mouth (e.g., gum, candy) that could choke him or her as she relaxes. Also, many people wear contact lenses, and some contact lenses (e.g., hard lenses) are constructed in such a way that if the client closes his or her eyes even briefly (i.e., a few minutes) the lenses irritate the eyes to the point of becoming uncomfortable or even painful. Ask the client if he or she would like to remove his or her glasses, contact lenses, shoes, or whatever else might inhibit responsiveness.

Alcohol, Drugs, Medications

Alcohol and street drugs do not enhance a person's focus, rather they diminish it, and so are counterproductive to doing effective hypnotic work. Prescribed medications vary in their effects on people. Part of your initial assessment of your client is the quality of the person's attentional processes. If the person has adequate focus, then hypnosis should be helpful. If the person's quality of focus is impaired by the medications they're taking or by their symptoms (e.g., pain, depression, anxiety), hypnosis will be more difficult, but also more important to include in treatment as a means of both reducing symptoms and enhancing focus.

Other Physical Factors

Similar diminished responses can exist for the tired or exhausted client. Given how many people are working too hard and getting too little sleep, this is a commonly encountered impairing factor. Such tired clients may be easy to put to sleep (unintentionally, as they relax and then drift off, if you let them) but are difficult to get to focus internally.

The less you assume about your client, the more objective feedback you will want to seek about his or her condition. You cannot assume the person has normal hearing, normal physiology, no contact lenses, no gum in the mouth, no use of street drugs or alcohol on therapy days, and so forth. It takes only moments to ask, and your sensitivity to such issues can save you a lot of frustration later. The key here, as in the environmental conditions, is to use the spontaneous events that arise. If a client coughs, don't fret. Accept and utilize it by saying something such as, "As you clear your throat, your throat can relax . . . and then *you* can relax even more deeply." Or, you can offer some statement that is less direct, such as, "It's good to *clear the way* . . . in order to be able to swallow new ideas."

When a client coughs or sneezes, the session is far from ruined. You can acknowledge that the client's hypnotic experience has lightened at that particular moment, and then you can use it to help the person go deeper into hypnosis again. Realistically, no one ever nose-dives into deep hypnosis and then stays there anyway. The person's hypnotic experience is generally fluctuating throughout the sessions, lightening and deepening in intensity from moment to moment. That's normal and to be expected, which you probably know from your own experience by now. (That's why the old incantation of saying "deeper, deeper, deeper" to the client is a poor representation of the experience.)

Following the "suggestion chaining" format of tying "what is" to "what can be" is the key to coping with environments that aren't perfect and clients who sneeze, cough, laugh, or cry in the middle of your hypnotic process. It is important that you can get comfortable in tying spontaneous occurrences into your work. No environment is completely controllable—you just have to "go with the flow." Ultimately, skilled communication is a principal factor in successful hypnosis—not the chair you use.

LEGAL VARIABLES, ESPECIALLY INFORMED CONSENT

The climate for health care providers has been and still is undergoing a remarkable transition in recent years as malpractice suits, highly publicized ethical lapses, and even prosecutions for criminal behavior among clinicians is brought to the attention of the general public. As attorney and hypnosis expert Alan Scheflin wrote:

> Up until 1980 . . . there had not been a single appellate legal decision in all of the country (referring to the United States) involving a lawsuit against a therapist for the manner in which the therapy had been conducted, excluding cases of inappropriate physical contact or sexual intimacy . . . In the 1980s, however, the legal climate turned inhospitable to the practice of therapy. By the 1990s, nearly 1,000 lawsuits had been filed against . . . mental health professionals, challenging the therapies practiced, and even the realm of psychotherapy itself. (2001, p. 158)

The legal issues associated with responsible clinical practice in general obviously also apply to the use of hypnosis as well. However, the use of hypnosis in one's clinical practice adds additional potential legal liabilities of which you must be aware. These grew to especially dramatic proportions in the wake of the repressed memory/false memory controversy. The majority of the lawsuits Scheflin refers to above directly or indirectly involved hypnosis that was charged with being applied inappropriately by ignorant (rarely malicious) clinicians.

In this section I will address only one of these issues, but it is enough to highlight to you the vital importance of your checking with your particular state's (or country's, as the case may be) laws about treatment issues with *and* without hypnosis. The issue is informed consent.

INFORMED CONSENT

In the medical context, the doctrine of informed consent governs the physical treatment of patients. Patients are not to be touched without it. Informed consent gives patients the power to collaborate in their own treatment as knowledgeable participants. Doctors are required to explain treatment options (e.g., surgery, medications) and provide helpful data about the chances for successful intervention with the various options in order to help guide the patient's choices.

Does the medical model apply to the context of psychotherapy? How much information can a clinician provide without impairing the spontaneity and emotional power of his or her intervention? (Can you imagine saying to a client, "I'm going to do a paradoxical intervention now in order to indirectly encourage you to take a contrary position to my stated one because that's really the one I want you to take!"?) Despite informed consent obviously not fitting the psychotherapy context as well as a medical one, Scheflin described "a growing movement" in the legal community "to demand a new, specialized form of informed consent before any therapy is undertaken" (2001, p. 162).

Hypnosis faces a number of specific vulnerabilities to the need for informed consent. One especially important one, highlighted in this section, concerns what is known in the legal realm as a "per se exclusion rule" regarding hypnotically obtained testimony (Giannelli, 1995). Many courts throughout the United States have adopted a per se exclusion rule which excludes the testimony of any witness, other than the accused, who has been hypnotized. Courts have relied heavily on the testimony of hypnosis experts who have said in no uncertain terms that hypnotically influenced testimony is inherently unreliable and should therefore be precluded from being offered into evidence.

This is an unfortunate and exaggerated response: Hypnotically derived information *can* be unreliable, but is not *inherently* unreliable. More prudent courts think of hypnosis as much the same as any other means of getting information: Maybe it's wholly right, partly right, partly wrong, or wholly wrong, and needs additional validation in order to evaluate it.

How might the per se exclusion, if it operates in your state, affect your practice? Consider this realistic case scenario: A woman is attacked and badly beaten. She seeks therapy for her post-traumatic stress symptoms. The therapist, with the absolute best of intentions, does hypnosis with this woman to reduce her distress and catalyze her recovery. The therapist did not know about (or simply forgot) about the per se exclusion rule, nor did the therapist know the assailant had been caught and the woman was going to have to pick him out of a lineup and then testify as a witness against him in court. You can probably see where this is going. When the defense attorney finds out she has been hypnotized for her post-traumatic symptoms, he files for a dismissal based on the inadmissibility of her evidence because it is presumably hypnotically tainted. End of case. (Not really, though, because that same client is likely to sue the therapist for not providing an informed consent that by doing hypnosis with her it would preclude pursuing her claim.)

Informing the client about possible memory distortions from hypnosis remains a controversy within the field, and simply highlights the turmoil left in the wake of the repressed memory/false memory wars (Frischholz, 2001; Hammond, Scheflin, & Vermetten, 2001; Lynn, 2001; Spiegel, 2001).

Informed consent means patients must be informed about the treatment options available, the scientific merits of the treatments the clinician intend to provide, any untoward potential consequences of the chosen treatment (that builds positive expectations, doesn't it?), and the likely consequences of no treatment (Scheflin, 2001). Informing the client about the research evidence for hypnotic procedures is growing in acceptance as simply good practice, even if not (yet) legally required.

CONCLUSION

The context in which hypnosis is performed matters. The physical environment of the clinician's practice setting and the physical comfort of the client also matter. And, given the litigation-heavy nature of our culture, the legal context for doing hypnosis is an additional important consideration. It is hardly a burdensome one, though, as long as one stays cognizant of the legal and ethical principles that govern sound clinical practice. In chapter 22 I will discuss some of the other legal and ethical issues associated with doing clinical hypnosis.

For Discussion

1. What kind of physical environment for doing hypnosis would you create if cost were no barrier?
2. What is your opinion of the "computerized hypnosis" approach described in this chapter? Why do you feel that way?
3. How might ignoring an intrusion cause a client to pay even more attention to it?
4. Do you think suggestions from a computer or cassette tape can be as effective as those from a live person? Why or why not?
5. Do you think informed consent in psychotherapy should be mandated? Why or why not?

Things to Do

1. Make a list of the most common intrusions you are likely to encounter while doing hypnosis in the place where you work. Generate five suggestions for each intrusion that can help you make positive use of it whenever it arises during your hypnosis process.
2. Visit a variety of clinicians' offices who use hypnosis, noticing the type and physical arrangement of their furniture. What seems most practical to you?
3. Vary the arrangement of seats from practice session to practice session, ranging from very close together to far apart, from frontal to side-by-side. Do you notice any differences in people's level of responsiveness to you? How do you account for whatever differences you may observe?
4. Talk to clinicians about how they address the informed consent issue in their practices and how it affects the treatment process.
5. Consult attorneys known for their expertise in hypnosis in your state (or country) and find out the local legal issues there relevant to your use of hypnosis.

REFERENCES

Burns, G. (1998). *Nature-guided therapy: Brief integrative strategies for health and well-being.* Philadelphia, PA: Brunner/Mazel.

Frischholz, E. (2001). Different perspectives on informed consent and clinical hypnosis. *American Journal of Clinical Hypnosis, 43*, 3–4, 323–27.

Giannelli, P. (1995). The admissibility of hypnotic evidence in U.S. courts. *International Journal of Clinical and Experimental Hypnosis, 43*, 2, 212–33.

Hammond, C., Scheflin, A., & Vermetten, E. (2001). Comment on Lynn: Informed consent and the standard of care in the practice of clinical hypnosis. *American Journal of Clinical Hypnosis, 43*, 3–4, 305–10.

Lynn, S. (2001). Hypnosis, the hidden observer, and not-so-hidden consent. *American Journal of Clinical Hypnosis, 43*, 3–4, 291–92.

Scheflin, A. (2001). Caveat therapist. Ethical and legal dangers in the use of Ericksonian techniques. In B. Geary & J. Zeig (Eds.), *The handbook of Ericksonian psychotherapy* (pp. 154–67). Phoenix, AZ: The Milton H. Erickson Foundation Press.

Spiegel, D. (2001). Informed dissent regarding hypnosis and its not-so-hidden observers: Comment on Lynn. *American Journal of Clinical Hypnosis, 43*, 3–4, 303–04.

11

Structured Approaches to Assessing Hypnotic Responsiveness

There is perhaps no one domain within the field of hypnosis that divides researchers and clinicians more than their sharply differing viewpoints about the use of standardized tests to assess hypnotic responsiveness in people. This chapter explores the conflicting viewpoints and presents several of the more widely used instruments and approaches for assessing hypnotic responsiveness. While it is a relatively unanimous observation shared by almost everyone in the field that people differ substantially in their hypnotic abilities, the use of a standardized means for assessing individual responsiveness seems to be undesirable to most clinicians, who apparently would rather learn from direct experience with the client what his or her unique hypnotic talents might be. In one of the few studies of its kind, Sheldon Cohen (1989) surveyed faculty members teaching at an annual meeting of the American Society of Clinical Hypnosis (ASCH), the largest national professional hypnosis society in the world, regarding their use of formal measures of hypnotizability. Cohen discovered that only slightly more than half of respondents had *ever* used tests of hypnotic responsiveness, and of these fewer than a third were current users.

In recent years, however, the climate has changed. The pressure to perform formal hypnotizability testing has greatly increased from within the profession as its members strive to have hypnosis better recognized as a science. The pressure to define hypnosis in scientific terms has been a long time coming since experimental psychologist Clark Hull first brought hypnosis into the laboratory in the 1920s and published the first scientific book ever on hypnosis with his classic work, *Hypnosis and Suggestibility* (1933/2002). The pressure to define hypnosis as a science has increased exponentially in the last decade, as the push within the health care professions, especially psychology, has been to provide objective evidence for the effectiveness of specific forms of intervention. The intense demand from insurance companies, consumers, and allied professionals for proof that a method is an "empirically supported treatment" (EST) has catalyzed the demand from within the hypnosis community, primarily the researchers, for a more objectively measurable approach to the practice of clinical hypnosis. Many of the most influential people in the field have gone on record as strong advocates for not only the desirability but the *necessity* of formal assessment of hypnotic responsiveness (Laurence, 1997; Lynn & Shindler, 2002; Nadon, 1997). It is too soon to know whether or just how much the call for testing has changed the minds and practices of clinicians, who appreciate the science of hypnosis but also recognize hypnosis will always be primarily about clinical artistry (i.e., judgment, adaptability, creativity).

THE ARGUMENTS AGAINST STANDARDIZED TESTING OF HYPNOTIZABILITY

More than a few clinicians and researchers have publicly expressed doubts about the merits of hypnotizability testing. In this section I will sample but a few of the opinions voiced by well-known experts on the matter.

Psychologist Michael Diamond (1989), in the very title of his article, asked, "Is Hypnotherapy Art or Science?" In it he asserted that standardized tests can provide only a general index of general hypnotic ability, rather than objective measures of the specific abilities that will influence actual responses to therapy involving hypnosis. He further stated that little can be learned from a standardized test of hypnotizability that couldn't be better learned from more natural, less intrusive methods.

Psychologist Stephen Gilligan (1987) made a similar point about the limits of standardization as it specifically applies to hypnosis, though more colorfully: ". . . the standardized approach attributes both success and failure in the hypnotic encounter to the *subject*. The hypnotist is not that important. There are some major problems with this approach. First it assumes that a standardized induction, which essentially instructs a person to relax and imagine various things, is a valid way of assessing an individual's general hypnotic ability. This is like assessing dancing skill in terms of one's ability to do the fox trot. The point is that some people can disco but not waltz; others can square dance but not boogie, and so forth . . . A second problem . . . is that it defines hypnotic ability in terms of *behavioral* responses to test suggestions. While using external behaviors to assess an internal state is understandable, especially in the experimental domain, it shades a major point: trance is primarily an *experience*, like love or anger, which will be different for different individuals" (pp. 7–8).

Psychologist and past president of the Society for Clinical and Experimental Hypnosis (SCEH) Joseph Barber (1989, 1991) also made an important distinction between one's hypnotizability scores and actual hypnotic capacity. He believes that hypnotizability scores are not especially helpful in predicting clinical outcomes. He further believes, however, that such scores might help shape your approach to a client, suggesting that how direct or indirect you might be in offering suggestions may be influenced by the person's level and quality of responsiveness.

Unlike the others, who may not advocate for suggestibility testing but are not against it, psychologist Ernest Rossi (1989) was quite adamant in his dismissal of such tests when he said, ". . . sensitive and humanistically oriented therapists avoid subjecting their already wary and weary patients to yet another power-trip, thinly veiled as 'an objective measure of hypnotic susceptibility'" (p. 15).

The most widely used hypnotizability assessment instruments, considered the "Gold Standard" by many in the profession, are the *Stanford Hypnotic Susceptibility Scales* (Forms A, B, and C), co-developed by psychologists André Weitzenhoffer and Ernest Hilgard, names quite familiar to you by now. Thus, it may come as a surprise that Weitzenhoffer has publicly taken the position that the scales are largely irrelevant to clinical practice. He wrote:

> If there is no real reason, besides the time required by doing so, against using scales in the clinical situation . . . it remains to consider why a clinician might want to use them aside from scientific reasons for doing so. Apart from this last, there seems to be little reason for it. This may come as a shock, being said by the main developer of the leading modern scale, and it has shocked many of my colleagues.
>
> The fact is that for many years this writer's position has been that from the standpoint of the everyday clinical practice of hypnosuggestion, using scales on a regular basis is not particularly useful for purposes of doing effective hypnotherapy. I must emphasize this last because some of my colleagues strongly advocate that clinicians routinely use an approved scale and some have upbraided me for advocating otherwise. But to what purpose? To show that one is a scientist as well as a clinician? Nonsense! There is much more than that to being scientific. (2000, pp. 276–7)

Weitzenhoffer, commenting about the relationship between responses to test items and eventual responses to therapy, went on to say:

> For one thing, such scales as are available test for specific effects. It is only to the extent that one can generalize from the response to a specific test suggestion to an entire class of more or less like suggestions that a useful prediction can be made. There is little evidence this can be done effectively . . . In the end, one usually has to go directly to the production of the desired effect

to find out if it can be done . . . Either the effect can be done when the time comes or it cannot . . . Trial-and-error is most often the order of the day. (2000, p. 466)

The incongruity of attempting to define hypnosis as science when prominent experts continue to argue about how to define hypnosis; how to measure the hypnotic condition; what constitutes increased suggestibility; what constitutes a hypnotic response; why "hypnosis is a stable trait" that varies with expectancy, social and contextual conditions; why people generate hypnotic phenomena while they're active and alert and no induction has been performed, and dozens of other such "flies in the ointment" has not deterred those who advocate the scientific position. From within that position, formal assessment is considered fundamental.

THE ARGUMENTS FOR STANDARDIZED TESTING OF HYPNOTIZABILITY

Formal assessment of hypnotizability has been a primary means of identifying the now well-established fact that people differ in their level of response to hypnotic suggestions. As a means of studying differences between individuals and specific group populations, hypnosis assessment tools provide similar benefits to other standardized instruments that reveal differences on other characteristics of interest. Without a means of standardizing test instruments, we lose the ability to correlate hypnotizability with any other trait or characteristic we want to test, such as treatment responsiveness or intelligence.

As in the previous section, I'll let some of the experts who advocate for formal assessment speak for themselves.

Psychologists and researchers Steven Lynn and Kelley Shindler (2002) summarized many of the most pointed arguments in favor of testing when they wrote:

Assessment can contribute to an understanding of the various components of hypnotic responsiveness and thus play a role in optimizing responsiveness to hypnotic procedures . . . (another) reason to assess hypnotizability is if there are great costs associated with the failure to hypnotize someone, or if there are clear benefits associated with a positive response to hypnosis . . . (and) assessment of hypnotizability is important because research has established that a link exists between hypnotizability and certain disorders and conditions and their successful treatment with hypnotic interventions. (pp. 187–89)

Psychiatrists Herbert and David Spiegel, in their book *Trance and Treatment* (1978) which introduced another assessment instrument, the *Hypnosis Induction Profile* (HIP), discussed in some detail later, stated the rationale for such instruments clearly when they wrote: "Trance capacity, as measured by the Hypnosis Induction Profile, has a significant relationship to the total adult personality structure. . . . The assessment of hypnotizability is a useful diagnostic aid that can facilitate the choice of an appropriate treatment modality along the entire spectrum of mental health and illness." (p. 4)

Psychologist and researcher Ernest Hilgard was an especially strong advocate for formal assessment. He succinctly stated why when he said:

> The characteristic of an unscientific therapy is that there is only one disease and only one cure: such therapies imply that everyone can profit from the favored therapy regardless of the presenting problem. A scientific therapy is based on a diagnosis, which in psychotherapy means selecting the therapy of choice appropriate to fit the patient's condition. Hypnosis is only one of these choices, and its choice and the manner of its use can profit from some estimate of the individual's hypnotic responsiveness. (1982, p. 400)

Psychologist Ronald Pekala (2002) advocated for the use of formal assessments for quite a different reason when he suggested clients can benefit from knowing "where they stand" on the issue of hypnotizability. By knowing something about their own capacity as measured by a test, clients in therapy can live up to—or be motivated to even exceed—the measured capacity. Pekala wrote:

> Of course, if no actual assessment of hypnotizability is done before a treatment intervention, the client may not have a good idea as to how hypnotizable they actually are, because there are no salient clues to inform them of such. Some clinicians believe that without the clients' knowledge of their actual hypnotizability level, positive expectancy effects and placebo effects will engender positive therapeutic outcomes, regardless of hypnotic ability. Although this may be true with some clients, I believe it is better to have knowledge about a person's hypnotizability level and tailor a treatment plan to that level, instead of hoping that positive expectancy effects will do the rest. (p. 245)

Psychologists William Kronenberger, Linn LaClave, and Catherine Morrow (2002) acknowledge the value of an initial assessment such as those obtained through standardized instruments, but go a step further when they advocate for the use of formal assessment on a session-by-session basis. The value of measurement information obtained in an individual clinical hypnosis session led them to develop their instrument, called the Hypnotic State

Assessment Questionnaire (HSAQ). In describing the value of individual session assessment in addition to standard hypnotic responsiveness assessment, they wrote:

> Clinical hypnotic response quantifies a patient's behaviors and experiences in a single hypnosis session that is clinically focused, (usually) individually tailored to the patient's issues, and placed in the context of an extended treatment (usually involving multiple hypnosis sessions). The assessment of clinical hypnotic response typically is useful for such tasks as documenting a patient's response to a particular induction technique, evaluating the impact of a particular set of suggestions, keeping accurate and useful chart notes, monitoring change across sessions, and communicating with trainees about the response of their patients. (p. 258)

Attorney Alan Scheflin (2001) advocated for formal assessment for one simple reason: to reduce legal liability. By employing a standardized instrument, one's treatment plan can be viewed as being based on "scientific data about the patient" (p. 165). That may be a defensive recommendation, but in today's litigious environment, it is not an unreasonable one.

Clearly, there are wise and well-considered viewpoints advocating for virtually opposite positions on the use of standardized instruments for assessing hypnotic responsiveness. The environment in which you work, the degree of affinity you have for testing, the importance placed on it by colleagues and teachers you have, and many other factors will have to be weighed by you to decide whether testing will be important in your practice of hypnosis.

MY BIAS ON ASSESSMENT ISSUES

I will confess to you now that I do not use formal suggestibility tests in my clinical practice. *Philosophically, I am most aligned with the view of hypnotic capacity as a potential that can only emerge under the right personal, interpersonal, and contextual conditions.* All the research about "low hypnotizables" improving markedly under adaptive clinical conditions (Gearan, Schoenberger, & Kirsch, 1995; Spanos, 1991) highlights for me what I had already learned in practice: the test score is less important than the clinical response. Thus, I assume the inevitable presence of suggestibility on the part of my client. Instead of attempting to discover *if* my client is suggestible, I find it a much more practical use of my mental energy to discover how I can best structure my suggestions to increase the likelihood of their getting accepted. For the clinician who does not share this perspective, or for the clinician who does not yet feel experienced enough to assess a client's spontaneous communications for suggestibility dynamics, formal suggestibility tests may be a useful tool. As noted above, there *are* some very good reasons for wanting to use them. That is the basis for their inclusion in this book. (Continued on page 223.)

FRAME OF REFERENCE: ERNEST R. HILGARD, PH.D.

Ernest R. "Jack" Hilgard, Ph.D. (1904–2001), was one of the 20th century's leading psychologists, and when he turned his attention to the subject of hypnosis relatively late in his professional life, he helped propel hypnosis into the spotlight as an area worthy of serious inquiry. Dr. Hilgard received his Ph.D. in 1930 from Yale. His early career interest was in the area of learning. In 1933, he and his wife of two years, Josephine, who already had a Ph.D. in developmental psychology, moved to Stanford where he soon became a full professor in the Department of Psychology. His early works are classics, and include *Conditioning and Learning* (1940), *Theories of Learning* (1948), and his runaway best-selling introductory psychology textbook, *Introduction to Psychology* (1953). He stayed at Stanford University for the rest of his life and eventually retired as Emeritus Professor following a long and highly distinguished career. He was a past president of the American Psychological Association, and a member of the National Academy of Sciences.

Together with André Weitzenhoffer, Ph.D., Dr. Hilgard established a hypnosis laboratory at Stanford in which countless valuable studies on hypnosis were conducted. Together, they co-created the *Stanford Hypnotic Susceptibility Scales*, among the first and probably still the best objective measure of hypnotic responsiveness. Their widespread use in research continues to this day, and so directly and indirectly Dr. Hilgard has helped shape the nature of hypnosis research for all the years since he first tasked himself with trying to understand hypnosis and hypnotic phenomena. Dr. Hilgard is responsible for the Neo-Dissociation Theory of hypnosis, best articulated in his 1977 book, *Divided Consciousness*, including his influential concept of the "hidden observer," a part of the person that could remain at least somewhat objective about ongoing events during hypnosis despite whatever subjective experiences the subject might be having. Dr. Hilgard's findings on the differences in individual responsiveness to hypnotic suggestions led to his classic 1965 book, *Hypnotic Susceptibility*, and his subsequent research on pain control through hypnosis led to his highly influential 1975 book co-authored with his wife, *Hypnosis in the Relief of Pain*. Dr. Hilgard, through his warm, gentle, and respectful demeanor and his encyclopedic knowledge of psychology and hypnosis, represented the best the field had to offer. Dr. Hilgard was instrumental in making hypnosis a respectable and worthwhile phenomenon to study in the laboratory and to practice in health care settings.

On His Interest in Hypnosis: "I was at Yale as an instructor at the time that Clark Hull wrote his book on hypnosis and suggestibility, so I had some familiarity with it as a respectable topic for an experimenter. But, at the time I was interested in moving my career in other directions. I didn't really participate in his work, though I think it made a difference to know that it would be a reputable thing to do. So, I started rather late in my career, after I had been well established in general psychology and particularly in the psychology of learning. I had the feeling that much of psychology dealt with rather superficial aspects of mental life. I thought it would be interesting to go into something that had more psychology in it. I felt that, in some sense, hypnosis really had psychology in it. How to get the psychology out of it, that's our own problem!"

On the Use of the Stanford Scales in Therapy: "I think that if I take just a sociological or political point of view, a scale is really very useful, and is more useful for clinicians than they like to admit. Whenever it's been tried on anything severe, like severe pain, there's no question that you have greater success with a more highly hypnotizable as measured by the scale, not as measured by some external method. Not that a person without a scale couldn't arrive at it by using various kinds of tests for analgesia and that sort of thing. From my point of view, that's the same kind of item you have on the scale anyhow. But if you want to use other techniques or something of that sort or recovered memories, it's kind of nice to know how readily you can get genuine age regressions where they relive their entire childhood."

On Defining "Trance": "I never use the word 'trance,' so, in that sense it's fair to say I'm less traditional. But these things are a matter of gradation. My own position, which I have described in neo-dissociation terms, is that you could have dissociations of various degrees. . . . "[So] when people use the word 'trance' they should really use it for a pretty massive set of dissociations so that you sense the personality change or that the whole orientation to reality is somewhat changed."

On the Need for Hypnosis Research: "It's the same problem in another sense with psychoanalysis. They never really wanted to do any real research. They thought psychoanalysis was itself a research method. You studied the individual and in a sense that's what Ericksonian treatment is—it's a research method to try and get a plan for the individual and if it works—[good!] But that isn't the way science is built. So, if there's any message I have, it is to not get scientistic, you don't have to have analysis of variance and become a slave to statistics, [but at least have] just garden variety statistics: Here's half a dozen people that have these same symptoms; they've been treated in three different ways. Why were the different ways chosen? Was it just arbitrary? Why were some of them started in one way and then shifted to another? Put some little design into it."

On the Importance of Hypnosis in His Career: "I would say that I really found the hypnosis period the most satisfactory in my career. I have this feeling that almost every time, even just in giving a simple scale of hypnosis, I learned something. It wasn't something I was necessarily ready to verbalize, but I learned about different kinds of responses to amnesia, or to age regression, or to hallucinated voices, and so on."

Source: Personal communication, 1988

GENERAL FUNCTIONS OF SUGGESTIBILITY TESTS

The chief purpose of suggestibility tests is to determine the person's degree, if any, of hypnotizability. Hypnotizability is generally defined in testing conditions as behaviorally manifested evidence of having responded, in whole or in part, to the clinician or researcher's suggestions for various kinds of experiences. Suggestibility tests will be divided in the latter part of this chapter into two general categories: Formal and informal. Examples of each will be presented. Beyond determining hypnotizability, suggestibility tests can serve a number of other purposes as well, as some of those experts quoted above alluded to. For example, by using suggestibility tests to measure responsiveness, the test information can yield insight into what approaches may be best (i.e., easiest to relate to, most comfortable to assimilate) for a particular client. Specifically, should your approach be a primarily (not exclusively) direct or indirect one? Should your suggestions be primarily in a positive or negative form? Should your demeanor be a commanding, authoritarian one, or an easy-going, permissive one? I have placed considerable emphasis on the relationship dynamics between clinician and client, and suggestibility tests may be a useful tool to help you assess your approach with a particular client. This presupposes, of course, a willingness on your part to adapt yourself to each client. There are those clinicians who take the position that this is neither necessary or desirable. Obviously, I disagree.

A second positive purpose of the suggestibility test is to serve as a conditioning experience for entering hypnosis. The suggestibility test is, in a way, an abbreviated version of the hypnotic encounter. By having the client focus his or her attention on an induction process and then respond to requests to generate hypnotic behavior, you provide him or her what may well be his or her first "official" hypnotic experience. Use of the experience as a foundation for future similar experiences starts to condition the client to the experience of entering hypnosis while having his or her experience guided by the clinician. Thus, the client has an opportunity to build rapport in the relationship with the clinician, begin to build trust in the clinician, and begin to build confidence in his or her own ability to experience hypnosis.

A third helpful function of the suggestibility test is its ability to accomplish what I call "pre-work work." If the suggestibility test is introduced as merely a preliminary to the "real" therapeutic work to be done, it can be an opportunity to catch the client "off guard" and offer some therapeutic suggestions perhaps less subject to critical analysis by the client. This can be accomplished by offering a suggestion such as, "Before we begin, would you prefer to go into deep hypnosis in this chair or the other one over there?" This suggestion is considered an example of a "double bind" because both of the alternatives offered the client include going into deep hypnosis. When prefacing the bind with, "Before we begin . . . ," the client is not yet asked to actively participate and so may not be consciously critical of the bind the clinician has employed. Either choice the client makes presupposes the development of deep hypnosis, and the "pre-work work" of preparing the client for hypnosis is thus accomplished.

FORMAL ASSESSMENT OF HYPNOTIC RESPONSIVENESS

In a recent article, Weitzenhoffer noted that there were "at least 25 instruments variously called scales of 'hypnotic depth,' of 'hypnotic susceptibility,' of 'suggestibility,' of 'hypnotizability,' and variations thereof." Then he asked bluntly, "Why so many?" (2002, p. 209). Why, indeed? It is beyond the scope of this introductory text to name and describe the many instruments available. Instead, I will mention and acquaint you with three of the tests that are among the most widely employed by researchers and clinicians in the field.

THE STANFORD HYPNOTIC SUSCEPTIBILITY SCALES

In 1957, Ernest Hilgard and André Weitzenhoffer, as the principal investigators, began comprehensive studies of hypnotic responsiveness at Stanford

University. In 1959, they had developed two alternate forms of a scale that came to be known as the Stanford Hypnotic Susceptibility Scale (SHSS): Forms A and B (Weitzenhoffer & Hilgard, 1959). Two forms were developed in order to permit repeated measures without results getting distorted from a "practice effect." The scale consists of 12 items, with instructions for each item fully scripted for wording to be exact and replicable by whomever is administering the test. There were, of course, objective criteria for scoring each item, yielding an overall score reflecting hypnotizability.

In Form A, the items included a "postural sway" (suggestions of standing, swaying, and involuntarily falling backward), eye closure (suggestions for feelings of fatigue in the eyes and a desire for closing the eyes), hand lowering (arm extended, suggestions given for heaviness), a "finger lock" (fingers are interlocked and suggestions are given the hands will be difficult to pull apart), a fly hallucination (suggestions for an imaginary fly buzzing about), posthypnotic suggestion for changing chairs (suggestions given that after hypnosis, a pencil tap would lead the subject to change chairs and have no recollection of why), and several other items. When subjects respond within the allotted time and in the suggested way, they get a point for each item. "Very High" hypnotizables, as you would predict, score positively on all or nearly all the items (11 or 12). Forms A and B were generally well received. However, since most of the items involved motoric responses, and because it did not distinguish well more specific characteristics of the "highs," Weitzenhoffer and Hilgard went on to develop a third form of the SHSS, Form C (1962). It was intended to highlight more of the cognitive elements of hypnotic experience. It, too, features 12 items, but includes different items that examined distortions of perception and memory, and presents items in an ascending order of difficulty, with a point given for each positive response. All forms of the SHSS take approximately one hour to administer. "Very highs" score 11–12, "Highs" score 8–10, "Mediums" score 5–7, and "Lows" score 0–4.

The SHSS is probably the best researched and most widely used instrument for establishing norms within and across populations. It has also been modified for a variety of special purposes (see Weitzenhoffer, 2000, for a detailed consideration). As mentioned earlier, many consider it the "Gold Standard" by which other tests are measured.

HARVARD GROUP SCALE OF HYPNOTIC SUSCEPTIBILITY

In 1962, Ronald Shor and Emily Orne devised a group version of the SHSS:A, which they called the Harvard Group Scale of Hypnotic Susceptibility, Form A (HGSHS:A). It was designed to be able to administer to group sizes of up to 20 people simultaneously, and is still extremely popular with many researchers and clinicians. It's entirely possible that more people use this test than the SHSS:C. Like the SHSS:A from which it was adapted, it includes 12 items and takes about an hour to administer. Unlike any of the SHSS forms, the HGSHS:A is group administered by audiocassette. It was first designed as a preliminary screening tool, a nonthreatening way to get an initial impression of hypnotic responsiveness, but the time-saving factor of testing 20 people simultaneously in one hour instead of only one became a very attractive advantage to examiners.

HYPNOSIS INDUCTION PROFILE

The Hypnosis Induction Profile (HIP) was developed primarily by psychiatrist Herbert Spiegel, joined later by his son David Spiegel (1978). (David Spiegel is the subject of a Frame of Reference section in chapter 17.) Unlike other scales, the HIP was developed in a clinical setting with patients in treatment where the "motivation is likely to be greater because the patient is seeking help with a personal problem rather than exercising curiosity" (p. 38). They were dissatisfied with the SHSS and HGSHS: A because the length of time they took to administer, and they thought several of the items were potentially too embarrassing. The HIP involves items similar in structure to the SHSS and HGSHS:A (e.g., arm levitation and amnesia), but has the unique additional feature of the "eye-roll" test. Subjects are told to roll their eyes up as if looking through the top of their head (the "up-gaze" part of the test), and then strive to close their eyes (the "roll" part of the test). The amount of the sclera (whites of the eyes) showing as the eyes raise and then close, each rated on a 5-point scale, are added together to yield the "eye roll sign" score which indicates level of hypnotizability. The Spiegels hypothesized that the eye-roll sign is a manifestation of the way the brain hemispheres interrelate, and serve as a "biological marker" of hypnotizability. The HIP takes only a few minutes to administer, and the Spiegels suggest the test can even become the induction for therapeutic work in hypnosis, thereby giving a more flowing element to the clinical interaction. Curiously, however, the HIP does not correlate significantly with the SHSS or the HGSHS:A. Despite that, it remains a popular instrument for its convenience, short duration, and clinical foundation.

INFORMAL ASSESSMENT OF HYPNOTIC RESPONSIVENESS

As mentioned above, most clinicians do not employ formal instruments for assessing hypnotizability, for reasons ranging from they "feel" artificial, or they don't want to set up "pass-fail" situations needlessly, to the belief they don't reveal useful clinical information. Psychologist Brent Geary (2001)

summed up this viewpoint when he wrote,

> (my) premise is that everyone with intact mental processes can benefit from hypnosis to some degree. The extent to which this is possible is tested through clinical intervention rather than by the administration of a set procedure that yields a quantifiable result . . . the primary context for assessment . . . remains the patient's ongoing narrative and responsiveness in the psychotherapeutic relationship (p. 3).

Not unlike Weitzenhoffer's comment that, "Either the effect can be done when the time comes or it cannot" (2000, p. 466), Geary and other clinicians prefer to observe responses as they unfold in the "real life" context of the therapy. *Responsiveness is thus seen as existing in the context of the interaction rather than as a function of some innate characteristic of the client.* What are some ways to assess responsiveness from this more informal perspective, that is, besides the formal standardized tests already described? Some people use structured "mini-tests" such as the Chevreul's Pendulum, the "Hot Object," and the "Hand Clasp," described next. But the "Embedded Commands" and "Nonverbal Shifts," described after the "mini-tests," are the kind of nonintrusive forms of assessment that Geary referred to above.

CHEVREUL'S PENDULUM

If you have ever played with a Ouija board, you've experienced the Chevreul's Pendulum test. This is a structured "mini-test" administered before formal hypnosis as a simple means of helping the client get "acquainted with hypnotic-like responding" (Bates, 1993, p. 40). A pendulum is given to the subject with the instruction to hold the chain between thumb and forefinger (Coe, 1993; Watkins, 1987). The process can be made a bit more dramatic by having the subject hold the pendulum over the center of a circle containing intersecting lines drawn on a piece of paper. The circle may look like this:

The vertical axis was labeled "Y" arbitrarily to stand for our cultural head nod to respond "Yes." Likewise, I arbitrarily labeled the horizontal axis "N" to stand for our cultural head shake to respond "No."

Once the subject has the pendulum dangling over the center of the circle, suggestions such as the following can be given: "As you relax by breathing deeply, you can concentrate on holding the pendulum still . . . that's right . . . and now as you continue to concentrate you'll notice and allow the pendulum to take on a particular motion." Notice the lack of specificity about what motion the pendulum is to take. As you observe the pendulum begin to move, you can then begin to use suggestions to amplify the movement: "That's right . . . the pendulum can begin to swing more and more along the (N, Y) axis, from (left to right or to and fro), and it can do so without you really knowing how or why . . . the pendulum can move just by your concentrating on it, and you can concentrate on letting it swing wider and wider without any effort on your part. . . . " Then you can further suggest stopping it and switching directions to the other axis. The greater the degree of the pendulum's swing, the greater the degree of suggestibility.

As hokey as this old test may seem, it does illustrate well the transderivational search and ideomotor processes first discussed in chapter 3. As the client processes the meaning of "left to right" or "toward you and away from you," his or her body responds to the mental meaning and causes small muscle movements (called the "ideomotor response") outside of consciousness which cause the pendulum to move. Because the person's small muscle movements causing the pendulum's swing are unconscious, the pendulum test is often a genuine surprise to the client and thus serves as a convincer of his or her hypnotic skills—and yours as well.

THE "HOT OBJECT" TEST

Like most tests, this one involves translating suggestions into physical responses, specifically a sensory hallucination of warmth in an ordinary object. In this technique, the subject has his or her eyes closed and is given an object to hold in his or her hand. Then he or she is told it's going to begin to heat up. Suggestions might be given that the object has been treated with a special chemical, or is perhaps plugged into an electrical outlet, and that it will begin to heat up and get hotter and hotter until it becomes too hot to hold. (I have a video clip of Ernest Hilgard demonstrating this in his Stanford lab with a woman he hands an ordinary ballpoint pen to while she focuses her gaze elsewhere. He tells her it is a "heating element" that he is going to plug into the wall. He instructs her to tell him when it starts to get warm, which she readily does. Then he tells her it will get hot, too hot to hold, and drop it when it does. She breathes heavily trying to hold on as long as she can before she drops the pen. She had the subjective experience of the pen getting too hot to hold!) The length of time it takes to "heat up" and the degree of sensation associated with it are the measures of suggestibility in this test.

THE HAND CLASP

One of the subtests of the Stanford Scale, one that involves a challenge to the client to perform, the client is asked to sit comfortably, hands together and fingers interlaced. Some suggestions are offered about his or her hands being (tied, glued . . .) stuck together, coupled with suggestions that "the harder you *try* to pull your hands apart, the more tightly stuck together they become."

There is a play on words in this mini-test. It concerns the difference between "trying" and "doing." Trying implies expending energy, but not actually "doing." The key suggestion for this and other similarly structured tests is phrased, "The harder you try to (pull your hands apart, bend your arm, open your eyes), the more difficult it will be to do so." The tendency for literalism is what allows this technique to work (when it does). The next step then is providing the suggestions that "In just a moment I'll ask you to separate your hands (bend your arm, open your eyes) and let them drop into your lap . . . and you'll be able to do so quite easily, quite effortlessly . . . Now go ahead and separate your hands and let them drop slowly to your lap." Notice the difference between the "try" challenge mode versus the "do" mode.

Another variable in this and each of the challenge tests is the amount of time you give the person to "try." Let the person make the initial effort, find it takes more energy than expected, and then give him or her the suggestion to "stop trying now and just continue to relax." If you give the person more than a few seconds to feel that initial effort, of course he or she can eventually do what you've suggested couldn't be done. Be quick to let him or her stop trying!

The three informal tests described above are commonly used, structured ones that are obviously quite arbitrary and ritualistic in terms of the demands they make on the client. There are other, more spontaneous approaches to assessing suggestibility as well, two of which are described below.

EMBEDDED COMMANDS

Embedded commands are suggestions for specific responses that are integrated into the context of a larger communication. By being components of a larger context, they are suggestive but do not stand out as such and can more easily therefore escape conscious detection. For example, if I use my voice to accent (i.e., emphasize) slightly (e.g., through a change of voice tone or volume) the underlined words as I say the following sentences, I can embed suggestions for specific responses:

"Isn't it nice to . . . *close your eyes* . . . at the end of the day?" (I may get
   the eye closure response, an obvious indicator of suggestibility)
"I thought to myself I could . . . *take a deep breath* . . . and think it over."
"You can . . . *scratch the itch* . . . to succeed."

If you offer a suggestion so indirectly and the person takes a deep breath or
scratches an itch, you have a positive response. Any suggestion that's embedded has the potential to get a response: More spontaneous, less imposing and arbitrary than challenge tests or gimmicks like a pendulum,
embedded commands can be a more useful indicator of suggestibility because of their subtlety.

NONVERBAL SHIFTS

Nonverbal shifts in unconscious behavior can also be a very good indicator
of suggestibility. Part of attaining rapport is the "pacing" or "mirroring" of
client behaviors outside of their consciousness. Nonverbal shifts can take
place in many behaviors: posture, gestures, scratching, eye contact, and
breathing, just to name a few. If you mirror a client's body posture and then
shift your posture and your client shifts at that moment also, you have evidence of rapport and suggestibility at an unconscious level. In one of my
clinical demonstrations available on video, The Case of Mike (see Appendix B, page 563, for information about this session), as I orient Mike to
hypnosis, I unconsciously lean back and cross my legs. Just two seconds
later he does exactly the same! I knew at that moment that the rapport (i.e.,
connection) between us would likely help make the session useful to him,
which follow-up shows it was.

Mirroring someone is effective only to the degree that it remains out of
the client's consciousness. If perceived consciously, it's no longer called pacing; rather, it's called mimicking, and rapport will be lost. Therefore, I'd
advise that you be careful and respectful in using these types of indirect
techniques.

SOME TIPS ON PERFORMING ASSESSMENTS OF HYPNOTIC RESPONSIVENESS

Introducing and performing suggestibility tests requires as much skill in
communication as any other aspect of working with hypnosis. There are the
matters of timing (i.e., when in the relationship it is introduced), the explanation of a test's role in treatment, the style in which you offer it, your response to the client's response (or lack thereof), and how you end it and
move on to the next phase of interaction.

Some clinicians use suggestibility tests right away—even before the person's problem is presented, even before rapport is attained. I adamantly discourage that practice, but still, it's what some people do. To my way of thinking, rapport is essential and must be earned through clinical skill.

The suggestibility test should generally not be introduced to the client as a "test." The word "test" has immediate implications of a "pass or fail" situation, and can raise an already uncomfortable client's anxiety level even higher. I suggest you call them "responsiveness measures" or even "conditioning experiences." The idea of a pass or fail situation is a legitimate objection to the use of suggestibility tests, especially those that directly challenge the client in some way. To demand a specific response from someone is to run the risk of not getting it. Why set a client up to fail? My emphasis is on your role of suggesting possibilities, but respecting the client's final choice as to whether the suggestion is accepted or rejected. With suggestibility tests, challenging clients to have a certain suggested experience doesn't much respect their ability to choose for themselves.

CONCLUSION

The broad questions of why and how people vary in their hypnotic responsiveness have already received massive attention in the research literature. These are important though difficult questions that underscore the unifying principle for all researchers and clinicians interested in hypnosis: *We want people to benefit as much as possible from hypnosis, and we're each in our ways trying hard to find out how to make that happen.*

For Discussion

1. Have you ever played with a Ouija board? What was your reaction to it? How did you explain what happened?
2. How do you know when someone is open to your suggestions? What "body language" do you equate with open and closed mindedness? What exceptions are you aware of?
3. How responsive do you think you are to others' suggestions? What makes you think so? Do you view your level of responsiveness to others as an asset or liability? Why?
4. One person yawning reliably triggers the yawning response in others. What other suggestions are you aware of that people seem to react to automatically?
5. What does "unconscious rapport" mean? How do you know when you have it?

Things to Do

1. Get hold of the assessment instruments described in this chapter, and others as well, and spend some time studying them—their structure, their wording of suggestions, their assumptions, etc.
2. Engage several people in a Ouija game who have no background in hypnosis and, ideally, who have no experience with the Ouija board game. What do you observe? How do they explain what happened to them?
3. The next time you shop, engage salespersons in a discussion about a product you intend to buy, and one you have no intention of buying. What differences are you aware of in your internal experience in the two conditions? How does your behavior differ in the two conditions?
4. Practice each of the suggestibility tests on at least 10 different people. Alter your style from authoritarian to permissive, and notice each person's response to your guidance. What do you learn about differences in response style? What explanation do you have for these differences?

REFERENCES

Barber, J. (1989). Predicting the efficacy of hypnotic treatment. *American Journal of Clinical Hypnosis, 32,* 10–11.

Barber, J. (1991). The locksmith model: Accessing hypnotic responsiveness. In S. Lynn & J. Rhue (Eds.), *Theories of hypnosis: Current models and perspectives.* (pp. 241–74). New York: Guilford.

Bates, B. (1993). Individual differences in response to hypnosis. In J. Rhue, S. Lynn, & I. Kirsch (Eds.), *Handbook of Clinical Hypnosis* (pp. 23–54). Washington, D.C: American Psychological Association.

Coe, W. (1993). Expectations and hypnotherapy. In J. Rhue, S. Lynn, & I. Kirsch (Eds.), *Handbook of Clinical Hypnosis* (pp. 73-93). Washington, D.C: American Psychological Association.

Cohen, S. (1989). Clinical uses of measures of hypnotizability. *American Journal of Clinical Hypnosis, 32,* 4–9.

Diamond, M. (1989). Is hypnotherapy art or science? *American Journal of Clinical Hypnosis, 32,* 11–12.

Gearan, P., Schoenberger, N., & Kirsch, I. (1995). Modifying hypnotizability: A new component analysis. *International Journal of Clinical and Experimental Hypnosis, 43,* 1, 70–89.

Geary, B. (2001). Assessment in Ericksonian hypnosis and psychotherapy. In B. Geary & J. Zeig (Eds.), *The Handbook of Ericksonian psychotherapy* (pp. 1–17) Phoenix, AZ: The Milton H. Erickson Foundation Press.

Gilligan, S. (1987). *Therapeutic trances: The cooperation principle in Ericksonian hypnotherapy.* New York: Brunner-Mazel.

Hilgard, E. (1982). Hypnotic susceptibility and implications for measurement. *International Journal of Clinical and Experimental Hypnosis, 30,* 394–403.

Hull, C. (1933/2002). *Hypnosis and suggestibility: An experimental approach.* Williston, VT: Crown House Publishing.

Kronenberger, W., LaClave, L., & Morro, C. (2002). Assessment of response to clinical hypnosis: Development of the Hypnotic State Assessment Questionnaire. *American Journal of Clinical Hypnosis, 44,* 257–72.

Laurence, J-R. (1997). Hypnotic theorizing: Spring cleaning is long overdue. *International Journal of Clinical and Experimental Hypnosis, 45,* 3, 280–90.

Lynn, S., & Shindler, K. (2002). The role of hypnotizability assessment in treatment. *American Journal of Clinical Hypnosis, 44,* 3–4, 185–98.

Nadon, R. (1997). What this field needs is a good nomological network. *International Journal of Clinical and Experimental Hypnosis, 45,* 3, 314–23.

Pekala, R. (2002). Operationalizing trance II: Clinical application using a psycho-phenomenological approach. *American Journal of Clinical Hypnosis, 44,* 241–56.

Rossi, E. (1989). Mind-body healing, not suggestion, is the essence of hypnosis. *American Journal of Clinical Hypnosis, 32,* 14–15.

Scheflin, A. (2001). Caveat therapist: Ethical and legal dangers in the use of Ericksonian techniques. In B. Geary & J. Zeig (Eds.), *The handbook of Ericksonian psychotherapy* (pp. 154–67). Phoenix, AZ: The Milton H. Foundation Press.

Shor, R., & Orne, E. (1962). *Harvard Group Scale of Hypnotic Susceptibility, Form A.* Palo Alto, CA: Consulting Psychologists Press.

Spanos, N. (1991). A sociocognitive approach to hypnosis. In S. Lynn & J. Rhue, (Eds.), *Theories of hypnosis: Current models and perspectives* (pp. 325–61). New York: Guilford.

Spiegel, H. & Spiegel, D. (1978). *Trance and treatment: Clinical uses of hypnosis.* New York: Basic Books.

Watkins, J. (1987). *Hypnotherapeutic techniques.* New York: Irvington.

Weitzenhoffer, A. (2000). *The practice of hypnotism* (2nd ed.). New York: Wiley.

Weitzenhoffer, A. (2002). Scales, scales and more scales. *American Journal of Clinical Hypnosis, 44,* 3–4, 209–20.

Weitzenhoffer, A. & Hilgard, E. (1959). *Stanford Hypnotic Susceptibility Scale, Forms A and B.* Palo Alto, CA: Consulting Psychologists Press.

Weitzenhoffer, A. & Hilgard, E. (1962). *Stanford Hypnotic Susceptibility Scale, Form C.* Palo Alto, CA: Consulting Psychologists Press.

SECTION TWO

Practical Framework

12

Structuring Suggestions

The theoretical foundation for your understanding what Ernest Hilgard (1973) called "the domain of hypnosis" has, hopefully, now been established. Throughout the remainder of this book, the focus will be entirely practical: I will encourage you to evolve the fundamental skills to do hypnosis effectively with your clients, and to develop an awareness for many of the clinical issues associated with applying hypnosis insightfully. In this chapter, I will begin with the "nuts and bolts" of hypnosis, the way you deliver suggestions to your client.

SUGGESTIONS ARE INEVITABLE, BUT THERE'S NO GUARANTEE

If you enthusiastically recommend a restaurant you recently tried and enjoyed to a friend, and then he or she goes to that restaurant solely on the basis of your recommendation, you have clearly influenced his or her experience. Somewhere in that interaction was at least one basic element of hypnosis: you offered a suggestion, and it was accepted and later acted upon. How exactly did you phrase your recommendation? What was your tone of voice and body posture? What is your relationship with that person? Why was he or she receptive to your recommendation? What other factors can you identify that made your recommendation the basis for a new experience for someone?

Suggesting to someone that he or she go to a particular restaurant or movie (or likewise, that he or she avoid it) is a routine, everyday type of interaction. Despite its commonness, this kind of interaction can illustrate the nature of suggestion quite well. In making a recommendation of *any* sort, you are sharing information with someone about an experience you've had or a belief you hold. On the basis of your description, the other person forms an internal representation of your experience (i.e., perhaps vividly imagining what the restaurant looked like, what the atmosphere was like, how the service was, how the presentation of the food was, how the food tasted, etc.). If it is a powerful enough representation, it may motivate him or her to seek out and have a similar experience directly. In this example, sensory information about a restaurant is transmitted from one person to another, but the information does not have to be acted upon since it is only a recommendation or suggestion, not a command. If the information is inherently appealing, or is made to sound appealing in some way to the listener, then it is more likely to be accepted. *Any suggestion can be accepted or rejected, hypnotic or otherwise.* The power of hypnotic communication, i.e., communication that absorbs the person's attention and directs their experience, is in its ability to act as a catalyst for organizing and using more of the client's resources, both conscious and unconscious. The ritualistic nature of traditional hypnotic inductions is a good example of a specific means for occupying a person's conscious mind, allowing the unconscious to be more accessible for therapeutic suggestions. The person in hypnosis isn't unaware of the suggestions, of course, but is able to respond more experientially and multidimensionally.

The skill of an effective hypnotist is in his or her ability to formulate suggestions in such a way as to make them both acceptable and *usable*. Merely performing an induction of hypnosis is not sufficient: A deep hypnotic experience on the part of the client is no assurance that he or she will accept offered suggestions, even ones that are clearly in his or her best interest to accept. As you learned in previous chapters, numerous personal, interpersonal, and situational factors ultimately determine the degree of a person's responsiveness to suggestion. The focus in this chapter is on some of the communication variables of hypnotic patterns, specifically the range of communication styles and structures that can be used to form hypnotic suggestions. There are many different ways of communicating an idea to someone, and so the clinician can be deliberate in choosing a means of organizing and delivering a suggestion that carries the greatest chance of being accepted by the client.

Suggestions are dynamic, not static in their structure. They can range along a number of continua, sharing multiple, simultaneous traits. There is no time when all your suggestions will fit into only one category, nor will there be any time you won't want to move up and down on a particular continuum of suggestion as you offer a series of suggestions to someone. What are these continua? On one continuum of suggestion, we have *direct* and *indirect* suggestions occupying the poles. On a second continuum, we have suggestions ranging from *positive* to *negative*. On a third continuum, we have *process* and *content* suggestions. And on the fourth and last continuum we have possibilities ranging from *permissive* to *authoritarian* suggestions. In a related but separate category are *posthypnotic suggestions*, an essential and well-

Table 2. Suggestion Structures and Styles: Generic Forms

Direct Suggestions
  "You can do X"
Indirect Suggestions
  "I knew someone who experienced doing X"
Authoritarian Styles
  "You will do X"
Permissive Styles
  "You can allow yourself to do X"
Positive Suggestions
  "You can do X"
Negative Suggestions
  "You cannot do X"
Content Suggestions
  "You can experience this (specified sensation, memory, etc.)"
Process Suggestions
  "You can have a specific experience"
Posthypnotic Suggestions
  "Later, when you are in situation A, you can do X"

considered part of any clinical intervention. Let's consider each of them in turn.

DIRECT AND INDIRECT SUGGESTIONS

Hypnotic communications can be structured in direct and indirect forms. Not only are they not mutually exclusive, but it is neither possible or desirable to do an effective hypnotic process exclusively in one form or the other. Realistically, both styles will be evident in a given process at various times. Furthermore, each suggestion will vary in the degree of directness, as if on a continuum with "direct" at one pole and "indirect" at the other. Which style to use at a given moment depends on the nature of the suggestion (i.e., its complexity, novelty, potential for raising the client's anxiety or defenses, and other such factors) and the degree of responsiveness of the client.

DIRECT SUGGESTIONS

Direct suggestions deal with the problem at hand or the specific response desired overtly and clearly. Direct suggestions provide specific directions as to how to respond. Consequently, they are not known for their subtlety. The generic structure for a direct suggestion is, "You can do X." The form of a direct suggestion can vary within this generic structure, depending on your specific word choice.

To initiate the hypnosis session, the clinician will typically suggest that the client close his or her eyes. If the clinician chooses a direct approach, he or she might offer any of the following direct suggestions:

> Close your eyes.
> Please close your eyes.
> You can close your eyes.
> Let your eyes close.
> I would like you to close your eyes now.

Each of these suggestions *directly* relates to obtaining eye closure from the client as a specific response. There is no mistaking what the clinician wants the client to do. The statements are clear in their intent to get the client to close his or her eyes. The same direct suggestion structures, by changing their content (i.e., associated details) might be used to obtain virtually any desired response:

> You can go back in your memory and remember when you went to your first school dance. (Age regression)
> I want you to let your arm lift effortlessly and become weightless. (Sensory alteration and arm levitation)
> You will be able to make your hand numb in the next few seconds. (Analgesia)
> Experience each minute as if it were an hour. (Time distortion)

The desired response in each of these examples is apparent because the suggestions directly ask for it. Nothing is hidden from the client in terms of what is wanted from him or her. Each suggestion is intended to generate a specific response. Additional direct suggestions may then be offered in order to provide a concrete means (i.e., a strategy) for accomplishing the suggested response:

> Imagine you are in a time machine that is taking you back to your first school dance.
> You can feel that your arm is tied to a large helium balloon allowing it to float.
> Remember how your hand tingles when you get a shot of novocaine? You can have that same sensation of numbness in your hand now.
> Time passes so slowly when you are waiting for something special, and you can notice now how slowly the hands of time move.

Many clinicians employ a direct suggestion approach to hypnosis almost exclusively. For many, it was simply the way they were trained and so it's what they're comfortable with. Some have difficulty evolving the flexibility it takes to vary their communication style even though they perceive it might be beneficial to do so. Others haven't seen the need to evolve any other style besides a direct one because they haven't seen any evidence for other styles being either as effective or more effective than a straightforward style. The issue of one style being "better" than another is one of the lingering controversies in the field, and I will address it directly later in this section.

Training courses and books that offer standardized "one-size-fits-all" scripts for use with general problems are typically direct in their approach. They employ suggestions that represent a frontal assault on the presenting problem. For example, if a client presents the complaint of wanting to lose weight, a direct approach might offer suggestions such as:

> You want to lose weight, and you will lose weight. You will lose weight seemingly effortlessly because you will find yourself becoming choosier about what you eat and when you eat. Whenever you reach for either a fattening or unnecessary food you will instantly see the detailed image in your mind of yourself weighing your ideal weight, and it will feel so good and so motivating to you that you will find it much easier to choose not to overeat. You would rather lose weight than eat fattening foods. You will feel so good about yourself in this process that losing weight becomes easier and easier, and you'll find yourself being satisfied with less and less food. You'll feel extra energy as you lose weight and so you will also want to exercise more just to use your extra energy to get leaner and stronger. . . .

This kind of direct approach may work with some people—perhaps some very obedient, highly hypnotizable, and deeply motivated ones! It's not that such suggestions are bad, wrong, or destined to fail. In fact, for someone who wants to lose weight, they *will* have to do as suggested, that is, eat less and exercise more. But, that's the equivalent of telling a depressed person to "Cheer up!" It's correct, but not particularly effective. (I regularly encounter people who would rather be right than effective. That puzzles me.) For most people, more subtlety and less of an "in-your-face" approach is preferred. Supportive and not merely demanding suggestions are required, as well as a more highly individualized approach acknowledging the person as special in some way, which each person is. Telling others bluntly what to do does not show much clinical skill, nor does it show much respect for their intelligence and creativity. People typically already know what to do, they just don't have access to the resources that would allow them to do it. (Realistically, do you think there's an overweight person out there who *doesn't* already know he or she should eat less and exercise more?) Finally, such approaches don't involve as much of the person in the therapy process as a more collaborative effort would. Thus, direct suggestions can be greatly helpful, but familiarity and skill with both direct and indirect approaches are essential to the development of a broad and flexible practice of clinical hypnosis.

Here is an abbreviated "cost-benefit" analysis of direct suggestions: The advantages of direct suggestions include: (1) their direct relevance to the matters at hand (easing concerns in the client about your ability to deal directly with his or her problems); (2) their ability to keep the client's goal(s) well defined and in sight; (3) their direct involvement of the client in the process in an active way; and, (4) their ability to serve as a model for the resolution of this and any future problems that arise through the development of a deliberate problem-solving strategy.

The disadvantages of direct suggestions include: (1) their over-reliance on a conscious willingness to follow suggestions, making less use of unconscious resources; (2) their greater likelihood of engendering resistance in the client by dealing so directly and even bluntly with his or her problems, potentially a threatening experience; and, (3) their defining the client's role primarily as one of mere compliance rather than an as active participant in the therapy.

Appreciating the advantages and disadvantages of the use of direct suggestions is necessary to allow you to make an informed decision as to when their use will most likely result in a successful hypnotic experience.

INDIRECT SUGGESTIONS

Indirect suggestions relate to the problem at hand or the specific desired response in a covert (or, at least, less obvious) and unobtrusive way. They can be quite subtle and thereby escape a full awareness and analysis. Such suggestions usually do not relate directly to the person's conscious experience. Rather, they are indirectly related and thus require the client to interpret them in a proactive and idiosyncratic way in order to make meaning of them. The generic structure of an indirect suggestion is, "I knew someone who experienced doing X." By talking about someone else (or some other situation), the response is invited through an indirect means. Use of indirect suggestions can have the client wondering at a conscious level what you are talking about, or perhaps may simply occupy (amuse, entertain, fascinate) the person at a conscious level, while at the same time unconscious associations are generated that can pave the way for change to take place.

Consider as an easy example a child's fairy tale: When you tell a child the story of *The Three Little Pigs*, the child can easily be entertained and fascinated by the drama of the story and by the playful exchange when you both "huff and puff and blow the house down." But, beneath the content of the story (i.e., the characters and the things they say to each other), there is a deeper message you hope to impart: The importance of planning, discipline, and hard work in order to move through life choosing substance (i.e., houses of brick) over "flash" (i.e., flimsy ones made of wood and straw). People can transmit and receive deeper messages of substance through such indirect paths. We don't have to experience something directly in order to be influenced by it. Clinically speaking, every time someone provides you a successful case example, you may be interested in and become absorbed in the details of the case, but the inescapable yet indirect message to you is, "When you see this type of client, you can use this kind of an approach."

Indirect suggestions can take numerous forms, including storytelling, analogies, jokes, puns, homework assignments, role modeling, and disguised and embedded suggestions. Any communication device that causes or requires the client to respond without directly telling or asking him or her to do so involves some degree of indirect suggestion.

The use of indirect suggestion is a focal point of study in the "utilization approach" to hypnosis, largely due to the many creative ways they were used by Milton H. Erickson, M.D. Erickson was widely acknowledged for his skill and creativity in formulating successful interventions, often with seemingly "impossible" clients. When you read his fascinating and unusual cases, many of which he described in his own words in the book, *A Teaching Seminar with Milton H. Erickson, M.D.* (Zeig, 1980), many of his ingenius hypnotic and strategic interventions seemed to have absolutely no relationship to the presenting complaint, so indirect were they. Yet, his therapeutic effectiveness with hypnosis and indirect suggestions has inspired intensive analysis of his methods and forced an appreciation for the merits of indirect approaches in the field when others succeed similarly using his methods. Thus, an advanced study of clinical hypnosis is literally impossible without studying Erickson's work directly, as well as the writings about his methods by his many students and colleagues (including Erickson, Rossi, & Rossi, 1976; Erickson & Rossi, 1979, 1981; Gilligan, 1987, Haley, 1973, 1985; Lankton & Lankton, 1983; O'Hanlon, 1987; O'Hanlon & Hexum, 1990; Rosen, 1982; Rossi, 1980, and many others).

To contrast direct and indirect suggestions, you can refer back to the previous section's examples for obtaining eye closure through direct suggestions. If you suspect, on the basis of feedback from your client, that you would be more likely to get eye closure through indirect methods, you might offer any of the following suggestions:

A responsive client usually begins the hypnotic experience by closing his or her eyes.

Can you allow your eyes to close?

Many of my clients like to sit there with their eyes closed.

Isn't it nice not to have to listen with your eyes open?

I wonder what you will think of that will allow you to comfortably *close your eyes.*

Each of these examples seeks eye closure as a specific response, but it has never been asked for directly. The statements are general ones that the client must respond to in *some* way since even no response is a response. The clinician can learn quite a bit about how the person thinks and responds from the way he or she relates to such suggestions. For example, does the person take initiative in responding, or simply wait to be told exactly what to do?

One pattern of indirection may take the form of simply describing others' experiences, allowing the client to choose a similar response or else generate an independent one. Another indirect pattern is to have the client become aware of routine, everyday experiences where the desired response is a natural event. As the client becomes focused on and associated to such a situation, he or she can begin to re-experience it himself or herself as if in that suggested situation. The responses associated with the past experience can become a part of the current experience. For example, if you were to think of a time when you felt very romantic and loving toward someone, and really spent time recalling the details of that experience, those same feelings are likely to arise now through your recall (an ideoaffective response). Thus, instead of demanding the specific response of creating those feelings now in a direct way, I can get them less directly by simply describing a context where such feelings are likely to naturally occur.

As with eye closure, indirect suggestions can be varied in content to obtain virtually any response:

A close friend of mine has a daughter who went to her first school dance, and I don't know if you can remember yours, but it sure was an exciting time for her. (Age regression)

When you were in grade school you had to *raise your hand slowly* when you wanted to say something important, and sometimes it would rise as if it were weightless and you didn't even realize it. (Sensory alteration and arm levitation)

Can you imagine what it's like to have a barehanded snowball fight and have so much fun making and throwing snowballs you forgot to notice you weren't even wearing gloves? (Analgesia)

Time is so difficult to keep track of, and after all a minute can seem like 5 or 10 minutes sometimes; you've had that experience, where you can get so wrapped up in your thoughts that only a minute can seem so much longer. (Time distortion)

In each of the above examples, the client's immediate experience is seemingly less the focal point than someone else's, or the suggestion seems so general as to be impersonal and therefore not requiring a direct response. It is up to the client to adapt herself in her own unique way to the *possibilities* for certain responses raised by the clinician's suggestion. In this way, direct commands for obedience are avoided, and the client's own creative ability to form an individualized response is tapped. How he or she finds a way to accomplish the possible response suggested is as varied and creative as are people. My strategies for getting the response may not be as useful to the person as the possibilities he or she creates for him or herself. Essentially, through the telling of stories or some similar indirect technique, I am suggesting to the person that a change can be accomplished without telling the person "what" to do, inviting his or her participation in the creation of a solution.

Here, then, is an abbreviated "cost-benefit" analysis of indirect suggestions: The advantages of the indirect approaches include: (1) their greater utilization of unconscious resources in the client's own behalf; (2) their greater distance between the suggestion and its intended target emotion or behavior, reducing the need for resistant defenses; (3) their permissiveness in encouraging and allowing the client to interpret the suggestions in whatever way might be useful to him or her, demonstrating a greater respect for the client; and, (4) their defining the client's role in the treatment process as an active one going beyond mere compliance.

The disadvantages of the indirect style include: (1) the client's possible fear or anxiety that the clinician is either unable or unwilling to deal directly with his or her problem, and "if he or she can't, how can I?"; (2) the clinician may be viewed as evasive or incompetent (i.e., seemingly irrelevant in "talking around" issues), and the client may feel manipulated and even cheated; (3) the client's unconscious responses may allow for alleviation of the problem, but may leave him or her consciously wondering how the change occurred, as if therapy was done "to" rather than "with" him or her; and, (4) the problem may be solved but may not leave the client with a knowledge of and access to effective and self-managed patterns for solving future problems.

As with direct suggestions, appreciating the advantages and disadvantages of using indirect suggestions gives you an ability to make sensitive choices about their applications. One approach is not better than another. The goal is to use either approach flexibly in order to get the desired therapeutic result.

CHOOSING A STYLE: ARE DIRECT OR INDIRECT SUGGESTIONS BETTER?

One of the ongoing debates within the field concerns the issue of which form of suggestion, direct or indirect, is clinically superior. There have been numerous studies attempting to answer the question, and, as one might expect, they differ in their conclusions (Barber, 1980; Fricton & Roth, 1985;

Groth-Marnat & Mitchell, 1998; Hayes & Gifford, 1997; Lynn, Neufeld, & Mare, 1993; Yapko, 1983). Such research misses an obvious point: *No suggestion is inherently worth much; a suggestion only becomes meaningful when a client accepts, integrates, and responds meaningfully to it.* Thus, generalizations about the superiority of one form of suggestion over another may, at best, be academically interesting, but they have little bearing on what an individual client will respond well to. Thus, if you only know how to be direct, you will be at a distinct disadvantage when you encounter those clients who will respond better to less direct approaches. *The most sensible goal is to be fluent in all suggestive approaches and vary them as circumstances warrant.*

For many experts in the field, the recommendation on this issue is to formally assess hypnotizability, and use the client's profile ("low," "medium," or "high" hypnotizable) to determine whether you should even do hypnosis. The more hypnotizable the person, generally speaking, the more you can be direct in your methods.

There are others, though, myself included, who are less interested in scores on a standardized test and who are more interested in other factors that influence hypnotic responsiveness. Alternative guidelines for choosing a style, and the degree to which that style should be used, are based on two major factors: the degree of insight desirable or necessary to allow the intervention to work, and the degree of responsiveness of the client.

There exists a split among psychotherapists regarding the role of insight in the treatment process. Some claim that insight is both necessary and desirable to facilitate change. Others claim insight is not required in order for meaningful changes to occur and that insight may even delay change by giving people a better cognitive understanding of the hurtful patterns, fueling the defense of "intellectualization," with no vehicle for affectively or behaviorally changing them.

It seems there are few, if any, absolute "right" or "wrong" ways to structure therapeutic interventions. Rather, there are ways that are effective and ineffective with specific clients, and it grows ever more obvious from diverse yet successful interventions that there are *many* "right" ways. Each client is unique as an individual, and whether insight will work for or against the therapy is a factor to weigh in formulating your interventions. Some clients demand understanding what you're doing on a conscious level, asking "Why?" a lot. Others are much more interested in getting some change to occur in the problem no matter what it takes. The more a person seeks conscious understanding and tries to engage you on that level, the more an indirect approach may disrupt his or her normal pattern, increasing the likelihood of change. Yet, at the same time, a person who seeks conscious understanding may be put off by an indirect method, lose patience and motivation, and then dismiss the experience as useless. Only clinical experience will teach you to make skilled assessments about which style to use with a particular client.

The second variable to consider in assessing whether to use a direct or indirect style is the degree of responsiveness of the client (or, conversely, the degree of "resistance," traditionally considered a lack of responsiveness). A basic guideline you can use to determine which style to use is this: The degree of indirection should be directly proportional to the degree of resistance encountered or anticipated (Zeig, 1980). In other words, the greater the degree of inability or unwillingness to follow directives on the part of the client, the more the suggestions should be offered indirectly. If a client is compliant with and highly responsive to the clinician's requests, following them in an authentic (and not in a "resistant over-cooperation") and positively motivated way, then indirection is not necessary. Conversely, if a client is resistant to directives, is self-directed (i.e., following his or her own agenda despite your recommendations), then indirect approaches are more respectful and nonthreatening. Their distance from the intended target (such as the underlying dynamics to be resolved) may well increase the likelihood of their acceptance.

In sum, the degree of direction or indirection in offering suggestions will vary according to the unique responses of each individual you work with. As with all the hypnotic communication patterns presented in this book, what you do at any given moment will rely on the feedback you get from the client. After all, he or she is the determinant of what works. You can feel much more secure in your abilities to relate to a wider range of people if you have both direct and indirect approaches in your repertoire.

AUTHORITARIAN AND PERMISSIVE SUGGESTION STYLES

Suggestion style refers to the demeanor or posture of the clinician while offering suggestions. Styles can be described as if on a continuum with "authoritarian" at one pole and "permissive" at the other.

AUTHORITARIAN SUGGESTIONS

The authoritarian style is a domineering one in which the clinician literally commands the client to respond in a particular way. The generic structure for an authoritarian style is, "You will do X." Authority and power are the key variables the clinician relies on, and the response from the "good" client is compliance. Stage hypnotists, as an exemplary group, are necessarily authoritarian in style, requiring obedient responses from their subjects. In the authoritarian approach, a lack of compliance is evidence of "resistance," and, unfortunately, is viewed as a shortcoming of the client. Literature advocating authoritarian styles as a modus operandi typically suggests first confronting the client about his or her resistance to the procedures and then attempting to eliminate it by identifying its source and means of resolution. In chapter 21 on non-ideal responses to hypnosis, the detriments of this approach to managing resistance are elaborated, but you may anticipate how easily this confrontive approach can initiate a "power struggle."

Authoritarian approaches involve offering suggestions in the form of commands. The following suggestions are structured in an authoritarian mode:

> Close your eyes when I count to three. (Eye closure)
> When I snap my fingers, you will be six years old. (Age regression)
> When I touch your shoulder, you will go into deep hypnosis. (Deepening)
> You will find it impossible to bend your arm. (Catalepsy)
> You will not remember anything from this experience. (Amnesia)

Directing someone to respond in a specific way that minimizes personal choice does not show much respect for that person's needs or wants. Thus, a strictly authoritarian approach should generally be used sparingly. There are times, though, when such an approach is not only viable, but even desirable: When a vulnerable and confused patient needs a clinician who is clearly in charge and decisive, and when the quality of good rapport between you and the client makes what you have to say far more important than how diplomatically you say it.

PERMISSIVE SUGGESTIONS

At the other end of the continuum is the "permissive" style, one that is much more respectful of the client's ability to make choices in his or her own behalf about what he or she will and will not respond to. The permissive approach is one characterized by its emphasis on allowing the client to become aware of possibilities for meaningful responses, rather than making demands for such responses. The generic structure for the permissive suggestion is, "You can do X." The clinician offers suggestions of what the client *may* experience if he or she chooses to. The sensibility of a permissive approach is in knowing you can't make someone respond (e.g., relax or focus). You can simply *suggest possibilities* in such a way that the person, hopefully, chooses to avail him- or herself of those possibilities. Ultimately, the responsibility is on the client to make use of information that has been provided by the clinician in his or her own way. Any response is deemed an adequate or usable one by the clinician, respectful of the person's choice. In this way, "resistance" is much less debilitating a factor, since whatever response the person generates is deemed acceptable.

Permissive suggestions are intended to raise the possibility of a response, and the following examples may illustrate the point:

You can allow your eyes to close, if you would like. (Eye closure)
You may choose to uncross your legs. (Postural shift)
You might be willing to let yourself relax even more deeply. (Deepening)
It's possible to experience your body differently. (Perceptual shift)
Perhaps you can remember a time when you felt comfortable. (Age regression)

In these examples, the client is offered choices and then responds to his or her own choices. The clinician is simply saying, in one form or another, that the client can have an experience if he or she permits it. The client's response in any direction is thus a choice and must be respected as such. Such acceptance by the clinician can add to the rapport by demonstrating a respect for the client as a person capable of making choices for him- or herself. It may be implicit thus far but can now be stated explicitly that when the client's choices are deemed counterproductive to your treatment plan, your strategy needs to be revised. The idea of the permissive approach is to make the suggestions you offered clients acceptable through their personal choice. The skill required in such an approach is evident.

In sum, there are those who want to be told what to do and will follow instructions to the letter, and there are those who refuse to follow anyone's lead and will even go out of their way to reject others' input simply because they resist being "controlled." If someone is willing to follow directives obediently, an authoritarian approach may be successfully employed. With most people, however, it will tend to set up "power struggles." The permissive approach is good for creating possibilities in people who like to have a large measure of control in their lives by making their own decisions, but may frustrate the person who wants to be told in explicit terms *exactly* what to do in a step-by-step fashion. Both authoritarian and permissive styles have their place in doing hypnosis, and as with all forms of suggestion, it will enhance your effectiveness when you familiarize yourself with their usage.

POSITIVE AND NEGATIVE SUGGESTIONS

POSITIVE SUGGESTIONS

Positive suggestions are by far the most common, simple, and useful type of suggestion structure. Positive suggestions are supportive and encouraging, and are phrased in such a way as to give the client the idea that he or she can experience or accomplish something desirable. The generic structure for a positive suggestion is, "You can do X." (You'll recognize this as a permissive suggestion as well.) Since words call to mind the experiences that the words (as symbols of experience) represent, positive suggestions are phrased to create desired responses. The following suggestions are structured in positive and permissive ways:

> You can feel more comfortable with each breath you inhale. (Deepening)
> You can remember a time when you felt very proud of yourself. (Age regression)
> You are able to discover inner strengths you didn't realize you had. (Resource building)
> You can notice how good it feels to relax. (Deepening)
> You may notice a soothing feeling of warmth in your hands. (Sensory alteration)

These examples are positive suggestions to the client of things he or she *can* experience. These suggestions are meant to be empowering, creating positive possibilities without demanding anything specific to resist. Amplifying what's possible, meaningful, and helpful is the foundation of positive suggestions.

Many experienced clinicians claim that suggestions should be in the positive form in order for the unconscious mind to process them, and it is further claimed that the unconscious mind does not understand negatives. My own experience is consistent with these views for reasons I will elaborate in the following discussion on negative suggestion structures.

NEGATIVE SUGGESTIONS

Negative suggestions employ a sort of "reverse psychology" approach when used skillfully. Negative suggestions may be used to obtain a response by suggesting the person *not* respond in the desired way. The generic structure for a negative suggestion is, "You cannot do X." By telling the person what not to do, he or she still has to process and interpret what you say, and the various subjective associations surface as he or she does so. When used deliberately and in a skilled way, negative suggestions can be most useful.

The following are examples of negative suggestions. Notice what your internal experience is as you slowly read each of them.

> Do not think of your favorite color.
> Do not allow yourself to wonder what time it is.
> I would suggest that you not notice that sensation in your leg.

You shouldn't be thinking about your high school sweetheart right now. Please try not to notice which of your friends is the most materialistic.

Did you find yourself doing what was suggested that you not do? If so, why? If you were able to avoid doing what you were instructed to, how did you accomplish this? Did you have to distract yourself with some other thoughts? Would a client be able to prevent herself from following the suggestion if he or she didn't know about negative suggestions?

All too often, negative suggestions are employed naïvely and accidentally, generating an unwanted response that may leave the practitioner wondering what went wrong. If a clinician says (with great sincerity and the positive intention of comforting the client), "Don't worry about it, just put it out of your mind," the client is most likely to still worry and think about "it." If a lawyer says to a jury, "Don't think about the horrible crime my client committed. Instead judge him only as a scared, confused person," it is a safe bet the jury has just recalled all the gory details of the crime and the feelings they have about it. Accidental outcomes as a result of non-selective use of negative suggestions can undo in a sentence what might have taken considerably longer to accomplish. Use them carefully!

I mentioned in the previous section that many experts have formed the opinion that the unconscious is unable to respond or decipher negative suggestions in the literal way they are presented. Based on your experience of the examples of negative suggestions above, do you agree? If I ask you not to think of the taste of pizza, didn't you have to first think of it before erasing it from your mind in whatever way you might have done so? Your unconscious responds to a negative with a positive. How might negative suggestions be used deliberately to facilitate the experience of hypnosis? By suggesting to the client he or she not do the things you actually want him or her to do (assuming the appropriate client and situational variables), you are paving the way for the client to respond in a way that can only be defined as cooperative. For example, if I say to my client, "Don't let your breathing slow down as you listen to me, or else your muscles might relax," the client can now respond by either letting his or her breathing slow down and muscles relax, positive signs of the beginning of hypnosis, or he or she can continue in the current state, essentially complying with the literal suggestion, a cooperative response. Thus, either response is a cooperative one, directly or indirectly.

Other examples may include negative suggestions such as:

Don't even consider the possibility that there might be a positive way to solve this problem.
There's no reason why you should even think about how good it will feel to get this behind you.

Don't sit in a comfortable position if you can help it. I'd prefer that you don't discover that you can relax here, at least not yet.

Negative suggestions are a way of "short-circuiting" resistances, occupying the client with negativity while asking for positive responses indirectly. The typical response of the client is to ignore the negative and respond to the implicit positive suggestion.

CONTENT AND PROCESS SUGGESTIONS

How much detail in your suggestions should you provide the client? Should you lead the client step-by-step through some sequence of suggestions designed to culminate in some response? Or, should you keep the suggestions general, and let the client figure out how to make them meaningful? As you might anticipate, both approaches have merit in different circumstances.

CONTENT SUGGESTIONS

Content suggestions contain highly specific details describing feelings, memories, thoughts, or fantasies the client is to experience during hypnosis. The generic content suggestion structure is, "You can experience this (specified sensation, memory, etc.)." Providing details that describe every dimension of the suggested experience can have the desired effect of assisting the client to have the experience more completely and therefore with a greater degree of absorption and clinical usefulness.

Examples of content suggestions may include:

Think of a red rose with soft, velvet petals you can lightly brush against your nose as you inhale its gentle, sweet fragrance.

Imagine being at the beach on a bright, clear day, feeling the sun warming your skin, smelling the salt in the ocean breeze, and hearing the lapping of the waves upon the shore.

Can you remember how pleasing it is to bite into a juicy, wet orange, how your mouth waters, how the juice feels as it runs all over your fingers, and how tart it tastes?

Each of these examples provides specific details about exactly what you are to experience in thinking of a rose, the beach, and an orange. Perhaps those details allowed you to have the suggested experience more fully, in which case the details were helpful to you. However, these examples can also illustrate a potential hazard in using content-filled suggestions, namely that the details I directed you to notice may not be the ones you would have chosen to focus on. Or, at their worst, they may even have been details that negated the experience for you. If, for example, when I said "imagine the beach" you recalled a negative experience you had at the beach, or if you have never experienced being at a beach in your life, then the details will lead you to a negative memory or perplex you as to what I'm getting at (since there is no personal experience to relate to my suggestions) and be disruptive. The potential problem with content suggestions is simply this: The more details you provide, the greater the probability that something you say will contradict your client's experience. The end result is the client will sense that the clinician is not really "with" him or her, and so is less likely to benefit from the experience.

On the other hand, when you offer content to someone and the details you suggest actually fit with his or her experience, the details will enhance the experience. One way to increase the fit of content suggestions is to notice the many cues the client continually provides (such as style of language, sensory-based terms he or she spontaneously uses in speaking, and details he or she provides of experiences during the interview you can feed back later during hypnosis) about his or her experience. Another possibility is to do a general hypnosis session and ask for direct feedback about which suggestions helped deepen the client's involvement in the experience and which seemed less effective. Yet another solution is to use process suggestions instead of content suggestions, discussed in the next section.

PROCESS SUGGESTIONS

In contrast to the details provided in content suggestions, process suggestions provide minimal details at most, encouraging the client to provide his or her own. The generic structure for a process suggestion is, "You can have a specific experience." In response to the deliberate ambiguity in the suggestion, the client projects his or her own personal experiences and frame of reference into the suggestion in order to make meaning of it. Consequently, process suggestions are less likely to contradict the experience of the client. For example, if I would like the client to imagine being in a relaxing place, instead of me choosing the beach as a specific place to focus on and then providing lots of details (content suggestions) about what it's like to be at the beach, I can simply suggest to my client that he or she imagine being *somewhere* relaxing. I don't say where that place might be, and so he or she can choose the specific place and which particular details of that place he or she would like to focus on. Process suggestions are so general in nature that the client can project personal meaning into them and then relate to them in his or her own, individual way.

If you read newspaper horoscopes, you have a common example of process suggestions. The observations and predictions are so nonspecific that they can apply to virtually anyone. The following paragraph is an example of the point:

> You are a person who likes to be with those people you care about, but sometimes you prefer to just be left alone. Sometimes you get very frustrated with events in your life, and even lose your temper on occasion. You would like more people to appreciate you, and you often think you deserve to make more money than you do. Sometimes you think terrible things about people you really do care about and then feel guilty about it.

I think the above represents most of the human beings on the planet, but did you find yourself silently agreeing and wondering, "How did he know that?" Process instructions give clients the opportunity to use their own experience and details in the process, and therefore make what seems, at first glance, to be too general to be effective appear to be a highly individualized approach. As you will discover in your use of process suggestions, people take their projections *very* seriously. Even for something as silly as astrology, there are people who invest themselves in horoscopes as daily guides to action. People get even more serious when they project themselves into the *big* questions of life: Why are we here? What's the meaning of life? What happens after we die?

The following are examples of process suggestions:

> You can have a particular memory from childhood, one that you haven't thought about in a long, long time. (Age regression)
> You will notice a certain pleasant sensation in your body as you sit there comfortably. (Kinesthetic awareness)
> You may become aware of a specific sound in the room. (Auditory awareness)
> Can you remember that special time when you felt so good about yourself? (Age regression)

None of these suggestions specifies anything—that is, they do not say which specific memory, sensation, sound, or event the client is supposed to experience. The client chooses that aspect of the experience when he or she projects a response to the suggestion. Notice, though, the use of qualifiers such as "particular," "certain," "specific," and "special" in process suggestions. These can be employed to have the client sift all of his or her experience down to one particular one to focus upon. Which one the person chooses is the product of an interaction between conscious and unconscious choices. Typically, the client wonders how you knew what he or she was experiencing, not realizing how general your suggestion was because of how specific it seemed! The use of process suggestions is often harder to master because of the "groping-in-the-dark" aspect to them. But, their ability to sidestep contradictions between the details the clinician provides and the client's actual experience makes them imperative to learn to use well.

Process suggestions are especially valuable in doing group hypnosis processes, in which the opportunity to carefully watch each individual's responses to content suggestions is virtually impossible. Using process suggestions of a general yet specific-sounding nature allows each person in the group to have an entirely different experience in response to a single set of suggestions. Trying to make a group of people share a common, detailed experience is a set-up for failure. Thus, through process suggestions the diversity among people is acknowledged and encouraged.

The content versus process paradigm can be viewed in another way: Dealing with the details contained in the structure of an experience, or with the structure itself. Content-oriented therapies deal with details of the problem, while process-oriented therapies focus on the problem's structure. For example, many people seek out a certain type of person in a romantic relationship, one who fits some measure of desirability that may or may not be a conscious criterion. So, if a person has a succession of intimate relationships with someone tall and dark-haired, who is a fashionable dresser, tight-lipped about feelings, and domineering, and each time the relationship ends in disaster, then what can be concluded? People have patterns that guide their behavior, and these are generally unconscious. In the current example, the content is each specific person in the succession of partners. The names and faces change, but not the structure of how a relationship partner is chosen, that is, the type of person in the pattern. The content approach to therapy might deal with the reason(s) why this particular relationship isn't working out, while a process approach might consider the structure of the pattern for how partners are chosen. By altering the structure of the pattern of selection, a change in the details (content) must naturally follow.

Using process or content suggestions is simply another choice point for the clinician in formulating an intervention. Shifting spontaneously from one suggestion structure to another is an easy thing to do, so the decision about which structure to use is by no means a final one, a "sink-or-swim" proposition. If what you are doing isn't getting the desired response, then flexibly making a midstream shift in your approach is a good idea.

POSTHYPNOTIC SUGGESTIONS

Posthypnotic suggestions are those given to the client while he or she is in hypnosis that encourage particular thoughts, behaviors, and feelings he or she is to have in some other future context. Posthypnotic suggestions have the generic structure, "Later, when you're in situation A, you'll be able to do X." They are a standard part of nearly every therapy session, since you will almost always want the client to take something away from the session that he or she can use elsewhere in the course of living. Posthypnotic suggestions make it possible for the person to carry over into the desired context whatever new associations he or she has acquired during hypnosis.

Posthypnotic suggestions are a *necessary* part of the therapeutic process if the client is to carry new possibilities into future experiences. Without them, the learnings acquired during hypnosis will most probably be limited to the session itself. The reason for this is that hypnotic responses are generally "trance state-specific," meaning they are tied to the immediacy of the hypnotic experience, operating within the boundaries of that experience. Posthypnotic suggestions permit the learnings acquired during hypnosis to cross internal boundaries and become available in other locations and frames of mind. If the client can only have the desired experience (e.g., pain relief) during hypnosis, the value of hypnosis is limited. Its value increases exponentially when new resources are extended across contexts. Posthypnotic suggestions facilitate that possibility. Posthypnotic suggestion might involve suggesting to the client that when he or she finds him- or herself in a particular situation he or she has had trouble with, or when he or she has unwanted hurtful feelings, he or she can take some specific step suggested during hypnosis to remedy the problem. The following are examples of posthypnotic suggestions:

> When you come out of hypnosis in a few moments, you can enjoy the feeling that you rested to a more satisfying degree than you have in a long, long time.
> When you begin to take your examination next week, you can close your eyes for a moment that can seem much longer and take a deep breath, and you can notice all the anxiety leaving you as you exhale.
> After you go home tonight, you'll have a certain memory that will make you laugh, and it'll feel really good to let off some steam in such an enjoyable way.
> When you find yourself in the next argument with your boss, the feeling of comfort that she can disagree with you but still appreciate you will soothe you enough to handle the discussion calmly in a way you feel proud of.

Each of these examples suggests a behavior or feeling the client is to experience in some future time and place to be based on the suggestions given to him or her during hypnosis. Interestingly, some clients may have no conscious memory for the origin of the suggestion (amnesia), but act on it unconsciously nonetheless.

Posthypnotic suggestions can be used to facilitate future hypnotic work by offering the suggestion that in future sessions the client can experience hypnosis even more deeply and rapidly. Wherever you want to facilitate "carryover," you'll employ posthypnotic suggestions.

Posthypnotic suggestions are essential to assure that the desired response will likely become integrated into the person's everyday life, replacing dysfunctional or absent responses.

SPECIALIZED SUGGESTIONS

While the suggestion structures and styles described throughout this chapter thus far represent the core components of hypnotic suggestion, there are numerous other more specialized forms of suggestion that may be derived from the core components. Most of these specialized suggestion forms were first conceived of and described by Milton H. Erickson and his student and collaborator Ernest Rossi, and are contained in the books that involve Erickson training Rossi in hypnosis (See Erickson, Rossi, & Rossi, 1976; Erickson & Rossi, 1979, 1981) as well as the lectures and papers of Erickson (Erickson, 1983, 1985; Rossi, 1980). These specialized forms of suggestion are described briefly in this section.

ACCESSING QUESTIONS

Questions that encourage the client to respond at an experiential level rather than on only a verbal one are known as accessing questions. More than rhetorical questions, accessing questions focus the client on particular aspects of his or her experience, which are amplified simply through the way the question was asked. In other words, the question suggests a response. For example: "Can you recall how very soothing and relaxing it is to lie in the warm sun and feel it warming your skin?" The fact that questions can suggest responses has been a controversial area of inquiry in the questioning of witnesses in forensic investigations. "Interrogatory suggestibility" and "leading questions" are a legitimate basis for concern that witnesses might be contaminated and distort their testimony as a result of the way questions are asked. In the clinical domain, however, accessing questions are used to enhance treatment responsiveness.

AMBIGUOUS SUGGESTIONS

You can deliberately use ambiguity in a suggestion in order to encourage the client's projections, related to but slightly different from the nonspecific "process" suggestion. The ambiguity may surround the desired action on the part of the client, or the meaning of the suggestion. For example, to suggest that "One can be quite iron-willed and hardheaded in such matters" leaves it open to interpretation as to whether the clinician is praising perseverance or criticizing stubbornness.

APPOSITION OF OPPOSITES

Offering suggestions that create distinct polarities of experience within the client is making use of the apposition of opposites. For example: "As your left hand becomes pleasantly cold and numb, you'll notice your right hand becoming comfortably warm and responsive." The increased awareness of such marked differences can lead the client to believe, "Hey, I'm doing it!"— a positive response that reinforces further responsiveness.

BIND OF COMPARABLE ALTERNATIVES

Providing the client with a bind of comparable alternatives, a classic double-bind, creates a "forced choice" situation for the client in which both choices lead to an equally desirable outcome: "Would you enjoy a deep and satisfying hypnotic experience while you're sitting in this chair or in that chair?" For as long as the client noncritically accepts the bind and responds within the parameters of the suggestion, the bind can be effective. If, in another example, you say to a child, "Would you prefer to clean your room now or in an hour?" and the child says, "Neither!" the bind is useless.

CONFUSIONAL SUGGESTIONS

Suggestions deliberately constructed to disorient or confuse the client in order to build responsiveness, overload an overly intellectual demeanor, and facilitate dissociation are known as confusional. Confusional suggestions are one of the most advanced suggestion structures to employ because they aren't linear and logical, they generate uncertainty and even anxiety rather than comfort and clarity, and they require greater concentration on the part of the clinician to keep track of where the process is going. But, they are valuable in interrupting ongoing client patterns of thought and perception, perhaps paving the way for new possibilities. You can think you consciously understand the point of such suggestions, but your unconscious likes clarity, too, so if you consciously organize around conscious understandings that you unconsciously believe will consciously work for you in unconsciously structuring the conscious and unconscious patterns for knowing consciously at an unconscious level that you can overload someone's ability to comprehend, then ... you can just consider using confusional suggestions when they seem sensible to do so. More is said about methods employing confusion in later chapters.

COVERING ALL POSSIBILITIES

An effective way to enhance responsiveness in the client is to encourage any and all possible responses in your suggestion, defining any specific response as a useful, cooperative one: "You may find yourself recalling an important memory . . . perhaps one from quite early in your life . . . perhaps a memory that is very recent . . . or perhaps one from somewhere in-between a long time ago and very recent times . . ." Well, what other possibilities are there? Any memory will be from the past, obviously, whether recent, intermediate, or distant. Thus, any memory he or she retrieves is in line with the suggestion, thus assuring a positive response.

IMPLIED DIRECTIVES

An indirect way to encourage a response is through the use of implied directives. The first part of the suggestion structure is the indirect suggestion to do something from which the second half of the suggestion then directly suggests a response. For example: "When you experience your hand lifting in just a moment (indirect suggestion), you will notice that it feels very, very light" (direct suggestion).

INTERSPERSAL OF SUGGESTIONS

The frequent repetition of key words or phrases within an ongoing flow of suggestions is an interspersal approach. You can use an interspersal of suggestions to deepen the hypnotic experience, facilitate the experience of a specific hypnotic phenomenon, "seed" (implant) ideas for future reference, or simply to reiterate an important point. For example: "A *deep* thinker, that is, one who thinks *deeply*, can evolve a *deeper* understanding of the complexities of suggestions, and perhaps an even *deeper* understanding of him- or herself in gaining *depth* of knowledge about suggestion" (deepening technique).

METAPHORS

Metaphors have come to mean the use of stories in the literature of clinical hypnosis. Metaphors are considered one of the most powerful yet gentle means for communicating relevant information to a client, using the vehicle of the story to bring important points to life. The art of creating and telling effective stories in hypnosis for therapeutic purposes deserves special attention, and so will be addressed in greater detail in several later chapters.

PARADOXICAL SUGGESTIONS

Paradoxical suggestions contain what seem to be, at first glance, incompatible or even contradictory components contained within the same overall suggestion. For example: "You can take all the time in the world . . . in the next minute . . . to complete your inner work of integrating your new understanding."

PRESUPPOSITIONS

A presupposition assumes the suggested response will happen. It's not a question of *whether* the response will occur—it's simply a matter of *when*. For example: "How pleasantly surprised will you be when you discover that you understand presuppositions?"

PUNS

The use of humor as a reframing device can be a valuable way of engaging the client in the process while simultaneously establishing a friendly and warm emotional association to the experience of hypnosis. For example: "Some people like to do hypnosis with a slow and rhythmic style of delivering suggestions . . . even pacing suggestions to the rhythm of the client's breathing . . . but you know and I know that the rhythm method is not very reliable . . ." Can the hypnotized person appreciate humor and even smile or laugh during hypnosis without diminishing the value of the experience? Yes.

TRUISMS

A truism is a "common sense" observation that appears to be so obviously true and self-evident that it is virtually undeniable. Truisms are generally used to build an acceptance of the suggestion that follows it as the person evolves an agreeable mindset. Building receptivity in the client in this way is called establishing a "response set," and is considered in greater detail later. For example: "Every person is unique (truism), we all know that . . . which is why you can experience deep hypnosis in your own unique way."

CONCLUSION

Words are stimuli, and they can come to evoke the same or similar responses as the objects or concepts they represent. Therefore, your words have to be chosen carefully, as does the manner in which your words are spoken. This chapter has detailed the different styles and structures underlying diverse hypnotic communications. The clinical skill is in employing whatever approach will likely work best with your client, and not just using the ones you might happen to personally prefer. In the next chapter, we will explore some hints to further enhance hypnotic communication.

For Discussion

1. When a friend recommends a movie or restaurant to you, what factors determine whether or not you'll follow the recommendation?
2. Why do people reject suggestions that are clearly in their best interest? What differences can you identify between people who like to be told what to do and those who don't?
3. What changes have you made on the basis of insight? What changes have you made for no apparent reason? What do you think about the role of insight in the process of change?
4. How do you feel when someone tells you how you feel? How is the feeling different when he or she is right than when he or she is wrong?

Things to Do

1. Make a list of the most common hypnotic suggestions (e.g., "Relax," Sit comfortably," "Close your eyes," "Breathe at a comfortable rate," etc.) and write five suggestions in each style and structure to get that idea across. *This is one of the best exercises there is to develop flexibility in suggestion formation.*
2. In class, have each student make up an imaginary product, and have each attempt to sell it to the rest of the class. Which sales pitches were best, and why? Which were least effective, and why?
3. Read the horoscopes daily and identify the process suggestions employed. What do you discover about the generality of language? What sort of person (specify his or her cognitive style) would think horoscopes have merit?

REFERENCES

Barber, J. (1980). Hypnosis and the unhypnotizable. *American Journal of Clinical Hypnosis, 23*, 4–9.

Erickson, M. (1983). *Healing in hypnosis: The seminars, workshops, and lectures of Milton H. Erickson* (Vol. 1). New York: Irvington.

Erickson, M. (1985). *Life reframing in hypnosis: The seminars, workshops, and lectures of Milton H. Erickson* (Vol. II). New York: Irvington.

Erickson, M., & Rossi, E. (1979). *Hypnotherapy: An exploratory casebook.* New York: Irvington.

Erickson, M., & Rossi, E. (1981). *Experiencing hypnosis: Therapeutic approaches to altered states.* New York: Irvington.

Erickson, M., Rossi, E., & Rossi, S. (1976). *Hypnotic realities: The induction of clinical hypnosis and forms of indirect suggestion.* New York: Irvington.

Fricton, J., & Roth, P. (1985). The effects of direct and indirect hypnotic suggestions for analgesia in high and low susceptible subjects. *American Journal of Clinical Hypnosis, 27*, 226–31.

Gilligan, S. (1987). *Therapeutic trances: The cooperation principle in Ericksonian hypnotherapy.* New York: Brunner/Mazel.

Groth-Marnat, G., & Mitchell, K. (1998). Responsiveness to direct versus indirect hypnotic procedures: The role of resistance as a predictor variable. *International Journal of Clinical and Experimental Hypnosis, XLVI*, 4, 324–33.

Haley, J. (1973). *Uncommon therapy: The psychiatric techniques of Milton H. Erickson, M.D.* New York: Norton.

Haley, J. (Ed.) (1985). *Conversations with Milton H. Erickson, M.D.* (Vols. I–III). La Jolla, CA: Triangle Press.

Hayes, S., & Gifford, E. (1997). The trouble with language: Experiential avoidance, rules, and the nature of verbal events. *Psychological Science, 8*, 170–74.

Hilgard, E. (1973). The domain of hypnosis: With some comments on alternate paradigms. *American Psychologist, 28*, 972–82.

Lankton, S., & Lankton, C. (1983). *The answer within: A clinical framework of Ericksonian hypnotherapy.* New York: Brunner/Mazel.

Lynn, S., Neufeld, V., & Mare, C. (1993). Direct versus indirect suggestions: A conceptual and methodological review. *International Journal of Clinical and Experimental Hypnosis, 41*, 124–52.

O'Hanlon, W. (1987). *Taproots: Underlying principles of Milton Erickson's therapy and hypnosis.* New York: Norton.

O'Hanlon, W., & Hexum, A. (1990). *An uncommon casebook: The complete clinical work of Milton H. Erickson, M.D.* New York: Norton.

Rosen, S. (1982). *My voice will go with you: The teaching tales of Milton H. Erickson, M.D.* New York: Norton.

Rossi, E. (Ed.) (1980). *The collected papers of Milton H. Erickson, M.D., on hypnosis* (Vols. 1–4). New York: Irvington.

Yapko, M. (1983). A comparative analysis of direct and indirect hypnotic communication styles. *American Journal of Clinical Hypnosis, 25*, 270–76.

Zeig, J. (Ed.) (1980). *A teaching seminar with Milton H. Erickson, M.D.* New York: Brunner/Mazel.

13

Helpful Hints
for Performing Hypnosis

In the previous chapter, I described the general styles and structures for suggestion formulation. In this chapter, some general guidelines for your choice of particular words and phrases within those styles and structures will be provided. These guidelines are intended to help you form suggestions that are more likely to be accepted by the individual you are working with.

These guidelines are, for the most part, communication skills based on common sense. While these guidelines generally hold true for most hypnotic processes, you should, of course, be aware that each principle has exceptions that may be even more useful to apply with a given client. Therefore, a brief discussion of each principle is provided to encourage you to think critically about it. By thinking of particular cases where the principle might not apply, and thinking of an alternative that might be more effective, you will increase your range of choices in responding skillfully to a particular person.

KEEP YOUR SUGGESTIONS SIMPLE
AND EASY TO FOLLOW

Generally, the more complicated a set of suggestions or instructions you provide for someone to follow, the more the person must rely on conscious resources to help understand and respond to them. That's true in *or* out of hypnosis. The more the person must rely on conscious resources, the less the person can respond with unconscious ones, partially defeating one of the primary reasons for even doing hypnosis. Keeping your suggestions relatively simple allows the client to "go with the flow" of the process without having to critically, and therefore consciously, analyze, interpret, and judge the merits of your suggestions.

Table 3. Some Helpful Hypnotic Communication Patterns

Keep your suggestions simple and easy to follow.
Use the client's language as much as sensibly possible.
Have the client define terms experientially.
Use the present tense and a positive structure.
Encourage and reinforce the client's positive responses.
Determine ownership of the problem and the problem-solving resources.
Use sensory modalities selectively.
Keep your clients as informed as desired and as is necessary to succeed.
Give your clients the time they need to respond.
Only use touch selectively and always with the client's permission.
Use anticipation signals to announce your intentions.
Use a voice and demeanor consistent with your intent.
Chain suggestions structurally.
Use process suggestions to encourage projections.
Build response sets gradually.
If desirable, substitute other terms for "hypnosis."

Keeping your suggestions flowing smoothly and clearly is not as easy as you might think. I have seen experienced hypnotists engender a lack of responsiveness in people just by making their directions too complex to follow. For example, in one case, a clinician did a group hypnosis process involving many instructions for a wide variety of possible responses, all of which were contingent on other responses. Observing his group's responses, I noticed many of the individuals had come out of hypnosis simply because the instructions were too complex, and the hurried pace did not match the stated intent of helping people relax. Some of the participants complained later that the suggestions were as confusing as some board game instructions ("Spin the wheel, and if an even number comes up, you'll throw the dice, but if an odd number comes up on the wheel you'll choose one of three cards and if you choose the right card you'll have your choice of four numbers, one of which will be the correct number allowing you to match the . . . whew!"). It's too much work to try to follow complicated instructions, especially when someone is trying to relax, focus, and get some help.

The ideal hypnotic process is one that can elicit the desired responses in as brief yet easy and meaningful a way as possible. The more the person's conscious mind is involved in trying to develop unconscious hypnotic responses, the more difficult and lengthy the hypnosis session is likely to be. Essentially, it's like trying really hard to be spontaneous. Furthermore, depending on the person you're working with, too complex a process may turn him or her off not only to that session's work, but to future work as well.

To complicate matters, there is another side of this guideline which involves specialized techniques whose value is derived from their complexity rather than from their simplicity. These advanced techniques include confusion and overload techniques, in which confusing ideas and an overabundance of information are provided deliberately. These techniques involve placing an excessive burden on the conscious mind to the point where it can no longer keep up. When the person eventually gives up trying to follow, he or she essentially resigns him- or herself to noncritically allowing the experience to unfold, ultimately becoming dissociated and permitting the unconscious mind to respond more independently.

How, then, do you know whether your suggestions are too complex and working against your goals? Observe your client's responses. Every suggestion that lightens his or her experience of hypnosis, and every undesirable response to your suggestions, indicates that he or she may not be following you (which also means you may not have been following him or her as well as you might have). A more direct means for finding out how your client is doing is to simply ask the client neutrally, directly or indirectly, for specific verbal and nonverbal feedback about his or her experience during and again after the hypnosis session.

Keeping suggestions easy to follow isn't the same as being predictable and obvious about where you are going with the hypnotic process. If the person is able to guess where you're going and can too easily remain a step ahead of you, there is obviously considerable conscious analysis taking place, increasing (but by no means assuring) the likelihood of reduced responsiveness. If you become aware that you may have lost the client somewhere along the way, you can go back to a point in the process where you sensed he or she was with you (and, if you are as observant as you can possibly be, you won't have to go back very far) and go on from there, but obviously not in the same way.

Don't force the client to rely on conscious processes to follow you. Keep in mind that only your client can be the one to determine what he or she can and cannot follow. In other words, you may think your directives were explicit and easily understandable, but you're not the one following them—your client is.

USE THE CLIENT'S LANGUAGE
AS MUCH AS SENSIBLY POSSIBLE

One of the lessons from the field of hypnosis which has been especially helpful clinically is the idea of using the language of the client whenever possible. You have learned that words represent experience, and even though we use a common language, our individual experiences are necessarily different. Taking the client's words, then attaching your meaning to them, then translating them into the conceptual language you happen to use, and then, finally, communicating from your linguistic style are all steps that are arbitrary on your part, and thus increase the likelihood of miscommunication.

In using the language of the client, you don't assume, even for a moment, that you mean the same thing as he or she does in using it. You can use the same language as your client simply because it is his or her world you are dealing with, not yours.

In studying numerous clinical theories and interacting with a wide variety of clinicians representing various treatment approaches, I have been unfavorably impressed with how a client's communications about his or her experience get translated into the clinician's favorite theoretical jargon, and then get fed back to the client that way. Words are symbols of experience, not the experience themselves. They represent a distortion (i.e., a distillation) of real-world experience anyway, so why distort them even further with new labels of interest to the clinician? I have had clients that have "resolved transference issues," "built ego strength," "strengthened their armor," and "released energy blocks." They did these and lots of other things that pleased their therapists, yet they left treatment not feeling much better about themselves. The main advantage of using the client's language is in your ability to intervene in the client's problem as he or she experiences it, and not as you interpret it. Furthermore, the client can get the sense of being understood to a greater degree, engendering greater trust in the clinician. (Continued on page 269)

FRAME OF REFERENCE: JEFFREY K. ZEIG, PH.D.

Jeffrey K. Zeig, Ph.D., is a psychologist and the founder and director of the Milton H. Erickson Foundation in Phoenix, Arizona. He is a superb clinician and teacher in his own right, lecturing nationally and internationally to professionals. He is especially well known as a primary catalyst for bringing the pioneering work of Milton H. Erickson, M.D., into the world spotlight. Dr. Zeig studied directly with Erickson for more than six years. Dr. Zeig's vision and organizational abilities have given rise to extraordinary meetings sponsored by the Erickson Foundation that are widely considered the best conferences for clinicians offered *anywhere*. To date he has organized six International Congresses on Ericksonian Approaches to Hypnosis and Psychotherapy held every two to three years since the first one in 1980, four Brief Therapy Conferences, and he has organized the landmark Evolution of Psychotherapy Conferences every

five years since the first one in 1985. Each of these featured the true luminaries in the field, all assembled in one place at one time, for what some
have affectionately called the "Woodstocks of psychotherapy." He edited
each of the proceedings from these meetings in impressive published volumes that are must-reads for clinicians.

In addition to maintaining a private practice, Dr. Zeig is the editor
and author of 18 professional books and five monographs about Erickson
and about psychotherapy, including *A Teaching Seminar with Milton H.
Erickson, M.D.* (1980, Brunner/Mazel), *Experiencing Erickson* (1985a, Brunner/
Mazel), and *Milton H. Erickson* (written with W. Michael Munion, 1999,
Sage Publications).

On His Personal Experience of Milton Erickson: "I vividly remember how emotionally touched I was by the experience of being with
Erickson. On the second day of my visit, I watched him struggle to move
himself from his wheelchair to his office chair. Then he started speaking
to me through his obvious pain, intent on instructing me about how to be
more effective as a person and therapist. I remember feeling powerfully
moved that he would selflessly spend his limited energy to help me. No
powerful figure I had met before had such a moving impact. There was
something extraordinary about Erickson: Perhaps his profound effect was
due to his acute sensitivity, respect for the individual, intensity, verve,
uniqueness, and joie de vivre in the face of adversity. I saw him struggle to
bring out the best in himself and it inspired me to want to do the same"
(Zeig, 1985a, p. 167).

On the Mission of The Milton H. Erickson Foundation: "The
intention was to differentiate Ericksonian methods from other schools
and then quickly integrate them into the mainstream of psychotherapy,
which we accomplished. We did not want to establish Ericksonian therapy
as a distinct school. Erickson's contributions have relevance to psychotherapy in general and now have been incorporated into other approaches,
including cognitive behavioral therapy. Erickson's work advanced the field
of psychotherapy; he was more than a pioneer in hypnosis."

On How Erickson Is Widely Perceived: "Erickson was sought after by some of the great minds of the 20th century, including Margaret
Mead and Gregory Bateson. He was respected because of his genius, en-
deared because of his humanism. Now Erickson is widely acknowledged
as one of psychotherapy's most innovative pioneers. Erickson was one of
the most public therapists of his time, consistently showing what he did at
a time when demonstrations of therapy for the professional public were
not popular. His work is readily available for serious research and critique."

On Erickson in Retrospect: "I think Erickson was "on the spot" in pioneering the doctrine of utilization; tailoring therapy to the uniqueness of the individual; using confusion and multilevel communication; and in harnessing what have become well understood and well researched social psychological principle of influence. But, no amount of research will clarify the essential nature of hypnosis, just as no amount of research will clarify the essential nature of love. Erickson's artistry will not be lost because of research. Evolving research will shed light on the effectiveness of his clinical work. Erickson was the consummate social psychologist studying how situational effects alter behavior. Recent mainstream psychological research studies on effects such as priming have demonstrated that Erickson was right in applying the analogous clinical method of 'seeding,' one of Erickson's favorites."

On Encouraging the Personal Development of the Therapist: "I integrate methods from systemic therapy, Gestalt, and Transactional Analysis. I use much of what I learned from Erickson as a foundation, but I have my own style and perspective. The therapist is more the tool of change than the techniques the therapist uses. An evolving clinician can best facilitate patient evolution. Erickson was a "people-builder," not a technician. Similarly, I am more dedicated to help clinicians BE the best therapists than helping them to learn techniques to DO therapy. Therapist development, moreover, motivates and inspires clinicians and obviates burnout."

On What He Calls the "Gift-Wrapping" of Suggestions: "Patients "gift-wrap" their problems within symptoms and the therapist must unwrap the symptom to discover the problem. Similarly, therapists can gift-wrap solutions and suggestions within techniques such as anecdotes and metaphors, encouraging the patient to activate to realize the intended message. Hence, therapy is an exchange of presents (and presence)."

On the Artistry and Science of Hypnosis and Erickson: "The most widely known research on hypnosis focuses on the nature of the phenomena, not on clinical outcomes. The major hypnosis researchers of the 20th century were scientists, not clinicians. Erickson's first career was as a researcher and he was more like an anthropologist conducting field studies than a modern psychological researcher armed with an ANOVA. Because there is a lot to be learned, I hope that some of Erickson's research methodologies will be resurrected and modernized."

Source: Personal communication, January 15, 2003

Sometimes, using the language of the client is neither appropriate nor desirable. If the person's style of speech is too idiosyncratic, or is related to the client's particular ethnic group or other subculture of which you are not a member, your using the same language to try to make a positive connection may instead be viewed as mockery and insulting. Recovery from such a mistake is difficult.

Some clinicians have a personal bias against using the client's language. I had an interaction a while ago with a prominent sex therapist who believed that if a patient of his used common language to describe a problem, it was his duty to make a point of speaking back to the person with the proper scientific jargon. He gave the example that if a male patient were to present the complaint that he "couldn't get it up," his response would be to speak to the patient about his "erectile dysfunction and inability to perform coitus." Those seemed, to me to least, to be cold, sterile terms that really don't reflect his client's experience. When I offered my reaction for some discussion, the doctor said that, "I didn't go to medical school to speak like an ignorant layman." Well, I didn't go through all the schooling I did for that purpose, either. Might he reach a wider range of the people he works with by working with them in terms they naturally use and can understand instead of expecting them to come to his level? Probably. And, likewise, are there patients of his relieved by his treating so personal a problem more professionally and scientifically? Probably. The point I'm making is about the value of considering the use of the client's language to possibly enhance the interaction. It takes a lot of flexibility to want to do that, though.

There is another important aspect of noticing and using a client's language that has to do with the role of the unconscious mind in the person's language choice. A client's word choice can reflect dimensions of the problem's dynamics at an unconscious level. This is especially true where a word or phrase is used idiosyncratically. Noticing a client's word usage may be a significant factor in formulating an intervention based on an understanding of what the words mean to the client.

HAVE THE CLIENT DEFINE TERMS EXPERIENTIALLY

Since words are simply symbols of the experiences they represent, using the same words as your client doesn't mean you are describing the same experience. Therefore, it is imperative to have the client explain to you the experience he or she is presenting as significant as best he or she can, rather than him or her just using a word or two to represent the experience. Whatever words are used they will never give you a complete idea of what the person is subjectively experiencing, but the more definition and description of his or her experience you have, the more opportunity you have for meaningful intervention.

Some clinicians are afraid to ask the client for clarification, erroneously believing it will reflect a lack of understanding. Thus, when a client says, "I have this terrible depression, ya know what I mean?" the eager-to-prove-empathy therapist is likely to say, "Yes, I know what you mean." But, the client's experience of depression in this example is being hallucinated by the clinician. The clinician apparently knows what depression is from previous experience, personal and professional, and now puts this client into the same category as others termed "depressed." However, what this particular client is actually experiencing is unknown. A more effective response might be, "Can you describe what your experience of being depressed is like for you?" Having the client describe the experience in his or her own way can lead you to a better understanding of how and where to intervene.

This point is illustrated well in the following case example: A woman in her early twenties came for therapy for what she called "a terrific phobia of men." I thought the words "terrific" and "phobia" were odd ones to be connected, and I wanted to know what her experience was of what she called a "phobia." So, I asked her, "What do you mean by a phobia?" Her response was, "I have a phobia of men—you know, I just can't get enough of them, and that complicates my life."

If I had responded to her on the basis of my experience and understanding of what "phobia" means, I might have started asking her questions about her fears associated with men. And, in so doing, I would likely have caused her to believe that I really didn't understand her and probably couldn't help her. By having her describe her experience instead of getting sidetracked by the (inappropriate) label she chose to represent it, I was able to begin her treatment in a different direction, one much closer to meeting her needs. Even if a client uses a label appropriately, though, we are invariably striving to alter their actual experience, not the label they use to represent it.

In having clients define the meanings of the terms they use, the clinician can often help the person redefine the term and subsequently alter the experience it represents. This is the essence of a technique called "Reframing," in which an experience is changed by the use of a different term to redefine the experience. Thus "cheap" can be altered to "fiscally conservative," a "retreat" can be reframed as a "strategic military withdrawal," and "weird" can become "uninhibited and eccentric."

In one workshop I conducted, a participant said she would like to "not be so controlling." I asked her what she meant, and she responded she would like to "let others make a decision for me once in a while." Given her definition of control, that is, whoever makes the decisions for her, being in control all the time can certainly be burdensome. In hypnosis, I told her I thought her definition was an interesting one, but I define control in another way. I define control as having choices; someone who is in control has a lot of choices about what he or she will say or do, but someone who is not in control has no choices. "Sometimes, a person has only the illusion of being in control, and may not have enough actual control to choose to make no choices." When she deciphered what I said, her response was a look of relief and the statement, "That's true. I never realized it before, but I don't need less control—I need more, so I can choose sometimes not to have to choose. Having more choices will change everything!" A simple redefinition of "control" that allowed for more personal freedom changed her experience of herself in a positive way. Instead of "control" being something negative, it can now be associated with a positive experience of recognizing her choices at a given time, one of which may be to let someone else be responsible for a change.

Words are the medium of exchange between the clinician and client, and the more ambiguous the words, the greater the room for miscommunication. This point emphasizes the need to be aware of both the connotative and denotative meanings of your words. If a client takes literally something you intended to be taken figuratively, or vice versa, the result may be an undesirable one.

USE THE PRESENT TENSE
AND A POSITIVE STRUCTURE

Generally, suggestions should be phrased in the present tense and in terms of what the person is currently experiencing. Of course, most therapeutic suggestions are intended to influence future behavior in some way, but the hypnotic session is the bridge between what is happening now and what will, hopefully, be happening later. The basic structure of hypnotic suggestions is linking what is occurring now to what is desired: "As you experience this, you can start to experience that." Continuous feedback about the person's present state is necessary to make the bridge effective.

This point is especially true in the case of working directly with variables of time, such as in age regression. When you are working with memory, talking to the person in past tense terms of what occurred "then" will produce a different and much less profound response than will talking to the person as if he or she is experiencing that past situation now. Having as much of the client in the "here-and-now" (whether the here-and-now is actually a past or future context) gives the clinician working access to more of the person. Current needs, motivations, feelings, values, and behaviors are available for incorporation into the process. In part, this is where hypnosis as a tool derives its power. Instead of intellectually talking about a situation one is removed from, the clinician recreates that experience now and deals with the resulting issues as they arise now.

Negative suggestions were described in the previous chapter. Caution was advised then about its potential inadvertent misuse. In general, suggestions should be phrased in positive ways as to what the person *can* do instead of what he or she *can't* do. Remember the effect of me directing you not to think of the taste of pizza? Suggesting to someone what not to do has the same effect as being told what to do in part because of transderivational search and in part because it does not provide an alternative focal point. An analogy about learning through reward or punishment might be useful to elaborate this point. In simply punishing someone for doing something wrong, there is nothing provided to tell the person what the right thing to do is. The person merely learns what not to do, and receiving repeated punishment with no alternatives provided leads to frustration, anger, and finally a point where punishment is no longer effective.

Positive suggestions that assist the client in discovering what he or she can do are a principal goal of treatment. Negative suggestions can be effective when carefully used, but the overwhelming majority of suggestions you use will likely be of a positive nature.

ENCOURAGE AND COMPLIMENT
POSITIVE RESPONSES

Support for the client in the form of encouragement and compliments can go a long way in assisting the client to find resources within him- or herself. The process of encouraging a client is typically one of guiding the client into a position where he or she can identify and acknowledge personal strengths and resources previously overlooked in him- or herself. Typically, the person seeking help feels out of control and frustrated. Seemingly empty compliments that contradict the person's low self-esteem are easily disregarded (recall the earlier discussion of cognitive dissonance). Guiding the person into a position of self-acknowledgment (contradicting his or her own negative self-generalizations), and confirming and then complimenting that recognition has been a powerful intervention, in my experience. Having the client reach his or her own conclusion that he or she is better off than previously assumed can be a more profound experience for him or her than simply hearing me say so.

Some clinicians are of the belief that a client has to be "torn down" before he or she can be "built up." For them, therapy often consists of attack, negativity, and disrespect. I don't subscribe to such views, and believe that a client must be approached with respect. A client's behavior is not the client, rather it is a reflection of what choices the person perceives as available at a given moment. The clinician's role is to provide new alternatives that are more adaptive for the person. When the new choices fit the client well, and are provided with a recognition of the person's integrity, the process of change can be considerably smoother.

Another dimension of the suggestion to encourage and compliment the client relates to the notion of accepting the client's communications as a means for facilitating hypnotic induction and utilization of the hypnosis for therapy. This is known as the "utilization approach," and its underlying principle is "accept and utilize" client responses. The sophistication of the utilization approach lies in its accepting (rather than contradicting) the client's communications (i.e., beliefs, values, experiences), and then striving to discover a way of utilizing them to facilitate change. If a client presents the complaint that, "I'm a no-good crazy person" and the clinician responds, "No, you're not, you're a good person who is just confused," the clinician has not accepted the client's view of him- or herself. (Part of forming a meaningful response is determining whether such a self-effacing statement is a genuinely felt one or just a manipulation to get a free compliment). Accepting the client as he or she sees him- or herself ("You may think you're a no-good crazy person right now, but I couldn't help but notice how much sense your no-good craziness has made given your circumstances which means you have sense even you don't know about just yet . . .") is the first step toward attaining a position with him or her from which to effect meaningful changes. Furthermore, it allows for the message "What you are doing right now is fine, because that is exactly what will allow you to accomplish the change you desire." Accepting the current state of affairs without a critical reproach is desirable in order to encourage the client to use the bridge of the intervention to reach the desired goals.

DETERMINE OWNERSHIP OF THE PROBLEM AND PROBLEM-SOLVING RESOURCES

Different therapeutic approaches have different terminology to express this concept, each one addressing the need to guide the client into accepting a measure of responsibility for what he or she is experiencing. If the client feels he or she is a "victim," or if he or she is a "blamer" with no awareness of personal responsibility at all for his or her experience, then helping the client to change in some meaningful way is more difficult. If you believe you have no control over your experience, then attempts to demonstrate to you that control is possible will most likely be ignored or dismissed with the ever-familiar, "Yes, but . . ." excuses of why change is impossible. Helping people to discover that they have power to control the events in their lives, at the most, or, at the least, their reactions to the events in their lives, is a necessary component of therapeutic work.

The underlying goal is to empower people, a foundation for all health professionals in the work they do. People don't get better when they see themselves as victims. Rather, they get better when they sense they can influence the course of their problems or the intensity of their symptoms. Thus, it is an essential part of treatment that the person define him- or herself as a participant, an owner of problem-solving resources and not just the owner of a sense of victimhood.

USE SENSORY MODALITIES SELECTIVELY

visual, kinestatic, auditory

A useful concept originating in the Neuro-Linguistic Programming (NLP) model (Bandler & Grinder, 1979) concerns people's preferred style for gathering information, storing it, retrieving it, and communicating about it. Most people have a preferred sense that is more well developed and more heavily relied on in processing day-to-day experience. Some people are quite visual in terms of their preferred modality, meaning they tend to think in pictures, remember or imagine images more clearly, and process the visual portion of experience more completely. Other people favor the auditory modality, thinking in terms of internal dialogue, talking to themselves about their experience, remembering or imagining sounds and conversations with great clarity, and processing the auditory portion of ongoing experience more completely. Still others favor the kinesthetic modality, thinking in terms of feelings, remembering or imagining the feelings associated with various experiences with clarity, and processing the kinesthetic portion of ongoing experience more completely.

It is important to realize that each person processes experience in all of the senses all of the time. The issue of clinical concern here is which modality is dominant in a given context, particularly the symptom context. If a clinician can identify a person's favored system of sensory experience, he or she can choose to adapt communications to that favored system and possibly increase the likelihood of meaningful influence through the attainment of greater rapport.

The language a person uses spontaneously, particularly the predicates (including verbs, adverbs, and adjectives), reflects a person's favored information-processing style. Language, because it is structured for the most part at an unconscious level, reflects the unconscious patterns of thinking through the specific words chosen to reflect inner experience. Thus, if in the course of a discussion I make a point that the listener responds to by saying, "I *see* what you mean; that *looks* right to me," I can deduce a visual preference in the listener relative to my point. If the listener responds to my point by saying, "I *hear* what you're saying; that *sounds* right to me," I can deduce an auditory preference. If the listener responds, "I get a *feel* for what you mean; that idea *grabs* me," I can deduce a preference for the kinesthetic modality. In each case, I can use language that will appeal to the preferred style. For example, with a visually oriented person, using visual imagery techniques is likely to be effective, but is likely to be less effective with the person who has a strong kinesthetic orientation.

The inability to notice a client's language usage, particularly in the area of preferred sensory modalities, can be a source of resistance. Responding to a client who says, "I feel bad" with a sensorily mismatched statement like, "Can you see why you feel bad?" is not likely to get a meaningful response, at least not as useful as a matched statement might.

A study I published (1981) demonstrated the greater depth at which research subjects could experience hypnotic relaxation when the induction's predicates were matched to their preferred modality. The matching of predicates to facilitate hypnosis is simply another way of using the language of the client while acknowledging the uniqueness of each person. Furthermore, since all experience can ultimately be broken down into its sensory components, the use of language patterns that emphasize the sensations of an experience will have a more powerful effect than the use of more distant, intellectual terminology. Consider the effect of the following statement:

> Think of how pleasant a walk in the woods can be . . . so enjoyable, enlightening and peaceful . . .

Contrast that effect with a more sensorily rich statement:

> Can you remember taking a walk in the woods . . . seeing the tall, sturdy trees and bright green leaves contrasting against the sunny blue sky . . . hearing the soothing sounds of the birds chirping and singing and the leaves crackling under your footsteps . . . the gentle feelings of a comfort and peacefulness inside. . . . ?

The experience of hypnosis is one in which the client's emotions and sensory experiences can be amplified to higher levels, appropriate for making greater use of the person's resources in facilitating change. The greater power is in the use of emotional, sensorily descriptive language, instead of intellectual language that appeals primarily to the conscious mind, the lesser force in guiding human behavior.

The best sensory-based descriptions are those that influence the client's experience the most. Therefore, it is of great advantage to be able to listen to the client, identify his or her most relied-on modality for the experience under consideration (since the dominant modality changes from context to context), and adapt the hypnotic process to that modality. In this way, a greater rapport may be obtained, and the stage may be set for leading the client into a different sensory awareness. Such a lead may be accomplished by shifting at some point into using language of the sensory system(s) outside of the person's usual awareness. For example, with a person whose favored modality is visual, you can match with visual suggestions and then gradually lead into the kinesthetic area, altering the person's typical pattern of consciousness:

> As you see yourself sitting in that chair, you can see each breath you inhale soothing each muscle of your body... visualizing each muscle unwinding, loosening comfortably... and as you see each muscle relaxing you can begin to feel the tingle of comfort in the muscles of your arms... and feel the comfort growing and flowing to other parts of your body...

KEEP THE CLIENT AS INFORMED AS DESIRED AND AS NECESSARY TO SUCCEED

While it is a high priority to provide relevant information to clients, and the ethical practice of securing an informed consent is highly desirable, it is also clinically necessary not to provide too much information about one's interventions. Giving the client the opportunity to develop defenses by analyzing and criticizing what the clinician is doing is counterproductive to the aims of therapy. Rather than explain why I am doing whatever I'm doing, most frequently I just do it. The spontaneity from the experience of my communications is what has an impact on the person, not the explanation of what I am trying to do. If I say to a client, "I'm going to give you a negative suggestion now in a "reverse psychology" strategy so you'll think you're spontaneously doing what I tell you not to do," what is the likelihood of me getting the response I want? Answer: Zero.

Presenting and withholding information selectively can be an obvious ethical dilemma (Scheflin, 2001; Zeig, 1985b). How can a client provide informed consent if he or she doesn't know what the clinician is doing and why? Yet, if he or she knows exactly what the clinician is doing, then how can the intervention succeed? This is a matter that must be handled delicately on a case by case basis, as the clinician gets a "feel" for how much information the client wants and needs to succeed.

One of the most interesting dimensions of the work of the late Milton H. Erickson, M.D., was his ability to obtain compliance from his patients to demands he made on them that were sometimes nothing short of outrageous. Erickson lived in an era where a doctor's authority went virtually unchallenged, and so if he asked his patient to climb a mountain to symbolically gain a greater overall view of things, the patient usually would. A more likely response in today's therapy climate is, "Why? I think I'll get two other doctors' opinions." If Erickson explained why he wanted the patient to climb the mountain, would it have the same therapeutic impact? Yet, doesn't the patient have a right to know?

People often asked Erickson how he motivated people to do the things he wanted them do (Haley, 1973; Zeig, 1980). His answer was simple: "Because they know I mean it!" Trust, rapport, and respect for the client's integrity are key ingredients in the hypnotic interaction.

GIVE YOUR CLIENTS THE TIME
THEY NEED TO RESPOND

Each person does things according to his or her own personal pace. In hypnosis, this characteristic is amplified to the point of being a critical component of the interaction, one to be noticed and respected by the clinician. To pressure someone to respond to your pace of doing things just won't work in doing hypnosis. Instead, you have to allow the client to form the suggested response at the rate he or she chooses. Imposing a time limit on the client's responses is more typically a beginner's mistake, caused by uncertainty and a lack of experience. Often, students in my introductory courses who are first learning to do hypnosis might suggest an arm levitation, for example, and if the subject's arm doesn't immediately begin to lift, the student may get agitated and assume the subject is resisting or he or she is doing something wrong. If they start to repeat their suggestions, I will stop them and instruct them to simply wait. Almost invariably, after a short while, the subject's arm begins to lift and the student has now learned to be a bit more patient in letting the subject respond in his or her own time.

In the phase of guiding the person out of hypnosis, called "disengagement" or "alerting," this is especially true. I have always disliked using a count-up to guide the person out of hypnosis (e.g., "When I count to three you will awaken, open your eyes, and be alert and refreshed") because it forces the client to adapt to your arbitrary choice of when he or she should come out of hypnosis, instead of letting him or her choose for him- or herself. I prefer a general closure on the order of: "When you have taken the time to complete this experience, you can bring yourself out of hypnosis at a rate that is comfortable for you . . ."

Let the person take the time he or she needs to fully develop the responses you suggest. No need to hurry . . .

ONLY USE TOUCH SELECTIVELY AND *ALWAYS* WITH
THE CLIENT'S PERMISSION

Can you imagine what it's like to be deeply relaxed, feeling good, wonderfully absorbed in some important internal experience . . . and all of a sudden feeling a strange hand on you? I have seen so many sessions that were going well ruined in an instant because the clinician assumed enough rapport was present (if he or she even thought about it, which some "touchy-feely" clinicians never do) to touch the person. The touch was entirely innocent, a well-intended expression of support or empathy, yet was highly disruptive to the client. It is very important to get permission to touch the person for a number of reasons.

First, touch is associated to intimacy—a cross into personal space. Some clients may welcome it, but others hate to be touched and experience it as a violation of personal territory. With such persons, it can hinder or even destroy rapport.

Second, in hypnosis, the person is typically (not always) focused inwardly on some internal experience. To have to notice or respond to a clinician's touch means reorienting one's focus to the external world, which is generally counterproductive to the development and maintenance of a deeper hypnosis. If you use touch indiscriminately, you can thus unintentionally work against yourself.

Third, an unexpected touch may simply startle the person, even if he or she doesn't find it offensive. The person may be so lost in thought that he or she may even have forgotten that you are even there! To suddenly feel a hand on you can scare anybody, in *or* out of hypnosis.

Fourth, the media have played on the terrible misconception that hypnosis is a means for seducing vulnerable clients. The sexual implication of touching someone unexpectedly can easily trigger unnecessary problems in this domain.

It is always a good idea to politely ask the client for permission to touch him or her during hypnosis, for it certainly demonstrates a respect for his or her integrity. Whether you ask before your hypnosis session begins (e.g., "During this session I will want to touch the back of your hand to gauge your degree of analgesia . . . is that all right with you?") or at some time during the hypnotic process is a matter of personal preference (I prefer to do *both*), just so long as you secure permission before touching your client.

USE ANTICIPATION SIGNALS TO ANNOUNCE YOUR INTENTIONS

announcements of intention

For the reasons elaborated in the previous section, it is a good idea to avoid shocking your client out of hypnosis with an unexpected maneuver on your part. The best tool to prevent this problem from arising is called the "anticipation signal." Anticipation signals are announcements of your intentions, effectively letting your client know what action you are about to take so as not to startle him or her. They also serve the deepening function of keeping the client comfortable enough to not feel as though he or she has to pay conscious attention to everything you say and do. Such conscious analysis is generally counterproductive to hypnosis.

Anticipation signals are simple statements you make during hypnosis about what is coming next in the process. The generic structure for an anticipation signal is, "In just a moment, I'm going to (fill-in-the-blank)." For example, I may say, "In just a moment, I am going to take your left hand by the wrist and raise it above your head." Assuming I have received permission to touch the person (". . . and if that's all right with you, please nod your head"), I am now preparing the person for my touch rather than just taking his or her wrist and lifting it without warning. It is a much gentler and more respectful approach, and clients greatly appreciate that consideration. When you state, "In just a moment I'm going to . . .", and then follow through in a way that is entirely consistent with what you stated your actions would be, a new level of trust in you can be reached, aiding in your future work together.

From the client's perspective, it is very difficult to be relaxed and on guard simultaneously. Anticipation signals are a very quick, simple, and effective way to foster trust in the hypnotic relationship while giving the client a valuable sense of participation in the process.

USE A VOICE AND DEMEANOR CONSISTENT WITH YOUR INTENT

Your tools as a skilled communicator are your voice and body. Beyond your words, your nonverbal communications can serve to reinforce or even negate your suggestions. Paying attention to such factors as eye contact, body posture, gestures, touch, timing, use of space, tone and volume of voice, and facial expressions is necessary in order to maximize the value of the things you say. If you don't incorporate these nonverbal components of communication well, positive results will be slow in coming, if they come at all.

It helps immeasurably to have control of your voice and body in communicating, using yourself as the mechanism to drive a suggestion home. To have tension in your voice when you suggest to your client that he or she relax is an avoidable incongruity. To use a normal conversional tone of voice with someone you want to guide into a different internal state of experience is another avoidable incongruity.

It is a good idea to have a well-practiced calm tone of voice and relaxed body posture to model for your client what you want him or her to experience. To gradually shift from your usual tone of voice to one more soothing and hypnotic builds an association (what some call an "auditory anchor") in your client's mind between that tone of your voice and the implied invitation to the client to go into hypnosis. Establishing that association makes it a smoother transition into doing hypnosis in subsequent sessions. Once the client associates going into hypnosis with that tone of your voice, you don't necessarily have to formally announce, "Now let's do hypnosis." Instead, you can gradually lead into using the voice your client associates to entering hypnosis, effectively inducing hypnosis without a formal induction. Using a soothing, comforting voice throughout your process also serves the additional purpose of discouraging conscious analysis, calming the person, and reducing the need for defensive hypervigilance.

The nonverbal components of your communications are critical to generating successful hypnotic experiences in your clients. It can be helpful to make audio- or videotapes of yourself doing hypnosis in order to learn how you look and sound as you do so. Often, people have no idea of how they look or sound as they interact with others, so getting feedback from a variety of sources can be highly instructive.

CHAIN SUGGESTIONS STRUCTURALLY

Like most of the other communication patterns offered as guidelines in this chapter, this particular one is a constant in doing hypnosis. "Chaining suggestions" means linking the desired response to the client's present experience. The idea is to build a link (hence "chain") between what the client is currently doing and what you would like him or her to do. The generic suggestion structure for chaining suggestions is, "As you experience (this), you can start to experience (that)." For example, as you continue to sit there and read these words, you can begin to notice your left foot.

As Bandler and Grinder (1975) pointed out, there are three types of links between current and future experiences, varying in the strength of the linkages. As will be true with all three links, the first half of the statement matches (paces, accepts) the person's current experience while the second half suggests (leads, utilizes) a possible, but not current, experience.

The first link is the "simple conjunction." It is the weakest link, and simply suggests an association between what is and what can be. It employs such connecting words as "and" and "but." For example:

> You are looking at me *and* starting to feel comfortable.
> You can see the clock clearly *but* still allow time to slow down.

The second link, and a slightly stronger one, is called the "implied causative," employing such connecting words as "as," "while," and "during." For example:

> *As* you notice yourself relaxing, you can let your eyes close.
> You can listen to me *while* your conscious mind drifts off.

You can feel yourself growing more comfortable *during* your experience of vividly remembering your high school graduation.

(handwritten: 3) causative predicate)

The third, and strongest, link is the "causative predicate." It's the strongest because it claims that not only are the current and desired behaviors connected, but one actually causes the other. For example:

Breathing deeply will *make* you relax even more.
Shifting your body's posture will *cause* you to want to close your eyes.

Each of these links forms a bridge to get the client to respond in a particular way on the basis of what he or she is doing currently. A typical hypnotic process, using the "As you X you can Y" chaining formula, may sound something like this:

As you continue to look at me, you can take in a deep breath . . . and as you take in a deep breath, you can allow your eyes to close . . . and as your eyes close, you can let your mind drift back to a specific memory . . . and as your mind drifts back to a specific memory you can begin to describe the memory out loud . . . and as you begin to describe the memory out loud you can . . .

Structurally, each suggestion is chained to the response before it, starting with a statement feeding back to the client his current, undeniable reality, that is, that he or she was looking at me and in so doing could take in a deep breath. Looking at someone and taking in a deep breath are not usually connected, and in this example are only connected by an arbitrary link of my own creation. Each response is then fed back (paced, accepted) as the basis for the desired response (the lead, or utilization).

Suggestions linked in this way are the basis for the hypnotic process being a flowing one rather than a choppy, disconnected one in terms of delivery. Grammatically, of course, hypnotic phrasing is a strict grammarian's nightmare, but to the person in hypnosis, the clinician is smooth and easy to listen to.

USE PROCESS SUGGESTIONS
TO ENCOURAGE PROJECTIONS

If you refer back to the last chapter's section on process suggestions, you can recall the general principle that the more details you provide for someone's hypnotic experience, the more opportunities there are for contradicting it. For example, "Let your right hand feel warmer" as a suggestion for the specific response of hand warmth is easier to resist than is a more general process suggestion: "You may notice a particular change of temperature in one of your hands." In the latter suggestion, which hand was to change was not specified, nor was it specific whether the hand was to grow warmer or cooler. Whatever response the person has can now be defined as a cooperative one.

It is difficult, if not impossible, to avoid the use of detail in suggestions. And, it is not always desirable to do so because often it is the details you provide during the hypnotic process that make suggestions easier to follow. Learning to "be general specifically," that is, sounding specific but being general, can help you avoid some of the unnecessary rejections of your suggestions. Notice as early on as possible whether you are being too specific (or too general) on the basis of the client's responsiveness to you, and, if necessary, shift your style as you go on.

BUILD RESPONSE SETS GRADUALLY

As the hypnosis session begins and starts to develop focus and momentum, enhancing the client's responsiveness to your suggestions is a primary goal. The term "response set" refers to a pattern of responding. Not unlike always choosing "answer a" in a multiple choice test, the task of the clinician is to encourage the client to develop a patterned style of fuller and consistent responding to suggestions.

The most commonly used response set is one commonly known as the "Yes set" described by Erickson (Erickson, Rossi, & Rossi, 1976; Erickson & Rossi, 1979). A "Yes set" on the part of the client is a patterned response of accepting—in essence saying yes to—the suggestions you provide. Building an agreeable frame of mind is valuable at any time during the hypnosis session, but is especially important at the outset when you are first establishing the therapeutic alliance with the client.

The most common means of establishing a "yes set" is with the use of a series of truisms, the suggestions you learned in the last chapter that involve making statements that seem so obviously true there is no legitimate basis for rejecting them (e.g., "Sometimes people surprise themselves by knowing things they didn't know they knew . . ."). As you offer three or four truisms in a row, the client silently agrees with each. If you agree with statement number one, then again with statement number two, then statement number three, and then statement number four, what is your most likely response going to be to statement number five? Agreement.

In general, when doing hypnosis, you go from general to specific. Before you ask for *specific* hypnotic responses, such as an analgesia, you first have to build a momentum in the client's responsiveness that will facilitate such a complex response. So, you might first offer a series of general statements (such as truisms) about ways he or she can begin to think of her physical perceptions being malleable. For example: "The human body is so complex in its many organs and organ systems . . . and isn't it interesting how our perceptions of our bodies change from time to time . . . sometimes you feel warm, and sometimes you feel cool . . . and sometimes you feel tuned in to your body, and sometimes you feel distant from it . . ." Once a *general* sense of variability in physical perception has been established, the clinician can then go from general to specific in suggesting a *particular* change in physical perception, such as an analgesia.

The "yes set" is the most commonly used one for what are now obvious reasons, but there are others as well. There may be times when you want to deliberately encourage rejection of your suggestions (e.g., to foster greater independence) with a "no set." Or, there may be times when you want to encourage skepticism or uncertainty (e.g., with someone very confident but very wrong) with an "I don't know" set.

Most people, as you will discover, don't simply form an immediate response to a suggestion. The skilled clinician recognizes the importance of taking the time to build responsiveness in the client as the session progresses. *In fact, if you were to ask me what single stage of the interaction most influences the overall success of the hypnosis session, I'd say it's the stage of deliberately building a response set.*

IF DESIRABLE, SUBSTITUTE OTHER TERMS FOR HYPNOSIS

I don't have a particular fondness for the word "hypnosis," and so whether one calls it hypnosis or calls it something else isn't an issue of significance for me. As long as the suggestive dynamics are operant, regardless of the chosen name, hypnosis is present. Hypnosis is a part of virtually every therapeutic modality I am aware of, but almost always under another name and woven into a different conceptual framework. The key disadvantage to hypnosis being so disguised is that it might well make others' work more precise if they directly studied and utilized hypnotic principles and methods without diffusing or diluting them.

Since I have no real attachment to the word "hypnosis," if it serves the therapy to use all the same principles and techniques under a different, more acceptable, name, I will do so. If a cancer patient fears hypnosis, yet really wants to experience the anticipated benefits of visualization techniques, why get into a lecture on how visualization is a specific type of hypnotic technique? It may create resistance needlessly. Instead of developing a positive feeling for hypnosis, he or she might develop a negative feeling about visualization.

There are many clients for whom the word "hypnosis" inspires fears and doubts, yet these same clients are happy to learn "progressive relaxation," a specific hypnotic induction technique. It isn't terribly important to sell your clients hypnosis; it's only important to help them have positive and therapeutic experiences with it. If the client reacts negatively to your query about any experience he or she might have previously had with hypnosis, you might exercise the option of using another term to label your intervention. Some specific possible alternative labels are:

> Progressive muscle relaxation
> Controlled relaxation
> Guided relaxation
> Deep relaxation
> Visualization
> Visual imagery
> Guided imagery
> Guided fantasy
> Guided meditation
> Mental imagery

Do these terms all represent hypnosis? Technically, the answer is no. These approaches are each different in a variety of ways, and so the hypnosis purist will find it incorrect to equate them. And he or she would be correct to object. However, in clinical practice, quibbling about differences wastes time and creates unnecessary conflict when all we want to do is help empower the client to develop important personal resources.

Whatever variation you might use, as long as a focused state of attention is narrowed to suggestions offered, dissociated experience and influence occurs as a result, then hypnosis is present. Hypnosis may be in effect without necessarily identifying it as such. If it works to the client's advantage somehow to call it by another name, it would seem wise to do so.

CONCLUSION

While this chapter covered some of the fundamental components of hypnotic communication, it obviously could not cover all the subtleties inherent in doing hypnosis. You may be reminded that for each general principle discussed, there are also exceptions. If you are starting to feel just a little overwhelmed at how much there is to pay attention to in doing hypnosis, then I am succeeding in describing to you how complex an art the skilled use of hypnosis is. I'd suggest you feel overwhelmed just enough to learn to do sensitive and effective work.

For Discussion

1. How do you react to being touched spontaneously by people you don't know very well? How might a spontaneous touch be viewed as an invasion of territory even if it was well intentioned? Why do some people dislike to be touched?

vision 2. What, if any, is your most well-developed sensory modality for information-processing? What implications does this have for your style of intervention? What advantages and disadvantages does it pose in your life?

3. Is language formed at an unconscious level? How do you know?

pg 264 4. What communication patterns seem to help you experience hypnosis more fully? Why do they seem to have that effect on you?

5. What is "personal responsibility"? How far does responsibility for one's self go when others' behavior clearly influences us on a continuous basis? How do you know when someone isn't accepting personal responsibility?

Things to Do

1. Analyze a commercially available hypnosis tape for its communication patterns. What patterns seem especially effective to you? Which seem disruptive?

2. Make a list of five therapeutic approaches (e.g., cognitive, behavioral, psychodynamic) you find interesting or valuable and list the primary techniques associated with them. How is hypnosis a part of each?

3. List at least one context in which each of the patterns described in this chapter would not be applicable.

REFERENCES

Bandler, R. & Grinder, J. (1975). *Patterns of the hypnotic techniques of Milton H. Erickson, M.D.* (Vol. 1). Cupertino, CA: Meta Publications.

Bandler, R. & Grinder, J. (1979). *Frogs into princes.* Moab, UT: Real People Press.

Erickson, M. & Rossi, E. (1979). *Hypnotherapy: An exploratory casebook.* New York: Irvington.

Erickson, M., Rossi, E., & Rossi, S. (1976). *Hypnotic realities: The induction of clinical hypnosis and forms of indirect suggestion.* New York: Irvington.

Haley, J. (1973). *Uncommon therapy: The psychiatric techniques of Milton H. Erickson, M.D.* New York: Norton.

Scheflin, A. (2001). Caveat therapist: Ethical and legal dangers in the use of Ericksonian techniques. In B. Geary & J. Zeig (Eds.), *The handbook of Ericksonian psychotherapy* (pp. 154–67). Phoenix, AZ: The Milton H. Erickson Foundation Press.

Yapko, M. (1981). The effect of matching primary representational system predicates on hypnotic relaxation. *American Journal of Clinical Hypnosis, 23*, 169–75.

Zeig, J. (Ed.) (1980). *A teaching seminar with Milton H. Erickson, M.D.* New York: Brunner/Mazel.

Zeig, J. (1985a). *Experiencing Erickson: An introduction to the man and his work.* New York: Brunner/Mazel.

Zeig, J. (1985b). Ethical issues in hypnosis: Informed consent and training standards. In J. Zeig (Ed.), *Ericksonian psychotherapy, Vol. 1: Structures* (pp. 459–73). New York: Brunner/Mazel.

Zeig, J. & Munion, W. (1999). *Milton H. Erickson.* London: Sage Publications.

14

Formal Strategies
of Hypnotic Induction

People routinely enter conditions of experiential absorption, focus, and dissociated awareness spontaneously, that is, without any formal ritual of induction taking place. While it is arguable whether these spontaneous hypnotic experiences are the same as hypnosis produced in either the laboratory or clinical setting, at the very least they clearly share many common characteristics. Theoretically, then, inducing hypnosis in others shouldn't be a particularly difficult thing to do. In fact, usually it isn't all that difficult to do, yet it can be very difficult if the client has poor concentration, low motivation, negative expectations, fear of hypnosis, or if the interpersonal dynamics of communication and influence aren't skillfully applied in an appropriate context.

Having the ability to develop hypnosis and experience hypnotic phenomena on a spontaneous basis in the course of daily living is important for survival. Focusing on changing traffic conditions as you drive, concentrating on material you're reading and trying to understand and retain, or narrowing your focus to important information a loved one is sharing are all snippets of countless hypnotically based experiences that are core components of effective daily living. As essentially episodes of self-hypnosis of brief duration for attending to whatever stimulus captures our attention, there are none of the potential interpersonal resistances present. In contrast, however, experiencing hypnosis with another person who is in the role of a guide (i.e., the clinician) raises relationship dynamics such as issues of control, power, responsibility, and so on. Consideration of such dynamics is implicit in your choosing a style of suggestion formulation. For example, you assume more power over the client if you choose to offer authoritarian commands to him or her which require compliance rather than permissive suggestions which invite collaboration.

The phrase "inducing hypnosis" implies the clinician is doing something *to* the client. The language of hypnosis is sometimes limiting and even misleading, for the client is not simply a passive receptacle for the clinician's

Table 4. Stages of Hypnotic Interaction

1. Orienting to hypnosis and securing attentional absorption
2. Hypnotic induction and building a response set
                     (intensification)
3. Therapeutic utilization
4. Disengagement and reorientation

suggestions. Rather, the client is an active force in shaping the interaction, and the clinician must respond meaningfully to the unique responses of the individual. Guiding the person into hypnosis may be a more accurate representation of the clinician's role. In the capacity of guide, you cannot know the exact experience the client is having or is going to have, and so giving the client room to experience hypnosis in his or her own way is not only desirable but *necessary.* The process of guiding a person into hypnosis is a large responsibility to assume as you make yourself a primary focal point, for the client is now focusing him- or herself on the experiences you stimulate through your communications.

Hypnotic interaction can be thought of as taking place in at least four general stages, as Table 4 above suggests. Each stage can be broken down even further into subcomponents, and these involve the detailed considerations about doing hypnosis step-by-step which are presented throughout this book.

Prior to the first phase, orienting the client to hypnosis and securing his or her attentional absorption, the clinician has already introduced hypnosis to the client, explained its merits and purposes, and established a therapeutic alliance. When the clinician says some variation of, "All right, let's begin . . . you can arrange yourself in a comfortable position," to signal the induction process is about to begin, he or she has clearly oriented the person to hypnosis. He or she has also indicated that the client should now strive to narrow his or her focus to the clinician's suggestions and the immediate matters at hand. All of the preparations for the hypnotic experience discussed in previous chapters are parts of this particular phase: the discussion concerning personal motivation to change; conceptions about hypnosis; defining personal goals; identifying the specifics of the symptomatology (i.e., origin, course, and quality of symptoms); assessing client responsiveness (either from formal assessments or informally from the responses to your guidance in the interaction); choosing and applying a communication style; and moving through the interaction in a goal-directed fashion.

This chapter considers the second phase of the hypnotic interaction, the hypnotic induction and the intensifying ("deepening") of the client's hypnotic experience. The process of hypnotic induction serves several purposes:

1. It provides a concrete stimulus for the client to focus his or her attention on, serving as a *bridge* between the "normal waking state" and the experience of hypnosis.
2. It engages and occupies the person's conscious mind, and in so doing effectively dissociates it from other competing awarenesses while simultaneously amplifying the unconscious mind's associational abilities. In fact, this is the chief function of an induction: facilitating the dissociation of conscious and unconscious functions. The degree of dissociation achieved is a relative measure of the depth of the hypnotic experience.
3. It allows for the building of a "response set," a characteristic pattern of responding to the guidance of the clinician, discussed at length in the previous chapter.

The induction process as the stimulus for the experience of hypnosis obviously plays an important role in the overall quality of the interaction, and consequently, deciding which induction to employ is a matter worthy of extra consideration. There are as many induction methods as there are practitioners of hypnosis, and since it is neither practical nor desirable to list them all I have included only several of the more common and useful ones. I have divided the methods of induction into two general categories: formal, structured inductions; and informal, conversational approaches. This chapter will present some of the formal inductions, while some of the informal ones are discussed in the next chapter.

FORMAL, STRUCTURED HYPNOTIC INDUCTIONS

The formal, structured inductions in this chapter represent the more traditional approaches to doing hypnosis. In using the term "traditional" to describe these inductions, I have two meanings. The first is for the literal meaning of the word "traditional." These techniques have been effectively used for a very long time, handed down from generation to generation of hypnotists. My second meaning of traditional is for the association to a more traditional model of hypnosis in which the process of hypnotic induction is generally more highly directive and ritualistic. The traditional model emphasizes the value of a formal and standardized ritual of induction in order to clearly define the interaction as hypnosis, and to assess the hypnotic capacity of the client. The emphasis, therefore, is on determining how well a client can respond to an impersonal set of suggestions, a marked contrast to the notion of adapting the approach to the client. The Spiegels (1978, p. 28) described the basis for approaching hypnotic induction in this invariant and structured way as follows:

> By using a standardized induction procedure, which involves systematic questioning regarding physiological, behavioral and phenomenological responses, the variable influence of different operators on the trance performance is minimized and the trance capacity of a subject can be systematically documented.

Each of the formal, structured inductions, if not scripted word for word, has at the very least key phrases and key concepts that are integral to the technique, defining them. *Thus, these key phrases and concepts must necessarily be present in order for that technique to be employed.* In doing hypnosis for the purpose of catalyzing some therapeutic shift in the client's experience, a clinician might choose to employ a structured approach, yet still vary at least some of the wording according to the individual needs or characteristics of the client (Weitzenhoffer, 2000).

These techniques are invaluable in the practice of clinical hypnosis, and should be mastered as basic approaches to hypnosis. Experience will prove to you quite dramatically that you will get a wide range of reactions to the same exact technique, such is the tremendous variation among people. One of the most important skills in doing effective hypnosis is being observant enough to notice and use the responses you get in order to either amplify or shift away from what you are doing. If what you are doing isn't working for some reason, you can have the flexibility to smoothly shift to a different technique and/or style. Stopping midway through a particular technique is a perfectly acceptable and even desirable thing to do when that technique isn't getting the response you want. The key to making such a midstream switch smoothly is in the transitional statement you make to the client leading from where you were to where you are going. You should never comment, "Well, that wasn't working, so let's try this." Instead, you can offer something more accepting and natural such as:

> That's right . . . you can continue to feel yourself shifting in the chair, wanting to relax . . . and you can begin to realize that paying attention to me isn't really necessary to have as soothing an experience as you'd like, and isn't it nice to know that you don't have to listen to me . . . and so why not let your mind drift off to something else it finds even more comforting than the things I'm talking about. . . .

Such statements give the client permission to have his or her experience of hypnosis in his or her own way without confrontation of so-called resistance.

Each of the techniques presented in the remainder of this chapter will include a discussion of some of the basic concepts involved in the technique as well as a brief sample of the method.

BEGINNING THE HYPNOTIC PROCESS

In beginning an induction, there are generally certain minimal responses you will want from the client. None of these are essential, since people can even experience hypnosis and generate hypnotic phenomena while active and alert, but they are basic to clinical contexts where putting the client at ease and building receptivity are crucial.

Suggesting, directly or indirectly, that the client assume a comfortable physical position is a good starting point. The general immobility (catalepsy) and the extra effort it takes to readjust one's position while in hypnosis make it necessary to be sure the client is in a comfortable position he or she can remain in effortlessly over time.

A second consideration may be to suggest a comfortable rate of breathing; you may notice with experience that a sense of anticipation and fascination sometimes lead the client to breathe irregularly and even hold breaths unconsciously. It helps to relax people to encourage a slowed and more rhythmic breathing.

A third consideration is helping the client turn his or her focus increasingly inward, and so suggesting that the client close his or her eyes at the start is generally a good idea. Eye closure blocks out external distractions, encourages internal absorption, and thus facilitates the induction. (An exception to this is the "Eye Fixation" technique induction, described later in this chapter, which encourages eye closure as the basis for the induction itself rather than as a lead-in to induction.) Suggesting the client close his or her eyes can be done directly or indirectly. Generally, I just ask, "Can you . . . close your eyes?" (an embedded question) which people routinely take as a directive to do so and respond accordingly. Modeling eye closure is also a good technique; you can close your own eyes while suggesting to the client, "You can close your eyes . . . now . . . and allow yourself to relax comfortably." (Don't keep *your* eyes closed, though, because the only source of information about your client's responses is your client, and he or she will be much too difficult to see if your eyes are closed!)

The final consideration at this beginning point is to use whatever behaviors the client offers as the basis for going into hypnosis. This can be accomplished by commenting on them and tying them to suggestions of relaxation and entering hypnosis. For example, "each shift in your chair can make you more comfortable. . . . Each breath you take in can soothe and relax your body . . ."

With the client comfortable and growing more responsive to the clinician, the hypnotic induction can now get under way. Here, then, are specific techniques for eliciting hypnosis.

PROGRESSIVE MUSCLE RELAXATION TECHNIQUES

Relaxation reduces stress, anxiety, fear of change, and defensiveness, and provides a sense of empowerment to the client. Things can simply seem more manageable. Hypnosis is much, much more than just relaxation, but relaxation is commonly used as a therapeutic stepping-stone for all of these reasons (Murray-Jobsis, 1993).

The progressive muscle relaxation technique involves offering suggestions of relaxation of the various muscle groups of the body sequentially (Coe, 1993; Kirsch, Lynn, & Rhue, 1993). The body is divided into as few or as many specific muscle groups as you wish, depending on how long or short you think the induction process need be. You can start with the client's head and work downward to his or her feet, or vice versa, as a matter of personal preference. (One of the questions I am asked most often is where in the body to begin. Working downward carries an implication of going "down into hypnosis," but physical relaxation is generally easier to accomplish than is mental, and working upward leaves the person's mind last in the sequence. In my experience, it's six of one and half a dozen of the other in terms of which direction of sequencing is better.)

A progressive muscle relaxation technique may sound like this:

> In just a moment I will begin to describe the various muscles of your body . . . and as I describe them relaxing you can notice how easily those muscles begin to relax . . . and how much more comfortable you feel as they do . . . and as you continue to breathe comfortably at a slow and easy rate . . . you can notice how the muscles of your feet can relax now . . . you can feel the muscles of your toes, your arches, your ankles all relaxing wonderfully easily, even feeling the tingle of comfort soothing those muscles, relaxing you easily . . . and now you can notice how the muscles of your calves and shins relax, growing more comfortable moment by moment . . . and now the muscles around your knees can relax . . . and now the muscles of your thighs can feel more at ease and comfortable . . . and now the muscles of your hips and buttocks can relax . . . and now you can notice the muscles of your abdomen and lower back growing loose and comfortable . . . and as the muscles of your back and chest relax with each breath, you can feel more and more at ease . . . and then your arms can grow heavier and more comfortable . . . and now your neck muscles can grow loose and limp . . . and finally the muscles of your face and head can relax and leave you feeling so comfortable, more relaxed than you've been in a long, long time. . . .

The above example is an abbreviated version of what can be a lengthier and more drawn-out process. You can be as repetitious and as slow with your suggestions of comfort at each specific muscle group as the client may require. The pace at which you move through the sequence has to be based on the client's reactions. You can take longer if the client is quite tense, or move along at a faster pace if the client is able to get comfortable quickly. A client who is either hurried by too rapid a pace or bored by too slow a pace is likely to be too easily distracted and disengaged from the induction process. Remember, when your suggestions don't fit well with the client's ongoing experience, they are much easier to reject.

The progressive muscle relaxation technique can take a considerable amount of time to do (perhaps as much as 20 minutes), but usually only at first. With repetition, the association of relaxation is formed to your mere mention of bodily relaxation, and usually after a short while of the client practicing this technique, the relaxation response comes quite quickly. After a period of practice, simply going through the naming of the body parts in sequence without providing all the detailed suggestions of relaxation will still elicit the relaxation response from the client as a result of conditioning. This is what makes a lengthy, detailed technique in the beginning have practical value for later sessions; otherwise an inordinate amount of time would be spent on just doing an induction each session. It is invaluable to tape-record your inductions and provide the tape to your clients to speed up the conditioning process and to provide them a means of getting comfortable even in your absence.

A second variation on the progressive muscle relaxation technique involves the same conditioning or association principle. By using a count-down (i.e., associating a number to each muscle group, e.g., "10 . . . relax your feet . . . 9 . . . relax your calves and shins . . .") as part of the process, in later sessions you can simply count downward in the established sequence and each number can trigger the associated relaxation response for that particular muscle group.

A third variation of the progressive muscle relaxation technique is called the "Deep Muscle Relaxation" technique. In this technique, the sequential progression through the body is the same, but the client is additionally instructed to deliberately tense the muscles of the specific group under consideration. Have the client hold the tension in the muscles for 10 seconds or so, and then release it. The obvious relaxation of the muscles is both immediate and substantial. Try this yourself: Make a tight fist, and hold it tightly for 10 or 15 seconds. You'll quickly notice your hand getting warmer, then tingly, and after a short while it can actually begin to shake with the exaggerated tension you create. When you just can't hold the tension in your fist anymore, let go and allow your hand to relax. Feel how relaxed the muscles are? Now imagine how you would feel if you did that with every muscle in your body! The relaxation can be quite profound. This is an especially good technique for very concrete people who need direct and immediate experience of the contrast between tension and relaxation, and also for those who generally have difficulty relaxing. The tense-release protocol works, in part, because physiologically, when a muscle tenses, it *must* relax before it can tense again. The muscle enters a "refractory period." You can even preface the "sure success" of this technique with this explanation of muscle physiology to the client. (What you don't need to tell him or her, however, is that the refractory period lasts only a fraction of a second.)

The variations of the progressive muscle relaxation are among the easiest and most effective inductions to perform. One word of caution, though. Most people I know who use hypnosis tend to use inductions that they find personally pleasing. I recommend you do inductions with the client's needs in mind, and not according to which work best on *you*. *With each induction you learn, it would be wise to consider for whom the induction would be perfect, and for whom it would be lousy.* For example, progressive muscle relaxation focuses people on their body. Thus, using this body-oriented technique with someone in pain is not recommended. Can you see why?

RELAXED SCENE EXPERIENCE

This technique involves offering suggestions to the client to experience him- or herself in some special place where he or she can feel relaxed, secure, and have a general sense of well-being. As you describe details of that special place, the client can experience getting more and more absorbed in the suggested sensations of being there.

 To begin, you can directly ask the client if he or she has a special place where he or she likes to go to relax, escape from the daily stresses, or to simply be comfortable. If the client can provide such a place, then feeding back to the client suggestions to experience the soothing characteristics of that place may be used in the induction. A second possibility is for you to choose a place for the client that you're reasonably confident will be a relaxing place for him or her. This is a potentially hazardous choice to make blindly since you cannot know the client's experience of the place you've chosen unless you ask. If you choose the place for the client, it is important to ask, "Have you ever been to (the beach, the mountains, Disneyland . . .)? How would you describe your experience in being there?" Not asking for feedback in this way creates the possibility that you may take the client to a place *you* enjoy but your client does not. Of course, nonverbal feedback from your client is also valuable as you progress with your induction, but that develops after you have already begun rather than employing a preventative approach before you begin. A third possibility is to avoid the mention of a specific place at all in your induction process, using contentless suggestions to facilitate the experience. I'll say more about this alternative shortly.

In providing the details of the special place to the client, using the sensory-based terms the client uses in describing his or her experience of that place can allow him or her to get more deeply absorbed in the suggested experience since you're using the details the client has already told you are significant. Providing additional suggested experiences in other sensory modalities can round out the induction and allows for a fuller experience of being in that place for the moment. The more involvement the client has in the suggested experience, the more dissociated a state he or she is in, detached from the immediacy of current goings-on elsewhere, allowing for a more meaningful hypnotic experience.

The following is a sample of a content-filled relaxed-scene experience induction. The suggestions all relate to the experience of being at the beach, and begin with visually oriented suggestions which then lead into auditorily and kinesthetically oriented suggestions:

> . . . Sometime in your life you have had the experience of being very near to the ocean and seeing it in all of its beauty and vastness . . . and you can begin to see the ocean in your mind's eye now . . . huge and mysterious, and for as far as you can see the ocean covers the earth . . . and way out on the horizon you can see distant ships and boats that sail the waters . . . and you can see the rolling waves in front of you gently and rhythmically lap up on the beach . . . and you can even hear them as they softly roll back into the ocean . . . and the gentle sound of the waves is so soothing a sound . . . and you can feel the cool ocean breeze on your face . . . so refreshing and yet so relaxing . . . soothing and calming you so deeply. . . .

Whatever special place you happen to use, whether a beach, a forest, an art museum, or any place the client finds comfort in, that place is probably full of sensory delights that you can use to ease your client into hypnosis. Use as much sensorily descriptive language as you can in order to facilitate a full experience for the client. The more sensory details you provide that *fit*, the more the client has to associate him- or herself to that place. One word of caution, though. It is also true that the more detail you provide, the more you may unintentionally provide suggestions that *don't* fit.

The solution is to use process (contentless) suggestions for the relaxed scene experience. When you provide few or no details at all, the client must provide his or her own in response to your general suggestions, thus reducing the likelihood of mismatches. A disadvantage to the process form of this induction, however, is its briefer, more repetitious nature. Without the details of the experience, there is considerably less to talk about.

A contentless or process-based version of the relaxed scene induction might sound like this:

> As you continue to sit there comfortably with your eyes closed, you can let your mind drift back to the pleasurable memory of some special place, perhaps a special place that you've been to where you felt so good . . . so comfortable and secure and happy . . . or perhaps a place that you'd like to *create* and go to where you can fully sense how very peaceful you can feel inside when there . . . and you can allow yourself to go to that place right now, in your mind . . . you can feel yourself there, feeling the comfortable feelings you'd like to feel there . . . and you can notice the specific sounds of that relaxing place, soothing you . . . and you can see in your mind the images of that place, noticing how pleasing this special place is to you . . . and you can feel so good there. . . .

Going on and on about the sensory details of that place is possible without your having any idea where the special place is your client chose! Anywhere the client can feel comfortable is sufficient in order for this technique to be effective. Notice in the sample the suggestion for "a place you'd like to *create* and go to." In the event the client doesn't have a place in his or her experience where he or she felt good to go to (a common issue in working with people with a history of abuse), he or she can then imagine creating such a place. That "safe place" can be a very helpful tool in later sessions beyond hypnotic induction (Rhue & Lynn, 1993; Smith, 1993; Spiegel, 1993).

EYE-FIXATION TECHNIQUES

If not the oldest, certainly one of the oldest, techniques for inducing hypnosis is the classic "eye-fixation" method. Popularized in movies, and often employed by classical practitioners, this technique involves having the client fixate his or her gaze on some specific stimulus (Spiegel & Spiegel, 1978; Weitzenhoffer, 2000). The stimulus can be virtually anything: a spot on the ceiling or wall, the clinician's thumb, a dangling watch or crystal ball, a fireplace, a candle, an aquarium, an hourglass, whatever. Anything that holds the client's attention long enough for him or her to respond to the concurrent suggestions for relaxation will suffice in this technique.

As the client stares at the stimulus, suggestions are offered encouraging him or her to notice every observable detail, and that while fixing his or her gaze he or she can experience his or her eyes growing more relaxed and even tired. There is a little bit of trickery in this technique when done properly; the client's eyes should be elevated in their sockets as he or she stares at the stimulus, which then allows physiology to work in the clinician's favor. Eyestrain naturally occurs, and thus the client will, in fact, experience the heaviness and tiredness in his or her eyes just as the clinician has suggested. But, the client naturally attributes the sensations of fatigue to the clinician's suggestions, not physiology, and as a result the clinician's credibility can rise. Personally, I am not a fan of this technique, but it is so commonly used by so many I thought it necessary to include it in this text. In that way, you can be in a position to decide for yourself what is useful and what isn't. Why am I not a fan of this approach? Eye closure may take a while to get as a response with some clients, and so can unnecessarily become a battleground in the "test of wills" between client and clinician. Older literature has often devoted a great deal of consideration to what you should do when an inordinate amount of time has passed and the client has still not closed his or her eyes (generally recommending it be treated as resistance, analyzing and confronting it). I find it much easier to just suggest eye closure and get on with the rest of the induction process.

An eye fixation induction method might sound like this one, done permissively and contentlessly:

> As you listen to the sound of my voice, you can let your eyes search the room and find some spot or some thing that is of particular interest to you . . . And when you find that particular object you can let your head begin to gently drop down while you allow your eyes to look upward toward that object . . . That's right . . . And now you can continue to look at it, and you can notice every detail about the way it looks . . . and as you continue to relax and look at it, have you noticed how tired your eyes have become? . . . and as focus your eyes intently on that object. . . . Your eyes can grow more tired, your eyelids can seem to become heavier and heavier . . . and as soon as you realize that it takes too much effort to keep your eyes open, you can let them drop down . . . and as they drop down you can drop into a very comfortable state of physical and mental relaxation. . . .

Commenting on the client's blinking, pacing your words to the eye blinks, and even modeling eye closure can further enhance your suggestions for eye closure. If after a reasonable period of time (don't hurry!) the client still has not closed his or her eyes, you can either switch techniques or simply suggest he or she close his or her eyes in a relatively direct way, such as: "You can close your eyes . . . *now*." If you still do not get eye closure, you can ask the client about what he or she is experiencing: "You haven't closed your eyes yet, for some reason . . . and as you become aware of the reason . . . if you'd like you can tell me that reason . . . and thereby make it even easier for you to get comfortable . . ." Or, as another alternative, you can match the client by encouraging him or her "to keep your eyes open . . . as you learn something meaningful. . . . with eyes wide open . . ."

Even with his or her eyes open, the client can still be in hypnosis, as discussed earlier. Keen observation will tell you this and perhaps save you needless self-doubts or confrontations over whether the client is experiencing hypnosis "properly."

COUNTING METHODS

Counting methods of induction generally involve counting downward (implying "going down" deeper into hypnosis) and in between numbers steadily offering suggestions of relaxation and comfort (Erickson, Rossi, & Rossi, 1976). At first, the slower and more detailed the process between numbers, the better. As in the progressive relaxation techniques, the client can become conditioned through experience and posthypnotic suggestions to need fewer and fewer suggestions between numbers until deep hypnosis can be accomplished with just a simple countdown.

This technique is popular because of its simplicity, evidenced in the following sample:

> In just a moment I'm going to begin counting downward from the number 10 to 1 . . . and as I count slowly downward you can relax a little more deeply with each number . . . and when I eventually reach the number 1 . . . you will begin to discover how easily you can experience yourself as very relaxed and comfortable . . . and I'll begin now with the number 10 . . . relaxing comfortably and breathing in . . . and out . . . at a rate that's comfortable for you . . . and 9, relaxing even more comfortably, feeling the relaxation grow a little more with each moment that passes . . . and 8, feeling so much more at ease . . . and 7 times more comfortable than you were just a couple of minutes ago . . . and 6 . . . I can think of half a dozen good reasons to be even more comfortable . . . 5, etc., etc., 4, 3, 2, 1 . . .

A variation involves having the client do the counting out loud downward from 100 while the clinician intersperses suggestions of relaxation. Furthermore, the clinician can offer the suggestion that when the client "soon discovers it takes too much effort to first remember and then say the next number," he or she can stop counting and go even deeper into hypnosis. Rarely have I encountered someone who continued to count below the number 80.

A variation on the same theme is to complicate matters a little by having the client count backwards by 7 from 1,000 (or some comparable numbers) as you offer suggestions for relaxation. This ends up requiring so much mental energy that it is a relief to the client to be able to stop counting and just drop into hypnosis!

THE "AS IF" METHOD

Generally a good method for more "difficult" clients, this pattern involves no direct suggestion to the client to respond in a particular way, but rather to act "as if" he or she were responding in the way suggested (Edgette & Edgette, 1995). For example, "you can arrange yourself in a comfortable position *as if* you were going to relax deeply . . . and you can close your eyes *as if* you were going to focus inwardly . . ." In terms of the outcome, where the act ends and the reality of hypnosis begins is ambiguous since the responses are virtually identical (Sarbin, 1997; Spanos & Coe, 1992).

To provide an idea of how this technique might be used, here is a sample of Milton Erickson using a variation of it with Richard Bandler and John Grinder as they described in their book, *Frogs into Princes* (1979, p. 136):

> Milton said to me "You don't consider yourself a therapist, but you are a therapist." And I said, "Well, not really." He said "Well, let's pretend . . . that you're a therapist who works with people. The most important thing . . . when you're pretending this . . . is to understand . . . that you are really not . . . You are just pretending . . . And if you pretend really well, the people that you work with will pretend to make changes. And they will forget that they are pretending . . . for the rest of their lives. But don't you be fooled by it."

Suggesting that a client act "as if" he or she is comfortable, relaxed, thinking about a happy moment, or whatever, can pave the way for the client to experience the effects of the suggestions without having to respond to any real demands being made.

INTENSIFYING (DEEPENING) TECHNIQUES

The formal, structured deepening techniques presented in this section have traditionally been used immediately after the formal induction is performed in order to intensify the client's experience of hypnosis. The traditional models of hypnosis, which view the hypnotic capacity of the client as the primary factor in successful hypnosis, have placed a greater emphasis on depth of hypnosis than does the utilization approach. Just how deeply in hypnosis does the client need to be? A deeper hypnotic experience isn't necessarily a clinically more successful one, and so generally you only need an experience deep enough to be effective. Simply put, if the client is only lightly engaged yet integrates and applies what you offer, it was deep enough. Achieving deep hypnosis may not always be necessary, but it can allow for certain possibilities (e.g., fuller dissociations) that make familiarity with deepening techniques necessary.

THE STAIRS (OR ELEVATOR) GOING DOWN

In this deepening technique, the client is encouraged to imagine (i.e., see, hear, feel) him- or herself at the top of a flight of "special stairs" or on a "special elevator" (Watkins, 1987). As he or she imagines going "down the stairs slowly one step at a time, you can go down even more deeply into hypnosis." Or, "as you pass each floor while you gradually descend in the elevator, you can experience yourself going even more deeply into the comfort of hypnosis." Here's a brief sample of how this technique might sound:

> I wonder whether you can imagine yourself standing at the top of a set of very special stairs, the stairs of relaxation . . . and as you see and even feel yourself at the top of the stairs . . . you can be very comfortable . . . and you can take the first step down . . . and as you take a step down the stairs of relaxation, you can step down into an even deeper state of comfort . . . you can relax so very deeply . . . And now you can take another step down, going even deeper into a very comfortable, profoundly absorbed state of mind and body . . . and then you can take another step down going even deeper . . .

Each step down is emphasized as a "step down deeper" into hypnosis. It is a good idea to make sure beforehand that the client doesn't have any negative associations to going downstairs (e.g., childhood spankings in the basement) or riding in an elevator. If he or she does, then use a different deepener.

COMPOUNDING: VERBAL AND MANUAL

In the previous chapter on helpful communication patterns of hypnosis, I discussed "chaining suggestions," also called "verbal compounding." As you may recall, verbal compounding involves the tying of one suggestion to another according to the generic formula, "As you X, you can Y" (e.g., "As you close your eyes, you can take in a deep, relaxing breath"). Besides smoothing the delivery of the process, verbal compounding also serves as a deepener by continually building new responses onto the foundation of past responses, thereby intensifying the hypnotic experience.

"Manual compounding" involves the tying of verbal deepening suggestions to some suggested physical experience. It generally takes the form of offering suggestions for going deeper into hypnosis while experiencing physical sensations that reinforce the suggestions. For example, assuming permission has been obtained to touch the client, you can gently push downward on the client's shoulder(s) while suggesting "you can feel yourself sinking even more deeply into comfort." Or, you can raise his or her hand, and suggest: "As I slowly and gently drop your hand back down to your side, you can drop slowly and gently even deeper into hypnosis." The physical sensations of "down" (from the push down on the shoulder or the hand dropping) can amplify the verbal suggestions of "down" and make the experience a more profound one as a result.

THE MIND'S EYE CLOSURE

I had previously been hypnotized quite a few times and found the experience comfortable, but it wasn't until I was exposed to this particular technique that I experienced deeper hypnosis. This technique involves offering suggestions about imagining the presence of a "mind's eye" as the part of the mind remaining active in thinking and imaging even as the body relaxes. By being offered suggestions similar to the "Eye Fixation" suggestions of the "eyelids getting heavy" for the "mind's eyelid," the client can slowly close out stray thoughts and images as the mind's eyelid closes and thereby have a deeper experience. It might sound something like this:

> . . . Just as you have eyes that can see the world around you, you have an inner eye that you can call the "mind's eye" . . . and it can see images and process thoughts even as you relax deeply . . . and you can think of your mind's eye as having an eyelid . . . and like your physical eyes your mind's eyelid can gradually grow more tired and heavy, and it can begin to drop . . . and as it begins to close it slowly closes out stray thoughts and stray images and can leave your mind perfectly quiet and open and free to experience whatever you'd like . . . and it's closing more and more . . . and your mind grows more quiet, more restful . . . and now your mind's eye can close . . . and close out any stray thoughts or images you don't want to interfere with how relaxed you are. . . .

This technique is an effective way of "turning off" much of the distracting or even unpleasant internal dialogue that goes on continuously in many of us, thereby making deeper hypnosis easier to accomplish.

SILENCE

Silence can be a useful deepening technique if used skillfully. Following an induction, suggestions can be offered to the effect that the client can now "have some silent time to enjoy the deep relaxation of hypnosis and the wonderful quiet inside; you can even deepen your level of comfort."

You may wish to preface the period of silence with an indicator of how long you will be silent (e.g., "You can take 60 seconds of clock time to enjoy a silent period during which you can deepen your relaxation even more . . ."), or you may instead suggest that your client signal you when he or she is ready to proceed.

It is almost always a good idea to give some protective suggestion to the client in the form of an "anticipation signal" so when you begin to speak to the client again after a period of silence, your voice will continue to soothe the client and not startle him or her. During the period of silence the client can be so absorbed in his or her internal experience that he or she forgets anyone else is even there!

Here's a helpful hint: The use of silence as a deepener can also provide you with an opportunity to compose yourself and think of what the next step in the treatment plan is. In other words, it is a prime time in the process for the client to go deeper into hypnosis while you figure out what you'd like to do next!

POSTHYPNOTIC SUGGESTION AND RE-INDUCTION

This deepening technique, also called "refractionation," is the deepening technique of choice with those clients whose attention spans are diminished by their symptoms. That includes deeply depressed, highly anxious, pain and attention-deficit clients. Refractionation can help build a better attention span.

The technique involves giving the client already in hypnosis a posthypnotic suggestion that the next time you do hypnosis together he or she can go into hypnosis both more quickly and deeply. The person is brought out of hypnosis, then after brief discussion is invited to go back into hypnosis, ideally going into hypnosis more quickly and deeply as suggested. The clinician thus guides the person in and out of hypnosis several times in the same session, each time for just a little longer.

Stage hypnotists gain their greatest notoriety for the way they use this technique. A posthypnotic suggestion is given during the pre-show phase of suggestibility testing that when the hypnotist commands "Sleep!" or snaps his or her fingers, the subject will instantly re-enter hypnosis. Naturally, the audience is baffled and fascinated by the "power" of the hypnotist whose subjects enter hypnosis at an unbelievably rapid rate as the dramatic subjects even fall out of their chairs!

Some clinicians establish what is called a "cue word" or "cue symbol" that the client is to use as a rapid means for entering hypnosis. Building such a cue simply allows for less induction time and more time to use the hypnosis therapeutically. Thus, the use of posthypnotic suggestion and re-induction as a deepening technique is a useful one, with the qualification that if a "cue" is used it be one that is more gentle and respectful than a harsh command to "sleep" or a finger snap. The best cues, in my opinion, are the most subtle ones, such as a gradual change in your voice to the voice qualities associated with your "hypnotic voice." The association to entering hypnosis in response to the use of your voice in a particular way allows a gentle transition from one style of interaction to another. Once the client has become experienced with entering hypnosis with you as a guide, such experiences can serve as a foundation for future experiences. In fact, making use of a client's previous hypnotic experiences is one of the conversational approaches to induction discussed in the next chapter.

SUMMARY

This chapter featured some of the most common and useful methods for inducing and deepening the hypnosis involving formal, structured approaches. *Anything* that focuses the person's attention and facilitates feelings of comfort and well-being can be used as an induction, and those few presented here are intended to provide a foundation on which to build.

Practicing these techniques will allow you to develop the ability to deliver them in a smooth, flowing way. Choppiness is distracting and reflects uncertainty, an unsettling experience for a client looking for expert guidance.

Just as there are no clear dividing lines between the different levels of hypnosis, there are no clear dividing lines between the stages of hypnotic interaction; for example, what has been identified as a suggestibility test in this book does not have to exclusively be a suggestibility test—it may also serve as an induction or a deepener. The inductions can be employed as suggestibility tests or deepeners, and the deepeners can be suggestibility tests or inductions. For the sake of clarity in presentation, I have put the various techniques in the categories I did, but you can allow yourself the flexibility to use whatever will work when you need it.

In the next chapter on conversational inductions, the lines separating one phase of treatment from another get blurred a little more. They require more adaptation to the client than the processes in this chapter which strive to get the client to adapt to the methods chosen.

For Discussion

1. Should the clinician perform inductions he or she doesn't personally like? Why or why not?
2. How might a clinician find out whether he or she is moving too quickly or slowly for the client?

3. With what specific client populations should each of the inductions listed in this chapter *not* be used? Why?
4. What experiences of acting "as if" you felt a certain way have you had, and with what results?

Things to Do

1. Practice each of the techniques in this chapter on your classmates, shifting your style from person to person. What feedback do you get?
2. Research other approaches to hypnotic induction, and briefly outline each.
3. Develop a list of words and as many alternative words for each you will likely be using frequently in doing hypnosis. Include words such as "focus," "remember," "imagine," "relax," "deeper," and so on.

REFERENCES

Bandler, R. & Grinder, J. (1979). *Frogs into princes*. Moab, UT: Real People.

Coe, W. (1993). Expectations and hypnotherapy. In J. Rhue, S. Lynn, & I. Kirsch (Eds.), *Handbook of clinical hypnosis* (pp. 73–93). Washington, D.C.: American Psychological Association.

Edgette, J., & Edgette, J. (1995). *The handbook of hypnotic phenomena in psychotherapy*. New York: Brunner/Mazel.

Erickson, M., Rossi, E., & Rossi, S. (1976). *Hypnotic realities: The induction of clinical hypnosis and forms of indirect suggestion*. New York: Irvington.

Kirsch, I., Lynn, S., & Rhue, J. (1993). Introduction to clinical hypnosis. In J. Rhue, S. Lynn, & I. Kirsch (Eds.), *Handbook of clinical hypnosis* (pp. 3–22). Washington, D.C.: American Psychological Association.

Murray-Jobsis, J. (1993). The borderline patient and the psychotic patient. In J. Rhue, S. Lynn, & I. Kirsch (Eds.), *Handbook of clinical hypnosis* (pp. 425–51). Washington, D.C.: American Psychological Association.

Rhue, J., & Lynn, S. (1993). Hypnosis and storytelling in the treatment of child sexual abuse: Strategies and procedures. In J. Rhue, S. Lynn, & I. Kirsch (Eds.), *Handbook of clinical hypnosis* (pp. 455–78). Washington, D.C.: American Psychological Association.

Sarbin, T. (1997). Hypnosis as a conversation: "Believed-in imaginings" revisited. *Contemporary hypnosis, 14*, 4, 203–15.

Smith, W. (1993). Hypnotherapy with rape victims. In J. Rhue, S. Lynn, & I. Kirsch (Eds.), *Handbook of clinical hypnosis* (pp. 479–91). Washington, D.C.: American Psychological Association.

Spanos, N., & Coe, W. (1992). A social-psychological approach to hypnosis. In E. Fromm & M. Nash (Eds.), *Contemporary hypnosis research* (pp. 102–30). New York: Guilford.

Spiegel, D. (1993). Hypnosis in the treatment of posttraumatic stress disorders. In J. Rhue, S. Lynn & I. Kirsch (Eds.), *Handbook of clinical hypnosis* (pp. 493–508). Washington, D.C.: American Psychological Association.

Spiegel, H., & Spiegel, D. (1978). *Trance and treatment: Clinical uses of hypnosis.* New York: Basic.

Watkins, J. (1987). *Hypnotherapeutic techniques.* New York: Irvington.

Weitzenhoffer, A. (2000). *The practice of hypnotism.* (2nd ed.) New York: Wiley.

15

Informal, Conversational Strategies of Hypnotic Induction

The formal, structured hypnotic inductions presented in the previous chapter are based on the general assumption that the experience of hypnosis is distinct from other forms of subjective experience and can be induced through some special, if not arbitrary, process. While most in the field readily acknowledge that hypnosis can occur spontaneously and a ritual of induction is unnecessary for hypnosis to occur (Lynn, Kirsch, Neufeld, & Rhue, 1996; Watzlawick, 1985), many practitioners continue to employ induction procedures that provide a structure to which the client must try to adapt. When a client finds a way to respond to a counting method, for example, he or she is demonstrating an ability to get absorbed *despite* the absence of relevance for the numbers as a source of personal meaning or comfort. After all, what's so engaging about counting numbers? Yet, the counting methods, and other techniques similarly structured, actually work with many people, probably for the reasons Kirsch (2000) offered when he described the role of expectancy in responsiveness and further suggested that an induction is whatever the client thinks of and expects an induction to be.

The utilization approach to hypnotic induction (Erickson, 1958, 1959; Erickson, Rossi, & Rossi, 1976) rests on different assumptions about the experience of hypnosis, the nature of induction, and the goals in even doing hypnosis, that add a more complex and sophisticated dimension to working with hypnotic communication patterns.

In the utilization approach, hypnosis is viewed as a natural experience occurring routinely in people. In adopting this perspective, one of the tasks of the skilled clinician is to recognize hypnotic responses as they naturally occur in the course of ongoing therapeutic interaction and then build on them meaningfully in a spontaneous and conversational manner. Another

one of the tasks is to organize hypnotic processes around the unique attributes of the client, adapting the approaches to his or her subjective style
of relating, thinking, and behaving. Instead of saying, "I'm going to name
body parts while you focus on relaxing" (i.e., progressive muscle relaxation),
an example of an approach that requires the client to try to adapt him- or
herself to the clinician's chosen technique, the utilization approach instead
strives to elicit from within the client the images, internal dialogue, feelings, and behaviors that are personally meaningful and engaging as the basis
for the induction and therapy. Zeig described the process this way:

> Initiating hypnotic induction is a little like fostering love. One cannot elicit
> an emotional state, such as love, by intoning, "Go deeply into love." Simi-
> larly, one does not elicit hypnosis by commanding a passive patient, "Go
> deeply into trance."
>
> Note a key word in the previous sentence, *elicit*. Hypnosis is elicited,
> not induced (despite the label "induction"). . . . The hypnotherapist estab-
> lishes conditions that allow the patient to bring forth previously dormant
> trance components. (2001, p. 18)

In other words, the skilled clinician can elicit responses from hypnotic
patterns of communication that capture the client's attention and focus him
or her on experiences that will be personally and therapeutically significant. The instructions to the client in the conversational (Ericksonian, naturalistic, utilization) approach to hypnotic induction are typically more
individualized, permissive, indirect, and process-oriented than other, more
technique-oriented approaches. Furthermore, there is typically not as clear
a beginning, middle, or end to the induction compared to the clearer transitions from phase to phase of the hypnosis session found in the more structured, content-oriented approaches of the previous chapter.

The spontaneity required to "accept and utilize" a client's communications makes it nearly impossible to ritualize (i.e., standardize) the practice
of clinical hypnosis in the utilization approach. For some, the lack of a rigid
structure to the methods is a turn-off. For others that same trait is a turn-on,
for the challenge of how to elicit a meaningful and therapeutically effective
hypnotic experience in a particular person in a specific context is a formi-
dable challenge, indeed. Implicit in this approach is the role of clinician as
both guide and initiator of what is to happen. The clinician's responsibility
to the client is greater in the utilization approach because the client is assumed to be capable of a meaningful hypnotic experience if a more individualized and flexible approach is employed. This is a marked contrast to
the traditional practice of assuming successful hypnosis is more about the
client's level of hypnotizability as measured by a standardized test than the
quality of the therapeutic alliance or the flexibility of your approach.

The stimulus for the hypnotic experience in the utilization approach is in the unconscious associations (e.g., cognitive, sensory, emotional) the clinician triggers in the client through his or her communications. This perspective also differs considerably from the more traditional perspective that the power of the hypnotic suggestion is contained in the suggestion itself rather than in the way the client relates to it. The scripting of inductions parallels the current trend toward the manualizing of therapies, or the empirical "validating" of a therapy, as if what's therapeutic is inherent in the technique rather than in a person's response to the technique. *Any therapy can be iatrogenic or antitherapeutic for some people who respond in idiosyncratic and negative ways.* That's the key reason why keeping a focus on the individual and tailoring approaches to him or her is emphasized throughout this text as a means for minimizing negative responses, even when I discuss non-individualized approaches. Which specific associations of client experience will be triggered by your words cannot be predicted with certainty. Observing and using a client's responses as they arise will, of necessity, temper your approach.

Securing and maintaining the attention of the client is a beginning point for the hypnotic interaction. Talking about the issues that brought the person into treatment, telling engaging yet instructive stories that parallel the client's experience, and behaving in unexpected but goal-directed ways are three common techniques for securing a client's attention. As the client's focus is narrowed to the clinician, the clinician can begin to build on the client's responses by first acknowledging them and then suggesting (directly or indirectly) that these responses can serve to gradually expand his or her range of problem-solving resources. When the clinician notices hypnotic responses building (absorption, changes in breathing, a fixed posture, muscular tension dissipating, etc.), he or she can begin to engage the person in the process of induction and deepening through the naturalistic techniques described in this chapter.

The transition from routine conversation to hypnotic induction is a subtle one in this approach in comparison to the more formal, "OK, close your eyes now and let's do some hypnosis," approach. Induction is not necessarily announced to the client as a new phase the therapeutic interaction is entering, but can instead be eased into as a natural part of the progression of treatment. Whatever the client spontaneously does during this time is accepted and utilized as part of the process. Thus, the implicit message is, "What you're doing right now is what will allow you to deepen your experience further." Behaviors that seem "resistant" (e.g., fidgeting, smiling, interrupting . . .) are accepted and used as the basis for further suggestions, redefining them as acceptable and even useful responses.

The skilled manipulation of the nonverbal components of the clinician's communications is always a major factor in doing hypnosis, but in the utilization approach it is especially so. Deliberate changes in your tone of voice, your quality of eye contact, and other analogical communications while shifting into an induction may serve as potential associations to entering hypnosis in this and future experiences. For example, using your "hypnotic voice" (i.e., slower pace, quieter) selectively will predictably trigger hypnotic responses (i.e., communicate an invitation to your client to enter hypnosis) without having to say, "Now I'm doing hypnosis" because those voice qualities became associated with hypnosis when you used them from the very first induction onward. This is but one example of how you can obtain hypnotic responses without directly asking for them. Your body posture, gaze, and breathing patterns are further examples of potential patterns on which to build hypnotic response associations. Table 5 below offers further hints for performing naturalistic inductions more skillfully. Most of these have already been discussed at various times in the text while others will be presented here.

The methods for guiding a person into hypnosis described in this chapter are reliable ones. They have a structure, they have a vehicle for delivering the structure, but they are more spontaneous and conversational than more formal approaches. Each involves narrowing the person's field of attention to his or her inner experiences, specifically the associations triggered by your suggestions. Resources long dormant in the client can be reactivated, memories long forgotten can be rediscovered, feelings long buried can be re-experienced, and issues long troublesome can be resolved.

CONVERSATIONAL (NATURALISTIC) INDUCTIONS

USING PAST HYPNOTIC EXPERIENCES

The recognition of hypnotic experiences arising spontaneously in people allows for a smooth transition into the induction phase of hypnosis. All people

---

Table 5. Conversational Induction Principles

Utilization of client's reality (past or present)
Accessing questions to absorb and direct attention
Use of yourself as a model
Notice and amplify responses
Verbal chaining: "As you X you can Y"
Presuppositions: *How* to do X, not *whether*
Interspersal of suggestions
Framing responses (incorporation)
Shift in delivery style (nonverbal)
Orient to internal experience
Elicit and guide associations

have, at the least, experienced naturally occurring (i.e., spontaneous) hypnotic experiences that probably weren't thought of as being hypnosis yet can be identified as such by the clinician and used as examples of hypnosis to build upon in treatment (e.g., "highway hypnosis," unconscious or automatic behaviors). Many people, however, have experienced formal hypnosis at one time or another, perhaps in educational or clinical contexts, where it was clear that hypnosis was occurring. These formal experiences can be even easier to build new hypnotic experiences upon.

The induction method of "Using Past Hypnotic Experiences" involves two general categories of previous hypnotic experiences on which to build: (1) Informal experiences with hypnosis, specifically the "everyday hypnosis" experiences people have during the course of normal daily living; and, (2) Formal experiences with hypnosis, specifically the previous time(s) the client experienced hypnosis positively. Either approach may be offered in either a process-oriented or content-filled structure, described later in this section.

In the first approach of building on previous informal experience with hypnosis, the phase of attentional absorption typically involves some pre-induction discussion about the nature of hypnotic experience while exploring the client's associations to hypnosis. At some point, the clinician can begin to model increased attentiveness, immobility (i.e., catalepsy), slowed breathing, and can begin to hypnotically describe one or more natural situations in which hypnosis occurs. Such situations might include long drives, absorption in a good book or movie, during a massage or jacuzzi, daydreaming, praying, and any other situation in which the person has had the direct experience of being absorbed. The nonverbal shift from a normal pace and conversational tone of voice to one that is slower, quieter, and more meaningfully articulated is fundamental to guiding the person into the suggested memory of that natural hypnotic state he or she has experienced (Lankton & Lankton, 1983). Through the absorption in that memory, hypnotic responses (i.e., the ideodynamics) naturally begin to occur in the here-and-now, which the clinician can notice, accept, and utilize according to the "As you experience this, you can experience that" chaining formula. The client need not close his or her eyes in order to experience hypnosis, but the clinician may want to suggest eye closure by offering a direct or indirect suggestion to do so. The following is a sample of how this technique may sound, using a previous informal hypnotic experience of reading with indirect suggestions in the form of embedded commands to obtain specific responses:

> You said earlier you enjoy reading a really good book . . . I really enjoy reading, too, especially when I have some quiet time all to myself . . . a *time for quiet* when I know I won't be interrupted. . . . It's such a luxury to have some

time . . . to sit quietly . . . and not have to do anything . . . a time I can let
myself *relax so deeply* . . . *sitting* in a way that is *so comfortable* . . . and you know
what that's like, too . . . and how easy it is to *sit quietly* . . . just
thinking . . . *without moving* for what can seem like a long, long time . . . and
I like to read books that encourage you to *experience yourself differently* . . . that
absorb you in different ways of thinking . . . different ways of feeling . . . books
that allow you to expand yourself and *change in beneficial ways* . . . and you
probably know quite well what I mean . . . how *your mind can be so active in
learning* while *your body gets even more comfortable* with each page you turn . . . and
when you get too comfortable to keep on reading, you can *close your eyes and
drift off* . . . and I'd like to tell you about a book I read that may have special
meaning for you. . . .

The above induction starts out conversationally, then turns to a sharing of personal experience the client can relate to in order to build rapport
while simultaneously slowing down and building associations to entering
hypnosis. Then the shift takes place from "I" to "you," with an emphasis on
the client's experience building into a relaxed and focused state through
the tonal emphasis on suggestive phrases. As the client becomes absorbed
in the memory of relaxing and learning while reading, his or her responses
can start to build in the current context and become the basis for transitioning
into whatever hypnosis is to be done.

The above sample is obviously a content-filled one, providing details
specific to the experience of reading. A process-oriented approach could
also be employed, of which the following is an example:

Can you think of a time when you were so involved in some deeply absorbing experience that you *detached from* and even forgot to notice things going
on around you? Every person has had experiences like that where . . . you
find yourself immersed in some activity . . . and as *you relax* . . . and
remember . . . and think about that kind of an experience . . . you can remember a specific experience like that . . . one that was especially
pleasant . . . where you were so into it . . . you could *lose track of time* . . . and
forget to notice outside sights and sounds . . . and only your sensations and thoughts
were important . . . and you could *feel so wonderfully relaxed* . . . and isn't it
nice to know you can be so wrapped up in your thoughts . . . that people's
voices fade away . . . and you're alone with your thoughts . . . and *feelings of
comfort* . . . and it's at times like that . . . and like this . . . that *you can learn
something important.* . . .

In the above sample, the process of becoming absorbed in sensation
and thought is described, but no details of a specific context triggering such
experiences are provided. Rather, the client provides those details for him- or
herself when the suggestion is offered to choose a specific experience that
was pleasant.

In the second approach building on formal experience with hypnosis, the typical pre-induction phase discussion can focus the client's attention on the range of possibilities hypnosis allows, and how previous experience with hypnosis can make future experiences easier, more satisfying, and successful. It seems worthwhile to reiterate a point made in an earlier chapter about exploring the nature and quality of the client's previous hypnotic experience(s). If the client had a positive and meaningful experience with hypnosis, then the clinician has a solid, positive base on which to build. If the client had a negative experience with hypnosis, one that was unsuccessful at least or hurtful at most, then the clinician must exercise caution to refer back to the experience either as little as possible or in a detached way in the course of doing hypnosis. Questioning the client about techniques used and identifying the personal, situational, and interpersonal variables operating negatively at the time can save you from unwittingly duplicating a previously negative experience.

If the client has had a positive experience with hypnosis before, a content-filled approach to the use of the formal hypnotic experience can involve engaging the client in providing an ever-slowing, detailed account of the experience. This approach usually involves a large degree of interaction as the induction progresses, with the clinician simultaneously questioning the client, suggesting possible responses, and building on the client's responses as they occur. The mechanism of induction is structurally the same as in using informal previous hypnotic experiences; as the person becomes absorbed in the memory of hypnosis, the ideodynamic responses associated with that memory evolve in the here-and-now. The clinician notices, accepts, and utilizes those responses, building hypnotic responsiveness toward the goal of the interaction. The following is an example of this induction approach:

Clinician: You mentioned earlier that you experienced the comfort of hypnosis before, didn't you?

Client: Yes. A couple of years ago I saw a doctor who did hypnosis for another problem I was experiencing.

Clinician: As you begin to think back now, can you recall how soothing and calming an experience hypnosis was?

Client: Yes, I do remember feeling really relaxed. I didn't expect to be able to hear the doctor's voice, but I did. I wasn't sure I was hypnotized, but it felt really good.

Clinician: That's right . . . the experience of hypnosis can be so relaxing . . . so soothing . . . and you can remember how you were sitting then, can't you?

Client: I guess so . . . (Readjusts position).

Clinician: That's right . . . sitting very comfortably now . . . and do you remember how good it felt to *breathe deeply and close your eyes*?

Client: (deep breath, eyes flutter closed) Yes.

Clinician: And you can probably recall what you heard then that allowed
you to relax so deeply, can't you? And what did you hear that
reminds you that *you can be comfortable*?

Client: Just the doctor's voice . . . telling me to relax deeper and
deeper . . . that it was as if I was floating. . . .

Clinician: That's right, and you can remember what it's like to *have that
light, comfortable feeling everywhere in your body*. . . .

In a sense, the client is acting as his or her own hypnotist, giving
him- or herself the same suggestions from the past in the present, and the
clinician's role is a simple one of amplification. The client already knows
how to experience hypnosis, has defined it as helpful, and reminds him- or
herself in detail of the relaxed, floating nature of the hypnotic experience
and, in so doing, unconsciously recreates it. By framing the interaction as a
"discussion" about past experience rather than a set of current demands to
respond to, the suggestions to enter hypnosis are less direct, more permissive, more natural to the interaction, and the issue of resistance is therefore
largely avoided.

To use this kind of an approach in a process-oriented way, the interactional dimension of the induction can, if desired, be eliminated. The following is an example of the use of formal previous hypnotic experiences offered
in a contentless way:

> You mentioned earlier that you had an experience with hypnosis before that
> was a very relaxing and helpful one. If you'd like, you can begin to recall
> now many of the details of what that experience was like . . . remembering
> how *your body can be so comfortable* . . . how *your breathing can begin to slow
> down* . . . and I wonder whether you'll remember how comforting it can be
> to simply *sit quietly* . . . in a comfortable position . . . while you listen to some-
> one describe some ways that *you can begin to experience yourself differently* . . . and
> do you recall how good it felt to *close your eyes*? . . . and the memory of relax-
> ing so deeply is still a part of you . . . even if you haven't had time lately to
> notice it . . . and isn't it nice to *rediscover something familiar and calming* that
> can help you? . . . and perhaps you can remember the room you were in
> when you learned how to *feel good in this way* . . . you can see the furniture
> and you can hear the sounds of that place, and as you remember the details
> of then . . . *you can feel comfortable* about that experience right now . . .

The context in which the client had his or her previous formal experience with hypnosis is not known to the clinician, nor does it need to be as long as the clinician is certain the experience was, in fact, a good one for the client by his or her own description.

Making use of the client's previous experience with hypnosis, whether formal or informal, is one of the easiest yet most effective induction and deepening processes. It is a spontaneous, loosely structured approach that generates little resistance because "we're not talking about *now*, we're talking about *then*." The extra psychological distance makes a difference in increased comfort. In sum, the techniques involving use of past hypnotic experiences are reliable and flexible ones and, when well practiced, can be among the best inductions in your repertoire.

BUILDING AN INTERNAL FOCUS

The experience of hypnosis has been described as one involving absorption, an intense concentration on some stimulus to the exclusion of others. Usually, but not always, the absorption is internally directed. In doing hypnosis, guiding the client into hypnosis implies having the client selectively attend to the stimulus of the clinician's guidance, specifically becoming absorbed in the subjective associations triggered by the clinician's suggestions. By focusing intently on his or her internal experience, the client can suspend attentiveness to the external world, diminish reality-testing, and thereby subjectively experience a wider range of possibilities.

The clinician's role is to facilitate the process of building an internal focus through suggestion. In routine interaction, therapeutic or otherwise, people are expected to be more externally oriented and responsive to the other person. When one lapses into brief episodes of self-absorption in social situations, it is considered rude, inattentive, disinterested, or is even considered evidence of (passive-aggressive) hostility. Yet, such episodes of internal absorption are normal, natural, frequent, and to be expected. In fact, in learning and doing hypnosis, part of the difficulty some students encounter is developing the ability to stay externally focused on the client's responses as much as is humanly possible. If you are internally absorbed while doing hypnosis, you are going to miss a great deal of important nonverbal information communicated by your client during the process. Maintaining an attentive external focus on the client is the best way for the clinician to maintain a connection to the client by noticing and incorporating his or her responses into the induction.

The induction process of building an internal focus involves offering "pacing" statements of what *external* stimuli the client is currently aware of, coupled with "leading" statements describing *internal* responses the client may begin to develop (Gilligan, 1987; Grinder & Bandler, 1981). This can be done in any ratio of pacing to leading statements the clinician judges to be useful. In other words, how many externally oriented suggestions of experience you offer for every internally oriented suggestion of experience is dependent solely on the responsiveness of the client.

The assessment can be made early on in your interaction with the client as to how internally or externally absorbed he or she tends to be in the course of routine interaction. An internal or external orientation in relating to the world is generally a fairly stable characteristic of an individual, yet can and does vary markedly from situation to situation. Internal or external focus exists on a continuum, and no one can be exclusively one or the other in a fixed way. Assessing the client's direction and degree of focus is usually a simple process of observing how the person communicates about his or her experience. Does he or she see him- or herself as responsible for his or her problem, or is he or she a victim of evil forces beyond his or her control? Is he or she sensitive to others' feelings and perceptions or is he or she blissfully unaware of others' feelings and reactions to him or her? Is he or she easily distracted from your interaction by external but routine things like a phone ringing or a plane flying overhead? Is or isn't he or she insightful about his or her experience? Observations along these lines of assessment can allow you the opportunity to formulate an induction and intervention that will more likely be effective.

Once you've assessed how internally or externally focused the client is at the time you would like to begin your induction, you can make the judgment as to what ratio of external paces to internal leads you think would be effective, modifying it as necessary according to client response. Some clients are already so internally focused at the beginning point that you don't have to have much of an induction beyond, "You can go into hypnosis, now." Others may be so externally focused that they may require five or even ten external pacing statements before a single internal leading suggestion is offered.

As the induction progresses, fewer and fewer externally oriented statements are made while more and more internally oriented suggestions are offered. The following is provided as an example of this induction process with someone deemed moderately externally oriented at the start of the induction. To help you distinguish them, an (e) follows each externally oriented suggestion, and an (i) follows each internally oriented suggestion.

> You're sitting in that chair (e) and you're listening to me describe the experience of going into hypnosis (e) . . . and as you continue to look at me (e) you may notice the feel of the chair underneath you, supporting your body comfortably (e) . . . and as you notice the chair you can hear the phone ringing somewhere (e) . . . and *isn't it soothing* . . . to know you don't have to answer it and so *you can let yourself relax* easily (i) . . . and you can notice the

wall behind me with its interesting pictures (e) and you may notice the objects on my desk (e) . . . and as you look around the room you can hear the routine sounds of this environment (e) and you can hear the sound of the world busily going on around you (e) and *you can feel so good* in realizing that your body can grow more at ease (i) . . . and *your mind can begin to drift* back to a pleasant memory (i) . . . and as your mind drifts back you can feel the texture of the chair on your fingertips (e) and as you notice how that texture feels you can also hear the things I have to say (e) . . . and as you listen *you can become aware of a certain memory* (i) . . . one that you feel is important that you'd like to re-experience and learn from (i) . . . a memory that may remind you of something you'd like to know now (i) . . .

In the above example, the induction starts with a series of statements that are pacing what the client is currently aware of, feeding back aspects of what he or she *is* doing, then offering a general statement of what he or she *can* experience. The number of paces to leads shifts as the induction progresses, gradually leading the client into re-experiencing an important memory.

You may notice the use of sensory based terms in visual, auditory, and kinesthetic modalities. A way to further tailor the process to the individual is to deliberately choose the sensory modality of internal experience you want the client focused on. Many of the problems clients present clinically can be described in terms of internal or external focus on a particular sensory modality. The most obvious example is pain, which can be thought of as an intense internal awareness on the kinesthetic level. Management of pain may, as you might predict, involve shifting the client's focus from internal to external, or from the kinesthetic modality to another one.

Most hypnotic inductions involve building an internal focus, each according to a different method. This induction provides the barest of frameworks for helping the client experience hypnosis, since all that is provided here is a structured description of the process as shifting the client's focus from external to internal experience. Which externals and which internals you use in what combination in which modality and in which style and structure make for a huge range of possibilities. How successful your induction will be, as always, is determined primarily by how well you have assessed the client's response style and how well you can spontaneously adjust your approach according to the feedback you get.

METAPHORICAL INDUCTIONS
WITH EMBEDDED SUGGESTIONS

In the earlier section on using past hypnotic experiences as an induction strategy, I described how putting a little psychological distance between the desired experiences "now" by focusing on experiences from "then" can make for less resistance. The use of metaphor is an even less direct induction approach, and so is even less likely to arouse resistance in the client. Rather than use the client's personal past experience as the basis for induction, metaphors may describe some other person's (or animal's, or thing's) experience at some other time in some other place. Thus, the degree of removal is even greater and the possibility for personal threat reduced even further. As Jay Haley wrote:

> When a subject resists directives, one way to deal with the problem is to communicate in terms of an analogy. If the subject resists A, the hypnotist can talk about B, and when A and B are metaphorically related, the subject will make the connection "spontaneously" and respond appropriately . . . the analogic, or metaphoric, approach to hypnosis is particularly effective with resistant subjects, since it is difficult to resist a suggestion one does not know consciously that he is receiving. (1973, pp. 26–7)

In *Webster's Encyclopedia of Dictionaries*, a metaphor is defined as "a figure of speech which makes an implied comparison between things which are not literally alike." Metaphors in the therapeutic context may include anecdotes, jokes, analogies, or any other form of indirect communication that conveys a meaningful message to the client on conscious and/or unconscious levels. Metaphors provide an opportunity for the client to learn from others' experiences, allowing him or her to identify, to some degree, with the characters, issues, and resolutions of the metaphor.

Learning from the experience of others throughout recorded history has allowed human civilization to evolve. You do not have to experience something personally in order to know about it, and if you are reflective or thoughtful about others' experiences, you can understand and benefit from the meanings of their experiences on a personal level. In growing up, you heard and read classic fairy tales like *Snow White* and *Cinderella*, and you learned something from them about human nature. Your parents' stories about their childhood taught you about families and growing up. In reading books of all kinds, you gradually learned about different societies, different lifestyles, as well as different types of relationships. Even in watching television and movies, your sense of involvement in the story allows you to experience vicariously similar feelings and events as the characters in the story, broadening your range of experience and developing resources that may be drawn upon at some future time.

The popular use of metaphorical approaches in clinical treatment is a relatively recent development, catalyzed primarily by the work of Milton Erickson. His fascinating and often simple teaching stories were able to capture his patients' interest on a conscious level, while his embedded suggestions allowed the patient's unconscious mind to form new associations that could serve him or her in therapeutic ways (Rosen, 1982; Yapko, 2001; Zeig, 1980). More will be said about metaphorical approaches to therapy in the next chapter, while this section focuses on the use of metaphor in the induction phase.

You may recall the earlier discussion about how a client's symptoms may be viewed as metaphors of his or her experience. Clinicians have historically been trained to take a client's communications and "read between the lines" to uncover their "real" meaning relative to the person's overall experience. Once the real meaning has been uncovered, the clinician's role has been to offer interpretations and, through the interpretations, generate insights that would lead to new perspectives and, ideally, more adaptive behavior in the client. In other words, while a client is communicating a meaning on a conscious level, it is understood that there are deeper unconscious meanings being communicated simultaneously if one is perceptive enough to detect them. The multiple-level communication on the part of the client has historically been responded to by the clinician in a clear, single-level interpretation.

Erickson considered such interpretations as too simplistic, too reductionistic, to reflect accurately the complexity of any piece of human experience. Furthermore, Erickson had great faith in the unconscious mind's resources, and thus had a greater interest in techniques that could make use of them. Erickson also thought that if the client could communicate on multiple levels, why couldn't the clinician do the same? Erickson's greater utilization of the unconscious in the treatment process was also out of respect for the integrity of those he worked with. If a person's unconscious mind defensively kept some information out of his or her awareness (i.e., repression), was it necessary and respectful to bring the information into the person's conscious mind? Erickson thought not, and believed that insights may even impede the therapeutic process by keeping the person restricted to a safe, cognitive level of existence, widening the gap between intellect and emotion rather than bridging it. Haley described Erickson's views on these issues this way:

> Although Erickson communicates with patients in metaphor, what most sharply distinguishes him from other therapists is his unwillingness to "interpret" to people what their metaphors mean. He does not translate "unconscious" communication into conscious form. . . . He seems to feel that the depth and swiftness of that (therapeutic) change can be prevented if the person suffers a translation of the communication. (1973, pp. 28–9)

Among the safest of alternatives to working consciously with potentially reductionistic or even trite interpretations is the therapeutic metaphor. Relating a story that can capture the client's conscious interest while at deeper levels allowing him or her to learn new ways of thinking, feeling, and behaving is a respectful and flexible way of engaging the person in the treatment process. In the context of inducing hypnosis, metaphors can focus the client's attention on an experience that is interesting, while embedding suggestions for desired hypnotic responses into the story's framework.

When you formulate a metaphor for the purpose of induction, it helps to know something of the client's personal interests, values, and hobbies. Metaphors built around things that are already a part of the client's lifestyle are more likely to capture and maintain the person's interest. Of course, things of an intrinsically fascinating nature will also serve well. The broader the base of knowledge and experience the clinician has, the more sophisticated one's metaphors can be. The metaphor as an induction method can introduce the client to other clients' experiences, help them build a rapport with the clinician, build an identification with the character(s) of the story, confuse the client as to why the story is being told and thereby stimulate a search for meaning and relevance, all while building the internal focus and receptivity for the subsequent intervention (Zeig, 1980).

Perhaps the easiest metaphors are those that begin with "I had another client in a similar situation to yours . . ." When you describe the experience of some previous client, the client can come to identify with that person, and also build confidence in the clinician's experience in dealing successfully with such problems. If, for example, a client presented the complaints of excessive stress and a poor self-esteem, the induction might go something like this:

> You're describing to me how uncomfortably tense you feel much of the time, and I guess it isn't often . . . or often enough . . . that you *take the time to relax* . . . and I'd like to tell you about a client I worked with not long ago . . . a woman who is *not unlike yourself* . . . with many responsibilities . . . and she came to me feeling so tense . . . so unsure of herself . . . uncertain how she could continue to function on too little sleep with too much to do . . . and she didn't know that she didn't have to feel that way . . . and she wanted to *feel good* . . . *feel relaxed* . . . and when she sat in that chair you just happen to be sitting in, too . . . she actually took the time to *notice how comfortable that chair is* . . . and then she let herself *take in some deep breaths* . . . and she seemed to *just let go of the everyday concerns* . . . and she could *listen to me comfortably* . . . while her mind could begin to wander . . . and the memory of the last time she could *relax deeply* helped her realize she knew how to *relax so deeply* . . . and that she could and would take more time for herself . . . simply because she deserved it . . . and she learned how to re-evaluate her priorities . . . and she learned how to *say no more comfortably* to extra tasks she really didn't have time for . . . and she learned. . . .

The above example is simply an induction starting point for leading into more metaphors about possible ways to start to build confidence and better manage stress. As an induction, it begins by matching the client's concerns and then building the identification with another similar client who had a positive experience in some ways that may be of interest. There is ample room to maintain rapport by incorporating the spontaneous responses of the client into the metaphor.

To illustrate a metaphorical induction tailored to a specific interest of the client's, the following example of a metaphor was developed for a person who likes to watch television:

> You like to watch television when *you can take the time to unwind* . . . and watching television can certainly be an entertaining way to *spend some time relaxing* . . . and I like to watch TV sometimes . . . but not nearly as much as some people . . . there's someone I really think you should know about . . . who, like you, likes to watch television more than almost any other form of entertainment . . . and as a good means of *relaxing you and quieting your mind* . . . and he says he can learn a lot about life and a lot about people by watching television . . . and there was a show on once that he told me about . . . that he watched to be entertained . . . that did much more than that . . . it taught him a lot about himself . . . he didn't know that in that show there was *going to be an opportunity to have a pleasant learning experience* . . . sometimes *you discover important things* in the most unexpected places . . . and he learned something important . . . because in that show he watched, there was a man who . . . not unlike you . . . felt very badly about a problem he just couldn't seem to resolve.

In the above example, television as a learning device and a source of relaxation is used as a vehicle to lead the client into hypnosis. At the point where the example stops, the clinician can go into one or more metaphors about the client's problem and its potential resolution.

Almost any experience can serve as a metaphorical induction into hypnosis when the qualities of that experience are defined as absorbing, comforting, and meaningful. Engaging the person's attention on the content of the story allows for deeper messages embedded in the story's structure to stimulate the client's unconscious associations. Metaphors, because of their indirect style, create the possibility for a response, but whether one is obtained is dependent on the way the metaphor is introduced (called the "framing" of the metaphor), the appropriateness of the metaphor for that individual client, and the degree of rapport maintained throughout its telling. The metaphor must be introduced as potentially significant, either by some direct introductory remark such as, "This other client of mine I'd like to tell you about is someone I think you could learn something valuable from . . ."

or indirectly through the meaningful tone of your voice and quality of eye contact. The relevance of the metaphor was discussed earlier, and should involve something of interest to the client (unless you consciously choose to bore your client into hypnosis!). The rapport between you is maintained by incorporating feedback from the client spontaneously into the telling of the metaphor.

Storytelling seems to have become an art on the decline. Television has saturated our society and placed us in the role of passive viewers of experience. Interactions between people become fewer in frequency as more of us learn to "talk" to computers instead. Developing a skill in storytelling is fundamental to developing a balanced approach to the practice of clinical hypnosis. One way to do that is to reread the classic fairy tales, fables, and old mythology, for they are excellent starting points for rediscovering the wisdom of the ages that's been handed down in story form.

The specific dynamics of meaningful metaphor construction could fill volumes, and so can only be superficially presented in this book. For more in-depth consideration, see the work of Stephen and Carol Lankton (1983, 1989), Philip Barker (1985), D. Corydon Hammond (1990), and Peter Brown (1993), to name just a few of many good sources.

INDUCTION THROUGH NEGATIVE SUGGESTION

You may recall the discussion of negative suggestion structures, presented in Chapter 12. Negative suggestions, when used skillfully, can encourage positive responses in clients through their paradoxical effect (Grinder & Bandler, 1981). They can do so in part because of the transderivational search and ideodynamic processes, and in part because of their acceptance and utilization of client resistances. Resistance as a factor in the hypnotic interaction is discussed in greater detail later in chapter 21; suffice it to say here that few clients are blindly obedient to the suggestions of the clinician. Instead, each client maintains a sense of control, internal homeostasis, and autonomy through the rejection of input (evidence of "resistance" according to the clinician's way of thinking) even when the input is obviously intended to benefit the client.

In those clients where control is a sensitive personal issue, a tendency to respond negatively and in a contrary manner as a reliable response pattern is frequently evident. If the clinician says, "It's day," the client responding in an oppositional mode disagrees and says, "It's night." Such polar responsiveness is not necessarily aimed specifically at the clinician, rather may be a general response pattern that the person uses everywhere or nearly everywhere to his or her own detriment. You have undoubtedly experienced such people's ability to stir up conflict wherever they go, yet who often puzzle over why people don't relate to them very well. The need to defend against others' input in order to maintain what must be a precarious internal balance is a basis for such response styles. Someone with a greater sense of self can maintain a strong sense of personal identity even while selectively incorporating ideas from others.

In the hypnotic interaction, the negative response style can be accepted and utilized in the service of hypnotic induction and utilization. The principle underlying the use of negative suggestions is, "fight fire with fire." When negative suggestions are offered to the critical, controlling client, he or she can naturally reject them and respond in an opposite way. Knowing the client's tendency to respond in such a contrary manner, the clinician can deliberately use negative suggestions the client will reject in order to get the opposite response(s) that is actually desired. Beware, though, for offering negative suggestions will seem an obvious and demeaning trick unless they are offered in a congruent and meaningful manner.

Imagine, for a moment, a client sitting opposite you who is anxious, uncertain about you and your hypnosis techniques, uncertain about him- or herself, and who is struggling to maintain a sense of personal control. The following example of an induction through negative suggestion might be a useful one to employ.

> You've come here looking for help with your problem because you don't like the way you are feeling . . . and *you can feel differently* . . . but I don't expect you to know that yet . . . for right now . . . it's important to know . . . you can and perhaps even should reject anything and everything I say . . . you don't have to *listen to me* or anybody else . . . you have the right to ignore anything you want to . . . especially if it's different than what you already believe . . . you can't be expected to *be open enough* right away *to listen and learn* what you came here to . . . at least not yet . . . and for now you can't be expected to *change in a meaningful way* . . . until you've had the opportunity to continue feeling badly a while longer . . . so don't listen to me . . . and don't *give yourself the chance to feel more at ease* . . . and you can continue to squirm in your chair . . . I don't want you to relax here or now . . . I don't think there's any reason for you not to continue fidgeting . . . so don't sit still and don't let your muscles relax . . . and don't *let your eyes close* even when they can get so tired of staying open . . . and some people *feel good* when they know they don't have to listen to me . . . talking about all the ways you don't need to *notice opportunities to change* in a comfortable way . . . and don't *allow yourself the comfort of relaxing deeply* . . . because you might *start to feel better* . . . and it's much too soon for that to happen . . .

In the above example, suggestions for relaxing and changing were offered in the negative framework, "don't do this." To the client deemed negative and resistant, on the surface no demands have been made and so there really isn't anything to resist consciously. On an unconscious level, the ideodynamics associated with the transderivational search process assure you of some degree, however small, of responsiveness to your suggestions on which to build. You have to think of relaxing in order not to relax, you have to think of change in order to think of not changing, and so on. The key is to incorporate into the process whatever specific spontaneous responses arise in the person, redefining them as cooperative. For example, if you accept the client's fidgeting instead of labeling it a resistant behavior, it can be encouraged. By encouraging it, you define it as something useful in the interaction, even though the client's intention was to not cooperate. This technique of using negative suggestions to utilize the client's resistance is one more way of responding to resistance in addition to those described in chapter 21 on non-ideal responses from clients to your methods.

The use of negative suggestions in the induction phase of hypnotic interaction is intended to use a client's resistance to help guide him or her into hypnosis. At some point, the client realizes that all your suggestions about not relaxing, not letting go, not focusing internally, and so on, have had the indirect effect of facilitating the attainment of hypnosis. This can be, and usually is, a positive turning point in the relationship. The client has now had his or her experience guided by the clinician, and not only did he or she survive it but actually found it pleasant and relaxing. The relief that comes from not having to fight to maintain a sense of control can have a profound impact on the client, who has now started to learn from his or her own direct experience that he or she can still be in control without having to fight others off negatively. This initial hypnotic experience can then serve as a basis for future hypnotic experiences conducted in a more positive suggestive framework.

INDUCTION THROUGH CONFUSION TECHNIQUES

The process of eliciting hypnotic experience involves creating a somewhat dissociated condition in which the client's unconscious mind is able to function with a greater degree of autonomy than in the usual "waking" state. Confusion techniques are especially effective for facilitating dissociation and, therefore, hypnosis (Erickson, 1964; Gilligan, 1987). Confusion techniques are among the most complex hypnotic patterns to master because they are, well, *confusing.*

Human beings generally hate to be confused. Confusion creates an unpleasant internal state that motivates the person to clear up the confusion. Frequently, the person is so motivated to resolve the confusion he or she will jump to erroneous conclusions just to have a conclusion, *any* conclusion. Confusion techniques deliberately disrupt the client's everyday mental set in order to increase the likelihood of a suggestion getting in (Otani,

1989). Because people do not like to be confused and will hold erroneous, even self-destructive, ideas rather than allow an issue to remain unsettled, the clinician faces the task of dislodging old, hurtful thought patterns in order to build more adaptive ones. When you are certain about something, how likely are you to change your attitude about it? Not very likely, for the more certain you are about an idea or behavior, the more stable and thus resistant to change you are in that domain. When you aren't sure, though, you are much more likely to take in what others say and adopt their recommendations for as long as they seem credible to you.

Confusion deliberately causes uncertainty, and thus paves the way for a change in attitude and behavior. When people are confused, they STOP! And then they develop an internal focus (a spontaneous hypnosis) as they quickly sort through everything they know in order to resolve the confusion. While the person's conscious mind is so preoccupied with making sense of something, the unconscious is more readily available for any suggestion that will reduce the dissonance. In a nutshell, that's the mechanism of confusion techniques. The relevant principles are listed in Table 6 below.

Confusion techniques can take a variety of forms, but generally fall into one of two categories: pattern interruption strategies and overload techniques. Pattern interruption techniques involve saying and/or doing something to deliberately interrupt the person's routine response style in some area. One may strive to interrupt a person's experience of a thought, a feeling, or behavior, or some other pattern, depending on the desired outcome. Disrupting the pattern and shifting the person onto a "new track" can effectively break the old pattern long enough to let a new and potentially helpful experience have a meaningful impact.

Table 6. Assumptions Regarding Confusion Techniques

People value clarity and understanding

Confusion, or lack of clarity, creates an unpleasant internal state, i.e., dissonance

Dissonance motivates striving to attain understanding

Wanting to attain understanding motivates a search for meaning and an increased receptivity to satisfactory (even if incorrect) explanations

People's behavior is patterned, and carrying out familiar patterns is most comfortable

Blocking the carrying out (i.e., interruption) of familiar patterns requires generating a novel response

The time span required to generate a new response is a period of amplified responsiveness to external cues

Table 7. Pattern Interruption Strategies

Confusion
Surprise, shock
Humor
Reframing
Double-binds
Paradox, symptom prescriptions
Task assignments, behavioral directives joining the client's frame
     of reference (utilization)
Confrontation
Hypnosis and hypnotic phenomena
Ordeals
Metaphors
Amplifying polarities
Externalizations

Interrupting a person's pattern may be accomplished in a variety of ways as listed in Table 7 above.

Changing some of the environmental variables surrounding the pattern (e.g., where the person "does" the symptom), shifting the sequence of the pattern's subcomponents, altering others' responses to the pattern, exaggerating or emphasizing the implications of the pattern, surrounding the desired responses with confusing irrelevancies, and building new associations to the pattern through outrageous and/or incongruent clinician responses are just a few techniques available to interrupt client patterns. Furthermore, one can use gestures to interrupt a client, one can dramatize with nonverbals the client's position, and one can use language patterns that are so ambiguous or are even blatantly in violation of normal speech syntax that the client becomes entranced through trying to figure out how a clinician can behave in such an unpredictable, even odd, way.

The following is a transcript of Milton Erickson using a confusion technique on a patient experiencing pain (in Haley, 1967; p. 152). Part of Erickson's strategy involved the use of language patterns violating the routine patterns of meaningful communication while embedding therapeutic suggestions at a deeper level. The normal flow of consciousness in the client is interrupted in order to accommodate Erickson's unusual speech patterns, allowing the client's unconscious to absorb meaningful suggestions in a beneficial way.

> (. . . some family member or friend) . . . *knows pain and knows no pain* and so do you wish to *know no pain* but comfort and you *do know comfort* and *no pain* and as *comfort increases* you know that you *cannot* say *no to ease and comfort* but you *can* say *no pain* and *know no pain* but *know comfort and ease.* . . .

While the client's conscious mind focuses on trying to make sense at a cognitive level out of a linguistic mess, at the feeling level the associations triggered by the suggestions to feel good and feel no pain allowed Erickson's patient the desired comfort.

The above transcript also demonstrates elements of the other form confusion techniques may take, namely overload techniques. Overload as a means for creating confusion can take the forms of excessive repetition and sensory overload. In the transcript above, Erickson's repetition of the suggestions to feel comfort and feel no pain are so frequent and so excessive while embedded in other confusing statements that it would be difficult to resist each and every one on a suggestion by suggestion basis. Repetition of suggestions is extremely tiresome (and boring) for the client's conscious mind, yet repetition is a well-known enhancer of the unconscious mind's learning process. Embedded in a confusion technique, however, are suggestions that are clear and actually make some sense. These can stand out as if illuminated in neon compared to the confusing background, and thus draw greater attention and potential impact.

The other form of overload, sensory overload, involves so overloading the person's conscious mind with information coming in from multiple sources that it can't possibly keep up; as the conscious mind struggles to stay focused, the unconscious can respond to a greater degree. An example of a sensory overload technique is the "Double Induction" technique originated by Kay Thompson and Robert Pearson (see Thompson's Frame of Reference section in chapter 8), and described by Stephen Gilligan (1987). With two clinicians *simultaneously* doing hypnotic inductions on a single client, the client may initially attempt to follow both clinicians' voices, but he or she quickly learns that it's simply not possible to consciously keep up with both for very long. Whatever information is offered that escapes conscious detection and analysis might still be incorporated on an unconscious level, and for the beleaguered and overloaded client, hypnosis may be a nice, relaxing place to escape to.

Sensory overload can involve the use of multiple (two or more) hypnotists working on a single client, or multiple stimuli (sounds, smells, sights . . .) operating on different levels. If you do not have the luxury of another clinician around to try this technique, you can even make a general induction tape and play it during a session while simultaneously doing your more personalized approach "live." You can even suggest to your client that, "You can listen to me . . . or, you can listen to me!" Such overload techniques can be especially useful in the treatment of individuals in pain (Yapko, 1988).

Confusion techniques for the purpose of induction require clearheadedness on the part of the clinician, demanding he or she know what he or she is doing at each moment. It also requires some dissociation on the part of the clinician (as well as the client) in order to keep from getting caught up in the confusion he or she is creating! One can build confusion around virtually any dimension of experience, from the days of the week ("You can relax on Tuesday but not nearly as well as on Wednesday and if you remember on Sunday how good it felt to relax on Friday you can remember one day on a Monday to take in a deep breath and . . .") to remembering ("How can one forget how good it feels to *go deeply into hypnosis* when one remembers that to forget what one remembers only reminds one to forget remembering the comfort and peace of remembering to forget what you've forgotten to remember about forgetting tension and *remembering comfort* . . ."). Table 8 below lists the specific dimensions of experience at which one can aim confusion strategies.

By offering confusing suggestions in a manner generally regarded as meaningful, the clinician induces the client to search and find meaning at deeper levels. Confusion techniques are especially good for clients deemed highly cognitive, especially those who tend to intellectualize their problems or feelings. The intellect cannot keep up for very long with an abundance of irrationalities embedded with meaning, and so overloads can shift the intellectual client onto a more affective level of relating.

In sum, confusion techniques are among the most complex and difficult techniques to use skillfully, but when they work, they work well. (I'm clear about that!)

CONCLUSION

The approaches to induction presented in this chapter are among the most spontaneous and effective means for inducing hypnosis in a naturalistic and collaborative way. Their inability to be scripted in a word-for-word manner is actually their strength. Hypnosis scripts may make clinicians feel a little less insecure about what to say, yet they are a reliable means for becoming more rigid and less creative in your work. Clinicians who develop skill in the use of these loosely structured and spontaneous approaches will have

---

Table 8. Categories of Confusion Methodologies

Cognitive
Sensory
Relational
Temporal
Role
Identity
Affective
Spatial
Behavioral

done so only through multiple sessions of practicing careful observation of client responses while developing the flexibility to turn each obtained response into one that enhances the quality of the interaction.

For Discussion

1. How are transderivational search and the ideodynamic processes operating in each of the inductions described in this chapter?
2. How does one's general internal or external orientation in relation to the world around us evolve? What implications for either mode of relating are there for doing effective hypnosis?
3. How does one "fight fire with fire" in everyday contexts? Give specific examples and describe the dynamics operating in each.
4. Should a clinician attempt to induce hypnosis in a client without first announcing his or her intention? Why or why not?
5. What is the basis for Erickson's claim that "out of confusion comes enlightenment"? Is confusion useful for facilitating change? Why or why not? Are there times in your own experience you have had an "Aha!" experience? Describe it.

Things to Do

1. List 25 common everyday experiences where elements of hypnosis are evident. Outline a set of suggestions for each as if describing them were an induction procedure.
2. Have two peers talk to you simultaneously on two different subjects and try to follow each. What do you experience?
3. Describe to your class in as hypnotic a demeanor as you can (slowly, modeling absorption, using sensory descriptors, etc.) an ostensibly nonhypnotic experience in which you relaxed comfortably (e.g., riding a bike, hiking in the woods, sitting in a sauna). What is your audience's response?

REFERENCES

Barker, P. (1985). *Using metaphors in psychotherapy*. New York: Brunner/Mazel.
Brown, P. (1993). Hypnosis and metaphor. In J. Rhue, S. Lynn, & I. Kirsch (Eds.), *Handbook of clinical hypnosis* (pp. 291–308). Washington, D.C.: American Psychological Association.

Erickson, M. (1958). Naturalistic techniques of hypnosis. *American Journal of Clinical Hypnosis, 1,* 3–8.

—— (1959). Further clinical techniques of hypnosis: Utilization techniques. *American Journal of Clinical Hypnosis, 2,* 3–21.

—— (1964). The confusion technique in hypnosis. *American Journal of Clinical Hypnosis, 6,* 185–207.

Erickson, M., Rossi, E., & Rossi, S. (1976). *Hypnotic realities: The induction of clinical hypnosis and forms of indirect suggestion.* New York: Irvington.

Gilligan, S. (1987). *Therapeutic trances: The cooperation principle in Ericksonian hypnotherapy.* New York: Brunner/Mazel.

Grinder, J., & Bandler, R. (1981). *Trance-formations: Neuro-Linguistic Programming and the structure of hypnosis.* Moab, UT: Real People.

Haley, J. (Ed.) (1967). *Advanced techniques of hypnosis and therapy: Selected papers of Milton H. Erickson, M.D.* New York: Grune & Stratton.

—— (1973). *Uncommon therapy: The psychiatric techniques of Milton H. Erickson, M.D.* New York: Norton.

Hammond, D. (Ed.) (1990). *Handbook of hypnotic suggestions and metaphors.* New York: Norton.

Kirsch, I. (2000). The response set theory of hypnosis. *American Journal of Clinical Hypnosis, 42,* 3–4, 274–93.

Lankton, S., & Lankton, C. (1983). *The answer within: A clinical framework of Ericksonian hypnotherapy.* New York: Brunner/Mazel.

—— (1989). *Tales of enchantment: Goal-oriented metaphors for adults and children in therapy.* New York: Brunner/Mazel.

Lynn, S., Kirsch, I., Neufeld, J., & Rhue, J. (1996). Clinical hypnosis: Assessment, applications, and treatment considerations. In S. Lynn, I. Kirsch, & J. Rhue (Eds.), *Casebook of clinical hypnosis* (pp. 3–30). Washington, D.C.: American Psychological Association.

Otani, A. (1989). The confusion technique untangled: Its theoretical rationale and preliminary classification. *American Journal of Clinical Hypnosis, 31,* 164–72.

Rosen, S. (1982). *My voice will go with you: The teaching tales of Milton H. Erickson.* New York: Norton.

Watzlawick, P. (1985). Hypnotherapy without trance. In J. Zeig (Ed.), *Ericksonian psychotherapy, Vol. 1: Structures* (pp. 5–14). New York: Brunner/Mazel.

Yapko, M. (1988). Confusion methodologies in the management of pain. *Hypnos: Swedish Journal of Hypnosis in Psychotherapy and Psychosomatic Medicine, 15,* 163–73.

—— (2001). Revisiting the question: What is Ericksonian hypnosis? In B. Geary & J. Zeig (Eds.), *The handbook of Ericksonian psychotherapy* (pp. 168–86). Phoenix, AZ: The Milton H. Erickson Foundation Press.

Zeig, J. (Ed.) (1980). *A teaching seminar with Milton H. Erickson, M.D.* New York: Brunner/Mazel.

—— (2001). Hypnotic induction. In B. Geary & J. Zeig (Eds.), *The handbook of Ericksonian psychotherapy* (pp. 18–30). Phoenix, AZ: The Milton H. Erickson Foundation Press.

16

Hypnotic Phenomena: Eliciting and Utilizing Hypnotic Resources

Witchcraft, the supernatural, and hypnosis are frequently lumped together as "the dark side of the force" in the minds of some seriously misinformed people. Along with recent trends in America of fundamentalist religious revival have come occasional accusations sent my way about "doing the Devil's work" because of my use of hypnosis. If you have not personally experienced such fear and ignorance, consider yourself fortunate. It's hard to believe, but it's true that many people have an entirely irrational fear of hypnosis. How do hypnosis books still manage to work their way onto the shelf in the Occult Books section of some bookstores? The answer to that question lies in the many hypnotic phenomena that are, to the untrained observer, unusual at least and spooky at most.

The various so-called classic hypnotic phenomena that will be defined and described in this chapter are the basic ingredients for the therapeutic applications of hypnosis. Furthermore, they are the basic building blocks of *all* experience, differing from their clinical applications only in degree, not kind (Spanos, 1991; Wagstaff, 1991). Shades of hypnotic phenomena are found in ongoing daily experience, but they are most dramatic to observe (and experience) when distilled to their essence as in structured hypnotic processes. These hypnotic phenomena can be assembled in ways that may help or hurt, depending on their associated content. More will be said about this idea later, particularly in relation to hypnotic phenomena and symptom formation.

The various hypnotic phenomena represent valuable but typically underdeveloped capacities of human beings. Each person is capable of these hypnotic phenomena to one degree or another in the formal hypnotic interaction because these are, in a sense, clinically structured amplifications of everyday experiences. In fact, these capacities are a necessary part of our experience in order for us to function in a normal, healthy way (Bányai, 1991). To claim someone cannot be hypnotized is questionable, for if the person could not focus, remember, imagine, behave in automatic ways, and demonstrate other such hypnotic phenomena, he or she simply could not survive. Of course, people differ in these abilities, and some may have marginal ability at best, but finding someone who can't do any of these at all would be pretty rare.

When I describe the various hypnotic phenomena, I will also describe examples of everyday contexts in which they naturally or spontaneously occur. People generally do not think of these random experiences as related to hypnosis, but they are structurally identical. When they occur, people tend to dismiss them lightly with some variation of, "Gee, that's kinda strange." No further thought is given them, because they seem to "just happen." The average person senses no participation in or control over the experience. This is a primary reason for acquiring skills with hypnotic patterns: Rather than having such potentially useful experiences remain random and seemingly out of control, clinicians familiar with hypnosis can facilitate these experiences *at will* for meaningful reasons, instilling in clients a greater sense of control in their lives.

The recognition that hypnotic phenomena occur routinely in people is, in most ways, unique to the utilization approach. In other models of hypnosis, hypnotic phenomena are considered manifestations of the separate and distinct state called "hypnosis." Even when others have claimed hypnotic phenomena are concentrated forms of everyday occurrences, the techniques used to obtain such responses have incongruously only been ritualistic and artificial (Gilligan, 1987; Lankton & Lankton, 1983). The arbitrary and content-filled structure of these techniques separates them from the utilization approach, which emphasizes a more natural and personally meaningful style for facilitating these responses.

Table 9. Classical Hypnotic Phenomena*

Age Regression
Age Progression (pseudo orientation in time)
Amnesia
Analgesia
Anesthesia
Catalepsy
Dissociation
Hallucinations (positive, negative)
Ideodynamic responses (ideoaffective, ideomotor,
     ideosensory)
Sensory Alterations
Time Distortion

*Value as Building Blocks: Neutral

Both structured and naturalistic inductions have been presented in the two previous chapters, and consistent with my desire to acquaint you with the range of possibilities, both structured and naturalistic approaches to eliciting hypnotic phenomena will be presented in this chapter. Applications of these phenomena in clinical contexts will be discussed in later chapters.

The hypnotic interaction was described in chapter 14 as taking place in phases (i.e., attentional absorption, induction and deepening, therapeutic utilization, and disengagement). This and later chapters will focus on the third phase, the phase of therapeutic utilization where hypnosis is used to facilitate some therapeutic intervention. Realistically, there is no clear dividing line between the different stages of hypnosis, and therapy may therefore take place at any point in the process. Usually, however, therapy is done in this utilization phase following the induction process. The more structured the approach, the more the facilitation of hypnotic phenomena will be concentrated in this particular stage.

As you read each of the following sections, you might think of your own experience of that particular hypnotic phenomenon, specifically what happened and what the context was. Discovering the everyday aspects of hypnotic experience can allow you to notice more of the spontaneous hypnotic responses arising in your clients as you interact with them, broadening your capacity for therapeutic utilization. In fact, the familiarity with everyday contexts where hypnotic responses occur is the basis for the naturalistic utilization approaches (Yapko, 2001a; Zeig, 1980). The general approach involves finding and describing a routine situation in which the desired response is likely to naturally occur. The client can become absorbed in that suggested experience and may then naturally demonstrate the hypnotic phenomenon more easily with direct suggestions to do so or perhaps even without the clinician directly asking for it. It has long been known that simply imagining the occurrence of a movement can bring that movement about (Arnold, 1946). T. X. Barber, Nicholas Spanos, and John Chaves wrote in 1974 that hypnotic responses can be produced by imagining "a situation which, if it actually occurred, would tend to give rise to the behavior that was suggested" (p. 62). Similarly, emotions, perceptions, and fantasies can be suggested that will give rise to hypnotic phenomena.

Here, then, are the classical hypnotic phenomena, presented in alphabetical order for easy reference.

AGE REGRESSION

DESCRIPTION

Age regression is defined as an intensified absorption in and utilization of memory. Age regression techniques involve either guiding the client back in time to some experience in order to re-experience it (called "revivification") as if it were happening in the here-and-now, or simply having the person remember the experience as vividly as possible (called "hypermnesia"). In revivification, the client is immersed in the experience, reliving it in a close parallel to the way the memory was incorporated at the time it actually happened. In hypermnesia, the person is in the present while simultaneously recalling vividly the details of the memory.

Most people have an intuitive understanding of how profoundly our previous experiences affect our current thoughts, feelings, and behaviors. Certainly, psychology has amassed vast amounts of information to substantiate the point. Consequently, age regression is one of the most widely used hypnotic patterns in therapeutic work. Age regression as a clinical technique provides an opportunity to go back in time, whether it be into the recent or distant past, in order to recall forgotten memories of significant events that can serve to help redefine one's view of oneself, or to "work through" old memories in order to reach new and more adaptive conclusions. Memory is a process, not an event. *Memory is based on subjective perception, and is therefore malleable and dynamic.* Memories can change in quality over time, as new experiences mingle with and affect older ones. Memories can be influenced intentionally or unintentionally because of their subjective and suggestible nature (Loftus & Hoffman, 1989; Sheehan, 1988, 1995).

In defining age regression as the intense absorption in and utilization of memory, the everyday aspects of age regression can become apparent, for people drift into memories routinely. If a song associated with a high school sweetheart comes on the radio, the listener can become absorbed in that person's memory and recall vividly things they did together and events taking place in their lives at that time. For a period of time, the rest of the world fades from awareness while the person is deeply internally absorbed and focused on memories, even re-experiencing profoundly the feelings from that time in his or her life.

Age regression is as commonplace as that kind of experience. Any cue that triggers the person to go back in time to remember or relive some event is stimulating a "spontaneous age regression." Looking at photographs, hearing a certain song, seeing an old friend, and re-experiencing a feeling not felt in a long time are all examples of routine age regressions.

Age regressions can be structured to engage someone deliberately in some memory that seems to have relevance to the symptoms the person is experiencing. People literally define themselves according to their memories, especially those memories that are of highly charged significant emotional events. Many symptoms do, in fact, arise because of how people have interpreted the meaning of past events, and so exploring and addressing memories often becomes a critical part of treatment.

AGE REGRESSION AT THE HEART
OF THE FIELD'S BIGGEST CONTROVERSY

At this point, I must now raise the issue that represents what has been a most bitterly emotionally charged and divisive issue, not only in the field of hypnosis, but in the mental health profession as a whole. It has been known as the "repressed memory controversy," the "false memory debate," the "memory wars," and by a variety of far more inflammatory names. Unless you were in blissful oblivion somewhere during the latter half of the '90s, you were reading almost daily about high-profile trials, reading articles by experts vigorously arguing opposite positions, hearing experts on television vehemently arguing mutually exclusive "realities," all revolving around the issue of whether presumably repressed memories uncovered through therapy in general and hypnosis (i.e., age regression) in particular should be considered valid (Loftus, 1993; Terr, 1994; Yapko, 1993, 1994a).

There are many therapists who have been trained (either academically or self-taught) and who have come to believe that virtually all symptoms are necessarily a product of past experiences and even past traumas, almost invariably childhood sexual abuse, that need to be identified and "worked through." Thus, if someone is unable to recall a memory that would account for the type and severity of someone's symptoms, the assumption is that the memory has been repressed, that is, split off from consciousness as a psychological defense. It is further assumed that excavating the memory is necessary for recovery (Blume, 1990; Fredrickson, 1992). In searching for presumably repressed memories, the critically important questions are these: Are traumatic memories "locked away" and does finding the "key" (with hypnosis or other memory recovery techniques) open them up for accurate recall? Or, are the techniques used for locating and retrieving memories themselves capable of contaminating or distorting memories without either the clinician or client realizing it? To go a step further, can a well-meaning clinician and an unwitting client even *create* complex and emotionally charged memories that seem genuine yet are entirely fabricated (called confabulations)?

The answers to these questions are now reasonably well established, and the controversy has all but died away. The answer to the first question is yes, traumatic memories can be locked away only to emerge much later (Spiegel, 1993). This appears to be an uncommon phenomenon. However, what can only be addressed—but not necessarily answered—is the question of the accuracy of such memories. These memories can be entirely accurate, partly accurate, partly inaccurate, and entirely inaccurate. Without objective evidence to corroborate a memory, there is no known technology for determining its veracity. *Hypnosis does not reveal the truth.* (More detail in the narrative or a more emotional telling of the episode does *not* mean it is any more likely to be true.) Neither does so-called truth serum or a lie-detector test, which is why information obtained through these tools of inquiry is not generally allowed in our courts. Since a true recovered memory cannot be reliably distinguished from a confabulation, it becomes even more critical for a clinician to minimize his or her potential contamination of a memory through unwitting suggestion.

The second and third questions above, regarding the memory recovery techniques themselves distorting or even creating memories, can both be answered with a firm yes. Memories have been shown to be highly responsive to a variety of suggestive influences in *and* out of hypnosis (Labelle, Laurence, Nadon & Perry, 1990; Lynn, 2001; Lynn, Weekes, & Milano, 1989; McConkey, 1992; Orne, Whitehouse, Dinges, & Orne, 1996; Ready, Bothwell, & Brigham, 1997; Scheflin & Frischholz, 1999).

FOCAL POINT: CREATING FALSE MEMORIES

The ability to unwittingly create false memories is an issue of such great importance that it is being given this small but special place in this book. It is a difficult issue with many different complicating variables, and it must be well considered in order to avoid the potential harm of therapy in general and hypnosis in particular.

Let's sidestep the highly emotional issue of repressed memories of childhood sexual abuse for a moment. Instead, let's consider this letter advertising a workshop I received, reproduced here in edited form.

"Dr. Yapko:
    As bizarre as the following question seems, please take the time to read further and give serious consideration to the subject discussed. During a hypnosis session, have you ever had a client that believes that he/she has had an alien (extraterrestrial) abduction or encounter? Has this person experienced missing time or repetitive dreams about unusual night visitors? In the last four years there has been a 65% increase in reported abduction cases. Many of these reports have surfaced during hypnosis sessions.
    What would you do if information similar to this was revealed by one of your clients during a hypnotic session? How do you help this person? . . . Some of the people have had conscious recall of the event. However, the majority of them recalled the encounter while under hypnosis—which many had sought out to help them with other problems . . ."

What is your reaction to this letter? Do you believe people are genuinely being abducted by extraterrestrials, or is there something else going on here?

Let's look at the serious implications of this letter, especially as they relate to the practice of psychotherapy. One fact the letter doesn't mention is that a popular book called *Communion: A True Story* by Whitley Strieber (1995) came out and received substantial media attention. The book is an intelligent and articulate description of the author's belief he has had repeated experiences of being abducted by extraterrestrials. Prior to becoming aware of the abductions, all Strieber had were periods of time he was amnesic for, and unusual dreams of abduction in which he served as a human guinea pig for extraterrestrials' experiments. Not long after, Harvard psychiatrist and Pulitzer Prize winner John Mack wrote a book called *Abduction: Human Encounters With Aliens* (1997), describing his work with patients who uncovered lots of details of their extraterrestrial abductions which they revealed with great emotional intensity with his "help." A psychiatrist from Harvard, a title with considerable prestige and credibility, he seemingly believes in these accounts and sees no undue influence on his part in bringing such apparently repressed memories to the surface. Is it a coincidence that there is a "65% increase in reported abduction cases" following the release of these books and the associated media "buzz" around them? I think not.

If so many people can be convinced so easily of "trance channelers" (people who claim to go into a trance and become the medium through which other entities, perhaps as old as 35,000 years according to one, can share their "wisdom") and people who can communicate with the dead, thanks to their popular books and even their own television shows, then you can convince a percentage of the population of *anything*. Hypnotic past-life regression, hypnotic ESP, hypnotic aura-reading, and countless other "applications" of hypnosis are offered to those who are either open to or already have beliefs in such phenomena.

So what's the problem? The serious problem is that a seemingly benevolent clinician can suggest an experience that the individual accepts as literally "true." With extraterrestrial abductions, it is easy to dismiss the problem lightly. However, consider what happens if what is suggested instead is that, "You have symptoms that suggest to me you may have been molested as a child. Let's do hypnosis to find out."

I am aware of clinicians too numerous to count who have become "molestation specialists," "traumatists," "certified regression specialists," and adopted other similar titles, who have a rudimentary checklist of "signs of an abuse survivor." These include poor self-esteem, sexual avoidance or apathy, relationship difficulties, unresolved anger toward one or both parents, and other such symptoms. Don't these same "signs" show up in almost everyone? But, a clinician intent on finding molestation issues to resolve can unwittingly plant the suggestion in the client's mind of the possibility of such an experience in her background. (e.g., "Were you sexually abused as a child? No? Well, the fact that you can't remember it is normal, it's called repression"). Then, in hypnosis, the clinician can ask leading questions: "Are you alone with your (father, uncle, family friend . . .)? Is he touching you? Why is he touching you? Where is he touching you? Is it a touch, or does it feel creepy like a fondle? It's okay, you're safe now and you can remember . . . " The client can then "discover repressed memories" that can become the basis for a whole new identity—that of a molest victim. But, the memories *may* have no basis in reality.

What made this issue so deeply controversial and emotionally charged was a natural and sincere desire to hear abused people tell their devastating stories when for so long they had been suffering silently or else were disbelieved and marginalized. The momentum for therapists was in the direction of believing *all* such stories, regardless of the conditions leading up to their emergence. As cooler-headed researchers and clinicians made their respective points, it became clear that hearing and supporting traumatized people remains a critically important agenda for the mental health profession, but at the same time clinicians would have to take the responsibility to learn and put into practice the lesson that they were catalysts for the quality of the memories that came up in their clients. *Clinicians would have to acknowledge and implement the principle that they are part of the process, not just outside observers of the process.* (You learned this same principle about doing hypnosis, namely that your client's responses are not separate and distinct from the things you say and do.) The use of direct suggestions, or even just leading questions, amplified in age regression, can create a false memory that can become a pathological frame of reference for the client that may last a lifetime. But be reminded, formal hypnosis is not necessary for this to occur.

Just to clarify and reinforce the key point of this section: This controversy revolved around *suggested memories* of abuse given to the client *by the clinician* when the client had symptoms but no recollection of any such trauma. *If someone knows now and has always known he or she was abused, then the issue is moot: Such memories can be believed and considered as reliable as any others.*

To say this sensitive issue is complicated is a gross understatement. For the reader who wants to study this issue in greater depth, there are many excellent sources to refer to. These include the works of Baker (1992); Brown, Scheflin, and Hammond (1998); Ceci and Bruck (1995); Doris (1991); Gardner (1992); Loftus and Ketcham (1994); Lynn and McConkey (1998); McConkey and Sheehan (1995); Ofshe and Watters (1994); Schachter (1996); Spanos (1996); Terr (1994); van der Kolk (1994); and Yapko (1994b); all of which are listed in this chapter's reference section.

GENERAL STRATEGIES TO ELICIT AGE REGRESSION

In using age regression clinically, at least two general strategies can be employed, each giving rise to a variety of specific techniques. The first general strategy concerns the use of age regression to go back to negative, or even traumatic kinds of experiences. The intention is to allow the client to explore the event(s), release pent-up feelings ("catharsis") while simultaneously providing new ways of looking at that situation ("reframing") that may help him or her release or redefine whatever negative influences from that experience may still be affecting his or her life. In this strategy, either revivification or hypermnesia may be employed, depending on the clinician's judgment as to how immersed in or distant from the experience the client can be in order to receive maximum benefit. For example, if a client felt rejected by his or her mother, and feels worthless as a result, the clinician may want to take the client back in time through revivification to relive one or more of the interactions critical in developing that feeling. This could be done by helping him or her to relive the feelings and re-experience the sights and sounds of that event while supporting him or her in expressing those feelings. Then, the clinician can focus him or her on dimensions of that experience previously not consciously attended to by him or her. By adding new understandings and insights to the old memory, one can help the client to re-shape the memory. Maybe the client can be encouraged to feel loved and cared for by a mother who was, perhaps, guilty of nothing more than expressing her affection in a distant way (or not at all) because of her own emotional limitations, rather than because of the daughter's presumed lack of worthiness.

Reaching a new conclusion about an old experience can change your feeling about yourself quite dramatically. Having the client immersed in the experience allows for its powerful emotional impact. In contrast, if one were working with a woman who had the terrible experience of being raped, putting her back in that intense situation through revivification is generally an undesirable alternative. She may be better helped through the more psychologically distant technique of hypermnesia. In this approach, she can *safely* be in the here-and-now while working through the trauma of the past (Smith, 1993).

The second general strategy of age regression is one of accessing and amplifying client resources, and is compatible with and easily integrated with the first. The strategy involves identifying and making use of specific problem-solving abilities the client has demonstrated in past situations but is not currently using, unfortunately to his or her own detriment. Often, the client has positive abilities he or she doesn't recognize, and because he or she doesn't have an awareness for them and a means to access them, they lie dormant. In using age regression, the clinician can help the client rediscover in his or her own past personal experience the very abilities that will allow him or her to manage the current situation in a more adaptive way. For example, if someone were complaining of difficulty in learning something new, the clinician might guide the person back in time to a variety of past experiences of initially feeling frustrated in learning something, and then showing how each frustration eventually led to mastery of that information and greater self-confidence in that area. Learning to get dressed, to read and write, to drive a car, and countless other experiences all started out being intimidating new experiences and later became routine, automatic abilities. Immersing the client in the experience of the satisfaction of mastering learnings that once seemed difficult can help him or her build a more positive attitude (i.e., frustration tolerance) toward the present challenges.

APPROACHES TO ELICITING AGE REGRESSION

Any pattern of suggestion that helps the client subjectively experience going back in time is an approach to age regression. One general approach to age regression employs suggestions that involve the use of structured and imaginative imageries as the trigger to recapture past experiences. Other approaches involve more naturalistic, everyday approaches to immersion in memory. Either approach can be a good one, depending on the client's response style.

Patterns that make use of the client's imagination include the various "special vehicle" approaches (e.g., train, plane, time machine, space ship, elevator, and the like) that can transport the client back in time to the event under consideration. The special vehicle imagery is an artificial, concrete, and content-oriented means for structuring the experience, and thus requires a considerable amount of detail in order to facilitate the regressive process for the client. The following is an example of an age regression approach (initiated after induction and deepening) using a "special train":

> ... and now that you can experience yourself as comfortably relaxed ... you can let yourself have the experience in your mind ... of going to a special train station ... a train station unlike any you've ever experienced before ... where the trains that run are so unusual in their ability to take you back in time ... and you can go back in time ... to important experiences you haven't thought about in a long, long time ... and you can walk over to one and see yourself getting onto the most interesting-looking train ... and you can easily find your way to a seat that is so comfortable to sit in ... so soft you can rest there ... deeply resting ... and then as you feel the train begin to move in a gentle and pleasant way ... you can experience the distinct movement of the train's motion ... going backward in time ... slowly at first ... then faster ... building a powerful momentum ... and as you look out the window ... and see the events of your life

moving past you like so many telephone poles you pass on the way, the
memories of yesterday . . . then the day before . . . and the day before . . . and
the day before . . . and all the days before . . . can drift through your mind as
you go further and further into the past . . . when way back then becomes
now . . . and then the train begins to slow down . . . and then it comes to a
stop . . . and now you can step off the train to find yourself in that situation
that was so important to you . . . and being in that situation now, you can
see the sights, hear the sounds, and feel the feelings of that time and
place . . . *this* time and place. . . .

At this point, dialogue between the clinician and client may be initiated, in order to elicit the details of the memory he or she is re-experiencing. Asking the client where in time he or she is, who else is present in the
memory, what exactly is occurring, what he or she is thinking, feeling, or
doing, as well as any other relevant questions can lead the clinician to better
understand how the experience was incorporated by the client as a memory
so that a differing perspective, one that may be more adaptive, may be offered as part of the therapy.

If the client knows when a certain significant event occurred, the clinician can regress the client back to that specific time. Often, though, the
client has no idea when a certain feeling, thought, or behavior started. In
such instances, the clinician can offer some process-oriented suggestions,
such as in the special train example above in which no particular age or
context for the regression were specified. In that example, it was left entirely to the client to choose an experience to focus on as representative of
his or her presenting problem's evolution. The clinician must ask the client
to verbalize the details of his or her experience at some point so he or she
can assist the client in having access to as much of the memory as possible
and in order to determine where and when to intervene.

Whatever approach you choose to employ as the catalyst for the age
regression experience, the use of more details to associate to encourages a
greater involvement in the experience. To accomplish a more personally
distant experience of the past event, suggestions can be provided that the
client is present (dissociated) in the secure here-and-now, and it can be "as if
you are watching a movie of an experience . . . and as you watch comfortably . . . you can learn something important from yourself over there . . ."

More naturalistic approaches to age regression involve offering indirect suggestions to become engaged in memory without the formality of
saying, "Now you can go back in the past." Patterns include asking accessing questions to orient the person to his or her own past personal history,
and conversationally sharing learnings from past personal or professional
experiences. Asking questions to orient the person to his or her own past
experiences as an approach involves the client in a search through his or her
past in order to recall the appropriate events necessary to respond meaning-

fully. Such a search can start out as a more distant memory simply being cognitively remembered, but then skillful further questioning can begin to immerse the client in the memory in order to actually re-experience it. The following is an example of such a pattern:

Clinician: Can you remember your fourth-grade teacher? (Orienting the client to age nine or ten)

Client: Sure, it was Miss Smith. As I recall, she was a really nice teacher. (Starting to remember that teacher and some associated childhood experiences)

Clinician: Fourth grade can certainly be an interesting time in one's life . . . many changes can take place in a person's thinking . . . I wonder if you can remember which event of that time in your life was especially important to you? . . .

Client: Well . . . there was a time once when I got into trouble at school and my mother . . . (Relates the story's details)

Clinician: Can you . . . *see yourself clearly in that experience*? . . . as you see yourself in that experience, you can remember how you felt, can't you . . . and those feelings are feelings that are still a part of you . . . even though you haven't thought about them in a long while . . . and you can see the other people and how they look . . . how they are dressed . . . and you can hear what they say that is so important to you . . . and what do they say? . . .

As the clinician asks the client to fill in the details of the memory, the client naturally becomes more and more immersed in it to the point of starting to re-experience it (notice the changing of tenses from past to present). This type of regression is a routine part of many psychotherapies, particularly those that focus on the past as a means of better understanding and altering the present. Such gradual immersion in the memory is a smooth and natural approach for focusing on the past. The involvement becomes greater and greater as the clinician involves more and more of the person in all the sensory components of the memory to as great a degree as possible.

In order to make the experience of going back into the past less personally threatening, the clinician can indirectly facilitate regression by describing his or her own relevant past learnings, or the relevant past learnings of others. When the experience of others is described, the client naturally tends to project him- or herself into that situation, imagining how he or she would feel or act in that situation. Talking about the experiences of others as children, for example, can build an identification for the client on the basis of his or her own experiences as a child. Thus, the regression occurs indirectly through identification and projection, and the client can go back in time to recall or re-experience the relevant memories. The following is an example of such an approach, offered to a client who felt guilty unnecessarily and unjustly about her parents having divorced when she was only six years old. The regression involves taking the client back to that time in order to re-experience the irrational feeling she that she was somehow responsible for her parents' divorce. This metaphorical example stops before the point of making the hurtful decision, and does not go into the actual re-decision therapy for such a problem.

Clinician: Children are quite remarkable, don't you think?

Client: Yes, I do.

Clinician: Sometimes kids think the whole world revolves around them . . . like life is a universal game of "peek-a-boo" . . . that the whole world stops for a while . . . and goes away to someplace else . . . who knows where . . . maybe someplace really calming and beautiful . . . when the child closes her eyes and the world disappears . . . how well can you remember being a child . . . and closing your eyes . . . and wondering where everyone went? . . .

Client: I used to play hide-and-seek a lot as a child, and I can remember worrying sometimes I'd be all alone, that when I closed my eyes everyone would be gone and I'd never find them again . . . but, of course, that's just a child's silly fears.

Clinician: That's interesting, because a child I'm working with described that same feeling . . . she's almost seven years old now, and she's feeling very proud of being in the first grade . . . excited and thrilled . . . the way almost all kids once were . . . you can remember that, can't you? . . . about being in school and learning to learn about how much there is to learn . . . and that there is a huge and complex world out there . . . a world much bigger than the world of a six-year-old . . . but the six-year-old doesn't know that yet . . . she still has to learn to read and write . . . about science and math . . . about adults and other kids . . . about falling in and out of love . . . and the six-year-old's world is always changing and growing . . . but not so fast as she thinks . . . because part of her still thinks the world revolves around her . . . and that she can cause big things to happen . . . and she won't learn until she's older . . . that the world doesn't revolve around her at all . . . that she's just six . . . and, understandably, afraid of being alone . . .

In the above example, the clinician is matching the part of the client that is feeling overly responsible at age six with the thoughts and feelings of a six-year-old. When these are described in a way that can allow the client to recapture her similar thoughts and feelings, she can age regress in a more spontaneous and naturalistic way. Furthermore, the seeds for the subsequent therapy are being planted simultaneously when the therapist points out in a nonthreatening way the distorted perceptions of a six-year-old. This can pave the way for the client to accept that her thoughts at that time might have been distorted also, and may therefore be more easily transformed.

Other techniques for age regression include: (1) Affect or somatic bridging, where the client's current feeling or awareness is linked ("bridged") to the first time, or one of the first times, he or she had that same feeling or awareness (". . . and as you continue to be aware of that 'abandoned feeling' you've described, you can drift back in time and recall the first time you ever had that same feeling"); (2) Temporal disorientation, in which confusional suggestions are employed to disorient the client from "now" and reorient the person to "then" ("What happens now and then is that remembering then now reminds you now of then when then is so important and when then becomes now because yesterday led to today and you can remember yesterday as if it were now because now and then remembering then as if it were now can be so important . . ."); and, (3) Age progression and regression, in which the client is first guided into the future at which time he or she can remember the things that have happened in his or her past ("Look forward to the times that you can look back . . ."). By orienting to the future first, an even greater emotional distance is created from past experiences, making them easier to recapture and use therapeutically.

Age regression is one of the most widely used and beneficial applications of clinical hypnosis. The clarity of long forgotten memories that can be elicited or the power of constant, intrusive memories that can be restructured are common components of clinical work in general and the use of hypnosis in particular. Knowing the mechanisms of memory, including its

---

Table 10. Age Regression Strategies

Direct regression to a specific time or situation
Affect or somatic bridging
Imagery, special vehicle techniques
Indirect associational suggestions
Metaphorical approaches
Gradual regression
Temporal disorientation
Age progression and regression

strengths and limitations, is vital to sound clinical practice. If you haven't yet made a study of memory, I'd encourage you to do so before your next client walks in and says some variation of, "When I was ten, here's what happened to me . . ."

AGE PROGRESSION

DESCRIPTION

In contrast to age regression's utilization of memory, age progression involves a utilization of projections of the future. Age progression involves guiding the client subjectively into the future, where he or she may have the opportunity to imagine and experience the consequences of current or new choices, integrate meanings at deeper levels, rehearse new patterns of thought, feeling or behavior, and, in general, obtain more of an overview of his or her life than a narrower focus on day-to-day living typically affords. You can think of it as encouraging hindsight while it is still foresight.

Projecting on the basis of current trends what is likely to develop in the future is not just a pastime for futurists. Foresight is a vital skill to possess, and is quite probably the best tool of *prevention* that therapists could be teaching their clients, if only more of them would be far-sighted enough to do so. People have a part of them that can plan and allow for the possibilities of future experience. It is a resource that, with practice, can become more skilled and efficient. But, even in basic form, people have a sense of how today relates to tomorrow. Common remarks like, "See you there next week," "I'll read that tomorrow and get it back to you by next week," "I'd like to enroll in that new program next year," and "When I retire I'd like to spend my time traveling," are all statements of intent regarding future experience. In order to make such statements realistically, the person must project some portion of him- or herself into that experience and imagine in some detail what it would or will be like. Any suggestive communication strategy that orients the client experientially to future events is an age progression pattern.

There are differing theoretical views on the dynamics of future orientation. Some hold the view that a client's future projections are purely fantasy material that have little or no relationship to the actual life experiences that will unfold over time. Such projections are considered useful in the same way as Rorschach inkblot responses might be—as interesting reflectors of unconscious dynamics only, with little true bearing on the future. Others hold the view that the unconscious has within it a "pre-programmed destiny" (acquired early in life through socialization according to believers with a social-learning orientation, acquired genetically according to believers with a biological orientation, or acquired through the evolving soul for those with a spiritual or philosophical orientation). The destiny of the person is thought to become available to the person through hypnotic patterns of age progression, when the "all-knowing" unconscious is tapped by the clinician.

My perspective is that age progression is an extrapolation of personal trends, including one's motivations, feelings, behaviors, and interactional patterns. The client in hypnosis can examine and extrapolate relevant trends and, depending on his or her degree of insight into them, can anticipate eventual outcomes. Many personal patterns, conscious or otherwise, are quite predictable. You don't have to be a psychic to predict someone's reactions or behaviors accurately when you know something about how they tend to see things. That applies to predicting yourself as well. But, age progression is more than just predicting. It's about becoming *absorbed in the future as if it's now*, giving rise to understandings and emotions not easily accessible in other ways.

STRATEGIES TO ELICIT AGE PROGRESSION

Age progression can be used in at least two general, complementary ways. One is as a therapeutic intervention, and the other is as a check on one's clinical work. Both applications involve guiding the client into a future orientation, but for different purposes.

Age progression for therapeutic purposes can be structured in many ways. Most clinicians are well aware of the "self-fulfilling prophecy," the unconscious alignment of behavior with an expectation. One way to think about age progression is as the deliberate creation of a therapeutic self-fulfilling prophecy, that is, an expectation of change that can be the foundation for the client adopting new adaptive behaviors. Irving Kirsch's view of hypnosis as a "non-deceptive placebo" is a parallel construct highlighting the vital role of expectancy in hypnosis and psychotherapy (1993, 2000). Most important of all in age progression is the ability to experience some of the benefits of implementing the changes encouraged in the client through the therapy. To "jump ahead" and preview and even feel the positive consequences of making important changes helps motivate the client to go ahead and actually do so. It takes the changes out of the realm of theory and gives them some life, some substance in the mind of the client. Other therapies (such as cognitive therapy's use of a "success imagery" strategy in which the client mentally rehearses the desired behavior leading to successful results) also recognize the value of lifting the client out of the moment and orienting him or her to future benefits, but hypnosis can make this process more intense and multidimensional (Torem, 1992).

Utilizing an age progression for the purpose of checking on one's work is one way of assessing two very important dimensions of therapeutic intervention. Specifically, one can assess whether the intervention's results will likely be lasting ones, and what impact on the client's life system the intervention will ultimately have. Even though the change under consideration may seem an obviously beneficial one, there may be less obvious factors (personal, situational, or interpersonal) that can work to keep the client from fully succeeding in his or her endeavors. Age progression allows the client to project into the future how he or she looks and feels after the change, how he or she looks and feels handling old situations in new ways, how others will likely react to his or her change, what areas might continue to be difficult for him or her, and, in general, which areas of his or her life have been affected positively and which negatively. Such information can be invaluable to the clinician in formulating the intervention while simultaneously checking on the impact of his or her work.

If a client experiences age progression and still has the presenting complaint well into the future, clearly the therapy isn't over. For example, if after working with a client who wants to stop smoking the clinician senses he or she has guided the client into accepting that he or she no longer needs or wants to smoke, and then the clinician does an age progression technique and the client still experiences him- or herself a month (a day, a week, whatever) into the future as a smoker, then the therapy cannot have been successful. Questioning the age-progressed client about various dimensions of his or her "recent" experience (post-therapy) can help the clinician discover what factors might play a role in the client restarting or continuing to smoke that had not been adequately addressed in the intervention. If the age-progressed client claims he or she wasn't smoking after therapy until he or she got into an argument with her boss, the clinician now knows he or she must provide some tools for effectively managing such a situation without smoking. Thus, age progression can serve result-checking as well as strategy planning purposes.

Milton Erickson had a little sneakier, albeit sophisticated, use for age progression which he called a "pseudo-orientation in time" (Erickson, 1954, 1980). By having his patient go forward in time and relate to that time as the present, Erickson could ask his patient how he or she got over the problem—specifically what Erickson said or did for the patient—or what the patient learned or decided that helped him or her overcome his or her problem. When the patient gave him the details of the "past" therapy that had helped him or her, Erickson facilitated amnesia for having done so, and thereby obtained his therapeutic strategy directly from the patient him- or herself!

Posthypnotic suggestion necessarily involves age progression, and sometimes amnesia as well. A suggestion is given for the client to respond in a particular way in some future context, and in order for the client to accept such a suggestion, the client must experience some degree of future orientation. In fact, orienting the client to positive future possibilities is a necessary part of *any* psychotherapy. Even therapeutic approaches emphasizing insights into the past can encourage some future orientation when such insights are expected to generate new possibilities in the client's future.

APPROACHES TO ELICITING AGE PROGRESSION

Patterns for facilitating age progression can range from structured, direct approaches to less direct and more conversational communications such as presuppositions. The direct approaches for facilitating age progression closely parallel the direct approaches described for age regression. These might include a "special vehicle" to take you into the future, a movie screen on which to watch or even step into a movie of the future, a book in which to read about your future and how it *happened*, or the imagery of a photograph collection of future events to view are all structured approaches to facilitate a future orientation or projection. As you can tell, the approaches to hypnosis are as varied as your imagination allows.

A simple, direct, permissive suggestion approach to age progression is exemplified in the following paragraph:

> ... and now that you've had the opportunity to discover something very important about yourself, I wonder how many ways you'll find to use this new ability of yours creatively in your own behalf ... and it can be as if a long time has passed since this session ... a few days ... and time passes so quickly ... then a few weeks ... and a few months ago we spent some time together where you learned that you could feel so good ... and you had a thought at that time that allowed you to look at yourself differently then ... and feel differently now ... and as you look back over all the time that has passed since then, how has that thought affected you? ... How are you different? ... What can you do now that you couldn't do back then? ...

In the above example, the client is encouraged to integrate some new thought or learning into his or her life in a way that will prove beneficial. Suggesting directly to the client that it is "as if a long time has passed" orients him or her to the future as if it were now, a time to reflect on the recent change and its consequences. Questions such as those in the above example require increasing involvement in the "then is now" experience, and can provide concrete ideas to the clinician about other factors to include in the overall intervention.

Indirect suggestions for future orientation may include: (1) metaphorical approaches (e.g., "I'd like to tell you about a client I worked with who could clearly imagine herself two months after our session doing exactly what we're talking about now and when she saw herself that way she discovered ..."); (2) embedded commands (e.g., "I sometimes like to look around and *wonder what will happen in the future* when you can *look back at and feel good about all the changes* you have made . . ."); (3) presuppositions (e.g., "I wonder exactly where you will be and what you'll be doing when you happily realize you haven't smoked in days . . ."); and, (4) indirect embedded questions ("You can tell me about how you will *describe the way you solved this problem* to your friends, can't you?"). Each of these approaches and examples demonstrates a capacity for guiding the client into a mental set for developing positive expectations for the future. Positive expectations about improving one's condition are fundamental to success in virtually anything, but are especially important in the healing arts. Why go through treatment if you don't expect some benefit? Age progression patterns are the bridge to get from here to there, from now to later. If the imagination doesn't create new directions, the will doesn't have anyplace to go but around and around.

Table 11 below contains a general age progression strategy that may be adapted to individual needs in the context of psychotherapy. This strategy illustrates the idea of sequencing steps in a hypnotic process in an effort to facilitate the greatest degree of responsiveness in the client.

The general strategy involves 11 steps, described as follows: Step 1 involves an induction of any type. Step 2 involves offering a set of *verifiable* suggestions that establish a momentum for responding positively to the clinician. Step 3 involves offering at least two metaphors regarding the future (e.g., changes will happen in science, in medicine, in society, and so forth), indirectly orienting the client to future possibilities. Step 4 involves identifying specific resources (e.g., intelligence, sensitivity, perseverance) existing in the client that are valuable. Step 5 involves identifying specific future situations the client will be facing that are a basis for concern. Step 6 involves associating the existing client resources to the likely future contexts where they would be helpful. Step 7 provides an opportunity for a "rehearsal"

Table 11. A General Age Progression Strategy

1. Induction
2. Building a response set
3. Metaphors regarding the future
4. Identifying positive resources
5. Identifying specific future contexts
6. Embedding the positive resources identified in #4
7. Rehearsal of behavioral sequence
8. Generalization of positive resources to other selected contexts
9. Posthypnotic suggestion
10. Disengagement
11. Reorientation to waking state

of the future sequence as if it were happening now. Step 8 provides a chance to identify several other contexts where that same new application of a skill would also be helpful. Step 9 involves specific suggestions to use the skill in contexts wherever it would be helpful. Step 10 brings the future-oriented work to a close and re-establishes the ties to the current context. The final step is guiding the individual out of hypnosis.

Hopelessness and helplessness are routinely found in clients in distress. Age progression as a means of building a *realistic* sense of hope, and as a way of empowering the person to take charge of his or her life, is a vital component of good therapy.

HYPNOTIC AMNESIA

DESCRIPTION

Hypnotic amnesia is a suggested loss of memory, and can be most simply described as the experience of forgetting something. In both hypnosis research and clinical practice, hypnotic amnesia generally involves the inability to recall items specifically suggested (either directly or indirectly) to be unavailable for recall, and subsequent recall when the amnesia suggestion is reversed (Dixon & Laurence, 1992). The quality of the amnesia may be broad in scope (e.g., childhood memory before age nine) or may be specific to a certain type or category of information (e.g., what happened during the robbery). As Theodore X. Barber (2000) described in his discussion of the "amnesia prone" individual, the quality of a person's amnesia and the proneness toward amnesia may be important both diagnostically and therapeutically.

Hypnotic amnesia has been the subject of considerable research in the domain of experimental hypnosis. Suggested and reversible amnesias hold the potential to reveal much about the cognitive basis for memory and other unconscious processes. There have been many different viewpoints developed over the years, ranging from the view of hypnotic amnesia as a socially prescribed role enactment (Spanos, 1986; Spanos, Radtke, & Dubreuil, 1982), an "unmotivated" but prescribed forgetting (Bowers & Davidson, 1991), and a prescribed breakdown of specific memory mechanisms (Kihlstrom, 1980, 1987).

Whenever you try to remember something, you attempt to bring information from somewhere in your unconscious into conscious awareness. Until you read this sentence, you were very probably not thinking of your old neighborhood where you grew up. That memory, however, is in your unconscious until you gain conscious access to it. Not all memories are available to be brought into conscious awareness, though. Some experiences were too superficially attended to and were not incorporated into long-term memory, while others had no personal meaning and thus were not integrated into memory in any recoverable way (Johnson, 1991; Parkin, 1993). Still others were so personally threatening that they had to be defended against. The classic defense mechanism called "repression" operating in tandem with dissociation are the primary mechanisms of hypnotic or structured amnesia. Repression and dissociation refer to the mind's ability to "split off" threatening thoughts, experiences, feelings, and impulses in the unconscious, allowing the person the opportunity to avoid consciously having to acknowledge and deal with the threat (Spiegel, 1986, 1993). Therapeutically, the goal of many forms of treatment involving such traumatic memories has been to uncover and "work through" them. The delicate issues surrounding amnesia have already been described.

In everyday living, examples of forgetting that parallel hypnotic amnesia are abundant. Lost keys, forgotten phone numbers, missed appointments, forgotten names of people you know you know, missed assignments, showing up on the wrong day for a meeting or date, forgetting details of significant experiences, and forgetting where you hid something important are common examples. There are countless opportunities in daily life to observe people forgetting things that may, on the surface, seem unforgettable. There are conditions which serve to enhance memory, and there are conditions which serve to interfere with memory. Some of these are biological in nature, as Ernest Rossi described in his considerations of state-dependent learning (1996, 1998, 2001), and some are social and situational. Structuring someone's experience hypnotically to create the conditions in which information can be "split off" in order to deliberately create an amnesia may occasionally be a goal in the course of treatment. Why might a clinician want to foster amnesia in a client?

There is often a detectable motivation for the act of forgetting, a reason why, even though the reason may objectively seem a poor one. Classic psychoanalysis is a long-term process of recovering repressed memories, particularly those of childhood, and bringing them into conscious awareness as "insights." Having insight into one's motivations and associated intrapsychic dynamics is thought to be the primary vehicle of change by a number of different schools of psychodynamic psychotherapy, primarily those in which the conscious mind's role is considered to be the most significant in the process of change (Nash, 1991). Herein lies a fundamental difference between the utilization approach to hypnosis and other therapeutic approaches which emphasize developing greater conscious awareness. The utilization approach emphasizes the greater positive potentials of unconscious processes, and thus makes considerable use of amnesia whenever possible (Haley, 1973; Zeig, 1980). The unconscious is considered to be an active and capable part of each person, able to integrate memories and learnings into patterns of living that allow the person to cope. It is important to point out that a coping mechanism may allow a person to manage without it necessarily being adaptive for him or her (evidenced in the self-destructive coping mechanisms people commonly use such as excessive alcohol intake, overeating, and so forth). Is the unconscious really capable of organizing responses and patterns of coping independent of conscious understanding? It is tempting to think of an unconscious that can be trusted to generate positive responses to life stressors, but clearly such a one-dimensional view of the unconscious isn't tenable, as discussed earlier. However, there are responses formed at unconscious levels that are, in fact, helpful to the individual. Thus, the use of amnesia to split off conscious awareness to focus on the unconscious may have therapeutic utility.

When the unconscious is able to integrate new information that has special significance, perhaps because of its point of origin (e.g., the suggestions of a trusted therapist) and its relevance, synergistically added to the motivation to change, the client can undergo changes seemingly with little or no awareness for how the change took place. For example, are you conscious of specific reasons why you no longer either like or wear that expensive piece of clothing you bought just a short while ago that you thought was so great at the time? Probably not. The change in your attitude "just happened."

Milton Erickson was a firm believer that the unconscious can be more powerful in generating changes than any other part of the person, and that if the appropriate information is provided to the client's unconscious from within his or her frame of reference, ideally with minimal interference from the conscious mind, the unconscious could effect rapid and lasting change. Consequently, Erickson developed a variety of ways to facilitate amnesia in order to promote change at an unconscious level (Zeig, 1985). By inducing the client to consciously forget the various suggestions and experiences provided, one can enable the client's unconscious to form its own unique response, free to use the hypnotic suggestions and experience as creatively and idiosyncratically as it desires. More often than not, the client's solution catalyzed by the clinician's suggestions is more creative than the clinician's.

Beyond offering therapeutic suggestions to the unconscious mind for it to use its hidden resources for problem-solving, amnesia can be and frequently is used more directly to deliberately help repress and dissociate hurtful memories if deemed appropriate to do so (Lankton, 2001). Caution must be exercised in facilitating repression by assuring the client that the memory is not gone forever, that it is only going to be "stored in a safe place . . . where it need not interfere with your daily living . . ." In the event that, for whatever reason, the client needs to have access to that memory, it can be available since it has only been set aside, not eliminated (remember, the mind is not a computer whose "tapes" can be erased). Suggestions for amnesia in such cases are likely to be accepted only when some healing (i.e., resolution, catharsis) has occurred first (Dolan, 1991; Murray-Jobsis, 1995).

Additional suggestions that dissociate the intense feelings from the memory can also be offered. (See the section on "Dissociation" later in this chapter.) Then, in the event the client does re-experience the memory, it can be without all the intense emotions previously associated with it.

Amnesia is a common characteristic of deeper hypnotic experiences. When the client emerges from hypnosis, he or she may have little or no recollection for what the hypnotic experience involved, even if no direct suggestion for amnesia was offered. Such amnesia is referred to as "spontaneous amnesia" for obvious reasons. If amnesia is a specific response the clinician wants the client to develop, gambling on spontaneous amnesia is not a certain bet; rather, playing a more active role in facilitating amnesia increases the likelihood of obtaining the amnesia response in the client.

Amnesia is not automatic with hypnosis, as many erroneously believe. In fact, for those who rely greatly on intellectual means of self-control, paying careful attention and remembering everything that happens may reduce anxiety. Inducing amnesia in such persons, as might be expected, is a bit more difficult. If a client is motivated to remember suggestions and experiences, he or she will. When spontaneous amnesia occurs, it is, in part, a reflection of the client's trust in the clinician's skills. It indicates the client didn't feel the need to scrutinize everything the clinician did.

Deciding what things a client should and shouldn't be aware of is one more area of responsibility on the part of the clinician. Ultimately, of course, the client is free to accept or reject whatever suggestions he or she chooses, but the clinician can influence the client in undesirable ways, as you may recall from the earlier discussion of human suggestibility. Amnesia can be a very tricky process, and its power, like that of the unconscious, is easy to underestimate.

STRATEGIES TO ELICIT AMNESIA

Amnesia, more than any of the other various hypnotic phenomena, is less likely to be obtained the more directly the clinician suggests it. Suggesting to someone that he or she "forget everything that took place during this time" can be very threatening, even to a responsive and obedient client. In facilitating amnesia in clients, the indirect approaches are much more palatable to people, in my experience.

If a direct approach to amnesia is employed, it is probably more likely to be accepted if offered in a more permissive manner. The following is an example: "You can choose to forget about that experience now, because it no longer has a place in your life . . ."

Indirect approaches may take a variety of forms, including indirect suggestions, attentional shifts, and confusional suggestions. Indirect suggestions for amnesia create the possibility of amnesia occurring without

your overtly asking for it as a specific response. The following is an example
of an indirect and distracting approach to amnesia:

> . . . and as you continue to relax, each breath soothing you . . . I wonder how
> much attention you have paid to the different thoughts floating through
> your mind . . . your mind can be so active while it relaxes . . . and then you
> can realize how difficult it is to remember what I was talking about exactly
> seven minutes ago . . . and you could try to remember what I was saying
> nine minutes ago, or what you were thinking four minutes ago, but doesn't
> it seem like much too much work to try and remember? . . . it takes more
> effort than it's worth . . . and so why not let yourself relax comfort-
> ably . . . knowing you don't have to remember when it's too much work to . . .

The above example is indirect because it doesn't specifically suggest to
the client he or she forget, it only describes the difficulties of remembering.
Another indirect suggestion for amnesia is: "You can remember from this
experience what you choose to remember . . ." This suggestion carries the
unspoken implication that, "You can forget what you choose to forget." I
view this suggestion as a respectful way of offering amnesia as a choice for
the client to make without me demanding it.

Another indirect approach to facilitating amnesia is the "attentional
shift." The mechanism for this approach is easy to understand when you
consider a routine interaction: You say to your friend, "I have something I
have to tell you." Your friend says, "Well, I have something to tell you, too,
and it's really important so let me tell you first." You agree, and so you listen
and then respond to your friend's concern. Finally, when he or she is through,
he or she says, "OK, now what were you going to tell me?" and you say, "Uh,
well, gee, I uh . . . forgot." The irritating but predictable response from the
other person then is, "Well, it must not have been very important!" What
actually took place? Your attention was on a particular "track," a particular
line of thought. But when you leave that track in order to attend to your
friend's input, the flow of thought was interrupted and was difficult to retrieve, thus creating a temporary amnesia. The reverse phenomenon happens as well: You have information "on the tip of your tongue," but the
harder you try to remember it the more elusive it is. Only when you divert
your attention away from deliberate effort to recall it does it eventually float
back into awareness.

Shifts in attention obviously have an impact on how information goes
back and forth between the conscious and unconscious minds. Deliberately
shifting the client's attention away from his or her hypnotic experience is
one way to get him or her to "jump tracks" and thereby develop amnesia for
the hypnosis. To do this, when the client is disengaging from hypnosis, the
clinician can gracefully and congruently distract him or her by having him
or her respond to something totally irrelevant to the content of the hypnosis

session. For example, the clinician can look bothered and say something like, "Oh, I just remembered. I needed to ask you which tests you had done at your last physical examination. Do you recall?" By encouraging the client to abruptly shift into thinking about his or her last physical examination (or whatever), you give the client no opportunity to consciously analyze the hypnotic experience he or she just had, and it can therefore integrate at an unconscious level. (You won't know whether the person's unconscious has integrated *anything*, however, until subsequent meetings when you have the opportunity to find out if anything has changed, and what degree of conscious awareness the person has for *how* things changed.) Discouraging conscious analysis inhibits opportunities for the client to pick apart or reject dimensions of the hypnotic experience that such conscious analysis might deem irrational. (Hypnosis sessions often involve suggesting experiences, such as "floating peacefully through space and time," that may be emotionally powerful but are logically impossible.) The unconscious can respond meaningfully to things that make very little sense to the conscious mind, a point which leads me to the next approach for facilitating amnesia.

Confusion as an induction technique was discussed earlier. Confusional suggestions may also be used to facilitate the various hypnotic phenomena, and can be especially useful in obtaining amnesia. In responding to confusional suggestions, the client becomes increasingly focused on trying to make sense of them. As in the previous approach, the client's attention shifts from where it was to the current confusing inputs, but the added element of the person's motivation to form a meaningful response can make for an even more powerful approach to eliciting amnesia. The following is an example of a confusion technique for the purpose of facilitating amnesia:

> . . . and now that you've had the opportunity in this session to discover new possibilities . . . while you can learn from past experiences . . . your conscious mind can begin to wonder . . . how it will know which things to remember . . . and which things only your unconscious need know . . . and then you can remember . . . to forget . . . or you may choose to forget to remember . . . but when you remember to forget what you've forgotten to remember . . . your memory of forgetting forgets what it has forgotten . . . but you can only forget what you've forgotten when you realize it's too difficult to remember anyway . . . and then you can forget all the confusion and relax even more deeply.

As more of the client's attention is engaged to sort out the confusion, the unconscious can respond to the suggestions for forgetting. Whereas the attentional shift is typically used at the close of the hypnosis session (although not necessarily so), the confusion approach can be easily integrated at any point in the hypnotic process.

Table 12. Techniques of Hypnotic Amnesia

Indirect Suggestion
Distraction
Structured/Direct
Confusion
Metaphor
Seeding

DISSOCIATION

Other approaches to facilitating amnesia include: (1) Metaphors, in which stories are told with embedded suggestions for forgetting ("... and when she opened her eyes it was as if from a deep sleep, barely able to remember anything but the good feelings of a restful night . . ."); (2) Seeding, in which advance hints are provided of the amnesia suggestions to come later ("Some people experience such deep or meaningful hypnosis that when they reorient later it's surprising how little there is to remember . . . and it's so interesting how they change for the better even though they don't necessarily remember how . . ."); and, (3) Dissociation, in which suggestions can be offered about remembering and forgetting as separate mechanisms that can function independently ("Your ability to remember is complemented by your ability to forget . . . and when your thoughts remember that situation, your feelings can forget to be there because they are remembering someplace else to be of greater importance and comfort . . .").

Observation of your self and others in various situations where memory is on display can teach you a lot about the routine nature of remembering and forgetting. Further study of the nature of human memory is also recommended to guide one's developing skills in the use of amnesia. (For a particularly good consideration, see Daniel Schachter's 1996 book, *Searching for Memory: The Brain, The Mind, and The Past.*)

ANALGESIA AND ANESTHESIA

DESCRIPTION

Hypnotically induced analgesia and anesthesia exist on a continuum of diminishing bodily sensation. Hypnotic analgesia generally refers to a reduction in the sensation of pain, allowing other sensations (e.g., pressure, temperature, position) that orient the client to his or her body to remain. Hypnotic anesthesia generally refers to a complete or near complete elimination of sensation in all or part of the body. Applications and approaches for analgesia and anesthesia overlap to a great extent, and so for the sake of simplicity only the term "analgesia" will be used in this discussion of these hypnotic phenomena.

Hypnotically induced analgesia is truly one of the most remarkable capacities human beings have. The potential to reduce pain to a manageable level or even eliminate it altogether is one of the most meaningful applications of clinical hypnosis. Given the large number of people suffering with chronic and debilitating pain, and the potential for any of us to suffer pain from injuries and medical conditions, the value of any tool for managing pain effectively is obvious. Consequently, pain relief through hypnosis may well be the most intensively studied of all the hypnotic phenomena, and may also be the most empirically well-supported application of hypnosis.

In a recent meta-analysis evaluating the merits of hypnotically induced analgesia conducted by Montgomery, DuHamel, and Redd (2000), hypnosis provided significant pain relief for about 75% of the population. Further analysis indicates that hypnosis appears to be at least as effective as other nonphysical approaches, such as cognitive-behavioral pain management approaches (Syrjala, Cummings, & Donaldson, 1992). And, there is evidence that when hypnosis is added to standard patient-controlled sedation, hypnosis affords significantly greater pain relief than does conscious sedation alone (Lang et al., 2000). Hypnosis is not addictive; it is empowering to the patient, and it encourages a healthy proactive role in managing pain (Chaves, 1989; Chaves & Dworkin, 1997).

Hypnosis has been used successfully in the treatment of all kinds of painful conditions, including headache (J. Barber, 1996a; Olness, MacDonald, & Uden, 1987; Spinhoven, Linssen, Van Dyck, & Zitman, 1992), burns (Ewin, 1983; Patterson, 1996; Patterson & Ptacek, 1997), cancer (Genuis, 1995; Levitan, 1992; Lynch, 1999), dental conditions (Hassett, 1994; Mulligan, 1996), surgical procedures (Bejenke, 1996), irritable bowel syndrome (Galovski & Blanchard, 1998; Gonsalkorale, Houghton, & Whorwell, 2002), and many, many other conditions.

The use of hypnosis in pain management necessarily involves eliciting hypnotic analgesia or anesthesia. Unlike chemical anesthesia, hypnosis involves a perceptual, and therefore mental, component. How exactly hypnotic analgesia works continues to be a mystery. It does not appear to be either placebo or mere stress inoculation, nor does it seem to involve the brain's natural opiate receptors, endorphins (Goldstein & Hilgard, 1975; Spiegel & Albert, 1983). Ernest Hilgard developed his neodissociation model, based in part on his studies of hypnotic analgesia, well described in the classic text, *Hypnosis in the Relief of Pain* (Hilgard & Hilgard, 1994). Hilgard was able to show in his experiments that subjects who successfully developed hypnotically suggested analgesia still had an awareness for their pain (1986). Subjects reported their pain was reduced to easily managed levels and dissociated from their awareness enough to be considered insignificant.

Working with clients in pain requires a broad base of understanding of hypnotic principles, human physiology, psychological motivations, human information processing, and interpersonal dynamics (Eimer & Freeman, 1998). Clients in pain are, in some ways, easier to work with because of their (usually) high level of motivation. In other ways, however, such clients are exceptionally difficult to work with because of the intensity and pervasiveness of the negative impact of the pain on their lives. Therefore, approaching the person in pain must be done sensitively, with an appreciation that the pain is usually more than only pain: It is also a source of anxiety, feelings of helplessness and depression, increased dependency, and restricted social contact. Even pain emanating from clearly organic causes has psychological components to it, particularly how the suffering person experiences the pain and its consequences. It is the psychological dimension of the pain that is most overtly affected by hypnosis for a variety of reasons that all seem to stem from the greater self-mastery hypnosis affords. Fear and anxiety, feelings of helplessness, and negative expectations can all be reduced with the use of hypnosis. The physical components of the pain are also addressed by the use of hypnosis, as evidenced in the various healing strategies employing hypnotic patterns (Barber, 1996b).

As mentioned earlier, to date no specific mechanism has been identified that can adequately account for the physical effect of hypnosis on the person in pain. Helen Crawford and her colleagues (1998) have described the general analgesia process as involving attentional focus and attentional shifts "in that persons inhibit incoming sensations from awareness while often simultaneously deploying their attention elsewhere" (p. 1). This is a general description suggesting an ability to inhibit attentiveness and responsiveness to incoming pain stimuli. How exactly this happens and how such attentional attenuation leads to diminished sensory awareness is a mystery. Understanding and explaining how hypnosis physiologically reduces pain is one of the most fascinating and highly researched areas of inquiry in the field of psychophysiology.

Fortunately, effective use of hypnotic analgesia is not contingent on having its neurophysiological mechanism(s) defined. The person in pain is capable of using his or her mind to change the perception of the pain in ways that will be described shortly, and this ability is amplified with hypnosis.

Hypnotic analgesia is one of the classical hypnotic phenomena that people react to with the most skepticism, asking, "If a person is in pain from cancer or some other physical cause, how can something psychological make a difference?" Most people even go a step further and hold the misconception that if the person's pain is reduced or eliminated through hypnosis, "then it must have been all in his or her head in the first place." Nothing is further from the truth. First, hypnosis and the various hypnotic phenomena (including analgesia and anesthesia) are evident, at least in part, in everyday experiences. Second, as was pointed out earlier, pain that is primarily physical in origin also has very real psychological components. The relationship between pain and anxiety and/or depression is an intense, circular one. Pain causes anxiety and/or depression, which intensifies the pain, which intensifies the anxiety and/or depression, and so on. By merely facilitating the relaxation hypnosis affords, one can interrupt the cycle (Eimer, 2000).

Consider routine experiences that closely approximate the experience of hypnotic analgesia. You can probably recall a time when you were very involved in an activity (perhaps while playing a sport, fixing a car, moving furniture, gardening, or the like), and only after the activity's completion did you notice you had cut or bruised yourself—and only then did it begin to hurt! Your awareness was distracted away from noticing genuine physical damage—the essence of hypnotic analgesia. The injury was real, but how much you noticed it and how much it affected you varied with your focus either on or away from it. Employing hypnosis to facilitate analgesia can give one at least partial control over the experience of pain through a deliberate procedure, rather than such useful distraction being only a seemingly random event. The fact that pain is modifiable through hypnosis is not indicative that the person's pain is psychogenic. Instead, it is indicative that our experience of our bodies is malleable and even negotiable.

Using hypnosis in the management of pain is advantageous for some very important reasons. First, and foremost in my opinion, is the opportunity for greater self-control and, therefore, greater personal responsibility for one's level of well-being (Daniel, 1999; Hornyak, 1999). Feeling victimized, whether by pain, circumstances, or other people, puts one in a helpless position from which it is difficult to do any real healing. Having some degree of self-control is extremely important to the person in pain, and hypnosis facilitates its acquisition (Bejenke, 1996; Ginandes, 2002). Second, because the ability to experience hypnosis is a natural one existing within the person, pain medications may be reduced or even eliminated. Hypnosis has no negative side effects, nor is it addictive. Pain is reduced in differing degrees in different people, but whatever the quality of result, it is obtained safely and naturally. Third, hypnosis permits a higher level of functioning and enhances the healing process in persons who utilize hypnotic patterns (Barretta & Barretta, 2001). Remaining as active as one's condition allows is important at all levels, and can make a significant difference in its course. The expectation of wellness, the experience of comfort, and the diminished anxiety and fear can all be important factors in facilitating recovery at most, or retarding decline, at least (J. Barber, 1996b).

Developing the ability to help your clients by offering effective approaches to pain management can be invaluable, but a few words of caution are in order. First, pain is a warning sign that something is wrong. Appropriate medical evaluation must necessarily be the first step well before hypnosis is applied. The various hypnotic approaches should be regarded as essentially "Band-Aids,"™ for while they may assist the client in being more comfortable, their healing abilities remain uncertain. Yes, there is some evidence that hypnosis promotes healing, and a cautious optimism is reasonable, but procedures and results across people are quite variable and do not justify telling clients anything that approximates "hypnosis will heal you" (Kalt, 2000; Rossi, 2001).

A person's pain must be viewed as a danger sign, and appropriate medical evaluation and treatment are not only encouraged, they are *demanded*. Harm can too easily be done if the pain is transformed hypnotically with little or no knowledge of its cause. *Delaying or discouraging appropriate medical care is tantamount to malpractice.* Second, if you are not either medically licensed or medically supervised, you should not be working with pain at all. Period. Practicing outside the realm of your qualifications is also tantamount to malpractice. Third, simply working with a person in pain without recognition for the meaning of the pain in the person's life is a potentially dangerous oversimplification of the problem. Each person's life can be thought of in terms of its many components. The underlying needs (i.e., motivations, dynamics) as well as the pain's impact on a variety of levels (personal, familial, professional, etc.) must be acknowledged and considered in the formulation of each person's treatment plan (Ginandes, 2002; Zeig & Geary, 2001).

In sum, hypnosis can offer physical relief and an emotional wellspring of positive possibilities to the person in pain. Over time and with practice, such persons can benefit greatly from the increased self-control and self-reliance hypnosis may afford.

STRATEGIES TO ELICIT ANALGESIA AND ANESTHESIA

Analgesia can be a deliberate and directly stated goal for hypnosis sessions, and directly suggested as a desired response. And, analgesia can be an indirect consequence of hypnosis since it often arises spontaneously during hypnosis for the client who is sufficiently absorbed in the experience and experiences a sense of detachment (i.e., dissociation) from his or her body. When people experience detachment, and when they are so absorbed they don't even move (i.e., catalepsy), analgesia is likely to be present as well. Therefore, any approach that successfully shifts the person's awareness away from the bodily sensation(s) under consideration (ranging from specific locations to the whole body) can have an indirect analgesic effect. With training and reinforcing practice sessions, the client in pain can learn to distract him- or herself, and then refocus on positive ideas, feelings, memories, or whatever he or she chooses as a focal point. The teaching of self-hypnosis is essential in order for this approach to the management of pain to extend beyond relief obtained in the clinician's office.

A considerable number of direct and indirect strategies can be employed to facilitate analgesia (Chaves, 1993; Eimer, 2000; Weitzenhoffer, 2000; Zeig & Geary, 2001). Table 13 below lists the most common forms of hypnotic pain management. The few presented in detail in this section include direct suggestion of analgesia, glove anesthesia, pain displacement, and physical dissociation. The rest are mentioned at the end of this section.

Direct suggestion of analgesia as an approach involves offering suggestions for the lack of sensation in the specific part of the client that is painful. If, for example, a client is experiencing pain in his or her abdomen, a direct analgesia approach might be structured as follows:

> ... and as you feel your arms and legs getting heavier ... you can see the muscles in your abdomen loosening ... relaxing ... as if they were guitar strings you were slowly unwinding ... and as you see those muscles in your abdomen relax ... you can feel a pleasant tingle ... the tingle of comfort ... and whenever you have had a part of you become numb, like an arm or leg that fell asleep ... you could feel that same tingle ... like the pleasing tingle in your abdomen now ... tingling more ... and isn't it both interesting and soothing to discover the *sensation of no sensation* there? That's right ... the sensation of no sensation ... a tingling, pleasing *comfortable feeling of numbness there.*

When you suggest the "sensation of no sensation" directly in the client's abdomen, he or she can experience diminished sensation and direct relief in the troublesome area. However, there is also likely to be greater resis-

---

Table 13. Approaches to Pain Management with Hypnosis

 1. Direct suggestion
 2. Indirect suggestion (e.g., interspersal, metaphor)
 3. Amnesia
 4. Sensory alteration (e.g., analgesia, anesthesia, shifting primary representational system)
 5. Symptom substitution
 6. Symptom displacement
 7. Dissociation (e.g., generalized, localized)
 8. Reinterpretation/reframing
 9. Confusion (e.g., sensory overload, pattern interruption)
10. Gradual diminution
11. Regression to pre-pain period
12. Pseudo-orientation in time
13. Time distortion

tance attached to the troubled area. Therefore, going after the analgesia response directly in the afflicted area may, with some individuals, be less likely to be effective. Directly suggesting numbness or the feeling of just having received an injection of Novocaine will likely be effective with the more responsive clients (J. Barber, 1996b; Crawford et al., 1998; Eimer, 2000).

Another (slightly less) direct approach is the "glove anesthesia." In this sensory alteration process, the client is given suggestions to experience full numbness (i.e., anesthesia) in either or both of his or her hands. Most people seem to be able to do this, if not fully, at least in part. When the glove anesthesia has been accomplished, further suggestions may be given that the anesthesia can be effectively transferred to whatever part of his or her body he or she chooses. Glove anesthesia permits a mobility for the anesthesia when the clinician suggests that a touch of the anesthetized hand to any part of the body will directly transfer the sensation of numbness to that spot. (In contrast, a direct suggestion for analgesia does not have such mobility, since it is localized to a specific, fixed spot.) This is particularly helpful when the location of the person's pain varies: today it is here, but yesterday it was there. Suggestions for glove anesthesia might take the following form:

> ... and in a moment, when I take your hand with your permission, I'm going to place it in a position it can stay in easily and comfortably (clinician takes the client's hand and props it up on the elbow) ... and you can easily hold your hand in this elevated position ... and as you do so you can notice how ... this hand begins to feel different from your other one ... more distant and even removed from you ... more distant ... and while the rest of you remains warm and comfortable ... this distant hand can begin to experience a sensation of coolness ... almost as if a cold wind were floating over your hand ... cooling it, chilling it ... and as your hand gets comfortably colder ... and still colder ... while the rest of you remains comfortably warm ... the pleasantly cool feelings in your hand get stronger ... cooler ... colder ... and as your hand continues to get comfortably colder ... it can tingle pleasantly with a cool numbness ... and when I touch your hand ... you can realize that the only sensation you feel is a cool numbness ... and you can place your hand anywhere else on your body you'd like to feel that same cool pleasant numbness. ...

In the above example of glove anesthesia, the sensation of numbness is built around a suggested change in perception of temperature, that is, the coolness of the hand. Descriptively suggesting in sensory detail the experience of making snowballs bare-handed, or the experience of reaching into the freezer for a tray of ice cubes, can help facilitate the experience of coolness and numbness.

Another approach to elicit analgesia involves the displacement of the pain. This might mean "moving the pain" (shifting the perception of the location of pain from one area to another more easily tolerated one), or it might mean restricting the perception of the pain to a smaller and less inconvenient area. For example, a client experiencing pain in his or her arm might be given the following suggestions for displacement:

> ... as you start to recall how you learned long ago about your body ... as all people eventually must ... you might begin to remember learning how delicately but wonderfully balanced the body is ... a muscle that allows you to bend your leg has a counterpart that allows you to straighten your leg again ... and while there are muscles that let your head lift ... there are also muscles that ... let your head drop down ... deeply relaxed ... and there is a part of you that can *feel comfort* where there was once discomfort ... and as the *comfort flows into the area where you'd most like it* ... and dislodges the discomfort, letting it flow down ... and as you feel it flowing down your arm ... you can feel it collecting in your baby finger ... so small there ... and so easy to forget about. ...

Transferring the pain of an arm to a baby finger can allow for a higher level of functioning and less preoccupation with discomfort since it can become confined to such a small and more easily managed part of the body. Essentially, this is a strategy of "symptom substitution," the deliberate creation of a new "outlet," one that is now within better control.

The next approach to analgesia involves a variable that is operating in each of the other analgesia approaches as well as in hypnotic patterns in general. That variable is "dissociation," and it involves the capacity to divide one's attentional and behavioral abilities. Physical dissociation causes the subjective experience of feeling separated from all or part of one's body, including the pain. Have you ever felt, however briefly, as if your body was going through something you really weren't a part of? Even though intellectually you knew you were "all together" at the time, you may have felt distant and removed from the physical experience. That kind of detached experience is representative of dissociation. After receiving chemical anesthesia, for example, you can watch yourself get stitches; you know the doctor is sewing your skin together, but since there is no feeling present, the experience can just appear to be a curious procedure you watch but from which you feel removed.

Physical dissociation as an approach to eliciting analgesia can involve guiding the client into the subjective experience that his or her mind and body exist on two different levels. Suggestions are given that there can be sufficient distance between them for the client not to notice (or feel) what his or her body is experiencing. The following sample illustrates this approach:

> ... and when your thoughts begin to travel faster than your body can keep

up with . . . you can rediscover how *your mind can travel so far* and so fast . . . and you can wonder about things that exist in the universe . . . the size of the mighty ocean . . . the age of huge trees that seem to fill the sky . . . and the number of stars in the sky . . . things you have probably wondered about from time to time . . . and you can *let your mind float freely* to the place you find yourself drawn to . . . while *your body stays here* . . . comfortably here . . . no need to move it . . . no need to let it hold your mind back . . . you can just enjoy the freedom of letting your mind float freely . . . to the places you most enjoy . . . and while *your mind is there* . . . *and your body is here* . . . it can be so comforting to know that your body is here . . . waiting . . . comfortably . . . patiently for as long as you'd like to float freely . . . without having to notice it . . . because your mind can comfortably go anywhere it wants to go. . . .

Suggesting that the mind "go somewhere" encourages a physical dissociation when the body isn't invited to go along. Such separation can be maintained beyond the formal hypnosis session when posthypnotic suggestions are offered that tie the capacity for physical dissociation to events in everyday living. Posthypnotic suggestions for comfort even after the hypnosis session is a vital consideration in planning your pain management strategies for your clients.

As a final approach to the hypnotic management of pain, one can refer back to the transcript of the confusion technique by Milton Erickson in the previous chapter on conversational hypnotic inductions. In that transcript, Erickson used a verbal confusion between "know pain" and "no pain" in order to facilitate the experience of comfort in his patient. Confusion captures the client's attention, leaving less awareness for discomfort (Erickson, 1966; Yapko, 1988).

Other approaches to eliciting analgesia include: (1) amnesia, in which the client is offered suggestions to forget having had pain, at least at times. This can interrupt the experience of the pain being continuous, and thus paves the way for suggesting intermittent and increasing periods of comfort as far as the client can remember; (2) gradual diminution, in which suggestions are offered that the discomfort decreases slowly over some specific span of time; (3) pseudo-orientation in time, in which the client is age progressed to a period post-recovery; (4) time distortion, in which moments of comfort can be expanded in subjective perception (see the later section in this chapter on time distortion); and (5) regression, in which the person is age regressed back to a period that is prior to the pain's onset to recapture feelings of comfort.

As a final note on the hypnotic management of pain, the wording of suggestions is especially important. The word "pain" has a strong negative emotional attachment to it, for it represents both a physical condition and an emotionally charged experience that is most unpleasant. Use of the word "pain," therefore, should be avoided whenever possible. (When you read

"The Case of Vicki" in chapter 20, a session for pain management with a terminal cancer patient, you may notice I never used the word "pain" during our session, even though that's why she was there.) You can substitute less charged words like "pressure," "discomfort," or "uncomfortable sensation" in place of the word "pain."

Integrating hypnotic analgesia with other therapeutic modalities can make for a well-balanced intervention for the client in pain, regardless of the pain's source. I have been encouraged in recent years by the number of medical and behavioral medicine practitioners discovering the viability of hypnosis as a tool in the overall treatment of the pain patient. Working hypnotically with patients in pain can be a specialty in itself, and is a most humane means for helping such patients cope with one of the most distressing and devastating human conditions.

CATALEPSY

DESCRIPTION

Catalepsy is defined as the inhibition of voluntary movement associated with intense focusing on a specific stimulus. The degree of catalepsy evident in a hypnotized individual has historically been considered to be directly related to the degree of hypnotic depth or experiential involvement. The degree to which the client is focused on the subjective associations triggered by the clinician's suggestions is the degree to which the client can demonstrate cataleptic responses. Such responses may include a fixed gaze, general immobility, the "waxy flexibility" usually associated with the catatonic patient who maintains his or her limbs in whatever position the clinician places them, muscular rigidity, unconscious movements, and the slowing of basic physical processes such as breathing, blinking, and swallowing (Weitzenhoffer, 2000). Signs of catalepsy can be relied on to a large extent as indirect indicators of hypnosis (both formally induced and spontaneous), or they may be directly suggested for specific therapeutic reasons to be described shortly. Catalepsy must be considered one of the most basic features of hypnotic experience, for it is associated directly or indirectly with virtually every other hypnotic phenomenon. Catalepsy is the behavioral result of focusing intently on a new and different reality, whatever it may be. Catalepsy helps pave the way to let go of the "old" reality long enough to create a therapeutic experience of age regression, analgesia, sensory distortions, or whatever.

As Ernest Rossi pointed out in his discussion of catalepsy (Erickson & Rossi, 1981), the so-called everyday trance (i.e., spontaneous hypnosis in the course of daily living) is a period of catalepsy where the person is daydreaming, self-absorbed, enthralled, captivated, but always preoccupied to the point of temporary immobilization by the intensity of the focus. Routinely over dinner, for example, people stop mid-reach for the pepper (or whatever) when the conversation turns intense and absorbing for the moment. Similarly, people will stand rigidly fixed in one spot, in one position, when more and more of their mind is called on to make sense out of a situation that seems to require a meaningful response.

Stage hypnotists typically demonstrate a "full body catalepsy" by suggesting the volunteer develop extreme stiffness of the entire body (e.g., "It is as if your body is a long, thick piece of wood") and then suspending the subject's rigid body between two chairs. Some add a little more dramatic flair to the demonstration by standing on the subject while he or she is suspended in that way. Suggestions to the client for a part of the body to be stiff and rigid, such as an arm (e.g., "Your arm is so stiff and rigid that you will find yourself unable to bend it"), is a demonstration of "arm catalepsy," if those suggestions are accepted. Suggestions to the client that "the eyelids or eye muscles of your closed eyes are so rigid or relaxed as to prevent your eyes from opening" may be accepted by the client, resulting in "eye catalepsy."

Suggestions of catalepsy are frequently used to assess a client's responsiveness to suggestion, as you may recall from the discussion of suggestibility tests. Responses to arm levitation procedures and the special "Handshake Technique" that Milton Erickson developed (Gilligan, 1987), as well as to various other pattern-interruption approaches are overt demonstrations of catalepsy. Arm levitation as a suggested response shows a catalepsy of the arm suspended in mid-air. The Handshake Technique involves initiating a routine handshake with someone, then interrupting the usual sequence of making hand contact by doing something else at the moment (e.g., bending over to tie one's shoes) just before hands would have touched. The other person's hand is left suspended in air, and the individual is now more externally oriented and responsive as he or she tries to make sense out of such an unusual situation.

For a long time, catalepsy was considered to merely be a passive response on the part of the client, but then again so was hypnosis in general (Watkins, 1987). In order for someone to focus so intently on the suggestions of the clinician, the demonstration of catalepsy must be viewed in the same way as hypnotic responses in general—as an active and dynamic process requiring the proactive formulation of meaningful responses. Catalepsy implies an intense internal absorption on one or more levels that also indicates a high degree of activity and receptiveness to the guidance of the clinician on other levels. This is why a client focused on one level may have his or her arm placed in a position and leave it there, literally too preoccupied with other more immediate things to think about than expending effort to move it (J. Barber, 1996b).

There are numerous therapeutic purposes for eliciting catalepsy, but they can be described in two general ways. Catalepsy can either serve to facilitate further hypnotic involvement through the client's recognition of his or her own unconscious mind's ability to respond in automatic ways, or it can be a target response in itself. Catalepsy as a target response may be used, for example, to assist any client whose physical movements need to be minimized in order to recover more quickly and comfortably (e.g., back injuries, burns). As a catalyst of further hypnotic experience, catalepsy can be a basis for securing and maintaining attention (thus serving as an inducer "as you discover yourself getting more mentally focused and your body becomes too heavy to move"), facilitating greater independent activity of the unconscious mind and increasing the degree of involvement or focus of the client (thus a deepener).

STRATEGIES TO ELICIT CATALEPSY

Anything that captures the intense interest of the client can facilitate cataleptic responses, including interesting stories, surprises or shocks, and confusion. Thus, catalepsy can and typically does arise as a spontaneous hypnotic phenomenon even if you don't suggest it. Eliciting catalepsy as a response from the client can be accomplished directly or indirectly, verbally and nonverbally, as desired. Direct suggestions for arm catalepsy are evident in the following suggestions for arm levitation:

> . . . as you continue to breathe in . . . and out . . . at a rate that's comfortable for you, . . . you can start to notice which of your arms is beginning to feel lighter than the other . . . light, almost weightless . . . and your hand can begin to float easily and effortlessly . . . rising . . . that's right . . . lifting without any effort on your part . . . your hand and arm can float in the air as if attached to a very large helium balloon, . . . and you can be surprised to discover how pleasurable it is to experience your arm floating straight out before you . . . as if it were completely weightless, . . . and it can stay there effortlessly while you begin to notice another sensation that can be of even greater interest to you. . . .

An indirect way to encourage catalepsy is to offer general suggestions for relaxation and immobility, such as in the following:

> . . . it can feel so good to you to know your body knows how to take care of itself . . . it knows how to *breathe comfortably* . . . in, and slowly out . . . effortlessly . . . and it knows how to *relax deeply* . . . and you will keep on breathing effortlessly . . . as your mind drifts off to some special memory . . . a memory you haven't thought about in a long, long time . . . and it also knows how to *sit quietly still* while you *get absorbed in enjoying that memory* . . . and isn't it comforting . . . and soothing . . . to know *your arms can rest heavily on the chair* with no need to move them? . . . and it takes more effort than it's worth to move when you are so comfortable. . . .

Both of the above examples are obviously examples of verbal approaches for eliciting catalepsy. The use of gestures and touch can facilitate catalepsy on a nonverbal level. You can model catalepsy as you begin your induction, showing a fixed gaze and a reduction in movement as you proceed.

Many beginning students of hypnosis feel anxious and pressured to "make something happen" when they first learn to perform inductions. This may show up as trying too hard, showing exaggerated gestures, speaking quickly and with dramatic flair, and the like.

In facilitating catalepsy, the best thing you have going for you is yourself. Using your body as a model, you can deliberately shift from the animated patterns of routine conversation to a demonstration to your client of the potential immobility of hypnosis. By gradually focusing yourself intently on your client, suspending bodily movement, and verbalizing your suggestions in an increasingly slow, absorbed, "hypnotic" way (employing the communication patterns described throughout), you are modeling to your client the possibility for catalepsy. If the rapport is adequate, your client can follow your leads. Often, the only barrier to effective hypnotic induction and utilization is the clinician's distracting demeanor! As a client, it is difficult to get into a relaxed, focused state when your guide is continually shifting positions, flailing his or her arms, gesturing, note taking, and so forth. Using yourself as a model for catalepsy can be a powerful means for facilitating the hypnotic experience for the client. You can even go a step further in modeling by gesturing slowly and deliberately stopping mid-gesture at well-chosen times as if preoccupied, thereby demonstrating the possibility of being so absorbed in thought as to lose track of voluntary motions.

Catalepsy takes a variety of forms, and as a constant feature of the hypnotic experience is a necessary hypnotic phenomenon to understand. Many advanced techniques build on the unconscious responses associated with catalepsy, particularly those that emphasize mind-body healing (Rossi & Cheek, 1988). While general immobility is the typical application or sign of catalepsy, remember that catalepsy has been defined as the inhibition of voluntary movement, which leaves ample room for involuntary or unconscious movement. The client in hypnosis may move in unconscious ways that are considered cataleptic, discussed later in the section on ideodynamic responses.

DISSOCIATION

DESCRIPTION

Dissociation is defined as the ability to break a global experience into its component parts, amplifying awareness for one part while diminishing awareness for the others.

Most clinicians learn about dissociation in the course of their clinical training, but almost invariably in the context of psychopathology, as in the dissociative disorders (such as Dissociative Identity Disorder, Psychogenic
Amnesia, fugue states, and the like). Dissociation is considered to be a basic
response of people in trauma (e.g., a rape victim reporting she was floating
above her body during the attack, an experiential detachment), and dissociation is thought to be so extreme in some instances that a person can
dissociate and develop amnesia for intense and prolonged trauma (Cardeña,
1994). Dissociation defensively applied in such a way has been linked to the
onset of the dissociative disorders (T. Barber, 2000; Spiegel, 1993). In fact,
however, dissociation, like the other hypnotic phenomena, is neutral, capable of being applied for positive or negative purposes. Dissociation to
repress trauma that deteriorates into a dissociative identity disorder is clearly
an unhealthy adaptation. In contrast, in the earlier section on analgesia,
you learned about dissociation as a pain management strategy, a potentially
helpful application of the same principles. It's important to appreciate that
what defines the positive or negative value of some process is the outcome it
generates, and not the process itself.

In the domain of clinical hypnosis, dissociation relates to the more
autonomous functioning of the conscious and unconscious minds in contrast to their normal, more integrated functioning. Dissociation allows for
the separation of different mental controls as Ernest Hilgard described in
his neodissociation model of hypnosis, briefly described in chapter 3
(Hilgard, 1986, 1992). Dissociation as a hypnotic phenomenon allows for all
the intriguing possibilities hypnosis as a tool affords.

Dissociation is a natural experience, for all persons are capable of processing and responding to information in ways they are not even aware of.
On a daily basis, people talk to disembodied voices through an instrument
called the "telephone." Physical processes go on routinely (e.g., blinking,
swallowing, adjusting the body, breathing, etc.) without any conscious involvement whatsoever. Each person has had the experience of feeling divided within him- or herself, as if simultaneously both participant and
observer in some experience. Even common cliches reflect dissociated states:
"I'm beside myself with joy," "Part of me wants to go, but another part of
me doesn't," "I'm out of my head to do this."

Through dissociation, people do not have to be attached to their immediate experience, involved, and "present." They can "go through the motions," but not really be "there." The conscious mind can drift off somewhere,
preoccupied with whatever else has its attention, and therefore the person's
unconscious is freer to respond in whatever way it chooses. The deeper the
hypnotic experience, the greater the degree of dissociation and the greater
the opportunity for non-conscious responses. Hypnosis is by its very nature

a dissociative experience. And, dissociation is the defining characteristic of hypnosis: You can be in hypnosis without being relaxed, but you can't be in hypnosis without *some* degree of dissociation being evident.

Dissociation may be used in a wide variety of ways. Splitting an integrated experience into parts can make for some very interesting possibilities. For example, one might split the intellectual component of an experience from the emotional component. Helping someone who is confused to distinguish their beliefs from their feelings would be helpful.

This particular thought/feeling dissociative phenomenon is demonstrated routinely in many stage hypnosis shows. The stage hypnotist suggests to the subject that he or she imagine (positively hallucinate) watching the funniest movie he or she has ever seen. The subject complies and begins to laugh uproariously. Then the stage hypnotist has the subject hallucinate seeing the saddest movie he or she has ever seen, and now the subject begins to cry, often with real tears. Many stage hypnotists then ask the subject, "What is so funny or sad about the movie?" and the typical subject responds by saying, "I don't know!" The subject isn't merely reluctant to describe what events transpired in the movie to generate such apparently intense emotions. Rather, the subject simply doesn't know, as he or she truthfully stated. *The stage hypnotist has suggested experiencing the emotion of funny or sad, but the feeling is not associated with a particular memory; it is a feeling dissociated from a particular context.* The fact that a (dissociated) feeling can exist without being attached to a situation is something too many therapists involved in the repressed memory controversy didn't understand. If a client reported, "I have the feeling I might have been abused, but I have no such memories," therapists erroneously assumed that wherever there's a feeling, there's a situation associated with it to account for it. Then they went looking for situations that would justify the feelings, often unwittingly creating them in the process through the process of confabulation (i.e., filling in gaps in memory with imagined experiences that are virtually indistinguishable from authentic memories). Hopefully, you now have much better insight into the relationship between memory, trauma, and suggestibility through your study of hypnosis.

Dissociation allows for the automatic, or spontaneous, responses of the client to occur; the forgotten memory can be remembered, the hand can lift unconsciously, the body can forget to move or notice sensation, and so forth. Facilitating the expression of a specific part of a person can have profound therapeutic impact. Finding and treating the part of the client that has felt weak and powerless, for example, when other parts of the person feel strong and able enough to take meaningful risks can give the clinician an opportunity to help the client resolve a troublesome problem that has existed "for no apparent reason." As another example, addressing the unconscious part of the person who is feeling weak, powerless, and angry in the context of an intimate relationship can allow him or her to fortify that part in a way that is adaptive. Giving that part the opportunity to express itself more directly can help rid him or her of that part's previous symptomatic mode of expression (Hornyak, 1999). Hypnosis in conjunction with ego state therapy has been an especially well-developed model for working in this way (Frederick & Phillips, 1995; Hartman, 2001; Phillips & Frederick, 1995; Watkins & Watkins, 1997).

Countless other examples of dissociation can be found in the literature on hypnosis, but the best examples are those of daily living. What situations do you observe people responding to in an automatic way? When are people least integrated in terms of mind and body? Intellect and emotion? Past and present? Optimism and pessimism? Masculine and feminine? The more polarities or "parts" you generate on a variety of levels (i.e., physical, mental, emotional, and spiritual) to describe the range of experiences people are capable of, the more you can appreciate how many different interrelated parts there are of human beings; each is capable of being dissociated and amplified for clinical use.

Too often, people have personal resources they could be using to help themselves, but these resources are either hidden from them or they simply don't know how to access them. In that sense, the parts of the person that may have appropriate skills for problem resolution are already present but dissociated. The clinician's role is to build new associations (i.e., cues, triggers, bridges) that will give the client access to more of his or her own abilities in the desired context. Dissociation is thus a valuable stepping stone in the process of recovery.

STRATEGIES TO ELICIT DISSOCIATION

Suggestions that facilitate divisions of experience are suggestions for dissociation. For example, an induction can generate a conscious-unconscious dissociation (Lankton & Lankton, 1983) simply by emphasizing the client's ability to experience things and learn things effortlessly and automatically (e.g., "Your conscious mind is listening to me while your unconscious is doing something even more important at a deeper level than you might realize"). The conscious mind is given ideas and experiences to focus on while the unconscious is encouraged to respond in other ways and learn at levels beyond awareness. In addition to eliciting dissociation during hypnotic induction, dissociation can be facilitated through a variety of approaches, including direct suggestions for dividing experience into parts, Erickson's "middle of nowhere" technique, and indirect suggestion of subjective divisions.

Direct suggestions for division let the client discover (or rediscover, as the case may be) that it is possible to have experiences on different levels, and that these experiences can occur spontaneously, automatically, and with no planning. Suggestions for hand levitation exemplify such a dissociation, as do the other nonvolitional cataleptic movements. Suggesting analgesia by "feeling your body resting comfortably here while you see that small part of your body that was uncomfortable way over there" is another direct suggestion for division. (You'll notice many such suggestions in The Case of Vicki in chapter 20.) Suggesting age regression by saying, "Your feelings can go back to age six while the rest of you remains an adult with me in the here-and-now," is yet another example of direct suggestion of dissociation. Anything you say that fits the pattern of the general dissociative suggestion statement that "part of you is experiencing this while another part of you is experiencing that" is a direct suggestion for dissociation. Further examples are evident in a variety of models of psychotherapy that make abundant use of dissociation without ever really identifying it as such, including Gestalt (which emphasizes the integration of parts) and Transactional Analysis (which dissociates each person into "Parent-Adult-Child" states).

A technique of dissociation that Milton Erickson often used is called the "middle of nowhere" (Zeig, 1980). Since one is guided to someplace called "nowhere," the paradox has the effect of dividing the person between the experience of being someplace but also being no place. An example of this approach might sound like this:

> . . . and when you sit that way it can become so easy to recognize that *a part of you is here* . . . but when *the rest of you drifts away* . . . and it *can* drift away . . . and you really don't know where it goes, do you? . . . to the middle of nowhere . . . where there is no time . . . and there is no place . . . in the middle of nowhere . . . there can just be my voice . . . and your thoughts . . . and nowhere is such a fine place to be . . . because nowhere else can one be so free to be nowhere . . . after all, you always have to be somewhere, sometime . . . but not now . . . nowhere is fine . . . and the middle of nowhere is a very pleasant place to be, isn't it? . . .

In this example, the client is encouraged to let him- or herself go to nowhere in particular, with no need to have any ties to anyone, any place, or any thing. As the client experiences him- or herself splitting her awareness between "here" and "there," the dissociation is intensifying.

Dissociation is indirectly suggested whenever suggestions for a particular hypnotic phenomenon are offered. Use of metaphors, confusion, and other forms of indirect suggestion all may facilitate dissociation. Metaphors are essentially stories that encourage you to leave here-and-now and go into the context of the story. Confusion as a facilitator for dissociation is an indirect technique in which the conscious mind attempts to make sense of communication that seems nonsensical. Confusion preoccupies the conscious mind struggling for clarity to the point of leaving the unconscious less well defended and more open for suggestion.

Indirect suggestions for dissociation are contained in the following metaphorical example:

> ... and I thought it might interest you to learn that I had a similar experience to the one you described ... an experience that taught me a lot about myself and others ... that I'd like to tell you about ... and isn't it amazing how you can learn important things from other people's experiences that ... on the surface ... seem so routine? ... sometimes you can listen so intently ... it's as if a *part of you is experiencing it, and another part of you is watching yourself go through the experience* ... wondering what will happen ... and how you'll feel when it's over ... and then the things that were so confusing at one level are made clear by the parts of us that understand ... at a much deeper level ... how to think creatively ... and there's a creative part in everyone, I'm sure you'd agree ... and in the experience I had, I found myself in a situation. ...

In this example, dissociation is suggested on a number of different occasions. A part is created that "experiences," another part that "observes," another that will "wonder," another that can "feel," another that can "clarify," and still another that can be "creative." Each of these parts can now be isolated, addressed, and utilized to accomplish some therapeutic goal. Each of these parts can be identified by the client as present in him- or herself, even though the suggestions are offered indirectly as comments by the clinician about him- or herself or as comments about people in general.

In facilitating dissociation, the final consideration for the clinician is related to the process of reintegration. Should the dissociated part(s) be reintegrated fully? Partially? Or not at all? Certainly an area of pain is best left dissociated, at least in part. Positive parts, such as the creative or adaptive parts, would probably need to be fully reintegrated. The task here for the clinician is to have some insight into the needs and motivations of the client in order to know what beneficial or harmful consequences might be associated with dissociating or reintegrating parts of the person. You may recall that age progression as an approach can be useful to help in this process (Torem, 1992).

Given the numerous daily experiences each of us has with hypnosis and dissociation, it should be apparent that all clinical applications of hypnosis involve making use of the processes that people use routinely to create their subjective ideas of reality. Developing insight into the multifaceted nature of dissociation can have an enormous impact on the future of your clinical interventions, for in every psychological disorder known to me, an element of dissociation is present. Clinical artistry often involves re-directing dissociative processes in more adaptive directions.

HALLUCINATIONS AND SENSORY ALTERATIONS

DESCRIPTION

Residents of state psychiatric hospitals will, given the chance, patiently explain to you the cultural biases against hallucinating. Generally, people find it a bit unnerving in daily life to encounter someone who is experiencing things that no one else is. Comedian Lily Tomlin asks the question, "Why is it that when I talk to God I'm praying, but when God talks to me I'm schizophrenic?" Hallucinations that are involuntary or are utilized as a coping mechanism (albeit a highly dysfunctional one) are considered either neurological aberrations or projections from the psychotic patient's unconscious, depending on one's point of view. In any case, they are maladaptive and nonvolitional.

Hallucinations created hypnotically are suggested experiences the client can have that are also removed from current, more objective realities, but they are structured to be adaptive and the client can accept or reject suggestions for experiencing them. Hypnotic hallucinations allow one to step outside conventional reality in order to have some beneficial experience that could not otherwise occur. For example, one therapeutic application might be to have a client go back in time (age regression) and have a meaningful conversation with a parent now deceased in order to settle some lingering personal issues.

A hallucination is, by definition, a sensory experience that does not arise from external stimulation. Simplistically, there are at least five senses in the normal human being; hallucinations may therefore exist in any or all of the sensory systems. For the sake of simplicity, the kinesthetic sense in this discussion will include separate but related sensory systems capable of detecting pressure, temperature, muscle feedback, that orient one to one's body and position in space, and to changes in motion. It is possible to hypnotically facilitate visual, auditory, kinesthetic (tactile), gustatory, and olfactory hallucinations (Edgette & Edgette, 1995). Hallucinations can be further characterized as being either "positive" or "negative." These terms do not refer to the emotional impact of the hallucinations on the person experiencing it. Rather, these terms refer to the structure of the hallucinations.

A positive hallucination is defined as having the (visual, auditory, kinesthetic, olfactory, gustatory) experience of something that is not objectively present. For example, you can take in a slow, relaxing breath, and as you inhale you can smell the fragrance of baby powder . . . and as you smell the fragrance of baby powder, you can realize that you have just had a positive olfactory hallucination. (That didn't hurt a bit, did it?)

A negative hallucination is not experiencing something sensorily that is objectively present (the flip-side of the positive hallucination). As you read this sentence, your awareness can drift to a sound in your environment that you didn't notice until just now . . . and as you become aware of that sound, and the feeling of surprise that you didn't notice it earlier, you can realize that you have just had a negative auditory hallucination.

In facilitating hallucinations, the clinician is altering awareness for sensory input. Many hallucinations associated with hypnosis arise spontaneously, others are suggested either directly or indirectly. For example, hypnotic analgesia can be thought of as a diminished sensory awareness for the kinesthetic level of experience. It may arise spontaneously simply because of the catalepsy associated with hypnosis. Another way to describe the same analgesic phenomenon is to say that, as you become increasingly absorbed on other sensory levels, perhaps experiencing vivid visual imagery, you dissociate and negatively hallucinate kinesthetic experience. As a second example, hypnotic amnesia can be described as the conscious forgetting of experience, but another way of describing the same phenomenon is to say the client negatively hallucinates the components of the experience. Specifically, a client might not remember what was said to him or her during hypnosis because he or she was so subjectively involved on another level that he or she negatively hallucinated the voice and suggestions of the clinician.

Positive and negative hallucinations occur routinely in the course of everyday living. Everyday examples of positive hallucinations include having a taste for food you crave, feeling itchy all over when you find an insect on or near your body, thinking you see someone you're trying to avoid wherever you turn, hearing someone call your name when no one is around, and thinking you smell something burning when nothing is. Everyday examples of negative hallucinations include not hearing the doorbell ring because you're engrossed in something, not noticing something on your way to work and then seeing it one day and exclaiming, "Wow! Where did that come from?" and not noticing that the milk you're drinking has gone sour until someone else tastes it and says, "Yecch!"

Sensory alterations and hallucinations are distinct but closely related terms. *Sensory alterations are defined as changes in sensory awareness, either magnified or diminished in some way.* The overlap between them exists because in order to facilitate hallucinations, the clinician must alter the client's sensory awareness, and in altering the client's sensory awareness, sensory hallucinations will be created. The client will have one or more of his or her senses made more or less sensitive, and more or less active, depending on the desired outcome.

Hallucinations may be used therapeutically to immerse the client in a situation that can't be reproduced in the "real" world. Guiding the client into a situation where he or she can experience him- or herself, or the world, differently in some meaningful way obviously increases the range of his or her experience and can thus instill valuable new resources. When one gets absorbed and hallucinates the details of the experience vividly, the suggested reality can become almost as real and powerful as "real" life. The client can then have the experience of hearing words he or she longed to hear, experiencing feelings he or she missed feeling, seeing places and people he or she needed to see, and so on. Through suggested hallucinations, the client can have structured experiences that can facilitate his or her personal growth and development. The "believed-in imagination" of hypnosis is especially potent in this application (Sarbin, 1997).

STRATEGIES TO ELICIT HALLUCINATIONS AND SENSORY ALTERATIONS

Hallucinations can and often do arise spontaneously during the course of hypnosis sessions. Negatively hallucinating one's body (e.g., "I felt disembodied") or the voice of the clinician (e.g., "I didn't hear you after a while") are common experiences for the client in hypnosis. Also common are experiences of seeing and hearing faces and voices from the past during hypnosis, perhaps even smelling the remembered person's cologne.

To deliberately facilitate the experience of hallucinations, both direct and indirect approaches can work well. Stage hypnotists demonstrate a direct approach to positive visual hallucinations when they suggest to their subjects that they can laugh uproariously when they "see the audience nude." A direct suggestion to experience something (e.g., "You can open your eyes and see yourself over there having that special experience") is usually sufficient; generally by the time a clinician attempts facilitating hallucinations, they have already attained sufficient rapport with and responsiveness in the client.

Suggestions for hallucinations, whether positive or negative, should generally be offered in a positive suggestion structure so the client knows what he or she is striving to experience. As an example, you can refer back to the earlier part of this section in which I offered you a direct suggestion for the positive olfactory hallucination of smelling baby powder. I let you know in a very direct and specific way what kind of experience you could have. In working hypnotically with a client, the more details the clinician provides, the more sensory experiences the client can have. Thus, extending an earlier example, if you want the client to see his or her deceased mother in the chair opposite him or her in order to have the meaningful conversation that never took place, the positive hallucination will be enhanced by having the client see his or her mother's clothing, smelling her perfume, touching her shoulder, seeing her physical position, and hearing her voice, all in as much detail as possible. All of these suggestions can be directly offered, immersing the client in the experience more and more intensely with each suggestion. In general, positive hallucinations are fairly easily accomplished through direct suggestions, of which the following are some examples:

> . . . You can look over there and see someone you've wanted to see whom you haven't seen in a long, long time . . . and how does she look? . . .
> . . . You can hear a voice telling you something you really shouldn't not know . . . and whose voice is it? . . . and what does it say? . . .
> . . . You can smell the aroma of the coffee perking . . . and that smell brings you back to a situation you haven't remembered in a long, long time . . . and where are you? . . .

In the above examples, while the sensory modality in which the positive hallucination is to occur is specified (i.e., see, hear, smell), the content of the hallucination is not. The person, the voice, and the situation to be experienced by the client in the above suggestions are left to the client's projections. You can now recognize these as process suggestions for hallucinations. If the clinician wanted to, it would be just as easy to suggest that the client see a specified person, hear a specified voice, or experience a particular situation, providing all the appropriate sensory details.

Indirect suggestions may also be used to facilitate hallucinations. Suggesting that the client be aware of his or her arm is an indirect suggestion to not notice her leg. Referring back to the earlier discussion on negative suggestions, it should be apparent why the negative suggestion, "Don't notice the pain in your neck" as a suggestion for a negative kinesthetic hallucination won't likely work. Thus, indirect suggestions for hallucinations usually take the form of positive suggestions for experiences that would preclude the unwanted experience. For example, rather than directly suggest, "You won't know anyone else is present," in order for the client to negatively hallucinate other people in the vicinity, such a negative hallucination is indirectly accomplished by directly suggesting, "You can be alone" or by the indirect suggestion embedded in the question, "Where did everyone else go?"

The following suggestions exemplify indirect suggestions for hallucinations:

> . . . and how does it feel to see yourself standing over there as a child? . . .
> . . . and whose voice is that that you're hearing? . . .
> . . . and why didn't you notice earlier that your hands were floating effortlessly? . . .
> . . . and when I went to the woods to hear the silence and smell the

fragrance of pine needles, and I'm sure you know those sensations, too. . . .

In the above examples, suggestions in the form of presuppositions are used to facilitate seeing one's self, hearing a voice, and feeling floating hands. By asking the client how it feels to see the child, whose voice it is he or she hears, or when he or she noticed his or her hands floating, the clinician presupposes the client is having these experiences, an indirect suggestion to do so. The last example is a metaphor with embedded commands to indirectly suggest certain sensory experiences. "Hearing the silence" is also an indirect suggestion to negatively hallucinate ongoing auditory stimuli.

Since the client tends to suspend reality-testing during hypnosis, he or she can more readily get absorbed in suggested realities. As you've learned, the person generally retains some sense of objective reality (recall Hilgard's "hidden observer"), but only if the person is aware of a more objective reality. Sometimes a client will get absorbed in hallucinations and not know he or she is hallucinating, as in the confabulations that lead people to believe they were abducted by hostile extraterrestrials. Thus, a clinician would have to be quite astute in making sure that sessions structured to provide hallucinatory experience are not going to inadvertently amplify or promote psychosis (Argast, Landis, & Carrell, 2001).

As for sensory alterations, simply consider under what conditions you might want to enhance or diminish someone's sensory capacities. Suggesting less auditory sensitivity to tinnitus (i.e., ringing in the ears), or greater auditory sensitivity to hearing the stress in a spouse's voice in order to encourage more empathy are examples of appropriate suggestions for auditory sensory alterations.

IDEODYNAMIC RESPONSES

DESCRIPTION

In chapter 3 I discussed the perspective of hypnosis arising as a result of triggering the subjective associations between words and experience. You may recall that in that section I briefly described the intense mind-body relationship, which was exemplified in a later discussion of the physical reactions associated with mental experiences when describing suggestibility tests. The powerful effects of conditioning can be observed in a lot of different ways in daily life since so much of our daily functioning is done on an automatic, unconscious level. If you had to pay attention to every single thing you did each day, by the time you got showered and dressed and ready for work it would be time to call it a day! Our automatic functioning frees the conscious mind to involve itself in higher-order activity. The automatic functions that humans are capable of exist on at least four different levels: cognitive, motoric, sensory, and affective. Collectively, these are the "ideodynamic responses"; individually, the responses are the "ideocognitive response," the "ideomotor response," the "ideosensory response," and the "ideoaffective response." *Each is an automatic response generated at an unconscious level in response to a stimulus, either external or internal.*

The ideocognitive response is what cognitive theorists might call an "automatic thought." These are the unconscious cognitive associations triggered in the client's thought processes in response to the clinician's suggestions. Hypnotic processes employ all kinds of procedures to encourage so-called cognitive distortions, irrational beliefs, and unrealistic expectations as self-limiting ideocognitions to come to the surface for identification and correction. This is especially the case when hypnosis is used in conjunction with cognitive-behavioral approaches (Yapko, 2001b; Zarren & Eimer, 2001).

The ideomotor response is the physical manifestation of mental experience, or, in other words, the body's unconscious physical reactions to one's thoughts. The Chevreul's Pendulum (described in chapter 11) is a hokey but useful demonstration of this relationship (Coe, 1993). Being a passenger in a car and moving to hit the brake is also an example. So-called body language is an entire category filled with thousands of examples (the body moves unconsciously as an analogue to what is thought or verbalized) of ideomotor responses.

The body's movements are usually slight—so slight that they remain out of awareness (hence, unconscious), but they can usually be observed by the naked eye. Certainly they are most easily measured with devices such as the polygraph which can measure variables such as heart rate, galvanic skin response, and level of muscular tension. The polygraph is an obvious example of the ability to detect measurable changes in the body that the test subject is generally unaware of as he or she responds to questions from the examiner.

Ideomotor responses may be facilitated for diagnostic and/or therapeutic purposes. Diagnostically, the clinician may suggest to the client an automatic physical response to questions. For example, one might suggest that if the response to the question is "Yes," the client's head will slowly nod automatically and effortlessly, and if the answer is "No," the client's head can shake involuntarily from side to side. It is not uncommon for a client to verbalize the "Yes" response while simultaneously indicating the "No" response with his or her head. Which would you believe? (If you would be prone to believe the verbal response, I have some real estate I'd like to talk to you about purchasing . . . nothing wrong with it, it's just under a few feet of water . . .) While the ideomotor response is certainly not a lie-detector, it can provide evidence of the existence of multiple cognitive controls and conflicting feelings within the client (Cheek & LeCron, 1968).

Therapeutically, the ideomotor response can be used to facilitate dissociation, to deepen hypnosis, as an indicator of responsiveness, and even as a means for exchange between clinician and client when such techniques as "automatic writing" or "automatic talking" are employed. Automatic writing refers to the ability of the client to write (or draw) without conscious involvement in doing so (Hilgard, 1992). Signing your name and doodling are examples of automatic writing and drawing. Automatic talking involves having the client speak without a conscious involvement in doing so (Watkins, 1987). Talking to one's self, reading aloud, and absentmindedly carrying on a conversation are examples of automatic talking. Direct but permissive suggestions are given to the client, for example, that he "can write and wait with eagerness to see what was written by your hand." The cataleptic client can move in automatic, usually jerky, movements as he or she carries out ideomotor responses such as hand levitation, finger signals (suggested to the client so he or she can provide information or to indicate when he or she has finished a thought, retrieved a memory, is ready to go on, or whatever), and head nods.

Ideosensory responses are automatic experiences of sensation associated with the processing of suggestions. Having the normal range of sensation and a kinesthetic memory for what the experience of the sensation was provide the basis for the ideosensory response. When someone suggests that you recall the experience of having peanut butter stuck to the roof of your mouth, the sensation can come back to you quite automatically as you make sense of what was asked of you. The taste and feel of peanut butter in your mouth is immediately available to you only because of your past experience with it. The suggestion would have no effect if you had never tasted peanut butter (or if you do not have a mouth). Describing in elaborate detail the various sensory components associated with an experience allows the client to reexperience those sensations to a degree determined by the amount and type of past personal experience with it, and the degree of kinesthetic awareness the person generally has.

Ideoaffective responses are the automatic emotional responses attached to the various experiences each person has. People have a diverse range of emotional responses to life's events, each differing in the types as well as degrees of intensity of response. It is difficult, if not impossible, to feel entirely neutral about something. Therefore, as the client experiences the suggestions of the clinician, different feelings associated with the ideas contained in the suggestions come to the surface. Buried negative feelings of hurt and despair can arise in a flash, as can positive feelings of joy and pleasure. The emotional intensity of people's responses to suggestion often catch both the client and the clinician off guard. Be ready!

Ideodynamics are simply structural components of a total experience. Every experience you have occurs on a variety of levels, each adding to the overall experience in a different and complementary way. In doing hypnosis, the ideodynamics are important variables for two important reasons. First, they reflect the inner experience of the client at the unconscious levels where change is sought. Second, they are a part of the current therapeutic experience, and will be the thought, action, feeling, and sensory-based components of the therapy that the person will recall and rely on as the basis for change in the future.

STRATEGIES TO ELICIT IDEODYNAMIC RESPONSES

Unlike many of the other hypnotic phenomena, ideodynamics will occur no matter what you do. There is virtually no way the client can prevent unconscious body movements or thoughts, or keep from reexperiencing feelings and sensations. In facilitating ideodynamic responses hypnotically, the issue becomes one of whether the client responds well to suggestions for specific automatic responses or not. The thoughts, feelings, sensations, and movements that the clinician suggests will be responded to more easily the greater the degree of dissociation present, since ideodynamics are defined as unconscious responses. Therefore, facilitating dissociation is a necessary first step before attempting procedures like automatic writing or finger signaling.

Direct suggestions offered permissively are useful for facilitating ideodynamic responses. The following suggestions are examples of this type:

> . . . as you listen to me describe that experience, I wonder what thoughts will pass through your awareness that might surprise even you . . . (ideocognitive response)
> . . . as you let your body relax . . . your head begins to slowly drop downward . . . and let it do as it wishes. . . . (ideomotor response)
> . . . and as your muscles continue to relax . . . you can feel the tingle in that spot . . . (ideosensory response)
> . . . while you remember that picture of yourself as a child . . . you can notice the feeling that the picture recreates within you. . . . (ideoaffective response)

Each of the above suggestions directly suggests an automatic experience not consciously created. They "just happen" as the client follows the suggestion, and the client doesn't have to will them to happen at all.

Indirect suggestions for ideodynamic responses are also very useful, as long as the clinician chooses words carefully since the words used will engender the specific response obtained. Examples of indirect suggestions for ideodynamics include:

> . . . as a reflex you can think you're to blame for that event happening, but a new thought will occur to you to make you seriously doubt it (ideocognitive response)
>
> . . . I don't think your conscious mind will know your unconscious knows about that event until your finger has lifted. . . . (ideomotor response)
>
> . . . I wonder whether you can recall how good it feels to cool off by jumping into a cool swimming pool after feeling hot and dried out from the heat of the sun. . . . (ideosensory response)
>
> . . . It can be a great relief to find out that what you thought would be a major car repair is only a minor one. . . . (ideoaffective response)

Preoccupying the client with the content of the suggestion facilitates the ideodynamic response, for while the client projects him- or herself into the described situation and attempts to make meaning of it, his or her unconscious is already responding. Identifying the idiosyncratic patterns of nonverbal communication each person uses unconsciously can be a rich source of information about that person. Noticing such patterns and interpreting them are two different things, however, and while I encourage noticing patterns, I am not as quick to encourage their interpretation. Saying a gesture "means" this or a posture "means" that is a gross oversimplification and is more likely to be only a projection of the observer's unconscious than anything else.

Ideodynamic responses are responsible for the most direct contact you will have with your client's unconscious. Doesn't that *automatically* entitle them to careful consideration?

TIME DISTORTION

DESCRIPTION

The experience of time is a purely subjective one, meaning you experience the passing of time in your own way at any given moment. Everyone has had the experience of doing something pleasurable and fun, and discovering that what seemed like a short period of time was actually a relatively long one: "Time flies when you're having fun." Likewise, you have no doubt had the experience of being in situations that were difficult or boring, and after checking your watch and waiting . . . for what seemed like three days . . . you then checked your watch again and found, much to your distress, that only 5 minutes had gone by. *The subjective passing of time can seem much longer or much shorter than is objectively true, depending on your focus of attention.* Such distortions of time take place in all people's experience, and like all other experiences that are subjective, the experience of time can be significantly altered in deliberate ways hypnotically with appropriate suggestions (Cooper, 1952; Edgette & Edgette, 1995; Erickson & Erickson, 1958).

Facilitating the distortion of time in a client's perception can make for a very useful therapeutic experience. Think of situations where it would be helpful to lengthen or shorten one's sense of time: When a client is in pain, for example, condensing a long period of painful existence into what seems like a very short period of time can be a most humane intervention (Bejenke, 1996). Expanding the perception of time of comfort in between the contractions of a woman in labor can make the birthing experience a much more comfortable one. Having a long work day subjectively seem shorter can make a difficult job a little easier to take. Having only a short period of clock time in which to take an examination and yet subjectively experiencing plenty of time can allow for better performance. These are but a few potential examples of useful applications of the hypnotic phenomenon of time distortion.

STRATEGIES TO ELICIT TIME DISTORTION

Approaches for facilitating time distortion can range from your "simply getting out of the way" and letting time distortion arise spontaneously to the offering of direct and indirect suggestions for its deliberate elicitation. Time distortion tends to arise with no suggestions for it at all, for once someone closes his or her eyes and becomes absorbed in internal experience (e.g., thoughts, memories, sensations, etc.), the "real" world recedes into the background, the passage of time is generally unimportant, and the chance to make a realistic assessment of how much clock time has elapsed is more difficult. Try this yourself: Check the time, let your eyes close, and then let your mind drift to wherever it happens to go. Open your eyes again after what you feel is five minutes of clock time. How far off are you? Did you under- or overestimate? Most people in this brief exercise would think more time had elapsed than actually did. If you ever had to be silent for an entire minute as a child in school, you know how only a minute of forced silence can seem like an hour! For the client in hypnosis, though, who is relaxed, absorbed in meaningful and helpful experience, and enjoying the experience, the tendency is to underestimate the passage of time. The client typically thinks that a 20- or 30-minute session was only 5 or 10 minutes long. It's often a convincer to people that they were, in fact, hypnotized when they discover the big difference between what the clock on the wall says and what their "inner clock" told them.

Direct suggestions for time distortion, especially when offered permissively, can facilitate the experience well. The following are examples of direct suggestions for time distortion:

> . . . and it can seem to you as if a long period of time has gone by . . . and that you have had many hours of high-quality rest. . . . (time expansion)
>
> . . . an hour can seem like a minute . . . and time can pass so quickly . . . when each thought passes through your mind at a rate so fast that it's easier to just let your thoughts pass quickly by than try to catch one. . . . (time condensation)
>
> . . . your mind and body have been so busy here . . . and it takes so much time to do everything you've done . . . hours might seem to have passed by while you have been so preoccupied. . . . (time expansion)

Indirect suggestions for time distortion gently plant the notion that the experience of time can be altered. Indirect suggestions (e.g., "I wonder how few minutes have gone by during this time . . ."), stories containing examples of experiences where time was distorted (e.g., "I was so busy I didn't even notice how much time had elapsed"), conversational postulates (e.g., "Are you surprised at how much you've accomplished in just a few minutes?"), and double-binds (e.g., "Did it seem like a very long time or just sort of a really long time to you?") are all capable of facilitating time distortion. The following suggestions provide another example of each:

> . . . keeping track of time is so difficult sometimes . . . and right now it's hard to know whether 5 minutes or 6 minutes have gone by . . . and how can anyone really know whether only $5\frac{1}{4}$ minutes have gone by or $5\frac{1}{2}$ . . . or $5\frac{6}{8}$ or $5\frac{7}{8}$ minutes have gone by . . . (indirect suggestion for an expanded experience of time)
>
> . . . I worked with a client not long ago who felt so uncomfortable when she first came in . . . her problem bothered her a lot . . . but when she closed her eyes and let herself listen to me . . . deeply . . . she forgot to notice how much time went by . . . and she let herself relax so deeply . . . it seemed like hours of comfort . . . soothed her mind and body . . . and she felt so good . . . for a long time afterward . . . (metaphor regarding an experience of time distortion)
>
> . . . and you've been so comfortable sitting and listening to me, haven't you? . . . That's right . . . and it isn't easy to know how long . . . very long . . . a period of time has passed, is it? . . . (conversational postulate)
>
> . . . and now I wonder whether you realize how fast and short this period of time has gone by . . . and you can guess if you'd like . . . would you say it's been only 5 minutes or would you say it's been as much as 7? . . . (forced choice orienting the person to a specific time span)

In the first example above, by getting so specific about how much time has elapsed and framing all the choices within a short period of time, one can help the client become oriented to that time frame and thus feel as if a lengthy process actually took only 5 to 6 minutes. If the clinician wants to expand time, the frame used can be an exaggerated one (e.g., for a 10-minute hypnosis session, the clinician can suggest how difficult it is to know if 20 or 20½ minutes went by . . .). In the second example, a metaphor is offered that lets the client know he or she can be comfortable for what feels like a long time by being in hypnosis through the building of an identification between him or her and the person in the story. In the third example, the conversational postulate is employed; by asking the client to realize how difficult it is to assess the length of elapsed time, the presupposition is that a long time has passed. In the last example, the client is forced to choose between two times that are both much shorter than the actual time elapsed. Time can be expanded by making the forced (double-bind) choices much longer than the actual time elapsed.

When clients disengage from hypnosis and discover how distorted their perception of time has been, they know they have experienced something out of the ordinary. The result can be a new respect for the complexity and sophistication of their own inner world. A boost in self-esteem accomplished so easily is one of the most positive dimensions of doing hypnosis.

ENDING THE HYPNOSIS SESSION (DISENGAGEMENT)

As good as it feels to be in hypnosis, eventually you have to disengage from the hypnotic experience and move on with your day. Disengagement is the final stage of hypnotic interaction. The client may indicate a readiness to disengage through a diminished focus of his or her attention and by beginning to move and stretch. The clinician has to make a decision at the moment of observing such signs as to whether the work is done for that session or whether the client's initiation of disengagement is some form of avoidance that can be addressed therapeutically.

The clinician is directing the therapy session, and should generally be the one to decide when initiating disengagement is appropriate, just as he or she decides when the induction of hypnosis is appropriate. In deciding when disengagement is appropriate, the clinician can also decide on what the manner of disengagement will be. When and how to disengage is a matter of individual clinical judgment, based on the overall treatment plan and the accomplishments of that specific session. The clinician has, by this time, employed a suggestion style and structure in his or her approach to the client, and the disengagement can be consistent with these. If the clinician has been relatively direct throughout, he or she can offer such suggestions as the following for disengagement:

> . . . You can bring yourself out of hypnosis at a rate that is comfortable for you . . . taking as much time as you'd like to in order to comfortably complete this experience for yourself. . . .
>
> . . . When you're ready, you can open your eyes and reorient yourself to the here-and-now, feeling relaxed and refreshed. . . .
>
> . . . When you open your eyes in about 1 minute and rediscover the outside world . . . you'll be able to notice how good it feels to have been in hypnosis. . . .

Most direct approaches to disengagement (traditionally called "awakening") have employed an authoritarian counting method, e.g., "I'm going to count to three and snap my fingers and you will then be wide awake . . ." Such an approach is not particularly respectful of the client's need to disengage from the hypnotic experience at his or her own rate. Expecting a client to respond to an arbitrary count and come out of hypnosis simply because you want him or her to does not allow the client whatever time he or she may want to complete the experience for him or herself. Furthermore, expecting *any* human being to respond to a finger snap is simply degrading and undesirable.

If the hypnosis session has been an informal, spontaneous one, the clinician can choose to be consistent in his or her approach by offering indirect suggestions for disengagement. The following suggestions are exemplary of such an approach:

> . . . and I wonder whether you've realized how comfortable it has been to let your mind consider that possibility . . . and that can certainly be an *eye-opening* experience. . . .
>
> . . . and after a nice rest such as the one you've just had you can certainly *alert yourself* to the joys of living. . . .
>
> . . . did I tell you how I learned about that? . . . I was so preoccupied with myself that I didn't notice things around me much . . . but one can *become less self-absorbed* and *move around* in the world and *notice things outside yourself* . . . *opening your eyes* to new possibilities. . . .

In deciding on the when and how of disengagement, the clinician can consider such factors as whether amnesia is desirable to suggest and what type(s), if any, of posthypnotic suggestions might be offered. How the hypnotic experience is concluded will have a significant impact on the client, since human memory is generally stronger for the most recent events (the "recency effect"). In other words, the feeling the client has as he or she disengages from hypnosis are the feelings he or she is most likely to associate with the whole hypnotic experience. This is another reason why it is usually the best option to allow him or her the time he or she wants or needs to complete his or her processing of the events of the hypnosis session. Letting the client disengage at his or her own chosen rate allows him or her the opportunity to feel relaxed and unhurried under your care.

CONCLUSION

This chapter has described in detail the most basic building blocks for the therapeutic applications of hypnosis. Clinical interventions will always involve some or all of these hypnotic phenomena, and it is therefore imperative that you be clear about what each of these subjective experiences is really about. Before you can apply them in meaningful ways, it may be most helpful to you to first spend some time observing these experiences as they arise in daily living, particularly if you attempt to uncover what served as the trigger for the phenomenon. Such careful observation of the range of human experiences occurring routinely can make their use in hypnosis easier to accomplish.

As building blocks, the various hypnotic phenomena can be arranged and rearranged in an unlimited number of configurations. The process of planning a specific intervention for a particular client can involve the development of a hypnotic strategy. You can decide which hypnotic phenomena would be useful experiences for the client to have. More specifically, you can decide the type(s) of orienting ideas to be presented, the type and style of induction to be used, which hypnotic utilizations (therapeutic strategies) to use with special consideration for their content, style, and degree of complexity.

With the various hypnotic phenomena serving as the foundation on which to build the intervention, the task of the clinician—to organize such experiences in a meaningful way—is a complicated one. This task is considered in greater detail in the next chapter.

For Discussion

1. What is your reaction to discovering some of the everyday aspects of hypnotic phenomena? Does it make it easier or harder for you to think of hypnosis as something special in therapy?
2. What is your opinion about past-life regression (regressing someone hypnotically

to a previous incarnation), hypnotic ESP (amplifying extrasensory perception hypnotically), and other paranormal applications of hypnosis? What is the basis for your opinion?

3. How can each of the hypnotic phenomena be seen in the various mental disorders? (For example, a dissociative identity disorder involves the dissociation of personality parts, and may also involve amnesia for the existence of each part.)

4. In what instances, if any, might facilitating any of the various hypnotic phenomena be contraindicated? Explain your reasoning.

5. How might you use age progression to assist your learning of hypnosis?

Things to Do

1. List 10 routine contexts in which each of the hypnotic phenomena arise. What factors seem to precipitate these phenomena arising?

2. During an age regression process, have your subject write his or her name while at different ages. Do you observe differences in writing style that seem age-appropriate? What do you conclude?

3. Make a list of the 20 most significant events in your development. Which ones would you characterize as being positive; which negative? Which ones seem to have the most emotion attached to them? Why? Does this make them easier or harder to recall for you?

4. Check with local hospitals to find out what their policies are regarding the use of hypnotic anesthesia in their operating rooms. What do you find out? Locate and arrange to interview any local physicians who do surgical procedures employing hypnotic anesthesia.

REFERENCES

Argast, T., Landis, R., & Carrell, P. (2001). When to use or not to use hypnosis according to the Ericksonian tradition. In B. Geary & J. Zeig (Eds.), *The handbook of Ericksonian psychotherapy* (pp. 66–92). Phoenix, AZ: The Milton H. Erickson Foundation Press.

Arnold, M. (1946). On the mechanism of suggestion and hypnosis. *Journal of Abnormal and Social Psychology, 41*, 107–28.

Baker, R. (1992). *Hidden memories: Voices and visions from within.* Buffalo, NY: Prometheus.

Bányai, É. (1991). Toward a social-psychobiological model of hypnosis. In S. Lynn & J. Rhue (Eds.), *Theories of hypnosis: Current models and perspectives* (pp. 564–98). New York: Guilford.

Barber, J. (1996a). Headache. In J. Barber (Ed.), *Hypnosis and suggestion in the treatment of pain* (pp. 158–84). New York: Norton.

—— (1996b). A brief introduction to hypnotic analgesia. In J. Barber (Ed.), *Hypnosis and suggestion in the treatment of pain* (pp. 3–32). New York: Norton.

Barber, T. (2000). A deeper understanding of hypnosis: Its secrets, its nature, its essence. *American Journal of Clinical Hypnosis, 42*, 3–4, 208–72.

Barber, T., Spanos, N., & Chaves, J. (1974). *Hypnosis, imagination and human potentialities.* Elmsford, NY: Pergamon Press.

Barretta, N., & Barretta, P. (2001). Hypnosis: Adjunct to medical maneuvers. In B. Geary & J. Zeig (Eds.), *The handbook of Ericksonian psychotherapy* (pp. 281–90). Phoenix, AZ: The Milton H. Erickson Foundation Press.

Bejenke, C. (1996). Painful medical procedures. In J. Barber (Ed.), *Hypnosis and suggestion in the treatment of pain* (pp. 209–66). New York: Norton.

Blume, S. (1990). *Secret survivors.* New York: Ballantine.

Bowers, K., & Davidson, T. (1991). A neodissociative critique of Spanos's social-psychological model of hypnosis. In S. Lynn & J. Rhue (Eds.), *Theories of hypnosis: Current models and perspectives* (pp. 105–43). New York: Guilford.

Brown, D., Scheflin, A., & Hammond, D. (1998). *Memory, trauma treatment, and the law.* New York: Norton.

Cardeña, E. (1994). The domain of dissociation. In S. Lynn & J. Rhue (Eds.), *Dissociation: Clinical, theoretical, and research perspectives* (pp. 15–31). New York: Guilford.

Ceci, S., & Bruck, M. (1995). *Jeopardy in the courtroom: A scientific analysis of children's testimony.* Washington, D.C.: American Psychological Association.

Chaves, J. (1989). Hypnotic control of clinical pain. In N. Spanos & J. Chaves (Eds.), *Hypnosis: The cognitive-behavioral perspective* (pp. 242–72). Buffalo, N.Y.: Prometheus.

—— (1993). Hypnosis in pain management. In J. Rhue, S. Lynn, & I. Kirsch (Eds.), *Handbook of clinical hypnosis* (pp. 511–32). Washington, D.C.: American Psychological Association.

Chaves, J., & Dworkin, S. (1997). Hypnotic control of pain: Historical perspectives and future prospects. *International Journal of Clinical and Experimental Hypnosis, 45,* 356–376.

Cheek, D., & LeCron, L. (1968). *Clinical hypnotherapy.* New York: Grune & Stratton.

Coe, W. (1993). Expectations and hypnotherapy. In J. Rhue, S. Lynn, & I. Kirsch (Eds.), *Handbook of clinical hypnosis* (pp. 73–93). Washington, D.C.: American Psychological Association.

Cooper, L. (1952). Time distortion in hypnosis. *Journal of Psychology, 34,* 247–84.

Crawford, H., Knebel, T., Kaplan, L., Vendemia, J., Xie, M., Jamison, S., & Pribram, K. (1998). Hypnotic analgesia: Somatosensory event-related potential changes to noxious stimuli and 2. Transfer learning to reduce chronic low back pain. *International Journal of Clinical and Experimental Hypnosis, 46,* 1, 92–132.

Daniel, S. (1999). The healthy patient: Empowering women in their encounters with the health care system. *American Journal of Clinical Hypnosis, 42,* 2 108–14.

Dixon, M., & Laurence, J-R. (1992). Two hundred years of hypnosis research: Questions resolved? Questions unanswered! In E. Fromm & M. Nash (Eds.), *Contemporary hypnosis research* (pp. 34–66). New York: Guilford.

Dolan, Y. (1991). *Resolving sexual abuse: Solution-focused therapy and Ericksonian hypnosis for adult survivors.* New York: Norton.

Doris, J. (Ed.) (1991). *The suggestibility of children's recollections: Implications for eyewitness testimony.* Washington, D.C.: American Psychological Association.

Edgette, J. H., & Edgette, J. S. (1995). *The handbook of hypnotic phenomena in psychotherapy.* New York: Brunner/Mazel.

Eimer, B. (2000). Clinical applications of hypnosis for brief and efficient pain management psychotherapy. *American Journal of Clinical Hypnosis, 43*, 1, 17–40.

Eimer, B., & Freeman, A. (1998). *Pain management psychotherapy: A practical guide.* New York: Wiley.

Erickson, M. (1954/1980). Pseudo-orientation in time as a hypnotherapeutic procedure. *Journal of Clinical and Experimental Hypnosis, 2*, 261–83. Reprinted in Rossi, E. (Ed.) (1980), *The Collected Papers of Milton H. Erickson on Hypnosis* (Vol. 4) (pp. 397–423). New York: Irvington.

Erickson, M. (1966). The interspersal hypnotic technique for symptom correction and pain control. *American Journal of Clinical Hypnosis, 8*, 198–209.

Erickson, M., & Erickson, E. (1958). Further considerations of time distortion: Subjective time condensation as distinct from time expansion. *American Journal of Clinical Hypnosis, 1*, 83–88.

Erickson, M., & Rossi, E. (1981). *Experiencing hypnosis: Therapeutic approaches to altered states.* New York: Irvington.

Ewin, D. (1983). Emergency room hypnosis for the burned patient. *American Journal of Clinical Hypnosis, 26*, 5–8.

Frederick, C., & Phillips, M. (1995). Decoding mystifying signals: Translating symbolic communications of elusive ego states. *American Journal of Clinical Hypnosis, 38*, 2, 87–96.

Fredrickson, R. (1992). *Repressed memories.* New York: Fireside.

Galovski, T., & Blanchard, E. (1998). The treatment of irritable bowel syndrome with hypnotherapy. *Applied Psychophysiology and Biofeedback, 23*, 4, 219–32.

Gardner, R. (1992). *True and false accusations of child sex abuse.* Cresskill, NJ: Creative Therapeutics.

Genuis, M. (1995). The use of hypnosis in helping cancer patients control anxiety, pain, and emesis: A review of recent empirical studies. *American Journal of Clinical Hypnosis, 37*, 316–25.

Gilligan, S. (1987). *Therapeutic trances: The cooperation principle in Ericksonian hypnotherapy.* New York: Brunner/Mazel.

Ginandes, C. (2002). Extended, strategic therapy for recalcitrant mind-body healing. *American Journal of Clinical Hypnosis, 45*, 2, 91–102.

Goldstein, A., & Hilgard, E. (1975). Lack of influence of the morphine antagonist naloxone on hypnotic analgesia. *Proceedings of the National Academy of Sciences, 72*, 2041–3.

Gonsalkorale, W., Houghton, L., & Whorwell, P. (2002). Hypnotherapy in irritable bowel syndrome: A large scale audit of a clinical service with examination of factors influencing responsiveness. *American Journal of Gastroenterology, 97*, 4, 954–61.

Haley, J. (1973). *Uncommon therapy: The psychiatric techniques of Milton H. Erickson, M.D.* New York: Norton.

Hartman, W. (2001). The utilization of ego state patterns of self-expression in the treatment of aphonic conversation reactions. *Hypnos: Swedish Journal of Hypnosis in Psychotherapy and Psychosomatic Medicine, 28*, 1, 4–10.

Hassett, L. (1994). Summary of the scientific literature for pain and anxiety control in dentistry. *Anesthesia Progress, 41*, 48–57.

Hilgard, E. (1986). Divided consciousness: Multiple controls in human thought and action (rev. ed.). New York: Wiley.

—— (1992). Dissociation and theories of hypnosis. In E. Fromm & M. Nash (Eds.), *Contemporary hypnosis research* (pp. 69–101). New York: Guilford.

Hilgard, E., & Hilgard, J. (1994). *Hypnosis in the relief of pain*. New York: Brunner/Mazel.

Hornyak, L. (1999). Empowerment through giving symptoms voice. *American Journal of Clinical Hypnosis, 42*, 2, 132–9.

Johnson, G. (1991). *In the palaces of memory*. New York: Vintage Books.

Kalt, H. (2000). Psychoneuroimmunology: An interpretation of experimental case study evidence towards a paradigm for predictable results. *American Journal of Clinical Hypnosis, 43*, 1, 41–52.

Kihlstrom, J. (1980). Posthypnotic amnesia for recently learned material: Interactions with "episodic" and "semantic" memory. *Cognitive Psychology, 12*, 227–51.

—— (1987). The cognitive unconscious. *Science, 237*, 1445–52.

Kirsch, I. (1993). Cognitive-behavioral hypnotherapy. In J. Rhue, S. Lynn, & I. Kirsch (Eds.), *Handbook of clinical hypnosis* (pp. 151–171). Washington, D.C.: American Psychological Association.

Kirsch, I. (2000). The response set theory of hypnosis. *American Journal of Clinical Hypnosis, 42*, 3–4, 274–292.

Labelle, L., Laurence, J-R., Nadon, R., & Perry, C. (1990). Hypnotizability, preference for an imagic-cognitive style and memory creation in hypnosis. *Journal of Abnormal Psychology, 99*, 222–28.

Lang, E., Benotsch, E., Fick, L., Lutgendorf, S., Berbaum, M., Berbaum, K., Logan, H., & Spiegel, D. (2000). Adjunctive non-pharmacological analgesia for invasive medical procedures: A randomized trial. *Lancet, 355* (April 29), 1486–1500.

Lankton, S. (2001). A goal-directed intervention for decisive resolution of coping limitations resulting from moderate and severe trauma. In B. Geary & J. Zeig (Eds.), *The handbook of Ericksonian psychotherapy* (pp. 195–214). Phoenix, AZ: The Milton H. Erickson Foundation Press.

Lankton, S., & Lankton, C. (1983). *The answer within: A clinical framework of Ericksonian hypnotherapy*. New York: Brunner/Mazel.

Levitan, A. (1992). The use of hypnosis with cancer patients. *Psychological Medicine, 10*, 119–31.

Loftus, E. (1993). The reality of repressed memories. *American Psychologist, 48*, 5, 518–37.

Loftus, E., & Hoffman, H. (1989). Misinformation and memory: The creation of new memories. *Journal of Experimental Psychology: General, 118*, 100–104.

Loftus, E., & Ketcham, K. (1994). *The myth of repressed memory: False memories and allegations of sexual abuse*. New York: St. Martin's Press.

Lynch, D. (1999). Empowering the patient: Hypnosis in the management of cancer, surgical disease and chronic pain. *American Journal of Clinical Hypnosis, 42*, 2, 122–30.

Lynn, S. (2001). Informed consent and uninformed clinical practice: Dissociation, hypnosis and false memories. *American Journal of Clinical Hypnosis, 43*, 3–4, 311–21.

Lynn, S., & McConkey, K. (1998). *Truth in memory*. New York: Guilford.

Lynn, S., Weekes, J., & Milano, M. (1989). Reality vs. suggestion: Pseudomemory in hypnotizable and simulating subjects. *Journal of Abnormal Psychology, 98*, 137–44.

Mack, J. (1997). *Abduction: Human encounters with aliens.* New York: Ballantine.

McConkey, K. (1992). The effects of hypnotic procedures on remembering: The experimental findings and their implications for forensic hypnosis. In E. Fromm & M. Nash (Eds.), *Contemporary hypnosis research* (pp. 405–26). New York: Guilford.

McConkey, K., & Sheehan, P. (1995). *Hypnosis, memory, and behavior in criminal investigation.* New York: Guilford.

Montgomery, G., DuHamel, K., & Redd, W. (2000). A meta-analysis of hypnotically induced analgesia: How effective is hypnosis? *International Journal of Clinical and Experimental Hypnosis, 48,* 2, 138–53.

Mulligan, R. (1996). Dental pain. In J. Barber (Ed.), *Hypnosis and suggestion in the treatment of pain* (pp. 185–208). New York: Norton.

Murray-Jobsis, J. (1995). Hypnosis and psychotherapy in the treatment of survivors of trauma. In G. Burrows & R. Stanley (Eds.), *Contemporary international hypnosis.* W. Sussex, UK: Wiley.

Nash, M. (1991). Hypnosis as a special case of psychological regression. In S. Lynn & J. Rhue (Eds.), *Theories of hypnosis: Current models and perspectives* (pp. 171–94). New York: Guilford.

Ofshe, R., & Watters, E. (1994). *Making monsters: False memories, psychotherapy, and sexual hysteria.* New York: Scribner's.

Olness, K., MacDonald, J., & Uden, D. (1987). Comparison of self-hypnosis and propranolol in the treatment of juvenile classic migraine. *Pediatrics, 79,* 593–97.

Orne, E., Whitehouse, W., Dinges, D., & Orne, M. (1996). Memory liabilities associated with hypnosis: Does low hypnotizability confer immunity? *International Journal of Clinical and Experimental Hypnosis, 44,* 4, 354–69.

Parkin, A. (1993). *Memory: Phenomena, experiment and theory.* Cambridge, MA: Blackwell.

Patterson, D. (1996). Burn pain. In J. Barber (Ed.), *Hypnosis and suggestion in the treatment of pain* (pp. 267–302). New York: Norton.

Patterson, D., & Ptacek, J. (1997). Baseline pain as a moderator of hypnotic analgesia for burn injury treatment. *Journal of Consulting and Clinical Psychology, 60,* 713–17.

Phillips, M., & Frederick, C. (1995). *Healing the divided self: Clinical and Ericksonian hypnotherapy for post-traumatic and dissociative conditions.* New York: Norton.

Ready, D., Bothwell, R., & Brigham, J. (1997). The effects of hypnosis, context reinstatement, and anxiety on eyewitness memory. *International Journal of Clinical and Experimental Hypnosis, 45,* 1, 55–68.

Rossi, E. (1996). *The symptom path to enlightenment: The new dynamics of self-organization in hypnotherapy.* Pacific Palisades, CA: Palisades Gateway.

—— (1998). Mind-body healing in hypnosis: Immediate-early genes and the deep psychobiology of psychotherapy. *Japanese Journal of Hypnosis, 43,* 1–10.

—— (2001). Psychobiological principles of creative Ericksonian psychotherapy. In B. Geary & J. Zeig (Eds.), *The handbook of Ericksonian psychotherapy* (pp. 122–53). Phoenix, AZ: The Milton H. Erickson Foundation Press.

Rossi, E., & Cheek, D. (1988). *Mind-body therapy: Methods of ideodynamic healing in hypnosis.* New York: Norton.

Sarbin, T. (1997). Hypnosis as a conversation: "Believed-in imaginings" revisited. *Contemporary Hypnosis, 14,* 4, 203–15.

Schachter, D. (1996). *Searching for memory: The brain, the mind, and the past.* New York: Basic.

Scheflin, A., & Frischholz, E. (1999). Significant dates in the history of forensic hypnosis. *American Journal of Clinical Hypnosis, 42*, 2, 84–107.

Sheehan, P. (1988). Memory distortion in hypnosis. *International Journal of Clinical and Experimental Hypnosis, 36*, 296–311.

Sheehan, P. (1995). The effects of asking leading questions in hypnosis. In G. Burrows & R. Stanley (Eds.), *Contemporary international hypnosis* (pp. 55–62). West Sussex, UK: Wiley.

Smith, W. (1993). Hypnotherapy with rape victims. In J. Rhue, S. Lynn, & I. Kirsch (Eds.), *Handbook of clinical hypnosis* (pp. 479–491). Washington, D.C.: American Psychological Association.

Spanos, N. (1986). Hypnotic behavior: A social-psychological interpretation of amnesia, analgesia, and "trance logic." *Behavioral and Brain Sciences, 9*, 449–67.

—— (1991). A sociocognitive approach to hypnosis. In S. Lynn & J. Rhue (Eds.), *Theories of hypnosis: Current models and perspectives* (pp. 324–61). New York: Guilford.

—— (1996). *Multiple identities and false memories.* Washington, D.C.: American Psychological Association.

Spanos, N., Radtke, H., & Dubreuil, D. (1982). Episodic and semantic memory in posthypnotic amnesia: A reevaluation. *Journal of Personality and Social Psychology, 43*, 565–73.

Spiegel, D. (1986). Dissociating damage. *American Journal of Clinical Hypnosis, 29*, 123–31.

—— (1993). Hypnosis in the treatment of posttraumatic stress disorders. In J. Rhue, S. Lynn, & I. Kirsch (Eds.), *Handbook of clinical hypnosis* (pp. 493–508). Washington, D.C.: American Psychological Association.

Spiegel, D., & Albert, L. (1983). Naloxone fails to reverse hypnotic alleviation of chronic pain. *Psychopharmacology, 81*, 140–43.

Spinhoven, P., Linssen, A., Van Dyck, R., & Zitman, F. (1992). Autogenic training and self-hypnosis in the control of tension headache. *General Hospital Psychiatry, 14*, 408–15.

Strieber, W. (1995). *Communion: A true story* (Revised edition). New York: Avon.

Syrjala, K., Cummings, C., & Donaldson, G. (1992). Hypnosis or cognitive behavioral training for the reduction of pain and nausea during cancer treatment: A controlled clinical trial. *Pain, 48*, 137–46.

Terr, L. (1994). *Unchained memories: True stories of traumatic memories, lost and found.* New York: Basic Books.

Torem, M. (1992). "Back from the future": A powerful age-progression technique. *American Journal of Clinical Hypnosis, 35*, 81–88.

van der Kolk, B. (1994). The body keeps the score: Memory and the evolving psychobiology of PTSD. *Harvard Review of Psychiatry, 1*, 253–65.

Wagstaff, G. (1991). Compliance, belief and semantics in hypnosis: A nonstate, sociocognitive perspective. In S. Lynn & J. Rhue (Eds.), *Theories of hypnosis: Current models and perspectives* (pp. 362–96). New York: Guilford.

Watkins, J. (1987). *Hypnotherapeutic techniques: The practice of clinical hypnosis* (Vol. 1). New York: Irvington.

Watkins, J., & Watkins, H. (1997). *Ego states: Theory and therapy.* New York: Norton.

Weitzenhoffer, A. (2000). *The practice of hypnotism* (2nd ed.). New York: Wiley.

Yapko, M. (1988). Confusion methodologies in the management of pain. *Hypnos: Swedish Journal of Hypnosis in Psychotherapy and Psychosomatic Medicine, 15*, 163–73.

—— (1993, September/October). The seductions of memory. *Family Therapy Networker*, 17, 5, 30–37.

—— (1994a). Suggestibility and repressed memories of abuse: A survey of psychotherapists' beliefs. *American Journal of Clinical Hypnosis, 36*, 163–71.

—— (1994b). *Suggestions of abuse: True and false memories of childhood sexual trauma.* New York: Simon & Schuster.

—— (2001a). Revisiting the question: What is Ericksonian hypnosis? In B. Geary & J. Zeig (Eds.), *The handbook of Ericksonian psychotherapy* (pp. 168–86). Phoenix, AZ: The Milton H. Erickson Foundation Press.

—— (2001b). *Treating depression with hypnosis.* Philadelphia, PA: Brunner/Routledge.

Zarren, J., & Eimer, B. (2001). *Brief cognitive hypnosis: Facilitating the change of dysfunctional behavior.* New York: Springer.

Zeig, J. (Ed.) (1980). *A teaching seminar with Milton H. Erickson, M.D.* New York: Brunner/Mazel.

Zeig, J. (1985). The clinical use of amnesia: Ericksonian methods. In J. Zeig (Ed.), *Ericksonian psychotherapy. Volume I: Structures.* New York: Brunner/Mazel.

Zeig, J., & Geary, B. (2001). Ericksonian approaches to pain management. In B. Geary & J. Zeig (Eds.), *The handbook of Ericksonian psychotherapy* (pp. 252–62). Phoenix, AZ: The Milton H. Erickson Foundation Press.

17

Designing and Delivering Hypnotic Interventions in Treatment

Knowing the basic forms of suggestion structure, the fundamentals of hypnotic induction, and the potential shifts in experience associated with various hypnotic phenomena, we can now focus more specifically on developing hypnotic and strategic approaches to treatment. In this chapter, I will consider some of the practical foundational principles for introducing and integrating hypnosis into the therapeutic context. How will you decide what exactly to say to a client who is suffering when you know that each word, each phrase, you employ has the potential to make a positive difference?

The key word in the previous sentence is "potential." There should be no illusion on your part that if you say everything just "right," *as if you could even if you wanted to*, you will be successful. As you have learned in previous chapters, there are many factors influencing the outcome of an intervention, hypnotic or otherwise. Some of these factors are in your control (e.g., your choice of wording and your sense of timing) and some of these factors are *not* in your control (e.g., your client's idiosyncratic interpretation of your meaning, medication side effects, and the residuals of your client's past treatment history). This chapter is meant to provide some guidance in helping you control the things you can in order to increase your potential effectiveness in applying hypnosis in treatment. Clinical skill counts for a lot (even though it doesn't account for everything), and many of the considerations in this chapter are meant to enhance your clinical skills in applying hypnosis.

DOING HYPNOSIS VERSUS *BEING* HYPNOTIC

There are many practitioners of hypnosis who know how to perform hypnotic techniques. However, I believe there is an important distinction to make between *doing* hypnosis and *being* hypnotic. Someone reading an impersonal script to a client may be doing hypnosis, but I don't believe he or she can necessarily be considered hypnotic (although he or she might be). Someone who is detached from the client and the process, who has the idea that what he or she says is less important than the person's susceptibility measure, is not likely to be very hypnotic. Being hypnotic means being able to fully engage the person, being so attuned and connected to the client that you are difficult to ignore or take lightly because what you're doing and what you're offering is so relevant and absorbing.

Think about those people that grab and hold your attention—the people that you don't want to take your eyes off. What about them grabs you and holds your attention? Whatever that quality is, *that's* hypnotic, even though the person isn't necessarily doing hypnosis. When are *you* hypnotic? Are you aware of those special times in therapy when your clients seem riveted to your every word?

In doing hypnosis, it's a distinction between moving a client through an arbitrary procedure that has no inherent meaningfulness, such as an utterly arbitrary method like a "countdown induction method" (what's meaningful or absorbing about counting numbers—unless you're an accountant?), versus stimulating personally meaningful associations in a client through individualized suggestions that acknowledge and incorporate his or her uniqueness (Rossi, 1980; Zeig, 2001).

Being hypnotic means engaging purposefully with people, accepting the responsibility for being an agent of influence and change, and striving to use your capacity for influence intelligently and sensitively. Being hypnotic also means knowing that the capacity for being absorbing, engaging, and influential doesn't only happen when formal induction takes place. Being hypnotic simply means incorporating hypnotic principles of focusing people and introducing positive possibilities to them into your very way of being, and is thus revealed through each interaction to one degree or another.

THE SKILLS OF A CLINICIAN

The skills needed to be an effective clinician, in contrast to those needed to merely perform an induction, are substantial. These include a broad knowledge of current clinical literature, an ability to relate to the client and form a therapeutic alliance, and an ability to organize and direct a well-structured intervention. These are all complex skills which require significant investments of time and effort to develop.

Who we are as people is the foundation onto which the veneer of our clinical training is later glued. Consider for a moment why you structure your clinical practice the way you do. What does it say about you as a person that you maintain your individual philosophy of treatment, are attracted to and strive to practice well a particular style of therapy, and practice in such a way as to even try to lead your clients to believe as you do, however directly or indirectly you may do that?

This is hardly a new concept. We've known for a very long time that we get attracted to and practice therapy, including our hypnotic interventions, on the basis of what we subjectively find appealing. Someone goes to a hypnosis workshop and learns about and experiences an "inner sage" induction technique, for example, discovering some previously untapped inner wisdom, and thought it was an inspiring experience. So, he or she goes back to work with a new enthusiasm and starts doing "inner sage" techniques with almost every client. Or, someone goes to a conference on the new and controversial "XYZ Disorder" and then starts seeing it in clients never previously known to have "it." As you've already discovered in the Frames of Reference sections throughout this book, the gifted experts each have their own viewpoint, just as you have yours. And yours will be the determining factor in whether and how you apply hypnosis.

Ideally, our personal backgrounds and interests should not be the primary basis for designing and delivering our interventions, hypnotic or otherwise. In the "real world," however, all of our clinical training prepares us to focus in on "this" but not "that" when we interview our clients, so we may understand what's going on "this" way and then treat it "that" way. Having a philosophy or belief system to provide you a foundation is both necessary and desirable. Perhaps where clinicians sometimes err, though, is when they only see things one way and don't stretch themselves to consider how other perspectives might help in understanding and addressing the problem. Almost any problem can credibly be understood and treated from many different viewpoints. It seems important, to me at least, to distinguish between the facts of a case and the interpretations or inferences you might make when designing your intervention so your inferences don't become dogma.

THE PRELIMINARIES TO HYPNOTIC INTERVENTION

As I have stated previously, the value of a specific therapeutic technique or a generic tool like hypnosis is largely determined by the context in which it is applied. *Any approach has the potential not only to fail, but even be damaging to the client if the therapeutic context doesn't support its use.* It goes well beyond the scope of this introductory textbook on clinical hypnosis to try to address all the salient clinical skills needed to establish a therapeutic context, but I can at least draw your attention in a general way to some of them.

Some of the preliminary considerations include: your defined professional domain (which encompasses your academic credentials and appropriate licensure to legally and ethically do whatever you do), how you obtain referrals, how you represent the nature of the work you do to potential clients and to referral sources, your agreed-upon fee for service, the length of your sessions, the frequency of your sessions, the type and amount of intake information you want (including any formal testing, whether for hypnotizability or some other dimension of the client's experience), the nature of your proposed interventions and the underlying rationale for wanting to employ them, the building of a therapeutic alliance with the client, the means for assessing progress, other avenues of treatment that may be desirable or necessary during or after your treatment, the criteria for termination and the schedule for follow-up (Lynn, Kirsch, & Rhue, 1996).

The rest of this chapter proceeds with the necessary assumption that you have created a therapeutic context in which your client is amenable to participating in therapy in general and hypnosis in particular. Now we can focus more directly on how to design and deliver effective hypnosis sessions.

STRATEGICALLY DESIGNING HYPNOSIS SESSIONS

In doing psychotherapy with people for nearly three decades now, and having conducted who knows how many hypnosis sessions, my thinking about therapy has become simpler rather than more complex over time. Having originally been trained in psychoanalytic methods, and having been, at first, an admirer of the minds that could dream up such complicated models of human personality and treating psychopathology, it took me what seemed like a very long time to *un*learn all those concepts that, to me personally, seemed to interfere with being able to actually *do* something purposeful to help someone. When I began to study the works of clinicians who were more interested in results than theories, I couldn't help but notice, in general, how much simpler and more practical their ideas and methods were.

With simplicity in mind, there are four basic questions I pose to myself when I am working with a client. There are obviously many more I pose as well, but there are four questions in particular that help me develop a clearer focus on what I want to address in treatment and how I want to address it. Here are the four questions I find helpful in organizing my therapies:

1. What are the client's goals? And, as a corollary, what is an appropriate order (i.e., sensible and with a likelihood of success) for addressing them?
2. What are the resources the client will need in order to be able to accomplish the goal(s)?
3. Does the client already have the necessary resources in his or her repertoire or in his or her history and primarily needs help mobilizing him or her? Or, does the client not have those resources and needs assistance in first identifying and then building them?
4. How will contextualization be accomplished, i.e., how will the resource(s) be made available in the appropriate context(s)?

The first question is about goals. Hypnosis is a directive approach, and its use presupposes a purpose, a goal to strive for. In the next section I will focus on the issue of goal setting since it is the first step in the process and creates the framework for all else that follows.

The second question is about resources. Addressing this second question skillfully presupposes that you know what skills would be necessary in order to accomplish some goal. Unfortunately, the language of therapy is often so abstract that clinicians sometimes lose track of precise meanings and the concrete actions necessary to produce a desired effect. We speak the "psychobabble" that employs phrases such as " building self-esteem," "increasing ego strength," "building permeable boundaries," and then act as if these phrases actually mean something. They represent experiences, and it is essential to know what experiences they represent. The task for me in answering this second question is having a concrete definition of what exactly the person needs to be able say or do (within themselves and/or out in the world) that would make achieving the goal possible. *If there aren't specific steps to follow, then it isn't a goal.* It's merely a wish.

The third question is about where the necessary resources will come from once they've been identified as necessary. Can anyone do anything if they just have the proper motivation, that is, "where there's a will, there's a way?" I think that is a potentially destructive notion because it defines all problems in terms of motivation alone. It would be more accurate to say, "Where there's a will, *maybe* there's a way." Motivation without the necessary abilities frustrates people. *Both motivation and ability matter in treatment, and neither alone will get the job done.* Thus, I first want to assess what abilities the client might have he or she isn't using to his or her detriment, and then I want to create a bridge to them that makes them accessible. Such "bridge-building" is a prime use of hypnosis. If the client doesn't have the necessary abilities to accomplish what they want or need to accomplish, then it becomes my task in treatment to provide a structured means for teaching those skills and making them learnable. Teaching skills is another prime use of hypnosis.

The fourth question is about contextualization. Having resources is one thing; using them in an effective way at the appropriate time is another. As you learned when studying posthypnotic suggestions, the chief function of the posthypnotic suggestion is to establish an association, a link, between the desired response and the context for that response. Of course, there are also other ways of building this association besides the posthypnotic suggestion. You can employ role-playing strategies, cognitive rehearsals (e.g., success imageries), and homework assignments for the same purpose. The goal at this stage is simply to take what is being learned in hypnosis and therapy and be able to apply it in the course of living.

Each of the four questions above naturally raises many others in the treatment process that are also helpful to consider. I find these questions especially helpful in helping me to get clear about what I want to say to my client during the hypnosis session, the first step in designing hypnotic interventions. Perhaps you'll find them helpful, too.

HYPNOSIS AND THE TARGETS OF TREATMENT

Clients routinely present to clinicians statements such as, "I just want to feel better," or "I just want to have a good relationship." Statements such as these are so global as to be nothing more than mere wishes. They are not well-defined targets for clinical intervention. If a clinician is unclear as to what he or she specifically needs to address, the intervention will likely go nowhere. As someone wise once said, "If you don't know where you're going, you'll probably end up somewhere else." Yet, somehow a culture of magical thinking has arisen around hypnosis, promoted by those who are attracted to the rather idealistic (and self-flattering) notion of an organized and benevolent unconscious mind: Clinicians are told to "trust your unconscious" to (magically) develop an appropriate intervention, while the client is told to "trust your unconscious" to (magically) learn what is relevant (Barber, 2000; Gilligan, 1987; Matthews, 2001).

I don't suggest you rely on a "trust your unconscious" approach. Instead I think there should be specific information you gather about the client's experience, well-defined goals you articulate and agree upon, and sensible strategies to employ in reaching them. In my opinion, the times hypnosis in particular and therapy in general work best are when there is a target to be hit and a well-defined means for doing so within the context of a good therapeutic relationship. (Continued on page 403.)

FRAME OF REFERENCE: DAVID SPIEGEL, M.D.

David Spiegel, M.D. (1945–), is associate chair of the Department of Psychiatry and Behavioral Sciences and Willson Professor in the School of Medicine at Stanford University. He is also the director of the Psychosocial Treatment Laboratory and medical director of the Center for Integrative Medicine. He has been on the academic faculty at Stanford since 1975. Dr. Spiegel earned his bachelor's degree at Yale and completed his medical and psychiatric training at Harvard. He is a gifted researcher and teacher, and a powerful presence in the field as he advocates for doing scientifically informed hypnosis and psychotherapy.

Dr. Spiegel is the author of more than 350 publications, including his 1989 landmark study on the effects of psychosocial treatment on the survival of patients with metastatic breast cancer. This research suggested that supportive and expressive group therapy in women with terminal disease improved their quality of life and, even more dramatically, increased their survival time. As Spiegel himself points out, this research has had mixed results in replication attempts, but is an important line of inquiry. His ongoing research in this critically important domain eventually led to his popular 1994 book, *Living Beyond Limits: New Hope and Help for Facing Life-Threatening Illness*, which provided further data and perspective, as well as coping skill guidelines for women living with breast cancer and their families. His most recent book is called *Group Therapy for Cancer Patients* (2000) and is co-authored with Catherine Classen, Ph.D. Dr. Spiegel likes to remind people that his work shows that survival is not merely mind over matter, but that mind *does* matter. His research has earned him many prestigious awards, and the highest respect from his peers.

Dr. Spiegel is at the forefront of research in the fields of psychosomatic medicine and hypnosis. His professional interest in hypnosis began early in his career, influenced in part by his well-known psychiatrist father, Herbert Spiegel, M.D., whom he had seen demonstrate hypnosis on many occasions. He took his first course in hypnosis while at Harvard, and in 1978, soon after completing his residency and postdoctoral fellowship, he co-authored with his father a book that many in the hypnosis community consider a classic called *Trance and Treatment*. In this volume, the Spiegels described a diagnostic system and means for evaluating hypnotic responsiveness called the Hypnotic Induction Profile (HIP), described in chapter 14, as well as diverse clinical applications of hypnosis. Dr. Spiegel co-authored a paper published in the *American Journal of Psychiatry* in August 2000, that received an extraordinary amount of attention for the extraordinary findings: Hypnotized research subjects given suggestions to hallucinate color while viewing black-and-white photographs had the parts of their brain used for color processing "light up" in brain scans. This remarkable finding suggests strong neurophysiological processes evident in hypnotic responsiveness, helping move the field a step closer to understanding the neuroscientific underpinnings of the phenomenon of hypnosis.

On Hypnotizability Testing: "Hypnotizability testing turns an induction into a deduction. You acquire useful information about a person's ability to respond to hypnosis in five minutes or less. By standardizing your input, you maximize what you can learn about the variance in responses to it, and use this to direct your approach to the patient and teach the patient about their responsiveness. You also reduce tension in the initial hypnotic encounter—your role is to assess rather than talk the person into a trance, and they are exploring their ability, rather than either complying or resisting."

On Spontaneous Hypnosis and Hypnotic Ability: "Hypnosis occurs spontaneously, even without a formal induction, as research on absorption indicates. Moments of "flow," peak performance, and intense pleasure have self-altering and intense attention as one component, and are thus hypnotic-like. While many people have such peak experiences, and some have dissociative experiences, not everyone does. Research indicates that hypnotizability is as stable a trait as IQ, and involves intense and focused attention. There is no reason why human mental experience should be any more equally distributed than human physical traits."

On Psychosocial Support, Hypnosis and Breast Cancer: "There is evidence from some but not all studies that participation in group therapy increases survival time with breast cancer. It has not been proven that hypnosis is a key component to this effect. However, hypnosis is extremely helpful in reducing cancer-related pain and anxiety. Cancer can be understood as a stressor, and focused attention coupled with dissociation is very helpful in managing stress, ranging from anxiety about dying to getting through difficult medical procedures with less pain and anxiety and even more rapidly."

On Different Hypnotic Styles: "While each clinician needs to sample various approaches and find one that makes sense and seems most useful to patients, I feel an obligation as an investigator and teacher to find and test the crucial elements in treatments that work. I feel there has been much mystification of hypnosis over the centuries, and that it is most likely to be used (and used well) in medicine when we distill the crucial elements and use them. I find that patients make good use of clear and direct approaches that invite their collaboration through facilitating their understanding of the treatment approach."

On Clinical Skills Underlying the Use of Hypnosis: "It is crucial for clinicians to have basic skills in diagnostic assessment and knowledge of various treatment approaches that can be utilized both with and without hypnosis. It is crucial to be a primary professional (psychiatry, psychology, dentistry, etc.) rather than a hypnotist. Then it is most helpful to learn to communicate clearly and compassionately, and use your relationship with the patient as a therapeutic tool."

On Excitements and Disappointments with the Field: "I have been excited to discover, along with other colleagues, the profound effects hypnosis can facilitate in affecting brain function, e.g. processing color perception and pain, and body function, e.g. asthma, gastric acid secretion, warts. My biggest disappointment is the enervating battles over socio-cognitive vs. state explanations of hypnosis and other unnecessary turf battles. The phenomenon is resilient and interesting enough that there is room for many approaches to compete productively for explanatory power."

Source: Personal communication; August 5, 2002

DESIGNING INTERVENTIONS:
WHERE TO FOCUS FIRST

In real world circumstances, unlike participants in traditional therapeutic efficacy studies who may be excluded from the research if they have additional problems beyond the single condition being investigated, clients have multiple problems, even multiple diagnoses. Clinical judgment, an artistic evolutionary development, requires making a decision about where to begin. Not all problems are equal. Some symptoms are generalized throughout the client's life, and some are specific to particular situations. Some are merely annoying, but some are clearly dangerous. Some are relatively easy to resolve, and some are refractory.

The first priority, of course, is what's urgent, and urgency is governed by hazard potential. Suicidal ideation, drug abuse, and reckless behavior that endangers one's self or others, are just a few examples of when clinicians must establish an order of priority for intervening that one might not otherwise choose if the symptoms or problem behaviors posed no immediate danger.

DESIGNING INTERVENTIONS: BUILDING
THERAPEUTIC MOMENTUM AND RESPONSE SETS

Where to begin, though, if no symptoms or behaviors are in urgent need of immediate attention? Generally, it is best to begin where you can generate some rapid symptom relief and thereby start to build a positive momentum in treatment. One of the most underemployed but useful constructs in applying hypnosis is called the "response set" (Erickson & Rossi, 1979), discussed previously.

Building a response set means building a momentum of responsiveness. For example, if I offer someone four consecutive statements I know he or she will agree with, what is that person's most likely response to my next statement? For example, if I say, "Each person is unique as an individual; . . . human experience is often complex; . . . people frequently have more resources than they realize; . . . sometimes it feels good just to sit and relax . . ."—all agreeable statements—where does the momentum of responses carry the client? Most likely into the realm of agreement for the next statement.

In the practice of clinical hypnosis, then, effectively utilizing this principle means structuring interventions to go from general to specific. Thus, before I give someone a specific suggestion to develop an age regression, for example, I would first offer a series of general suggestions about memory that I know he or she would agree with, such as: "Each person is capable of remembering many different experiences . . . some memories are much more vivid than others. . . ." , which gradually lead the client in the direction of later remembering or even reliving (i.e., revivifying) a specific memory.

Response sets can only be effectively designed and delivered when the session's goal is relatively clear. If you can't clearly state the hypnosis session's goal or your primary therapeutic message in 25 words or less, then it may be best not to do the session (unless the goal is to simply "go fishing," which may occasionally be a reasonable choice). An unfocused session which yields little can too easily de-motivate the client for participating in further hypnosis sessions.

DESIGNING INTERVENTIONS: RISK FACTORS
AS INTERVENTION TARGETS

Comprehensive treatment must take the risk factors for other problems and for relapses into account as well as current symptoms. A risk factor is any factor that increases the probability of a particular disease or disorder occurring. The risk factors to be targeted in treatment, along with their associated symptoms, represent some of the deeper applications of hypnosis and psychotherapy. To ignore underlying risk factors and focus only on the client's symptoms is a relatively superficial intervention, addressing only the problem's content but not its structure. (The content refers to the details—the *what*—of the problem, while the structure refers to the process—the *how*—of *how* the symptom is produced.)

Key risk factors to address include such self-organizing factors as: (1) Cognitive style (Abstract or concrete? Global or linear? Attributional style?); (2) Response style (Self or other-directed? Open or guarded?); (3) Attentional style (Focused or diffuse? Focused on saliency or irrelevance?); and, (4) Perceptual style (Focuses on similarities or differences between experiences? Magnifies or diminishes events or perceptions?) (Yapko, 1988). Risk factors may be addressed singly or in combination.

The heart of therapy, it seems to me, is in teaching clients to identify which subjective patterns will work best in a given context and then use your interventions to deliberately associate them to those patterns. It requires people to read situations accurately in order to know what the situation requires (e.g., an impersonal response) and what specific resources one has to meet those demands (e.g., an effective strategy for reminding oneself the criticism isn't personal based on clear criteria).

This is precisely what people *don't* do, however, to their own detriment. For example, they want to self-disclose ("Let me tell you what I think of this job") but they don't read the context well in order to recognize this isn't a safe place for self-disclosure (i.e., it'll get back to the boss and I'll likely be punished). Misreading or simply ignoring the situational cues can thus be very costly.

"Relating to the context" means adapting to situations flexibly. Facilitating flexibility in clients while simultaneously encouraging them to be more observant (therefore less internally and more externally oriented) and critical in their thinking are primary goals of effective therapies. Hypnosis can help magnify the key learning underlying adaptability that *every pattern is valuable somewhere, but no pattern is valuable everywhere* (Yapko, 2001).

DELIVERING INTERVENTIONS: WHAT ABOUT USING HYPNOSIS IN THE FIRST SESSION?

Having interviewed the client and obtained a symptom description and history and medical history, and having assessed the psychosocial factors operating in this person's life, the clinician might well have enough information to formulate a meaningful hypnotic intervention, even in the very first therapy session. Some clinicians claim one should have a strong rapport and therapeutic alliance built over many sessions *before* doing hypnosis out of the fear that hypnosis might be introduced too early in the treatment process and somehow harm the alliance. I believe that position is too limited.

I would suggest instead that one can often use the hypnosis itself as a means to build the necessary rapport and therapeutic alliance with a client. In fact, I demonstrate this very process with Vicki, a woman I had just met for the first time, in chapter 20.

When someone is in distress, feeling hopeless and overwhelmed, it seems both cruel and entirely unnecessary to say, "give me more of your history" and "I'll start helping you next time." Why shouldn't the client begin to get some help right away? Given the typically low-frustration tolerance of the distressed individual, who wants and hopes for some immediate relief, why not provide some if possible when this is one of the things hypnosis does best? The ability of hypnosis to provide anxiety reduction, lowered agitation, and reduced ruminations are some of the best reasons to use hypnosis early on in treatment as a means for demonstrating to the client that his or her symptoms are malleable, effectively building positive expectations for therapy (Kirsch, 1990, 2000, 2001). The clinician's responsibility, even in the very first session, is to facilitate hope and meet the need for at least some relief as quickly as possible. Hypnosis can help you do both.

DELIVERING INTERVENTIONS: INTRODUCING HYPNOSIS TO THE CLIENT

Making the transition from clinical interviewing and establishing rapport with the client to beginning an actual hypnotic intervention is easier than many people seem to think. One can interview a client, and then 20 or 30 minutes into the session, assuming you want to do hypnosis with the client, say something such as the following as a lead-in to the hypnosis:

> I've been *listening intently* to you now for the last half hour or so, describing your symptoms and problems, and how *absorbed* you have been in just trying to manage. I've been impressed by your suffering and despair, and it's obvious to me that *you want things to change.* Having been so *focused on and absorbed in* all the most hurtful thoughts and feelings, it seems obvious to me how valuable it would be for you to *start to consider and then get absorbed* in *different thoughts and feelings* that can help you feel better. You came here knowing it would be important *to get absorbed in a different way of looking at things*, and to help you *start to get absorbed* in a different way of thinking and feeling you can just let your eyes close and focus yourself on some of the possibilities I want to describe to you. . . ."

And thus the hypnosis session begins. I cannot think of a single instance in all my years of practice in which a client refused to participate or was even reluctant to join the process when I introduced the purpose of focusing to them in this way. Clients are typically looking for direction and feedback, knowing *something* has to change, but they are typically unclear as to what.

There is another style for introducing hypnosis to the client, of course, a much more conventional and structured one in which the clinician asks the client whether he or she has worked with hypnosis before and how he or she would feel about working hypnotically in the therapy. The clinician draws out existing attitudes about hypnosis, identifies and corrects any misconceptions, establishes both cooperation and expectancy by describing what hypnosis is, how it feels to be hypnotized, what the potential benefits of hypnosis are in his or her particular case, and so on (Kirsch, Lynn, & Rhue, 1993). Some clinicians even go so far as to have the client sign a release form authorizing hypnotic treatment as tangible evidence of informed consent.

DELIVERING INTERVENTIONS: CHOOSING YOUR HYPNOTIC STYLE

This section briefly addresses the issue of hypnotic style, encouraging you to consider whether you want to be more direct or indirect, more positive or negative, more content or process oriented, and more authoritarian or permissive in the way you deliver your suggestions to a specific client. I recommend you choose your style based on the client's patterns of self-organization, described above, and not from some invariant formula. The idea is to be fluent in *all* styles, and to draw upon them flexibly as client patterns dictate.

There is a division in the field of hypnosis, as you know by now, over the issue of hypnotizability as a relatively fixed trait of responsiveness, based on standardized tests. *That people differ in their responsiveness to hypnosis is a given. What that means to clinical practice, however, is still wide open for discussion.* Therapy is more art than science, a condition that is unlikely to ever change as long as therapy remains an interpersonal process involving subjective clinical judgment and considerable social skill (Covino, 1997). Hypnosis is even more artistry than science, utilizing subjectively created hypnotic phenomena such as regression or dissociation that arise from suggestive influences within the hypnotic relationship.

I choose to land on the side that strives to improve the artistry of clinicians using hypnosis. More efficacy data won't help us be better humans doing clinical work. There is simply no substitute for having the range to formulate direct *and* indirect suggestions, positive *and* negative suggestions, process *and* content suggestions, and authoritarian *and* permissive suggestions. Having the range, the flexibility, to impart information and perspective in a variety of ways is what clinical artistry is about (Haley, 1973; Zeig, 1980). Disavowing client uniqueness by summarily believing that "if he or she is hypnotizable, it won't matter how you phrase a suggestion," allows ineffective suggestions to be attributed to client limitations. It makes some clinicians feel better to do that, apparently, but I'd caution against anyone really believing it. Instead, believing the client can respond to *some* degree, and expecting to find and striving to find a channel for meaningful shared communication is a great way to initiate hypnotic interventions.

Thus, arguing over whether direct or indirect suggestions are superior is a colossal waste of time when we should already have reached the understanding that *no* suggestion, direct *or* indirect, is powerful or useful until a client *chooses* to respond to it. The divisiveness in the field over this and other such academic questions that are clearly of no interest to the client seeking treatment is something we cannot be proud of if we want to be socially relevant.

DESIGNING INTERVENTIONS: A GENERIC STRUCTURE FOR A HYPNOSIS SESSION

The structure of hypnosis sessions varies far less than their content. If we consider the structural elements necessary for a *formal* hypnosis session to take place, we can create a "generic structure" of primary components. Such a generic structure is contained in Table 14 below.

As you can see, the generic structure provides a skeleton framework for your session, and your decisions as to session content (e.g., which induction to employ in what style of suggestion, or what problem to address with which kinds of suggestions) produce the variations in one client's treatment compared to another. So, even though you may be treating five different people for depression, what you actually say to each will vary dramatically depending on what their individual needs and patterns of self-organization

---

Table 14. A Generic Structure For a Hypnosis Session

Orient the client to hypnosis
Perform induction procedure
Build a response set
Introduce therapeutic theme #1 (i.e., problem, goal)
Provide suggestions addressing the theme
Ask about derived meanings
Introduce therapeutic theme(s) # 2 (#3, etc.)
Provide suggestions addressing the theme(s)
Ask about derived meanings
Provide post-hypnotic suggestions (contextualization)
Provide closure
Suggest disengagement

are (Yapko, 1988, 1992, 2001). Let's go through the generic structure, component by component, so you may be clear about what's happening at each stage of the process.

Orient the Client to Hypnosis

If you intend to do hypnosis with your client, at some point in the interaction you will want to shift the person's attention away from wherever it has been focused, and you will want to redirect it in the direction of creating a state of readiness to begin the process of hypnosis. A statement as clear and direct as, "Now that you've had some time to talk about this problem, it seems like a good time for you to start to focus on getting comfortable so we can do some hypnosis" is usually a good way to start the process.

Perform Induction Procedure

Encouraging the client to position him- or herself comfortably, breathe comfortably, let his or her eyes close, focus and listen, and simply relax are all the stepping stones to beginning the induction. Which induction you use is, of course, a matter of judgment based on all the considerations detailed in previous chapters. Whatever secures and directs the attentional processes of the client will be a perfectly fine induction.

Build a Response Set

The importance of building a momentum of responsiveness cannot be overstated. Most people simply can't produce hypnotic phenomena (e.g., analgesia or regression) instantly on demand. But, given time and an atmosphere which encourages exploration, people can usually develop hypnotic responses sufficient for therapeutic purposes. Paying attention to the deliberate building of response sets is simply a way of increasing the likelihood—not guaranteeing—a positive response to the hypnotic experience. Before asking your client for a specific response, you present ideas in a general and irrefutable way that indicate such a response is humanly and even personally possible. Thus, before attempting to generate an analgesia in a specific part of the person's body later in the session, for example, it is helpful to first get the person comfortable with and attuned to the notion that noticing or even creating variations in your perception about your body is possible (e.g., "Sometimes your body feels tired, and sometimes it feels well rested . . ."). In this example, the response set centers on orienting the client in a general way to the subject of variabilities in bodily perception, serving as a stepping stone to the larger goal of the session, namely, creating a specific variability in sensation with an analgesia. The response set moves the client in the direction of the larger therapeutic goal without yet demanding a specific response from him or her.

Introduce Therapeutic Theme #1

The advice I gave earlier was to distill your message to the client down to 25 words or less when you're planning your session so *you* can be clear about the session's purpose. What do you want to say to this person that is meant to be helpful? What is the client's misperception or self-limiting belief you want to address? What empowering resource(s) do you want to associate the client to? When you are clear about what the message you want to convey is, then you have established the topic of your therapeutic theme (McNeilly, 2001). For example, if you have a client who believes he or she is a victim of circumstances and seems oblivious to proactive beneficial choices he or she could make, if you simply say to the person, "You could make proactive beneficial choices," the client will likely be entirely unimpressed. Employing hypnosis, however, you have the opportunity to get that same important point across in a much more focused, experiential, and powerful way. So, you might introduce the salient therapeutic theme "the importance of knowing what's controllable" to the client, with the goals in mind of motivating the person to make deliberate choices and teaching the skills of recognizing what's in his or her control as a precursory step in the direction of being proactive in living life well. The message you want to get across in 25 words or less is "Quit acting like you're a victim and take charge of your life!" But to help soften that too abrupt and emotionally threatening message I need to say it in a way that's more comfortable and easier for the client in a victim mindset to absorb. So, I might introduce that theme more gently by saying something such as:

> . . . *As I continue to talk to you about different ideas and different possibilities you might well become aware of how different people experience life in very different ways . . . Some people think life is just whatever happens to them, while others think they can create whatever kind of life they want . . . Isn't it interesting how some people think they have control over the quality of life and others feel they don't . . . Sometimes people overestimate how much control they have and try to control things they really cannot . . . While others sometimes underestimate how much control they have and don't try to control things and make good choices they really could . . . It can be very confusing to know what's in your control and what isn't, don't you think? . . .*

I have now introduced the theme and focused the person's attention on the therapeutic issue of controllability. A more direct approach at this stage would be to say something such as, *"You see yourself as a victim in the circumstances of your life, as if you have no control over what goes on in your life. You have more control than you realize, you are not merely a victim, and I want to talk to you about ways you can begin to take charge of your life."* The next step in the process then builds on whatever therapeutic theme you have introduced to your client at this stage in the process.

Provide Suggestions Addressing the Theme

Once you have introduced the therapeutic theme and drawn the client's attention to whatever the problem is you intend to address with your suggestions, the next step is to address the theme by offering suggestions that can help resolve the problem and/or accomplish the therapeutic goal. This is the stage at which your therapeutic strategy is implemented. Are you going to try to teach the client a specific skill that can empower him or her? Attack a self-limiting belief or misconception he or she holds as true? Share a meaningful observation or philosophy about life you believe he or she can benefit from? Try to alter a perceptual process he or she engages in? Whatever your intended use of hypnosis, hopefully you have some strategy in mind for how to achieve the goal of your session. Will you make an emotional appeal by telling a moving and inspiring story of someone else's success? Or make an indirect threat as to what terrible things will happen if continuing on in the same way? An appeal to logic? A promise of great personal rewards for changing?

Whatever strategy you decide on determines the kinds of suggestions you will use to address the therapeutic theme. Direct suggestions to "stop doing that and start doing this" (e.g., telling a smoker, *". . . whenever you feel the urge to smoke you can go outside and slowly and deliberately take in some deep breaths of cool, clean air and you can enjoy knowing you're gradually making yourself healthier than you have been in a very long time . . ."*) are probably the most commonly used approaches. Indirect suggestions, most commonly through the use of storytelling, are also used quite commonly to suggest new ways of thinking about and responding to old problems (e.g., *". . . when the townspeople started suffering strange symptoms, they finally realized the damage the smokestacks of the factory were doing to them and their families . . . and even though it was hard for them because the factory employed so many of them . . . they realized they had to shut the factory down so they could start breathing in clean air again . . . and get their health back . . . because what good is a job if you're sick or the people you care about are sick? . . ."*).

The suggestions you employ in addressing the therapeutic theme are meant to associate some new response(s) to the problem context. Your suggestions may also be used to give the client a preview of homework you may be assigning later. You can do this by orienting him or her to the idea of what can be learned through experience, a process commonly known as "seeding," and later assigning that experience as homework (Geary, 1994; Zeig, 1990).

Interaction Regarding Derived Meanings

This is the "check-in with your client to find out what's going on" phase of the hypnosis session. No matter how direct and/or indirect your suggestions might be, regardless of however clear or relevant you think your suggestions are to the client, communication is a two-way street. Whatever the intention of your message, what your client actually receives may be quite different. As you've already learned, meaning is not in the words you use, rather *meaning is in the person* who relates to your words in idiosyncratic ways. Thus, you can give someone a direct suggestion to go take a walk outside when they feel themselves getting stressed, and all the person heard was "take a hike!" Or you can tell someone a story about another client with a similar problem and all he or she hears is that you talk about other clients in your examples. Then he or she gets wrapped up in anxiously wondering whether you'll be using him or her as an example, and thus never hears whatever the point of your story is!

Instead of talking *at* the client and hoping he or she absorbs some intended message, at this stage of the session you have offered suggestions of one type or another to help the client and now you need some feedback as to what, if anything, he or she received from your input. The easiest way to do this is to simply say to the client, "*In just a moment I'm going to ask you to describe what you're aware of right now in terms of what's different in your (understanding, body, perception, feelings), and you can describe to me quite easily what you're aware of.*" (Did you notice the therapeutic presupposition in that suggestion?) The client can then verbalize what, if anything, is different, and you now have the opportunity to reinforce it if it's useful or contradict it if it isn't. *But, only by checking in with the client during the session can you have any sense as to whether he or she is deriving anything useful from your session and thereby have the chance to make midstream corrections to your approach if necessary.*

Introduce Therapeutic Themes #2, 3, and so on

How many topics or themes can you address in a single hypnosis session? It depends on the client. Specifically, how much does it take for this person to feel appropriately stimulated (i.e., challenged, supported, enlightened), and how much does it take for the person to feel overloaded? Some people will do best if you give them a single new concept to chew on, and others will be bored silly if you don't give them lots of new ideas to chew on. You have to assess this person's focus, stimulus need, level of distress, openness to the process, and other such variables that help you decide just how much to pack into a single session. However many themes you choose to address, you will obviously be *providing suggestions* and hopefully *checking in with your client* each step of the way.

Provide Posthypnotic Suggestions (Contextualization)

By this stage in the session you have already introduced the ideas, perspectives, and methods that are meant to help your client, and you've "checked in" and received some indication he or she developed some new possibilities. The challenge now is how to help the client integrate these new possibilities you've suggested into his or her life. You may want to *summarize key concepts, insights, or suggestions from other parts of the session* at this point in the process as a precursor to linking them to ongoing life experience. Then, using the generic structure for posthypnotic suggestions you learned previously ("Later, when you're in situation X, you can do Y and Z"), you can offer fairly direct suggestions that build those links to the person's everyday life (e.g., *"The next time . . . and each time . . . you feel someone is trying to take advantage of you by imposing their wishes upon you . . . you can remind yourself that while other people may want what they want . . . which is quite natural . . . you now have a new choice . . . instead of just giving in to them . . . you can say yes or no to their demands depending on what you decide is best for you and best for the circumstances . . . and enjoy feeling stronger as a result"*).

Provide Closure

The session is now complete, and the process of generating closure begins. It is important to give the client the amount of time he or she needs to process what has happened during the session. Some people process things very quickly and are ready to bring the session to an end, and others are slower in assimilating new ideas and need some time to absorb it all. Most people, regardless of their rate of processing, simply enjoyed being so relaxed and comfortable, they are in no hurry to end the session. So, it is a good idea to first orient the person to the idea of closure (e.g., *"You can review and absorb whatever important new possibilities you wish to as you prepare to bring this session to an end"*) before suggesting actual closure, and then you can suggest they begin to bring themselves out of hypnosis at a comfortable rate (*"And when you're ready to, you can start the process of bringing yourself out of hypnosis at a rate that is gradual and comfortable"*). No one likes to be hurried out of hypnosis, and it can be quite disorienting, even uncomfortable, if the client is encouraged to come out of hypnosis too quickly. By letting the client control the rate at which he or she re-orients, you can avoid the mistake of hurrying somebody.

Suggest Disengagement

The final step in the process, the client is encouraged to slowly re-orient and open his or her eyes (*"And when you're ready to, you can fully re-orient yourself, and let your eyes open whenever you'd like, fully re-oriented, becoming fully alert"*). The first moments after the person has opened his or her eyes are particularly sensitive ones as the person thinks about the session while "reconnecting" with you. Waiting silently until the person feels like speaking is generally a good idea, although you can also quietly offer further suggestions consistent with your goals at this time, since the client is still usually partially in hypnosis. Re-orienting is a process, not an event.

DELIVERING INTERVENTIONS: FOLLOWING UP THE SESSION

When the hypnosis session has ended, the opportunity exists to do some debriefing with the client about the session. As with every other aspect of the treatment process, this requires some thoughtful planning. On one hand, detailed de-briefing about the session (e.g., "How was that for you? What was your experience like?") can provide you with valuable feedback about how the client responded (i.e., thought, felt) that can be important in shaping future sessions and even the overall direction of the treatment. On the other hand, some of the things that happen during hypnosis sessions, such as fantasy imagery that has no logical basis (e.g., visualizing being a carefree child) can create powerful emotional responses that are very helpful to the person to have, yet they would fall apart under conscious scrutiny. *So, you have to give thought as to how much of the session you want to analyze without such an analysis being detrimental to the session's results.*

The next opportunity for follow-up is in the next session. This is when the clinician has the chance to find out what, if anything, is now different in the client's experience. Has anything changed? If so, what? Does the client seem to have absorbed and made use of suggestions given during the hypnosis session? If so, is the client aware of having done so, or does whatever is different seem outside of his or her awareness? The times hypnosis is most mysterious and compelling are when the person has made changes in obvious response to the suggestions you have offered, yet the person seems to have no awareness for the connection between what you suggested and what he or she is doing differently. It gives hypnosis that "magical" quality, which is fascinating, but which may also be clinically undesirable. *If we want to empower people, having them make changes without any sense of personal connection to those changes simply reinforces a disempowering belief that these things happen to them instead of being caused by them.* I'm a strong fan of taking the magic out of the process and replacing it with a sense of deliberateness on the part of the client, emphasizing that he or she did actively participate in some way to make changes possible. You can do that by linking new behaviors with improved conditions, asking about and reinforcing "what's different and better."

What if the person comes back for the next session and nothing is different, or worse still, if things have actually gotten *worse*? There are many different possibilities as to why an intervention of *any* type, including hypnosis, can fall flat. Some of the possibilities have to do with the client (e.g., negative expectations, inadequate motivation, misapplying suggested concepts), some have to do with the clinician (e.g., too emotionally threatening, too controlling, too condescending), and some have to do with the interaction between the two (e.g., inadequate rapport, conflicting goals). De-briefing the client under these circumstances becomes even more important for the clinician. Did the client listen to the tape of the session again (I tape my sessions routinely and provide them to the client as a means of reinforcing our work), and if so, what did and didn't fit for them? If something didn't fit, why?

I want to know what I can do differently in subsequent sessions to be more helpful, even if it's the client's issues (e.g., negative expectations) getting in the way. I want to address those limitations and try to resolve them as part of the therapy. But it means backing up a step or two to address those issues before going on in a different way. If it's my approach that needs adjusting, I'll do my best to adjust it. If it's the quality of our interaction, I'll do what I can to change what I do there, too. The important point is that feedback allows for the possibility of change, wherever in the process a change may be indicated. It may be easier to simply blame the client for his or her lack of progress, of course, but as you can tell, I'm not inclined to blame the client for what he or she doesn't know how to do. I'd rather strive to create a context where he or she can explore the possibilities and learn to choose wisely.

THE ART OF DESIGNING AND
DELIVERING HYPNOSIS SESSIONS

Conducting good clinical interviews that yield significant information and insight into the structure of the person's problems is an art. Establishing rapport and a good therapeutic alliance with a client is social artistry. Adapting your style and demeanor to the client (what it takes to impress a young child you're going to treat is quite different than what it takes to impress an adult) is artistry in behavioral flexibility. Designing a session to acknowledge and incorporate the unique attributes of the client while keeping an eye on the goal is organizational artistry. Communicating an expectation of success and encouraging the client to discover new possibilities is an art of building a therapeutic context.

In this chapter, many of the nuts and bolts of clinical intervention involving hypnosis have been assembled into a general framework for evolving the art of doing clinical hypnosis. No book, no person, no scientific study can tell you exactly what to say, or when and how to say it best to a particular client. The single person that can give you the most feedback about "what works" is your client. And, as you probably already know, what works for one may be quite different from what works for another. Perhaps ironically, hypnosis, a highly directive approach, is simultaneously among the most respectful and client-centered of approaches.

For Discussion

1. Who do you think of as "being hypnotic" and why? Does the person intend to be hypnotic, or is it simply something about the way he or she is as a person?
2. What does it mean to have your clinical training be a veneer that overlays who you are as a person? What specifically do you bring to the therapy context that is uniquely you?
3. Do you make a distinction between a wish and a goal? How would you distinguish them for a confused client?
4. How is your style of therapy a reflection of you at least as much as the problem you hope to solve?

Things to Do

1. With the emphasis on therapy being more empirically based, it will be important to keep current with research in your area. Pick a particular symptom you encounter and read some of the latest findings on what it takes to address it effectively. Then develop a set of hypnotic suggestions for resolving it.
2. Write out briefly three events in your life that were somehow significant to you. List your personal resources that led you to respond as you did.
3. Make a list of common symptoms. If a client presented you with several of them, which would you focus on first and why? Ask others and compare your answers.

REFERENCES

Barber, J. (2000). Where Ericksonian legend meets scientific method: A comment on Matthews. *International Journal of Clinical and Experimental Hypnosis, 48*, 4, 427–32.

Covino, N. (1997). The integration of clinical and experimental work. *International Journal of Clinical and Experimental Hypnosis, 45*, 2, 109–25.

Erickson, M., & Rossi, E. (1979). *Hypnotherapy: An exploratory casebook.* New York: Irvington.

Geary, B. (1994). Seeding responsiveness to hypnotic processes. In J. Zeig (Ed.), *Ericksonian methods: The essence of the story* (pp. 295–314). New York: Brunner/Mazel.

Gilligan, S. (1987). *Therapeutic trances: The cooperation principle in Ericksonian hypnotherapy.* New York: Brunner/Mazel.

Haley, J. (1973). *Uncommon therapy: The psychiatric techniques of Milton H. Erickson, M.D.* New York: Norton.

Kirsch, I. (1990). *Changing expectations: A key to effective psychotherapy.* Pacific Grove, CA: Brooks/Cole.

—— (2000). The response set theory of hypnosis. *American Journal of Clinical Hypnosis, 42*, 3–4, 274–92.

—— (2001). The response set theory of hypnosis: Expectancy and physiology. *American Journal of Clinical Hypnosis, 44,* 1, 69–73.

Kirsch, I., Lynn, S., & Rhue, J. (1993). Introduction to clinical hypnosis. In J. Rhue, S. Lynn, & I. Kirsch (Eds.), *Handbook of clinical hypnosis* (pp. 3–22). Washington, D.C.: American Psychological Association.

Lynn, S., Kirsch, I., & Rhue, J. (1996). Maximizing treatment gains: Recommendations for the practice of clinical hypnosis. In S. Lynn, I. Kirsch, & J. Rhue (Eds.), *Casebook of clinical hypnosis* (pp. 395–406). Washington, D.C.: American Psychological Association.

Matthews, W. (2001). Social influence, expectancy theory, and Ericksonian hypnosis. In B. Geary & J. Zeig (Eds.), *The handbook of Ericksonian psychotherapy* (pp. 31–42). Phoenix, AZ: The Milton H. Erickson Foundation Press.

McNeilly, R. (2001). Creating a context for hypnosis: Listening for a resource theme and integrating it into an Ericksonian hypnosis session. In B. Geary & J. Zeig (Eds.), *The handbook of Ericksonian psychotherapy* (pp. 57–65). Phoenix, AZ: The Milton H. Erickson Foundation Press.

Rossi, E. (Ed.) (1980). *The collected papers of Milton H. Erickson, M.D., on hypnosis* (4 vols.). New York: Irvington.

Yapko, M. (1988). *When living hurts: Directives for treating depression.* New York: Brunner/Mazel.

—— (1992). *Hypnosis and the treatment of depressions: Strategies for change.* New York: Brunner/Mazel.

—— (2001). *Treating depression with hypnosis: Integrating cognitive-behavioral and strategic approaches.* Philadelphia, PA: Brunner/Routledge.

Zeig, J. (Ed.) (1980). *A teaching seminar with Milton H. Erickson, M.D.* New York: Brunner/Mazel.

—— (1990). Seeding. In J. Zeig & S. Gilligan (Eds.), *Brief therapy: Myths, methods and metaphors* (pp. 221–46). New York: Brunner/Mazel.

—— (2001). Hypnotic induction. In B. Geary & J. Zeig (Eds.), *The handbook of Ericksonian psychotherapy* (pp. 18–30). Phoenix, AZ: The Milton H. Erickson Foundation Press.

18

Hypnotic Patterns Commonly Employed in Psychotherapy

Throughout this book there have been numerous descriptions of ways to apply hypnosis in a variety of clinical contexts. The goals for each session and the steps toward those goals will naturally vary across clients, but there are specific themes that frequently recur in psychotherapy. Some examples are: encouraging people to take responsibility for themselves; encouraging people to be proactive on their own behalf; helping people develop a better sense of both their uniqueness and personal boundaries; and, helping people adjust to difficult circumstances. There are, of course, many, many others.

In the same way there are common problems across client populations, there are common patterns of hypnosis for addressing them. In this chapter, I will describe some of these common patterns of hypnotic intervention. And, in the same way I have described the importance of treating individuals rather than diagnostic categories, I will encourage in this chapter the importance of tailoring the approach to the individual. *The patterns here represent ways to intervene in certain types of problems, but none of these techniques, in fact, no techniques, are likely to be successful if the therapeutic alliance and/or therapeutic context doesn't fully support their use* (Cummings & Cummings, 2000).

In the first section of this chapter, I'll describe how to use hypnotic phenomena for both diagnostic purposes and therapeutic treatment planning. Then I'll describe some of the most basic patterns of hypnotic intervention. In this chapter's latter section, some of the most common problems you are likely to encounter are briefly described, with emphasis on how hypnosis may be employed in the treatment process. These descriptions are all necessarily general and superficial, appropriately so in an introductory text, but they will expose you to the kinds of issues and methods that a deeper exploration of the research and clinical literature can provide. The

Table 15. Assumptions Inherent in Hypnotic Psychotherapy

Influence is inevitable; all therapy is directive to some degree
The clinician is a catalyst for change
The client wants change to occur
The problem is in the client's perceptions, not the client
The client has utilizable resources for change
No one is completely helpless
Each person is making the best choice available
Choice is better than no perceived choice

assumptions associated with the use of hypnosis in psychotherapy are presented in Table 15 as a way of orienting you to this chapter's subject matter.

SYMPTOM STRUCTURES AND HYPNOTIC PHENOMENA

I have previously described hypnotic phenomena as the building blocks of experience. In varying combinations and degrees of purity, the various hypnotic phenomena comprise ongoing experience, whether good or bad (Araoz, 1995). Developing the ability to view everyday experiences in terms of the associated hypnotic phenomena can help you develop the ability to more easily identify the structures of experiences (i.e., how the problem pattern is organized), not just their content (i.e., what the symptoms are) (Gilligan, 1987, 2001).

In the context of conducting therapy, identifying the hypnotic phenomena associated with a client's symptoms permits you a more rapid and comprehensive understanding of the problem. Knowing the sequential steps involved in the creation of the symptom(s) permits you the opportunity to choose at what point in the symptomatic sequence you may introduce an intervention that alters it in some beneficial way (Lankton & Lankton, 1983).

Consider the example of someone with a fear of flying. How does someone generate such a fear? What is the symptom producing internal sequence? Despite individual variations, there is a general sequence most airplane phobics follow: They visualize in great detail the airplane they're sitting in taking off, and that soon after takeoff, the engines flame out. They visualize with horror the plane going down and crashing at top speed, and then they see twisted metal and body parts scattered all over the hillside. Imagining yourself on an airplane that is imminently going to crash and kill you is a horrific sequence of images. With such disturbing imagery, it is easy to appreciate how a fear of flying is generated (Wilson, 1996). Asking why someone would visualize this sequence of events is unnecessary; it's self-evident, given the reality that planes do crash, albeit relatively rarely.

There are many different ways of treating such individuals, from deeper symbol-laden interventions to more overt cognitive-behavioral strategies. Hypnosis can be integrated with any and all of them, suggesting alternative images and ways of thinking about flying. Even the most superficial hypnosis approach would at least offer suggestions to think about flying comfortably, seeing detailed images of the wonderful things to be experienced at the destination and framing flying as a liberating experience that can enlarge your world. In essence, the clinician is saying, "Here. Visualize these relaxing images instead of those terrible images." While the content of the visual imagery changes in such an intervention, both the solution and the problem are comprised of images of the future (i.e., elements of age progression) that feel real in the present.

In the same way that age progression (in the form of a fear of bad things that might happen in the future) is generally evident in anxiety disorders, it is possible to similarly characterize other problems according to associated hypnotic phenomena. Table 16 below provides some relevant principles and examples.

Consider the average smoker from the perspective of how hypnotic phenomena are evident in the pattern of smoking. Smoking is a terribly self-damaging habit, yet despite the warning labels and the laws passed to discourage smoking, more than 50 million Americans continue to smoke. Most of them began as teens, and despite getting sick the first few times, they endured and became dependent on cigarettes. For individuals to smoke, what must they do to make it possible to inhale smoke and gas containing hundreds of deadly toxins and even proclaim to enjoy it? They are typically unaware of the immediate stress and damage to their body with each puff of the cigarette. They do not feel their heart rate and blood pressure increase as their body fights for oxygen, nor do they feel the toxins circulating through their body. They don't smell the foulness of their clothes, hair, breath, or surroundings (car, home, office), and, generally speaking, they tend to be quite oblivious to the many effects of their smoking.

Table 16. Symptom Phenomena as Hypnotic Phenomena

1. Identify hypnotic phenomena evident in symptomatic pattern(s), for example:
   Overweight: physical dissociation, sensory alteration
   Smoking: physical dissociation, sensory alteration
   Depression: age regression, catalepsy, sensory alteration
   Anxiety: age progression, time distortion, sensory alteration
2. Use complementary hypnotic phenomena in interventions
3. Contextualize responses through experiential approaches, such as task assignments and behavioral prescriptions

Do you know when many people decide to quit smoking? When the elevator at work breaks! Taking the stairs highlights very quickly their degree of physical (un)fitness. Or as a result of some other similar situation where the negative effects of their smoking is dramatically brought into their awareness.

Clearly, a smoker is in a physically dissociated state. How else could one be oblivious to the physical damage associated with breathing toxic fumes? The main idea in identifying hypnotic phenomena underlying symptom phenomena is that it provides you with some understanding of the kind of experience you want to encourage hypnotically. *As a general principle, therapy takes the form of providing complementary experiences, helping people develop either undeveloped or underdeveloped personal resources.* In smoking, for example, *dissociation* is a large part of the problem. Thus, *association*, the complement to dissociation, is going to be a large part of the solution (Lynn, Neufeld, Rhue, & Matorin, 1993). Building associational cues (triggers) to encourage an increased body and sensory awareness is a likely path to the successful treatment of smokers (Zarren & Eimer, 2001; Zeig, 1980). Tying both these cues for better health and the redefinition of yourself as a nonsmoker to the specific contexts through the use of posthypnotic suggestions is the final step of the treatment.

Notice how the intervention described here for smokers is not based on an interpretation of the "meaning" of the smoking. Such an interpretation of the meaning of smoking could only be my personal projection. Thus, interpreting smoking as a suicidal wish, a socially defiant behavior, an oral gratification representing a fixation at the oral stage of psychosexual development, or any other such assignment of meaning is both arbitrary and unprovable. What is clear, however, is that the smoker is dissociated, for *whatever* reason, and he or she needs to build new healthy associations to his or her body as well as develop the other resources necessary to move forward in life without cigarettes (Bayot, Capafons, & Cardeña, 1977; Capafons & Amigo, 1995).

The dissociative aspect of people's symptoms is an especially noteworthy point to appreciate. Clients routinely describe how the symptom "just happens," meaning it is not a voluntary response on the part of the individual. I generally define therapy as a process involving *pattern interruption* (i.e., getting the person to stop doing one thing) and *pattern building* (i.e., getting the person to do something else), as virtually all therapies must do. As discussed early on, hypnosis by itself cures nothing—it's what happens *during* hypnosis that has the potential to be helpful. The role of the clinician is to establish new positive associations to modify the client's dysfunctional or self-limiting behaviors, thoughts, and feelings. Such associations can best be built through direct experience, such as hypnotic processes or structured learning opportunities (e.g., role plays, homework assignments, behavioral experiments, etc.).

The key points, then, of this section are twofold. First, utilizing hypnotic phenomena as a reference point can be a useful means for understanding symptom structures. Second, when such hypnotic phenomena are evident in the problem structure, a solution can take the form of building new associations through the use of complementary hypnotic phenomena.

As was done in the examples listed in Table 16 above, it may be useful for you to identify which hypnotic phenomena are evident in the type(s) of disorders you tend to treat most frequently.

PATTERNS OF HYPNOTIC INTERVENTION

Applications of hypnosis are as diverse and creative as the number of clinicians who work with it. There is no human problem that can be solved in all people through a "one size fits all" formula. Giving simple and direct suggestions to your hypnotized client for a problem's resolution is one possible form of intervention since such an approach can work with some people. But, the patterns described in this section are based on the recognition that most people need something a little more multidimensional than direct suggestions of symptom abatement.

Individualizing treatment is always a necessity, in my opinion, and that means tailoring general patterns of intervention to the specific needs of the client. Patterns range from relatively simple and obvious to very complex and subtle. The following are some of the more basic and common hypnotic patterns for intervening in client problems. More complex and specialized approaches are readily available in the literature contained in the reference sections throughout this book. The patterns described here are listed in alphabetical order for easier reference.

CHANGING PERSONAL HISTORY

The pattern of intervention called "Changing Personal History" has been used routinely in clinical intervention over many years, in a variety of forms and with a variety of names (Eisen, 1993; Lankton, 2001; Phillips, 1988). As you can gather from its name, the purpose of the intervention is to help people redefine their view of their own personal history. So often in treatment, people have come to see themselves as victims of the past, as damaged and unchangeable. This strategy is appropriate to use with such clients, particularly when a client is presenting a problem that has its origins in a hurtful episode where the person made some negative life decision that perpetuates his or her distress. For example, if a client had the experience of being abused as a child and made the decision (i.e., formed the generalization) that the world is an abusive place and people are not to be trusted or related to in a positive way, the clinician might take the client back in time (i.e., age regression) to his or her earliest memories and suggest they be "rewritten" in order to facilitate the (imaginary) experience for him or her of feeling loved, cared for, and protected by others (Murray-Jobsis, 1996). The resources of affection and caring can be provided through imagined but realistic suggested interactions, such as his or her mother expressing love and approval when he or she brings home a good report card. The client is then guided forward through time while having a subjective sense of love and caring present across all his or her life experiences. In doing so, his or her feelings about him- or herself and others can change in a healthier direction.

Here's a case example illustrating the pattern: In the case of a man I worked with whose mother had died when he was a boy of seven, he had "decided" (not consciously) that "women were not to be trusted and gotten close to because they leave you." Through age regression to the time of his mother's death, he remembered feeling abandoned, angry, and hurt and he decided then that the best way to prevent such emotional pain was to never get close to anyone, especially women. His life, as you can imagine, has been lonely and painful.

The strategy of changing personal history was used with him. When he was age regressed to his fondest memories of his mother (times when he felt her closeness and love), it was possible to make those good feelings of having her around more readily available to him for recall when he wanted them. This was done through the building of an "anchor," or association, to those good feelings; specifically, he could vividly "see" her and "hear" her voice respond to him in his thoughts whenever I touched his arm. The next step was to suggest amnesia during the session for the reality of his mother's death. Once this was established, we could examine his life experiences, both good and bad, and have him "recall" sharing them with his mother as if she had really been there. In hypnosis, she could grow older with him and be there for him in the way he had needed her. The experience of having his mother "with him" in a variety of very specific life situations (e.g., preparing for his first job, getting his driver's license, graduating from high school) through the years allowed him to redefine his view of her and his relationship with her. Suddenly, his mother hadn't abandoned him and women weren't so unreliable. It served to alter his feelings and behavior toward women, especially when he had the insight that "dying probably wasn't her idea, anyway."

In helping "change" his personal history through hypnosis, I provided a means to allow him to experience each of his life experiences with the "missing piece," allowing him to feel, hear, and see life from a different perspective. Did he know the life experiences with his mother that he had re-written were imaginary? Yes, he did. Were they emotionally powerful anyway? Yes, they were. It is the power of hypnosis to help people get absorbed in experiences that are not objectively "real" that makes therapeutic interventions with hypnosis potentially so therapeutic.

CRITICAL (TRAUMATIC) INCIDENT PROCESS

One can't go through life without experiencing trauma of one sort or another. Cars crash, people die, wars are fought, and people seem to evolve innovative ways of hurting each other. In addition to these harsh realities, "everyday" traumas can often have a serious impact: The mean kid in class who made fun of your freckles, the practical joke at your expense that left you standing there wanting to die of embarrassment, and the thoughtless and cruel comment by a loved one that should never have been said are all examples of the "everyday trauma" (i.e., non–life threatening) that can have a profound impact on one's life. Years later such traumas may even seem silly and irrational on a logical level, yet they can still carry a big emotional wallop. In persons who have suffered a trauma of some sort (as defined by them), the traumatic event may well have been a turning point in the person's life. If it was a turning point for the worse, which not all traumas are, then the critical incident process may be an appropriate treatment strategy (Erickson & Kubie, 1941; Spiegel, 1993, 1996).

This is an emotionally powerful hypnotic process, intending at its initial stages to release pent-up emotions associated with a traumatic event ("catharsis"). *If the client has conscious memory for the content of the critical incident, you may simply proceed in a relatively straightforward way. However, if the traumatic incident seems to have been dissociated and forgotten in whole or in part, the process is hazardous.* How does one know there's a hidden trauma, since you cannot reliably infer this merely from symptoms? Yet, it is often the case that people were traumatized and because they minimized and rationalized, they don't even recognize themselves as traumatized until the therapist says some version of, "My God! How did you endure such horrific treatment?" You are advised to exercise extreme caution in dealing with trauma, and study considerably more in-depth material than that provided here before embarking on trauma treatment when the client has no clear memories of the trauma. In such an instance, you can still do a critical incident process, but you must be careful to let the client work at his or her own rate and not push the client to deal with something directly he or she feels unable to (Dolan, 1991; Lankton, 2001). Ideomotor questioning (e.g., finger signals to provide responses) may help assess whether the client is ready, willing, and able to deal with the traumatic experience and/or the consequences in their life.

Table 17 below provides a general structure of the critical incident process.

Table 17. General Structure of a Critical Incident Process

Induction, establish anchor to comfort
Age regression to context
Exploration of context
Elicit affective associations
Identify central distortion(s)
Catharsis
Dissociation of affect
Dimensional shifting of representation/reframing
Restructuring of focus and memory content
Amplification of alternate representation(s)
Age progression with new resource
Posthypnotic suggestion for future accessing
Reorientation

The critical incident process as a treatment strategy involves an age regression (either hypermnesia or revivification, depending on the appropriate level of emotional intensity needed to re-work the situation) back to the time of the traumatic experience. Generally, it is a good idea to first do a regression to a positive experience, demonstrating to the client that he or she can trust the clinician's guidance, find comfort (or *something* positive) within him- or herself, and control the hypnosis experience.

Once the client has become immersed in the experience, and describes it aloud so the clinician can know what's happening and how the person is interpreting the meaning of what's happening, the clinician's primary role is to offer him or her support for exploring the episode. Simultaneously, the therapist identifies and amplifies a part of the experience the client had previously not attended to, such as how insecure (angry, sick, hurt . . .) the other person involved might have been, or how well he or she coped in the face of adversity, or some such thing that can be used as a pivot point to start to redefine the way the traumatic episode is stored and remembered. One might strive to change the history of the situation by adding something new to the interaction to make it easier to bear (e.g., successfully fighting off the attacker). By supporting the client's expression of emotional pain, the clinician can usually guide him or her to a point where he or she can start to feel differently about the situation. Frequently, just having the chance to tell the story that has never been told and release some pent-up emotion in a supportive atmosphere has ample therapeutic value (Phillips, 2001; Phillips & Frederick, 1995). But, the strongest part of this process is in guiding the client into a new awareness or new understanding of the meaning of the experience, redefining its place in his or her life in an empowering way. To complete the process, the client can be age progressed, integrating into the future the changes in thoughts and feelings associated with the release of the hurt, bringing with him or her new conclusions about both the critical incident and him- or herself (Watkins & Watkins, 1997).

One can also use the critical incident process to revivify an experience that was critical in the client's life in a *positive* way. With the growing emphasis on a "positive psychology" in the field, this choice can be an especially powerful means of helping people get and stay connected to the best parts of themselves. Typically, though, the experiences that wreak the biggest emotional havoc on people and that send them into treatment are traumatic ones, requiring a great deal of sensitivity on the part of the clinician. It is vital, especially when considering the excesses of the battles over the issue of repressed memories, to be judicious in one's use of trauma-focused therapies. Many clinicians I am aware of are "emotional voyeurs" who want or need to help their clients "get in touch with the pain." The reality is that if you look for people's pain, you will always find it. However, that isn't necessarily therapeutic and may actually be *antitherapeutic*. A lot of people have suffered considerably by the time they consult the clinician; guiding the client through the traumatic incident process with no precise goal in mind beyond "finding the pain" is capable of amplifying hurt needlessly. Caution is advised.

HOMEWORK ASSIGNMENTS

Many therapeutic approaches regularly make use of "homework," educational tasks the client is given to carry out in between therapy sessions (Cummings & Cummings, 2000). These are intended to encourage new behaviors, test out the accuracy of one's perceptions, and amplify particular thoughts, feelings, and behaviors that the clinician judges important in the therapy. Homework assignments operate on the level of actual direct experience, a more powerful level than the merely intellectual. Homework helps people integrate new learnings on multiple levels. And, by assigning homework, the client has to expend effort, increasing the likelihood that they will value the therapy more (Lynn & Sherman, 2000).

The homework assignment isn't hypnosis, but it is hypnotic in its absorbing people in new frames of mind and developing deeper understandings of themselves and their life circumstances. Homework can also be thought of as an *experiential metaphor* in the treatment process. Prescribed properly, homework will address unconscious dynamics of the presenting problem(s). When the client engages in an activity that will cause him or her to experience him- or herself differently while confronting self-limiting thoughts, feelings, and behaviors, new associations are formed and the desired change may be accomplished (Lankton & Lankton, 1983, 1989).

In one case example involving homework while working with a depressed client, at one point in the therapy I wanted to target this woman's depressing patterns of making negative comparisons between herself and others. She assumed and really *believed*, "Everyone else is happy, I'm not," "Everyone else has fun, I don't," "Everyone else's life is easy, mine's hard," and on and on. She virtually never strayed outside her immediate comfort zone to go anywhere interesting or try anything new, and it's fair to say she was exceptionally dull. Simply telling her, "You know, you assume way too much about things at the expense of actually checking out whether things are as you think they are," is an intervention that will likely fall flat. She believes herself too easily. So, to make the point more experientially, I instructed her to go to a nearby state park and hike a mountain trail there called the Azalea Glen Springs Trail. Sounds beautiful, doesn't it? Can you picture the fields of beautiful azaleas? Can you imagine the clear mountain springs spilling over the rocky terrain? Well, don't. There are probably four azaleas you see on the hike, and the "spring" is little more than a metal pipe dripping water out of the side of a hill! This particular client, as part of her depressed mental set, built things up way beyond what they really are in a way that always put her at the bottom. In instructing her to hike the trail, I knew she'd imagine flower fields and the springs as abundant, beautiful and flowing water. I also knew she'd be in for a big surprise when she got there after several miles of moderately difficult hiking and found such a disappointing sight. And, I knew that when you hardly ever leave your living room, the experience would be dramatic. It was.

When I saw her the day after her hike, she was by far the most animated she'd been since I'd met her. At the start of the hike, she was annoyed with me for telling her to go, and she was annoyed with herself for agreeing to go. She couldn't understand what she could learn on a trail that she couldn't learn more easily in my office. But, she stuck with it, to her credit. When she finally arrived at the Azalea Glen Springs, anticipating all she anticipated finding, at first she was confused. But then she found it very, very funny that after all her hiking and high level of expectation all she found was a dripping pipe coming out of the ground! During her descent she thought very hard about why I would ask her to hike such a disappointing trail. After a while she had the realization that *she had set herself up for disappointment* by building the springs up into something special in her mind when, in reality, the springs weren't at all the way she had imagined them. She broadened her thinking, and had the "big *aha*!"—that she is almost always building things up to be better than they really are, and *making herself worse* than she really is. On the spot, she decided to make greater effort to find out the true value of things from her own direct experience, rather than from assumptions rooted in her insecurity.

This homework assignment provided her a much more intense experience of herself than would my saying to her (in or out of hypnosis), "You build things up in your mind to be better than they really are and you make yourself out to be worse than you really are so stop doing that!" The hike served a number of therapeutic purposes: It symbolically matched her "going uphill against the world" feelings, it got her physically active (a great tool in dissipating depression), it caused her to confront her unconscious pattern of maximizing everything and everyone else while minimizing herself, and it boosted her self-esteem by giving her a greater feeling of being in control of herself, for she had accomplished something meaningful all by herself.

Assigning homework or task assignments that will address the client's concerns can take a variety of forms. In addition to the symbolic task described above, another type of assignment can involve "making the symptom inconvenient" for the person. Typically, a symptom is coddled and catered to, for the client adapts his or her life to its presence. Having the client do something that will make the symptom exceptionally inconvenient can effect a surprisingly rapid and lasting change. It can mobilize resistance against the symptoms themselves (Haley, 1973, 1984).

For example, one client I treated indirectly using the approach of making the symptom inconvenient was a girl, age nine, who refused to sleep in her own bed because she wanted to be with her parents in their room at night as they watched television. Consequently, she was up late, couldn't get up on time to go to school, and was tired and inattentive much of the time.

The girl's parents fought with her to go to bed in her own room, but to no avail. When they consulted me as to what they should do with her, I told them that I did not need to actually see their daughter if they would follow my instructions. I told them to *kindly and affectionately* send her on frequent errands *after* she had settled comfortably into their bed: "Mommy wants a glass of water, will you please go downstairs and get me one?" or "Daddy forgot to check the front door, will you go downstairs and make sure it's locked?" and so forth. Each time she came back and got comfortable, they lovingly sent her somewhere. It took only three nights for her to come to the conclusion that being with mom and dad wasn't so much fun after all, and that she could be a lot more comfortable in her own room!

Homework assignments involve more dimensions of the person in the therapy than does verbal dialogue alone. It also allows the interventions to generalize to times and places outside the clinician's office, allowing changes to be more easily integrated into the client's life. My tendency is to want to avoid pathologizing people. I'd generally prefer to find a way to help people that focuses on what's *right* with them rather than what's wrong. This is illustrated in my intervention with the girl described above. This was a girl who simply didn't want to miss being with her parents. She's not "sick." She just doesn't want to miss anything. But, more traditional interventions might have overtly focused on pathological separation anxiety, inadequate individuation, dysfunctional family issues, parental double binds through tacit encouragement of the symptomatic behavior, and so forth. If you think about it, these very issues *were* addressed, though indirectly, and with greater speed and less trauma to her integrity. Homework assignments can make a point on a variety of levels simultaneously, both directly and indirectly, and when used skillfully are an art form in their own right.

REFRAMING

The meaning of an event or a communication is determined to a large extent by the context in which it appears (Watzlawick, Weakland, & Fisch, 1974). For example, a single word such as "no" can actually mean a wide variety of things ranging from a firm, clear "no" to a wishy-washy "I don't know" to an affirmative, "I guess so," depending on one's tone of voice, body posture dynamics, and the social context.

Changing the context of a communication changes its meaning and value. A behavior may be perfectly acceptable in one situation, but not in another. Consider the act of stealing as an example. Stealing money from a blind beggar is an act no one would condone. Stealing a serum that will cure your mother's terminal cancer from a greedy neighbor who wants a million dollars so you don't have to buy the cure is the same act of stealing, yet it stimulates empathy in most people rather than anger and a desire to punish the offender. Lying by the government to the public is considered a betrayal, unless it's for "national security." A man who acts strangely is "crazy" if he's poor, but "eccentric" if he's wealthy.

The various euphemisms that abound in the English language are all simple and effective "reframings." Reframing means changing the meaning by changing the context which defines the way an event is perceived (Watzlawick, 1978). *Psychotherapy in whatever form it happens to take at a given moment necessarily involves reframing.* Liabilities are turned into assets, traumatic events are converted into learning experiences, weaknesses are turned into strengths, and so forth. Reframing can be accomplished with a single remark, or can involve a lengthier, more experientially absorbing hypnotic experience. Any approach that encourages the client to have a different perspective on the problem involves a reframe. As soon as you say, "Look at it this way . . . ," you're attempting a reframe.

There was a highly gifted speaker on the subject of "Love" that I (and millions of others) enjoyed named Dr. Leo Buscaglia, whose numerous books all managed to find their way onto the bestseller list. Dr. Buscaglia did a wonderful and emotionally powerful reframe in one of his televised lectures when he somberly observed that each of us human beings has experienced hurt, sadness, and loneliness. He paused dramatically, then burst into a big smile and cheerfully asked, "Isn't that wonderful?" When he described hurt, sadness and loneliness as "wonderful," it forced listeners to look at those feelings differently. He challenged us to find a sensible basis for his describing them so peculiarly. When we realize, as he intended us to, that it is those negative feelings, as well as positive ones, that unite us all as human beings by allowing us to share common emotions, such feelings *can* legitimately be viewed as wonderful. I doubt, though, that anyone in Dr. Buscaglia's audience would have thought of sadness as wonderful before his reframe.

Humor involves reframing as the vehicle for the joke. The punch line inevitably causes us to look at the incidents in the story differently. Consider this joke told to me by one of my clients: A police officer spots an old, deteriorated van driving down the street and notices it doesn't have license plates. Upon pulling the driver over, and walking up to him to ask him where his license plates are, the officer notices fifty penguins standing in the back of the van. The officer, not expecting to see penguins in a van, yells at the driver: "I pulled you over because you don't have any license plates, but now I want to know what the heck you're doing with these penguins in your van. No, actually I don't want to know, just *take them to the zoo*. You got it, mister? *Just take these penguins to the zoo!*" As the van driver pulls away, the police officer shakes his head and mutters to himself "Well, now I've seen it all." The very next day while on patrol, the officer sees the same van driving along and decides to pull it over again, this time to address the license plate problem. When he steps up to the driver's window, he sees the fifty penguins still in the van—only this time they are all wearing sunglasses! Furious, the officer says, "Mister, I thought I told you to take those penguins to the zoo." The driver's response was, "Well, I did. And, today, I'm taking them to the beach!"

Humor softens hard times, gives us emotional distance from despair, and provides us with a means to make something big much smaller and easier to handle. For example, after the national trauma of 9/11, how healing it was to have our comedians make us smile again. Reframing through humor made life bearable again.

The clinical skill involved in reframing is to suspend the client's self-limiting belief system long enough for him or her to consider an alternate viewpoint. Turning the "half empty" glass into a "half full" one is an obvious example of how a negative viewpoint can be transformed into a positive one. Reframing can work in the other direction, too. An action a client engaged in that he or she felt fine about until the clinician said, "How could you let yourself do that?" could rapidly turn his or her comfort into pain. Most interventions, though, are intended to transform pain into comfort. The underlying assumption in doing reframing as an intervention strategy is that *every experience (i.e., thought, feeling, behavior) has some positive value somewhere.* By taking an experience that the client views as a negative one and commenting on how and why that same experience might actually be an asset to him or her somewhere, one can change the client's attitude about that experience, allowing the negativity to be discharged.

As another example, a woman complained that her husband's habit of snoring was disturbing her sleep. She was told an emotionally charged story by a widowed friend she happened to complain to. The widow described her loneliness since her husband died, how much she felt the weight of her husband's death on her every experience, and how much she longed to hear her deceased husband's snoring, something she said she'd hated about him when he was alive. The impact on the woman complaining about her husband's snoring was to instantly develop an appreciation for her husband's snoring, because it was clear evidence he was still alive and well. It actually became comforting to her. Her husband's snoring behavior was the same, only her attitude about it was changed. That's a successful reframe.

Finding a way to turn a minus into a plus (or vice versa, if appropriate) is a basic part of clinical work. Learning and using the techniques of reframing, with or without formal hypnosis, can make the transformation of a client's personal reality a more efficient and deliberate process.

SYMPTOM PRESCRIPTION

Symptom prescription is a paradoxical therapeutic strategy which involves the direct or indirect encouragement of the client's symptom(s). When the client is encouraged to continue to do what he or she is already doing, but in a way that is slightly different through some adjustment requested by the clinician, the habitual symptom generating sequence is interrupted (Foa & Wilson, 1991). The symptom is no longer a puzzling thing that "just happens." It happens in response to the clinician's direction, only now it happens differently, in a way easier to see as both arbitrary and unnecessary rather than as important and inevitable. Consequently, symptoms lose their original meanings and associations (Haley, 1973; Madanes, 1981, 1984).

Symptom prescription, in a sense, is a sort of "reverse psychology" approach. For example, in the case of a woman I treated for depression, I prescribed that this woman lie in her bed continuously for four hours a day, specifically in the middle of the day when she was more likely to be active in her daily activities. Lying in bed was something she was already doing as part of her depression, but it was at her leisure. I adjusted her behavior by instructing her to get up early in the morning, shower, dress, have breakfast, do a few chores, and then go back to bed for the prescribed four-hour period. After following my instructions for several days, she found the bed that was once a haven of comfort was now "feeling like a prison." She "had to" be there, by "doctor's order." She reacted very emotionally to her bed, and later pleaded with me to not have to lie in bed anymore. As a final prescription, I instructed her to have a "leaving bed" party, complete with hats, balloons, cake, and the presence of her family. It symbolized for her a genuine transition, a "coming out" from her depression, especially when her party "guests" sat on her bed to be with her. Bed just wasn't the desirable place to be that it once was. As a result, this particular client has been able to actively get on with her life in a very positive way. My symptom prescription strategy encouraged the symptom, made it inconvenient, encouraged a search for better alternatives, and encouraged her to abandon an avoidant behavior that reinforced her depression.

Encouraging people to do what they are already doing robs their action of spontaneity and personal ownership (i.e., it's not "theirs" anymore). When the pattern loses spontaneity and personal ownership, it provides no gratification for continuing to engage in that behavior. A key to having symptom prescription work lies in the rationale you provide with the prescription. If the rationale doesn't meet the client in his or her frame of reference, he or she will not be likely to follow the prescription. Furthermore, there are multiple dimensions of a presenting problem (its associated feelings, thoughts, behaviors, relational components, symbolic components, etc.) and the symptom prescription must be offered carefully in order to address the appropriate dimension(s). Finally, the modification in the sequence culminating in the symptomatic behavior that the clinician introduces in the prescription is a key element, since it is this modification that will, when used successfully, alter the entire symptom pattern.

The potential applications of the symptom prescription paradigm are broad in scope. Encouraging a "resistant" person to "be resistant" then redefines that resistance as cooperation. Encouraging a client to have a prescribed relapse redefines a relapse (unless the client resists and refuses to have one, which is better yet) as an acceptable and required part of the treatment process. Encouraging clients to do what they are already doing can give what seems like an uncontrolled symptom some concrete defining limits that make it a little easier for them to be dealt with effectively.

THERAPEUTIC METAPHORS

Stories as teaching tools have been the principal means of educating and socializing people throughout human history. Metaphor, in the world of hypnosis, has come to mean the use of stories in the treatment process. The use of metaphor is a core component of most hypnotic processes. Building and telling stories as a vehicle for imparting therapeutic messages is a complex and powerful therapeutic skill to develop (B. Erickson, 2001; Haley, 1973; Rosen, 1982). Therapeutic metaphors can be created in such a way as to parallel the client's problems, and may be told in such a way as to absorb the client in the metaphor. As Australian psychologist and colleague George

Burns points out in his excellent book of metaphors, *101 Healing Stories: Using Metaphors in Therapy* (2001, Wiley), the client may project meanings into the story that the clinician didn't even intend to communicate, and these may have greater impact than the intended meanings!

The best metaphors are usually those found in the client's own personal experience. Naturally, these are more personal, more immediate, and easier for the client to relate to in a meaningful way. If you take the time to review incidents in the client's life that had special significance for him or her, usually because they taught him or her something valuable about life, you can have immediate access to a wealth of potentially meaningful metaphors. Likewise, your own background and personal history reflect important learning experiences, and these may be used as the basis for therapeutic metaphors as well. *The more you participate in life, the more experiences you have to draw upon when constructing therapeutic metaphors.* Cases you have worked on or read about that illustrate worthwhile points are also a good source of metaphors. Other sources include storybooks, movies, jokes, anecdotes that illustrate important points about human nature, newspaper stories, television programs, and virtually any other milieu from which you have the opportunity to learn important lessons about living life well from considering other people's experience.

Learning to tell stories in a hypnotic manner (i.e., meaningfully, in a way that focuses and absorbs the person's attention, accepting and utilizing the client's responses, embedding suggestions, with an expectancy of the person learning something important, etc.) is a skill for doing hypnosis that is vital to develop. The necessity of formally inducing hypnosis diminishes as the client becomes absorbed in the telling of a story. The natural ability of the client to drift in and out of hypnosis as he or she listens to the clinician can be tapped and amplified by the clinician wanting to use a metaphorical approach (Brown, 1993).

Metaphor is obviously an indirect way of suggesting possibilities to the client. Instead of saying, "Do this," you say, with exaggerated simplicity, "Once I had a client who faced a problem similar to yours and one day he tried this and it helped." The client can be encouraged to learn from others' experiences, whether to apply a specific suggested solution or, more generally, to simply be willing to experiment with new possibilities. The use of metaphor isn't a heavy-handed approach. It is a respectful way of suggesting possibilities without demanding much from the client. A common consequence of this approach is that change can sometimes seem relatively effortless, as if it "just happened," a possibility that the clinician can allow for. Without offering magical interpretations about the wisdom of the unconscious, I can simply say metaphor has a way of stimulating the client's internal associations and directing them toward problem-solving in a way that not only makes sense, but *works*. And, to be sure, some changes *do* take place rather "spontaneously," with no real internal tug-of-war apparent. For an example out of your own life, consider those foods you hated as a child that you now enjoy. These are probably not foods you forced yourself to learn to like. Your tastes changed, they evolved—and they changed effortlessly.

Obviously, not all or even most changes take place so effortlessly, making the process of therapy uneven in both practice and rate of success. But the therapeutic metaphor as a means of imparting valuable messages in a memorable context (i.e., the drama of the storyline) stands a very good chance of facilitating such seemingly spontaneous changes. Spend a day or two just noticing the things that happen in life that illustrate principles of effective living; practice telling people about those events while leading them to discover the principle the story reveals, and you'll be well on your way to evolving skills in designing and delivering therapeutic metaphors.

SUMMARY

Each of the half-dozen patterns of intervention described in this section have been presented in a general way in order to acquaint you with some of the possibilities inherent in the process. Many of these patterns will be evident to you when you read them in the sample hypnotic transcripts in the next chapter.

There are numerous components of each process and each must be considered and properly integrated in order for it to be effective. For a more complete understanding of the concepts and techniques of these and the hundreds, if not thousands, of ways to structure hypnosis sessions, other writings in these areas are invaluable. (Many of these are contained in the reference sections at the end of each chapter.) While the patterns included here are representative of some of the best (i.e., most effective and reliable) hypnotic interventions, there are many other therapeutic patterns involving hypnosis.

ADDRESSING COMMON CLINICAL CONCERNS HYPNOTICALLY

In clinical practice, therapists encounter a wide range of presenting concerns. Some problems are rare, others quite common. This section contains a brief and superficial consideration of six of the most common clinical concerns and some quick ideas for how hypnosis might be used directly or indirectly in their treatment. Referring back to last chapter's ideas on designing treatment plans, it would be helpful as you think about people's problems to not only think of *what* their symptoms are, but of *how* they generate them. As described earlier in this chapter as well, the more you understand about how the person generates symptoms, the more targets for effective intervention you will have.

The next chapter contains full transcripts of hypnosis sessions performed with actual clients.

ANXIETY, STRESS

Some have called this the "Age of Anxiety," and there is considerable justification for doing so. The demands placed on each person today in order to live effectively are more numerous and more complex than at any other time in the past. Personal safety, a core issue in anxiety, is uncertain when acts of terrorism can occur at any time in any place. Just as soon as we get used to one technological advance, it becomes obsolete, requiring us to readjust. Traditional values holding society together have been and are continuing to deteriorate, emphasizing individualism and personal gain over social responsibility, and making even the most important relationships seem only transient. Gender roles are much less specific, and committed marital and family relationships are taking second place to making strategic career moves, confounding many people trying to figure out how to make their relationships work. Finding work and staying employed is a more demanding and complex task than ever before as people matter less to companies than does the company's "bottom line," threatening economic security. The number of potential sources of stress in our lives keeps growing, and most people will struggle with these issues to one degree or another at some point in their lives (Regier & Robins, 1991).

Stress and anxiety are inevitable whenever someone faces a circumstance that requires adapting. Stress cannot be prevented, only managed, because life throws all kinds of things at each of us. But, as often as not, stress isn't generated by external circumstances, it's generated by unrealistic expectations (such as perfectionism), a need for things to be orderly and predictable when too little of life is that way, or any of a variety of ways people torment themselves with their own internal issues. Hypnosis can be used to address any and all of these sorts of issues, teaching more realistic thinking, greater flexibility, and better problem-solving skills.

There is one particular aspect of anxiety that bears special consideration, if only briefly. It has to do with the foundation of anxiety. There are two separate but related structural components of most people's anxiety: The tendency to overestimate the risks one faces, and the tendency to underestimate one's resources or abilities to manage those risks successfully (Barlow, 2000). Thus, teaching people how to more realistically assess the risks they face and how to cope with them skillfully can go a long way in reducing people's anxiety. The reality is, no place is truly safe, and many life experiences are inherently ambiguous, requiring us to manage them skillfully as they arise. Trusting yourself to do exactly that, rather than getting overwhelmed and fearful, is critical to keeping anxiety within normal limits. Using hypnosis to teach such critically important skills as risk assessment and personal resourcefulness are vitally important applications.

Hypnosis in its most superficial yet still helpful application in managing anxiety can help one build relaxation skills and an increased sense of self-control. Teaching clients the skill of self-hypnosis (hypnotic inductions and utilizations they can perform on themselves whenever they'd like to) is a necessary part of using hypnosis in clinical contexts. Simply knowing you have the ability to relax deeply and reorganize your thoughts, feelings, and behaviors can have a powerful effect in helping you better manage stress and anxiety. Managing anxiety effectively allows for better concentration, clearer thinking and problem-solving, better self-esteem, better time management, better job performance, greater receptivity to new ideas, and better just about everything.

DEPRESSION

Depression has been a major focus of my professional life, having been my area of specialization in clinical practice, and the subject of many of my books (1988, 1989, 1992, 1997, 1999, 2001a, 2001b), book chapters, articles, and clinical trainings. Depression is a very complex, multidimensional problem that, despite the development of effective psychotherapies and antidepressant medications, continues to grow in prevalence. It is estimated that 20–25 million people in the United States currently suffer depression severe enough to require treatment, yet the majority of them will not receive the treatment they need. The World Health Organization (WHO) recently declared depression currently the world's fourth most debilitating human condition (behind heart disease, cancer, and traffic accidents), and predicted that it would grow to become the *second* most debilitating condition worldwide by the year 2020 (Murray & Lopez, 1997).

There are numerous theories or models describing why people get depressed, but virtually all of them recognize three primary domains of contributing factors: biological, psychological, and social. In what must be seen as a triumph of marketing over science, the biology of depression has been overstated, leading too many people to believe depression is the result of a shortage of serotonin in the brain which requires medication to correct. Given the massive evidence that psychological and social factors are huge contributors to depression, focusing on neurochemistry alone is too one-dimensional and overly simplistic. It's not wrong—it's just that this view is only a part of the depression story, and not even the greater part of the story.

Studies of therapeutic efficacy make it clear that active psychotherapy approaches that teach specific skills, especially in clear thinking, effective behavior, and building positive relationships, match and, in some ways, outperform medications in terms of both symptom management and relapse rates (Antonuccio, Danton, & DeNelsky, 1995). Psychotherapy for depression should be considered an essential aspect of treatment, since no amount of medication can teach coping skills, problem-solving skills, social skills, build a support network, or do all the other things that are known to not only reduce depression but minimize the potential for relapses. Antidepressant medications can be valuable, to be sure, but should not generally be considered a sole form of intervention.

Hypnosis can be used in many different ways in treating depressed individuals. Many of the possibilities are addressed in considerable detail in my books *Hypnosis and the Treatment of Depressions* (1992) and *Treating Depression with Hypnosis* (2001a). Possible targets for intervention might include the depressed person's negative and de-motivating expectations (i.e., hopelessness), the perception that no amount of effort will yield success (i.e., helplessness), cognitive distortions, faulty attributions, ineffective behavior, poor social skills, low frustration tolerance, poor coping skills, and any of the other many subjective patterns of thinking, feeling and behaving that can help form and exacerbate depression. Empowerment is a basic theme in treating depression, and in that respect, hypnosis can be an invaluable part of the treatment process.

RELATIONSHIP PROBLEMS

Considering the fact that the majority of marriages in this country end in divorce, as well as the fact that more people today live alone than ever before, the indication is quite clear that people are having a harder time building and maintaining healthy relationships with others than ever before. Why? There are many reasons: The still-changing roles of men and women, the diversity of family structures that might be convenient but may not always best serve their members, the increasing technological advances that keep diminishing our need for contact with others (i.e., more time on the computer than with people), the ease of divorce, the lack of good role models teaching the skills good relationships require (consider the role models on trashy television) and the still-casual attitudes about sex despite the spread of herpes, AIDS, and other sexually transmitted diseases are just some of the factors affecting each person's ability to relate to another in a positive and balanced way.

Good relationships don't just happen. There is much, much more to them than just "good chemistry." They require nurturing, and a considerable range of skills including empathy, compassion, tolerance, impulse control, problem-solving, negotiation, communication, self-sacrifice, and an attitude of protectiveness to name just a few (Gottman, 1999; Weiner-Davis,

2001). In intervening in relationship problems, factors to consider include the quality of each person's expectations (a primary determinant of one's level of satisfaction such that when the other person does as you think he or she should you're happier with him or her), the quality of their communication skills, and their subjective views on issues like "power" and "intimacy." Often, the partners in a relationship have inadequate communication skills, poorly defined or even inappropriate expectations, more interest in being "right" than effective, more investment in advancing themselves than the relationship, and other such barriers to building an effective relationship.

When working with couples and families, you are less likely to employ formal hypnosis, although hypnotizing one member in front of the others or hypnotizing the whole group can easily be done if you think it an appropriate intervention. Much more likely, however, is the use of informal hypnosis, using hypnotic strategies (e.g., metaphor, imagery, symptom prescription, or role playing) to focus and absorb family members on ideas and perspectives you present to them that are meant to empower them to be more effective in their relating to one another (Haley, 1973; Kershaw, 1992; Parsons-Fein, 2001; Robles, 2001). Many clinicians will see couples or families as a unit and then see the members individually. Hypnotic strategies may then be employed to clarify expectations, increase the level of motivation to resolve differences respectfully and skillfully within the relationship, enhance communication skills, and address self-limiting patterns that interfere with the growth of the relationship (i.e., increasing empathy, frustration tolerance, impulse control, etc.).

Even when partners and other family members are not available to do couples or family therapy, you can still do what can be called a "systemically informed" intervention, taking the roles and effects of others into account in the therapy. Healthy relationships serve as a buffer against all kinds of disorders, emotional and physical, and so are an important consideration in multidimensional treatment. Using hypnosis to enhance the client's relationships can also enhance the therapy.

SELF-ESTEEM PROBLEMS

Your self-esteem is your subjective assessment of your value as a human being. It is formed in part by the feedback we get from others, but it is formed to an even larger extent by our beliefs and how they serve as filters for the feedback we get. You may recall the earlier discussion of cognitive dissonance and its implication for the experiences a person will and will not permit him- or herself (Festinger, 1957). If you think you're no good, then other people telling you that you are good will not likely change your view of yourself. Cognitive dissonance leads you to filter out feedback that contradicts your belief about yourself, serving as the perceptual mechanism for maintaining an unfortunate status quo.

Self-esteem has been the target of many therapists' interventions. They have believed that most problems stem from poor self-esteem, and thus made raising a client's self-esteem a primary therapeutic goal. Self-esteem in this regard has been vastly overrated. Self-esteem is a statement as to how you feel about yourself. Good self-esteem doesn't mean you're more socially aware or skilled, or a better more compassionate person, or more skilled in any way. It just means you feel good about yourself. Some of the most seriously disturbed or malicious people (e.g., full-blown sociopaths) on this planet have quite good self-esteem. They are dysfunctional or destructive people who just happen to feel good about themselves.

Helping people become more skilled is a more expedient path to raising self-esteem, though, than is simply telling people how "special" they are. I want my clients to be able to move through their day being effective in what they do, allowing them to say to themselves many times during the day, "I like what I did there. I like the way I handled that." Self-esteem rises as people develop and notice their skills in living.

When you work with self-esteem issues hypnotically, the client can be encouraged to take control of situations by planning and implementing a deliberate and effective course of action. The person can learn that their problems are not caused by fatal flaws, but by a lack of salient skills, ones that can be learned. Absorbing the person in learning alternative ways of addressing the issues in his or her life, and solving problems while also teaching broader skills in problem-solving, are fundamental components of good therapy. Hypnosis enhances skill acquisition, encourages a willingness to try new behaviors, and empowers people to feel better about themselves as they come to better "own" the changes they make. Hypnosis can also help the client learn to generalize skills to other areas of his or her life. (For a thorough and practical consideration of self-esteem as a target of intervention, see Andreas, 2002.)

SUBSTANCE ABUSE

Some of the most serious and pervasive problems in our society today are directly and indirectly related to substance abuse. Excessive use of alcohol and other drugs, cigarette smoking, and overeating are all examples of substance abuse. In each case, the person is experiencing feelings, consciously or otherwise, that are uncomfortable (e.g., fear, loneliness, boredom, depression, etc.). Instead of dealing with the uncomfortable feelings directly and effectively, the person employs what is known as an "avoidant coping style." Avoidance is an inherently disempowering strategy, placing one in the "victim" position by saying, in essence, "I can't handle this." The substance is turned to as a way of altering one's feelings, making them more manageable, even if only for a few moments.

Substance abuse also has a strong social component. People build their relationships around the substance, and perhaps their identities as well. Treatment has to be as multidimensional as the problem. Using hypnosis to teach better problem-solving skills, increase impulse control, resolve underlying depression and/or anxiety, enhance a stronger sense of commitment to sobriety or abstinence, and many other such empowering skills are just some of the possible approaches in addressing substance abuse (Alman & Lambrou, 1992; Bell-Gadsby, 2001; Levitt, 1993).

On a different level of consideration, substance abusers typically are in a physically dissociated state to some degree, with a markedly diminished awareness of the negative effects of the substance on their bodies. Furthermore, substance abusers gradually build their lives around the substance: Cigarette smokers don't take the stairs, and obese people don't look at their bodies in the mirror. Each wants to avoid situations that will force them to confront (i.e., associate to) the physical effects of their habit, and so dissociation from the body helps to allow the pattern to continue.

Hypnosis can be used to cultivate greater body awareness, a more positive attitude of self-protectiveness, and a greater sense of independence such that whatever situations are encountered can be dealt with more effectively without self-abuse.

SEXUAL DYSFUNCTIONS

Engaging in sexual relations with someone you love can be one of the nicest of all hypnotic experiences, wouldn't you agree? Not for many people, though. For them, sexual activity is inhibited or even eliminated because of sexual problems. The various sexual dysfunctions (e.g., erectile dysfunctions, premature ejaculation, disorders of sexual desire, etc.) can occur for a wide variety of reasons, including: (1) misinformation about human anatomy or sexual functioning in general; (2) negative feelings about sex because of past negative experiences with it, such as guilt from a conservative religious upbringing or an abusive partner; (3) poor self-esteem and body concept; (4) poor quality relationships based, in part, on inappropriate expectations; and, (5) organic problems resulting in impaired functioning, as well as other less common reasons (Klein, 2002).

A thorough physical examination is the first step in dealing with this and all the other problems present that may be organically based. Once the organic reasons for impaired or absent sexual functioning are ruled out, the clinician's task is to assess what psychosocial factors may be causing and/or contributing to the sexual problem(s). Some people can discuss sensitive sexual issues directly, in which case the clinician can also discuss them directly. But others are embarrassed, afraid, or otherwise reluctant to discuss delicate matters directly, and so a clinician might reasonably decide to be less direct, at least initially, in his or her approach. In such cases, metaphors about other clients' problems can be useful in helping diagnose the client's problem (the observant clinician can observe the ideodynamic changes in response to different parts of the story), as well as in offering therapeutic suggestions and directives.

People with sexual problems are generally in a dissociated state relative to their sexual functioning, rather than being fully associated to the pleasure of the experience (Araoz, 2001). There is a part of them attempting to engage in sexual activity, but their focus may instead be on other parts of themselves that distract or even distress them, such as a part that is observing and criticizing their sexual performance, or perhaps a part remembering past failures with the associated feelings of humiliation, or maybe a part that feels guilty remembering the shame of their religious upbringing, or even a part that simply feels angry with their partner for some real or imaginary hurt. The result is diffuse concentration, mixed feelings, and a discomfort that dissipates the hypnotic aspects of the experience necessary to function well sexually.

Hypnosis may be employed to address and resolve past hurts, educate the client about sexual matters, and facilitate the process of reintegration so that all of the person may more easily be in the "here and-now," more fully experiencing and enjoying the sexual activity (Araoz, 1998). Another type of intervention is even more basic: altering sensory awareness by heightening kinesthetic sensitivity hypnotically. This is essentially an amplified "sensate-focus" technique that sex therapists routinely employ in the treatment of sexual dysfunction.

Anxiety about sexual performance is a primary target for hypnotic interventions in cases of sexual dysfunction. Anxiety causes poor performance, which causes more anxiety, which escalates the probability of poor performance, and so on in a vicious circle. Using the comfort of hypnosis to allow the client to "let go" is a good model for "letting go" during sexual activity, which is fundamental to sexual enjoyment. Teaching self-hypnosis in order to help the client control anxiety can allow the relaxation to generalize to the sexual context where he or she would like to have it.

Reframing sex as a natural, healthy function is an important suggestion that can be amplified hypnotically in sexual therapy. Giving the paradoxical directive (i.e., symptom prescription) to "avoid sex at all costs this week" can facilitate the "I'll show you by doing it!" attitude in the mildly defiant client (Haley, 1973). Changing personal history to teach a positive attitude toward sex (in the place of a negative one) while growing up is also a viable treatment strategy. Age progressing the client to see him- or herself as sexually active and satisfied is yet another potential application of hypnosis built on establishing positive expectancy.

As you can probably tell, hypnosis and sex therapy are two highly compatible and easily integrated approaches to the treatment of sexual dysfunction. Given how sexual difficulties can strain even the best of relationships, this is an important area to address if we are to support good marriages and healthy families.

CONCLUSION

Hopefully, this chapter gave you some good exposure to some of the many ways hypnosis may be creatively and meaningfully applied in psychotherapy. Learning how, when, and where to apply the many different potentially therapeutic experiences available through hypnosis requires many years of practice and study. The deeper your understanding of the numerous components that are a part of each and every symptom, the greater the respect you can have for the overall integrity of the finely balanced system called "the client." And, the deeper your understanding of how to define problems as solvable and treat them effectively, the greater will be your sense of skill and satisfaction with your chosen work.

For Discussion

1. What are the advantages and disadvantages of individualizing treatment? Do they offset each other? Why or why not?
2. Can you identify a belief you hold to be true about yourself that has prevented you from having certain experiences? How did it do that? With what effect?
3. What evidence do you have that reality is subjective? Is there an objective reality? How do you know?
4. When, if ever, should a client be forced to deal with something directly that is intensely painful? Why do you say so?
5. Discuss what you think these statements mean: (a) Personal problems are a result of negative self-hypnosis; (b) All change involves hypnosis to some degree. Do you agree? Why or why not?

Things to Do

1. Research a wide variety of therapeutic interventions in your field. How is hypnosis directly or indirectly a part of those interventions?
2. Have each member of the class identify as many euphemisms as he or she can (e.g., it's not a "used car"—it's a "pre-owned automobile"). How is "reframing" evident in each? What euphemisms exist in your field?
3. Have each member of the class tell a personally meaningful story of an experience in which a significant life lesson was learned. What is your internal experience as you listen? How does it compare to simply hearing the story's key point stated outright?

REFERENCES

Alman, B., & Lambrou, P. (1992). *Self-hypnosis*. New York: Brunner/Mazel.

Andreas, S. (2002). *Transforming your self: Becoming who you want to be*. Moab, UT: Real People.

Antonuccio, D., Danton, W., & DeNelsky, G. (1995). Psychotherapy vs. medication for depression: Challenging the conventional wisdom with data. *Professional Psychology: Research and Practice, 26*, 574–85.

Araoz, D. (1995). *The new hypnosis*. Northvale, NJ: Jason Aronson.

—— (1998). *The new hypnosis in sex therapy*. Northvale, NJ: Jason Aronson.

—— (2001). The hidden symptom in sex therapy. In B. Geary & J. Zeig (Eds.), *The handbook of Ericksonian psychotherapy* (pp. 432–42). Phoenix, AZ: The Milton H. Erickson Foundation Press.

Barlow, D. (2000). Unraveling the mysteries of anxiety and its disorders from the perspective of emotion theory. *American Psychologist, 55*, 1245–63.

Bayot, A., Capafons, A., & Cardeña, E. (1997). Emotional self-regulation therapy: A new and efficacious treatment for smoking. *American Journal of Clinical Hypnosis, 40*, 142–52.

Bell-Gadsby, C. (2001). Addictions. In B. Geary & J. Zeig (Eds.), *The handbook of Ericksonian psychotherapy* (pp. 362–73). Phoenix, AZ: The Milton H. Erickson Foundation Press.

Brown, P. (1993). Hypnosis and metaphor. In J. Rhue, S. Lynn, & I. Kirsch (Eds.), *Handbook of clinical hypnosis* (pp. 291–308). Washington, D.C.: American Psychological Association.

Burns, G. (2001). *101 Healing stories: Using metaphors in therapy*. New York: Wiley.

Capafons, A., & Amigo, S. (1995). Emotional self-regulation therapy for smoking reduction: Description and initial empirical data. *International Journal of Clinical and Experimental Hypnosis, 43*, 1, 7–19.

Cummings, N., & Cummings, J. (2000). The essence of psychotherapy: Reinventing the art in the new era of data. San Diego, CA: Academic Press.

Dolan, Y. (1991). *Resolving sexual abuse: Solution-focused therapy and Ericksonian hypnosis for adult survivors*. New York: Norton.

Eisen, M. (1993). Psychoanalytic and psychodynamic models of hypnoanalysis. In J. Rhue, S. Lynn, & I. Kirsch (Eds.), *Handbook of clinical hypnosis* (pp. 123–49). Washington, D.C.: American Psychological Association.

Erickson, B. (2001). Storytelling. In B. Geary & J. Zeig (Eds.), *The handbook of Ericksonian psychotherapy* (pp. 112–21). Phoenix, AZ: The Milton H. Erickson Foundation Press.

Erickson, M., & Kubie, L. (1941). The successful treatment of a case of acute hysterical depression by a return under hypnosis to a critical phase of childhood. In E. Rossi (Ed.) (1980), *The collected papers of Milton H. Erickson, M.D., on hypnosis* (Vol. 3, pp. 122–42). New York: Irvington.

Festinger, L. (1957). *A theory of cognitive dissonance.* Stanford: Stanford University Press.

Foa, E., & Wilson, R. (1991). *Stop obsessing! How to overcome your obsessions and compulsions.* New York: Bantam.

Gilligan, S. (1987). *Therapeutic trances: The cooperation principle in Ericksonian hypnotherapy.* New York: Brunner/Mazel.

—— (2001). The problem is the solution: The principle of sponsorship in psychotherapy. In B. Geary & J. Zeig (Eds.), *The handbook of Ericksonian psychotherapy* (pp. 398–415). Phoenix, AZ: The Milton H. Erickson Foundation Press.

Gottman, J. (1999). *The marriage clinic: A scientifically-based marital therapy.* New York: Norton.

Haley, J. (1973). *Uncommon therapy: The psychiatric techniques of Milton H. Erickson, M.D.* New York: Norton.

—— (1984). *Ordeal therapy.* San Francisco: Jossey-Bass.

Kershaw, C. (1992). *The couple's hypnotic dance.* New York: Brunner/Mazel.

Klein, M. (2002). *Beyond orgasm.* Berkeley, CA: Celestial Arts.

Lankton, C., & Lankton, S. (1989). *Tales of enchantment: Goal-oriented metaphors for adults and children in therapy.* New York: Brunner/Mazel.

Lankton, S. (2001). A goal-directed intervention for decisive resolution of coping limitations resulting from moderate and severe trauma. In B. Geary & J. Zeig (Eds.), *The handbook of Erickson psychotherapy* (pp. 195–214). Phoenix, AZ: The Milton H. Erickson Foundation Press.

Lankton, S., & Lankton, C. (1983). *The answer within: A clinical framework of Ericksonian hypnotherapy.* New York: Brunner/Mazel.

Levitt, E. (1993). Hypnosis in the treatment of obesity. In J. Rhue, S. Lynn, & I. Kirsch (Eds.), *Handbook of clinical hypnosis* (pp. 533–53). Washington, D.C.: American Psychological Association.

Lynn, S., Neufeld, V., Rhue, J., & Matorin, A. (1993). Hypnosis and smoking cessation: A cognitive-behavioral treatment. In J. Rhue, S. Lynn, & I. Kirsch (Eds.), *Handbook of clinical hypnosis* (pp. 555–85). Washington, D.C.: American Psychological Association.

Lynn, S., & Sherman, S. (2000). The clinical importance of sociocognitive models of hypnosis: Response set theory and Milton Erickson's strategic interventions. *American Journal of Clinical Hypnosis, 42,* 3–4, 294–315.

Madanes, C. (1981). *Strategic family therapy.* San Francisco: Jossey-Bass.

—— (1984). *Behind the one-way mirror: Advances in the practice of strategic therapy.* San Francisco: Jossey-Bass.

Murray, C., & Lopez, A. (1997). Global mortality, disability, and the contribution of risk factors: Global burden of disease study. *Lancet, 349,* 1436–42.

Murray-Jobsis, J. (1996). Hypnosis with a borderline patient. In S. Lynn, I. Kirsch, J. Rhue (Eds.), *Casebook of clinical hypnosis* (pp. 173–92). Washington, D.C.: American Psychological Association.

Parsons-Fein, J. (2001). The hypnotic language of couples. In B. Geary & J. Zeig (Eds.), *The handbook of Ericksonian psychotherapy* (pp. 458–68). Phoenix, AZ: The Milton H. Erickson Foundation Press.

Phillips, M. (1988). Changing early life decisions using Ericksonian hypnosis. In S. Lankton & J. Zeig (Eds.), *Ericksonian Monographs, 4,* 74–87.

—— (2001). Ericksonian approaches to dissociative disorders. In B. Geary & J. Zeig (Eds.), *The handbook of Ericksonian psychotherapy* (pp. 313–32). Phoenix, AZ: The Milton H. Erickson Foundation Press.

Phillips, M., & Frederick, C. (1995). *Healing the divided self: Clinical and Ericksonian hypnotherapy for post-traumatic and dissociative conditions.* New York: Norton.

Regier, D., & Robins, L. (1991). *The NIMH epidemiologic catchment area study.* New York: Free Press.

Robles, T. (2001). Indirect work with couples. In B. Geary & J. Zeig (Eds.), *The handbook of Ericksonian psychotherapy* (pp. 443–57). Phoenix, AZ: The Milton H. Erickson Foundation Press.

Rosen, S. (1982). *My voice will go with you: The teaching tales of Milton H. Erickson, M.D.* New York: Norton.

Spiegel, D. (1993). Hypnosis in the treatment of posttraumatic stress disorders. In J. Rhue, S. Lynn, & I. Kirsch (Eds.), *Handbook of clinical hypnosis* (pp. 493–508). Washington, D.C.: American Psychological Association.

—— (1996). Hypnosis in the treatment of posttraumatic stress disorder. In S. Lynn, I. Kirsch, & J. Rhue (Eds.), *Casebook of clinical hypnosis* (pp. 99–111). Washington, D.C.: American Psychological Association.

Watkins, J., & Watkins, H. (1997). *Ego states: Theory and therapy.* New York: Norton.

Watzlawick, P. (1978). *The language of change.* New York: Basic.

Watzlawick, P., Weakland, J., & Fisch, R. (1974). *Change.* New York: Norton.

Weiner-Davis, M. (2001). *The divorce remedy: The proven 7-step program for saving your marriage.* New York: Simon & Schuster.

Wilson, R. (1996). *Don't panic: Taking control of anxiety attacks* (rev. ed.). New York: HarperPerennial.

Yapko, M. (1988). *When living hurts: Directives for treating depression.* New York: Brunner/Mazel.

—— (Ed.) (1989). *Brief therapy approaches to treating anxiety and depression.* New York: Brunner/Mazel.

—— (1992). *Hypnosis and the treatment of depressions: Strategies for change.* New York: Brunner/Mazel.

—— (1997). *Breaking the patterns of depression.* New York: Random House/Doubleday.

—— (1999). *Hand-me-down blues: How to stop depression from spreading in families.* New York: St. Martins.

—— (2001a). *Treating depression with hypnosis: Integrating cognitive-behavioral and strategic approaches.* Philadelphia, PA: Brunner/Routledge.

—— (2001b). *Psychological 911: Depression.* Leucadia, CA: Yapko Publications.

Zarren, J., & Eimer, B. (2001). *Brief cognitive hypnosis: Facilitating the change of dysfunctional behavior.* New York: Springer.

Zeig, J. (1980). Ericksonian approaches to promote abstinence from cigarette smoking. In J. Zeig (Ed.), *Ericksonian approaches to hypnosis and psychotherapy* (pp. 255–69). New York: Brunner/Mazel.

19

Treatment Dynamics and Sample Hypnosis Session Transcripts for Common Problems

THEMES OF THERAPY

There has been a clear distinction made between the content (i.e., the details) and the structure (i.e., the form) of hypnotic suggestions. Similarly, such a distinction can be made between the structure and content of a client's problem. For example, someone may have a series of unsuccessful romantic relationships and report that he or she continually gets involved with the same type of "wrong" person (e.g., each was alcoholic, or abusive, or emotionally distant, or "wrong" in some other way). Even though the names and faces are different (i.e., the content) from bad relationship to bad relationship, the way (i.e., the structure) the person chooses someone to get involved with remains hurtfully the same.

Should the clinician focus on the details of each failed individual relationship that the person attempted, and assume the person has some unconscious personal pathology that leads him or her to sabotage relationships? Or, should the therapist acknowledge that the person is motivated to have a relationship (he or she keeps trying despite painful failures) but clearly lacks the relevant skills? Shouldn't the clinician focus on the need to teach relationship skills, including how to choose and how to be a healthier relationship partner?

I almost invariably choose those approaches that not only help solve a problem, but also teach the process of problem-solving. To do this, spending an inordinate amount of time sifting through all the content-related

447

details of a problem, in this case the client's specific difficulties in each individual failed relationship, is simply not necessary. *If you introduce new and more effective ways to address a problem, and make it practical for people to absorb and apply new concepts and methods (e.g., how to make insightful and competent relationship decisions) on a structural level, the content must also change as a direct and predictable consequence.*

When you think along these lines, considering *how* someone does something even more than *what* they do, it becomes possible to identify the common structures, or themes, that repeatedly surface in the problems clinicians are asked to treat. Consider, for example, the range of problems that people can experience when their problem theme is "letting go." Learning to "let go" is a necessity of life. Many things that happen in life are inherently transient in nature, and can't be held onto forever: Your first job is not meant to be your lifelong career, nor is your first "crush" (i.e., romantic interest) meant to be your lifelong love. *Knowing insightfully when and how to "let go" as a basic life skill permits you to cleanly end one involvement whose time has come to an end in order to begin another.*

For those individuals who show an impairment of the ability to "let go," the symptoms can be quite diverse: staying in a relationship that is pathological or abusive, staying in a job that is unchallenging and unrewarding, smothering a child with overprotection to the point of blocking his or her ability to achieve a healthy independence, compulsively accumulating unnecessary or even trivial things (e.g., he or she can't throw anything away), an inability to get over a death or relationship breakup, and many other such common problems. Thus, while the content of these examples of problems that clients present may differ markedly, each shares a common theme of the afflicted individual having a problem in "letting go." It is essential in treatment to teach the client not only to "let go" in the immediate problem situation at hand, but also to extend the learning of appropriate "letting go" skills (i.e., clear signs it's time to "let go," ways to "let go") to the many other life situations where the individual will need that same ability. By extending the learning into other contexts, perhaps some that are not yet problematic, there can be a sophisticated preventative element to the therapeutic intervention.

It is a major decision point in the therapy process as to whether you would like to intervene on the level of content, the level of structure, or on both. *In general, interventions addressing only the content level tend to produce the most transient results.* Focusing on content can be useful, but only to the extent that it facilitates rapport and helps identify associated problem structures ripe for intervention.

Table 18. Functions of Metaphors in Psychotherapy*

Diagnosis

Establishing Rapport

Treatment
- To make or illustrate a point
- To suggest solutions
- To get people to recognize themselves
- To seed ideas and increase motivation
- To embed directives
- To decrease resistance
- To reframe and redefine a problem

*Based on Zeig, 1980

USING THERAPEUTIC METAPHORS IN HYPNOSIS

There are many themes common to human experience that surface in the therapy context. This chapter will provide you with a few of them as they relate to particular clients with whom I did hypnosis. As you will note, these hypnotic processes make use of both direct and indirect suggestions, as well as of all the other suggestion styles and structures identified earlier. They also include the use of therapeutic metaphors, that is, stories I tell the client during hypnosis. From what you have already learned about metaphors in treatment, you know they are meant to first elicit and then guide the client's internal associations in the direction of some therapeutic goal. Metaphors as a form of indirect suggestion can have the multiple functions listed in Table 18 above.

Metaphors are both engaging and nonthreatening to the client because they are only indirectly related to his or her sensitive issues; this can make it easier for the client to learn the relevant therapeutic principle(s) in a less emotionally charged atmosphere (see Table 19 below).

Table 19. Principles of Metaphorical Communication

Symptoms may be viewed as metaphorical communications

Metaphors may be therapeutic in their ability to match the client's
    indirect communication style

Metaphors contextualize learnings, bringing them to life

Metaphors allow for accessing of personal resources

Metaphors encourage a search for relevance, projection

Metaphors can be created quite readily when the underlying theme of the presenting problem has been identified. Table 20 below provides some guidelines for the creation of therapeutic metaphors.

In general, the metaphors that tend to be the most meaningful to the client are those that come directly out of his or her own experience. For example, teaching skills in "letting go" as a goal of treatment can be made easier by referencing the fact that the client has previously experienced making a geographic move from one place to another in his or her life. As he or she is oriented to the subject of "moving" through a metaphor, he or she can be reminded of and focused on the resources associated with moving and "letting go," such as how moving involves giving up the known for the unknown, leaving the past for the future, how the process of moving involves getting rid of burdensome accumulations of items no longer necessary or meaningful, and so forth. Associating those resources to the current problem situation establishes a progressive new emotional framework for moving and "letting go."

Perhaps the easiest metaphors begin with, "Once I had a client, not unlike you, who . . ." Such metaphors are encouraging to most clients, who seem to appreciate knowing they are not alone in their problems and also that you have previously successfully treated similar problems. If the client comes to identify with the person in the story, the positive associations to therapeutic solutions can be more easily established. That is not always the case, however. As I discussed in *Treating Depression with Hypnosis* (2001), clients

---

Table 20. Structuring Therapeutic Metaphors

1. Gather information including:
   - significant persons involved
   - characteristics of the problem, situation
   - the desired outcome
   - available resources to be accessed
   - dimension(s) to be addressed (i.e., physical, cognitive, etc.)
2. Acknowledge previous attempts to problem-solve, frustrations
3. Build metaphor or task analogous to problem
   - select a context based on client interest
   - isomorphic (structurally similar) characters, plots
   - reframing of problem
   - direct or indirect resolution suggestions
   - discovery of alternate responses
4. Mapping Metaphors
   - number and sequence of metaphors on a theme

absorbed in feelings of personal helplessness tend not to be inspired by others' success stories. Rather, they may feel *worse* as they conclude, "See, everyone else can do it but me."

Keep in mind that the use of metaphors is not a "given" in doing clinical hypnosis. All the guidelines provided previously about suggestion formulation must be taken into account. If you launch into a story with a client without carefully evaluating the person's style and demeanor, you could create an avoidable problem for yourself when he or she confronts you about wasting time talking about other people's problems instead of about his or hers! The subsequent loss of rapport can hinder further treatment results.

SESSION TRANSCRIPTS

I have repeatedly emphasized throughout this book that the effective use of clinical hypnosis involves tailoring your approach to the unique characteristics of each client. However, I also recognize the value of modeling as a teaching tool. So, the remainder of this chapter contains some samples of hypnosis sessions that may serve to help you more easily integrate all the information about hypnosis contained in this book. The following session transcripts are derived from hypnosis sessions done with actual clients seeking help for a variety of problems. I hope you will study them with a deep consideration of the personal, interpersonal, and contextual variables that led to the creation of the therapeutic suggestions made. You will be given some background on each of the clients, an explanation as to the goal(s) for that particular hypnosis session, and how the session relates to the larger goal(s) for the client's therapy.

As a final point regarding these sample transcripts, I have chosen to present in this chapter only those things that I said to the client in order to illustrate the various forms hypnotic suggestions may take. In reading the following transcripts, your learning of hypnotic patterns can be enhanced by actively considering the suggestions offered and reasoning out the rationale for their inclusion. In contrast to the one-sided hypnosis presented in this chapter, the next chapter contains *The Case of Vicki*, a complete session transcript with commentary and analysis for a woman with terminal cancer seeking pain relief through hypnosis. That session provides a fuller representation of how doing clinical hypnosis is a cooperative, interactional, and individualized process.

One other note: These sessions are timeless in almost all ways but one: I used to use the terms "hypnosis" and "trance" interchangeably, and so I frequently referred to "trance" responses in the course of these sessions. As you know, I have subsequently dropped the use of the word "trance" in my sessions and writings, simply because it is too vague a term and now strikes me as even being too esoteric as we accumulate more data about the hypnotic experience. (Change happens . . .) So, feel free to substitute the word "hypnosis" for "trance" in your mind as you read these transcripts.

CASE 1: SELF-DEFINITION AND
TAKING CARE OF SELF

The client is a woman in her early sixties who initially sought treatment for nightmares, recurring traumatic images associated with childhood episodes of molestation, poor self-esteem, and an inability to effectively set limits in her relationships with others. Supporting her working through the feelings associated with her traumas was one obvious and necessary part of her treatment plan. Another part of her therapy focused on her lack of a sense of Self—what many clinicians call a lack of "ego boundaries." Assertiveness and limit-setting capabilities are possible to achieve later in a therapy sequence, after sense of a Self is first defined. This woman was so global in her self-understanding and so adaptive to whomever was around her that she knew very little about her own thoughts and feelings. The following transcript represents part of one hypnosis session conducted quite early in her therapy addressing the theme of building boundaries and evolving a clearer definition of Self.

All right, Molly, you can begin by taking in a few deep . . . relaxing breaths . . . getting yourself comfortable . . . getting yourself oriented now . . . to enter into internal experience for a while . . . so that you can really enjoy the balance between conscious awareness and unconscious awareness . . . let each breath relax you . . . let your thoughts run loose for a while . . . until they tire themselves out . . . and then little by little, they can slow . . . becoming very slow . . . so that more and more of your mental energy can be spent on learning . . . at the deepest levels within yourself . . . of the experience of comfort . . . about the experience of being so distant . . . from all the usual focal points of your awareness . . . so that you really can know deeply . . . that all the inner terrain . . . your inner landscape . . . can be traveled comfortably . . . looking at this natural formation . . . and that natural formation . . . the feelings and thoughts . . . the historical markers . . . your curiosity . . . and a very deep recognition . . . of inner capabilities . . . and it's interesting to observe the evolution . . . what the experience of development is like . . . to see a newly born baby . . . and no one really knows *whether* the baby thinks or *what* the baby thinks . . . and to watch an infant discover its own fingers, its own toes . . . to see the amused look on an infant's face . . . when it discovers that it can make a finger wiggle . . . at will . . . and little by little . . . that infant learns . . . this is *my* body . . . and it is separate and distinct from any other part of the world . . . from all other people and places and things . . . and each square inch of your skin . . . is a boundary . . . between your inner world . . . and the outer world . . . and it really isn't possible for you to jump out of your skin . . . you are *self-contained* . . . and it's interesting . . . that there are some people who don't have a home in which to live . . . who believe that the sky is their roof . . . that the earth is their home . . . and then there are others who mark off huge territories, acres of land . . . they clearly mark that it is theirs . . . and each wall . . . keeps something in and keeps something out . . . and there are walls of stone . . . walls of wood . . . steel-reinforced walls . . . and there are the walls . . . that you can build for yourself . . . deliberately and happily . . . that are permeable walls . . . the kind that can selectively let things in and let things out . . . and it's that kind of a wall . . . that allows just enough distance from discomfort . . . to be able to drive down a freeway . . . comfortably . . . it is the kind of permeable wall . . . that when someone makes a comment during a conversation . . . that perhaps you can relate to . . . that permits a comfortable distance . . . a protective . . . distance from which to consider each bit of input . . . and you can feel secure that each person's feedback to you will have to check in at your front gate . . . before you decide to let it in or not . . . before you decide *whether* to react or not . . . and *if* you react . . . to decide *how* you'll react . . . based on what works . . . and feels good at the deepest levels within yourself . . . so, why not have a construction party? . . . and build a pretty wall . . . and a creative wall . . . and I wonder what colors you'll use . . . what materials you'll use . . . and what does the check-in gate look like? . . . and how very much room is there . . . for lots and lots of growth . . . and the walls . . . can always be moved when you so desire . . . they can be built up or built down . . . you can put in peep holes and panoramic windows . . . after all, the walls are yours . . . and all I know is that the ability . . . to walk into an open space . . . has at one level . . . unlimited freedom . . . but at another level . . . where's the structure to guide experience meaningfully? . . . and when I moved into this particular office that I'm in now . . . it was a huge space . . . I had to draft a plan . . . detailing how many walls I wanted . . . and where I wanted them . . . how many outlets . . . and how many doors . . . and did I want the doors opening in or opening out . . . how many "on" switches and how many "off" switches . . . and there's a part of you that knows very well . . . that designing uses for space . . . is a real art . . . and you discovered over time . . . that each part of you . . . all the parts of you . . . have some space . . . and how you want to use that space . . . is certainly a matter of individual design . . . and the aesthetics . . . of a high wall here, or a low wall there . . . more space for this part and less space for that part . . . and you can really enjoy . . . the incredible clarity . . . that comes along . . . with increasingly sophisticated designs . . . movable and removable walls . . . and what a relief to know . . . that nothing that you experience need necessarily flow right through all of you . . . that you have lots of *inner protection* . . . walls of *inner strength* . . . and you've seen pictures of the Great Wall of China . . . and you've heard of the Wailing Wall . . . and you've read about the Berlin

Wall . . . and you know about Wall Street . . . and maybe you've even heard about Wall Drug, South Dakota . . . and the natural wall of the Rocky Mountains . . . the sheer cliff walls of La Jolla . . . and with all the different possibilities . . . your unconscious mind can . . . without any real effort on your part . . . it can plan . . . and build . . . and if you were to work for the Border Patrol . . . you'd really know about the importance of enforcing and protecting the walls that separate inner from outer . . . twenty-four hours a day . . . seven days a week . . . one really must protect one's borders . . . and there are a lot of deeper meanings . . . that I really know . . . you can absorb and use . . . a day at a time . . . and so take your time . . . to process . . . to architect . . . and then . . . when you feel like you want to . . . and when you're ready to . . . that's when you can re-orient . . . and open your eyes when you are ready. . . .

Multiple sessions were conducted with Molly emphasizing inner awareness, the recognition and acceptance of her own uniqueness, the ability to make positive choices in her own behalf, and the ability to deal with past traumas so as to permit future growth.

CASE 2: PAIN MANAGEMENT

The client is a woman in her late thirties who suffers chronic pain in her neck and shoulders, a consequence of a car accident in which she was rear-ended while stopped at a red light. She had several neurological evaluations prior to consulting me, and was told that the pain would most likely eventually diminish, though not in the near future. The client is a professional woman who, as a result of her injuries and residual pain, is currently unable to work. She is married, and in all other respects is a high functioning, competent woman. She did not evidence depression or anxiety beyond what would be considered normal for her circumstances. Thus, other than instructing her in the use of dissociative techniques of hypnotic pain management over the course of a few sessions, further therapy was deemed unnecessary. The following transcript was from the fourth of five sessions.

. . . Okay, Madeline . . . Are you comfortable? . . . (Nods) . . . Good . . . you can begin by taking in a few deep, relaxing breaths . . . and then whenever you're ready . . . you can just allow your eyes to close . . . so that you can begin now . . . to go inside . . . to be able to explore within yourself . . . find those most comfortable . . . thoughts . . . and feelings . . . that can allow you that very, very relaxed state . . . of mind and body . . . and you might remember . . . that you've experienced trance with me before . . . and so I know from at least those experiences . . . as well as other trance experiences you've had . . . both on your own and with others . . . that you know from your own direct experience . . . what it's like to *breathe comfortably* . . . and to *sit comfortably* . . . what it's like to get so absorbed in your own thoughts . . . that for a little while you forget . . . that the rest of the world is going about . . . its usual business . . . and one of the most soothing, relaxing recognitions . . . is that you really don't have to pay attention . . . to anything other than what pleases you for the moment . . . and the nature of the conscious mind is such . . . that it will naturally drift . . . from here to there . . . and to nowhere in particular . . . and wherever your conscious mind drifts to at any moment . . . is just fine . . . whether you notice the routine sounds of the environment . . . or your own thoughts . . . or your own reactions to the different things that I say . . . or *the changes that take place in your body* . . . as your mind drifts . . . to the different awarenesses . . . and it can be very comforting to know . . . that that is the nature of the conscious mind . . . it can drift in . . . and out . . . it can notice and not notice . . . it can think and enjoy not having to think . . . or having to analyze critically . . . and so it can accept easily . . . the different possibilities . . . and while your conscious mind is certainly capable of processing . . . whatever it happens to notice . . . the part of you that is infinitely . . . more interesting and powerful is your unconscious . . . the part of you that can listen . . . and respond . . . even when your conscious mind drifts elsewhere . . . and your own unconscious mind . . . has abilities that your conscious mind sometimes forgets about . . . and when you're conscious of your unconscious mind's abilities . . . and can consciously analyze and access . . . the unconscious awareness . . . of what your conscious mind knows and doesn't know . . . and what's easier to understand consciously than unconsciously . . . that's when you can appreciate the comfort of recognizing . . . how the mind and the body . . . can work so closely together sometimes . . . when that's important . . . and how other times . . . the conscious mind and the unconscious mind . . . can drift off elsewhere . . . and the mind's greatest ability is the freedom . . . to go wherever imagination wills it . . . and some people like the freedom of having their minds float through space and through time . . . others like to drift back in time to the comfort . . . of a very special soothing place . . . that's prominent in their memory . . . and is vivid in their senses . . . and the fact *that your mind can drift off* . . . way over there . . . while *your body rests* . . . over here . . . is certainly an interesting experience . . . and sometimes people forget . . . how when their mind is drifting there . . . and their body is resting here . . . that their body can continue . . . to take care of itself . . . the automatic, unconscious . . . self-preserving . . . nature of your body over here . . . can give your mind the comfort over there . . . that allows a comfortable distance . . . that gives you the freedom to simply know how differently . . . you can feel . . . and when your mind drifts . . . that's when it's easy to not notice things that change . . . and I don't know whether you know that your breathing has changed . . . that your pulse rate has changed . . . and what it feels like to have . . . your body somewhere . . . close enough . . . to use if you want it or need it . . . but without impinging on the freedom . . . to float freely and comfortably . . . that light . . . airy feeling . . . and as you experience that interesting sensation . . . it can be very interesting to discover . . . how easy it is to forget . . . to notice where your left foot is relative to your right . . . until I draw your attention to it . . . what it feels like to wear a wristwatch on your left wrist . . . it's easy to forget . . . what it feels like . . . to have earrings in your ears . . . or to have the chair supporting your body comfortably . . . and you know and I know . . . that the mind and body . . . are closely related . . . and so are thoughts and feelings . . . and so is past and present . . . but you're also very aware that things change . . . and that awareness offers . . . a buffer . . . a comfort zone . . . that leaves just enough room between the present and the past . . . to make the present of comfort a gift that you can enjoy for months to come . . . and the comfort zone . . . between the present and the future . . . where the present can be just comfortable enough . . . to allow a future of feeling better . . . a day at a time . . . and you know that sometimes . . . people don't understand the relationship between past and present . . . anymore than they understand the relationship . . . between thoughts and feelings . . . but you have a feeling that your thoughts matter . . . and your thoughts about your feelings can allow your feelings some distance . . . a safe, comfortable distance . . . between what you experience now and what you felt then . . . and what you're going to think tomorrow . . . but you'll have to wait until tomorrow . . . for your conscious mind to know . . . what your unconscious has already discovered . . . that it takes far more effort than it's worth . . . to move your hand . . . when it's so much easier . . . *you can be so much more comfortable sitting beside yourself so much more comfortably* . . . when your mind is here . . . and your body is here . . . and it's just enough distance to be *so much more comfortable than you thought you could be* . . . and you can be very aware . . . of that interesting sensation . . . of being separate from your body . . . and having all of yourself . . . in the experience of deep trance . . . and you know and I know that as distant as your body feels on one level . . . it also feels close enough on another level . . . to be aware of its need to continue to breathe . . . in . . . and slowly out . . . so effortlessly . . . and so comfortably . . . and as your mind continues to float there . . . and your body continues to rest comfortably over here . . . your conscious mind can certainly be curious . . . about the *comfortable sensations of feeling the separation existing* . . . and you don't really have to analyze too carefully which part of you is the most comfortable at the moment . . . you can simply allow yourself instead . . . to enjoy the comfort that goes along . . . without really being sure . . . exactly . . . where your fingers are . . . or where your hair is . . . it can be very soothing to know that you can drift back . . . into an awareness of your body when you choose to . . . and that for the moment . . . you can simply enjoy the choice . . . of letting your mind be there . . . while your body rests comfortably over here . . . and I know that doesn't make much sense to your conscious mind . . . but fortunately . . . even though your conscious mind is very smart . . . your unconscious mind is a lot smarter than you are . . . and all the learnings of your lifetime . . . allow you the *comfortable position now* of being able to drift freely . . . far enough away . . . yet close enough to your body . . . to be so comfortable . . . in ways your conscious mind is only beginning to discover . . . and each time that you listen to this tape or each time that you sit quietly with your eyes closed . . . your unconscious mind can add a new and interesting dimension to the experience . . . your overall awareness . . . of your ability to be as close to or as far away from . . . your body as you'd like to be . . . and when you recognize . . . powerfully within yourself . . . how much more control you have than you ever thought possible . . . then *you can enjoy the feeling of comfort* . . . that you really can rest comfortably . . . and that you really can heal surprisingly quickly . . . now that more parts of you have begun some work on the job . . . and so, Madeline . . . I'd like you to take your time . . . and reorient yourself to whatever degree that you wish to . . . in order to bring . . . yourself out of trance to whatever degree you wish . . . and by that, I mean that if you choose to keep your body in trance while you bring your mind out of trance . . . I can certainly understand that choice . . . or if you choose to bring your body out of trance . . . but leave the comfort intact to enjoy the rest of the day . . . I can certainly understand that choice . . . and whatever choice you make . . . you'll certainly be aware . . . that when you allow your eyes to open . . . you'll be ready to get on with the rest of today in a much more comfortable state of mind and body . . . and that will certainly be an eye-opening experience. . . .

The suggestion of being able to keep her body comfortably in hypnosis while in a "waking" state was one that Madeline found especially useful in helping her carry out routine activities. The many suggestions throughout for disorientation and dissociation (mind and body, conscious and unconscious, past and present, and body parts) facilitated a very deep experience of hypnosis that permitted substantial relief from pain during her lengthy recovery.

CASE 3: GOAL (FUTURE) ORIENTATION

The client is a man in his late fifties who presented the problems of "being stuck" in an unstable "on-again, off-again" relationship that he finds distressing, having high blood pressure, and procrastinating around issues of his career. He presented as "wanting to achieve enough personal growth to be able to move forward with my life." He did not have any specific goals in mind as to what would represent "moving forward." If the client's goal isn't well-defined and if there aren't specific steps to follow to achieve it, then it isn't a goal. It's only a wish. Thus, one goal in this client's treatment was to help him evolve a clear sense of direction in his life. During the course of treatment, hypnosis was utilized to encourage the development of a clear and specific sense of the future, enough to compel him to take some decisive courses of action in the present. The client is an educator who claimed to be well acquainted with clinical hypnosis in general and the work of Milton Erickson in particular. This transcript is from the third of a dozen sessions.

. . . Okay Jerry, you can begin by taking in a few deep, relaxing breaths . . . and little by little . . . you can let the various recollections . . . drift through your awareness . . . of what it's like to be in deep trance . . . in a way that's pleasing and comfortable . . . and it's been quite a while . . . since you last experienced . . . a formal trance process . . . with me as guide . . . but there was a time . . . not all that long ago . . . when you first became accustomed . . . to hearing my voice . . . get quieter . . . to hearing me . . . speak in a very slow . . . deliberate way . . . and it was during that initial experience . . . when you were first beginning to learn something about trance . . . and were open to much deeper possibilities . . . that you allowed yourself to experience . . . some of the most interesting dimensions . . . of doing trancework . . . and since quite some time from our first trance has elapsed . . . and since you've grown in so many ways since . . . it can certainly be much easier . . . to *drift into a deeper trance* . . . and a much more comfortable state of mind and body . . . moment by moment . . . and this is one . . . very worthwhile opportunity . . . to rediscover . . . your ability . . . to drift . . . in a way that's useful . . . in a way that's meaningful . . . and I know . . . that the various possibilities . . . as you explore your experiences . . . can certainly be most intriguing . . . as the various possibilities . . . allow you to rediscover . . . old awarenesses . . . that pave the way for new awarenesses . . . and as the new awarenesses drift . . . into your consciousness . . . that's when it's so easy . . . to discover how little attention . . . is necessary . . . to allow all kinds of comfort . . . that we can build upon . . . in a future experience . . . of each day . . . and I'm aware that your mind is drifting . . . to nowhere in particular . . . that the things that you think about at this moment . . . are tied . . . to past experiences . . . and future expectations . . . and you know and I know . . . that so often . . . if the seed . . . can get planted today . . . it generates the greatest amount . . . of worthwhile . . . future possibilities . . . and as Erickson correctly pointed out . . . you can't change the patient's past . . . you can only change his perspective of it . . . and how much the past relates to your future . . . you'll presently come to know . . . because it's the present that is connected to your past . . . and leads to your future possibilities . . . that you're willing to explore . . . and your presence here . . . confirms that . . . as you make yourself the present . . . of a positive future . . . that wisely incorporates learnings of the past . . . of things that you experience presently . . . and all that talk about past and present and future . . . isn't really meant to disorient you in any way . . . that might be worthwhile . . . but it certainly can help you . . . in seeing the perspective . . . that the impulses of the moment . . . can be looked at differently . . . as you discover . . . that the most worthwhile things to be made . . . you can make on the inside . . . from within . . . in your deep self . . . your deep self . . . and if you think back . . . through the worthwhile things that you've already experienced . . . few of them came easily . . . for the simple reason . . . that whatever you've obtained . . . you've worked for . . . and there were so many times . . . on your way to becoming a teacher . . . that it would have been so much easier . . . to skip class . . . and go play . . . to go to the beach . . . or to go for a run . . . and you certainly would have been justified in doing so . . . but you felt deeply . . . there was something more important to be gained . . . in the name of sacrifice . . . and every self-sacrifice for self-improvement really isn't much of a self-sacrifice . . . because when you think about the relationship between sacrifices and improvements . . . and you improve the sacrifice . . . and you sacrifice more than you improve . . . you really haven't sacrificed . . . you've just improved . . . and gone a step further . . . and the questions from within . . . that generate the momentum to grow . . . and experience . . . is a dwindling internal pressure . . . that each experience can comfort . . . each new opportunity . . . for growth . . . can be recognized for what is . . . and there's been so much that you've learned over time . . . so many ways that you've changed . . . and as each change equalizes the pressures outside . . . by responding deeply to the appropriate demands from inside . . . you've become so skilled . . . and the results have shown . . . and you can have a very powerful impact . . . when you allow yourself . . . to release . . . maybe to teach . . . in a sharing way . . . what you already know . . . and going to school is only one way . . . to evolve . . . and change . . . in a self-sacrificing way . . . that leads to a greater sense of self . . . than anything you've experienced before . . . and all through your past . . . there was self-sacrificing . . . that had an aura . . . of taking care of yourself . . . beneath them . . . and when one becomes a parent . . . it's apparent . . . that the selflessness of parenthood . . . is the shiny surface . . . of a selfish decision . . . to have children . . . that one hopes will reflect one's self . . . with pride . . . and accomplishment . . . and the debate about the selfish nature of the selfish decision to have children . . . continues . . . and the sacrifice . . . of a loving relationship . . . that gives you what you want . . . and you know what it means to give . . . in order to get . . . and whatever you may have to openly give . . . grows . . . easily . . . and as you understand more and more deeply within . . . that giving to get . . . is the greatest way . . . to build a solid relationship . . . especially with yourself . . . especially . . . with yourself . . . and so . . . why not . . . selfishly and selflessly . . . sacrifice a little bit of time each day . . . to give to yourself . . . in order to get from yourself . . . a much more comfortable . . . and *much less pressured* . . . way of doing things . . . a *much less pressured* . . . way of circulating blood . . . in a body that's so healthy . . . with comfort . . . and the ability to relax deeply . . . and you know from the people that you work with . . . that you can pretend that they're not listening . . . but you know that their unconscious mind is . . . and they can pretend they're not listening . . . but don't you be fooled by it . . . because there's a part of each person . . . no matter how educated or otherwise . . . that has the ability to learn . . . and to grow . . . and to change . . . and someone can work hard at staying the same . . . but you know and I know that *change is inevitable* . . . and so don't you be fooled by it . . . and I'm going to be silent for a minute . . . as you explore within yourself . . . the thoughts and feelings . . . that pass through your awareness . . . that become significant for you in ways that your conscious mind has yet to discover . . . and when I again speak to you in a minute . . . my voice can just relax you even more deeply . . . and the minute of silence begins . . . now . . . (one minute of silence) . . . that's right . . . you can just continue to relax . . . to continue to be at ease and resting comfortably . . . and you've allowed me to be aware . . . of the multiple purposes of our session . . . learning opportunities and personal growth opportunities . . . professional growth . . . and meaningful experiences . . . and I wonder how much you'll be able to discover . . . from these trance experiences . . . as you notice the different ideas and the different perspectives . . . and you can enjoy knowing . . . that each trance process . . . will have a different effect . . . and generate a different pattern . . . in ways that your unconscious mind . . . can allow . . . while your conscious mind looks forward . . . to discovering . . . the range of possibilities . . . a day at a time . . . and so, take what ever time you'd like to . . . to process your thoughts . . . the different dimensions of your experience . . . and to think about your expectations . . . and which learnings will be most appropriate to utilize . . . this week . . . and which learnings can wait until next week . . . and then, whenever you're ready . . . you can begin to re-orient yourself to here and now . . . this room and this place . . . and whenever you'd like to . . . you can slowly move to re-orient yourself . . . and then you can allow your eyes to open . . .

The client reflected on the basic truth that anything he had of value, he worked hard for. He was easily able to recall what seemed like a sacrifice at the time when he was in school taking classes while others were out enjoying recreational activities. The session motivated him to directly confront the aimlessness in each of the areas of his life, and led to later sessions addressing issues of goal-setting, setting aside immediate gratification while striving for worthwhile future possibilities, and being more responsive ("giving to get") in his relationship.

CASE 4: ADAPTABILITY

The following transcript is of a hypnosis session conducted with a psychologist in his mid-fifties attending one of my clinical hypnosis training courses. While he found the concepts and techniques of clinical hypnosis highly illuminating as a model for better understanding people's subjective experience relative to psychotherapy, he was having difficulty shifting his perspectives about doing therapy away from his previous psychodynamic model. During a demonstration session in the training, he asked to have a hypnosis session to help him better assimilate the new learnings and to evolve greater flexibility in his treatment approaches. Thus, this session was done before the other class members in a context defined more as educational than clinical. It was the first and only time I worked with this man.

. . . Ben, you can arrange yourself in the most comfortable of positions . . . and then a little at a time . . . you can orient yourself to the possibility . . . of being very relaxed . . . very comfortable . . . very much at ease within yourself . . . and I know that it was Ernest Hilgard . . . who formulated the idea . . . that a person's ability to be hypnotized . . . to go into deep trance . . . was a fixed characteristic . . . one that really wouldn't change much over time . . . and I wonder whether you're discovering . . . a good and satisfying basis for disagreeing with Hilgard . . . perhaps discovering that *people can go into deeper trances* . . . reaching deeper levels more quickly . . . through practice . . . through experience . . . and you may be interested in knowing . . . just how *deeply into trance* you can go . . . or just how quickly you can reach . . . a very comfortable level . . . within yourself . . . it really doesn't matter much . . . whether you focus on depth . . . or speed . . . or Hilgard . . . or yourself . . . all that really matters . . . is the enjoyment that goes along . . . with discovering that at all levels within yourself . . . that *you really can be comfortable* . . . and I know that it's important to you to have your mind be active . . . to think and to analyze . . . and to always be oriented . . . to as much as what's going on around you as you can . . . that's the pattern . . . that you've evolved through a lifetime of learning . . . and you know and I know . . . as mental health professionals . . . that sometimes people are the masters of what they learn . . . and other times . . . people are the victims of what they learn . . . and each time that you take time to learn something new . . . you have a chance . . . to integrate it with what you already know . . . deeply . . . and I don't know how much you know . . . about what you know . . . about what Milton Erickson knew . . . about what he knows . . . and how people know what they know . . . and don't know about what they don't know . . . and a famous humorist once said . . . it's not what you don't know . . . that's the problem . . . it's what you know that ain't so . . . and Milton Erickson . . . a gentlemen that you're by now familiar with . . . didn't really believe in formal theories of personality . . . Milton wouldn't be the one to describe your patterns as . . . obsessive or compulsive . . . he wouldn't be the one to label a person with a particular name . . . and yet . . . some people insist on doing exactly that . . . and I worked in a hospital long enough . . . to know . . . that doctors will say . . . how's the broken leg in room 210? . . . how's the manic in room 325? . . . where's the depressive in room 104? . . . as if no one has a name anymore . . . no one is a person . . . just a label . . . and it was Erickson's belief system . . . and I wonder just what you think . . . deeply . . . in reaction to Erickson's observation . . . that while your unconscious mind has . . . ample resources that can be used to help facilitate changes . . . in yourself and in others . . . it's the learned limitations . . . the learned limitations . . . that reinforce what Erickson referred to as rigidity . . . of patterned behavior . . . that a person learns a certain sequence . . . a certain style . . . a certain response pattern . . . and then that's what he does over and over again . . . in a very rigid sort of way . . . and when you suggest a deviation from that pattern . . . you may get resistance . . . and when you suggest that someone step outside . . . the boundaries of his patterns . . . you may get resistance . . . and it isn't until someone breaks his own pattern . . . by responding to the same old situation . . . in a new way . . . that the most meaningful changes occur . . . and there are rigid thought patterns . . . rigid emotional patterns . . . rigid behavioral patterns . . . rigid social patterns . . . rigid therapy patterns . . . dynamically speaking . . . stereotyped responses in specific situations . . . and why not step outside . . . the usual boundaries . . . why not demand a new response from yourself in an old situation . . . why not do something differently . . . and enjoy the new results . . . and enjoy discovering . . . that *you really can be flexible* enough . . . *to respond differently* . . . in ways that are only first being discovered . . . by your conscious mind . . . and I wonder how many new things you can do today . . . and how many out of character responses you can generate today . . . and can you be flexible enough . . . to respond differently . . . and when your usual level of tension gives way to the deep relaxation you have now . . . that's a change in pattern . . . and when discomfort becomes comfort . . . that's a change, also . . . and little by little . . . you're beginning to discover . . . new possibilities in old situations . . . in ways that can feel so good . . . on all levels . . . and why not . . . allow yourself . . . a different response . . . in that situation where it would be most helpful . . . and least restrictive . . . opening the door to new possibilities . . . and closing the door . . . on outdated learnings . . . a day at a time . . . and so take your time . . . process the part of my message that your conscious mind can understand . . . safely . . . and pretend that there aren't any deeper meanings . . . for your unconscious to learn . . . and then when you feel like you're ready to . . . and want to re-orient to here and now . . . you can begin that process . . . of bringing yourself . . . to a different level of responses . . . and when you're ready to . . . you can just allow your eyes to open. . . .

After the hypnosis session, the demonstration subject reported being aware of an important reframing that had taken place for him during the session. He claimed he had not thought of his therapy approaches as "rigid." Rather, he had simply thought of them as "proper procedure." In hearing his patterns described as "stereotyped responses" and absorbing the idea that growth comes from "stepping outside the usual boundaries," he reported feeling a freedom to experiment he had not previously felt. Over the course of the remaining days in the course, he commented several times on the "liberating effect of having more ways to conduct therapy."

CASE 5: WEIGHT MANAGEMENT

The client is a woman in her early forties, employed as a computer programmer, who presented the concern of wanting to maintain the weight loss she had succeeded in obtaining through a program she participated in. She had been able to gain control over all of her dysfunctional eating habits, with the exception of snacking on bread, particularly French sourdough baguettes. She wanted to be able to develop moderation in her bread intake, much as she had with the other foods in her diet. She is a woman who values logic, and has a long history of being fairly dissociated from her feelings. This transcript represents the second of three sessions.

... All right Gerda, ... you can take in a few deep, relaxing breaths ... and orient yourself now to inner experience for a while ... somewhere ... a little deeper than rationality ... somewhere beneath ... logic ... somewhere to the right of your left brain ... somewhere above ... everyday living ... and when you're above and below ... the right of things that are left ... then every direction provides a new opportunity or deeper sense ... of comfort ... and for a very long time ... you've had many experiences of being able to think rationally ... to relate at a deeper level ... to the logic of computers ... the sequencing of programs ... all exercises ... for the intellect ... but you know and I know ... that the true balance of things ... rests ... on continuous movements ... continuous minor adjustments ... in daily experiences ... that move us from balance to imbalance ... back to balance ... hoping and adjusting ... and all of that ... about *imbalance is very heavy* ... and balance is light ... red light ... blue light ... white light ... light feelings ... light beer ... light air ... light thoughts ... and what makes something that's heavier than air ... float ... and *which part of your body is lighter?* ... left side ... or right side ... top half ... or bottom half ... the front of your back ... the back of your front ... you really don't know ... but when you experience ... the kind of uplifting experience ... that really raises your awareness ... for how distant one part of you can seem ... while another part seems to float ... right in front of you ... and if thoughts are over here ... and feelings are over there ... then you might ... be oriented to a disorienting experience ... and whether it's temporal disorientation or physical disorientation ... being oriented to how disoriented your body can be ... then you're oriented to thought ... and have you noticed how disoriented your thoughts can be when you're *so oriented to your body* ... and it can seem so close and yet so far ... and you can think you understand and that you know what you hear ... but if you don't know what you hear when you're here then maybe you know what is there ... and when you play ... that light ... carefree feeling returns ... and your thoughts can smile ... and what a sensation when your body giggles ... and which part ... experiences humor? and what about ... being disoriented to the usual cues ... the usual patterns ... that you'd really like to scale down ... and *lightening up* allows for that possibility ... and remember once I described that the ocean has the ability to maintain itself ... and at a much deeper level ... your unconscious is learning nature's way of maintaining a body ... of water ... and how much of the body is water? ... and you know when there's chemistry ... which molecule ... and which atoms ... have a natural attraction ... and what is the chemical makeup ... of sourdough bread in comparison to rye? ... and when they bag it (baguette) ... to take it home ... any change in your deeper structure provides an interesting opportunity for growth ... and that's an awful lot to digest ... in one sitting ...

but when the conscious mind is overloaded . . . that's when the unconscious gets to enjoy the spotlight for a while . . . and that's when it can really shine . . . and I don't know if anybody really knows why that's true . . . all I know is . . . you have a conscious mind . . . that's very smart . . . and an unconscious mind . . . that's even smarter . . . and I remember . . . a colleague of mine named Jeff Zeig telling me once . . . that Erickson told him once . . . that variety . . . is the spice . . . of life . . . but he said it a little differently . . . he sat Jeff down . . . and he said that each person enjoys meals differently . . . some really enjoy seven course dinners . . . and which course is the right first course? . . . some enjoy soup . . . followed by salad . . . some prefer it the other way around . . . and one might enjoy . . . something to cleanse their palate with . . . and which side dish goes with which main dish? . . . and I knew one individual who enjoyed dessert first . . . which I thought was a very heavy decision to make . . . but with each person there are differences . . . and Erickson droned on and on describing . . . *how many different ways there are to eat in a way that's healthy and satisfying* . . . he finally led to the conclusion that if man cannot live by bread alone . . . then a woman probably shouldn't either . . . and when Jeff was working too hard . . . Erickson reminded him . . . there's more to life than protein . . . and how does an unconscious mind understand deeper messages? . . . and translate them into *subtle changes that really feel good* . . . well, let your conscious mind chew on that for a while . . . and if you ever have the experience of being crusty and discovering yourself taking it too seriously . . . there will come an opportunity to remind yourself . . . that when you don't understand why you do what you do . . . that's the time for the services of a good trance— later . . . or perhaps a trance now . . . I don't know which . . . but I do know . . . that it could be the feeling . . . of amusement guiding you . . . it doesn't detract from the significance of what you've learned . . . it can be the lingering feeling . . . long after . . . of feeling good about what you've done . . . and whether you'll remember that . . . consciously or unconsciously . . . or both . . . you really won't know . . . until you re-orient in a moment . . . and find your eyes opening . . . to discover what you know . . . that's different . . . take your time . . . before you have that eye-opening experience. . . .

The client's response to the confusional suggestions was an amused detachment that highlighted to her how impactful things on a nonrational level could be. Given her usual emphasis on logic, a pattern which did not assist her in losing weight or keeping it off, she found it meaningful to discover how subjective and malleable her experiences really are. She made frequent use of the tape of this session that was given to her, and found the phrase "woman cannot live by bread alone" coming back to her in a light-hearted way when passing by the bakery where she normally stopped and bought bread. The use of humor in the session associated a positive emotional tone to the content of the session. As with all patterns, humor must be used selectively.

CASE 6: STRESS MANAGEMENT

The client is a man in his mid-thirties who presented the problem of "too many things raining down on me to cope with." He was undergoing a major shift in responsibilities in his job as an administrator in a construction company, his first child (age four) was suffering health problems, and his wife was pregnant with their third child. He felt as though every domain of his life was unsettled and a source of stress, and wanted to learn to manage stress more effectively in order to prevent any debilitating effects. He shared his fantasy of escaping to a Caribbean island, and wished there was a way to prevent stressful events from happening in his life. The following transcript represents a hypnosis session done in the first of seven sessions.

> . . . Alright Ken, you can begin by taking in a few, deep relaxing breaths . . . and you can begin now to orient yourself . . . to the possibility of feeling . . . very comfortable . . . and very relaxed . . . and little by little as the world goes on around you . . . why not make yourself really comfortable . . . of course the more absorbed you get . . . in your own inner experience . . . the less it really matters what's going on in the world around you . . . everybody needs a little bit of time away . . . a little bit of a break . . . to turn their attention in a different direction . . . and one of my favorite television shows is M*A*S*H . . . and I don't know if you're a fan of that show or not . . . but it will happen from time to time . . . that the M*A*S*H hospital . . . will be shelled by the enemy . . . and numerous explosions take place . . . as the shells rain down . . . and everyone runs around scared and overwhelmed . . . unsure if they'll be able to survive . . . and you can imagine . . . how fighting for your life . . . can be a very serious battle . . . and then what always happens at some point along the way . . . is that the shelling stops . . . and someone will offer the comment . . . to *listen to the silence* . . . (pause) . . . and in living life each day . . . the shelling takes a lot of different forms . . . the shelling can be hassles with other people . . . concerns about the environment . . . doubts with one's self about what one should do . . . the battles can be inside . . . they can be outside . . . they can be brief . . . they can be tolerable . . . they can be inspirational . . . they can cause growth . . . they can foster creativity in finding ways to see beyond the moment . . . but there come quiet times . . . times when all the hoopla is over . . . when the noise stops . . . when your thoughts slow down . . . and when nothing really seems to matter very much . . . and it's *those quiet times that prepare you so well* . . . for the times that aren't so quiet . . . the few seconds that can feel like a lot longer period of quiet . . . they restore comfort . . . and balance . . . that strengthen you . . . for any . . . and all future occasions . . . where patience and understanding . . . might work quite well . . . and right now you're in one of those periods of silence . . . and the world is so unpredictable . . . it's hard to know . . . whether things will still be quiet . . . next week . . . next month . . . next year . . . and it really doesn't matter . . . all that really matters . . . is how you use your quiet period

now . . . whether you *use the time to strengthen yourself* . . . and *pamper yourself* . . . to *congratulate yourself* . . . and to *appreciate your ability to grow* and do much more than just survive . . . and for a while when I was much younger . . . I had the experience of living on the island of Jamaica . . . I lived in a very small village . . . on the west end of the island . . . where very few Americans actually go . . . and nobody there knew how to read . . . nobody knew how to write . . . nobody was informed about world events . . . the Jamaicans were shocked and disbelieving . . . when I described to them how Americans had put men on the moon . . . and brought them back safely again . . . and despite their ignorance . . . there was a certain satisfaction . . . in understanding the island on which they lived . . . where most of the time the sky is so clear and blue . . . but as is typical of the tropics . . . every once in a while . . . huge clouds would roll in . . . and there would be heavy rain and thunder and lightning . . . and then the clouds would roll out again . . . and at first I found it very unsettling . . . that unexpectedly . . . my enjoyment of the sunshine . . . could be interrupted at any moment . . . and obviously, I had no control . . . over thunder . . . and rain . . . and you learn very quickly . . . that the loudness . . . can be so well appreciated by the counter balance of quiet . . . and that it's the loudness . . . that makes the rain forest come alive . . . and allows the growth to take place . . . and sometimes it's inconvenient . . . sometimes it seems unnecessary . . . but the fact of the matter . . . is that the darkness of rain . . . leads to the lush vegetation's growth . . . that permits the pleasure . . . and all things are balanced . . . and how good it feels for you to be settled comfortably . . . and how well it prepares you for periods of being unsettled . . . just as periods of being unsettled . . . allow you to really appreciate . . . settled, comfortable times . . . like now . . . and why not enjoy . . . quiet times . . . and appreciate what they have to offer . . . and why not accept the inevitable . . . that rain falls . . . and people change . . . and things get better . . . a day at a time . . . as you *grow more tolerant* . . . and *enjoy greater periods of comfort and stability* . . . it can grow easier and easier . . . to move flexibly and fluidly . . . through the rain and through the shine . . . whether you're in Jamaica or San Diego . . . Europe or Africa . . . the sunshine on the inside . . . makes it easy to deal with the rain on the outside . . . and someone once said . . . no news is good news . . . but you'll have to make your mind up about that for yourself . . . and taking the time to *enjoy feelings of comfort* . . . to enjoy the quiet inside . . . how good it feels . . . to know . . . that the shelling has stopped . . . and experiencing the comfort . . . is certainly a privilege . . . and so why not carry it with you everywhere . . . everywhere that comfort is permitted . . . and share some of it and keep some of it . . . let some go . . . hold on to some . . . and as you begin the process of reorienting yourself . . . bring just enough back with you . . . to enjoy the quiet . . . and then when you feel like you're ready to . . . you can quietly open your eyes. . . .

The client found the hypnotic process "a good break" from the routine pressures he faced, and found it interesting that I would reference *M*A*S*H*, which is one of his favorite programs. He thought of Hawkeye in particular, and how he uses humor to stay sane in an insane situation. He decided that he would act similarly, and gave himself the assignment of making a point of telling jokes to people as a way of easing tense situations. He thought that approach to be a positive stress-management tool in addition to the self-hypnosis he was taught, and related it further to things he had read about humor and healing. Subsequent sessions involved addressing specific problems needing his attention.

CONCLUSION

Each of the six transcripts included in this chapter was provided for the general purpose of illustrating what forms a hypnotic process might take. You may have noticed how each session was constructed according to characteristics of the individual client being treated. It is precisely for this reason that these transcripts are not likely to be useful to anyone else, even someone with a similar problem, without considerable re-tailoring. Thus, the inability to standardize utilization approach interventions should be more readily apparent to you. Hopefully, though, your creativity is stimulated by thinking about what you might have said and done differently in working with such clients. *There are lots of right ways to do clinical hypnosis, and it's the result you get that lets you know whether you were on the right track or not.* An interesting or elaborate hypnotic process doesn't mean much if it doesn't generate the desired responses for you and your client.

For Discussion

1. Do you think it would be useful to have a book of prepared scripts to use for specific client problems? Why or why not?
2. What do you think about the idea of common themes of human experience relative to therapy interventions?
3. Do you like learning from others' experiences? What limits, if any, are you aware of in employing metaphors as a teaching tool?

Things to Do

1. For each transcript, identify the stages of induction, deepening, utilization, and disengagement. Do you see clear dividing lines between stages?
2. Identify the suggestion structures and styles in each of the sessions.
3. Find the places where metaphors, confusion, ambiguity, puns, and other such mechanisms are employed. How are they introduced and utilized?
4. Identify and list the most common (repetitive) themes in the client problems you encounter. What themes of therapy can you identify as relevant to treatment?

REFERENCES

Yapko, M. (2001). *Treating depression with hypnosis: Integrating cognitive-behavioral and strategic approaches*. Philadelphia, PA: Brunner/Routledge.

Zeig, J. (Ed.) (1980). *A teaching seminar with Milton H. Erickson, M.D.* New York: Brunner/ Mazel.

20

The Case of Vicki: Hypnosis for Coping with Terminal Cancer

This chapter presents a moving and highly instructive single-session intervention I conducted with a 42-year-old woman named Vicki. You first met Vicki in the opening lines of this book, which you may want to re-read before going any further.

Analysis of and commentary about the session are provided side-by-side with the session transcript in order to elaborate more clearly the aims and methods of the session. You may find it helpful to view the actual session sometime as you read along. (Information for obtaining a copy of the session is available in Appendix B.)

BACKGROUND OF THE SESSION

Vicki was referred to me for a single hypnosis session by her co-therapists, Lillian and Harold. She had been in treatment with them over the course of several years and, as you will see, greatly benefited from her work with them. She had progressed from apparent emotional instability with no real focus in life to becoming a highly successful graduate student eventually pursuing a career in counseling. Her new life plan came to a screeching halt, however, when she was formally diagnosed as having advanced-stage cancer throughout her body, with a very short time to live.

Lillian and Harold, associates from a mutual university affiliation, referred Vicki to me for a hypnosis session with the hope that hypnosis might be useful in helping her manage both the emotional shock and the physical discomfort associated with her terminal condition. Lillian was the one who contacted me by phone and asked if I could see Vicki. As it so happened, I would be unable to see her for an individual session in the immediate future because of a scheduled teaching trip. I volunteered, however, to do a session with her if she was willing to do it in the context of an advanced hypnosis course I was teaching. Lillian's immediate reaction was positive; she believed that the opportunity for Vicki to work some things out in a group context would be of great benefit to her.

When I am referred a new client, I typically prefer not to hear the diagnostic impression of the person making the referral. I much prefer to arrive at my own diagnostic impressions without the influence of someone else's judgment. Thus, when Lillian began to describe Vicki, I asked her to share only minimal information about her, specifically the goals associated with the referral. When I see someone more than once, I am then likely to call the referring clinician after the first session and ask for whatever additional data he or she may have regarding the client.

So, at the outset of the session, I knew only Vicki's name, her general goal of wanting to cope as well as possible with truly tragic circumstances, and the fact that she was held in high regard by Lillian and Harold. When I called Vicki to suggest a time and describe the context in which we could meet—she was to be a demonstration partner in a clinical hypnosis course with others present—she agreed with no apparent hesitation. No further discussion took place during that phone contact.

CONTEXT OF THE SESSION

The session was held in my group training room the day after I called Vicki to set up the appointment. She agreed to my invitation; I would conduct the session before a group of psychotherapists learning to utilize hypnosis. In fact, there were 10 observers present, all of whom were instructed to be silent so as to not interrupt the natural flow of the session.

Vicki arrived on time (after lunch) for the session and was seated in a chair opposite me. I had asked Lillian and Harold not to say much about what she could expect in working with me, but as it turns out, she had already heard of me from other sources. Her expectations for the session were clearly positive, and it evidently helped her when I defined the context as more of an educational one than a clinical one.

The transcript of this session, both the interview and the intervention, is unedited, preserving its integrity. You may wish to read the verbatim transcript in entirety first, and then read it a second time with reference to the analysis and commentary. Some follow-up and final comments are provided immediately following the session transcript.

THE CASE OF VICKI

| **Verbatim Transcript** | **Commentary and Analysis** |

The Interview

V: My greatest concern at the moment is, because I know that I have a very short time to live that I don't want to spend it being zonked out on drugs. And, so I would like to have some way of coping with the pain without being . . . I'm not afraid of becoming an addict. I can live being an addict, I suppose, but I don't want to miss the time that I have left. I would like to have . . . my interest is in being able to alleviate pain without drugs.

Vicki's beginning remarks orient me to her goal of managing her condition naturalistically. Notice her immediate emphasis on the issue of "time," a dominant theme which becomes a core dimension of the hypnosis session.

M: I really know very little about what's going on with you and in your life right now. Can you give me a little bit of background?

V: I have cancer that is, they don't even know where the primary is, but it's throughout my body. I have it in the brain, in the bone, in the lung, in the adrenal glands, in the lymph system—everywhere. And they say—my doctor says I'll be surprised if you don't live a month. I'll be astounded if you live a year and we think we're talking three to four months." And I'm okay with that . . . I'm not, the death part is not the hard part. The hard part is being able to get done all that I want to get done in the time that I have left, and make sure that everybody's dealing with it, which is the second hardest part.

Vicki's time frame has been established by the physician giving her the prognosis. She speaks in terms of "parts," distinguishing one part of her experience from another. This is a clue that she will be able to benefit from an approach that emphasizes dissociation, since she is already used to thinking in terms of "part of me is experiencing this while part of me is

My family wants to stick their head in the sand and they don't want to deal with it and I keep saying "You have to because you don't—I don't have time to wait for you and do it your own way. You have to do it my way now, you know." So time is the thing and being drugged, and they want right away to put you on very heavy drugs, and I'm very sensitive to drugs, and it just makes me sleep which I don't want to sleep my time away, you know. I have a lot of things to say and a lot of things to do and I want to be able to do those things in the time that I have.

M: How long ago were you diagnosed, Vicki?

V: Three weeks ago.

M: Okay.

V: Anger's another thing that I wish I had time to deal with, because I have a lot of anger, because I've been going to doctors for four years, saying I'm sick, I'm very sick, I'm sick, and they say "No, you're a hypochondriac. You just think you're sick. You're making yourself—" all these things and even doctors that refused to examine me. And I have a lot of anger at doctors because if I had been diagnosed, if they would have listened to me as I was listening to my body tell me that I was sick it would have been a different trip. So I have a lot of anger at doctors, but I finally decided that I just don't have time to deal with that so I'm going to skip that part.

experiencing that." Further interviewing will permit me to determine just how adept at dissociation she really is. The issue of "time" is reiterated as she introduces the "power struggle" she experiences with her family.

Vicki lets me know she wants to be active during this time, saying and doing the things she feels are necessary.

Vicki acknowledges she has angry feelings, but indicates she does not have the time to deal with her feelings—a realistic choice to make given the shortage of time.

Vicki states clearly that she is able to dissociate from her angry feelings out of necessity. This needs to be acknowledged, but it is not yet known

M: You're saying that you presented physical complaints to doctors, and basically they ignored it?

V: Yeah, I could tell you a lot of horror stories about that but, you know, even doctors that just refused to examine me, which at that point, my idea was even hypochondriacs get sick! I at least deserve an examination and was told "No." I mean a lot of really bad . . . Even seven months ago, I went so far as to have a biopsy done and the doctor missed it, because he was going on vacation that day and he was in a hurry and he was . . . You know all these just really coincidental things, kind of things that—you can't really put—I mean everything has its explanation but the whole thing makes a real ugly package, you know. So a lot of anger there that I'm just kind of trying not to—I'm just saying that I don't have time. You have to prioritize and you have to say what's really important and getting my family okay with this and getting my affairs in order and dealing with it spiritually and physically is more important than kicking butts.

M: Can you tell me a little bit about your family and what the family situation is right now?

V: I'm in the process of divorce which is being a real complication for me because my husband has decided that, well he's figured out that—we were very close to making a financial agreement—we haven't lived together for five years and he has

whether she is truly able to dissociate her feelings to the extent she claims.

Further acknowledgement of angry feelings she attempts to dissociate from. She also shows an ability to prioritize and sequence her involvements, evidence of a more concrete and linear style of thinking—important diagnostic information for the construction of an appropriate hypnosis session.

Information is sought regarding her support network and associated relationship issues.

Vicki identifies her husband as a source of distress.

another family—and we were very close to coming to a financial agreement which was substantial but he's figured out now that if he prolongs, he gets it all. So he's decided that he's not going to participate in any way financially and that he's just going to drag it off and . . . That was a real shock, that was a real shock for me because I think if he would have called me and had been—this is the hard part (*becomes tearful*)—I would have helped him and he won't help me but that's only financial consideration, puts me in a financial bind because I'm not eligible for aid because I'm married and his income is considered, but he won't give me any of it, so I'm stuck. He thinks I should go to Balboa Hospital, and the one thing I don't want is to spend the rest of my life sitting in a waiting room at Balboa Hospital, that's the one thing I don't want to do. So that part of my family is not, the rest of my family is very supportive. I have a lot of very supportive friends and I have a daughter that's twenty-three and she wants to run and hide and I'm not letting her and it's being difficult for her and that, she's probably my number 1 concern. Just a lot of friends that are being real supportive and that helps a lot. I'm amazed at how many people are—I think that is a really amazing thing to learn how many people go away and how many—the ones who go away and the ones that stay. A lot of people that I grew up with, I grew up with kind of a large gang of people; we all ran around together for years in San Diego and I was the youngest of the

Vicki identifies her daughter as a source of distress.

group and it's being real hard for them because it's, all of a sudden their own vulnerabilities are coming through and they're having to deal with feelings of their own that are making it difficult for them. There's a lot to deal with.

M: Are they talking with you about those things?

V: The hardest thing—everybody reacts different and—a few years ago I lived in Colorado and my family called me and said my uncle who I was very close to was dying of cancer and if I wanted to see him I should come and I did. And when I got here they said, "Now, we don't talk about it to him." And I went along with that because it was my family's wish and all the while that he died, he never mentioned to them that he was dying and they never mentioned to him and everybody, I mean it was so stupid and when I got back to Colorado I thought the worst thing that I did was not to sit down with him and say, "You want to talk about it?" So I did a lot of thinking at that time about it and now, to me, I have to talk about it and some people find that really difficult to deal with. It's just the way that I have to do it. I have to. And the more that I do it, the more okay I feel and not only that but the more I do it, the more I know that other people are okay and if other people are okay, I feel better. So it has kind of a circular benefit for me. It's scary to some people, like my daughter is not a very verbal person and she wants to stick

Vicki makes it perfectly clear that she wants to and needs to talk about her situation. Thus, the pace of the interaction will be tailored to her need, respecting its value to her.

her head in the sand and it's real hard for me to get through to her. We're managing to do it, but it's hard.

M: What would you want her to know? What would you want her to understand?

V: Something really–like a miracle happened the other day because when she first found out, she took off and went to Mexico and really running. I keep sitting her down saying, "This is serious. You can't run away. We don't have time to play games. You have to, we have to deal with it." "Well, what do you want me to do, what do you want from me?" She's really confused about it and, for some reason I'm able to get across to other people what my needs are, but I can't to her because she's so afraid. And the other day she got back from Mexico and she was at my house and she was sitting on the bed and she was giving me this "what do you want from me?" and "I don't know what you want from me," and I just, I didn't know what to say and in popped one of her friends that she'd had ever since she was real little, popped in the door and ran in the bedroom and plopped down on the bed and said "My God. Tell me what it's like to know you're going to die." You know, my daughter's sitting there and this is her friend and . . . So Linne and I started to talk and I started to tell her, and then she'd say, "And then what does it feel like? Does it hurt?" Just asking this whole, the kind of questions that you don't know how to ask and here's this kid sitting there asking and my daughter kind of curled up on the pillows and was a little mouse and said ... We asked, we went on for about two hours, and we asked her, no participation at all, she was like the mouse in the room. We talked about her like she wasn't there and Linne said "What's your greatest fear?" and I said that my greatest fear is that I won't be able to sit and talk to her the way, or talk to Carrie the way I can talk to you. Still there was nothing required of her at all. But things changed after that, things changed. You know, it was like all of a sudden she had at least some understanding of what my needs were and how communication can work beneficially and openness is necessary as I don't have time to play games. Everybody keeps saying to me, "You have to let her accept it in her own way, in her own time." And I was saying, "That's fine. I've known that for years." And everything we come across, in your own time and in your own way you will accept. Right now, I don't have time so I have to push and maybe I'll push too hard and it'll hurt her more than help her but I have to take that chance because I don't have the time. So it's . . .

A good example from her life of the value of indirect communication. As in couples or family therapy, talking to person A in the presence of person B influences B despite the lack of direct interaction.

M: Do you have the sense that there are things that you want to say to her and she to you?

Time is reiterated as a vital issue.

V: My biggest fear is that five years down the road she's not going to be able to deal with it because she's going to say "I stuck my head in the sand and I should have sat down and

Vicki shows an ability to have foresight that is of an immediate and realistic quality.

talked." It's more urgent for her than for me. I don't have trouble verbalizing; I say what I feel and what I think and I don't feel . . . There's a lot of things I feel like I want to say, you know, "Put your seat belt on" and stuff, but things that I would like to share, family things, but the urgency in my mind is in her ability to deal with it herself after it's over; that she can say we spent quality time, that we did the best we could do for each other in whatever time we had, that she doesn't feel guilty, and that she doesn't have this after thing that's going to make it harder for her to facilitate the rest of her life.

M: So when you were talking earlier about family members sticking their head in the sand, were you referring specifically to her or others as well?

V: Her father—my first—my husband that I'm trying to get a divorce from— I've been married fifteen years—her father I was married to years ago and we've been really close friends all these years and he was at the hospital when they did the diagnosis and he took off and hasn't been seen since. I mean, he's the one that taught her how to do this. And he's not dealing with it, and that's okay. I'm not really too concerned with him. Another one that I'm really concerned with is my mother. My mother's sixty-nine and, but really she's ninety-nine. I take care of her totally and so, and I think in my mind the hardest thing in the world to do would be to lose a child. I've never been close to my mother, my

Vicki identifies her mother as a source of distress.

mother and I have never been close. And we're becoming that now. She's trying very hard to understand my philosophies which—she's never listened to me and now she's listening and she'll get my philosophy books and she'll bring them and want me to read to her and she asks me questions and she talks to me. I think that's a neat thing that's happening. I feel much closer to her. I have a son, this is another sad part, I have a son that is in trouble and my husband has turned him against me and he hates me. That hurts me a lot. I expect probably not to see him again and if I did see him again I think it would be a difficult time. He's a strange boy and he would come to me and he would say "I love you," and a lot of things that he doesn't feel. He's not bonded to me very much and he, you know, I do better, I do better with people that put it out just the way it is: "I don't feel very close to you but I wish I'd had a chance to get to know you," or something like that, rather than "I love you and I can't stand losing you" and all the stuff that's just crap, you know. I don't want any crap. If I do get a chance to see him again I think that that's going to be very difficult to deal with. He doesn't have the emotional—he's a very immature, emotionally immature person who just needs a lot of, lot of time to get it together. So I don't, I really—that's a hard one and I don't know what's going to happen with that. I have an aunt that doesn't speak to me, that . . . My family were taught, my mother and all of my family were taught when they

Vicki emphasizes how she values being listened to, a dominant theme throughout her presentation.

Vicki identifies her estranged son as a source of distress.

Vicki has an aunt who is a source of distress, who embodies the "if you're angry, clam up" approach that Vicki feels is a waste of valuable communication time. By now, it is clear that were very young that when you got angry at someone you quit talking to them. I don't know who ever thought that one up, but I guess years ago that was the way that you dealt with a lot of things.

M: Instead of talking it out and working it through.

V: You don't talk at all. I mean if you, if I don't like the way, something you said to me today, just something you said to me, I might stop talking to you for five years. I mean that's the way they do it. And my aunt hasn't spoken to me for about nine months because of one day I said something that she didn't like. It's so ridiculous I can't believe it. Now, she's frantic, she's panicky. She won't come to me and talk to me; she won't make an overt gesture to me. But she like sends me cookies under the counter. I send them back and my mother says that I'm being really ugly and not understanding and I am, I suppose, but I think that if I accept the cookies under the table, that's all I'll ever get. I think for both of us it's important that she comes. I think she has something to learn if she would come and talk to me and so I won't take the cookies. She's really panicky. I've decided that I'm not going to die and leave her with her guilt but I'm not going to just take the cookies either. I'm going to play it out a little bit. There's a streak in me.

M: What do you expect to happen? That she will come see you?

Vicki has few, if any, conflict-free relationships; thus, relationships as a focal point for hypnotically building comfort would seem an unlikely path.

Vicki sees herself as competent in dealing with things directly, a relevant piece of information for later formulating suggestions.

Vicki's sense of urgency about resolving things is not evident here, further evidence of an ability to compartmentalize experience.

V: I don't know. Either she'll go farther away or she'll come and talk to
me. I think that she's a very controlling person; she always wants to have
control of everything and if she was
in my life right now she'd say, "Now
what are we going to do with this?
And, who's going to take care of
this?" and all these things—she'd
want to take over and control everything. I won't let people control me
and so we conflict there. See, she
wants to run the show, she wants to,
so that's where the conflict is. So if
she was in my life right now, she
would be causing conflict in my life
right now, there's no doubt about
that. She's going to have to come to
a place where she can say, she's got
to let me make my own decisions
about my own life and my own way
that I want to die and not tell me, try
to tell me how to do it. I don't let
people do that, and that's why we
don't get along. I think that that'll
work out eventually. I'm not too concerned about that.

Acknowledges tendencies to engage
in power struggles, letting me know
that if I want to succeed, it will be by
treating her as an equal, not as someone to direct.

M: So you really have your own mind
and it's just trying to get these people to understand that . . .

Rapport-building confirmation that
I've heard the message about respecting her need to maintain control.

V: Yeah, I know what I want. No
doubt about it.

M: How have you dealt these last
three weeks with getting the prognosis?

V: That was really the easy part because I knew I was sick. I knew I was
dying. I knew it a long time ago. I
just couldn't get any doctor to con-

Another reference to a "part" (either
easy or hard, in this case "easy").

firm that. So it's something that I've been dealing with a long time and . . .

M: Are you saying that it was almost a bit of relief to have some confirmation?

V: Well, it certainly wasn't what I wanted to hear.

M: I wouldn't think so.

V: I wanted to hear that I had something curable. But it was a relief to have some kind of diagnosis. It's an awful thing to know that you're awfully sick and have people tell you that you're not. To be in the kind of double bind or that kind of conflict is really an awful place to be, and I've been there for four years. Pretty soon you start to believe that you're crazy. Then you start to act crazy, and then you become crazy and then you fall into all the patterns; people categorize you and you're labeled and then you have no hope of getting out. That's an awful place to be. There's no way to dig out of that kind of a hole, until it's too late like it has . . . I think that's one of—In the medical profession, even the psychological profession, we tend very much to categorize people and label them and expect them to behave and do according to what their labels are and that's so wrong because there's so much more. Everybody's different, everybody's an individual. We get going so fast and we never stop to listen and really look at people the way, for who they are and their differ-

Vicki introduces her very, very strong opinions about being labeled, clearly a reflection of the emotional intensity that could only be a direct by-product of having been hurt by such a process.

She started to say that it was too late for her, but blocked it; acceptance is' not fully achieved, which is probably to her advantage.

Vicki warning me of what *not* to do in treating her, as well as what *to* do.

ences, people don't fit into little boxes.

M: What do you think somebody who would have been a little bit smarter, a little bit more perceptive, a little bit more sensitive would have done? What do you think the best way would have been to have responded to you?

Asking for clarification of exactly what position she would like me to take in dealing with her.

V: Just listen to me. I got a diagnosis only because of my own tantrum. One day I threw a tantrum. You see, I knew that there was something in my lung and, like I said, six or seven months ago I had a lung biopsy, and then I kept going back to doctors and going back and they kept saying "It's not your lung. We did the lung, right? We had a biopsy on your lung, we checked your lung. It's not your . . ." I said "But it *is* my lung. I lived in this body forty-two years. I kind of got to know it a little bit. Something is wrong in my lung." "No, it's not your lung because we've done all the tests on your lung." So we go off, we go off, and I went through the seven months and then one day I just had a tantrum. I said "Can't somebody at least do a chest x-ray? What the hell is it going to hurt to do a chest x-ray?" "All right, if you'll just shut up we'll do it." And then it was a tumor about this size (the size of a golfball) that shows up in my lung. And if I hadn't had that tantrum that day they would've never even at this time had a diagnosis. So I think that people, doctors don't listen and we tend to let them not listen which is a big mistake because they're gods and

Vicki letting me know not to hurry her, not to label her, and to treat her respectfully as an individual who needs to be listened to.

Vicki has moved into "preacher" mode to make sure that all present are mandated with the task of listening to their patients.

they know what they're talking about and they went to school and they know all this stuff and they don't. If you have a doctor that's not listening, you should find another one because they may know scientifically but they don't live it. If you know your body, you live in your body, you have more, you know more about your body than they're ever going to know because they don't live there. They think that most people aren't smart enough to know that, I guess. I don't know.

M: What is the medical intervention at this point? What has been prescribed for you? What are you supposed to be doing?

I want to know what her treatment plan is and whether she knows what to expect.

V: At the moment, I'm doing a lot of radiation therapy. I'm not into heavy therapies and I'm more the kind of person who would rather die with dignity. I'm not going to, I don't want to spend the rest of my life being sick to death. I'd rather have a shorter life and not be sick than a long life, but I did consent to the radiation therapy which is about the only thing they had to offer me anyway. We're way beyond surgery, we're way beyond chemotherapy. Radiation therapy can, they tell me that it's not going to increase the length of my life but maybe the quality of my life. And I've had a few days where I doubted that, because it did make me sick. Now, I'm beginning to believe it. I had a very large tumor in my shoulder and I lost all the use of my right arm and it was very painful and they said that if I didn't do something about it, it

She asserts the value of quality of life rather than quantity.

was going to explode my shoulder. It was a real toss up. They did the radiation therapy and it was a real toss up whether there was going to get to be enough radiation, if the radiation was going to be beneficial before it exploded. It came, I mean I could tell, it came right to the very line and then the tumor did start to decrease and the pain decreased so I know that by doing that I saved my shoulder and now I'm even gaining some use of that. The tumors in my brain which they said radiation therapy is going to probably decrease the amount of seizures and so forth that I will have, so it seemed reasonable to me to try that. Also in the lung, the tumor presses on the vena cava which is where all the blood drains from the . . . and that's the real dangerous part of that, so if it can decrease it somewhat, to cause that—it's not going to extend my life, it's just going to make it more comfortable probably, for a longer time.

M: Are you currently taking any drugs?

V: I'm real selective about that. They want to always keep putting me on more and more drugs and I, like I say, I don't want to miss anything.

Vicki reasserts her desire to minimize the influence of drugs on her functioning.

M: Some of the drugs seem to have a mental effect?

V: I tell you. When you get to this place you, this is a drug addict's dream. You just tell them what you want, anything you want, they . . . morphine, the whole shmear. I just,

I did Tylenol III for a while, and then
when the shoulder got real bad I went
to Percocet, and now I'm cutting
back because it's not as painful and
so I'm back to Tylenol III now, and
I'm trying to maintain on that. But I
haven't closed my mind, I don't want   Drugs are an acceptable last resort,
to be, you know I'm not a martyr; I   but the first choice is self-
don't want to be, I can't enjoy and   management.
do the things that I want to do if I'm
in terrible pain so it's a real balance
for me and I'm hoping that this is
going to make it easier to stay awake
and still not be in pain. I don't like
pain, so I'm not into pain, but I'm
not into being drugged up either. It's
a balance that I have to maintain and
just decide as I go. I have this whole
dresser full of pills; some make you
not throw up, and I'm also doing
some mega-vitamin kind of stuff so—
the radiation, in the next week all of
my hair is going to fall out and I'm
going not to be able to eat solid food   This mention of difficulty eating is
for about a week because the irrita-   noted as something to address in the
tion to the esophagus, so I figure that   hypnosis session.
next week is going to be a real tough
one to get through and then I'll be
okay. So you have to kind of see as
you go along, what you need to do as
far as medicine is concerned. But as   Her need for control is reiterated.
long as I'm making the decisions, I
feel okay about it. I've been looking
into hospice care because I have this
really strong thing about I don't want
to die in a hospital and I don't want
to be hooked up to machines and I
want, I'm looking into hospice kind
of situations and I like a lot of what
they have to say and then they get to
the bottom and they said "Who's
your doctor?" and I told them and
they said "He won't cooperate with

us." I said then we have to find a new doctor because I'm not going to die in a hospital and I'm not going to die hooked up to a machine, with a doctor that's going to keep me alive that way. I don't want that. And the legal situation being what it is, that's—you really need to know that before, because it depends on the doctor. So I'm working on those kinds of things.

M: Are you currently experiencing any discomfort in your body?

The first reframe—pain as "discomfort," a less charged term.

V: At this moment? My shoulder I suppose. It's a lot better than it has been but it's uncomfortable. I can't raise my arm.

M: On a day-to-day basis, over the last few days, has the discomfort been limited to your shoulder or do you experience it in other places as well?

I am asking how localized or generalized her experience of pain is.

V: My chest. I'm getting more and more uncomfortable in my chest. The more and more pain in my, the more radiation they do to my chest, the more irritated the esophagus becomes, and like I said, for a week I won't be able to eat solid foods, so it becomes quite irritated.

M: Can you describe what that means—irritated?

I want a sensory description of what she expects in order to address it in the hypnosis session, since eating and maintaining body weight are important.

V: They call it, they say it's like esophagitis. You get a real bad sore throat and you can't swallow things. I've been having difficulty swallowing for some time, but I do anyway because I'm a little pig. Not much makes me stop eating so, but just like having a bad ulcer is what it's going to be like. It just kind of hurts. But it's temporary. That part is temporary. It'll go away when the treatments end. Like hair grows back.

M: Can you describe a little bit what the sensation in your shoulder is like?

V: My shoulder is so much better but it's like it's just a lot of pain. There was a lot of pain in my shoulder and it does, it feels just like there's something huge inside the joint which is exactly what it was, and it's pressing, pressing, pressing, pressing so hard that the bone was getting ready to explode, and it's just growing, growing, and there's no room for it to grow so it just, and that's the kind of pain it is. Not only that but it makes me unable to move my arm in certain ways. I can't lift my arm. I can't go up. I can use my fingers, and I can do—it's funny the things that, you know, because I'm right-handed, so it's been really kind of a hard thing to deal with and there's—it feels like somebody hit me in the shoulder with a baseball bat and it's just this horrible bruise. There's no bruise, but it feels like, if you looked there'd be black and blue everywhere. It's getting a lot better. I suppose there's a considerable amount of chest pain, but I've been dealing with that for a long time so it's kind of . . . See, I learned, it's kind of a strange thing because for four years I've had a lot of pain. It started in my joints and my muscles, all over my body. Like terrible arthritis, and I kept going to doctors and they'd say there's no ar-

Vicki's ability to recognize the situation as changeable is a powerful deterrent to her giving up.

More sensory descriptions to use in the hypnosis session.

thritis here. Of course it wasn't, it was cancer but they didn't look past and they kept telling me that there wasn't anything that could be causing that pain and so I finally got to the point where I said "Okay. I'm a full-time student; I'm a very active person; I can't get slowed down by pain and so there just won't be pain." So I spent a lot of time teaching myself how not to perceive the pain or how to let my brain override the pain to some degree. And now that I have a diagnosis I find myself feeling the pain, allowing myself to feel the pain. So it's a real different kind of thing for me to do and now that I've allowed myself to feel the pain I'm trying to find this place in between where I, because I know that the mind controls so much of what you feel, there must be a place where I can, I don't want to be totally unaware of it, but I want to be able to deal with it because I got so confused in this period where you feel pain and people are telling you there's no pain. It gets you real confused. I don't know exactly what I'm feeling is what I'm feeling. Know what I mean? Well, my level of feeling is, may not be, what's real. I don't know where "real" is anymore.

M: That must be pretty confusing.

V: That part is. Yeah, I think that I got to the point where I'd say "No it doesn't hurt," when it really did hurt. Because doctors convinced me that there wasn't anything there and I didn't want to be crazy so I went along with it. It does strange things to your head.

Vicki describes an ability to use mental mechanisms to overcome pain, a potentially meaningful indicator of what ability or abilities to amplify hypnotically.

Vicki's references to confusion reflect the antitherapeutic aspects of confusion. Since certainty and clarity at all times is not possible, given the advanced state of her illness, it seemed important to be able to establish a new association to the experience of confusion that would make it tolerable. Thus, confusional suggestions were planned into the session.

The previous experience of confusion has a negative association to being out of touch with reality to her own detriment.

M: All that time that you said that basically, you didn't let yourself experience the pain—how did you do that?

V: I just didn't focus on it mostly. I learned not to focus on it. I had a lot of things going on in my life. I had a lot of important things to do and I would just focus on other things.

M: Being in school?

V: Being in school.

M: Family relationships? Other kinds of things? Were you working?

V: No. Well, I was for a while. That was too hard. I did get to the point where I knew that I wasn't able to do all that I used to be able to do and I did cut back. I was working full time and going to school full time and that became way, way too much for me. So I stopped. I worked and saved as much money as I could and then I dropped out of work and went to school full time and that was just really exciting for me. But I spent a lot of time resting. I did meditation things, I did a lot of relaxation—I learned to do a lot of relaxation things that helped me not focus on it.

M: I'd like to hear a little bit more about that—the relaxation, the meditation, some of the things that are probably going to parallel a little bit what we're going to be doing. Can you tell me a little bit about those things that you've already learned?

I want to identify what method—the sequence of steps she took to psychologically manage her pain.

She lets me know it was through distraction.

Vicki lets me know she has previous hypnotic experiences to access in the form of meditation and relaxation procedures, and that these were helpful. Thus, they can safely be referenced in the hypnosis session.

I want the specifics of what she has experienced in order to know which parts to amplify and which to gloss over.

V: One thing that I'm doing right now that's really exciting to me is guided imagery. I think that's really exciting.

M: You're working with someone, doing that?

V: Lillian and Harold. And I think that's really exciting. I'm really into the—all my whole life has kind of centered around how much control the mind has over your body. I kind of always believed that you could make yourself sick and you could make yourself not sick. I don't think I believe it so much anymore. I've always kind of thought along those lines. I know that you can control an awful lot with your mind and so I've always been interested in learning how to do that.

Vicki professes to have held an attitude of "mind over matter" that is now untenable.

M: And so Lillian and Harold are doing formal guided imagery sessions with you? What kinds of things and how are you responding to it?

More specifics are needed if I am to make meaningful references to their work.

V: I guess you don't ever know really how you could respond to it but it's a kind of white light kind of melting away the tumors. I have tornadoes that come down—white tornadoes that come down and get rid of—and I can get into it. I really get into it. I see it. I try to do it quite a bit every day and I spend time on that radiation—getting radiation therapy is like going and putting yourself in a giant microwave and turning it on is how I visualize it. I try to do it while I'm there but it's such an awesome place to be it's kind of hard to do there.

Vicki is being taught methods of visualization that she claims to benefit from.

Sometimes I can do it, sometimes I can't. There's a big switch on the wall that says "Emergency Shut Off" and I look at it and I just want to get up and shut it off. I suspect very strongly that radiation is the cause of my problems. I was radiated as a child in an experimental kind of thing and most of the people that had this radiation as children are coming up with this kind of . . . It's hard to imagine that radiation is the cause and radiation is how we diagnose and how we treat. Those things are hard to put together. To put yourself in a microwave is kind of a difficult thing to do. But other places it works a lot better. It feels good to me. I don't know if it's working or not but it feels good to me and so I do it.

M: So you're able to relax and you're able to get into it? Great.

I am seeking to amplify her capability.

V: Sometimes. Depending where I'm at. Sometimes it's easier than other times. Sometimes it's just really fantastic. I also do meditation which I've done for a long time and that's always helped me and so I hang onto that. I haven't really done too much other kind of relaxation. For a while, I was doing it but now that they've got me on—Tylenol III puts me in a place that's never-never land. I don't really need to relax for that reason. I think that I'm really probably much more relaxed than most people. My doctor says that he never had anybody fall asleep on the radiation table before and every once in a while I fall asleep, and my arm will fall off in all positions. I've always been the kind of person that you give an aspirin to and I go to sleep, so I react very strongly to these drugs.

M: What is your experience with the Tylenol III in terms of what it does to you mentally? You're saying that's one of the drugs that you want to get away from, or at least reduce.

I want specifics of the mental effects she is wanting to minimize or eliminate, since these are instrumental in her seeking my help in the first place.

V: Well, it has codeine and I'd like to not have to take drugs that dull my— they're doing radiation to my brain. Radiation destroys good cells as well as bad cells. My area of study is physiological psychology so I know a little bit of physiology and I know that the brain cells don't regenerate. Now, they radiate my shoulder and I know that they destroy the good cells as well as the bad cells and that they can regenerate to some degree. But I know my brain cells can't so I'm very much afraid of losing my brain cells and I find myself not thinking good, not remembering things, talking to someone on the phone one day and the next day not remembering. A lot of memory stuff leaving and it makes me feel a bit panicky. I don't know if it's the radiation or if it's just that I have so many things on my mind and my mind is so totally occupied with all that's going on. I have this really silly thing ever since I can't remember how old—I've never been able to throw anything away. A little piece of string—somebody in the world needs this little piece of string and I'm not going to take it to the dump, I'm going to save it for this person who might need it and maybe I'll

Vicki shares that a lack of clarity and an impairment of memory are the things she fears.

Vicki introduces an ongoing issue in her life of "letting go." She will burden herself on the chance that someone may want the item, defining herself as a provider to others. This issue is an important one, since making plans surrounding death—the ultimate "letting go"—is a necessary task. Thus, "letting go" is a theme to be integrated into the hypnosis session.

have a garage sale some day and sell it for a penny.

So all my life I've saved all these things and I know if I die everybody's going to take all my junk and put it in the garbage can and that just kills me. One of my real goals is I have to have, I finally have to have my yard sale. I also have to look at each and every thing that I have that I love and care about—I have these little stickers that I'm sticking on the backs of—I have to figure out who's going to love this thing the most. So I have all these things to do, so I have a lot of things on my mind. It could be that just the mind is so full that it doesn't have time to remember who I talked to on the phone yesterday. Maybe the radiation isn't the only thing that's killing my mind. Maybe it's just too full.

M: The burden of thinking about everything, and everybody.

V: But I do worry about that. I don't want to destroy my brain. I want my brain to survive.

M: How long will the radiation continue?

V: One more week at this point, and then, of course, they have to keep watching because what they expect is—they expect that it's in a lot of places in my body that they haven't been able to detect yet and so it's just a matter of keeping up with that. I'm only doing it—they're not going to even touch my adrenal glands,

She wants people to value what she does.

Vicki introduces the solution of a "yard sale" as a means to "let go"; this solution is noted, and is later referenced during the hypnosis session.

Reinforcing a nonpathological basis for her memory lapse in order to minimize counterproductive anxiety.

they're so far gone. It's not a vital organ or—you can have it real bad in your adrenal glands before it's going to kill you. That's not what's going to kill me. So that each time that it shows up somewhere else then it has to be re-evaluated to see what and I have to learn enough to be able to evaluate myself and decide whether I want to go through the therapy— sometimes the cure is worse than the disease. I'm afraid of that, so each thing has to be evaluated on its individual kind of basis.

M: You said that you had been working and then you stopped working and went back to school. That's a pretty major change. How did that come about?

Moving away from pathology, I am interested in identifying and accessing specific resources she has that have been employed in previous transitions.

V: I've wanted to go to school all my life and I put my husband through school and I raised a family and it always got put off.

M: Sort of time to do something for yourself.

Validating the worth of the investment in herself.

V: I got to a point where I figured out that I had some value and I had some worth. I lived fifteen years in a violent marriage. My husband was a very violent person and I spent most of my life thinking that I wasn't very deserving and wasn't very—that I was worthless, very low self-esteem. It's taken the last five years, I've really gotten that turned around and figured out that I had a lot of value and a lot of worth and knew where I wanted to go and what I wanted to do, exactly what I wanted. A lot of

Being goal-directed is only a recent development, but she shows an ability to effectively operate in that way.

very definite goals and even have it
all figured out how I'm going to get
there. I'd been carrying a 4.0 average at school and so I've been feeling very good about myself. At first I
thought I feel real sad that I'm not
going to reach my goals but then I
decided that maybe the important
thing was to figure out that I could
and that I had the worth and the   An interpretation of the "meaning"
value and maybe that's the lesson I   of her disease.
had to learn.

M: That's a pretty amazing discov-   By accepting her interpretation, she
ery.   is permitted to focus on her progress
                                           rather than on the frustration of
                                           never reaching her goal.

V: To get there wasn't the main thing.   She accepts that ratification.
To just discover was the main thing.

M: How did you find that after all   I am asking her to identify her
those years of being in such a diffi-   method—the sequence of steps used—
cult relationship?   to effect a significant transition. She
                                           may identify a usable resource for the
V: Well, it's a long story. Twenty years later hypnosis session.
ago I had, my husband put me in a
psychiatric hospital and I was diag-
nosed catatonic-schizophrenia, a   Here are some of the specifics that
back ward patient that would never   led to the earlier sermon about label-
be out of the hospital again and that's   ling.
an awfully hard label to overcome.
Two months ago I went out into the
community and I wanted to get into
a women's group, a women's support
group, I guess about four months
ago, and I started interviewing clinicians because I learned to do that.
So if they interviewed me, I interviewed them. And this woman I hit
with some of my background be-
cause I've been in and out of hospi-   Another personal rejection on the
tals a good part of my life and she   basis of an impersonal label.

told me that I was too sick to be in her group. After one hour of talking to me, and then charging me for the session which I thought was kind of crummy. There's so much of that that goes on that I use it as kind of a tester now. If you see my labels faster than you see me then I can just get up and walk away. I don't need you in my life anymore. That's a real dangerous thing that happens. I progressed, I fought and I never gave up and I overcame all those things, mostly . . . Another thing that I think was important in my history is that they, of course at that time, drugs were coming in, psychotropic drugs and they gave me so many psychotropic drugs and I had such horrible side effects from them. I would try to tell people I'm . . . and nobody would listen to me and they would say "You need more Thorazine." The more they gave me, the sicker I got. I kept trying to tell people, nobody listened. That's when I first learned that people don't listen. My husband kept me in this kind of mindset. I guess it's pretty awful but I overcame it, that's the thing.

She identifies "fighting and never giving up" as the relevant resources for her changes.

M: I'm amazed. It's obviously against all the odds . . .

V: That's why my interest is in physiological psychology because I had just had a complete hysterectomy. There was a lot of physiological things going on in my life at the time that this happened and I really truly believe that there's so much to the chemical brain structure. I really do. I think it was my biggest problem

She is attributing her emotional difficulties to a chemical imbalance.

beside the fact that my husband stole away my person or I let my husband steal my person. And that I had such low self-esteem. I think the chemical makeup of my body at the time was a real key factor and so that's why my interest of study was in that area. I thought that I wanted to make some discoveries that—I knew what it felt like to be on the inside. I knew what it felt like to be in a psychiatric hospital where nobody listened. Have you ever read that study, I forget who did it, where the psychologists all admitted themselves and they . . . Well, that was my life. People don't hear you. You're a nonentity and that's such a horrible thing to be.

What she learned in therapy—to accept responsibility—is given lip service, but she clearly has not yet internalized the lesson. In her situation, that is actually an advantage since a more internal attribution would likely lead to depression.

M: Did you have the idea that you could be a 4.0 student? Go back to school and accomplish these things all that time?

V: Not all that time. No.

M: You got in touch with that much later?

I am wanting to amplify her ability to pleasantly surprise herself with abilities she did not know she had.

V: There came a point where I—one day I was living with my husband on the East Coast and my husband's a commander in the Navy. He was stationed in the East. And the anger grew and grew with him and I found myself standing over him one night with a fireplace poker and I knew that I was going to kill him if I didn't get away from him. The next day I found myself standing on a bridge, the Brooklyn Bridge or one of those bridges, and I was going to jump and

I said "What is it that I'm sorry I didn't do?" Is there any thing that I'm sorry . . . I just couldn't take it anymore, and I said, you know, I always wanted to go to Colorado and I never did. Then I thought, what the hell. Why don't I go to Colorado and if I can't—if it doesn't work out then I'll jump off a mountain. So I went home and I packed myself a backpack and I got in my husband's wallet and I got about $400 out and I took off and I went to Colorado and that's when things turned around for me, because—it was the middle of winter, I slept—I lived on the street. I had a hard time but I began to realize that there was a "me" and I could function totally without him, that I didn't need someone to tell me that I was okay or I wasn't okay. It also goes back to childhood. My father was killed when I was a year old, in the War. My mother was an alcoholic and a drug addict. I had no siblings. I never lived with any one family more than just a few months. I mean I was never—I didn't have a family life so I didn't know how to do that. I never had any . . . So I was used to people who didn't love me and it was like this super goal to find people who don't know how to love and make them love me. My husband never knew how to love; he was incapable of loving. He isn't capable of loving and yet, just somebody who could easily love me wasn't what I needed. I needed the mother who couldn't, the husband that couldn't, I needed all the couldn'ts to do it. That became my whole life's goal. Well, that's a stupid goal. I mean I

The benefits of her therapy are showing in these insights about her life patterns.

wasted my whole life trying to do that and it doesn't work. So I learned that. That was one thing that I learned. That if you want somebody to love you, you have to find—first of all it has to come from within. You're your own best parent, that you have to love yourself, which is such a cliche that unless you really get inside yourself and learn that it sounds so stupid. For years I thought "love yourself," people keep saying that but how stupid, what a stupid thing to say. But it's real and I got to the place where I did. And then . . .

Vicki is letting me know that individuation and self-validation were the keys to her reaching for and achieving more substantial goals.

M: You really feel that now?

Testing the strength of her convictions.

V: Yes. Oh, yes, absolutely. But it's a— it sounds so stupid when you're telling someone who doesn't know what you mean.

M: Almost any feeling sounds a little trite when you say it but if you really feel it and it's strong, that's what matters.

Joining her viewpoint, and validating her right to feel as she does.

V: Yeah, so I learned that probably just by being with myself and I started getting it together in Colorado and I became sick in Colorado, that's where I was. I loved Colorado. It was like my world. I made this world. I lived twelve thousand feet high, in the country, way out in the woods and it was like the happiest time of my life. But I started getting sick and I had to get out of the altitude so I came back here. Also to take care of my mother. But also because I wanted to go back to school. And I thought that I couldn't. I was afraid

to try. I'd been told for so many years
that I was stupid and that I couldn't
do anything right. It's awfully hard—
you know, just one day believe it and
then the next day not believe that this
whole long process that goes
on . . . But I knew that if I didn't try
I was never going to find out so I
signed up for six units. I took two
classes just to see that if maybe,
maybe I could and I did.

M: Must have been a thrill to find
out you could.

Amplifying the feeling of accomplishment following the uncertainty
of taking a risk.

V: Yeah, it was. And it got, and then
each time I started adding more units
until I was up to sixteen and still carrying a 4.0 and that felt good. I mean
it was like super high then. I was just,
but it was also, it made me understand that if I would have tried to do
it when I was seventeen or eighteen
when I got out of high school, I would
not have done it. That there's something that drives you when you want
the information. You have to want
that information or it doesn't work.
I go to school and I compete with
these eighteen- nineteen-year-olds
and I thought "Oh, they're so used
to studying, it's going to be so hard."
They don't want to be there and so
it's really easy competition, but you
have to want to and you have to be
studying something that you're interested in and want the information
and it's not any work at all. You just
soak it in, just love to . . .

M: Have you been seeing Lillian and
Harold all this time or how has that
been working?

How much of your gains have been
made all on your own, how much
with the support of your therapists?

V: Lillian came into my life through my son who doesn't do very well. I finally got my son away from my husband, got him out here with me and got him into seeing Lillian but he's really kind of too far gone to do anything and then Lillian just became a very close friend. I have a close, close relationship with Lillian and Harold both, mostly through some therapy, just friendship, and they're just very special people in my life.

M: She said the same about you. She said "Michael, this lady's a knockout. You'll love her" and I can see why she said that. So you've known her for a while?

Sharing my positive regard for her.

V: Four years.

M: Well, the guided imagery things that you've been doing with them Lillian told me very little—she just said that the guided imagery was something that you had been working with a little bit. She told me basically what you told me, that part of what you were looking for was some more naturalistic way of keeping yourself clear, keeping yourself as comfortable as you can be and I understand that, I wonder now if you think there's anything else I might need to know?

Sharing what was told to me about her, and confirming to her that I have heard what she wants.

V: I don't know. What do you need to know?

M: It was interesting to me to hear you say that you could keep yourself comfortable by focusing on other things even though there was pain at

Amplifying the resource within her of being able to benefit from distraction; amplifying also that she

different times, doctors weren't pick-
ing anything up, but that you were
uncomfortable and that you found
ways to deal with it. It wasn't anything formal that you were doing; it
was just part of your lifestyle to get
yourself to work on other things and
not really pay that much attention to
it. Have you ever had any formal experience in learning specific techniques for managing discomfort?

could experience pain reduction naturalistically despite the apparent absence of a formal strategy for doing
so.

Asking whether she has had any previous formal experience with pain reduction methods.

V: No. Well, that's not true. I did, for
a while, biofeedback. I even tried
some hypnosis with someone
that . . . and it didn't work, which I
probably should have told you before
I came here. I think it had a lot to do
with . . . I wasn't very trusting of the
person. Again, he did his thing and
his thing was his thing and he wasn't
listening to what my needs were and
that's such an important thing for
me. I didn't trust because I kept, I
have a lot of—it goes back to psychologists—and I had some experiences
where psychiatrists mostly have
made big blackouts in my life. I'm
afraid of that and I think I got afraid
of that in the hypnosis because I
wanted to record the sessions and he
wouldn't let me. I was afraid of that
blackout and I think I was fighting
it. They've done a lot of sodium
amytol kinds of things with me and
wouldn't ever tell me what happened
during those periods of blackout and
I don't like that. I don't like people
stealing part of my life away from me
and not sharing it with me.

She reports previous hypnosis experience that was unsuccessful. Details
are needed in order to avoid accessing any part of that experience.

She lets me know that a lack of trust
was the divisive factor, fueled by his
lack of listening to her.

She associates a lack of memory with
negative experience; thus, amnesia
during or after the hypnosis is contraindicated.

The fact that our session was being
conducted before a group was no
doubt of comfort to her. As is typical
of my sessions, the session was also
being recorded on both video- and
audiotape with the promise having
been made that she would receive a
copy of the tape.

M: A little bit scary to lose pieces of
what's going on.

Joining her perception.

V: Right. And I was afraid this guy was doing that and so I wasn't very successful because I think that I was fighting.

M: Was that here in San Diego?

V: Yes.

M: Recently?

V: About a year ago, year and a half ago.

M: Do you remember specifically what it was he was saying or what it was he was doing that you were finding difficult to relate to?

Here I am asking for the details of what went on so that I could be sure to do things differently.

V: I think that it was just the general . . .

M: The atmosphere of what was happening?

V: It was something general about him that didn't listen. There was something general about not letting me record, like what are you hiding? I wasn't trusting that. Not explaining things to me. I have to be super-explained to and if you explain something to me fourteen times and I don't understand it, then I'll ask you again and if you don't explain it to me sixteen times then, I mean sometimes it takes a while to soak in but I've got to have that information in order to process whatever I process. And he was getting annoyed with me that I was asking the same kind of questions over and over and I don't know, I went for a long time. I went

Again, the emphasis is made on needing to be heard.

Vicki lets me know that she values understanding and participation. To not utilize these values—that is, to expect her to just follow directions blindly—would undoubtedly meet with her resistance. As is generally true, much of the "resistance" of therapy arises from the clinician's inability to recognize and utilize the client's values and capabilities. Thus, resistance can be defined as interpersonal as well as intrapersonal.

for five to six months before I finally said "This is a waste of my money and your time and I don't think we're getting anywhere." It was also interlinked with the biofeedback and he was putting these things on my forehead and I was having so much pain in other places in my body, I didn't understand why it was on my forehead. Sure, there was a good reason for that but I didn't understand it. He wouldn't explain it to me. Also he was into—he got off the track and he was into a lot of regression. Now, I'm into regression and once he found out that I was into that, then that was his focus and it wasn't my focus. I would like to have done that as a side line, kind of an interest area of my very own, but not for the therapeutic thing that I was trying to get at at the moment. Once he found out that I had that interest, then the whole thing switched to that area and I couldn't get him back over here to the therapeutic kind of thing. So I thought that he was using me, that he was doing it for his own little bag because he found somebody that would allow him to do regressive therapy. My spiritual interests—a lot of my spiritual interests are in reincarnation and he was doing some previous lifetime kind of regression with me which is very fascinating and very interesting and I'm into it, totally into it, but at that moment in time it wasn't what I wanted to pay him to do. And he got stuck there so . . . It may have been my fault.

M: I think it's a valid concern to want the work to be along the lines of what

Whether these aspects of her treatment are "true" is less relevant than the fact that this is how she incorporated the experiences into her memory. If true, here is another example of a clinician not listening to his or her client, fueling Vicki's obviously strong need to be heard. The client is the source of information. She knows her internal world better than anyone else ever will.

Her belief in reincarnation is noted as a possible association to use later.

Vicki acknowledges she may not have been entirely a helpless victim.

Validating she is entitled to get what she wants, providing assurance of that in her interaction with me.

your needs are instead of what his interests are.

V: At the time my financial situation is kind of balancing and I felt like I had to spend my money where the most benefit was to be had. You can spend so much money on fun and games . . .

M: But the work's got to be done sooner or later. Have you talked with Lillian at all about what I do? What you could expect here? What the possibilities were?

Attempting to have Vicki define her expectations of me, first by asking about the information accompanying the referral by Lillian.

V: Uh-uh.

She asserts that Lillian said little to her about me.

M: Lillian and I work together at the university. That's how we know each other.

Helping her understand my connection to Lillian, referencing her positive association to Lillian and the university—both positive forces in her life.

V: Yeah, she told me that.

M: And I work a lot with hypnosis and . . .

V: The reason I was interested is that I've been asking around about hypnosis and everybody that it seemed like I talked to said they had studied under you and she came up with you and I thought that was just a greater idea than coming to somebody that studied under you. Go right to the source. I haven't got time to fool around.

Vicki shares with me that she has had exposure to my reputation from multiple sources.

The issue of "time" is reiterated.

M: Makes sense to me. Well, certainly one of the things that's so fascinating about the mind is its ability to control what goes on in the body the way that you were describing earlier.

Amplifying her awareness for her beliefs about the mind-body relationship, and referencing the previous discussion of absorption and distraction as a natural means of pain

The ability to focus on discomfort or focus on other things and lose track of discomfort is one of the capabilities and it seems to me that part of what you're asking for, at least, is to be able to develop a way to be able to experience yourself more comfortably, more naturally.

reduction within the scope of her experience.

We can do that. The kinds of guided imagery things that you've been doing with Lillian are hypnotic procedures. I don't know if she's ever described them that way before but it's a form of hypnosis.

As a preliminary to formal induction, I am feeding back to Vicki what she has expressed an ability to do, a desire to do, and identifying a mechanism to do it.

Positive expectancy.

Visual imagery is one form of hypnosis and it involves, obviously, images and so it's very much a visual kind of process. Some people are real visual. They can form . . .

Reframing her previous successes as based in hypnosis, directly relating them to our work, thus amplifying the expectation of being able to succeed with me.
Reframing her known methods of comfort as hypnotic, and assessing her true ability to visualize, since so much of her spontaneous speech would indicate a kinesthetic primary representational system.

V: I don't consider myself a real visual person.

She validates my doubt that her visual ability is her most well developed one.

M: Would you consider yourself more of a feeling kind of person?

V: Feelings? Yes. And even a little more auditory than visual. I get into the imagery. I think it's because I want to so much but I do find that feelings are the number one and maybe auditory number two.

M: And so even though visual imagery is not first on the list you've still been able to make use of it.

Amplifying for her that her motivation really does enhance her ability.

V: Oh, I want to so much. Normally, visual things haven't worked for me too much in the past, so I was surprised that this is, I'm getting into this so much but it's not my best mode I don't think.

M: Are there times during the day that you are comfortable?

I am looking for the exceptions to her painful times in order to amplify them.

V: They vary a lot. You know, some days I do okay—the radiation therapy makes you very, very, very exhausted. It takes, drains all your energy. So I've gotten to the point now where I say "Okay, I can do my treatments and one other thing." Then I spend the rest of the time resting. My doctor said next week therapy, no more. Just go home and go to bed. I try to keep my mind okay, that's not the way I want to do it. I've got to be able to function and do things, but it's only going to be another week. Sometimes that's hard to remember.

Vicki's hope rests on having one difficult week followed by periods of normal activity.

Sometimes, for a while it was like I was being very sick in the morning and then in the evening I was feeling better, and then it got where I felt great in the morning and then I felt sick. So it kind of starting to switch around a lot.

She does not have awareness for any predictable pattern of good or bad times. Given her desire for control, the unpredictable nature of time relative to her illness sensitizes her even more to time-related suggestions.

M: There's no set pattern to it?

Double-checking for the possibility of relevant patterns.

V: Right. So I'm kind of just going with it. Just kind of going with it. I have one more week—it's hard for me to remember that the sickness, the really—the day before yesterday morning my daughter stayed all night with me. I'm not allowed to stay alone anymore, at night. And now they've decided even in the day I'm not supposed to be alone because of the threat of seizures. But most of the time I feel good. Well, the morning before yesterday, my daughter got up and went to work and I thought I'd be fine until my aunt came to help me take a shower and take me to my treatment, and I could get my bowl of cereal which I was going to have and everything went to hell. I got up, I didn't make it to the bathroom in time. I messed myself and I started throwing up and I threw up all over the house and I got the bowl of cereal and I dumped it on the floor and pretty soon I just found myself sitting in the middle of the floor, saying "I'd rather be dead." And when you get that kind of moment, when things come just (*raspberry*), it's so hard to grab hold of that string that says "It's the treatments. In a week it's going to get better; you're going to feel better. It's not going to go like this for the rest of the time." There are going to be good days and there's going to be productive days, so you really have to grab hold of that and sometimes it's hard to hold onto but it doesn't usually go away for too awfully long. I have a pretty good grip on it.

M: It sure sounds that way to me. Well, I've been asking you all kinds of questions. I wonder if you have any for me.

V: I don't know. I can't think right now.

Her ability to see the situation as unstable (changeable) is obviously vital to her ability to maintain.

Validating her positive view of her ability to manage.

The basic framing of our work has already been established, rapport is excellent, and she has been sufficiently heard.

The Hypnosis Session

M: Well, then let me describe a little bit of what I'd like to be able to do. Having worked with imagery before, and having worked with meditation and the different kinds of relaxation processes, you know what it's like to be able to close your eyes, go inside, have different kinds of experiences internally. Basically I'm going to talk about different ideas, different possibilities. There isn't really anything that you have to do, Vicki. All I really want you to do is give yourself the opportunity to experience whatever it occurs to you to experience. I'm going to be talking about different possibilities, different potentials, and it's really going to be for you to take what makes sense to you, leave behind what doesn't make sense to you, and that's about it. Different ideas. But you'll hear everything, know everything, everything will be real clear for you, because that's what you're looking for, that kind of clarity in your thinking, that kind of clarity in your perception. But certainly one of the things that will become real clear to you is how you can use your own thoughts to create sensations in yourself that you find real comfortable, other kinds of sensations that you feel real interesting, and it will be for you to pick and choose what you want to experience.

If you feel like you're ready to, arrange yourself in a position that's comfortable.

Assuming a more active position to begin directing the course of the remainder of the session. Referencing the methods she knows and likes and utilizing parts of them to begin building the response set necessary for hypnotic induction and utilization.

Defining my role as someone simply offering possibilities, emphasizing her control in being able to choose what she does and does not take in. Giving her the freedom to experience herself in whatever way occurs to her, rather than imposing any specific demand on her.

Reassuring her she will not be unaware of what transpires, given her negative associations to amnesia.

Reassuring her that she will have the mental clarity she defined as a primary goal of treatment.

Reaffirming her ability to maintain control of the interaction.

V: I have a hard time to sit up straight and put both feet on the floor. Harold says everything works better that way. So I've been trying it that way.

Vicki presents a previous learning that is rigid, unnecessary, and worst of all, inhibits her ability to respond well.

M: You can sit any way you want to. In all my years of study I have yet to find the one right way to sit, so just whatever is most comfortable for you.

Again she is given permission to be in control and choose what is best for her. If I give her that control, then who is in control?

V: I've been having, I think the next place that's going to show up is in my feet and legs because I've been having a lot of pain in my feet and legs. I'm kind of suspicious of that area.

She informs me that her legs are currently in pain and that she has negative expectations for them.

M: (*Shifting positions*) Are you comfortable?

Indirect suggestion to get comfortable.

V: Except that I just had this huge big Mexican dinner and I think the beans are going to get me. My digestive—I have a little bit of heartburn.

Another somatic sensation to take into account.

M: Let's make that one of the sensations that we work with.

Begin by taking in a few relaxing breaths . . . and when you feel like you're ready to, Vicki, you can just . . . let your eyes close . . . so that you can go inside for a little while . . . That's right. And certainly you know from previous experience how you can relax . . . what kinds of things that you like to experience that you find the most soothing . . . what kinds of experience make the most sense to you . . . and as you pointed out, there isn't anyone who knows you the way that you do . . . so is there anybody that's in a more comforta-

Permissive suggestion for eye closure.

Building an internal focus.

Accessing previous hypnotic experiences.

Accepting her need to be the authority over herself.

ble position to know what's right for you, to know what's good for you? . . . If you want to . . . you can . . . *listen very carefully to the things that I talk about,* but you really don't need to, Vicki . . . You can allow yourself . . . that's right . . . the exquisite luxury of letting your mind travel or relax . . . It can do a lot or it can do nothing . . . It can listen and it can not listen . . . But you can certainly allow yourself the experience of being very comfortable within yourself . . . and certainly you know from previous experiences . . . that sometimes *you can get so absorbed* in interesting possibilities . . . it doesn't really matter whether it's white lights or deep breathing . . . or an interesting voice, or soothing sensation . . . because as someone who's been studying psychology . . . you certainly know enough about the complexity of the mind, the complexity of physiology . . . to know that there is an automatic sort of pattern . . . that allows for the rhythmic rise and fall of breathing . . . the kind of balance of each breath in and each breath out . . . and because the mind is so complex, it's really convenient, really a *comfort* to know that while the conscious mind tends to notice whatever captures its attention for the moment . . . that there's a *deeper* part of you that can really *experience a surprising level of relaxation and comfort* . . . It's really not unlike having the rest of the world drift for a while . . . It's there but it's not there . . . It's here but it's there . . . It's right here, close by, and it's so far off in the distance . . . and to be able to

Utilizing her desire to be the authority on her own experience. Embedded command for attentiveness.

Permissive suggestion for dissociation.

Covering all possibilities.

Permissive suggestion for comfort. Accessing previous hypnotic experiences.
Embedded suggestion for absorption.

Encouraging flexibility in that there is a variety of ways to experience hypnosis meaningfully.

Utilizing her interest in psychology and her newly enhanced self-image derived from her education.

Suggesting an amplification for an appreciation of unconscious control mechanisms.

Marking the word "comfort."

Marking the word "deeper."

Embedded commands.

Introducing spatial dissociation—separating specific locations in space.

get absorbed in the interesting sensations of what it feels like to have a watch on your wrist . . . or a necklace around your neck . . . or the feel of the chair . . . each an interesting sensation in its own right . . . Close . . . Distant . . . And how far away is far enough? And I really don't know which sensations are the most soothing . . . because that varies so much from individual to individual . . .

Embedded command while reframing sensations as "interesting." External kinesthetic focal points to shift away from internal kinesthetic focal points to begin facilitating pain relief. Dissociation of sensation suggestions.

Some people really enjoy the sensation of looking at an unusual cloud that can seem so out of place against a blue sky . . . Some really enjoy the sensation of a very well-written piece of music that has just the right rhythm, just the right blend of instruments . . . And if you've ever had the experience of a particularly enjoyable melody . . . that sort of floats through your mind . . . and you catch yourself humming that song . . . or all of a sudden realizing that you're singing that song and you really don't know why that song seems so important . . . Sometimes it's a corny song; sometimes it's a real favorite . . . And it's interesting how some lyrics remain unforgettable . . . and I bet you know what the eighth word in the national anthem is . . . But when you take time to . . . *sit quietly* . . . and you experience the sensation of a particularly enjoyable and soothing voice that might be your own as you talk to yourself . . . It might be mine as you listen . . . I really don't know . . . All I know is you have a conscious mind that can be very aware of the things that seem the

Encouraging redefining sensations in her awareness as "soothing" while utilizing her belief in the uniqueness of each person.

Visual suggestion, distracting from kinesthetic awareness.

Auditory suggestion, distracting from kinesthetic awareness.

Amplifying auditory absorption.

Unconscious involvement.

Memory can remain intact.

Preoccupying her on an auditory level with a distracting reference. Auditory focus.

Auditory focus, soothing internal and external dialogue.

Reassuring her that she can be as aware as she needs or wants to be.

most important . . . Isn't it interesting how something can seem so important at one time and seem so unimportant at another time? . . . And time . . . how a minute can seem like an hour . . . how a day can be an interesting one to experience . . . When you think about all the things you've accumulated, it really reminded me of what basements are for and what attics are for . . . Old issues of *National Geographic,* out-dated *Time* magazines, and a string here, marble there, and isn't it interesting . . . because I was working with a young boy not long ago who taught me a very important lesson as sometimes only kids can . . .

And it was a lesson that I really think has a wider spread value than what I might even understand now . . . because it's a little boy who's lived here in San Diego all of his life, all eight years of it . . . And kids being what kids are, he really has a very difficult time understanding that there are other places to live . . . But when he was told that he was going to be moving soon he really didn't understand that things were going to be a little different . . . He wanted to take his entire house and he wanted to take his school and all of his friends and teachers and that part was the easy part . . . The hard part came when his mother told him "You're really going to have to clean out your drawers and closet. You're not going to want to take all that junk with you." And how do you decide which baseball cards to throw away or give away? That's really interesting be-

A truism regarding the inevitability of change.

Time distortion, expansion.

Referencing her issue of "letting go" by addressing the subject of accumulating things.

A "time" reference of outdated, no longer relevant things.

Introducing a metaphor on the general theme of "letting go."
Referencing children as a source of learning, perhaps establishing a new association to her own children.
Learnings can increase in value over time.

The egocentricity of a child's thinking is amplified to encourage sensitive handling of her children.

The absurdity of "wanting to take it all with you," reframing "holding on" as undesirable.

Easy and hard parts, feeding back her framing of experience in those terms.

Indirect suggestion to "let go."

On re-evaluation, "letting go" was

cause what he discovered was that all these things that seemed so important, weren't important anymore . . . The favorite toy that he had when he was three wasn't much fun when he was eight . . . There aren't a lot of eight-year-olds I know that enjoy little Peg Boards and rattles . . . And it gave him an incredible sense of accomplishment, a powerful recognition of how much he had grown, that he had outgrown all these things, and it was an uplifting experience for him to discover that being a little older and a little wiser allowed for different possibilities now . . . And I really don't know how, I really don't know why, but then again, eight-year-old boys really have mysterious ways . . . But going through the drawers and closets showed him how much he'd grown and changed without even trying . . . and what it really meant to him was that he could move on comfortably, comfortably, and there might be a . . . deeper . . . meaning. Sometimes it's hard to know; sometimes it really pays to listen at a deeper level . . . And you know that . . .

easy because what mattered once didn't matter anymore.

Amplifying a positive feeling for "letting go," reframing it as clear evidence of growth.

Incorporating Vicki's head lifting.

Reinforcing that change in the absence of insight is possible.

Marking.
Marking.

Validating her knowledge.

And I wonder whether you've noticed that your breathing has changed . . . how much effort it takes to move . . . how absorbed all of you can be in the comfortable experience of right now . . . And now becomes later, and later you really can be comfortable . . . And one of the most interesting dimensions of experiencing deep comfort . . . is that sensations seem different because there is a disorienting effect when you get so

Ratifying hypnosis through evidence of a visible physical change. Indirect suggestion for catalepsy.

Time distortion, extending comfort into the future.

Physical disorientation, preliminary

comfortable . . . it becomes hard to know which side is more relaxed. . . . Is it your left side or is it your right side? . . . and if your left side drifts off comfortably . . . then which side is left? And if it's your front, then do we really know if it's the front of your back that's comfortable or the back of your front? . . . And it's very difficult to know whether it's your top half or the bottom half, or the middle half of the back or the front half that's the most comfortable. . . . That's right. And I knew one person who was exceptionally skilled at being able to experience this part of the body as very comfortably distinct from that part of their body which seemed disconnected over there, even though they had the peculiar feeling that there was something here that they just weren't really in touch with . . . But I know this much . . . that when you take in a breath . . . and when your mind is curious . . . and you're really not sure which part's here and which part's there . . . and which part's left or right, and you have the right to know what's left . . . it can take a different turn for the better . . . and that's something that you really can be clear about. . . . But there's something that you might really want to know about the sensation of comfort that grows more profound moment by moment . . . And what's so interesting is that your legs haven't moved and your arms haven't moved and you know and I know that you could move them if you could think of a good reason to . . . but how much more enjoyable to experience the

to a confusion technique.
Associating comfort to disorientation.

Left/right disorientation, dissociation.

Front/back disorientation, dissociation.

Top/bottom disorientation, dissociation.

Metaphor for physical dissociation.

Embedded command for dissociation and comfort.

Diminished kinesthetic awareness.

Uncertainty and dissociation.

Uncertain perceptions about her body but mentally clear there is an improvement.

Increased comfort.

Catalepsy is evident and is fed back to her, amplifying it.

Reaffirming she is in control of the experience.

luxury of a very relaxed body . . . a very comfortable experience of being here, being fully here mentally, of being over there physically . . That's right . . . And without disturbing your relaxation . . . you might find it a particularly interesting experience to have your throat and voice so comfortable and relaxed that you could describe to me what you're experiencing, and why not verbalize what you're aware of right now, Vicki?

Suggestions for mental and physical dissociation.

Protective suggestions to remain comfortable preceding the suggestion to speak.
Throat comfort, later extended to next week (when she anticipated it being painful).

Suggestion to verbalize while remaining in hypnosis.

V: Heartburn is gone.

M: You can say that again.

I didn't hear what she'd said, and so I suggested she repeat it.

V: My heartburn is gone.

M: Good. Your body's comfortable.

Reinforcing her experience of comfort.

V: It feels soft.

M: Is it a good experience?

Amplifying its positive value.

V: Yes.

M: Good. It's an interesting experience, isn't it? To have your body in trance . . . To have your mind comfortable . . . And how far away is your body from where you are?

Reinforcing the dissociation of mind and body.

Presupposition of having accomplished the dissociation.

V: Not far.

M: Just close enough for when you need it . . . That's right. And just far enough to really be comfortable . . . And what an interesting experience to know that you can be so comfortable . . . Can you describe what it feels like to be just far enough away from your body to really be comfortable?

Framing her response as a good one.

Reframing comfort as "interesting," associating comfort to even mild mental experiences.
Questioning to deepen the experience of dissociation.

V: Nice. Safe.

M: Good . . . That's right . . . That's
right . . . It's that nice, safe, comfortable feeling that you really can memorize in very intense, vivid
detail . . . Very comfortable . . . And
what your unconscious mind might
really want to know is that you can
be so comfortable whenever you
want to be . . . And it's interesting,
very interesting . . . how the most everyday experiences can be the most
profound reminders of what it's like
to have a mind here and a body
there . . . what it's like to notice a
cloud . . . or a moving van . . . or an
eight-year-old boy . . . or hands that
rest comfortably in a lap of
luxury . . . and you really never
know . . . because sometimes it's
looking at your watch that reminds
you that *it's time to be comfortable* . . .
Sometimes it's kicking off your shoes
to remember that you're two feet
ahead of yourself when you're here
and there comfortably. . . . Sometimes it's giving yourself a hand, in
the most simple and elegant of
ways . . . I really don't know . . . I
know one individual who tends
to . . . *eat with a real gusto* . . . because
she really likes the strong sensations
of being well-fed . . . and somehow
she has it in her mind that every time
she opens the refrigerator door, she
has that cool comfort . . . and the
little light goes on . . . and I don't
know what it is about white
lights . . . and I really don't know
what it is about food . . . but the
interesting thing is that it really
works for her. . . . And she really can

Feeding back her terms for the experience.
Amplifying a clear memory of the
experience of comfort to use as a later
reference point.
Affirming the ability is hers and that
it can be applied at later times of her
choosing.
Associating the experience of comfort to everyday experiences ("an-
choring").
Dissociation of the mind and body
as a vehicle for everyday comfort.
Everyday cues referencing the hypnotic process and recreating comfort.
Reinforcing that just sitting as she is,
with her hands in her lap, she can be
comfortable.
Associating time–and the everyday
experience of looking at her watch–
to comfort.
Embedded suggestion.
Associating taking off her shoes to
the experience of dissociation.
Self-help as a means of obtaining
comfort.

Metaphor for appetite enhancement.
Embedded command.

Positive association to eating.

Associating comfort and appetite to
opening the refrigerator.
Utilizing her "white light" association for comfort.

Embedded command, association of
comfort to specific places.

be comfortable standing up in a kitchen, and sitting down in a . . . *living* . . . room, and napping and talking seem to really regenerate the feelings of comfort . . . but I don't think that I need to remind you that you can relax . . . that you can be safe and comfortable anywhere. After all . . . you're here with me and you can hear with me . . . and you can hear with you . . . and you can hear you talking to yourself . . . in the strangest of places you can hear you, soothing, comforting, distancing . . . keeping close the feelings of comfort . . . and everything else can fade into the distance . . . into the distance, like baseball cards and string . . . And there really is no reason that I'm aware of to limit one's thinking to believe that a yard sale has to be in a yard, when you can have one inside, as many times a day as you'd like to . . . And you can be a yard which is three feet away from yourself . . . being here but three feet over there . . . experiencing comfort now and later . . . front and back . . . top and bottom . . . left and right . . . and the right to comfort is what's left. . . . And that's what I'd really like you to know . . . and why not look ahead to a little bit later . . . or a lot later . . . or something in between a little and a lot . . . and as you look forward, can you see how comfortable you are? . . . (*Nods*) . . . Good. . . . And you know that a week passes quickly . . . and you know that a week passes slowly . . . depending on point of view . . . and since it's you and your point of view . . . you might as well know that

Marking.

Extending comfort through all routine activities.
Extending comfort to *any* context.

Internal dialogue can be comforting and meaningful, regardless of where she finds herself.

Amplifying comfort, distancing anything else.
Referencing and amplifying "letting go" what is no longer necessary.
Referencing her idea of a yard sale as a vehicle for getting rid of what she no longer needs, including internal feelings or thoughts she finds distressing.
Dissociation.

Associating comfort to the previous disorientation and dissociation suggestions.

Future orientation (post-hypnotic suggestions) to include comfort.

Time distortion, either expansion or contraction as she wishes.

it's fully up to you . . . to have a fast
day and a slow day depending on *your*
choice . . . because twenty-four hours,
seven days in a row, or sixteen hours,
ten days in a row, or thirteen hours,
thirteen days in a row, really don't
matter, but when it's two weeks
of . . . *feeling so strongly* . . . about how
time has been well used, . . . you really can look back when you're looking ahead at yourself looking
back . . . feeling   good . . . and
safe . . . and comfortable . . . And
that's a *strong feeling* to hold on to,
isn't it? (*Nods*) . . . Good . . . And
since you can look forward to that
experience of comfort, why not have
that be the feeling that you hold onto
tightly? . . . When I ask you to reorient in just a moment . . . the one
thing that I really want you to know
is that you have done marvelously
. . . and why not enjoy the sense of
pride in discovering that *you can use
your head to be comfortable,* and you can
use your body to *alter sensation, comfortably* . . . in the way that you'd like
to . . . *and let that be the guiding memory
and experience for this experience of comfort that you really can hold onto–here,
there and everywhere that you go* . . . and
when you know that you can do
that . . . and when you feel the
strength and comfort that you can do
that . . . that's when you can begin to
slowly reorient yourself mentally . . .
but you may want to keep the physical disorientation of being here and
being there . . . using your body but
letting it come close and drift away
as you see fit . . . So take whatever

Time expansion through confusion.

Embedded suggestion.

Time disorientation; comfort embedded throughout.

A suggestion for strength.

Posthypnotic suggestion for later
comfort, extending the current experience into later contexts.
Anticipation signal regarding disengagement.

Reinforcing her having succeeded in
this context.
Reinforcing that she has successfully
done what she set out to do. Redefining her relationship to her body.

Establishing success as the memorable association to this experience.

Maintaining comfort and generaliz-
ing it to the rest of her life.
Integrating the learnings and new associations.

Suggesting the possibility of maintaining the dissociation as a means
for remaining comfortable.

time you'd like to, Vicki, to process your experience and feelings, and then when you feel like you're ready to and when you want to . . . that's when you can bring back every comfortable sensation . . . for today, and tomorrow, and all your tomorrows that become todays. And when you're ready to, you can let your eyes open. (Pause). You did great!

Suggesting obtaining closure on the experience before disengaging.

Maintaining comfort post-hypnosis. Future comfort.

Permissive disengagement.

V: (Difficulty opening her eyes). It's bright. (*Closes her eyes again.*)

M: Take a moment. No need to reorient fully . . . just yet. That's right . . . Discover each comfortable sensation.

V: (Long pause before opening her eyes and moving). I like that.

M: Good. You sat just right!

Validating her responses and posture humorously.

V: I didn't even know I was sitting.

Confirmation of the extent of her physical dissociation.

M: It's nice not to know, isn't it?

Reframing uncertainty as pleasant.

V: Um-hum. The part that I—something that I liked very much that I never thought of before was "time." Some days do go fast, and some days go slow. It never entered my mind that I could have some control over that, so that's something new to think about. I liked that part.

The issue of "time" was so central to her, it's little surprise that she latched onto a mechanism to control her perception of it.

M: How are you feeling?

V: I liked that a lot. I got very much in touch with being over there and being over here. I hope I don't forget.

Confirmation of her positive regard for the session, and her experience of physical dissociation. She expresses concern for her memory of the session.

M: You're going to have a tape of this that I'm going to give you right now and then as you requested I'll be happy to make a copy of the video and then if you'd like I could either mail it to you or maybe we'll get together again sometime and give it to you then. But you'll have an audio-tape right now and a videotape a little bit later, so that way . . . you'll always have a reminder.

Immediate reassurance that she has full and ready access to the experience via her memory as well as the tape of the session.

V: It was a very nice experience.

Embedded suggestion, referencing all the posthypnotic suggestions given throughout the session.

M: Good. Would you be willing to . . .

V: Yes!!

She cut me off to quickly agree to whatever I would ask of her! I think that is fairly good evidence for a high level of rapport!

M: . . . answer some questions? (*Turning to class*) Are there any questions? (*To class*) You can come out of trance now!

V: (*Surprise*) Does it really affect everybody, really?

M: (*Laughs*) They pretend that it doesn't, but I know better!

Playful closure to the session.

V: I don't know how it could not.

Orienting to the others and beginning to engage with them.

The session concludes with Vicki responding to specific questions about her experience during the hypnosis session as well as her remarkable personal history. After about 15 minutes of questions, she left. We parted most amiably.

FOLLOW-UP AND FINAL COMMENTS

Sadly, Vicki passed away less than eight weeks later. I never had the chance to see her again. I received a warm thank-you note from her a few days after our session, and spoke to her once on the phone for some follow-up. She reported that she was using the audiotape of our session that I had provided, and found it very helpful. She was able to make use of the physical dissociation and time distortion techniques, which helped her cope with the most recent round of radiation she was receiving. She reported feeling pleased she was managing her daily regimens without pain medications. She managed to function reasonably well for a short while after our meeting, but after just a few weeks her illness became too severe to self-manage.

After Vicki left, the group of clinicians in attendance was noticeably quiet. It took us all awhile to open up and process the session, each of us dealing with our own vulnerable feelings about encountering a remarkable woman so courageously facing death, as well as our hurt feelings about how badly some clinicians had treated her. After so much pain in her life, Vicki was in the process of first discovering her uniqueness and strength, while evolving her first real vision of what she had the potential to become. How cruel that just as Vicki was getting her life together, her life was lost. Yet, you can recall her saying that even though at first she was sad her dreams wouldn't happen, she could feel good discovering some of her own potential. That attitude was nothing short of remarkable. Vicki was easy to admire, and I was deeply saddened by her death.

I cannot imagine a more dramatic way to get across the message to helping professionals to "listen to your client" than to be exposed to Vicki. She had so much to say, but her voice was drowned out by the labels some people gave her. *Too many clinicians seemed to forget that we treat people, not labels.*

Ironically, Vicki, who desperately wanted to be heard by her doctors, has been listened to by more doctors and other health professionals now, through my clinical trainings, than she could have ever imagined. She has inspired them, chastised them, and challenged them to be better clinicians. What an extraordinary gift she has given all of us.

21

When People Respond in Non-Ideal Ways

By now you have most likely had the experience of performing hypnotic inductions, facilitating hypnotic phenomena, and structuring and delivering suggestions to other people during hypnosis that were meant to be helpful to them. As you have no doubt discovered from your direct experience, peoples' responses to your hypnotic processes can range from minimal to dramatic. You can now better appreciate why assessing hypnotizability has been the subject of serious inquiry as researchers and clinicians attempt to understand why people differ so substantially in their abilities to respond. Hypnosis as a vehicle for delineating individual differences is a very active and interesting domain of research into the areas of human personality and cognition.

The main focus of this chapter, though, is addressing these two questions: How shall we interpret either a lack of responsiveness to hypnotic suggestions (i.e., an inability to manifest a particular suggested hypnotic phenomenon or an inability to integrate and apply a suggested resolution to a problem) or, worse, a negative response? And, how might we effectively respond to those individuals who are not particularly responsive to our hypnotic procedures?

Clinicians' responses to minimal or negative responses to their hypnotic suggestions have ranged from labeling unresponsive clients "resistant" to labeling the clinicians inept (or worse). These extreme views reflect interesting attributions (i.e., explanations) that reveal a pattern called "attributional style," a person's characteristic way of explaining the meaning of life events (Seligman, 1989; Yapko, 1992). An *internal* attribution is one that suggests the reason something happened the way that it did is somehow "because of me." An *external* attribution says, in essence, that it happened the way it did "because of the other person" or "because of the circumstances."

In the realms of hypnosis and psychotherapy, the attributions that clinicians make for unsuccessful hypnosis sessions or therapies tend to be external, that is, it was the client's fault. Clinicians routinely say things like, "The person wasn't ready for change," "The person was getting too many secondary gains," "The person was too threatened by the therapy," and the ever-popular, especially in hypnosis, "The client isn't hypnotizable," or, "The client is resistant." Might any of these external attributions for a lack of client responsiveness be true at times? Yes. But, might they also be blaming the client unfairly at times for what may be a limitation in the clinician's approach? Yes. I strongly encourage clinicians to recognize, *before* they reflexively declare a client resistant, that they may have played a bigger role in the client's responses than they at first realized. *When there are two people (or more) in an interaction, there is a shared responsibility for the outcome.* This point is true enough to discourage entirely internal attributions as well, that is, "It's totally my fault the person reacted that way."

RESISTANCE IN HYPNOSIS

The literature pertaining to clinical hypnosis has generally had quite a lot to say about the issue of client resistance. Historically, resistance was considered to be a manifestation of the client's defenses for coping with sensitive or unresolved intrapsychic conflicts, and thus perceived as a psychological vulnerability of the client's (Greenleaf, 2001). "Proper" treatment was a confrontive inquiry about the appearance of the resistance, first acknowledging it, next attempting to uncover its origin and function, and then collaborating on its resolution. Weitzenhoffer summarized this viewpoint succinctly when he wrote, "*Unconscious* resistance . . . always has its source in the psychodynamics of the subject, and overcoming or circumventing it is frequently dependent upon understanding these psychodynamics and acting accordingly . . . At a conscious level, he may want hypnosis, but may be very much threatened by it at an unconscious level" (2000, pp. 204–5).

From this perspective, resistance was always the client's problem. When it interfered with the progress of therapy, as it inevitably did, the client was blamed as the saboteur. Accusations and interpretations were thrust at the client who obviously "really didn't want to change," or perhaps was "too resistant to succeed."

Resistance can be described, for all intents and purposes, as a force that works against the aims of therapy. Resistance has long been recognized as an integral and unavoidable component of the therapeutic process, and virtually every therapeutic approach I am aware of has roughly equivalent recognitions of its existence. Only the rationale for its presence and the techniques for its acknowledgment and treatment differ from approach to approach.

Describing resistance as a force that works against the aims of therapy doesn't place blame on either the clinician or client. Rather than view people who come in voluntarily (dealing with persons in treatment involuntarily differs in some ways) for help as not really wanting help when we try things that don't work very well, it seems much more practical to view resistance as a communication from the client about his or her limitations in relating to the world (of which the clinician is obviously a part). *In other words, resistance isn't a fixed property of the client, but rather can be viewed as a dynamic communication indicating the limits of what the client can and cannot do.* Rather than blame the client, the communication can be accepted as a valid indication of the person's experience of him- or herself (Zeig, 1980).

Placing this general perspective in the context of doing clinical hypnosis, resistance is not necessarily an indication of unconscious sabotage on the part of the client. It is frequently the case that the client is simply making a choice at some level not to respond in the desired way to suggestions for any of a variety of other reasons, each of which has a common denominator: *The suggestion simply does not fit with the person's experience, and, in fact, may even contradict it.* Resistance may be viewed as an *inter*personal statement that says that whatever therapeutic strategies and maneuvers are being performed are not acceptable at some level(s) to the client.

Resistance is a real force to reckon with in treatment, and can be tied to one or both of the two main areas of treatment: resistance to hypnosis, and/or resistance to therapeutic progress.

RESISTANCE TO HYPNOSIS

Undesirable responses to hypnosis can be manifested in a variety of ways. The client may actively or passively refuse to go into hypnosis, or may enter hypnosis but refuse to respond to the suggestions of the clinician. Examples of potentially contrary behaviors include, but are not limited to: fidgeting, smiling, laughing, crying, interrupting, spontaneous disengagements, polar (opposite) responses, over-cooperation, coughing, and direct or passive-aggressive hostility aimed at the clinician (Weitzenhoffer, 2000). Responses such as these are not necessarily resistant. They may be idiosyncratic responses that occur without interfering with the course of treatment (Gilligan, 1987).

Origins of resistance to hypnosis can be numerous. One of the most common is the fear of what will happen during hypnosis. If the client is misinformed about the nature of the hypnotic experience, he or she may fear it. All the misconceptions discussed in detail in chapter 2 may be all that someone knows about hypnosis. If you thought you might divulge sensitive information, be coerced into doing things against your will, or be controlled by someone you really don't know much about, would *you* want to be hypnotized?

Resistance to hypnosis may also arise because of past failures associated with it, either from personal experience or the experience of credible others. Furthermore, resistance may also arise from negative feelings toward the clinician (thus highlighting the value of rapport), and from contextual variables such as the immediate environment, the client's mood, health, and even the weather (e.g., sinus headaches triggered by weather conditions).

Some of the resistance to hypnosis, however, is attributable to the quality of the clinician's suggestions, specifically how well they match the client's experience (Zeig & Rennick, 1991). If I give a client a suggestion to feel his or her muscles relaxing, and he or she isn't experiencing that sensation, then my suggestion does not fit with his or her experience and is easily rejected. To impose arbitrary suggestions on a client that he or she experience something you want him or her to experience (e.g., arm levitation) that has little relationship to what he or she is experiencing or wants to experience is a legitimate basis for him or her choosing not to follow your suggestion. Furthermore, your client may be in so comfortable a state of mind and body that your suggestions for specific responses, simple as they may seem, are too much a strain for him or her. Even beyond that, your client may be giving him- or herself suggestions that are more meaningful than yours! Why shouldn't the client be free to have that experience without being deemed "resistant"?

Hypnosis increases, rather than descreases, the range of a person's control. Suggestions that don't fit well, by mismatching experience or by placing too much demand on the person, can be and usually are rejected. *A clinician can offer possibilities to the client, and can respond respectfully to the choices the client makes.* To expect unquestioning obedience on the part of the client is wholly inappropriate in the clinical context, where collaboration in the service of therapeutic goals is vital.

RESISTANCE TO THERAPEUTIC PROGRESS

Resistance to the aims of therapy has an extensive overlap with the dynamics of resistance to hypnosis. Such resistance may be manifested by such contrary behaviors as appointments being missed, cancelled, or arrived at tardily. Assigned tasks ("homework") not being carried out, setting up a "power struggle" with the therapist for control of the relationship, clock-watching, frequent interrupting, terminating treatment prematurely, over-cooperation, inappropriate gift-giving, and requests for special favors may be further evidence of treatment blocks.

Origins of resistance to the aims of treatment can be numerous. Blocks may arise because of the client's intrapsychic conflicts, that is, ambivalences, that have been described in detail in analytic writings, particularly in the realm of object-relations theory. They may arise because of the fear of change, since for many people change is considered a risky, scary process of giving up the known for the uncertainty of the unknown. Small changes can gradually give rise to big changes in one's life, and for many that is a frightening prospect. The reluctance to let go of the old, albeit dysfunctional, but familiar is a classic sign of resistance.

For this reason, the clinician, in order to intervene successfully, needs to understand the impact of the client's symptom(s) on his or her world. Symptoms can be viewed as a metaphor, or symbol, of the person's experience. They reflect limitations the person is experiencing in relating flexibly to the world around him or her. And, symptoms have consequences: They affect the client's self-image, social network, behavioral possibilities, emotional realm, physiology, and spiritual makeup. Sometimes these consequences are deeply connected to the symptom's reason for being, and sometimes they're merely fallout. To attempt removal of a symptom without appreciating its role in the person's universe, though, is potentially hazardous. Symptoms may even serve protective functions at times, and the client's holding on to symptoms may look like resistance, but the resistance to the clinician's efforts is merely a side effect. Teaching better coping, that is, without symptoms, is obviously necessary, and becomes a clearer therapeutic goal when the protective function of the symptom is understood.

Resistance to therapeutic progress may also be attributed to the type of intervention employed if it involves strategies and maneuvers that are unacceptable to the client. Furthermore, if the clinician is working at a faster or slower rate than the client, resistance can surface. Resistance may also arise from negative feelings toward the clinician, or their opposite—that is, idealized, romantic feelings that place a clinician on a pedestal he or she must inevitably fall from. Finally, contextual variables play a role as well, including such factors as environmental conditions, client disposition and health, and so forth. It should be apparent that all the sensitivity that goes into performing effective hypnosis is just a part of the larger therapeutic picture, for all the same guidelines apply. (Continued on page 532)

FRAME OF REFERENCE: JAY HALEY, PH.D. (HON.), M.A.

Jay Haley, Ph.D. (Hon.), M.A. (1923–), is one of the most influential figures in the field of psychotherapy and is recognized as such by all those who have had even just a passing interest in hypnosis, systems theory, family therapy, and strategic psychotherapy. His contributions to the clinical world are profound in helping us to understand problems in interpersonal terms and in stressing the need to intervene actively and strategically for our clients' benefit.

Dr. Haley has written 19 books on therapy, including *Strategies of Psychotherapy*, *The Power Tactics of Jesus Christ*, and perhaps his most well-known work, *Uncommon Therapy*. It was this latter book that rocketed the innovative nature of Milton Erickson's strategic approaches into the forefront of systemic thinking, and simultaneously revealed the crispness and incisiveness of Dr. Haley's thinking about the complex process of psychotherapy. It remains "must" reading for clinicians. Dr. Haley's work continues as he and his wife, the anthropologist and filmmaker Madeleine Richeport-Haley, Ph.D., work on producing training videos on therapy.

Dr. Haley was the co-founder of the Family Therapy Institute of Washington, D.C., he was a research associate at Stanford University and the Mental Research Institute, and he was the founding editor of *Family Process*. He is the first recipient of the Lifetime Achievement Award of the Milton H. Erickson Foundation, which also held a *Festschrift* in his honor in 1999. The many papers and accolades offered in Dr. Haley's honor were published in a volume edited by Jeffrey Zeig called *Changing Directives: The Strategic Therapy of Jay Haley*. In recognition of his lifelong contributions to humankind, Dr. Haley was awarded an honorary doctorate in June 2002 by Alliant International University in San Diego.

Dr. Haley is a modest man with some strong opinions. His dry wit and ability to sense and articulate the ironies of the therapy business are simply unparalleled.

On Types of Hypnosis: "I tend to think of three different hypnoses: (1) the personal hypnosis, where you go through a yoga experience or meditation experience, or whatever; (2) research hypnosis, where you're trying to find the limits of influence of hypnosis in various ways—in terms of deafness, color-blindness, or whatever; and, (3) clinical hypnosis, where you're trying to change someone—and I don't think that has anything to do with the other two hypnoses . . . It's so different changing someone; the person's motivation is different, the responses are different."*

On Hypnosis and Double-Binds: "In hypnosis we found the first double-bind. (Gregory) Bateson had this idea of the double-bind, but we couldn't find one. And I remember when I realized that a hypnotist was directing a person to behave spontaneously—that was the double-bind, a classical paradoxical conflict."*

On Defining Problems in Social Terms: "I think a lot happened in the 1950s. Therapy became more social and began to change and transform. Things are still changing, and we are still exploring. I think the most important idea that came in this (20th) century was that the individual wasn't the appropriate unit of study, rather it's the individual and others together. As Gregory Bateson said, "The mind is outside the person."**

On Defining Problems in Biological Terms: "I'm not an enthusiast for attributing so much to an individual's biochemistry. I think that is important for certain problems, but I think that the overselling of medications is one of the worst problems in the field, and it is getting worse all the time. Some psychiatrists now don't even seem able to talk to people—they only listen to decide which medications to prescribe. It's a shame."**

On Family Therapy Today: "I think the state of family therapy is still developing, but it still has a number of people trying to haul it back into an individual theory. I think the problem is that most teachers are still trained in doing individual therapy and they try to draft the theories of family therapy to fit an individual model."**

On the Diversity of Therapies: "I think we have been too lenient in many ways. One of the problems is that there is no longer any orthodoxy in the field. When there is no orthodoxy, you can't be a deviant. So, what used to be condemned as deviance years ago is not being condemned now. If they do something a little different in therapy, they immediately form a school with powers of influence, rather than saying it is just one more technique that a therapist should be able to use when necessary."**

On "Impossible" Cases: "Well, I can't think of one. Certainly, not on the basis of any category, because the category isn't the person. And you're dealing with the person—not a set of ideas . . . If you're a competent therapist, you're going to win some and lose some. It doesn't mean they're incurable, it just means you haven't found a way to cure them!"*

On His Most Significant Contribution: "I think my most significant contribution is breaking therapy down to a practice of specific skills—of simple ideas, skills and techniques. This is quite different from the non-directive ideology the field had when I first got into it."**

*Sources: *Personal communication, 1988*
***Personal communication, 1999*
Note: Full transcripts of Michael Yapko's interviews with Jay Haley are published in Changing Directives: The Strategic Therapy of Jay Haley *(Zeig, 2001).*

RESPONDING TO RESISTANCE

How to deal with communication deemed "resistant" is, of course, a function of how you conceptualize it. How you define resistance and who you reflexively assign responsibility for it to will determine whether you tend to view resistance as a property of the client, a property of the clinician, or an interactional outcome of the two. Listed in Table 21 below are some of the many ways to respond to resistance.

Accepting resistance as a valid communication from the client prevents having to ascribe blame to one or the other person in the relationship. More important, it paves the way to elevate the relationship to a new level of collaboration through what Milton Erickson called the "utilization of resistance" (Erickson, Rossi, & Rossi, 1976; Erickson & Rossi, 1979). Erickson's unique perspective on resistance makes a great deal of sense. Better yet, it *works* by diffusing and re-directing people's resistance to hypnosis and therapy.

The basic utilization formula of "accept and utilize" applies here. In practice, it takes the form of being able to skillfully *accept* the client's response as a valid one while developing a way to *utilize* the response in service of further suggestions. For example, if Erickson was performing an arm levitation on someone, offering suggestions for his or her arm becoming lighter and lighter, and the person reports experiencing his or her arm as getting heavier and heavier, Erickson would say something like, "That's right, that's fine, and your arm can get heavier still." *By accepting the client's response as a valid one, it can be built upon, redefining a seemingly resistant behavior as a cooperative behavior.* If the goal was to get an arm levitation, that is, a sensory alteration in the person's arm, then a "heavy arm" is an acceptable alternative in the same realm of response. It just wasn't a compliant one

---

Table 21. Potential Responses to Resistance

1. Ignore
2. Examine
3. Encourage
4. Prescribe
5. Confuse
6. Dissociate
7. Associate
8. Intersperse
9. Deflect
10. Diffuse
11. Confront
12. Redefine
13. Interpret

with the clinician's arbitrary demand for a levitation. If the clinician defines everything the client does as cooperative, then where is the resistance? Finding a way to make the nonconforming behavior seem an asset to the person can also change the feeling he or she has attached to it in favorable ways (Gilligan, 1987).

Another technique for managing resistance is more of a preventative one: Employing process suggestions, that is, suggestions without specific content. By not asking for a specific response and covering all the possible responses, whatever the client does is cooperative. For example:

> You can notice the temperature in one of your hands, and as you continue
> to breathe in and out at your own comfortable rate, you may notice how
> your hand becomes warmer, or perhaps cooler, or you may notice how the
> temperature remains the same ...

The person's hand is going to either get warmer, cooler, or stay the same. What other possibilities are there? Therefore, *any* response the client generates can be accepted and utilized as a cooperative one.

Erickson was of the belief that clients need to be able to resist directives in order to maintain a sense of autonomy, rather than adopting a position of mere obedience to authority (Erickson & Rossi, 1979; Zeig, 1980). Thus, one of the strategies he often employed was offering the client multiple directives simultaneously so that the client could resist one and accept the others. For example, I may direct a client to, "Sit down, close your eyes, uncross your legs, take a deep breath, focus on my voice, and remember an experience from childhood you can talk about." By offering so many directives at the same time, the probability is I will get most or all of the desired responses. Even if the client resists one, I will have gotten the other responses and can re-suggest the other in a different form later if I care to.

Notice also in the above suggestions the phrase "... an experience ... you can talk about." The implication to the client is that he or she can refuse to talk about some experiences, allowing him or her to resist telling me something while simultaneously following my guidelines.

Another technique for managing resistance is the strategy pioneering family and directive therapist Jay Haley (1973) described as "encouraging resistance." When you encourage resistance, usually with an intentional use of negative suggestions, in order for the client to resist resisting, he or she must cooperate (sort of a "reverse psychology"). For example, if I'd like the client to sit down, but anticipate that a straightforward directive to do so will be met with resistance, I can instead suggest:

> You don't have to (pause) *sit down.* I don't expect *you can make yourself comfort*
> *able* (embedded command) here. It will be much better for you to stand just
> as you are.

By encouraging him or her to resist sitting and remain standing, the person's resistance to me can now allow him or her to be seated. Either way, sitting or standing, the person's behavior is defined as cooperative (sitting is what I want him or her to do, standing is what I've directed him or her to do).

Responding to a client's resistances in a way that is accepting and nonconfrontational requires considerable flexibility and respect for the integrity of the client. Flexibility refers to the ability to have a variety of ways to get a point across without having to beat the client over the head with it. Flexibility means being willing to go the extra distance to meet the client on the client's level, joining his or her reality instead of expecting or demanding him or her to come to yours. It also means not having so rigid a set of expectations and procedures that your approach wouldn't allow for unique, individual responses. You can see a sharp division on this point between different schools of hypnosis, given how some approaches emphasize the importance of *invariant* procedures as a means of assessing client differences.

It is important not to build resistance in your client by doing things the way you think they should be done with little or no regard for your client's expectations, beliefs, values, and unique talents. If you attempt a strategy that fails or offer a suggestion that is responded to unfavorably, don't do the same thing over again a little more emphatically! Shift your approach smoothly, and perhaps even compliment the person's resistance if you care to comment on his or her ability to make *effective* choices in his or her own behalf. Then, *do something different.*

Not many people like to be told exactly what to do, so commanding someone to respond obediently, as in direct authoritarian suggestions (i.e., "You *will* do this"), generally encourages resistance. A helpful guideline is this: *The more resistance you anticipate getting or actually derive from the client, the greater the need for permissiveness and even indirection in your approach.* As Jeffrey Zeig (Zeig, 1980; Zeig & Rennick, 1991) pointed out, if a client is going to be obedient and highly responsive, the use of indirect techniques isn't really necessary. But when you have someone who is wary, or uncomfortable with hypnosis and/or therapy, or simply isn't very cooperative for *whatever* reason, then permissiveness and indirection become invaluable mechanisms for attaining increased responsiveness.

CONCLUSION

Resistance to change seems a basic feature of humankind. We spend so much of our lives trying to build a ritualized pattern of behavior so as to expend the least amount of physical and mental energy, and after developing such a pattern we frequently complain of "being stuck in a rut."

Resistance doesn't always show up in detectable ways (some forms are so unconscious and subtle), and resistance can't always be used in the service of change. Some clients simply will not change, others only slightly. The discussion of resistance in this chapter is intended to present the idea that much of resistance which has usually been thought of as *intra*personal is actually *inter*personal, arising from a demanding, or somehow incompatible approach to the client. Interventions have a better chance of succeeding when you are able to flexibly get a single point across in a number of different ways, using the feedback from each unique individual you treat to adapt your methods accordingly.

For Discussion

1. What personal change(s) would you like to make that you have had difficulty changing thus far? How would you react to someone who suggested to you that you must not really want to change it or else you already would have? Do you believe "where there's a will, there's a way"? What resistances to change can you identify as underlying your inability to change thus far?
2. What reasons can you suggest for why people both seek change and avoid it?
3. Can all people change whatever trait they wish to, or are some aspects of people unchangeable? Why or why not? How does your belief in response to this question influence your work?
4. How is resistance a reflection of one's limitations?
5. What examples can you cite for how people work to get into a predictable pattern and then complain about "being in a rut"? When is a predictable pattern an asset? A liability?

Things to Do

1. In a "Hand Dance" exercise with your study partner, sit opposite each other, eyes closed, and hands held up to each other as if to play "Pattycake." Silently, one will begin to move his or her hands in all directions with the other person following, all the while keeping your hands together with your partner's. When a minute or so has gone by, switch so the other person leads the "hand dance." What feelings come up as you lead and follow? Did you experience resistance? Why?

2. Research ways resistance has been considered over the years. Who gets blamed for it? How is it treated?
3. Go through the list in Table 21 of possible ways to respond to resistance and generate a suggestion for each one.

REFERENCES

Erickson, M., & Rossi, E. (1979). *Hypnotherapy: An exploratory casebook*. New York: Irvington.

Erickson, M., Rossi, E., & Rossi, S. (1976). *Hypnotic realities: The induction of clinical hypnosis and forms of indirect suggestion*. New York: Irvington.

Gilligan, S. (1987). *Therapeutic trances: The cooperation principle in Ericksonian hypnotherapy*. New York: Brunner/Mazel.

Greenleaf, E. (2001). Transference/countertransference. In B. Geary & J. Zeig (Eds.), *The handbook of Ericksonian psychotherapy* (pp. 93–111). Phoenix, AZ: The Milton H. Erickson Foundation Press.

Haley, J. (1973). *Uncommon therapy: The psychiatric techniques of Milton H. Erickson, M.D.* New York: Norton.

Seligman, M. (1989). Explanatory style: Predicting depression, achievement, and health. In M. Yapko (Ed.), *Brief therapy approaches to treating anxiety and depression* (pp. 5–32). New York: Brunner/Mazel.

Weitzenhoffer, A. (2000). *The practice of hypnotism* (2nd ed.). New York: Wiley.

Yapko, M. (1992). *Hypnosis and the treatment of depressions: Strategies for change.* New York: Brunner/Mazel.

Zeig, J. (Ed.) (1980). *A teaching seminar with Milton H. Erickson, M.D.* New York: Brunner/Mazel.

Zeig, J., & Rennick, P. (1991). Ericksonian hypnotherapy: A communications approach to hypnosis. In S. Lynn & J. Rhue (Eds.), *Theories of hypnosis: Current models and perspectives* (pp. 275–300). New York: Guilford.

22

Hypnotic Hazards and Ethical Guidelines

In chapter 2, I addressed common misconceptions about hypnosis, often the basis for people's fear about hypnosis. One of the misconceptions I discussed briefly concerned the potential harm to a client undergoing treatment through hypnosis. I made the point then that hypnosis could be applied skillfully and helpfully, or it could be misused and potentially cause harm to the client. In this chapter, I will consider more carefully the hazards associated with doing hypnosis that make it absolutely essential to exercise caution and sensitivity in its use.

I have left this discussion until near the book's end. I have clearly mentioned many times the responsibilities a clinician has to a client, and the range of skills necessary to function competently and ethically. I have tried to inspire rather than frighten you with scary hypnosis stories. Are there such stories? Yes, there are. And when you hear them, you will likely recognize that when problems have arisen, they haven't been due to hypnosis itself, but rather to the way someone who was either ignorant or malicious applied it. I cannot emphasize this point enough.

It is the measure of a field's maturity, in my opinion, when it can perform self-examinations with an openness to discovering the truth, even if the truth isn't all that pleasant. Due in large part to the repressed memory controversy, the field of psychotherapy has had to come to terms with the reality that well intended psychotherapists can cause devastation to the lives of individuals and families. There is a much greater willingness to explore the issue of the untoward effects of bad therapy, and the increased effects of self-monitoring with greater objectivity is helping us realize the problems in other domains as well, such as the negative effects of over-medicating patients and the number of patients coming out of hospitals sicker than when they came in.

The field of hypnosis is maturing as well. Historically, the hazards of hypnosis were rarely discussed, and when they were, the focus was a narrow one on the issues of whether hypnosis could be used to coerce people into engaging in antisocial behavior, and whether hypnosis would cause psychological harm to emotionally unstable people, perhaps precipitating suicide or a psychotic reaction in them (Frauman, Lynn, & Brentar, 1993; Kleinhauz & Eli, 1987; Stanley, 1994). More recently, the concerns about hypnosis have become more diverse, and clinically more relevant (Lynn, Martin, & Frauman, 1996). Generally, the reports of negative effects from hypnosis were minor ones occurring very rarely, such as anxiety or panic (Judd, Burrows, & Dennerstein, 1985), difficulties in disengaging or re-orienting (Orne, 1965), and physical discomfort such as headache, dizziness, or nausea (Coe & Ryken, 1979; Hilgard, 1974). With such reports as these, and others that I will consider shortly, it is no wonder that hypnosis has seemed at least a little bit risky to some.

Are these issues and reports something you should be concerned about? The answer is yes and no. Yes, there are potential hazards in doing hypnosis for you to be concerned and educated about. No, there is no evidence whatsoever that hypnosis causes psychosis, precipitates suicide, strips people of their defense, or otherwise harms people. *There is a high level of consensus after all these years amongst hypnosis researchers and practitioners that hypnosis holds no inherent dangers when used appropriately by a well trained clinician* (Barber, 1995; Conn, 1981; Orne, 1965; Perry, 1990). The hazards that exist are identical to those that apply to conducting a clinical practice, and dealing with diverse, vulnerable people in distress. However, the greater intensity of the therapeutic alliance hypnosis affords can also intensify the relationship dynamics between a client and a practitioner (see Barber, 1995, for an excellent discussion of the interpersonal boundary issues in hypnosis), and between a client and him- or herself.

The relationship a client has with him- or herself, that is, his or her psychodynamics, coping skills, quality of thought, and so on, is magnified in hypnosis as the client's attention is focused inwardly on his or her issues, problems, symptoms, and other aspects of his or her subjective world. What you focus on, you amplify. Might there be some negative effects as a result? Yes, and these are what require an advanced knowledge that comes from appropriate academic and clinical training.

The lack of a serious credentialing or licensure for hypnosis attesting to at least some minimal standards of training has been harmful to the reputation of hypnosis (Stanley, 1994). The evidence is simply too substantial that when misapplied, hypnosis can be a problem. Paraphrasing Martin Orne (1965), the guideline should be that *if you're not qualified to treat the problem* without *hypnosis, then you're not qualified to treat the problem* with *hypnosis.*

The potential hazards people most associate with hypnosis, rightly or wrongly, include: spontaneous regressions and abreactions, symptom substitution, confabulations, and failure to remove suggestions. I will address these hazards and whether and how each might be a legitimate concern. Before you begin to fantasize unspeakably horrible possibilities, let me assure you of one thing: If you are aware and respectful of the innate integrity of your client, you will avoid the potential pitfalls.

SPONTANEOUS REGRESSION AND ABREACTION

The topic of this section represents the most common hazard of doing hypnosis, and it isn't a question of *whether* you will encounter it, but *when*. If you have been practicing your skills in hypnosis with different people, then you probably have had the experience of discovering that people respond in unexpected and even unusual ways even to the most straightforward, seemingly one-dimensional hypnotic suggestions. *The fact that people will interpret what you say from their own frame of reference, and will therefore associate meanings to what you say that you never intended, is a given in doing clinical hypnosis.* It's to be expected, planned for, accepted, and utilized. Sometimes the unexpected responses you get are actually *better* than what you had hoped for: The person finds a simple word, phrase, or concept you mentioned deeply enlightening and transformative, and radiates that wonderful perception. When that happens, it's *wonderful*. Other times, however, the unexpected responses you get are almost the opposite: The person finds something you said offensive, threatening, insensitive, or merely irrelevant. Sometimes it's because what you said really *was* offensive, threatening, insensitive, or irrelevant.

More often, though, the person's association to what you said was unique (i.e., idiosyncratic), and simply couldn't have been predicted by you or anyone else. For example, you might offer suggestions for the purpose of inducing hypnosis employing imagery, meant to be soothing, of being at the beach. As the person begins the process of relaxing, he or she nearly has a panic attack, simply because you didn't know that he or she had nearly drowned in the ocean as a young child. And that's even after you had the foresight to ask, "So, would it be all right to begin this process by having you focus on relaxing at the beach?" and the person replied, "Yes, that's fine." Could the person really have forgotten that drowning episode, only to have it come up seemingly out of nowhere as you start to do hypnosis? Yes.

Memories can come up through structured age regression sessions, but most often they simply arise spontaneously for people during hypnosis, hence the term "spontaneous regression." That's natural and to be expected. After all, the events in a person's personal history have shaped their very lives. Sometimes the memories are pleasant ones, but sometimes what comes up are unpleasant memories that surface dramatically and with considerable emotional intensity (Fromm, 1980; Lynn, Kirsch, & Rhue, 1996). These are termed "abreactions."

The terms "spontaneous regression" and "abreaction" are not synonymous terms, but rather are so closely related in their association that I have chosen to discuss them together in this section. Together, these two account for the unexpected and often intense emotionalism that potentially makes hypnosis powerful in shaping the client's experience. When the emotions are positive and bring pleasure, it's not much of a concern to clinicians. But when the feelings are painful, involving hurt, grief, fear, rage, or whatever, the need for the clinician to know how to skillfully and therapeutically manage such feelings cannot be overstated (Lynn, Kirsch, & Rhue, 1996).

A spontaneous regression back to some unpleasant memory is an indicator of what is commonly called "unfinished business," personally significant experiences which didn't reach an adequate resolution and thus require further attention. Sometimes the suppression or repression of significant memories is so great that the material remains out of consciousness even during hypnosis and instead of there being an overt abreaction, the person complains of a headache or some such discomfort during or after hypnosis.

Even the most skilled clinician cannot know what land mines are in the client's unconscious waiting be tripped in doing therapy or hypnosis. What seems like a neutral term to one person may be the trigger to some intense personal experience for another. Therefore, the possibility of doing hypnosis without ever experiencing an abreaction is unlikely. Be ready by having good training in handling intense affect, the kind of training you are most likely to receive in advanced clinical workshops on working with people who have endured traumas of one sort or another.

Some clinicians, on the other hand, actually instigate abreactions in their clients in order to deliberately bring painful memories up and attempt to resolve them therapeutically. This can be an invaluable treatment strategy if done skillfully. If done poorly, it can place the already vulnerable client in greater emotional distress, not to mention wasting an opportunity to do some real healing. If a clinician is uncomfortable in dealing with strong emotional associations that may be triggered by what was originally intended to be the most soothing of hypnotic experiences, the choice exists to either get comfortable or avoid doing any work of real emotional impact (i.e., doing therapy in an entirely detached, intellectual style).

Abreactions can manifest themselves in a variety of ways, including crying, hyperventilation, trembling of the body (or specific body parts), premature disengagement from hypnosis, hallucinations, delusions, and autistic-like rocking motions. Each of the above behaviors is not automatically indicative of an abreaction, but should be responded to cautiously and sensitively. *Any* sign of discomfort on the part of the client signals a need for you to clarify what's going on with him or her. "Checking in" with the client as I have encouraged you to do many times is a good thing to do anyway, since one of the things well established through the research of Sheehan

and McConkey (Sheehan, 1992; Sheehan & McConkey, 1982) is that someone can report being distressed even while maintaining an outward appearance of seeming calm and comfortable.

The first and foremost thing to remember in dealing with spontaneous
regressions and abreactions is this: *You can feel comfortable directly asking your
client to describe his or her experience.* Give protective suggestions, and be supportive of his or her experience, using the general "accept and utilize" formula. *Allow the abreaction, but be calming and helpful to the client in helping him or
her reach a new perspective on the experience.* (After all, that's what therapy is for,
isn't it? One can't change the past, only attitudes toward it.) Use calming
suggestions, make sure your voice is soothing and confident, and move in a
casual way as opposed to abrupt, rapid movements. In general, the best
thing you can do is use hypnosis to resolve the situation and attain some
closure. You do that by first supporting the emotional release, and then
guiding the client's attention in the direction of considering new perspectives, developing necessary coping and transcending resources, and helping
the person to integrate them. Even if your client's hour is up, your responsibility to that person isn't over. Make certain he or she can leave in a collected manner.

The specifics of how to do all that are beyond the scope of this introductory text, so I again encourage you to take more advanced clinical training with experts in this domain. If a client opens up with some sensitive
information that you are simply not equipped to handle for whatever reason, I suggest that you make sure the client is immediately referred to an
appropriate helping professional (thus the value of a good referral list). A
suggestion such as the following may be employed in such instances:

> . . . And you've become aware now of some feelings that are very strong and
> some memories that are needing some attention . . . and you can know com-
> fortably that as these images and feelings drift into your awareness that they
> can be handled skillfully and that you can help yourself by keeping this
> information in a safe place within you until they can be brought out with the
> person best able to help you with them, and so you can let these images and
> feelings drift to the safe place within you until you are ready to share them
> when the time is right. . . .

Essentially, the suggestions above are telling the client that he or she
can "put the information away safely for now and deal with it later" in a
context that is more appropriate. Such protective suggestions can have a
very soothing effect on the person, and can build even greater trust for your
open acknowledgment of your limits in intervening. Follow-up to make sure
the person gets in to see someone qualified right away is critically important, as is staying aware of and supporting his or her overall well-being.

SYMPTOM SUBSTITUTION

Historically, the most common criticism leveled against the use of hypnosis concerned the potential for "symptom substitution." Symptom substitution refers to the onset of a new symptom, perhaps, but not necessarily a worse one, in the place of the old symptom removed during treatment. For example, Rosen (1960) reported that one patient treated with hypnosis to relieve phantom limb pain later developed schizoaffective disorder, and another patient treated for smoking developed overeating and then alcoholism. He did not provide assessment data or the specifics of his treatment plan, so we do not know if hypnosis had anything to do with his patients' difficulties.

In order for one to charge hypnosis with this potential liability, hypnosis must be viewed as a symptomatic treatment as opposed to a more dynamic or depth-oriented approach. The dynamic theory is that there is a psychic energy associated with internal conflicts that is relieved by the development of a symptom—an outlet for the energy. By removing the outlet, the energy must be re-directed elsewhere and a new outlet developed (Weitzenhoffer, 2000). Other "symptomatic" approaches, most notably behaviorism, have faced this same charge.

In the case of hypnosis, there is a twist that makes the response to the criticism somewhat complex. Hypnosis *can* be used superficially and symptomatically (scripted approaches, for example), and, in my opinion, is used this way all too often. Simple, direct suggestion aimed at a target symptom can be used by untrained laypeople and poorly trained professionals with no real understanding of the deeper issues presented in this chapter in particular and this book in general. There have been many times, especially in these later chapters, I have encouraged making the distinction between the content of a person's problem and its underlying structure, encouraging you to address the structure. Furthermore, without an understanding of the role of a symptom in a person's life and the related dynamics, symptom substitution can be (but isn't necessarily) an unwanted, unexpected outcome.

The primary issues associated with the potential for unwanted symptom substitution are first, a symptom's function (*if* it has one, and it is not safe to assume it always does), and second, the associated secondary gains, *if* any.

The idea of a symptom frequently, but not always, serving a useful purpose even though it may be uncomfortable to a person is probably not a difficult idea to grasp. To view it as a way of coping, a way of controlling others, a way of getting what one wants, a way of avoiding responsibility, and a way of maintaining a stable position in an erratic world are all ways of giving the symptom a special respect for its value instead of derogating it as stupid and meaningless (Frauman, Lynn, & Brentar, 1993). If the function or value of a symptom is not considered, how is that same need in the person to be managed more constructively through the therapeutic alternatives you provide?

Here's a personal example of the point: In the psychiatric hospitals I have worked in, the staffs did something I considered to be a bit odd. It is a purely subjective estimate on my part that 98.36% of psychiatric patients are cigarette smokers and most are chain-smokers (only a slight exaggeration). Cigarettes entertain them in what can often be a boring environment, they are a medium of exchange in the patient barter system, they are a status symbol, but mostly they just help the patients manage their anxiety by giving them a series of temporary focal points. Staff members, noticing the value of cigarettes, often use them for leverage to get the patients to do whatever the staff wants them to do. "Difficult" patients lose their smoking privilege and must earn the right to smoke. This ploy works enough times to keep it going, but some patients don't react well to it: A short time after the cigarettes are taken, the patient ends up in seclusion for "acting out." This is what I mean when I talk about the value of a symptom. In this example, cigarette smoking is not just a bad habit—it's the glue holding the fragile patient together. Removing an outlet and providing no better alternative can lead to rapid deterioration. Of course, the patient teaches the staff not to do that again. In emotionally healthier people, this process is not nearly as extreme, but a similar potential exists. The idea of responsible treatment is to acknowledge the function of the symptom and to develop alternatives that will satisfy the underlying dynamics in a more constructive way.

Closely related is the issue of "secondary gain." Secondary gain refers to the "payoff" for a symptom, that is, the advantages the symptom allows the person. The payoff is rarely, if ever, a conscious one. Rather, it is an unconscious system which supports the symptom's existence. Realistically, the symptom has an impact on the person's personal and interpersonal worlds, including his or her family, friends, spouse, therapist, and whoever else might be in the sphere of the symptom's influence. If the impact is one that encourages the symptom, the symptom is easier to maintain. In fact, one of the better strategic approaches to addressing secondary gains is making the symptom inconvenient, that is, making it easier to give the symptom up than to keep it. I described this pattern previously in chapter 18. Haley described a similar approach in detail in his 1984 book, *Ordeal Therapy*.

Symptom substitution need not occur if the client is educated about treatment, and if the symptom's purpose(s) and secondary gain(s), if any, are identified and resolved within the treatment process. Whether these issues should be presented to the client as "insights" or not (perhaps choosing to address them indirectly) is a matter of professional orientation and clinical judgment. It is impressive, though, that Barabasz and Sheehan in an unpublished 1983 study (reported in Barabasz & Barabasz, 1992) obtained data from over 600 patients treated on a hypnosis and psychosomatic medicine unit in a hospital and had only one patient report mild, transient difficulties associated with his treatment. Their conclusion, which I support, is that psychoeducation and psychological evaluations (including mental status exams) overwhelmingly precluded negative effects from hypnosis (Barabasz & Barabasz, 1992).

If symptom substitution should arise for some reason, the new symptom can be addressed more directly in terms of its origin, purpose, secondary gains, and meaning to the client. It can be removed through suggestion, through techniques like age progression, or Bandler and Grinder's "ecology check" (1979), described below.

Age progression was discussed in detail in chapter 16. Suffice it to say here that taking the client forward in time (through fantasy projection) allows the person to assess realistically the impact of the proposed changes. Such assessment consists of evaluating whether alleviation of the symptom has been helpful or hurtful, and in what specific ways.

The "ecology check" is a more sophisticated technique based on the systemic perspective that each person is composed of multiple, interrelated parts. A change in one part of the person is necessarily going to have an impact on the other parts, hopefully positive, but perhaps not. The "ecology check" is a way to gauge the client's perspective on the impact of the symptom's removal. The check essentially involves establishing direct communication, verbal or otherwise, with the client in hypnosis, having him or her implement the change under consideration, and noticing the changes that result in the person's experience as a consequence. Specifically, the person is directed to notice whether the change is an acceptable one at all levels. If so, the person is asked whether the part of him or her that was formerly responsible for the old symptom can now be responsible for integrating the new alternative(s) provided in treatment into the desired context. (See Bandler & Grinder, 1979, for a more detailed description and examples.)

As a final point, there may be occasions when symptom substitution may be a desirable alternative as a deliberate part of the treatment plan. In other words, intentionally creating an "acceptable" symptom may be a choice a clinician and client make together. Channeling a client's physical pain from one part of his or her body and concentrating it in his or her little finger, for example, may be a desirable alternative for the patient (Chaves, 1993).

Developing an appreciation for the complexity of these therapeutic issues will facilitate not only clinical hypnosis in particular, but therapeutic intervention in general. The issue of symptom substitution associated with the use of hypnosis has declined in recent years as clinicians better understand treatment dynamics as well as the dynamics of clinical hypnosis. Not only is symptom substitution not inevitable, it should be regarded as a rare phenomenon.

CONFABULATIONS

Having described the vulnerability of memory processes to suggestive influences previously in a number of places, but especially in chapter 16, it seems unnecessary to go into great detail about this particular hazard. I do, however, want to reiterate some of the key points anyone doing hypnosis should know about this issue.

When someone doesn't remember some event or some fact, he or she may fill in the memory gap with misinformation (i.e., fantasy material, inferences, misremembered information, etc.) without realizing he or she is doing so. The material projected into the memory gap is called a confabulation (Schachter, 1996). Confabulations may be self-generated, or they may be suggested memories that are incorporated as real. In the course of hypnosis, when the lines separating fantasy from reality may be even more blurred, the danger is increased that someone will mistake a confabulation for truth. This misperception can be a problem in therapy at any time, but it has been an especially serious one as clinicians struggle with the issue of how to best address the population of people who may have abuse (whether sexual, physical, or emotional) in their background. Such individuals may suffer a variety of memory problems as a direct result of the trauma (Spiegel, 1993, 1996). Gaps in memory may even be taken by some clinicians as evidence of abuse when in fact no such memories exist and there was no such actual history (Belli & Loftus, 1994; Lynn & Nash, 1994; Yapko, 1994).

There is a general sequence in the development of false memories when the therapist is the source of the contamination. First, the client has distressing symptoms of unknown origin he or she presents to a therapist. The therapist believes and then directly suggests to the client that the symptoms are evidence of a history of abuse. The client denies any such abuse took place, which the therapist then uses as confirming evidence that there was abuse and that it is repressed. Next, the therapist suggests that the "root causes" of the symptoms must be brought to the surface for resolution, even suggesting that remembering and "working through" the memories is essential to recovery. The therapist is sincere, persuasive, and seen as a credible expert. So, the client agrees to undergo a memory recovery process of one sort or another (perhaps called hypnosis, or perhaps called by other names such as imagery, visualization, primary processing, etc.). The client undergoes the process, the holes in his or her memory become especially evident to both the clinician and him- or herself (e.g., "I can't remember!").

The therapist frames this inability to remember as resistance ("You have to face this even though it's painful!") and "helpfully" suggests details of abuse (e.g., "Notice where your father is putting his hands . . . don't you feel terribly violated and angry?") which the person comes to believe actually happened. A new identity, that of an "abuse survivor," is born.

It bears repeating that this terrible scenario is most likely to occur when the therapist is the one to suggest the memories of abuse as a means of helping the client explain symptoms and fill in memory gaps. This is a minority of cases, since *most people who have been abused know it now and have always known it*. They might not ever have talked to anyone about it before, but they have known about it. Repression to the point of a full amnesia for abuse is possible, but it is a most uncommon phenomenon.

The means to avoid making the mistakes associated with the suggested memory problem should be obvious: Don't infer a history of abuse where none is stated, don't offer leading suggestions to a client in hypnosis about what and how to remember, don't assume a "root cause" for every problem, do know the workings of human memory, do know the limits of hypnosis, do know that memories can be detailed and emotional and still be wrong, and be clear about the distinction between supporting versus validating your client's memories (Loftus & Yapko, 1995; Lynn, Kirsch, & Rhue, 1996).

Be reminded, there is no technology currently available to distinguish between truth and confabulation. No clinician doing hypnosis should hold the terribly erroneous belief that hypnosis will reveal the truth.

FAILURE TO REMOVE SUGGESTIONS

A common fear expressed to me by students new to the field concerns the failure to remove suggestions. With all the things there are to occupy your mind while doing hypnosis (formulating meaningful suggestions while closely observing and utilizing your client's responses), what happens if you forget to remove a suggestion? Will your client stay age-regressed indefinitely? Will your client stay anesthetized and live life "comfortably numb"? The answer is no. But why isn't the failure to remove suggestions a serious concern?

Actually, it *is* a serious concern. It is possible that a suggestion may have a delayed or hidden effect, and so your suggestions to the client, if meant to be temporary, should be structured to say that they are temporary. André Weitzenhoffer has probably written the most about this phenomenon, and described the issue clearly when he wrote:

> It is not well-recognized that when the response to a suggestion is not allowed to be completed or is prevented from taking place there may be a lingering effect that may unexpectedly manifest itself sometime in the fu-

ture. Furthermore, while it is usually assumed that if a response does not take place, this indicates the suggestion had no effect, this can be a quite erroneous conclusion. A related effect may take place also unexpectedly at some future time. While this may not be a frequent occurrence, it does occur. For this reason, I terminate or annul any suggestion that I do not plan to have an ongoing effect. (2000, pp. 53–4)

While Weitzenhoffer acknowledged it is rare for a suggestion to linger beyond the time it is needed, his advice to deliberately annul suggestions is wise. Why are hypnotic responses generally temporary? Because they are "state specific" (Rossi, 1996, 2002). In other words, they are operative only as long as the person is in hypnosis. There is little or no carryover of the hypnotically obtained responses into the client's "waking" state unless there has been a suggestion to do so.

You may remember that the purpose of the posthypnotic suggestion is to allow the responses obtained during hypnosis to generalize to other contexts. Without the posthypnotic suggestion (either from the client to him- or herself or from the clinician) to carry the hypnotic response over to some other context, the response is just an interesting one observable only temporarily during hypnosis. Thus, if you forget to remove suggestions given during hypnosis at the end of the hypnosis session, the suggestion is highly likely to dissipate automatically upon disengagement.

If the exception occurs and the client continues to experience a suggestion that was not intended posthypnotically, it is a safe bet the client has given him- or herself the posthypnotic suggestion to do so (perhaps by simply assuming the suggestion was supposed to endure). Hypnosis may be re-induced and the suggestion directly removed if so desired.

Another possibility to consider in such instances is that the suggestion might have some special significance to the client or he or she would not have maintained it. Hypnosis may be re-induced in order to explore its significance. Suggestions are generally followed only as long as they are appropriate, that is, beneficial.

The point to remember is that any suggestion can be accepted or rejected, and the maintenance of a suggestion not intended to exist outside of the hypnotic experience represents a choice at some level by the client. Suggestions will most probably dissipate on disengaging from hypnosis, but in the exception where this does not occur, the client may be re-hypnotized and the suggestion removed in whatever manner is deemed appropriate.

It bears repeating that the best way to avoid any of the potential hazards described in this section of the chapter is by respecting the integrity of each person, regardless of their symptoms, age, or background. I can think of no one who models this attitude better than one of the field's most well respected experts, and one of its best voices of conscience, Dr. Karen Olness. (Continued on page 551.)

FRAME OF REFERENCE: KAREN OLNESS, M.D.

Karen Olness, M.D., (1936–) is professor of pediatrics, Family Medicine and International Health at Case Western Reserve University. She is also director of Rainbow Center for International Child Health. Dr. Olness has specialized in pediatric medicine since receiving her medical degree from the University of Minnesota in 1961. Actually, she chose her specialty much earlier, first declaring at age 6 that she wanted to be a doctor. Later, at age 12 she wrote an essay titled, "Why I Want to Be a Pediatrician." Her dedication to the needs of children has been extraordinary, serving as president of the Northwestern Pediatric Society and as president of the Society for Developmental and Behavioral Pediatrics.

Dr. Olness has had a long-time interest in clinical hypnosis, and her work in the field has been highly visible and influential, especially through her classic text, *Hypnosis and Hypnotherapy with Children*, now in its third edition and co-authored with pediatrician Daniel Kohen, M.D. (Guilford Press, 1996). She is also the author of the book *Raising Happy Children* (Meadowbrook Press, 1977), as well as more than 50 articles and nearly two dozen book chapters. She is the incoming president of the International Society of Hypnosis, and she is a past president of the American Society of Clinical Hypnosis (ASCH), the Society for Clinical and Experimental Hypnosis (SCEH), and the American Board of Medical Hypnosis. I can think of no one who is more knowledgeable in the applications of hypnosis with children.

Even more remarkable than her many professional accomplishments are her many humanitarian contributions. Dr. Olness is medical director and co-founder of Health Frontiers, a volunteer faculty outreach in international child health. Through Health Frontiers and other humanitarian organizations (such as the International Rescue Committee) she has helped set up a pediatric residency program in Laos, helped support HIV research in Uganda, consulted to faculty in Turkey regarding the effects of earthquakes on children, helped in Albania with Kosovo refugees, helped in El Salvador with hurricane survivors, and helped refugees in Rwanda and Afghanistan. She brings a strength and kindness to the field that is exceedingly rare and precious.

Dr. Olness has been recognized for her remarkable efforts with many honors and awards. She has received the Outstanding Physician Award from the Minnesota Association of Women in Medicine, the Aldrich and Christopherson Awards from the American Academy of Pediatrics, and the Distinguished Service Award from the International Health Medical Education Consortium. Recently, Dr. Olness was elected to the Cleveland Medical Hall of Fame, and named one of the Distinguished Women in

Health Care in Cleveland. She may belong to Cleveland, but she is world class.

On how the field of hypnosis has changed since the late '60s, when she began using hypnosis: "I think that induction techniques are less authoritative. It is encouraging that there has been substantial research to document physiological changes (including brain changes) and mechanisms associated with hypnosis. In spite of this, there do not seem to be greater numbers of health professionals who study or use hypnosis. For example, membership in both the ASCH and the SCEH is substantially less than 20 years ago. On the other hand, some other professional organizations have developed regular hypnosis workshops, and there are more articles about hypnosis published in nonhypnosis journals. Nurses are using hypnosis in increasing numbers and doing a great deal of research using hypnosis; however they call hypnosis guided imagery or visualization."

On what any student new to the field of hypnosis should know about doing hypnosis with children: "It is fun to work with children. It is also a joy to give them the gift of self-hypnosis and to follow them over years. I now hear from adults in their twenties and thirties who still use their self-regulation skills, acquired when they were young children. I believe that all children with chronic conditions such as hemophilia, cancer, diabetes, and sickle cell disease should have the opportunity to learn self-hypnosis as soon as possible after the diagnosis is established."

On implications of her research in which schoolchildren used self-hypnosis to change immune responses, including both humoral and cellular responses: "Dr. Hewson Bower in Australia repeated our work and took it into the clinical realm. Her carefully done thesis demonstrated that children who learn and practice self-hypnosis have reduced numbers of respiratory infections, and fewer days of illness when they do contract a respiratory infection. There is substantial evidence that various stressors suppress immune responses. It would seem a good idea to teach all children how to use self-hypnosis to cope with stress."

On how average children can use hypnosis to change the temperature in their fingertips or their electrodermal activity: "There are now many monitoring systems, ranging from a bioband which cost a few dollars to biofeedback units costing thousands of dollars. Both children and adults enjoy seeing graphic evidence of their ability to control body responses. In general, I use a biofeedback monitor when teaching children self-hypnosis, as an adjunct, to encourage them to recognize their own self-control."

On the evolution of her "mind body machine" for children: "I had long had the idea that it would be helpful if there could be an easy way to give young children an experience which would make it clear that "thinking changes body responses." Ten years ago we developed a touchscreen computer program which is driven by a sensor that measures galvanic skin resistance. This unit was in the Cleveland Health Museum until just recently when the museum closed for major renovations. Thousands of schoolchildren responded to the instructions for using this program. Basically, they can choose a favorite animal on the screen. As they follow instructions to imagine themselves in a safe, favorite place, the animal will smile. My computer engineer colleague has now modified the program so it is available on a CD-ROM for home computers. I have one of these programs on a laptop and use it frequently in the clinic and hospital."

On how hypnosis can help children with depression: "Teaching children self-hypnosis can facilitate a sense of self-control and mastery which is important for depressed children. Often children who are depressed also have depressed parents. I think we cannot expect good results in working with depressed children unless the parents are involved in the treatment."

On how doing hypnosis with children compares technically and relationally to hypnotizing adults: "First, I tell children and adults that I serve as their coach or teacher to facilitate self-hypnosis for them. I avoid the term "hypnotizing," because it implies external control. In general, children remain close to their imagination and like to play. These characteristics make it easy for them to learn and enjoy self-hypnosis. They also lack abstract reasoning skills (most until at least age 16 years) and do not analyze themselves or the process to the extent adults do. I tell adults to "pretend you are eight years old" when you practice self-hypnosis."

On how her knowledge of hypnosis influences her personal and professional values and volunteer efforts: "Basic principles in working with displaced persons and with developing country projects are to encourage persons in their personal coping skills, to develop ownership in programs, and to facilitate sustainability. When one thinks about these concepts, they are consistent with the goals in teaching self-hypnosis. Ninety percent of children are born into the developing world. What does or doesn't happen for them, especially in the crucial first 3 years, will impact everyone else in the world. We should all care, either from an idealistic perspective (which I prefer) or from a pragmatic perspective."

Sources: 1. Personal communication, November 27, 2002
2. Interview with Dan Short in the Milton H. Erickson
Foundation Newsletter, Winter 1998.

ETHICAL GUIDELINES

The descriptions of potential difficulties that may arise in the use of hypnosis indirectly comment on the need for formal education in the dynamics of human behavior, patterns of mind-body interactions, the intricacies of treating various clinical conditions, and the need to be deeply self-aware of one's own issues, needs, and motivations, as well as knowing one's own limits in providing therapeutic interventions to others.

There are many ways to get into trouble in clinical practice, virtually all of them avoidable by being well-educated enough and emotionally intelligent enough. Every professional association in the United States, and as far as I know, internationally as well, has a code of ethics. The code of ethics spells out what constitutes appropriate and inappropriate conduct in exhaustive detail, and each person is tasked with knowing and honoring the code.

I assume that you are a helping professional and that you have only the best of intentions for your clients. I also assume, therefore, that the understandings of human nature and the capacity for interpersonal influence you learn here will be used in benevolent and even noble ways. Therefore, there is only a superficial coverage of the most basic ethical guidelines provided here.

1. The number one priority is to help, not hurt. If you feel that, for any reason, you are unable to work well with either the person or problem presented to you, then evaluate honestly whether it would be best to refer that person elsewhere, and do so when appropriate. There are few factors, if any, more important than the therapeutic alliance in determining treatment outcomes (Cummings & Cummings, 2000; Duncan, Miller, & Coleman, 2001).

2. A professional's responsibility is to educate, not show off. Hypnosis lends itself to both. It is my sincere hope that the hypnotic phenomena you are learning to induce are used and/or demonstrated only in appropriate clinical or educational settings. Furthermore, I would hope you are able to distinguish between your personal interests and what you teach your clients.

For example, there is no legitimate basis for anyone to bring into clinical practice their interest in conducting past-life regressions or other such esoteric procedures. The goal of any treatment is to empower people, not disempower them by encouraging magical thinking.

3. Have your relationship with your client(s) as clearly defined as possible, including the nature of the intervention, the duration, the cost, the expectations, evaluation points, and so on. Involving and educating your client will almost certainly make for a better, more productive relationship, and will also meet the legal requirement for an informed consent to treatment (Frauman et al., 1993; Scheflin, 2001).

4. Do not go beyond your range of expertise, or misrepresent yourself. Human problems are very complex and can't be reduced to a paragraph of dynamics. If you feel you are out of your league when presented with a problem, refer the person to someone better able to meet his or her needs. Discussing cases with colleagues, continuing to get your information updated, and having peer supervision may help you keep your boundaries clear (Barber, 1995).

5. Presenting misinformation and/or the use of indirect techniques will sometimes be judged to be the best clinical approach. Be careful—such approaches can help a client, but they can also backfire. Have alternatives prepared every step of the way by thinking your intervention strategy through and taking all steps necessary to prevent untoward effects. In other words, be prepared!

6. Always involve, when appropriate, the proper qualified health professionals (Cummings & Cummings, 2000). When working on a physical symptom, for example, unless you are a physician you should have a medical referral and medical clearance to work with the problem. Practicing medicine (psychology, nutrition, etc.) without a license or without advanced clinical training, knowledge, and backup is illegal, unethical, and irresponsible.

There are many, many other considerations that go into conducting a competent, legal, and ethical clinical practice. Clinicians are generally well-intentioned people who want to do the highest quality work with their clients, but they sometimes get into trouble when they underestimate the complexity of what they're dealing with, or when they don't know the hazards of a particular type of problem or treatment approach, or when they overestimate their skills.

CONCLUSION

The issues and approaches presented in this chapter rank as some of the most important in this book. I hope they have sensitized you to the complex issues associated with the responsible practice of hypnosis, and also provided you with some comfortable guidelines for managing them well.

Working with hypnosis is inspiring in what it highlights about people's hidden resources, but there aren't many miracles to be had. There are just well-informed, well-designed clinical interventions that work.

For Discussion

1. Have you ever experienced an abreaction? If so, in what context? What factors allowed the abreaction to occur? What effect did it have?
2. Have you ever experienced symptom substitution? If so, why? Have you been cured of symptoms that did *not* resurface in other forms? How?
3. When the secondary gain of a symptom doesn't seem adequate to cover the "cost" of the symptom in terms of pain or inconvenience, what else do you think maintains the symptom's presence?
4. What steps can you take to "expect the unexpected"?
5. What differences are you aware of between something being "legal" and "ethical"? How and where is the dividing line drawn for you as an individual?

Things to Do

1. Interview some traditionally oriented psychologists and psychiatrists, and ask them what dangers they associate with the use of hypnosis. Do you feel their responses reflect current knowledge? Why or why not?
2. Develop a strong referral list of a number of competent professionals in as many areas of health care as you can. Contact these professionals directly in order to be certain you know when a referral to them is appropriate and what their system for providing care is.
3. As an individual, but preferably as a class, create a list of ethical guidelines specifically for the practice of clinical hypnosis based on case examples contributed by each class member.

REFERENCES

Bandler, R., & Grinder, J. (1979). *Frogs into princes*. Moab, UT: Real People.

Barabasz, A., & Barabasz, M. (1992). Research designs and considerations. In E. Fromm & M. Nash (Eds.), *Contemporary hypnosis research* (pp. 173–200). New York: Guilford.

Barber, J. (1995). Dangers of hypnosis: Sex, pseudo-memories, and other complications. In G. Burrows & R. Stanley (Eds.), *Contemporary international hypnosis* (pp. 13–26). West Sussex, UK: Wiley.

Belli, R., & Loftus, E. (1994). Recovered memories of childhood abuse: A source monitoring perspective. In S. Lynn & J. Rhue (Eds.), *Dissociation: Clinical and theoretical perspectives* (pp. 415–33). New York: Guilford.

Chaves, J. (1993). Hypnosis in pain management. In J. Rhue, S. Lynn, & I. Kirsch (Eds.), *Handbook of clinical hypnosis* (pp. 511–32). Washington, D.C.: American Psychological Association.

Coe, W., & Ryken, K. (1979). Hypnosis and risks to human subjects. *American Psychologist, 34*, 673–81.

Conn, J. (1981). The myth of coercion through hypnosis. *International Journal of Clinical and Experimental Hypnosis, 29*, 95–100.

Cummings, N., & Cummings, J. (2000). *The essence of psychotherapy*. San Diego, CA: Academic Press.

Duncan, B., Miller, S., & Coleman, S. (2001). Utilization: A seminal contribution, a family of ideas, and a new generation of applications. In B. Geary & J. Zeig (Eds.), *The handbook of Ericksonian psychotherapy* (pp. 43–65). Phoenix, AZ: The Milton H. Erickson Foundation Press.

Frauman, D., Lynn, S., & Brentar, J. (1993). Prevention and therapeutic management of "negative effects" in hypnotherapy. In J. Rhue, S. Lynn, & I. Kirsch (Eds.), *Handbook of clinical hypnosis* (pp. 95–120). Washington, D.C.: American Psychological Association.

Fromm, E. (1980). Values in hypnotherapy. *Psychotherapy: Theory, Research and Practice, 17*, 425–30.

Haley, J. (1984). *Ordeal therapy*. San Francisco: Jossey-Bass.

Hilgard, J. (1974). Sequelae to hypnosis. *International Journal of Clinical and Experimental Hypnosis, 22*, 281–98.

Judd, F., Burrows, G., & Dennerstein, L. (1985). The dangers of hypnosis: A review. *Australian Journal of Clinical and Experimental Hypnosis,13*, 1–15.

Kleinhauz, M., & Eli, I. (1987). Potential deleterious effects of hypnosis in the clinical setting. *American Journal of Clinical Hypnosis, 29*, 155–59.

Loftus, E., & Yapko, M. (1995). Psychotherapy and the recovery of repressed memories. In T. Ney (Ed.), *Handbook of allegations of child sexual abuse* (pp. 176–91). New York: Brunner/Mazel.

Lynn, S., Kirsch, I., & Rhue, J. (1996). Maximizing treatment gains: Recommendations for the practice of clinical hypnosis. In S. Lynn, I. Kirsch, & J. Rhue (Eds.), *Casebook of clinical hypnosis* (pp. 395–406). Washington, D.C.: American Psychological Association.

Lynn, S., Martin, D., & Frauman, D. (1996). Does hypnosis pose special risks for negative effects? *International Journal of Clinical and Experimental Hypnosis, 44*, 7–19.

Lynn, S., & Nash, M. (1994). Truth in memory: Ramifications for psychotherapy and hypnotherapy. *American Journal of Clinical Hypnosis, 36*, 194–208.

Orne, M. (1965). Undesirable effects of hypnosis: The determinants and management. *International Journal of Clinical and Experimental Hypnosis, 13*, 226–37.

Perry, C. (1990). Some conditions of compliance and resistance among hypnotic subjects: Comment: Coercion by hypnosis. *American Journal of Clinical Hypnosis, 32*, 242–43.

Rosen, H. (1960). Hypnosis: Applications and misapplications. *Journal of the American Medical Association, 172*, 683–87.

Rossi, E. (1996). *The symptom path to enlightenment: The new dynamics of self-organization in hypnotherapy.* Phoenix, AZ: Zeig, Tucker, & Theisen.

—— (2002). A conceptual review of the psychosocial genomics of expectancy and surprise: Neuroscience perspectives about the deep psychobiology of therapeutic hypnosis. *American Journal of Clinical Hypnosis, 45*, 2, 103–18.

Schachter, D. (1996). *Searching for memory: The brain, the mind, and the past.* New York: Basic Books.

Scheflin, A. (2001). Caveat therapist: Ethical and legal dangers in the use of Ericksonian techniques. In B. Geary & J. Zeig (Eds.), *The handbook of Ericksonian psychotherapy* (pp. 154–67). Phoenix, AZ: The Milton H. Erickson Foundation Press.

Sheehan, P. (1992). The phenomenology of hypnosis and the experiential analysis technique. In E. Fromm & M. Nash (Eds.), *Contemporary hypnosis research* (pp. 364–89). New York: Guilford.

Sheehan, P., & McConkey, K. (1982). *Hypnosis and experience: The exploration of phenomena and process.* Hillsdale, NJ: Erlbaum.

Spiegel, D. (1993). Hypnosis in the treatment of posttraumatic stress disorders. In J. Rhue, S. Lynn, & I. Kirsch (Eds.), *Handbook of clinical hypnosis* (pp. 493–508). Washington, D.C.: American Psychological Association.

—— (1996). Hypnosis in the treatment of posttraumatic stress disorder. In S. Lynn, I. Kirsch, & J. Rhue (Eds.), *Casebook of clinical hypnosis* (pp. 99–111). Washington, D.C.: American Psychological Association.

Stanley, R. (1994). The protection of the professional use of hypnosis: The need for legal controls. *Australian Journal of Clinical and Experimental Hypnosis, 22*, 39–52.

Weitzenhoffer, A. (2000). *The practice of hypnotism* (2nd ed.). New York: Wiley.

Yapko, M. (1994). *Suggestions of abuse: True and false memories of childhood sexual trauma.* New York: Simon & Schuster.

Postscript

I don't know who originally made the observation, "The more you know, the more you know how little you know." Whoever it was, I wonder if he or she was talking about hypnosis at the time. Well, probably not. But, it holds true for the study of hypnosis nonetheless. I hope that by the time you have reached this postscript you have discovered the enrichment and empowerment that clinical hypnosis can provide in the service of improving the quality of human life. And I hope you have also discovered the complexities associated with using hypnosis skillfully, making ongoing study and practice a welcome necessity in your professional life.

THE NEXT STEP

One of the most frustrating things to people in the field of clinical hypnosis is the fact that people with far less education in hypnosis than this book provides are engaged in providing services to the public that they are not qualified to provide. All I can do about this issue is appeal to each person to get the education and credentials it takes to practice responsibly. It's a vitally important next step in taking seriously the responsibilities associated with providing health care to people.

A second source of frustration to those in the field of clinical hypnosis lies in the observation that many people take courses in hypnosis and then, when the course is over, the skills they started to acquire are not immediately utilized and soon fade into the past. The more hypnosis seems removed from mainstream practice, the easier it is to abandon. I hope through your learning process that you have seen elements of hypnotic experience all around you, and see their immediate relevance to every clinical interaction. My goal was not and is not to transform readers of this text into "official hypnotists." Rather, my goal has been to provide you with an introduction to a dynamic and evolving field that emphasizes concepts and techniques which can significantly expand the range of both your communication and clinical skills. Even if you never formally induce hypnosis again in your life, my guess is that you'll reflexively think twice before saying something like, "Don't think about what's bothering you."

From this introduction to the field, I hope that you are sufficiently intrigued by the range of possibilities hypnosis has to offer to want to continue developing your skills with it. There are many ways to take that next step.

As you've seen from the extensive list of references throughout this book, there are more books and articles published on the subject of clinical hypnosis than any of us can read in a lifetime, and every day the list of publications grows. Staying current with the literature is a valuable way of staying connected to the evolution of the field. The sources listed in this book can provide you with a starting point for meaningful reading and, of course, the bibliography in each reference can provide further sources for learning.

Getting connected to other professionals who share a common interest in hypnosis is another wonderful way of staying current with the field as it continues to evolve. There are organizations for professionals all over the world, and information about some of these is contained in Appendix A. Many of them publish scientific journals dedicated to hypnosis research, and some of these are also listed in Appendix A.

CLOSURE

In preparing this third edition, my approach to the subject of clinical hypnosis has been a little different compared to the first two editions. I still emphasize clinical artistry in hypnosis, obviously, but I also emphasize the value of clinical research in informing and shaping artistry. There is so much more to say now about clinical hypnosis than ever before. This made it all the more difficult for me to decide what to include. I frequently found myself wanting to say more about each of the topics presented, but felt obligated to preserve this text's integrity as an introductory one.

There is much more to learn about the human mind, personality, communication, and the potentials of clinical hypnosis to enhance the human condition. Our current understandings in these domains are ever-expanding, and there appears to be no upper limit as to how much more can eventually be known. I look forward to all that is possible with curiosity and hope.

Appendix A

HYPNOSIS ORGANIZATIONS FOR PROFESSIONALS AND JOURNAL INFORMATION

AMERICAN PSYCHOLOGICAL ASSOCIATION, DIVISION 30, SOCIETY OF PSYCHOLOGICAL HYPNOSIS

The American Psychological Association (APA) is the national organization for psychologists in America, with a large membership well exceeding one hundred thousand members. It is divided into dozens of components, each with a specialized focus within the domain of psychology. Division 30 is called the Society of Psychological Hypnosis. Once a member of APA, you are eligible to join the component division branch(es) of your choice. When you join Division 30, you will receive an informative bulletin three times per year of events within the field in general and within Division 30 in particular. Clinical issues, news updates, literature reviews, and other informative and helpful information is included. Furthermore, at the large annual meetings of APA, the Society of Psychological Hypnosis holds specialized programs with prominent members sharing their latest research and clinical insights. For membership information, you can contact APA directly.

Website: www.apa.org.
For Division 30 information write: The American Psychological Association
                                       P.S.O./Division 30
                                       750 First Street NE,
                                       Washington, D.C. 20002-4242.
Phone number in the U.S.:   (202) 336-5500.

AMERICAN SOCIETY OF CLINICAL HYPNOSIS (ASCH)

ASCH is the largest of the national professional hypnosis societies in the world. ASCH holds smaller, more topically focused regional workshops several times a year around the United States, and a large annual meeting with an impressive array of topics and presenters. ASCH also has component branches in most of the major cities across the United States. Components vary in their level of local activity. Many hold monthly meetings and annual workshops.

Website: www.asch.net
E-mail: info@asch.net
Journal: The American Journal of Clinical Hypnosis (AJCH)—published
             quarterly and included with membership in the organization
             along with a quarterly newsletter.
For Membership Information write: American Society of Clinical Hypnosis
                                   140 North Bloomingdale Road
                                   Bloomingdale, Illinois 60108-1017
                                   U.S.A.
Phone number in the U.S.:   (630) 980-4740

INTERNATIONAL SOCIETY
OF CLINICAL HYPNOSIS (ISH)

ISH is the umbrella organization for dozens of component society branches all over the world. ISH holds tri-annual meetings, each time in a different location somewhere around the world, that feature many of the world's premier researchers and clinicians presenting their latest findings. The contact information is provided below in order to learn about ISH activities and the specific member countries.

Website: www.ish.unimelb.edu.au
Newsletter: ISH quarterly newsletter featuring informative articles,
             interviews, meeting information, and component activity
             updates is included in membership.

For Membership Information write: ISH Central Office
                                   Level 3, Gentaur Building, A&RMG,
                                   Repatriation Campus, Locked Bag 1
                                   West Heidelberg, VIC 3081
                                   AUSTRALIA

SOCIETY FOR CLINICAL & EXPERIMENTAL HYPNOSIS (SCEH)

SCEH is a prominent American organization for hypnosis professionals, both clinical and research oriented, that places especially heavy emphasis on research. The International Journal of Clinical and Experimental Hypnosis is one of the most respected and most frequently cited scientific journals in all the behavioral sciences, and reflects the high standards of SCEH. SCEH holds an annual conference that features papers, workshops, and panels on latest developments within the field, presented by many of the most well-known and respected people in the field.

Website: http://sunsite.utk.edu/IJCEH/scehframe.htm
Journal: The International Journal of Clinical and Experimental
           Hypnosis (IJCEH)—published quarterly and included with
           membership in the organization along with a quarterly
           newsletter.

For Membership Information write: The Society for Clinical and
                                    Experimental Hypnosis
                                    Washington State University
                                    P.O. Box 642114
                                    Pullman, Washington 99164-2114
                                    U.S.A.
Phone number in the U.S.:   (509) 335-7504

For journal subscriptions only, write to: Sage Publications
                                             2455 Teller Road
                                             Thousand Oaks, California 91320
                                             U.S.A.
Phone number in the U.S.:   (805) 499-0721

On-line database for researching topics in hypnosis: www.hypnosis-research.org.

THE MILTON H. ERICKSON FOUNDATION

This organization is very active in advancing psychotherapy in all its forms, but is especially dedicated to the advancement of Ericksonian approaches to hypnosis and psychotherapy. The foundation is not a society and does not have a membership. They organize major internationally attended annual meetings most often on Ericksonian approaches but also on Brief Therapy and the Evolution of Psychotherapy. These meetings are held over 4–5 days and feature stellar faculties conducting workshops, clinical demonstrations, and other presentation formats. The foundation also holds many smaller meetings throughout the year around the United States. The foundation is the core of an international network of Erickson Institutes around the world (more than 100 to date) that also strive to advance the work of Dr. Erickson. Each institute varies as to its length and frequency of trainings. Contact the foundation for the various institute locations.

Website: www.erickson-foundation.org
E-mail: office@erickson-foundation.org
Newsletter: published three times a year, free in the United States, a small mailing fee for international mailing

For General Information write: The Milton H. Erickson Foundation, Inc.
                                    3606 N. 24th Street
                                    Phoenix, Arizona 85016-6500
                                    U.S.A.
Phone number in the U.S.:   (602) 956-6196

Appendix B

SUPPLEMENTAL MATERIALS FROM
MICHAEL D. YAPKO, PH.D.

Readers of this book may be interested in some of the audiotapes and video-tapes featuring Dr. Yapko's clinical interventions. These are described below.

VIDEOTAPES

"The Case of Vicki: Patterns of Trancework
with a Terminal Cancer Patient."

This clinical demonstration features Dr. Yapko's profoundly moving single-session intervention with a 42-year-old woman named Vicki who is dying of cancer. Vicki requests help in learning to manage pain without the use of medication so that she may remain clear-headed for the little time she has left to live. This session is transcribed in chapter 20 of this text and is available on DVD.

"Breaking Patterns of Depression: Hypnosis
and Building Resources."

Transcribed with commentary and analysis in chapter 8 of Dr. Yapko's book *Treating Depression with Hypnosis: Integrating Cognitive-Behavioral and Strategic Approaches* (Brunner/Routledge 2001), this elaborate, professionally produced and edited demonstration shows a single session with a moderately depressed man named Mike who has a history of severe physical abuse. Includes discussion and follow-up, (90 minutes, DVD).

"Hypnosis and Exploring Options."
Transcribed with commentary and analysis in chapter 7 of Dr. Yapko's book *Treating Depression with Hypnosis: Integrating Cognitive-Behavioral and Strategic Approaches* (Brunner/Routledge 2001). This beautifully filmed session shows Dr. Yapko's hypnotic and strategic work with Consuelo, a psychologist from Italy, who experiences herself as "feeling stuck" in her inability to write. The teaching value of the session is enhanced by the addition of explanatory subtitles and commentary throughout the hypnotic intervention. Includes follow-up information. (60 minutes, video—NTSC format)

"Hypnotically Generating Therapeutic Possibilities."
This session was described in chapter 4 of Dr. Yapko's book *Treating Depression with Hypnosis: Integrating Cognitive-Behavioral and Strategic Approaches* (Brunner/Routledge 2001). It features Dr. Yapko's use of hypnosis with Bob, a therapist new to the field, who is feeling overwhelmed and insecure about his new career. Some emotionally powerful material emerges during hypnosis about his relationship with his father that is utilized in the therapy. Includes explanatory subtitles, commentary, and follow-up information. (60 minutes, video—NTSC format)

AUDIOTAPES/COMPACT DISCS

"Focusing on Feeling Good"
Designed as an experiential supplement to Dr. Yapko's clinical writings on depression, this program is a professionally produced and innovative series of skill-building sessions involving the use of formal hypnosis in treating depression. There are seven hypnosis sessions, each targeting a different issue or symptom commonly associated with depression. The topics are listed below. Each side (except the first) is approximately 25 minutes long and provides a brief discussion of the topic followed by a hypnosis session.

1. Depression as a Problem: Hypnosis as a Solution (Overcoming depression)
2. The Power of Vision   (The value of goals)
3. Try Again . . . But Do Something Different (Developing flexibility)
4. Is It in Your Control? (Discriminating controllability)
5. You're the Border Patrol (Developing boundaries)
6. Presumed Innocent But Feeling Guilty (Resolving guilt)
7. Good Night . . . and Sleep Well (Enhancing sleep)
8. Prevention Whenever Possible (Thinking preventively)

Available on four Compact Discs (CDs).

ORDERING INFORMATION

Items can also be ordered securely on-line by visiting Dr. Yapko's website at www.yapko.com.

Author Index

Subject Index